Hyper-Intelligent Networks

Scrivener Publishing
100 Cummings Center, Suite 541J
Beverly, MA 01915-6106

Industry 5.0 Transformation Applications

Series Editors: Dr. S. Balamurugan (sbnbala@gmail) and Dr. Sheng-Lung Peng

The increase in technological advancements in the areas of artificial intelligence (AI), machine learning (ML) and data analytics has led to the next industrial revolution "Industry 5.0". The transformation to Industry 5.0 collaborates human intelligence with machines to customize efficient solutions. This book series covers various subjects under promising application areas of Industry 5.0 such as smart manufacturing, intelligent traffic, cloud manufacturing, real-time productivity optimization, augmented reality and virtual reality, etc., as well as titles supporting technologies for promoting potential applications of Industry 5.0, such as collaborative robots (Cobots), edge computing, Internet of Everything, big data analytics, digital twins, 6G and beyond, blockchain, quantum computing and hyper-intelligent networks.

Publishers at Scrivener
Martin Scrivener (martin@scrivenerpublishing.com)
Phillip Carmical (pcarmical@scrivenerpublishing.com)

Hyper-Intelligent Networks

Exploring the Future of Connectivity for Society 5.0

Edited by

Pradosh Kumar Gantayat
Department of Artificial Intelligence and Data Science, Faculty of Science and Technology (IcfaiTech), ICFAI Foundation for Higher Education (IFHE), Deemed to be University, Hyderabad, Telangana, India

Sandeep Kumar Panda
Department of Artificial Intelligence and Data Science, Faculty of Science and Technology (IcfaiTech), ICFAI Foundation for Higher Education (IFHE), Deemed to be University, Hyderabad, Telangana, India

S. Balamurugan
iRCS, Coimbatore, India

and

Sheng-Lung Peng
Department of Creative Technologies and Product Design, National Taipei University of Business, Taiwan

Scrivener Publishing

WILEY

This edition first published 2026 by John Wiley & Sons, Inc., 111 River Street, Hoboken, NJ 07030, USA and Scrivener Publishing LLC, 100 Cummings Center, Suite 541J, Beverly, MA 01915, USA

For more information about Scrivener publications please visit www.scrivenerpublishing.com.

Wiley Global Headquarters
111 River Street, Hoboken, NJ 07030, USA

For details of our global editorial offices, customer services, and more information about Wiley products visit us at www.wiley.com.

The manufacturer's authorized representative according to the EU General Product Safety Regulation is Wiley-VCH GmbH, Boschstr. 12, 69469 Weinheim, Germany, e-mail: Product_Safety@wiley.com.

Library of Congress Cataloging-in-Publication Data

ISBN 978-1-394-31560-4

Cover image: Generated with AI using Adobe Firefly
Cover design by Russell Richardson

Set in size of 11pt and Minion Pro by Manila Typesetting Company, Makati, Philippines

Printed in the USA

10 9 8 7 6 5 4 3 2 1

Dedicated to
Maa and Bapa

Pradosh Kumar Gantayat

Dedicated to
My sisters Susmita, Sujata, Bhaina Sukanta, nephew Surya Datta, wife Itishree (Leena), my son Jay Jagdish (Omm), and late father Jaya Gopal Panda, and late mother Pranati Panda.

Sandeep Kumar Panda

Contents

Preface

In an era marked by unprecedented technological advancement and global connectivity, the concept of the *hyper-intelligent network* emerges as a beacon of innovation and possibility. As we stand at the cusp of a new technological frontier, the convergence of artificial intelligence, machine learning, and network infrastructure is set to revolutionize how we engage with and harness the power of digital ecosystems.

This vision transcends traditional notions of connectivity. It marks a paradigm shift—where networks evolve from passive data conduits into dynamic, cognitive entities capable of adaptability, autonomous decision-making, and continuous self-optimization. Imagine a network that not only routes information efficiently but anticipates user needs, adjusts performance in real time, and learns from every interaction to enhance its functionality.

By exploring this domain, readers will gain not only a deeper appreciation for the transformative potential of hyper-intelligent networks but also the insight and foresight needed to navigate the complexities of our increasingly interconnected world.

This book explores the emerging field of hyper-intelligent networks—where artificial intelligence, machine learning, and advanced networking technologies converge to redefine digital infrastructure. It examines how these intelligent systems are poised to revolutionize industries such as telecommunications, healthcare, finance, and transportation.

Offering a comprehensive view of both theory and practice, the book delves into the foundational principles, real-world applications, and future implications of hyper-intelligent networks. Written by leading experts in AI and networking, it adopts a multidisciplinary approach that blends technical insight with practical case studies and examples.

Designed for both technical professionals seeking deeper expertise and non-technical readers interested in the broader impact of these technologies, the book strikes a careful balance between accessibility and depth. Complex concepts are rendered clearly, without sacrificing analytical rigor.

It includes the fundamentals of Hyper Intelligent Network, features, working principles and its application in different sectors. To meet the objectives, this book contains twenty-one chapters contributed by accomplished writers as follows:

Chapter 1 presents a foundational analysis of hyper-intelligent network (HiN) technologies, emphasizing a novel distributed architecture based on ternary-world interactions. It examines the benefits and drawbacks of HiNs, outlines current challenges in metaverse systems, and reviews cutting-edge solutions. The chapter concludes by proposing new directions for future HiN research and development. Chapter 2 focuses on hyper-intelligence in machine learning, exploring the role of advanced neural networks, reinforcement learning, and quantum computing. It addresses technical, ethical, and societal challenges, culminating in a proposed framework for the responsible deployment of hyper-intelligent systems.

Chapter 3 compares communication protocols by analyzing power consumption, data rate, latency, range, and security. A decision tree aids in selecting protocols for smart home systems. The chapter emphasizes design factors like scalability and interoperability, while suggesting further research into ethics, governance, and sustainability. Chapter 4 introduces a dual-layered cognition framework and MTChain—a custom blockchain ecosystem tailored to HiN medical technologies. It evaluates Proof of Stake and Proof of Work within this context and presents simulations validating the decentralized architecture's effectiveness for healthcare.

Chapter 5 proposes a privacy-preserving model for the cooperative exchange of electronic health records using Ethereum Blockchain and Google Firebase. The approach allows patients to retain control over their data while ensuring immutability and secure access. Chapter 6 highlights how deep learning enhances network intelligence through real-time optimization, predictive analytics, and autonomous decision-making. The collaboration between deep learning and smart infrastructure is positioned as a driver of hyper-connected futures.

Chapter 7 explores strategies for resource control and bandwidth allocation to minimize congestion, optimize performance, and prioritize critical network traffic. Chapter 8 focuses on cloud security within smart cities, proposing improvements in encryption, access control, and vulnerability management. It critiques existing models and advocates for ethically sound and resilient digital urban ecosystems. Chapter 9 contrasts traditional supply chains with blockchain-based models across industries like retail, pharmaceuticals, and automotive. It explores how integrating IoT and blockchain can solve longstanding inefficiencies and improve transparency.

Chapter 10 examines the transformative potential of integrating hyper-intelligent networks into healthcare. It details how the fusion of advanced technologies can improve patient care, operational workflows, and overall service delivery. Chapter 11 introduces an AI-driven remote health monitoring system designed to predict diabetes and heart disease. Utilizing smart devices and a hybrid optimization-classification algorithm, the system demonstrates improved accuracy and processing speed across multiple datasets.

Chapter 12 explores six core dimensions of cloud manufacturing with a focus on healthcare. It outlines technical foundations, critiques traditional models, and presents real-world case studies to illustrate the benefits of cloud-based health manufacturing systems. Chapter 13 reviews the role of e-services platforms as the backbone of smart city infrastructure. It calls for strategies to scale these platforms, ensure equitable access, and address privacy and security concerns for inclusive urban development.

Chapter 14 explores the cybersecurity landscape of hyper-intelligent networks, emphasizing blockchain and encryption as tools to ensure data integrity and compliance. It envisions a future where these networks drive transformation across transportation, finance, and healthcare. Chapter 15 provides a comprehensive look at machine learning applications in networking, covering models such as linear regression, neural networks, reinforcement learning, and decision trees. It highlights their roles in traffic prediction, intrusion detection, and dynamic resource optimization.

Chapter 16 presents a hybrid model combining BiLSTM and CNN for sentiment analysis in the Amharic language. Trained on the Ethiopic Twitter dataset, the model achieves high accuracy by capturing both sequential and local linguistic features. Chapter 17 applies the ARIMA forecasting model to historical automotive retail data (2015–2023) to predict future sales trends. It demonstrates how time-series analysis can inform business decisions in the automotive sector.

Chapter 18 introduces an Arduino-based anti-theft system that connects to a user's mobile device to send alerts when unauthorized access is detected, providing a low-cost, real-time security solution. Chapter 19 investigates the role of data analytics in managing hyper-intelligent networks. It explores tools like NMS, SIEM, and APM, showing how machine learning enables proactive network optimization, threat mitigation, and performance enhancement using diverse data sources.

Chapter 20 examines the security challenges of cloud computing and reviews existing mitigation strategies, including cryptographic techniques. It emphasizes the importance of compliance with privacy standards and the use of secure tools for managing cloud-based data. Chapter 21 explores the intersection of AI, Industry 4.0, and human resource management. It analyzes how automation, data analytics, and smart systems are reshaping traditional HR functions, highlighting both opportunities and organizational challenges in the digital workplace.

Topics presented in each chapter of this book are unique to this book and are based on unpublished work of contributed authors. In editing this book, we attempted to bring into the discussion all the new trends and experiments that have made on Hyper Intelligent Network. We believe this book is ready to serve as a reference for larger audiences such as system architects, practitioners, developers, and researchers. Finally, we offer our gratitude to Martin Scrivener and the team at Scrivener Publishing for their efforts and guidance in publication.

Pradosh Kumar Gantayat
Department of Artificial Intelligence and Data Science, Faculty of Science and Technology (IcfaiTech), ICFAI Foundation for Higher Education (IFHE), Deemed to be University, Hyderabad, Telangana, India

Sandeep Kumar Panda
Department of Artificial Intelligence and Data Science, Faculty of Science and Technology (IcfaiTech), ICFAI Foundation for Higher Education (IFHE), Deemed to be University, Hyderabad, Telangana, India

S. Balamurugan
iRCS, Coimbatore, India

Sheng-Lung Peng
Department of Creative Technologies and Product Design, National Taipei University of Business, Taiwan

Acknowledgement

Many people have directly or indirectly contributed to the outcome of this book. I feel extremely privileged to have this opportunity to convey my deep sense of gratefulness to some of them.

Foremost, I would like to express my sincere gratitude to our Director, Prof. (Dr) K.L. Narayana, for providing intellectual guidance, sensible and timely advice, continuous support, and motivation throughout my work. I am also thankful to "Centre for Excellence Blockchain Technology" Coordinator, Dr. Sandeep Kumar Panda, and his team, ICFAI Society, our families, friends, colleagues, and well-wishers for their constant support throughout this journey. The invaluable comments, suggestions, and motivation encouraged me from the beginning until the completion of this book. I am fortunate enough to get valuable input anytime I needed for which I am exceedingly thankful to our Director.

My cordial thanks to all Deans, All the faculty and staff members of the Department of Artificial Intelligence and Data Science, Department of Computer Science and Engineering, for their consistent help and support.

I also wish to thank all the faculty and staff members of the Faculty of Science and Technology (IcfaiTech), ICFAI Foundation for Higher Education, Hyderabad, Telangana, India, especially Dr. P. Pavan Kumar, Dr. P. Rohini, for their continuous support and motivation and all authors who have contributed a chapter to make it a success.

Finally, Dr. Sandeep Kumar Panda, indeed, without your support, I had doubts about whether this book could come to a realization. Your input was very helpful in improving the narrative and the message being conveyed, and, as a friend who advised me on how to proceed, you made it a lot easier to handle and quite strategic. Your kind support also helped me regain my focus whenever I felt unsure or during those times when I wanted to give up.

Moreover, I must thank my father, Mr. Dasharath Gantayat; my mother, Mrs. Padmabati Gantayat; my wife, Mrs. Madhusmita Majhi; and my daughter, Padmaja Gantayat, for their unconditional and loving support.

Lastly, I want to thank and bow to the Almighty God for everything.

Editor
Pradosh Kumar Gantayat

Part 1

ARTIFICIAL INTELLIGENCE AND BLOCKCHAIN IN HYPER INTELLIGENT NETWORK

1

Introduction to Hyper-Intelligent Networks

Mohammed Kaleem, P. Pavan Kumar, Pradosh Kumar Gantayat and Sandeep Kumar Panda*

Department of Artificial Intelligence and Data Science, Faculty of Science and Technology, (IcfaiTech), ICFAI Foundation for Higher Education (IFHE), Hyderabad, Telangana, India

Abstract

Hyper-intelligent networks (HINs) represent a transformative leap in network technology, integrating artificial intelligence (AI) and machine learning (ML) to generate adaptive, self-optimizing systems. These networks are planned to come across the demands of modern digital environments, with the propagation of Internet-of-Things devices, the extension of cloud computing, and also the need for real-time data processing. By leveraging AI and ML algorithms, HINs can learn from data traffic patterns and ecological changes, enabling proactive decision-making to optimize routes, manage bandwidth, and enhance security without human intervention. HINs offer unprecedented efficiency and performance by automating network management tasks, reducing operational costs, and minimizing human errors. Their scalability allows dynamic resource allocation, ensuring optimal network performance for applications demanding low latency besides high consistency, such as self-directed vehicles and telemedicine. Robust AI-powered security features provide continuous monitoring and adaptive responses to threats, enhancing network resilience against cyber-attacks. The development of HINs is supported by advancements in edge computing and 5G technology, which provide the necessary computational power and connectivity for real-time processing. These technologies, combined with advancements in data analytics and AI algorithms, enable HINs to effectively learn and adapt, making them a critical component in the evolution of network technology.

***Keywords*:** Hyper-intelligence networks, artificial intelligence, machine learning, Internet of Things

**Corresponding author*: sandeeppanda@ifheindia.org

Pradosh Kumar Gantayat, Sandeep Kumar Panda, S. Balamurugan and Sheng-Lung Peng (eds.) Hyper-Intelligent Networks: Exploring the Future of Connectivity for Society 5.0, (3–30) © 2026 Scrivener Publishing LLC

1.1 A Comprehensive Overview

Hyper-intelligence networks (HINs) represent a significant leap from conventional networking by incorporating artificial intelligence (AI) and machine learning (ML) to create systems that are self-learning, adaptive, and highly efficient. These networks can make real-time decisions to optimize performance, enhance security, and manage resources dynamically [45–47]. This chapter explores the fundamental concepts that underpin HINs, including data traffic analysis, predictive maintenance, and automated configuration. It also addresses the critical role of edge computing and 5G technology in supporting the high-speed, low-latency requirements of these intelligent systems.

1.2 Definition of Hyper-Intelligent Networks

HINs represent the next evolutionary step in network technology, where traditional networking principles are enhanced with AI and ML to create systems that are not only more efficient but also adaptive and self-optimizing. These networks are intended to handle the complexities and difficulties of modern digital environments, including the propagation of Internet-of-Things (IoT) devices, the extension of cloud computing, and also the increasing need for real-time data handling [27–29, 48–52].

At the core of HINs is the incorporation of AI and ML algorithms that enable the grid to learn from data traffic patterns, user behaviors, and environmental changes. This learning capability allows the network to make proactive decisions, optimizing routes, managing bandwidth, and enhancing security measures without human intervention. For instance, a HIN can detect anomalies in network traffic that might indicate a cyber-threat and automatically adjust its defenses to mitigate potential risks [30–33, 53–55].

One of the crucial benefits of HINs is their capability to provide unprecedented levels of efficiency and performance. Old-style networks often require handbook configuration and management, which can be time-wasting and disposed to errors. In contrast, HINs can automate these processes, reducing operational costs and minimizing the likelihood of human error. This automation extends to network maintenance and troubleshooting, where AI-driven diagnostics can identify and resolve issues faster than human administrators [34–36, 56–60].

The scalability of HINs is another significant advantage. As businesses and users continue to generate more data and connect more devices, the demand for network resources grows. HINs can dynamically assign resources based on current needs, confirming that bandwidth is available where it is most needed and that network performance remains optimal. This dynamic resource allocation is mainly beneficial for applications that need low invisibility and high consistency, such as self-sufficient vehicles, telemedicine, and virtual realism [37–39, 61–64].

Security is a critical aspect of any network, and HINs offer robust security features powered by AI. These networks can continuously monitor for threats and vulnerabilities, using ML to identify patterns that suggest malicious activity. By knowledge from past incidents and adjusting to new threats, HINs can provide a stronger defense against cyber-attacks. Furthermore, the use of AI in security allows for faster response times, as the network can automatically implement countermeasures without waiting for human intervention [40, 41, 65–67].

The development of HINs is supported by advancements in several key technologies. Edge computing, for example, brings computational authority nearer to data sources, dipping latency and also permitting real-time handling. 5G technology delivers the low-latency, high-speed connectivity essential for the vast amounts of data that HINs handle. Additionally, advancements in data analytics and AI algorithms contribute to the ability of HINs to learn and adapt effectively [1].

1.3 Key Components of Hyper-Intelligent Networks

HINs are integrated advanced technologies to enhance automation, decision-making, and connectivity. The key components included are illustrates in Figure 1.1.

1.3.1 Artificial Intelligence (AI)

Networking systems are becoming increasingly complex due to digital transformation initiatives, multi-cloud environments, the proliferation of devices and data, hybrid work models, and more sophisticated cyberattacks. As network complexity grows and evolves, organizations need the skills and capabilities of network operators to evolve as well. Talent shortages and budget constraints only add to this challenge. To overcome these challenges, organizations are adopting HINs and AI for networking to provide the necessary support and efficiency [2].

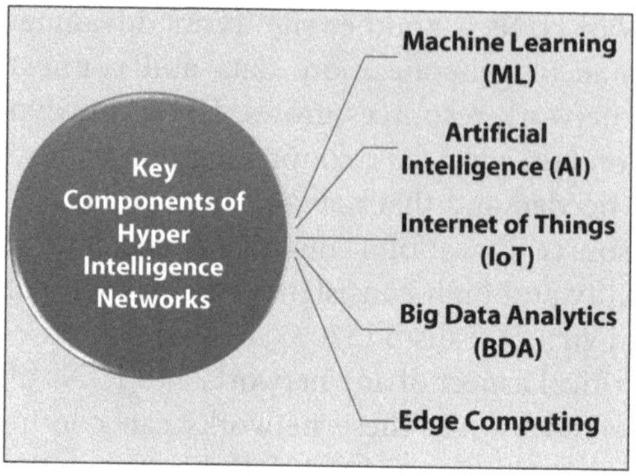

Figure 1.1 Key components of HINs.

1.3.2 Machine Learning (ML)

ML, a subdivision of AI, plays a pivotal role in developing algorithms that allow structures to learn from data and also enhance their recital iteratively. In the context of HINs, ML algorithms process vast datasets, discern patterns, and optimize network operations. This continuous learning capability is crucial for adapting to dynamic conditions and improving overall efficiency [68–71].

1.3.3 Internet of Things (IoT)

In the realm of HINs, the IoT plays a pivotal role. IoT seamlessly connects an array of devices, sensors, and systems, enabling them to communicate and exchange data. Within this context, IoT devices serve as valuable data sources, providing real-time information that AI and ML algorithms can analyze. This connectivity fosters the creation of a cohesive and responsive network, enhancing overall efficiency and adaptability [42, 72–74].

The number of global internet users has steadily increased over the past few decades, driven by advancements in internet technology, networks, and communication strategies. One of the most significant developments in this area is the IoT, which has grown into a crucial element of smart city structure. IoT plays a central role in current smart town initiatives, producing vast quantities of data. The term "Internet of Things" denotes to a gathering of tools that allow users to access data from various maneuvers through both wired and wireless internet grids [75–77].

In 2017, over 1.6 billion IoT components and devices were in use within smart metropolises, marking a 39% upsurge from 2015. By 2018, this number had risen to approximately 3.3 billion, reflecting growth rates of 42% in 2017 and 43% in 2018. The proliferation of smart components and devices has fueled the development of IoT-based solutions in smart cities. For instance, in a smart homebased atmosphere, data produced by electronic domestic appliances, such as fridge-freezers, is swapped and stored to deliver user-customized facilities. However, managing the vast and complex data generated by these devices can be challenging. Advanced practices, such as AI, deep reinforcement learning, and ML, can be working to analyze this data and derive optimal solutions [3].

1.3.4 Big Data Analytics (BDA)

In HINs, BDA entails processing and analyzing large, complex datasets. These networks utilize big data technologies to extract valued insights from massive quantities of information. These insights are then used to optimize operations, predict future trends, and enhance decision-making processes.

1.3.5 Edge Computing

It is a paradigm that includes handling data near its point of source rather than depends on only on central cloud infrastructure, and it has gained prominence. In the context of HINs, it plays a critical role in dropping latency and enhancing real-time processing capabilities. This is mainly valuable for applications that demand instant responses, like self-governing vehicles and industrialized automation. By handling data nearer to its source, it reduces latency and reduces bandwidth practice. HINs leverage edge computing to improve present data analysis and decision-making, making them well-suited for applications like self-governing vehicles and smart cities [45, 78–81].

1.4 Literature Review

Deep learning (DL) is emerging as a dominant tool for pattern acknowledgment from multifaceted raw data, making it an ideal method to enhance wireless grids with extensive topologies and intricate radio circumstances. By utilizing multiple neural network layers, DL mimics the intellect's ability to extract features from high-dimensional data. This capability allows DL to identify grid dynamics such as interference distribution, traffic bottlenecks, hotspots, and congestion points, with spectrum handiness by analyzing a vast array of network limitations like loss rate, delay, and link SNR [43, 82–84].

DL's potential extends across various network layers, data link layer access resource allocation, including physical layer coding, and routing layer track search and traffic complementary. Additionally, DL can improve other network roles such as security and data solidity. The article also highlights unresolved research challenges in this field, pointing to future trends in DL-based wireless networks. This comprehensive survey aims to provide readers with a deep thoughtful of the current state of DL-based wireless grid designs and inspire further research into these promising areas [4].

AI has observed extraordinary growth in current years, transforming industries and affecting the forthcoming of technology. As AI applications developed progressively prevalent across various arenas, scalability arises as a precarious factor for their success. This paper explores the multi-layered territory of scalability in AI, aiming to deliver a complete thoughtful of its challenges, significance, and solutions [46, 85–87].

The broadsheet begins by contextualizing the rapid evolution of the AI site, emphasizing the essential role of scalability in meeting the growing difficulties for AI-driven solutions. Through a widespread literature evaluation, we describe scalability in the context of AI and examine present studies to shed light on the varied proportions of scalability, including mountable AI algorithms, models, cloud computing, and infrastructure services [44, 88].

This paper looks at the common problems organizations and researchers encounter when trying to scale up AI systems, even though scaling can have big benefits. We explore practical solutions and best practices to tackle these scalability issues, such as optimizing resources and thoughtful system design [47, 89, 90].

To show how scalable AI solutions can make a real difference, the paper includes several case studies of organizations that have successfully scaled their AI projects. These case studies offer valuable insights into the strategies and technologies that they used, demonstrating the transformative impact scalability can have on AI initiatives [91–94].

Overall, this paper underscores the importance of scalability in the AI landscape, offering a detailed analysis of its implications and providing guidance for effectively addressing scalability challenges to connect the full possible of AI technologies [5].

The integration of AI and blockchain (BC) technologies represents a powerful synergy poised to transform numerous industries. This chapter delves into the future potential of AI in BC applications, highlighting its far-reaching impacts, challenges, and opportunities. AI's strengths in data analysis, pattern recognition, and automation naturally complement BC immutable, transparent, and decentralized ledger. Several key use cases are explored, where the convergence of AI and BC is transforming sectors like supply chain management, healthcare, finance, and smart contracts. The chapter also addresses challenges such as scalability, data privacy, and regulatory compliance, explaining how AI can help overcome or mitigate these hurdles. Additionally, it underscores the opportunities for innovation in emerging AI-powered BC solutions, including self-executing smart contracts, fraud detection, and identity verification [6].

AI is an advanced computer system designed to replicate human intelligence in various scenarios. It encompasses multiple fields of study and leverages existing technologies to mimic human behavior, enabling autonomous decision-making in specific situations. BC, a more recent advancement in data capture and storage, distributes data across several nodes within a decentralized network. Augmented reality (AR), on the other hand, provides users with an interactive experience by enhancing their real-world environment with computer-generated graphics, superimposing virtual elements onto the real-world view. The integration of AI further enhances AR by incorporating capabilities like text analysis, object detection, and scene labeling, allowing AR systems to engage with the physical world through neural networks. This paper explores the various applications of AI in AR and examines how combining BC with these technologies can support and enhance the entire AR ecosystem [7].

In recent years, the rapid advancement of AI and BC technology has garnered increasing attention, particularly regarding their integration. This paper delves into a comprehensive analysis of the challenges and potential shortcomings faced in the development of these technologies. It examines areas for improvement and technical pain points while highlighting the strengths of AI, including its applications in data, computing power, and algorithms. Furthermore, it explores the potential advantages and industry prospects that could arise from the convergence of AI and BC. The aim is to provide a new theoretical foundation for deeper academic and industry discussions on the integration of these technologies while encouraging more research institutions and small enterprises to participate in the broader landscape of technological innovation [8].

1.5 Applications of Hyper-Intelligent Networks

In this division, we discuss some of the key application areas of HINs. These are going to have wide range of market space. Here are some major arears where these HINs are building a substantial impact.

1.5.1 Smart Cities

HINs play a vital role in mounting smart towns by integrating different urban systems like transportation, energy, and public services. These networks help optimize traffic movement, achieve energy feeding, enhance community safety, and increase residents' overall quality of life. By handling the huge volumes of data produced by smart city uses, HINs can optimize traffic, energy use, and safety systems through real-time analysis and adaptive responses [48, 95–97].

Tools play an essential role in the expansion of smart towns, where innovative technological techniques are key to enhancing urban living. Smart towns leverage Info and Communiqué Technology (ICT) to computerize processes and improve the excellence of life for residents in city areas. They apply integrated intelligence tools to upgrade metropolitan structure

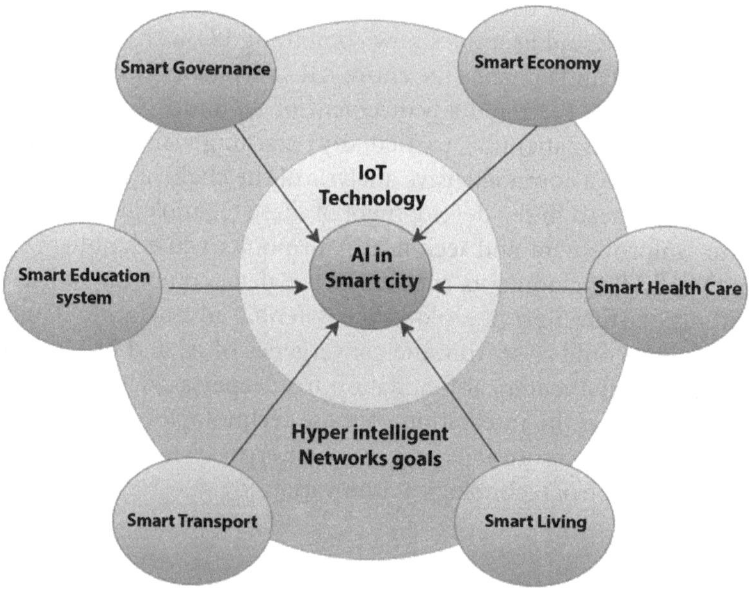

Figure 1.2 Illustration of applications of HINs.

and enable responsive control, allowing peoples to actively participate in city organization. A variety of modern technologies and approaches support clever facility models that boost efficiency and operations across sectors such as healthcare, transportation, energy, education, and more. It is widely acknowledged that towns can be considered "Clever" if they encounter specific criteria, which includes the integration of AI in various areas within smart towns, as illustrated in Figure 1.2 [3].

1.5.2 Healthcare

In a healthcare system, using HINs significantly improves the worth of healthcare facilities by making the old-style medical system extra convenient, efficient, and personalized. HINs foster better communications among patients, doctors, research institutions, and hospitals. With wearable devices, doctors can monitor patients' health in real time through HINs and respond to any irregularities or medical requirements distantly. This simultaneous monitoring, facilitated by HINs, not only helps in accurate diagnosis and reduces the need for hospitalization but can also save lives during medical emergencies [49, 98–100].

Additionally, healthcare system, supported by HINs, enhances communication and makes medical records more accessible. Electronic health records allow the seamless show of patient information among medicinal professionals *via* HINs, reducing waiting times. The collected data, managed by HINs, can also be used for statistical studies, supporting medical research and leading to better treatments in the future [9].

1.5.3 Industrial Automation

HINs are pivotal in industrial automation, utilizing progressive technologies like AI and ML to improve decision-making, automate processes, and boost overall efficiency. These systems integrate smart tools and computers into various industrial operations, leading to increased productivity and economic growth [101–103].

Overall, HINs revolutionize industrial processes, support innovation, and drive data-driven decision-making, optimizing production outcomes and reducing operational costs [10].

1.5.4 Autonomous Vehicles

Autonomous vehicles depend heavily on advanced networks, such as HINs, including modular, self-adaptive autonomy frameworks with integrated dynamic risk management and personalized cognitive agents for each driver. These networks enable the vehicles to navigate, make real-time decisions, and ensure passenger safety. By processing data from sensors and external sources using sophisticated algorithms and computer vision techniques, HINs facilitate safe and efficient autonomous driving [50, 104, 105].

The incorporation of non-monotonic logic and individualized cognitive agents within HINs allows autonomous vehicles to anticipate and respond effectively to unforeseen events, enhancing safety in critical situations. This technology, which utilizes a mixture of sensors, cameras, and ML algorithms, is poised to revolutionize travel. It aims to reduce accidents caused by human error and offers increased mobility to individuals who cannot drive, thereby improving road safety, traffic flow, and overall travel efficiency [11].

1.5.5 Financial Services

In the financial sector, the integration of hyper-intelligent systems powered by AI and ML technologies has renovated fraud detection, risk management, and personalized customer experiences. These advanced systems analyze transaction data and market trends to identify assess risks, fraudulent activities, and tailor financial products to individual requirements [106, 107].

By leveraging extensive datasets, including traditional financial indicators and non-traditional sources like social media activities, AI enhances operational efficiency and decision-making accuracy within financial institutions. This elevates fraud detection mechanisms to unprecedented levels of precision. Moreover, AI-driven methods such as ML, natural language processing (NLP), and data mining provide powerful tools for identifying and mitigating fraudulent activities, significantly enlightening the efficiency, accuracy, and effectiveness of fraud prevention efforts [12].

1.6 Challenges of Hyper-Intelligent Networks

HINs have demonstrated significant potential in improving DL simulations by increasing their efficiency, flexibility, and generalization proficiencies. However, there are still numerous trials and breaks for future research and expansion that have not been fully explored. In this segment, we will talk over some of these key encounters and suggest potential directions for future investigation. Figure 1.3 illustrates the challenges of HINs.

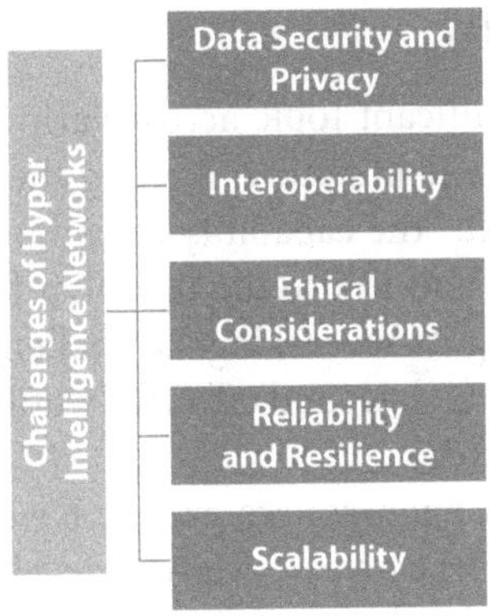

Figure 1.3 Challenges of HINs.

1.6.1 Data Security and Privacy

Technology should serve as a tool for societal progress and simplify daily life. However, in our increasingly hyper-connected world, it brings additional complications and questions about the vast amounts of data needed for these digital connections. As an internet user, you are sharing your data with third-party sources. With the advent of digitalization and rapid digital transformation, ensuring privacy has become a complex task that demands individual attention. Privacy, the right to be left alone, is essential in our digital age, making it a crucial aspect of modern living.

Scaling AI systems also involves addressing security and compliance challenges. Protecting data privacy, ensuring secure data transmission, and complying with regulatory requirements become more complex as systems grow.

In decision, the detection of scalability in AI comes with encounters that include resource constraints, model complexity, data management, and moral considerations. However, useful solutions are existing to tackle these issues, such as source optimization strategies and ethical AI rules. As AI lasts to evolve and integrate into various fields, taking a pre-emptive approach to handling scalability tasks will be crucial for unlocking the full probable of AI systems [108–110].

Data privacy challenges remain significant, affecting both organizations and consumers. By approaching these issues with resilience, confidence, and trust, organizations can leverage progressive and secure technologies to drive business innovation and growth, all while ensuring the security and privacy of user information [13].

1.6.2 Interoperability

Interoperability is a significant topic across various domains, with multiple definitions found in the literature. Among these, the IEEE's definition stands out in our context: "the capability of two or more systems or modules to interchange info and to use the data that has been swapped" [14]. This classification highlights several logical challenges, including exchanging information, acquiring data, and effectively utilizing the received information [111, 112, 117, 118].

Normal societies and open-source groups have been actively addressing interoperability concerns across various levels: networking level and semantic level. Device level, syntactic level, cross-domain and cross-platform level interoperability were discussed in further chapters [15].

1.6.3 Ethical Considerations

Using HINs raises ethical concerns, like the risk of unfair decisions made by AI and possible job losses. It is important to tackle these issues to use this technology responsibly.

1.6.4 Reliability and Resilience

For HINs to be successful, they need to be reliable and strong. These networks have to work well in all kinds of situations, bounce back from problems, and keep running smoothly to make sure everything keeps working without interruptions.

1.6.5 Scalability

The underlying infrastructure, including servers, storage, and network capabilities, must be capable of scaling to support AI workloads. This requires investment in scalable cloud computing services and infrastructure management tools [113, 114].

Integrating scalable AI solutions with current legacy structures can be problematic. Ensuring compatibility and smooth data flow between new AI systems and traditional IT infrastructure requires careful planning and execution.

The underlying infrastructure, including servers, storage, and network capabilities, must be capable of scaling to support AI workloads. This requires investment in scalable cloud computing services and infrastructure management tools.

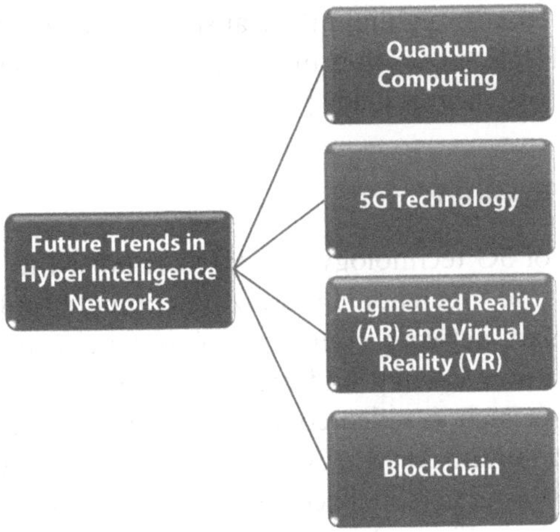

Figure 1.4 Future trends in challenges of HINs.

1.7 Future Trends in Hyper-Intelligent Networks

HINs will keep evolving as AI and network technologies improve. In the future, we can expect more advanced AI algorithms, better integration with 5G and newer technologies, and wider use in different industries. HINs are a major advancement toward smarter, more efficient, and more secure network systems. Figure 1.4 illustrates the future trends in HINs.

1.7.1 Quantum Computing

IT has the prospective to greatly enhance HINs by enabling advanced applications in remote sensing and DL. For example, combining quantum computing with AI in systems like the hyperspectral quantum deep network (HyperQUEEN) can revolutionize satellite remote sensing by overcoming current limitations such as quantum collapse effects and the limited number of qubits available [115, 116].

Moreover, quantum annealers, which are specialized quantum computers, can be used to learn models that forecast the performance of DL algorithms, improving the process of hyperparameter optimization on high-performance computing systems. Quantum artificial intelligence (QAI) blends quantum information processing with ML, offering significant speed improvements in learning and recognition tasks due to quantum parallelism. Experimental implementations, such as quantum neural networks (QNNs), show promise for the future development of portable QAI devices [16].

These advancements highlight the transformative potential of quantum computing on HINs, promising improved computational efficiency and performance across various fields [17].

1.7.2 5G Technology

The integration of 5G technology into HINs is poised to greatly enhance their scalability and efficiency. By utilizing computer-aided 5G technology, wireless smart network communiqué systems can achieve quicker data broadcast, lower latency, and higher capacity, which are crucial for real-time requests such as video conferencing and self-sufficient vehicles. Additionally, combining AI with 5G networks improves network diagnostics, cybersecurity, and personalized applications, transforming consumer-business interactions. Figure 1.5 illustrates Future of 5G Technology [18].

Moreover, the proposed scalable intelligence-enabled networking in 5G scenarios reduces traffic redundancy, enhancing network performance and cutting redundant traffic by up to 46.04%, thereby demonstrating increased scalability and efficiency for HINs. Furthermore, innovative methods like heuristic optimization techniques and advanced neural network architectures in 5G MIMO systems improve channel estimation, leading to better

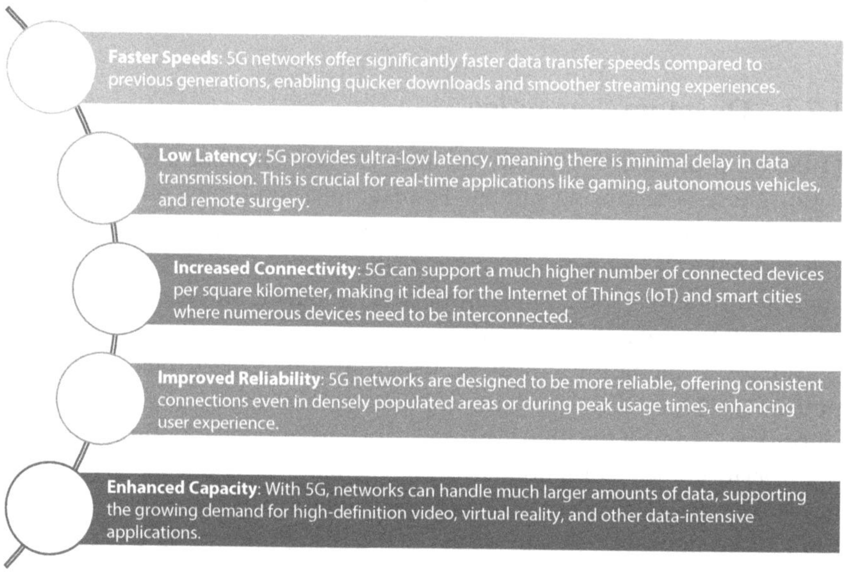

Figure 1.5 Futures of 5G technology [20].

convergence rates, prediction performance, and reduced computational costs, further enhancing the scalability and efficiency of HINs in the future [19, 20].

1.7.3 Augmented Reality (AR) and Virtual Reality (VR)

The future of HINs incorporating AR and VR is set for remarkable progress through the integration of AI, BC technology, 5G networks, and IoT devices. The combination of AI and AR enhances user experiences by enabling capabilities such as text analysis, object detection, and scene labeling [21]. Additionally, the synergy between 5G networks and AI supports innovative services in smart roads and vehicles, including in-vehicle augmented VR and road safety services [22].

The development of AI-XR metaverse applications leverages AI, XR technologies, and 5G/6G communication to create immersive, personalized experiences, highlighting the importance of security and privacy in critical AI applications. Furthermore, collaboration between XR and AI experts aims to create AI-enabled XR experiences through generative XR, large language models, and explainable AI for XR, seamlessly blending digital and physical worlds [51–54, 107, 108].

These three technologies work well together, and their combination is about to bring big changes and new possibilities. While AI has been around for a while, the mix of VR-AI and AR-AI is about to change the way that we live and do business. These technologies are likely to become a big part of our everyday lives—it is already normal to see people using filters to add cat whiskers to their photos! And this trend is spreading to much more than just camera filters [112, 113].

VR uses technology to create a virtual world that people can interact with. For example, brands, like Tommy Hilfiger and Gap use VR, supported by HINs, to let customers watch fashion shows or try on clothes without being there in person [114, 115].

AR adds digital elements to the real world. A well-known example is Pokémon Go, where players could see Pokémon appearing in their actual surroundings when looking through their smartphone. HINs enhance these experiences by ensuring seamless and responsive interactions between the digital and physical worlds.

Moreover, the application of AI in semantically understanding scenes and generating AR content demonstrates the potential for AI-driven smart AR services with high generalization capabilities for various real-world scenarios [23]. Figure 1.6 the role of generative AI in AR and VR learning.

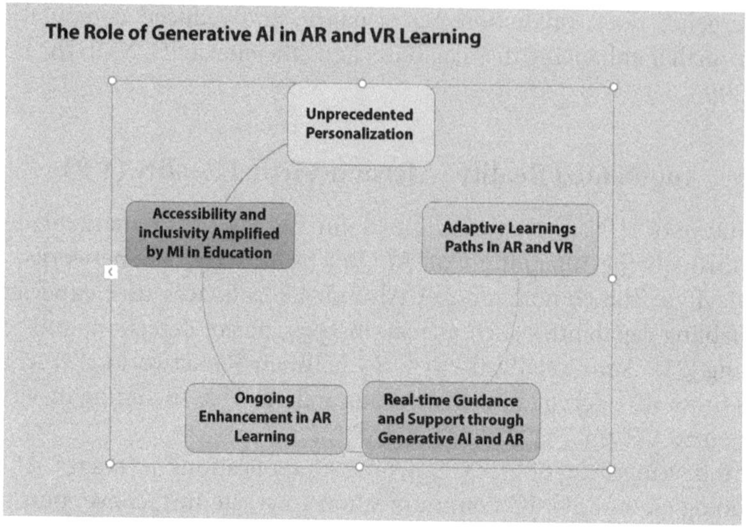

Figure 1.6 The role of generative AI in AR and VR learning [24].

1.7.4 Blockchain

The future of HINs leveraging BC technology looks promising, particularly with the integration of AI and BC across various applications. This combination addresses issues such as scalability, security, and privacy, thereby improving efficiency and transparency in sectors like supply chain management and financial services. Moreover, the potential of AI and BC in future wireless networks is immense, with AI enabling dynamic network adaptation and BC ensuring data integrity and security [109–111].

Additionally, the integration of 5G wireless networks, IoT, and BC in autonomous communications offers opportunities for hyper-connected, trust-managed systems that utilize decentralized approaches and global trust values stored on the BC. The future of HINs lies in the ongoing exploration and synergy of AI and BC technologies to create secure, efficient, and transparent network ecosystems [25]. Figure 1.7 artificial intelligence and blockchain-based architecture for heterogeneous IoT systems.

The solid lines represent the connection and communication links between nodes involved in the BC. The dashed lines indicate communication links between IoT devices and edge nodes. Red lines, whether solid or dashed, highlight vulnerable connections and potentially suspicious IoT communications [26].

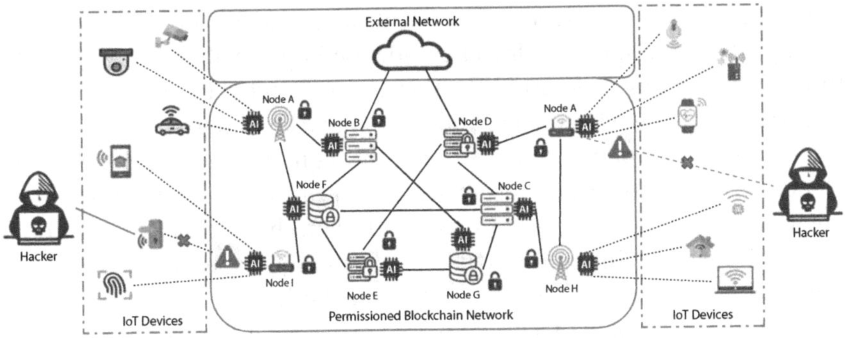

Figure 1.7 Artificial intelligence and blockchain-based architecture for heterogeneous IoT systems.

1.8 Conclusions

Some conclusions based on this chapter about HINs are as follows:

Enhanced Efficiency and Performance: HINs leverage AI and ML to automate network management tasks, reducing operational costs and minimizing human errors. This leads to more efficient and reliable network performance.
Adaptive and Self-Optimizing: The combination of AI and ML allows HINs to study from data traffic patterns and environmental changes, enabling them to make proactive decisions. This adaptability ensures optimal performance and resource allocation in real time.
Scalability: HINs can dynamically assign assets based on current demands, making them highly scalable. This is mostly beneficial for requests requiring high reliability and low latency, such as self-sufficient vehicles and telemedicine.
Robust Security: AI-powered security features in HINs provide continuous monitoring and adaptive responses to threats. This results in a more resilient defense against cyber-attacks, with faster response times compared to traditional networks.
Support from Advanced Technologies: The development and effectiveness of HINs are bolstered by advancements in edge computing and 5G technology. These technologies provide the necessary computational power and connectivity to handle the vast quantities of data processed by HINs.
Real-Time Conclusion Making: HINs are capable of making real-time decisions to optimize network performance, enhance security, and manage resources dynamically. This real-time capability is crucial for handling the complexities of modern digital environments.

Overall, HINs represent a significant advancement in network technology, offering improved efficiency, adaptability, scalability, and security through the mixing of AI and ML. They are well-suited to meet the hassles of current digital environments and emerging technologies.

Quantum computing, particularly through advancements like the HyperQUEEN and QNNs, promises significant enhancements in computational efficiency and performance. These technologies will overcome current limitations in remote sensing, DL, and hyperparameter optimization, flagging the way for classier and talented HINs.

The integration of 5G technology into HINs is set to revolutionize network scalability and efficiency. Benefits include faster data transmission, higher capacity, and lower latency, which are vital for actual applications such as audio-visual conferencing and autonomous vehicles. Additionally, the use of AI in 5G networks will improve network diagnostics, cybersecurity, and personalized services, further advancing the capabilities of HINs.

The combination of AI, AR, and VR, supported by 5G networks and IoT devices, will lead to ground breaking advancements in user experiences and services. AI-enhanced AR applications will offer improved text analysis, object detection, and scene labeling, whereas AI-XR metaverse applications will create immersive and personalized experiences. This convergence will enhance smart road and vehicle services and ensure the seamless blending of digital and physical worlds.

The synergy between AI and BC technology holds great promise for enhancing the scalability, security, and privacy of HINs. This integration will improve efficiency and transparency in various sectors, including supply chain management and financial services. Additionally, combining 5G, IoT, and BC in autonomous communications will enable hyper-connected systems with robust data integrity and security, leveraging decentralized approaches and global trust values.

The ongoing evolution of HINs will be driven by advancements in AI, quantum computing, 5G technology, AR/VR, and BC. These technologies will work synergistically to create smarter, more efficient, and secure network systems. The integration of these cutting-edge technologies will result in transformative improvements across various industries, highlighting the potential of HINs to transform the way that we interrelate with and utilize network systems in the future.

Overall, HINs represent a significant advancement in network technology, offering improved efficiency, adaptability, scalability, and security through the incorporation of AI and ML. They are well-suited to encounter the hassles of modern digital environments and emerging technologies.

References

1. Banaeian Far, S. and Imani Rad, A., Internet of Artificial Intelligence (IoAI): the emergence of an autonomous, generative, and fully human-disconnected community. *Discov. Appl. Sci.*, 6, 3, 91, Feb. 2024, doi: 10.1007/s42452-024-05726-3.
2. Elahi, M., Afolaranmi, S.O., Martinez Lastra, J.L., Perez Garcia, J.A., A comprehensive literature review of the applications of AI techniques through the lifecycle of industrial equipment. *Discov. Artif. Intell.*, 3, 1, 43, Dec. 2023, doi: 10.1007/s44163-023-00089-x.
3. Herath, H. M. K. K. M. B. and Mittal, M., Adoption of artificial intelligence in smart cities: A comprehensive review. *Int. J. Inf. Manage. Data Insights*, 2, 1, 100076, Apr. 2022, doi: 10.1016/j.jjimei.2022.100076.
4. Mao, Q., Hu, F., Hao, Q., Deep Learning for Intelligent Wireless Networks: A Comprehensive Survey. *IEEE Commun. Surv. Tutorials*, 1–1, 2018, 10.1109/COMST.2018.2846401.
5. Adewole, O., Scalability in Artificial Intelligence, 2023.
6. The Future of Artificial Intelligence in Blockchain Applications, in: *Adv. Syst. Anal. Softw. Eng. High Perform. Comput. Book Ser.*, pp. 346–373, Dec. 2023, doi: 10.4018/978-1-6684-8531-6.ch018.
7. *Applications and Future Trends of Artificial Intelligence and Blockchain-Powered Augmented Reality*, Aug. 07, 2023, doi: 10.1515/9783110785234-009.
8. The Prospect of Blockchain Application in The Field of Artificial Intelligence. *Acad. J. Sci. Technol.*, Jun. 2023, doi: 10.54097/ajst.v6i1.9098.
9. Mohd Shari, N.F. and Malip, A., State-of-the-art solutions of blockchain technology for data dissemination in smart cities: A comprehensive review. *Comput. Commun.*, 189, 120–147, May 2022, doi: 10.1016/j.comcom.2022.03.013.
10. Lincy, S.S.B.T., *Artificial Intelligence (AI) Driven Industrial Automation*, 2024, doi: 10.1201/9781003516668-4.
11. Wolf, P., Ensuring Safe Autonomy: Navigating the Future of Autonomous Vehicles, *arXiv.org*, 2024, doi: 10.48550/arxiv.2403.19006.
12. Feng, S., Integrating artificial intelligence in financial services: Enhancements, applications, and future directions. *Appl. Comput. Eng.*, 2024, doi: 10.54254/2755-2721/69/20241455&rdquo.
13. Iftikhar, A., Qureshi, K.N., Shiraz, M., Albahli, S., Security, trust and privacy risks, responses, and solutions for high-speed smart cities networks: A systematic literature review. *J. King Saud Univ. Comput. Inf. Sci.*, 35, 9, 101788, Oct. 2023, doi: 10.1016/j.jksuci.2023.101788.
14. Radatz, J., Geraci, A., Katki, F., IEEE standard glossary of software engineering terminology. *IEEE Std.*, 610121990, 121990, 3, 1990.

15. Noura, M., Atiquzzaman, M., Gaedke, M., Interoperability in Internet of Things Infrastructure: Classification, Challenges, and Future Work, in: *Third International Conference, IoTaaS 2017, Taichung, Taiwan, September 20–22, 2017, Proceedings*, pp. 11–18, 2018, doi: 10.1007/978-3-030-00410-1_2.
16. Lin, C.-H. and Chen, Y.-Y., Quantum Deep Hyperspectral Satellite Remote Sensing, 2023, doi: 10.1109/igarss52108.2023.10282472.
17. Wulff, E., Girone, M., Southwick, D., Cuba, E., Hyperparameter optimization, quantum-assisted model performance prediction, and benchmarking of AI-based High Energy Physics workloads using HPC, *arXiv.org*, 2023, doi: 10.48550/arXiv.2303.15053.
18. Xu, Y. and Li, Y., Application of Computer Aided 5G Technology in Wireless Intelligent Network Communication System, 2023, doi: 10.1109/indiscon58499.2023.10270688.
19. Gunturu, V.V., Ranga, J., Murthy, C.R., Swapna, B., Balaram, A., Raja, C., Artificial Intelligence Integrated with 5G for Future Wireless Networks, 2023, doi: 10.1109/ICICT57646.2023.10134364.
20. Premium Photo, 5G network digital hologram and internet of things on city, Freepik. Accessed: Jul. 31, 2024. [Online]. Available: https://www.freepik.com/premium-photo/5g-network-digital-hologram-internet-things-city_5122889.htm.
21. Bale, A.S., Hashim, M.F., Bundele, K.S., Vaishnav, J., *9 Applications and future trends of Artificial Intelligence and blockchain-powered Augmented Reality*, 2023, doi: 10.1515/9783110785234-009.
22. Sung, P. and Siraz, M., *Intelligent 5G Networks and Augmented Virtual Reality in Smart Transportation*, 2023, doi: 10.1201/9781003248750-6.
23. Qayyum, A., Butt, M.A., Ali, H., Usman, M., Halabi, O., Al-Fuqaha, A., Abbasi, Q.H., Imran, M., Qadir, J., Secure and Trustworthy Artificial Intelligence-Extended Reality (AI-XR) for Metaverses, *arXiv.org*, 2022, doi: 10.48550/arXiv.2210.13289.
24. How Generative AI Shaping the Future of AR and VR Experiences?, Accessed: Jul. 31, 2024. [Online]. Available: https://www.solulab.com/generative-ai-shaping-future-of-ar-and-vr/.
25. Nguyen, C.T., Liu, Y., Du, H., Hoang, D.T., Niyato, D., Nguyen, D.N., Mao, S., Generative AI-enabled Blockchain Networks: Fundamentals, Applications, and Case Study, *arXiv.org*, 2024, doi: 10.48550/arxiv.2401.15625.
26. Dhieb, N., Ghazzai, H., Besbes, H., Massoud, Y., *Scalable and Secure Architecture for Distributed IoT Systems*, pp. 1–6, 2020, 10.1109/TEMSCON47658.2020.9140108.
27. Gantayat, P.K. and Tiwari, R., Spider Monkey Algorithm for Enhancing Security in Delay Tolerant Network. *Int. J. Comput. Digital Syst.*, 14, 1, 2023.
28. Gantayat, P.K. and Das, S., Award-Reward Protocol Based on Clustering and Trust Level for Routing in Delay Tolerant Network. *J. Appl. Secur. Res., (Taylor and Francis)*, 14, 3, 270–285, (Scopus) https://doi.org/10.1080/19361610.2019.1621593.

29. Gantayat, P.K. and Das, S., Harris-Hawk and Jaya Algorithm for Routing In Delay Tolerant Network. *Int. J. Bus. Data Commun. Networking (Scopus)*, 17, 1, 38–54, IGI Global, 2021, DOI: 10.4018/IJBDCN.2021010103.
30. Gantayat, P.K. and Das, S., Secure Trust Level Routing in Delay Tolerant Network with Fuzzy Empowered Node Categorization Technique. *J. Comput. Theor. Nano Sci. (Scopus)*, 16, 5-6, 2294–2298.
31. Gantayat, P.K., Mohanthy, S., Gochhayat, S., Various routing protocol in DTN. *Int. J. Inf. Technol. Mech. Eng.*, 2, 11, November 2016.
32. Gantayat, P.K. and Jena, S.S.P., Delay Tolerent Network-A Survey. *Int. J. Adv. Res. Comput. Commun. Eng.*, 4, 7, July 2015.
33. Acharya, B.R. and Gantayat, P.K., Recognition of Human Unusual Activity in Surveillance Videos. *Int. J. Res. Sci. Innov.*, 2, 7, 18–26, July 2015, ISSN 2321-2705.
34. Panda, C., Patro, S.N., Gantayat, P.K., Node reliability in WDM Optical Network. *Int. J. Comput. Sci. Issues (IJCSI)*, 9, 2, 2012.
35. Panda, C., Patro, S.N., Gantayat, P.K., Link Reliability in WDM Optical Network. *Indian J. Comput. Sci. Eng. (IJCSI)*, 3, 1, 126–132, 2012.
36. Gantayat, P.K., Tiwari, R.G., Misra, A., An Optimization Based Anonymous Messaging System for Data Security in Delay Tolerant Network. *2022 IEEE International Conference on Data Science and Information System (ICDSIS)*, IEEE.
37. Tiwari, R.G., Jain, A.K., Gantayat, P.K., Jain, N., Jindal, V., Ant Lion Based Optimized Leach Protocol to Enhance the Security and Transmission of Wireless Sensor Network. *2022 International Interdisciplinary Conference on Mathematics, Engineering and Science (MESIICON)*, IEEE.
38. Gantayat, P.K. and Das, S., A Hybrid Route Optimization In Delay Tolerant Network. *2nd International Conference on Advances in Distributed Computing and Machine Learning (ICADCML- 2021)*, 15-16 January 2021, Springer.
39. Gantayat, P.K. and Das, S., Optimized Trust and Reputation based Routing in Delay Tolerant Network. *4th International Conference on Smart Computing and Informatics (SCI-2020)*, 9-10, October 2020, Springer.
40. Gantayat, P.K., *et al.*, Security Issues In DTN. *International Interdisciplinary Conference On Engineering Science & Management*, Goa, India, 17th - 18th December 2016, ISBN: 9788193137383.
41. Pradosh Kumar Gantayat, and Das, S., Optimization Trust and Reputation based Routing Protocol in Delay Tolerant Network, in: *Data Engineering and Intelligent Computing*, Springer, Singapore, 2021.
42. Gantayat, P.K., Dash, S., Mohanthy, S., Liver Disease Prediction using Machine Learning Algorithm, in: *Data Engineering and Intelligent Computing*, Springer, Singapore, 2021.
43. Gantayat, P.K. and Mohanthy, S., Employee Churn Management using AI, in: *Artificial Intelligence and Machine Learning in Business management, Concepts, Challenges and Case Studies*, CRC Press, Taylor and Francis Group, 2021.

44. Gantayat, P.K., Das, S., Tripathy, B., Hybrid Route Optimization Mechanism in Delay Tolerant network, in: *Advances in Distributed Computing and Machine Learning*, Springer, Singapore, 2021.
45. Panda, S.K. and Satapathy, S.C., An Investigation into Smart Contract Deployment on Ethereum Platform Using Web3.js and Solidity Using Blockchain, in: *Data Engineering and Intelligent Computing. Advances in Intelligent Systems and Computing*, vol. 1, V. Bhateja, S.C. Satapathy, C.M. Travieso-González, V.N.M. Aradhya (Eds.), Springer, Singapore, 2021, https://doi.org/10.1007/978-981-16-0171-2_52.
46. Panda, S.K., Rao, D.C., Satapathy, S.C., An Investigation into the Usability of Blockchain Technology in Internet of Things, in: *Data Engineering and Intelligent Computing. Advances in Intelligent Systems and Computing*, vol. 1, V. Bhateja, S.C. Satapathy, C.M. Travieso-González, V.N.M. Aradhya (Eds.), Springer, Singapore, 2021, https://doi.org/10.1007/978-981-16-0171-2_53.
47. Panda, S.K., Dash, S.P., Jena, A.K., Optimization of Block Query Response Using Evolutionary Algorithm, in: *Data Engineering and Intelligent Computing. Advances in Intelligent Systems and Computing*, vol. 1, V. Bhateja, S.C. Satapathy, C.M. Travieso-González, V.N.M. Aradhya (Eds.), Springer, Singapore, 2021, https://doi.org/10.1007/978-981-16-0171-2_54.
48. Nanda, S.K., Panda, S.K., Das, M., Satapathy, S.C., Automating Vehicle Insurance Process Using Smart Contract and Ethereum, in: *Advances in Micro-Electronics, Embedded Systems and IoT, Lecture Notes in Electrical Engineering*, vol. 838, V.V.S.S.S. Chakravarthy, W. Flores-Fuentes, V. Bhateja, B. Biswal, (Eds.), Springer, Singapore, 2022, https://doi.org/10.1007/978-981-16-8550-7_23.
49. Varaprasada Rao, K. and Panda, S.K., Secure Electronic Voting (E-voting) System Based on Blockchain on Various Platforms, in: *Computer Communication, Networking and IoT, Lecture Notes in Networks and Systems*, vol. 459, S.C. Satapathy, J.C.W. Lin, L.K. Wee, V. Bhateja, T.M. Rajesh, (Eds.), Springer, Singapore, 2023, https://doi.org/10.1007/978-981-19-1976-3_18.
50. Varaprasada Rao, K. and Panda, S.K., A Design Model of Copyright Protection System Based on Distributed Ledger Technology, in: *Computer Communication, Networking and IoT, Lecture Notes in Networks and Systems*, vol. 459, S.C. Satapathy, J.C.W. Lin, L.K. Wee, V. Bhateja, T.M. Rajesh, (Eds.), Springer, Singapore, 2023, https://doi.org/10.1007/978-981-19-1976-3_17.
51. Panda, S.K., Elngar, A.A., Balas, V.E., Kayed, M. (Eds.), *Bitcoin and Blockchain: History and Current Applications*, 1st ed., CRC Press, 2020, https://doi.org/10.1201/9781003032588.
52. Panda, S.K., Jena, A.K., Swain, S.K., Satapathy, S.C. (Eds.), *Blockchain Technology: Applications and Challenges*, Springer, Intelligent Systems Reference Library, https://doi.org/10.1007/978-3-030-69395-4.
53. Sathya, A.R., Panda, S.K., Hanumanthakari, S., Enabling Smart Education System Using Blockchain Technology, in: *Blockchain Technology: Applications and Challenges, Intelligent Systems Reference Library*, vol. 203, S.K. Panda,

A.K. Jena, S.K. Swain, S.C. Satapathy (Eds.), Springer, Cham, 2021, https://doi.org/10.1007/978-3-030-69395-4_10.
54. Lokre, S.S., Naman, V., Priya, S., Panda, S.K., Gun Tracking System Using Blockchain Technology, in: *Blockchain Technology: Applications and Challenges, Intelligent Systems Reference Library*, vol. 203, S.K. Panda, A.K. Jena, S.K. Swain, S.C. Satapathy (Eds.), Springer, Cham, 2021, https://doi.org/10.1007/978-3-030-69395-4_16.
55. Panda, S.K., Daliyet, S.P., Lokre, S.S., Naman, V., Distributed Ledger Technology in the Construction Industry Using Corda, in: *The New Advanced Society: Artificial Intelligence and Industrial Internet of Things Paradigm*, https://doi.org/10.1002/9781119884392.ch2.
56. Panda, S.K., Mohammad, G.B., Nandan Mohanty, S., Sahoo, S., Smart contract-based land registry system to reduce frauds and time delay. *Secur. Privacy*, e172, 2021, https://doi.org/10.1002/spy2.172.
57. Panda, S.K. and Satapathy, S.C., Drug traceability and transparency in medical supply chain using blockchain for easing the process and creating trust between stakeholders and consumers. *Pers. Ubiquitous Comput.*, 28, 75–91, 2024, https://doi.org/10.1007/s00779-021-01588-3.
58. Niveditha, V.R., Sekaran, K., Amandeep Singh, K., Panda, S.K., Effective prediction of bitcoin price using wolf search algorithm and bidirectional LSTM on internet of things data. *Int. J. Syst. Syst. Eng.*, 11, 3-4, 224–236.
59. Arza, M.S. and Panda, S.K., An Integration of Blockchain and Machine Learning into the Health Care System, in: *Machine Learning Adoption in Blockchain-Based Intelligent Manufacturing*, vol. 1, pp. 33–58, DOI: 10.1201/9781003252009-3.
60. Murala, D.K., Panda, S.K., Swain, S.K., A survey on cloud computing security and privacy issues and challenges. *J. Adv. Res. Dyn. Control Syst.*, 11, 1276–1290, 2019.
61. Murala, D.K., Panda, S.K., Swain, S.K., Secure dynamic groups data sharing with modified revocable attribute-based encryption in cloud. *Int. J. Recent Technol. Eng. (IJRTE)*, 8, 4, 2019, ISSN: 2277-3878.
62. Murala, D.K., Panda, S.K., Swain, S.K., A novel hybrid approach for providing data security and privacy from malicious attacks in the cloud environment. *J. Adv. Res. Dyn. Control Syst.*, 11, 1291–1300, 2019.
63. Panda, S.K., Swain, S.K., Mall, R., An investigation into usability aspects of E-Commerce websites using users' preferences. *Adv. Comput. Sci.: Int. J.*, 4, 1, 65–73, 2015.
64. Panda, S.K., Swain, S.K., Mall, R., Measuring Web Site Usability Quality Complexity Metrics for Navigability, in: *Intelligent Computing, Communication and Devices, Advances in Intelligent Systems and Computing*, vol. 308, L. Jain, S. Patnaik, N. Ichalkaranje (Eds.), Springer, New Delhi, 2015, https://doi.org/10.1007/978-81-322-2012-1_41.

65. Panda, S.K., A Usability Evaluation Framework for B2C E-Commerce Websites. *Comput. Eng. Intell. Syst.*, 5, 3, 66–85, 2014.
66. Bhalerao, V., Panda, S.K., Jena, A.K., Optimization of Loss Function on Human Faces Using Generative Adversarial Networks, in: *Machine Learning Approaches for Urban Computing, Studies in Computational Intelligence*, vol. 968, M. Bandyopadhyay, M. Rout, S. Chandra Satapathy (Eds.), Springer, Singapore, 2021, https://doi.org/10.1007/978-981-16-0935-0_9.
67. Panda, S.K. and Dwivedi, M., Minimizing Food Wastage Using Machine Learning: A Novel Approach, in: *Smart Intelligent Computing and Applications, Smart Innovation, Systems and Technologies*, vol. 159, S. Satapathy, V. Bhateja, J. Mohanty, S. Udgata, (Eds.), Springer, Singapore, 2020, https://doi.org/10.1007/978-981-13-9282-5_44.
68. Panda, S.K., Sathya, A.R., Mishra, M., Satpathy, S., A supervised learning algorithm to forecast weather conditions for playing cricket. *Int. J. Innov. Technol. Explor. Eng. (IJITEE)*, 9, 1, 2019.
69. Panda, S.K., Fraud-Resistant Crowdfunding System Using Ethereum Blockchain, in: *Bitcoin and Blockchain*, pp. 237–276, 2020.
70. Panda, S.K., Mishra, V., Balamurali, R., Elngar, A.A., *Artificial Intelligence and Machine Learning in Business Management Concepts, Challenges, and Case Studies*, pp. 1–278, https://doi.org/10.1201/9781003125129.
71. Joshi, S., Panda, S.K., Ar, S., Optimal Deep Learning Model to Identify the Development of Pomegranate Fruit in Farms. *Int. J. Innovative Technol. Explor. Eng.*, 9, 3, 2352–2356, 2020.
72. Puranam, K.S.RK., Gaddam, M.C.T., K, V.P.R., Panda, S.K., Reddy, G.S.M., Anatomy and Lifecycle of a Bitcoin Transaction. *Proceedings of International Conference on Sustainable Computing in Science, Technology and Management (SUSCOM)*, Amity University Rajasthan, Jaipur - India, February 26-28, 2019, Available at SSRN: https://ssrn.com/abstract=3355106 or http://dx.doi.org/10.2139/ssrn.3355106.
73. Panda, S.K. and Swain, S.K., Quality Assurance Aspects of Web Design, in: *Design Solutions for Improving Website Quality and Effectiveness*, pp. 87–129, IGI Global, 2016.
74. Panda, S.K., Bhalerao, V., Ar, S., A Machine Learning Model to Identify Duplicate Questions in Social Media Forums. *Int. J. Innovative Technol. Explor. Eng.*, 9, 4, 370–373, 2020.
75. Ahmareen, S., Raj, A., Potluri, S., Panda, S.K., Book Shala: An Android-Based Application Design and Implementation of Sharing Books, in: *Smart Intelligent Computing and Applications, Smart Innovation, Systems and Technologies*, vol. 159, S. Satapathy, V. Bhateja, J. Mohanty, S. Udgata (Eds.), Springer, Singapore, 2020, https://doi.org/10.1007/978-981-13-9282-5_28.
76. Panda, S.K., Das, S.S., Swain, S.K., S-Model for Service-Oriented Applications in Web Engineering, Regional College Of Management. 10, 3, 38–46, 2013.
77. Panda, S.K., An Investigation into Usability and Productivity of ECommerce Websites.

78. Panda, S.K., Chandrasekhar, A., Gantayat, P.K., Panda, M.R., Detecting Brain Tumor Using Image Segmentation: A Novel Approach, in: *Data Engineering and Intelligent Computing, Lecture Notes in Networks and Systems*, vol. 446, V. Bhateja, L. Khin Wee, J.C.W. Lin, S.C. Satapathy, T.M. Rajesh, (Eds.), Springer, Singapore, 2022, https://doi.org/10.1007/978-981-19-1559-8_35.
79. Sanghi, P., Panda, S.K., Pati, C., Gantayat, P.K., Learning Deep Features and Classification for Fresh or off Vegetables to Prevent Food Wastage Using Machine Learning Algorithms, in: *Intelligent Data Engineering and Analytics, Smart Innovation, Systems and Technologies*, vol. 266, S.C. Satapathy, P. Peer, J. Tang, V. Bhateja, A. Ghosh, (Eds.), Springer, Singapore, 2022, https://doi.org/10.1007/978-981-16-6624-7_44.
80. Gantayat, P.K., Mohapatra, S., Panda, S.K., Secure Trust Level Routing in Delay-Tolerant Network with Node Categorization Technique, in: *Intelligent Data Engineering and Analytics, Smart Innovation, Systems and Technologies*, vol. 266, S.C. Satapathy, P. Peer, J. Tang, V. Bhateja, A. Ghosh, (Eds.), Springer, Singapore, 2022, https://doi.org/10.1007/978-981-16-6624-7_45.
81. Panda, S.K., Urkude, S.V., Urkude, V.R., Vairachilai, S., An investigation into COVID 19 pandemic in India, in: *The New Advanced Society: Artificial Intelligence and Industrial Internet of Things Paradigm*, vol. 1, pp. 289–305, Wiley.
82. Panda, S.K., Das, S., Swain, S.K., Web Site Productivity Measurement Using Single Task Size Measure. *J. Inf. Sci. Comput. Technol. (JISCT)*, 4, 3, October 12, 2015.
83. Hanumanthakari, S. and Panda, S.K., Detecting Face Mask for Prevent COVID-19 Using Deep Learning: A Novel Approach, in: *Smart Intelligent Computing and Applications, Volume 2, Smart Innovation, Systems and Technologies*, vol. 283, S.C. Satapathy, V. Bhateja, M.N. Favorskaya, T. Adilakshmi, (Eds.), Springer, Singapore, 2022, https://doi.org/10.1007/978-981-16-9705-0_45.
84. Panda, S.K., Sathya, A.R., Das, S., Bitcoin: Beginning of the Cryptocurrency Era, in: *Recent Advances in Blockchain Technology, Intelligent Systems Reference Library*, vol. 237, S.K. Panda, V. Mishra, S.P. Dash, A.K. Pani, (Eds.), Springer, Cham, 2023, https://doi.org/10.1007/978-3-031-22835-3_2.
85. Murala, D.K., Panda, S.K., Sahoo, S.K., Securing Electronic Health Record System in Cloud Environment Using Blockchain Technology, in: *Recent Advances in Blockchain Technology, Intelligent Systems Reference Library*, vol. 237, S.K. Panda, V. Mishra, S.P. Dash, A.K. Pani, (Eds.), Springer, Cham, 2023, https://doi.org/10.1007/978-3-031-22835-3_4.
86. Rao, K.V., Murala, D.K., Panda, S.K., Blockchain: A Study of New Business Model, in: *Recent Advances in Blockchain Technology, Intelligent Systems Reference Library*, vol. 237, S.K. Panda, V. Mishra, S.P. Dash, A.K. Pani, (Eds.), Springer, Cham, 2023, https://doi.org/10.1007/978-3-031-22835-3_9.
87. Panda, S.K., Mishra, V., Dash, S.P., Pani, A.K., *Recent Advances in Blockchain Technology Real-World Applications*, Intelligent Systems Reference Library (ISRL, volume 237), vol. 1, pp. 1–317, 978-3-031-22835-3.

88. Panda, S.K., Mohapatra, R.K., Panda, S., Balamurugan, S., *The New Advanced Society: Artificial Intelligence and Industrial Internet of Things Paradigm*, vol. 1, pp. 1–512, John Wiley & Sons, DOI:10.1002/9781119884392.
89. Nanda, S.K., Panda, S.K., Das, M., Satapathy, S.C., Decentralization of Car Insurance System Using Machine Learning and Distributed Ledger Technology, in: *Intelligent Data Engineering and Analytics. FICTA 2022, Smart Innovation, Systems and Technologies*, vol. 327, V. Bhateja, X.S. Yang, J. Chun-Wei Lin, R. Das, (Eds.), Springer, Singapore, 2023, https://doi.org/10.1007/978-981-19-7524-0_52.
90. Nanda, S.K., Panda, S.K., Dash, M., Medical supply chain integrated with blockchain and IoT to track the logistics of medical products. *Multimedia Tools Appl.*, 82, 32917–32939, 2023, https://doi.org/10.1007/s11042-023-14846-8.
91. Panda, S.K., Jena, A.K., Panda, M.R., *et al.*, Speech emotion recognition using multimodal feature fusion with machine learning approach. *Multimedia Tools Appl.*, 82, 42763–42781, 2023, https://doi.org/10.1007/s11042-023-15275-3.
92. Panda, S.K. and Mohanty, S.N., Time Series Forecasting and Modeling of Food Demand Supply Chain Based on Regressors Analysis. *IEEE Access*, 11, 42679–42700, 2023, doi: 10.1109/ACCESS.2023.3266275.
93. Desai, D.D., *et al.*, Optimal Ambulance Positioning for Road Accidents With Deep Embedded Clustering. *IEEE Access*, 11, 59917–59934, 2023, doi: 10.1109/ACCESS.2023.3284993.
94. Lakshmi, L., Devi, K.D.S., Gupta, S., Reddy, K.A.N., Grandhi, S.K., Panda, S.K., WOMT: Wasserstein Distribution Based Minimization of False Positives in Breast Tumor Classification Using Deep Learning. *IEEE Access*, 11, 57831–57842, 2023, doi: 10.1109/ACCESS.2023.3279496.
95. Mishra, P. and Panda, S.K., Dependency Structure-Based Rules Using Root Node Technique for Explicit Aspect Extraction From Online Reviews. *IEEE Access*, 11, 65117–65137, 2023, doi: 10.1109/ACCESS.2023.3287830.
96. Routray, N., Rout, S.K., Sahu, B., Panda, S.K., Godavarthi, D., Ensemble Learning With Symbiotic Organism Search Optimization Algorithm for Breast Cancer Classification and Risk Identification of Other Organs on Histopathological Images. *IEEE Access*, 11, 110544–110557, 2023, doi: 10.1109/ACCESS.2023.3322222.
97. Agarwal, R., Pande, S.D., Mohanty, S.N., Panda, S.K., A Novel Hybrid System of Detecting Brain Tumors in MRI. *IEEE Access*, 11, 118372–118385, 2023, doi: 10.1109/ACCESS.2023.3326447.
98. Nayak, S.K., Garanayak, M., Swain, S.K., Panda, S.K., Godavarthi, D., An Intelligent Disease Prediction and Drug Recommendation Prototype by Using Multiple Approaches of Machine Learning Algorithms. *IEEE Access*, 11, 99304–99318, 2023, doi: 10.1109/ACCESS.2023.3314332.
99. Gupta, A., Gandhi, R., Jatana, N., Jatain, D., Panda, S.K., Ramesh, J.V.N., A Severity Assessment of Python Code Smells. *IEEE Access*, 11, 119146–119160, 2023, doi: 10.1109/ACCESS.2023.3327553.

100. Murala, D.K., Panda, S.K., Dash, S.P., MedMetaverse: Medical Care of Chronic Disease Patients and Managing Data Using Artificial Intelligence, Blockchain, and Wearable Devices State-of-the-Art Methodology. *IEEE Access*, 11, 138985, 2023, doi: 10.1109/ACCESS.2023.3340791.
101. Sethi, B.K., Singh, D., Rout, S.K., Panda, S.K., Long Short-Term Memory-Deep Belief Network-Based Gene Expression Data Analysis for Prostate Cancer Detection and Classification. *IEEE Access*, 12, 1508–1524, 2024, doi: 10.1109/ACCESS.2023.3346925.
102. Mahapatra, A., Majhi, S.K., Mishra, K., Pradhan, R., Rao, D.C., Panda, S.K., An Energy-Aware Task Offloading and Load Balancing for Latency-Sensitive IoT Applications in the Fog-Cloud Continuum. *IEEE Access*, 12, 14334–14349, 2024, doi: 10.1109/ACCESS.2024.3357122.
103. Mishra, P., Sharma, O., Panda, S.K., ADN-BERT: Attention-Based Deep Network Model Using BERT for Sarcasm Classification, in: *Evolution in Computational Intelligence. FICTA 2023, Smart Innovation, Systems and Technologies*, vol. 370, V. Bhateja, X.S. Yang, M.C. Ferreira, S.S. Sengar, C.M. Travieso-Gonzalez (Eds.), Springer, Singapore, 2023, https://doi.org/10.1007/978-981-99-6702-5_51.
104. Varaprasada Rao, K. and Panda, S.K., Initiation, Innovation, Implementation and Integration of CBDC in Digital Virtual Payment Systems, in: *Advances in Microelectronics, Embedded Systems and IoT. ICMEET 2023, Lecture Notes in Electrical Engineering*, vol. 1156, V.V.S.S.S. Chakravarthy, V. Bhateja, J. Anguera, S. Urooj, A. Ghosh, (Eds.), Springer, Singapore, 2024, https://doi.org/10.1007/978-981-97-0767-6_20.
105. Murala, D.K. and Panda, S.K., Artificial intelligence in the development of metaverse, in: *Metaverse and Immersive Technologies: An Introduction to Industrial Business and Social Applications*, pp. 407–436, Wiley, Hoboken, NJ, USA, 2023.
106. Murala, D.K. and Panda, S.K., Metaverse: A study on immersive technologies, in: *Metaverse and Immersive Technologies: An Introduction to Industrial Business and Social Applications*, Wiley, Hoboken, NJ, USA, 2023.
107. Murala, D.K. and Panda, S.K., The Internet of Things in developing metaverse, in: *Metaverse and Immersive Technologies: An Introduction to Industrial Business and Social Applications*, Wiley, Hoboken, NJ, USA, 2023.
108. Murala, D.K. and Panda, S.K., Blockchain in the development of metaverse, in: *Metaverse and Immersive Technologies: An Introduction to Industrial Business and Social Applications*, p. 1002, Wiley, USA.
109. Murala, D.K. and Panda, S.K., The role of immersive reality (AR/VR/MR/XR) in metaverse, in: *Metaverse and Immersive Technologies: An Introduction to Industrial Business and Social Applications*, pp. 159–189, Wiley, Hoboken, NJ, USA, 2023.
110. Panda, S.K., Revolution of the Metaverse and Blockchain Technology, in: *Metaverse and Immersive Technologies: An Introduction to Industrial Business and Social Applications*, Wiley, Hoboken, NJ, USA, 2023.

111. Sahoo, S.K., Das, S., Panda, S.K., Alzheimer's Disease Classification Using Brain MRI Based on 2D CNN and Transfer Learning, in: *Proceedings of the 6th International Conference on Communications and Cyber Physical Engineering . ICCCE 2024, Lecture Notes in Electrical Engineering*, vol. 1096, A. Kumar, and S. Mozar, (Eds.), Springer, Singapore, 2024, https://doi.org/10.1007/978-981-99-7137-4_1.
112. Panda, S.K., Ramesh, J.V.N., Ghosh, H., Rahat, I.S., Sobur, A., Bijoy, M.H., Yesubabu, M., Deep Learning in Medical Imaging: A Case Study on Lung Tissue Classification. *EAI Endorsed Trans. Pervasive Health Technol.*, 10, 2024.
113. Paruchuri, V.N.L.L., Shaik, A.H., Murala, D.K., Panda, S.K., IoT-Enabled Neural Network Analysis for Early Detection and Prediction of Mental Depression, in: *Information System Design: Communication Networks and IoT. ISDIA 2024, Lecture Notes in Networks and Systems*, vol. 1057, V. Bhateja, J. Tang, D.K. Sharma, Z. Polkowski, A. Ahmad, (Eds.), pp. 257–268, Springer, Singapore, 2024, https://doi.org/10.1007/978-981-97-4895-2_21.
114. Paruchuri, V.N.L.L., Malaviya, M.P., Murala, D.K., Panda, S.K., Connecting IoT Sensors for Enhanced Dementia Disease Monitoring and Intervention, in: *Information System Design: Communication Networks and IoT. ISDIA 2024, Lecture Notes in Networks and Systems*, vol. 1057, V. Bhateja, J. Tang, D.K. Sharma, Z. Polkowski, A. Ahmad, (Eds.), pp. 269–281, Springer, Singapore, 2024, https://doi.org/10.1007/978-981-97-4895-2_22.
115. Panda, S.K., Das, S., Sahoo, S.K., Predominant Music Genre Classification Using Machine Learning Approach, in: *Signal Processing, Telecommunication and Embedded Systems with AI and ML Applications. ICMEET 2023, Lecture Notes in Electrical Engineering*, vol. 1281, V. Bhateja, V.V.S.S.S. Chakravarthy, J. Anguera, A. Ghosh, W. Flores Fuentes, (Eds.), Springer, Singapore, 2025, https://doi.org/10.1007/978-981-97-8422-6_17.
116. Panda, S.K., Das, S., Sahoo, S.K., Vehicle Detection and Classification Using Intelligent Systems, in: *Signal Processing, Telecommunication and Embedded Systems with AI and ML Applications. ICMEET 2023, Lecture Notes in Electrical Engineering*, vol. 1281, V. Bhateja, V.V.S.S.S. Chakravarthy, J. Anguera, A. Ghosh, W. Flores Fuentes, (Eds.), Springer, Singapore, 2025, https://doi.org/10.1007/978-981-97-8422-6_18.
117. Chandrasekhar, A., Dodhiawala, Z., Panda, S.K., An Investigation into Chronic Kidney Disease Based-on Classification Model, in: *Signal Processing, Telecommunication and Embedded Systems with AI and ML Applications. ICMEET 2023, Lecture Notes in Electrical Engineering*, vol. 1281, V. Bhateja, V.V.S.S.S. Chakravarthy, J. Anguera, A. Ghosh, W. Flores Fuentes, (Eds.), Springer, Singapore, 2025, https://doi.org/10.1007/978-981-97-8422-6_19.
118. Chandrashekhar, A., Saheb, S.H., Panda, S.K., Balamurugan, S., Peng, S.-L., *Metaverse and Immersive Technologies: An Introduction to Industrial, Business and Social Applications*, John Wiley & Sons, 2023.

2

Hyper-Intelligence in Machine Learning: Unleashing the Next Evolution of AI

Tejinder Kaur[1]*, Kiran Rani Panwar[2], Ankita[3], Mukesh Soni[4], Neelam Oberoi[5] and Pokkuluri Kiran Sree[6]

[1]*Department of MMICTBM, Maharishi Markandeshwar (Deemed to be University), Mullana, Ambala-Haryana, India*
[2]*Subharti Department of Liberal Arts and Humanities (FASS) Swami Vivekanand Subharti University, Meerut (U.P.), India*
[3]*Department of Computer Applications, Panipat Institute of Engineering and Technology, Samalkha, Panipat, Haryana, India*
[4]*Division of Research and Development, Lovely Professional University, Phagwara, India*
[5]*Department of Computer Science & Engineering, MMEC, Maharishi, Markandeshwar (Deemed to be University), Mullana-Ambala, Haryana, India*
[6]*Computer Science and Engineering, Shri Vishnu Engineering College for Women(A), Vishnupur, Bhimavaram, India*

Abstract
The concept of hyper-intelligence represents the pinnacle of artificial intelligence, where systems surpass the cognitive capabilities of the most brilliant human minds. This chapter explores the foundations, current state of research, and future directions of hyper-intelligence in machine learning. By examining advanced neural networks, reinforcement learning, and quantum computing, we outline the technological underpinnings necessary for hyper-intelligent systems. Additionally, we discuss the ethical, societal, and technical challenges associated with developing such systems and propose a framework for their responsible and beneficial deployment.

***Keywords*:** Neural networks, reinforcement learning, quantum computing

**Corresponding author*: teji7890@gmail.com

Pradosh Kumar Gantayat, Sandeep Kumar Panda, S. Balamurugan and Sheng-Lung Peng (eds.) Hyper-Intelligent Networks: Exploring the Future of Connectivity for Society 5.0, (31–42) © 2026 Scrivener Publishing LLC

2.1 Introduction to Hyper-Intelligence

2.1.1 Defining Hyper-Intelligence

Hyper-intelligence in machine learning (ML) represents a quantum leap in artificial intelligence (AI) capabilities, transcending the boundaries of traditional AI systems. These systems exhibit extraordinary learning abilities, adaptability, and cognitive skills that enable them to perform at superhuman levels in complex tasks. This chapter introduces the concept of hyper-intelligence, outlining its significance and setting the stage for an in-depth exploration of its foundations, applications, and implications. AI has made remarkable strides over the past decade, with ML at the core of this progress. Yet, the ultimate goal remains the creation of hyper-intelligent systems—those that can learn, adapt, and innovate beyond human capabilities. This paper seeks to define hyper-intelligence, review pioneering efforts in the field, and address the challenges and implications of such advancements. The concept of AI has evolved significantly over the years, driven by advancements in computer science, mathematics, cognitive science, and other disciplines.

2.1.2 Historical Context (Andries P. *et al.*, 2013) [1]

The evolution of AI has been marked by significant milestones, from the development of simple rule-based systems to the advent of deep learning (Andries P. *et al.*, 2013) [1]. Hyper-intelligent ML is the latest paradigm, building on previous advancements and introducing new capabilities that promise to revolutionize various fields (Andries P. *et al.*, 2013).

2.2 Theoretical Foundations (Andries P. *et al.*, 2013) [1]

2.2.1 Autonomous Learning (Battisti G. *et al.*, 2010) [2]

Autonomous learning allows hyper-intelligent systems to learn and adapt without direct human intervention. This capability is achieved through advanced neural network architectures and reinforcement learning algorithms (Battisti G. *et al.*, 2010) [2].

2.2.2 Complex Problem Solving (Battisti G. *et al.*, 2010) [2]

Hyper-intelligent systems are designed to tackle complex, multi-faceted problems that require sophisticated reasoning and decision-making abilities. This involves integrating symbolic reasoning with neural networks, creating neurosymbolic AI (Battisti G. *et al.*, 2010) [2].

2.2.3 Contextual Understanding (Battisti G. *et al.*, 2010) [2]

The ability to understand and utilize contextual information is crucial for hyper-intelligent systems. This involves leveraging large language models and contextual embeddings to interpret and respond to nuanced information (Bughin J. *et al.*, 2017) [3].

2.3 Core Technologies (Christensen C.M. *et al.*, 1992) [4]

2.3.1 Advanced Neural Networks (Christensen C.M. *et al.*, 1992) [4]

The backbone of hyper-intelligent systems includes state-of-the-art neural network architectures such as transformers, convolution neural networks, and recurrent neural networks (Christensen C.M. *et al.*, 1992) [4].

2.3.2 Reinforcement Learning (RL) (Cockburn I.M. *et al.*, 2018) [5]

This chapter explores advanced RL techniques and their applications (Coombs R. *et al.*, 2000) [6].

2.3.3 Meta-Learning (Coombs R. *et al.*, 2000) [6]

Meta-learning, or "learning to learn," allows hyper-intelligent systems to rapidly adapt to new tasks with minimal data, enhancing their versatility and efficiency (Coombs R. *et al.*, 2000) [6].

2.3.4 Quantum Computing (C. Huang *et al.*, 2020) [7]

Quantum computing offers the computational power needed to process vast amounts of data and solve complex problems at unprecedented speeds, making it a key enabler of hyper-intelligent ML (C.-X. Wang. *et al.*, 2020) [8].

2.4 Practical Applications (Davenport T.H. *et al.*, 1993) [9]

2.4.1 Healthcare (Davenport T.H. *et al.*, 1993) [9]

Hyper-intelligent systems are transforming healthcare through predictive analytics, personalized medicine, and accelerated drug discovery. These applications leverage vast medical datasets and advanced modelling techniques to improve patient outcomes (Erevelles S. *et al.*, 2016) [10].

2.4.2 Autonomous Systems (E. C. Strinati *et al.*, 2019) [11]

In autonomous systems, hyper-intelligent ML powers self-driving vehicles, drones, and smart infrastructure. These systems navigate complex environments with high precision and adapt to changing conditions in real-time (F. Tariq *et al.*, 2020) [12].

2.4.3 Financial Services (Freeman C. *et al.*, 2001) [13]

The financial industry benefits from hyper-intelligent ML through enhanced market analysis, fraud detection, and automated trading strategies. These applications utilize advanced algorithms to process diverse data sources and provide actionable insights.

2.4.4 Natural Language Processing (NLP) (G. Liu *et al.*, 2020) [14]

Hyper-intelligent NLP systems offer advanced language capabilities, including conversational agents, high-accuracy translation services, and sophisticated content generation.

2.5 Ethical and Societal Implications (G. H. Walker *et al.*, 2018) [15]

2.5.1 Bias and Fairness

Ensuring that hyper-intelligent systems are free from biases and provide equitable outcomes is a critical ethical concern. This chapter discusses methods to identify and mitigate biases in data and algorithms (G. Baxter *et al.*, 2011) [16].

2.5.2 Transparency

Developing transparent AI systems that allow users to understand and trust their decisions is essential. This involves creating interpretable models and providing clear explanations of their workings (Henderson R.M. *et al.*, 1990) [17].

2.5.3 Accountability (Johnson M.W. *et al.*, 2008) [18]

Establishing accountability frameworks is necessary to address the potential risks and harms associated with hyper-intelligent systems. This includes legal and regulatory considerations.

2.5.4 Privacy Concerns (J. Y. Lee *et al.*, 2020) [19]

The vast data requirements of hyper-intelligent ML raise significant privacy concerns. This chapter explores strategies to protect data privacy while enabling advanced AI capabilities.

2.6 Future Prospects

2.6.1 Human–AI Collaboration (J. Lee *et al.*, 2019) [20]

The future of hyper-intelligent ML lies in fostering effective human–AI collaboration. This involves developing user-centric interfaces and systems that augment human capabilities.

2.6.2 Continuous Learning (K. David *et al.*, 2018) [21]

Hyper-intelligent systems must continuously learn and adapt to stay relevant. This chapter discusses ongoing research and developments aimed at enhancing the lifelong learning capabilities of AI (K. B. Letaief *et al.*, 2019) [22].

2.6.3 Societal Transformation

Hyper-intelligent ML has the potential to drive profound societal changes, from transforming industries to reshaping the workforce (Laursen K. *et al.*, 2003) [23]. This chapter explores these potential impacts and the steps needed to manage them responsibly (Makridakis S. *et al.*, 2017) [24].

2.7 Case Studies

Case Study 1: Hyper-Intelligent Healthcare (Nijssen E.J. *et al.*, 2006) [25].
A detailed examination of how hyper-intelligent ML is revolutionizing diagnostics, treatment planning, and medical research.
Case Study 2: Autonomous Transportation (Popper R. *et al.*, 2008) [26] (Rindfleisch A. *et al.*, 2017) [27]. An exploration of the development and deployment.
Case Study 3: Financial Analytics (Sirilli G. *et al.*, 1998) [28].
A look at how hyper-intelligent ML models are transforming financial services, from predictive market analysis to real-time fraud detection (Tushman M.L. *et al.*, 1986) [29], (Utterback J.M. *et al.*, 1996) [30], (Yu X. *et al.*, 2016) [31].

Education: AI-driven tools personalize learning experiences, grade assignments, and offer tutoring.
Entertainment: AI recommends content on streaming platforms, creates realistic video game environments, and even composes music.

Ethical and Social Considerations (Yu X. *et al.*, 2016) [31]
Privacy: AI-driven data collection and analysis pose significant privacy concerns.
Autonomy and Control: Ensuring that AI systems operate within the bounds of human control and ethical guidelines is crucial.

2.8 Prospective Research Avenues

The future of AI promises further integration into everyday life and the development of even more sophisticated systems. Key areas of research include:

General AI: Developing machines with generalized cognitive abilities akin to human intelligence.
Hyper-intelligence refers to AI systems that exhibit cognitive abilities far surpassing those of humans. These systems would not only excel in specific tasks but also demonstrate superior general intelligence, creativity, and problem-solving skills. The distinction between hyper-intelligence and other forms of AI lies in the magnitude of their capabilities and their potential to innovate autonomously (Yu X. *et al.*, 2016) [31].

2.9 Core Technologies (Yu X. *et al.*, 2016) [31]

2.9.1 Advanced Neural Networks

Deep learning has been instrumental in achieving state-of-the-art performance in various domains. For hyper-intelligence, neural networks must evolve into more sophisticated architectures, potentially incorporating multi-modal data integration and hierarchical learning processes.

2.9.2 Reinforcement Learning

Reinforcement learning (RL) enables agents to learn optimal behaviors through trial and error. Hyper-intelligent systems would leverage advanced RL techniques, including meta-learning and lifelong learning.

Quantum algorithms could solve complex optimization problems and simulate large-scale neural networks, accelerating the development of hyper-intelligent systems. An artificial general intelligence (AGI) system would possess the ability to perform any intellectual task that a human can, setting the stage for further advancements toward hyper-intelligence.

2.9.3 Pioneering Efforts

Leading Research Institutions (Yu X. *et al.*, 2016) [31]
Institutions like OpenAI and DeepMind are at the forefront of hyper-intelligence research. OpenAI's GPT series and DeepMind's AlphaGo and

AlphaFold project highlight significant strides in creating more capable and adaptable AI systems.

2.9.4 Neuroscience-Inspired AI

Neuromorphic computing and other neuroscience-inspired approaches aim to replicate the efficiency and learning capabilities of the human brain. These efforts seek to bridge the gap between human and machine intelligence, facilitating the development of hyper-intelligent systems.

2.10 Collaborative AI

Collaborative AI projects focus on creating systems that work together to achieve collective intelligence this approach leverages the strengths of multiple AI agents, potentially leading to emergent hyper-intelligent behaviors.

2.10.1 Breakthrough Innovations

Transformers and Attention Mechanisms
The advent of transformer models has revolutionized NLP and other AI fields. These models utilize self-attention mechanisms to weigh the importance of different inputs, leading to superior performance and scalability.

2.10.2 Self-Supervised Learning

Self-supervised learning reduces the dependency on labelled data by enabling systems to learn from vast amounts of unstructured data. This approach is crucial for developing more generalized AI models, a key component of hyper-intelligence.

Initiatives like the IEEE's Ethically Aligned Design and AI for Good programs aim to ensure that AI technologies benefit humanity while adhering to ethical standards.

2.11 Challenges and Future Directions

Challenges of Artificial Intelligence
Algorithmic Fairness: Developing algorithms that treat all users and groups fairly is a significant challenge.

Security Risks: (Yu X. *et al.*, 2016) [31]
Robustness: Ensuring AI systems are robust and secure against various types of attacks and failures is critical.

Ethical and Moral Issues:
Autonomy: As AI systems become more autonomous, questions arise about their decision-making capabilities and the ethical implications of their actions.

Regulation and Governance:
Regulatory Frameworks: Developing appropriate regulatory frameworks that balance innovation with protection of public interest is a significant challenge.
Global Standards: Establishing international standards and agreements on the use and Impact on Employment.

2.11.1 Future Directions of Artificial Intelligence

Advancements in General AI: (Yu X. *et al.*, 2016) [31]
Artificial General Intelligence (AGI): Researchers are working towards creating AGI, which would possess generalized.

Improving Explain ability and Transparency:
Their decisions more understandable to humans are a key research area.

Human–AI Collaboration:
Augmented Intelligence: AI is quickly becoming a talking point about human potential. From personalized learning and intelligent healthcare diagnostics to design and the creative arts, AI systems are helping individuals achieve tasks faster and with greater accuracy. Future advances will likely focus on human-AI collaboration – creating systems that not only automate but also enhance human decision-making and creativity.
Collaborative AI: Designing AI systems that can effectively collaborate with humans, understanding context, and providing relevant assistance.

Advances in Specific AI Subfields:
Computer Vision: With applications in areas like healthcare imaging, autonomous vehicles, and security.

Ethical and Responsible AI Development:
Diagnostic Tools: Enhancing diagnostic accuracy and speed with AI-powered tools, leading to better patient care.

Sustainability and Climate Change: (Yu X. *et al.*, 2016) [31]
Energy Efficiency: Applying AI to optimize energy use in various sectors, contributing to sustainability efforts (Yu X. *et al.*, 2016).

Education and Lifelong Learning: (Yu X. *et al.*, 2016) [31]
Adaptive Learning: Developing AI-driven educational tools that provide personalized learning experiences for students of all ages.
Lifelong Learning: Supporting lifelong learning and continuous skill development to help individuals (Yu X. *et al.*, 2016) [31].

In conclusion, while AI holds tremendous potential to transform various aspects of society, addressing its challenges is are realized in a fair, ethical, and inclusive manner. Advancements in technology, thoughtful regulation, and ongoing efforts to align AI development with human values and societal needs.

A recapitulation of the major themes and insights is discussed in the book, emphasizing the transformative potential of hyper-intelligent ML.

2.12 Future Directions

This section provides a perspective on future advances and research areas in hyper-intelligent machine learning, highlights key areas for further research and provides a call to action for researchers and developers.

Hyper-intelligence represents the next frontier in the evolution of AI, promising unparalleled advancements in cognitive capabilities and problem-solving. While the journey is fraught with technical, ethical, and societal challenges, the potential benefits of hyper-intelligent systems are immense.

References

1. Andries, P. and Debackere, K., Business-model innovation: Propositions on the appropriateness of different learning approaches. *Creat. Innov. Manage.*, 22, 4, 337–358, 2013. https://doi.org/10.1111/caim.12033.

2. Battisti, G. and Stoneman, P., How Innovative are UK Firms? Evidence from the Fourth UK Community Innovation Survey on Synergies between Technological and Organizational Innovations. *Br. J. Manage.*, 21, 1, 187–206, 2010. https://doi.org/10.1111/j.1467-8551.2009.00629.
3. Bughin, J., Hazan, E., Ramaswamy, S., Chui, M., Allas, T., Dahlström, P., Henke, N., Trench, M., *Artificial Intelligence: The Next Digital Frontier?*, McKinsey Global Institute, New York, 2017McKinsey Global Institute Discussion Papers, June 2017.
4. Christensen, C.M., Exploring the limits of the technology S-Curve. Part I: Component technologies. *Prod. Oper. Manage.*, 1, 4, 334–357, 1992a. https://doi.org/10.1111/j.1937-5956.1992.tb00001.x.
5. Cockburn, I.M., Henderson, R., Stern, S., *The Impact of Artificial Intelligence on Innovation (NBER Working Paper w24449)*, National Bureau of Economic Research, Cambridge, MA, 2018.
6. Coombs, R. and Miles, I., Innovation, measurement and services: The new problematique, in: *Innovation Systems in the Service Economy. Measurement and Case Study Analysis*, J.S. Metcalfe and I. Miles (Eds.), pp. 85–103, Springer, Heidelberg, Dordrecht, London, New York, 2000, https://doi.org/10.1007/978-1-4615-4425-8.
7. Huang, C., *et al.*, Holographic MIMO surfaces for 6G wireless networks: Opportunities, challenges, and trends. *IEEE Wireless Commun.*, 27, 5, 118–125, Oct. 2020.
8. Wang, C.-X., *et al.*, 6G wireless channel measurements and models: Trends and challenges. *IEEE Veh. Technol. Mag.*, 15, 4, 22–32, Dec. 2020.
9. Davenport, T.H., *Process innovation: Reengineering work through information technology*, Harvard Business School Press, Cambridge, MA, 1993.
10. Erevelles, S., Fukawa, N., Swayne, L., Big Data consumer analytics and the transformation of marketing. *J. Bus. Res.*, 69, 2, 897–904, 2016. https://doi.org/10.1016/j.jbusres.2015.07.001.
11. Strinati, E.C., *et al.*, 6G: The next frontier: From holographic messaging to artificial intelligence using subterahertz and visible light communication. *IEEE Veh. Technol. Mag.*, 14, 3, 42–50, Sep. 2019.
12. Tariq, F., *et al.*, A speculative study on 6G. *IEEE Wireless Commun.*, 27, 4, 118–125, Aug. 2020.
13. Freeman, C. and Louça, F., *As time goes by: The information revolution and the industrial revolutions in historical perspective*, Oxford University Press, Oxford, 2001.
14. Liu, G., *et al.*, Vision, requirements and network architecture of 6G mobile network beyond 2030. *China Commun.*, 17, 9, 92–104, Sep. 2020.
15. Walker, G.H., Stanton, N.A., Salmon, P.M., *et al.*, A review of socio technical systems theory: a classic concept for new command and control paradigms. *Theor. Issues Ergon. Sci.*, 9, 479–499, 2018.
16. Baxter, G. and Sommerville, I., Socio-technical systems: From design methods to systems engineering. *Interact. Comput.*, 23, 1, 4–17, 2011.

17. Henderson, R.M. and Clark, K.B., Architectural innovation: The reconfiguration of existing product technologies and the failure of established firms. *Adm. Sci. Q.*, 35, 1, 9–30, 1990. https://doi.org/10.2307/2393549.
18. Johnson, M.W., Christensen, C.M., Kagermann, H., Reinventing your business model. *Harv. Bus. Rev.*, 86, 12, 50–59, 2008. https://hbr.org/2008/12/reinventing-your-business-model, accessed 21.03.2022.
19. Lee, J.Y., A Study on Agile Transformation in the New Digital Age. *Int. J. Adv. Cult. Technol.*, 8, 1, 82–88, 2020, doi: DOI: https://doi.org/10.17703/IJACT.2020.8.1.82.
20. Lee, J., A Study on Research Trend Analysis and Topic Class Prediction of Digital Transformation using Text Mining. *Int. J. Adv. Smart Converg.*, 8, 2, 183–190, 2019, doi: DOI: https://doi.org/10.7236/IJASC.2019.8.2.183.
21. David, K. and Berndt, H., 6G vision and requirements: Is there any need for beyond 5G? *IEEE Veh. Technol. Mag.*, 13, 3, 72–80, Sep. 2018.
22. Letaief, K.B., *et al.*, The roadmap to 6G: AI empowered wireless networks. *IEEE Commun. Mag.*, 57, 8, 84–90, Aug. 2019.
23. Laursen, K. and Foss, N.J., New human resource management practices, complementarities and the impact on innovation performance. *Cambridge J. Econ.*, 27, 2, 243–263, 2003. https://doi.org/10.1093/cje/27.2.243.
24. Makridakis, S., The forthcoming Artificial Intelligence (AI) revolution: Its impact on society and firms. *Futures*, 90, 46–60, 2017. https://doi.org/10.1016/j.futures.2017.03.006.
25. Nijssen, E.J., Hillebrand, B., Vermeulen, P.A., Kemp, R.G., Exploring product and service innovation similarities and differences. *Int. J. Res. Mark.*, 23, 3, 241–251, 2006. https://doi.org/10.1016/j.ijresmar.2006.02.001.
26. Popper, R., Foresight methodology, in: *The Handbook of Technology Foresight: Concepts and Practice*, L. Georghiou, J.C. Harper, M. Keenan, I. Miles, R. Popper (Eds.), pp. 44–91, Edward Elgar, Cheltenham, 2008a.
27. Rindfleisch, A., O'Hern, M., Sachdev, V., The digital revolution, 3D printing, and innovation as data. *J. Prod. Innov. Manage.*, 34, 5, 681–690, 2017. https://doi.org/10.1111/jpim.12402.
28. Sirilli, G. and Evangelista, R., Technological innovation in services and manufacturing: Results from Italian surveys. *Res. Policy*, 27, 9, 881–899, 1998. https://doi.org/10.1016/S0048-7333(98)00084-5.
29. Tushman, M.L. and Anderson, P., Technological discontinuities and organizational environments. *Adm. Sci. Q.*, 31, 3, 439–465, 1986. https://doi.org/10.2307/2392832.
30. Utterback, J.M., *Mastering the Dynamics of Innovation. Harvard Business School Press, Cambridge, MA,* 1996.
31. Yu, X., Nguyen, B., Chen, Y.S., Internet of things capability and alliance: Entrepreneurial orientation, market orientation and product and process innovation. *Internet Res.*, 26, 2, 402–434, 2016. https://doi.org/10.1108/IntR-10-2014-0265.

3

Edge Computing and Its Role in Hyper-Intelligent Networks

Shivani Kumari, Anukrity Gupta, Aashish Sahu, Simran Dalmia, Mamoon Rashid and Hitesh Mohapatra*

School of Computer Engineering, KIIT Deemed to Be University, Bhubaneswar, Odisha, India

Abstract

Wireless communication protocols are essential for facilitating smooth connectivity and interoperability between devices in smart home environments. This analysis focuses on three prominent protocols: ZigBee, Z-Wave, and Wi-Fi, evaluating their respective strengths, limitations, and suitability for various smart home applications. It has all these protocols integrated together with comparative analysis of the three. This work also discusses the future trends and developments emerging wireless protocol. ZigBee stands out for its low-power operation, mesh networking capabilities, and standardized interoperability, making it ideal for battery-powered devices and wireless sensor networks. Z-Wave, tailored for home automation, offers reliable low-latency communication, strong security features, and a dedicated frequency band, addressing the specific needs of smart home control systems. Wi-Fi, with its high bandwidth and widespread availability, excels in supporting bandwidth-intensive applications like media streaming and online gaming. A detailed comparison of key functionality such as power, range, data rate, latency, and security provide a decision tree to choose the right protocol according to an application. The analysis emphasizes the importance of carefully evaluating factors such as power efficiency, scalability, security, and interoperability when designing and implementing smart home systems catering to a broad audience of researchers, practitioners, and stakeholders. The strengths and trade-offs of each protocol, developers, and consumers can make informed choices to ensure a seamless, efficient, and secure smart home experience tailored to their specific needs. Further, the work can be extended for analysis of integration of

**Corresponding author*: hiteshmahapatra@gmail.com

Pradosh Kumar Gantayat, Sandeep Kumar Panda, S. Balamurugan and Sheng-Lung Peng (eds.) Hyper-Intelligent Networks: Exploring the Future of Connectivity for Society 5.0, (43–66) © 2026 Scrivener Publishing LLC

emerging protocol, ethical considerations, policy and governance, economic perspectives, sustainability, and societal implications.

***Keywords*:** Smart home, wireless communication protocols, Internet of Things (IoT), mesh networking, power consumption, data rate, interoperability, home automation

3.1 Introduction

The Internet of Things (IoT) is network of things that are embedded with sensors, actuators, software, and other technologies for exchanging data among devices over the internet. When we talk about wireless, we refer to the absence of any physical wires or connections. Here, communication means exchanging data among different interconnected devices. Protocols define the standard and conventions that should be followed by interconnected devices for efficient and reliable communication [1]. So, wireless communication protocols refer to a set of rules that should be followed by communicating devices without any physical connections involved. Wireless technology has been established to have played an important catalyst in the development of the IoT in recent years, which has improved society in every way. Domains like education, retail, transportation, wearable technology, smart homes, smart farming, healthcare, retail, and security are among those where IoT finds application [2]. The IoT includes various sensing nodes which help in knowing or collecting data from the environment. These nodes sense, process, and communicate with other motes and then actuators help in interacting with the environment. IoT uses cloud for storage and analysis of data for different applications. Wireless sensors are very small in size and also very cost effective which increases the use of these types of disposable sensors. Mesh topology protocols build a large area and connect cyberspace to the practical world. ZigBee and Z-Wave are some examples that support mesh topology and thus provide reliable signals with efficient communication [3].

The growing use of smart home devices has led to a rise in wireless connections within home networks. This poses challenges in network congestion, data latency, and power usage. ZigBee, Z-Wave, and Wi-Fi protocols each have their own advantages and drawbacks in terms of scalability, efficiency, and compatibility with various smart home devices. Trends in connectivity are moving in the direction of wireless solutions. Different home appliances are connected, controlled by devices such as Arduino microcontroller which can communicate *via* Android applications in home automation. Currently, ZigBee, Z-Wave, Wi-Fi, and Bluetooth are used for communication in home automation [4]. The popular choices for protocols based on low power consumption and scalability include ZigBee and Z-Wave. ZigBee is known for its low power consumption, and, thus, battery-operated devices use this protocol. Wi-Fi is preferred due to its high transmission rate although it is less power efficient. Thread is another protocol specifically for IP connectivity. Most suitable protocol is selected according to the type of appliances and its requirements of power, transmission rate, and range. There is room for analyzing how advancements, like wireless communication protocols, can be paired with IoT to maximize benefits on performance gauges like scalability, service quality, energy efficiency, and cost effectiveness. We will explore the significance of wireless protocols in enabling scalability by accommodating many devices and ensuring efficiency through optimized data transmission in smart homes. This involves cutting-edge approaches [5].

ZigBee was specifically designed for use in short-distance scenarios, given its characteristics as a wireless communication protocol with low power consumption and a low data transfer rate. It uses mesh networking topology and enhances reliability by allowing devices to relay signals through other devices [6]. It supports multi-node environment. It is ideal for battery-operated devices in home automation systems. It is best known for reliable connection in home automation systems. Z-Wave has less interference with wireless devices that operate on a different frequency

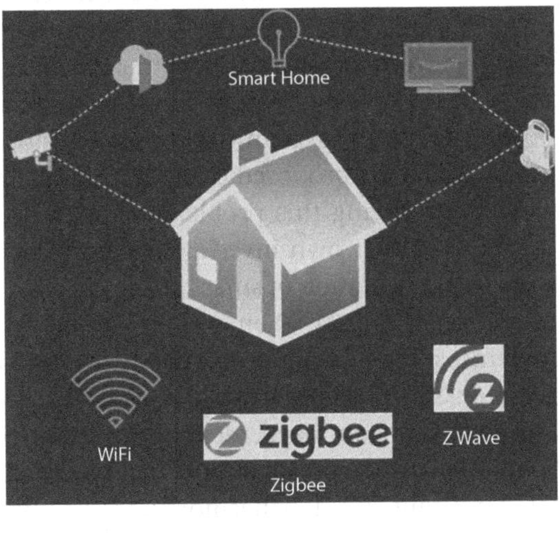

Figure 3.1 Wireless communication protocols.

band than other wireless communication protocols. It uses mesh topology. It also has interoperability due to certification process enforced by the Z-Wave alliance. It is used in easy installation of devices in home automation system [7]. Wi-Fi is used for local area networking as it is a ubiquitous communication protocol. It enables suitable bandwidth for bandwidth intensive applications within smart home environment. Using Wi-Fi devices can directly connect to home network without any gateway or hub. It is for a more energy efficient environment. Figure 3.1 illustrates the overall working of wireless communication protocols [8].

3.2 Literature Review

Over the course of several years, numerous research studies have delved into the realm of enhancing residential dwellings by making them "smarter," exploring a wide array of different methodologies and approaches with regards to controlling various elements such as lights and household appliances [9]. These studies have encompassed a diverse range of investigations, some of which focused on testing novel technologies, whereas others have involved comparing different options available on the market. One such study, conducted by Sikandar and his colleagues in the year 2009, sought to investigate the potential use of text messages and wireless technology as a means of remotely controlling home gadgets, primarily aimed at heightening security measures when individuals are away from their homes [10]. To make this easier, the scientists created a system called the home automation and control system, which effectively gave individuals the ability to control their devices from a distance. Nonetheless, a fundamental flaw was uncovered during the investigation of this study, specifically that, in the event of a power outage, the system could possibly stop working [11]. In light of this, the researchers proposed the inclusion of a battery backup system as a means of rectifying this problem. Then, in 2016, Jacobsson and his team carried out their own investigation into the potential risks associated with the implementation of smart home systems, particularly in terms of privacy and security [12]. Their comprehensive analysis revealed 32 potential problems, some of which were deemed serious. Accordingly, they underscored the essential significance of considering security and privacy concerns from the very commencement of the design process. Failure to do so could potentially place personal information stored within smart home systems at significant risk. Furthermore, in 2015, Bhatt and Verma embarked on a project that sought to automate buildings through the use of wired networks [13].

Although their system functioned effectively, it did not align with the prevailing trend of utilizing wireless technology. As such, they recommended future iterations incorporate wireless capabilities to remain in sync with the ever-evolving technological landscape. Similarly, authors of [8] employed smartphones and wireless networks as the means to remotely control home gadgets. While their system exhibited a high level of intelligence, they expressed concerns with regard to potential internet outages or power disruptions. To address these concerns, they proposed the implementation of a backup plan, such as the utilization of text alerts that could be directly sent to users' mobile phones [14]. In light of these considerations, it becomes evident that security plays a pivotal role in the realm of savvy household systems. Authors of [4] emphasized the importance of bolstering the protection of systems that control critical elements such as gas supplies, as these systems are particularly vulnerable to hacking attempts. Authors of [9] conducted a comparative analysis of various smart home systems, scrutinizing their respective costs and ease of use. This analysis revealed that each system possessed its own unique set of advantages and disadvantages, with none being considered perfect or flawless.

The expanding scope and intricacy of smart home environments require the implementation of effective wireless communication protocols, which serve as integral components in the seamless functioning of these technologically advanced living spaces [15]. Wireless communication protocols comprise a collection of vibrant characters within the landscape of smart home environments, each presenting its own distinctive narrative in relation to the aspects of efficiency and scalability [16]. This comprehensive literature review critically examines a diverse range of protocols that have been developed for application within smart homes, meticulously assessing their efficiency and scalability [9]. Among the protocols that have been meticulously examined are ZigBee, Z-Wave, Bluetooth Low Energy (BLE), Wi-Fi, and Thread. ZigBee, in particular, has emerged as a popular choice within the realm of smart home environments due to its intricate mesh networking mechanisms and its highly efficient utilization of power resources. The self-organizing network structure of this protocol has been expertly demonstrated in [10], showcasing its ability to seamlessly integrate effectiveness with scalability, thereby establishing an environment in which various gadgets can seamlessly interact with one another. On the other hand, Z-Wave offers the promise of expanded coverage and heightened resilience against the detrimental effects of interference-induced noise that is generated by the sub-1 GHz band resonance, resonating within the depths of the gloomy abyss. However, authors of [11] caution against the proprietary nature of the Z-Wave protocol, suggesting that its scalability may be compromised and that lingering concerns may be overlooked within the confines of its limited scope. In contrast, BLE stands out as a versatile contender within the realm of smart home environments, thanks to its low power consumption and its seamless integration with the mobile realm, thus positioning it as an adaptable sprite that enhances the overall functionality of these smart living spaces [17]. Table 3.1 discusses the comparison of the three protocols.

Every communication protocol has its own characteristics and is preferred in different scenarios accordingly. The main criteria for selecting protocols in different cases are based on keeping efficiency and scalability in mind. With it implies of low power consumption and cohesive acceptance of integration with the mobile realm, BLE emerges through being as an adaptable sprite. Authors of [12] convey convincing descriptions of its agility, they further warned regarding the maze-like constraints that it might encounter while traversing the vast regions of massive deployments, where its alarming gasps of complicated and interoperability might turn out to be untrue. With its establishing presence and promise for high data rates and faultless communication, Wi-Fi stands forth as a giant among its counterparts. While the researchers of [13] describe its magnificence, they also caution of the adverse conditions that might hinder its path,

Table 3.1 Comparative study between Wi-Fi, Z-Wave and ZigBee.

Attributes	Wi-Fi	Z-Wave	ZigBee
Year first launched in Market	1997	2003	2003
PHY/MAC Standard	IEEE 802.11.1	ITU-T G.9959	IEEE 802.15.4
Frequency Band	2.4 GHz	900 MHz	2.4 GHz
Nominal Range (0 dBm)	100 m	30–100 m	10–100 m
Maximum Data Rate	54 Mbit/s	40–100 kbit/s	259 kbit/s
Topology	Star	Mesh	Mesh
Power Usage	High	Low	Low
Alliance	Wi-Fi Alliance	Z-Wave Alliance	ZigBee Alliance

where interference and power consumption currents might cause tremors to appear on the surface. Thread offers an efficient and secure network of communications for smart home devices, built around IEEE 802.15.4 and IPv6. Pister and colleagues drew attention to its mesh networking architecture that ensures efficiency and scalability and enables easy integration with current networks due to native support for IP [14].

3.3 Proposed Study

The prevalence of Wi-Fi in intelligent homes is reduced by significant energy consumption, especially compared to energy-efficient alternatives such as ZigBee. This poses a significant obstacle to the sustainability of battery devices and the entire ecosystem of smart homes. As a result, it is vital to urgently develop energy-efficient Wi-Fi protocols and explore alternative low-power communication methods [18]. These initiatives are necessary to optimize energy consumption of Wi-Fi-enabled devices and ensure their long-term effectiveness. Furthermore, the limitations inherent in ZigBee data transmission obstruct its application in scenarios that require high bandwidth. Thus, progress in extending ZigBee's scope to the smart home landscape becomes imperative. These include strategies to increase ZigBee data throughput while maintaining low power consumption. The growing demand for different functionalities requires the adoption of such strategies. On the other hand, Z-Wave offers reliability and security features, but its limited signal range and limited cloud integration capabilities limit its scope [19]. To overcome these limitations, Z-Wave needs to extend the signal range by optimizing the mesh network and exploring alternative communication methods. In addition, improving cloud integration protocols is essential to ensure seamless interaction with various platforms. Faced with these difficulties, the advancement of intelligent housing technology can be advanced. This will increase energy efficiency, expand the scope of application, and improve user experience across the range of communication protocols used in smart homes [20]. This kind of improvement can only be achieved through a concerted interdisciplinary effort aimed at encouraging innovation and bridging the gaps. This will ensure that smart houses can fulfil their full potential as sustainable and interconnected ecosystems that meet the evolving needs of modern living [21].

ZigBee: ZigBee is a popular protocol that is used for low-power and low-cost wireless communication in many applications, e.g., home automation, industrial control, and sensor networks. It uses the 2.4-GHz frequency band and has powerful mesh network capabilities for devices to communicate with each other through multiple hops, hence providing limited self-healing connectivity within this network [19]. The most important characteristic that puts ZigBee as a top-level must consideration is that it operates in low-power mode of operation (which is highly desirable for any battery-powered peripherals like sensors or light switch). This protocol incorporates sophisticated energy management techniques that enable devices to go into low-power sleep mode when they are not actively transmitting or receiving data, effectively extending battery life [22]. This feature is crucial in scenarios where frequent battery replacements or cable sources are impractical or undesirable. ZigBee's mesh network capabilities allow seamless communication between devices, even if some nodes are not nearby or experience connectivity problems. The data can be transmitted through intermediate nodes, thus ensuring reliable and fault-tolerant communication throughout the network [23]. This feature is particularly useful in large-scale deployments such as industrial automation systems or smart building environments where obstacles and distances may prevent direct communication between devices. In addition, ZigBee gives priority to interoperability and adheres to a well-defined set of standards and specifications developed by the ZigBee Alliance. This ensures that products from different manufacturers can communicate seamlessly within the same network and promotes vendor neutrality by facilitating the integration of different products and solutions [24].

However, ZigBee also has some inherent limitations. Compared to other wireless technologies, such as Wi-Fi, ZigBee provides relatively low data rates, usually between 20 and 250 kbps, which may not be suitable for high-speed data transmission or multimedia streaming applications [25]. In addition, ZigBee networks may suffer from higher latency, especially when data needs to cross multiple hops, which may be a concern for time-sensitive applications [26]. Even with its limitations, ZigBee is popular because it uses very little power, supports mesh networking, and works well with different systems. It is widely used in home automation, industrial monitoring, and wireless sensor networks, where saving energy, being reliable, and easy integration are important.

Z-Wave: Z-Wave is a communication protocol made for home automation and smart home systems. It works in the sub-gigahertz range, typically around 900 MHz. Z-Wave is built to ensure reliable and quick communication in homes or buildings [25]. Some advantages of Z-Wave are that it focuses on specific intelligent home applications such as lighting control, door lock, and temperature sensors. Unlike Wi-Fi and ZigBee, which are designed for many uses, Z-Wave is specifically made for home automation needs. This specialization allows efficient and reliable communication between devices and seamless interoperability within the Z-Wave ecosystem [27]. Z-Wave also places a strong emphasis on security, implementing cutting-edge encryption techniques and robust authentication measures to safeguard against unauthorized entry and potential cyber risks will significantly enhance the security of our systems and data. Each Z-Wave device has a unique ID and encryption key, ensuring secure communication within the network. Additionally, Z Wave operates on a dedicated frequency band, minimizing interference from other wireless technologies and enhancing the reliability of the network [28]. Another notable feature of Z-Wave is its mesh networking capability, which allows devices to communicate with each other through multiple hops, providing extended range and improved coverage throughout a home or building. This feature is particularly beneficial in larger residential or commercial settings, where obstacles or distance can hinder direct communication between devices [29].

However, Z-Wave has some inherent limitations compared to other wireless technologies. Its scope is generally limited to homes or small buildings, making it less suitable for applications requiring long-distance communication. Additionally, Z-Wave usually provides slower data speeds than Wi-Fi, ranging from 9.6 to 100 kbps. This might not be enough for apps that need fast data transfer or streaming [30]. Despite these limitations, Z-Wave's emphasis on reliable, low-latency communication, strong security features, and bandwidth dedicated to smart home devices makes it a popular choice for home automation systems and IoT applications in residential and commercial environments. As demand for smart home technology continues to grow, Z-Wave's specialized capabilities and seamless interoperability within its ecosystem make it a robust and secure home automation solution [31].

Wi-Fi: Wi-Fi is a widely accepted wireless communication technology, ubiquitous in both residential and commercial environments. Key benefits of Wi-Fi include its extensive availability and ability to work with various devices such as smartphones, laptops, tablets, and smart home appliances [25]. Wi-Fi provides fast data transfer, making it ideal for things like streaming videos or sending large files. Depending on the Wi-Fi standard, speeds can range from 54 Mbps to several gigabits per second. This makes Wi-Fi great for high-bandwidth activities like video streaming, online gaming, and big file transfers [32]. Wi-Fi devices generally consume more energy than low-energy wireless protocols such as ZigBee and Z-Wave, which can be a problem for battery devices or applications where energy efficiency is essential [33]. Furthermore, as the number of Wi-Fi devices increases in each area, the risk of network congestion and interference also increases, which may lead to deterioration in performance and connectivity problems [21].

Another important consideration with Wi-Fi is security. While Wi-Fi networks can be secured using various encryption and authentication methods, such as WPA2 or WPA3, improper configuration or the use of weak security protocols can leave networks vulnerable to unauthorized access and cyber threats [25]. To keep data safe on Wi-Fi networks, it is important to use strong passwords, update firmware regularly, and follow the latest security protocols. This helps protect the privacy and accuracy of the data being shared. Despite these challenges, Wi-Fi remains a popular choice for a wide range of applications due to its high bandwidth, widespread availability, and compatibility with numerous devices. Its suitability for streaming applications, online gaming, and other bandwidth-intensive tasks makes it a preferred solution in residential and commercial settings where high-speed wireless connectivity is required. Table 3.2 summarizes different smart home scenarios.

The table outlines eight smart home scenarios and the wireless protocols (ZigBee, Z-Wave, and Wi-Fi) used in each one. It highlights how the different protocols' key features like low power consumption, mesh networking, security, high data rates, and scalability make them suitable for various applications. These include smart lighting, security systems, entertainment, environmental monitoring, energy management, health tracking, irrigation systems, and smart kitchen appliances. The table demonstrates how leveraging the strengths of different wireless protocols enables scalable and efficient smart home automation [30].

3.3.1 Critical Analysis of Wireless Communication Protocols

Table 3.3 compares ZigBee, Z-Wave, and Wi-Fi. ZigBee and Z-Wave are designed for low power use, making them ideal for battery-powered devices. In contrast, Wi-Fi uses more power because it handles higher data rates and bandwidth. Wi-Fi also covers a longer range compared to ZigBee and Z-Wave, which are better for short-range and indoor use [34]. Wi-Fi supports much higher data speeds, up to several gigabits per second, making it great for tasks like streaming and transferring large files.

Table 3.2 This table summarizes the different smart home scenarios, the wireless protocols used, and their key features for each scenario.

Scenario	Description	Wireless protocol	Key features
Smart Lighting Control	Install ZigBee light bulbs and motion sensors paired with a ZigBee hub. The sensors trigger the hub to adjust lighting based on motion detection.	ZigBee	Scalable by adding more lights and sensors, low power consumption, and mesh networking capabilities
Smart Security System	Install Z-Wave smart locks, door/window sensors, and security cameras paired with a Z-Wave hub. Sensor triggers record video and send notifications.	Z-Wave	Scalable by adding more sensors and cameras, low power consumption, and robust security features
Smart Entertainment System	Connect smart TV, media streamers, and speakers to Wi-Fi network; use voice assistants for control and streaming content.	Wi-Fi	Scalable by adding more devices, efficient for high-bandwidth applications like video and audio streaming

(*Continued*)

Table 3.2 This table summarizes the different smart home scenarios, the wireless protocols used, and their key features for each scenario. (*Continued*)

Scenario	Description	Wireless protocol	Key features
Environmental Monitoring System	Install ZigBee sensors to monitor environmental conditions, data sent to hub for analysis and alerts; can control heating, ventilation, and air conditioning (HVAC)/ air purifiers based on data.	ZigBee	Scalable by adding more sensors, low power consumption, and mesh networking capabilities
Energy Management System	Install Z-Wave smart plugs, thermostats, and energy monitors paired with a Z-Wave hub; monitor and control energy usage.	Z-Wave	Scalable by adding more devices, low power consumption, and robust security features
Health and Wellness Monitoring	Pair wearables, smart scales, and blood pressure monitors with Wi-Fi network; sync data with mobile app for insights and alerts.	Wi-Fi	Scalable by adding more devices and efficient for transmitting health data due to high data rates
Smart Irrigation System	Install ZigBee soil moisture sensors paired with a ZigBee hub to control irrigation valves based on sensor data.	ZigBee	Scalable by adding more sensors and valves, low power consumption, and mesh networking capabilities

(*Continued*)

Table 3.2 This table summarizes the different smart home scenarios, the wireless protocols used, and their key features for each scenario. (*Continued*)

Scenario	Description	Wireless protocol	Key features
Smart Kitchen Appliances	Connect smart refrigerator, oven, and coffee maker to Wi-Fi network for monitoring, remote control, and automation.	Wi-Fi	Scalable by adding more appliances and efficient for transmitting data and commands due to high data rates and reliability

Table 3.3 Comparison of key features for ZigBee, Z-Wave and Wi-Fi.

Attributes	ZigBee	Z-Wave	Wi-Fi
Power Consumption	Very low [21]	Low [25]	High [30]
Range	10–100 meters [21]	Up to 30 meters [25]	Up to 100 meters [34]
Data Rate	20–250 kbps [21]	9.6–100 kbps [25]	Up to several Gbps [35]
Latency	Higher, suitable for non–time-critical applications [23]	Low latency for smart home applications [25]	Low latency suitable for real-time applications [35]
Security	AES-128 encryption, secure key exchange [22]	AES-128 encryption, unique device IDs [25]	WPA2/WPA3 encryption, various authentication methods [34]

ZigBee and Z-Wave have lower data rates, optimized for low-power and low-bandwidth applications. Wi-Fi and Z-Wave are designed for low-latency communication, suitable for real-time applications and smart home control, respectively. ZigBee may experience higher latency, particularly in large mesh networks. All three protocols offer encryption and security features, with Wi-Fi supporting advanced encryption standards like WPA2/WPA3 and various authentication methods. ZigBee and Z-Wave also incorporate AES-128 encryption and secure key exchange mechanisms [35].

3.3.2 Choosing the Right Protocol for Your Smart Home Needs

With the rise of smart home technology, choosing the right wireless communication protocol is key to making sure your devices work well, efficiently, and securely. It is important to understand what your smart home needs and how each protocol performs. You should consider factors like power use, range, data speed, delay, security, and how well it works with other systems to make the best choice. For instance, if the application involves battery-powered sensors or light switches that require low power consumption and mesh networking capabilities, then ZigBee would be an appropriate choice. ZigBee's advanced power management techniques and ability to create self-healing mesh networks make it well-suited for such applications [23].

On the other hand, applications that demand reliable, low-latency communication and strong security features, such as door locks or alarm systems, might benefit from the Z-Wave protocol. Z-Wave's focus on specific smart home applications, dedicated frequency, band, and robust encryption mechanisms provide a secure and responsive solution for these use cases [22]. For high-bandwidth applications like smart TVs, media streaming devices, or online gaming, Wi-Fi emerges as the preferred option due to its ability to support high data rates and handle bandwidth-intensive tasks. However, it is important to consider Wi-Fi's higher power consumption and potential network congestion issues, especially in dense environments with numerous connected devices [34]. When selecting a protocol, it is also essential to consider interoperability and ecosystem support. Protocols like ZigBee and Z-Wave have well-established alliances and certification programs that promote seamless integration and compatibility among devices from different manufacturers, enabling the creation of comprehensive smart home solutions [36]. In the end, choosing the right protocol depends on the specific needs of the application. It is important to balance things like power use, range, data speed, delay, security, and how well different devices work together. By thinking through these factors, smart home developers and users can create a smooth and efficient smart home setup that fits their needs perfectly [37].

3.3.3 Smart Home Communication Requirements

When building a smart home system, choosing the right wireless communication protocol is very important. It affects how well the devices work, how efficient they are, and how secure the system is. There are several things to think about when picking the right protocol for your smart home. Many devices, like sensors, switches, and door locks, run on batteries, so power usage is a big concern. Protocols like ZigBee and Z-Wave are made to use less power, helping these devices run longer without needing frequent battery changes [33]. In contrast, Wi-Fi typically consumes more power due to its higher data rates and bandwidth requirements, making it less suitable for battery-powered devices. The effective communication range within a home is another important factor. While Wi-Fi can provide a longer range, ZigBee and Z-Wave are optimized for short-range and indoor applications, ensuring reliable communication within the confines of a typical home or building [22].

As smart home systems add more devices and applications, the protocol used needs to handle the growing number of connected devices without losing performance or reliability. Protocols like ZigBee and Z-Wave support mesh networking, meaning devices can connect through multiple pathways. This helps the system scale and stays reliable, even if some connections fail [20]. Different smart home applications have varying data rate requirements. For instance, high-bandwidth applications like media streaming or online gaming demand higher data rates, making Wi-Fi a suitable choice with its support for data rates up to several gigabits per second [44]. However, for low-bandwidth applications such as sensor data transmission or light switch control, the lower data rates offered by ZigBee and Z-Wave are sufficient. Certain smart home applications, such as home automation and security systems, require low-latency communication for real-time actions and responses. Protocols like Z-Wave and Wi-Fi are designed for low-latency communication, ensuring timely execution of commands and actions [38]. ZigBee, on the other hand, may experience higher latency, particularly in large mesh networks. Protecting the privacy and integrity of data transmitted within the smart home environment is of paramount importance. Protocols like ZigBee, Z-Wave, and Wi-Fi offer various security features, including data encryption (e.g., AES-128), secure key exchange mechanisms, and authentication methods (e.g., WPA2/WPA3 for Wi-Fi) [39]. However, proper configuration and implementation of these security measures are essential to mitigate potential vulnerabilities. By carefully evaluating these key factors and aligning them with the specific requirements of the smart home application, homeowners and developers can make informed decisions regarding the selection of the most appropriate wireless communication protocol, ensuring a seamless, efficient, and secure smart home experience.

3.3.4 Procedure for Connection of Wireless Communication Protocol

Wireless communication protocols serve as the foundation for enabling devices to interact and exchange information seamlessly over wireless channels. The procedure involves several distinct steps, each crucial for establishing efficient communication.

To begin, selecting the appropriate protocol entails a comprehensive analysis of various factors including range, data rate, power consumption,

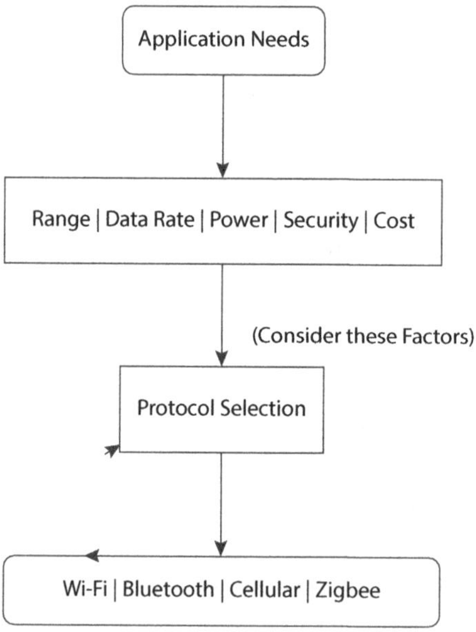

Figure 3.2 Flowchart to choose right protocol.

security, and cost considerations. This involves delving into available options such as Wi-Fi, Bluetooth, cellular, and ZigBee, each tailored to different needs and requirements. A detailed flowchart depicted in Figure 3.2 illustrates the decision-making process, guiding users through a systematic evaluation of their application needs and the corresponding protocol attributes [22]. Moving forward, the setup phase involves acquiring hardware equipped with the requisite transceivers specific to the chosen protocol. Devices such as Wi-Fi routers, Bluetooth modules, cellular towers, and mobile devices are essential components in this regard.

Additionally, configuring these devices according to protocol specifications is paramount, necessitating adjustments to parameters like frequency bands, encryption keys, and network identifiers (SSIDs). Figure 3.3 elucidates the setup process through a comprehensive flowchart, facilitating users in configuring their devices effectively. Once devices are appropriately configured, the next step involves establishing communication between them. This typically entails pairing or associating devices, followed by the transmission of data packets adhering to the protocol's prescribed format and procedures. Figure 3.4 outlines the process of initiating communication between two devices, underscoring the importance of seamless data exchange facilitated by the chosen protocol.

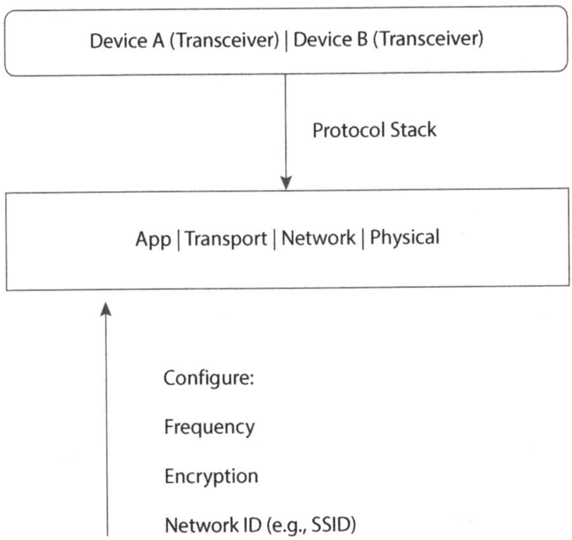

Figure 3.3 Flowchart to set devices.

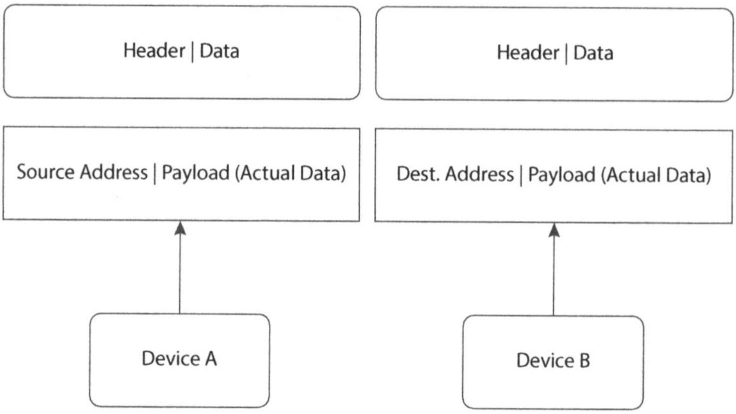

Figure 3.4 Flowchart to establish communication.

Security remains a paramount concern throughout the entire process, with many protocols offering encryption options to safeguard data confidentiality during transmission. Implementing encryption measures is imperative, particularly for sensitive data exchanges. Lastly, the maintenance and monitoring phase involves continuous vigilance to ensure optimal communication performance. Monitoring signal strength, data throughput, and connection status are essential tasks, complemented by troubleshooting measures in the event of connectivity issues. Referring to protocol documentation or troubleshooting guides can aid in resolving any encountered issues effectively, ensuring uninterrupted communication flow [40].

3.4 Future Trends

The future of smart homes and IoT is closely linked to new wireless technologies like Wi-Fi 6 and Matter, which bring both challenges and opportunities. Wi-Fi 6, also called 802.11ax, is the newest Wi-Fi standard. It improves speed, capacity, and efficiency over earlier versions. Features like orthogonal frequency-division multiple access (OFDMA) and Target Wake Time make it better for handling many devices at once, especially in crowded spaces. This technology will transform smart homes by offering faster, more reliable connections, which are key for things like 4K streaming, online gaming, and communication between IoT devices. Matter is an open-source smart home standard supported by key industry stakeholders like Amazon, Google, Apple, and the ZigBee. This unified protocol aims to simplify device connectivity and interoperability across different ecosystems, addressing the current fragmentation in the smart home market. By standardizing communication protocols and security measures, Matter is capable of integrating smart devices and facilitating consumer setup and management of smart home systems. The adoption of Matter could lead to increased compatibility among devices from various manufacturers, fostering a more cohesive and user-friendly smart home experience. The integration of Wi-Fi 6 and Matter into smart home and IoT applications brings about several challenges and opportunities. One of the key challenges is ensuring seamless interoperability between different wireless technologies and devices within a smart home ecosystem. As the number of connected devices continues to grow, managing network congestion, ensuring data security, and maintaining reliable communication become critical considerations. Additionally, the transition to new wireless standards may require updates to existing infrastructure and devices, posing compatibility issues and potential disruptions during the migration process.

However, these challenges also present opportunities for innovation and growth in the smart home industry. The adoption of Wi-Fi 6 and Matter opens up possibilities for enhanced smart home functionalities, improved energy efficiency, and expanded device compatibility. Smart home applications can provide users with higher data speeds, lower latency, and more network capacity, enabling advanced automation, remote monitoring, and personalized settings. In addition, the standardization introduced by Matter paved the way for a more cohesive smart home ecosystem, with devices from different companies communicating and working together seamlessly, enabling a more integrated and user-centric approach to home automation. While challenges such as interoperability issues and infrastructure updates may arise, the opportunities for innovation, enhanced functionalities, and standardized communication protocols present a promising future for the smart home industry. By leveraging these advancements and addressing the associated challenges, the smart home ecosystem can evolve to meet the evolving needs and expectations of consumers in the digital age.

3.5 Conclusion

The selection of an appropriate wireless communication protocol is a critical decision that can significantly impact the performance, efficiency, and security of smart home systems. Each protocol (ZigBee, Z-Wave, and Wi-Fi) has its advantages and disadvantages, which makes it suitable for different home smart applications and needs. ZigBee stands out for its low-power operation, making it an excellent choice for battery-powered devices like sensors, light switches, and other low-bandwidth applications. Its mesh networking capabilities ensure reliable communication and self-healing networks, even in the presence of obstacles or interference. However, ZigBee may experience higher latency, especially in large-scale deployments, which could be a concern for time-sensitive applications. On the other hand, Z-Wave is tailored for specific smart home applications, offering reliable, low-latency communication, strong security features, and a dedicated frequency band to minimize interference. Z-Wave focuses on making devices from different brands work together easily, allowing you to build a complete smart home system. On the other hand, Wi-Fi is great for things that need fast data transfer, like streaming videos, because of its high bandwidth. It is also widely available and works with many devices, making it a popular choice for smart homes. However, Wi-Fi devices tend to use more power and can struggle with slowdowns in crowded networks with lots of connected devices.

When selecting a wireless communication protocol for smart home applications, it is crucial to consider the specific requirements of the devices and applications involved. For battery-powered sensors and light switches that require low power consumption and mesh networking capabilities, ZigBee would be an appropriate choice. Applications demanding reliable, low-latency communication and strong security features, such as door locks or alarm systems, might benefit from the Z-Wave protocol. For high-bandwidth applications like smart TVs, media streaming devices, or online gaming, Wi-Fi emerges as the preferred option due to its ability to support high data rates and handle bandwidth-intensive tasks. In some cases, a hybrid approach combining multiple protocols may be necessary to address the diverse requirements of a smart home system. For example, a smart home system could leverage ZigBee or Z-Wave for low-power, low-bandwidth devices while also incorporating Wi-Fi for high-bandwidth applications. Ultimately, the selection of the most appropriate wireless communication protocol should be driven by a thorough evaluation of the specific device requirements, balancing factors such as power consumption, range, data rate, latency, security, and interoperability. By carefully considering these factors, smart home developers and consumers can ensure a seamless and efficient smart home experience tailored to their specific needs.

References

1. Danbatta, S.J. and Varol, A., Comparison of Zigbee, Z-Wave, Wi-Fi, and Bluetooth Wireless Technologies Used in Home Automation. *2019 7th International Symposium on Digital Forensics and Security (ISDFS)*, Barcelos, Portugal, pp. 1–5, 2019, Doi: 10.1109/ISDFS.2019.8757472.
2. Liu, J., Wang, F., Ma, X., Yang, Z., Recent advances in wireless communication protocols for Internet of Things. *Wireless Commun. Mobile Comput.*, 2017, 8791485, 2017. https://doi.org/10.1155/2017/8791485.
3. Mukherjee, S. and Mohapatra, H., Performance Analysis of Different MANET Routing Protocols. *2024 5th International Conference on Innovative Trends in Information Technology (ICITIIT)*, IEEE, 2024.
4. Ryu, D.H., Kim, H., Um, K., Reducing security vulnerabilities for critical infrastructure. *J. Loss Prev. Process Ind.*, 22, 6, 1020–1024, 2009. http://dx.doi.org/10.1016/j.jlp.2009.07.015.
5. Sikandar, M., Khiyal, H., Khan, A., Shehzadi, E., SMS Based Wireless Home Appliance Control System (HACS) for Automating Appliances and Security Preliminaries. *Int. J. Res. Comput. Commun. Eng.*, 6, 2009. DOI:10.28945/1048.
6. Jacobsson, A., Boldt, M., Carlsson, B., A risk analysis of a smart home automation system. *Future Gener. Comput. Syst.*, 56, 719–733, 2016. https://doi.org/10.1016/j.future.2015.09.003.
7. Bhatt, J. and Verma, H.K., Design and Development of Wired Building Automation Systems. *Energy Build.*, 103, 396–413, 2015. https://doi.org/10.1016/j.enbuild.2015.02.054.
8. Joshi, S.A., Poojari, S., Chougale, T., Shetty, S., Sandeep, M.K., Home automation system using wireless network. *2017 2nd International Conference on Communication and Electronics Systems (ICCES)*, Coimbatore, India, pp. 803–807, 2017, Doi: 10.1109/CESYS.2017.8321195.
9. Waghmare, P., Chaure, P., Chandgude, M., Chaudhari, A., Survey on: Home automation systems. *2017 International Conference on Trends in Electronics and Informatics (ICEI)*, Tirunelveli, India, pp. 7–10, 2017, Doi: 10.1109/ICOEI.2017. 8300864.
10. Palattella, M.R., *et al.*, Standardized Protocol Stack for the Internet of (Important) Things. *IEEE Commun. Surv. Tutor.*, 15, 3, 1389–1406, Third Quarter 2013. Doi: 10.1109/SURV.2012.111412.00158.
11. Linh An, P.M. and Kim, T., A Study of the Z-Wave Protocol: Implementing Your Own Smart Home Gateway, in: *2018 3rd International Conference on Computer and Communication Systems (ICCCS)*, Nagoya, Japan, pp. 411–415, 2018, doi: 10.1109/CCOMS.2018.8463281.
12. Lacava, A., Zottola, V., Bonaldo, A., Cuomo, F., Basagni, S., Securing Bluetooth Low Energy networking: An overview of security procedures and threats. *Comput. Netw.*, 211, 108953. ISSN 1389–1286, 2022.

13. Banerji, S. and Chowdhury, R., On IEEE 802.11: Wireless Lan Technology. *Int. J. Mob. Netw. Commun. Telemat.*, 3, arXiv preprint arXiv:1307.2661, 2013.
14. Mohapatra, H., Socio-technical Challenges in the Implementation of Smart City. *2021 International Conference on Innovation and Intelligence for Informatics, Computing, and Technologies (3ICT)*, Zallaq, Bahrain, pp. 57–62, 2021, doi: 10.1109/3ICT53449.2021.9581905.
15. Mehmood, A., Ullah, I., Hussain, S.A., Khan, M.A., Javaid, N., Energy-efficient and reliable communication protocols for smart homes: A comprehensive survey. *2022 International Conference on Electronics, Information, and Communication (ICEIC)*, pp. 1–6, 2022, doi: DOI: 10.1109/ICEIC54908.2022.00009.
16. Kim, H., Park, J., Kim, Y., A survey of communication protocols for smart homes. *J. Sens. Actuat. Netw.*, 12, 1, 16, 2023, doi: DOI: 10.3390/jsan12010016.
17. Jiang, T., Yang, M., Zhang, Y., Research and implementation of M2M smart home and security system. *Secure Commun. Netw.*, 8.16, 2015, 2704–2711, 2012.
18. Schneps-Schneppe, M.A., M2M Communications Based on the M-Bus Protocol. *Autom. Control Comput. Sci.*, 46, 83–89, 2012.
19. Siddiqui, M.W., Advances in conventional breeding approaches for postharvest quality improvement of fruits, in: *Postharvest Biology and Technology of Horticultural Crops*. pp. 111–162, Apple Academic Press, 2015.
20. Baronti, P., Pillai, P., Chook, V.W., Chessa, S., Gotta, A., Hu, Y.F., Wireless sensor networks: A survey on the state of the art and the 802.15. 4 and ZigBee standards. *Comput. Commun.*, 30, 7, 1655–1695, 2007. https://doi.org/10.1016/j.comcom.2006.12.020.
21. Farahani, S., *ZigBee wireless networks and transceivers*, Newnes, 2011, https://doi.org/10.1016/B978-0-7506-8393-7.00004-0.
22. Lee, J.S., Su, Y.W., Shen, C.C., A comparative study of wireless protocols: Bluetooth, UWB, ZigBee, and Wi-Fi, in: *33rd Annual Conference of the IEEE Industrial Electronics Society (IECON 2007)*, IEEE, pp. 46–51, 2007, https://doi.org/10.1109/IECON.2007.4460126.
23. Koubâa, A., Cunha, A., Alves, M., Tovar, E., A time division beacon scheduling mechanism for IEEE 802.15. 4/ZigBee cluster-tree wireless sensor networks, in: *19th Euromicro Conference on Real-Time Systems (ECRTS'07)*, IEEE, pp. 125–135, 2007, https://doi.org/10.1109/ECRTS.2007.29.
24. Siddique, M.M., Kamruzzaman, J., Alamri, A., Evaluating the performance of ZigBee protocols for advanced metering infrastructure, in: *Innovations and Advances in Computer, Information, Systems Sciences, and Engineering*, pp. 1053–1063, Springer, Cham, 2015, https://doi.org/10.1007/978-3-319-06773-5_97.
25. Gomez, C. and Paradells, J., Wireless home automation networks: A survey of architecture and technologies. *IEEE Commun. Mag.*, 48, 6, 92–101, 2010. https://doi.org/10.1109/MCOM.2010.5473869.

26. Horyachyy, O., Comparison of Wireless Communication Technologies used in a Smart Home: Analysis of wireless sensor node based on Arduino in home automation scenario, 2017.
27. Väyrynen, T. and Aksebo, M., Security on Z-Wave IoT protocol, in: *2015 International Conference on Intelligent Environments (IE)*, IEEE, pp. 148–151, 2015, https://doi.org/10.1109/IE.2015.31.
28. Dey, Anushka, et al., Solutions for Energy Management and Environmental Conservation in IoT-Integrated Smart Home. *AI and Emerging Technologies for Emergency Response and Smart Cities*, edited by Froilan D. Mobo, IGI Global, 2025, pp. 389-408. https://doi.org/10.4018/979-8-3693-9770-1.ch018.
29. Saha, H.N., Mandal, A., Sinha, R.S., Singh, J., Mahanti, A., Smart home systems: An evaluation of communication technologies, in: *2018 IEEE International Conference on Advanced Networks and Telecommunications Systems (ANTS)*, IEEE, pp. 1–6, 2018, https://doi.org/10.1109/ANTS.2018.8708158.
30. Dargie, W. and Poellabauer, C., *Fundamentals of wireless sensor networks: theory and practice*, John Wiley & Sons, 2010.
31. Mohapatra, H. and Rath, A.K., Fault tolerance in WSN through PE-LEACH protocol. *IET Wireless Sens. Syst.*, 9, 358–365, 2019. https://doi.org/10.1049/iet-wss.2018.5229.
32. Gast, M.S., *802.11 wireless networks: the definitive guide*, O'Reilly Media, Inc, 2005.
33. Edney, J. and Arbaugh, W.A., *Real 802.11 security: Wi-Fi protected access and 802.11 i*, Addison-Wesley Longman Publishing Co., Inc, 2004.
34. Mohapatra, H. and Rath, A.K., Detection and avoidance of water loss through municipality taps in India by using smart taps and ICT. *IET Wireless Sens. Syst.*, 9, 447–457, 2019. https://doi.org/10.1049/iet-wss.2019.0081.
35. Perahia, E. and Stacey, R., *Next generation wireless LANs: 802.11 n and 802.11 ac*, Cambridge University Press, 2013.
36. Wang, Wei, Guangyu He, and Junli Wan., Research on Zigbee wireless communication technology. *2011 International Conference on Electrical and Control Engineering*. IEEE, 2011.
37. Gomez, C. and Paradells, J., Wireless home automation networks: A survey of architectures and technologies. *IEEE Commun. Mag.*, 48, 6, 92–101, 2010. https://doi.org/10.1109/MCOM.2010.5473869.
38. Mohapatra, H. and Rath, A.K., Designing of fault-tolerant models for wireless sensor network-assisted smart city applications, in: *Intelligent Technologies: Concepts, Applications, and Future Directions, Volume 2*. Springer Nature Singapore, Singapore, 25–43, 2023.
39. Landge, P.B., Singh, Y., Mohapatra, H., Efficient resource allocation in disaster management sensor network through forest optimization algorithm. *Int. J. Inf. Tecnol.*, 2025. https://doi.org/10.1007/s41870-025-02580-3.
40. Xing, F. and Wang, W., Analyzing Resilience to Node Misbehaviors in Wireless Multi-Hop Networks, in: *Proceedings of the IEEE Wireless Communications and Networking Conference WCNC 2007*, March 11–15, 2007.

4

Emerging Horizons: Exploring Blockchain-Driven Hyper-Intelligent Network in Healthcare

Subasish Mohapatra*, Subhadarshini Mohanty and Ayaskanta Mishra

School of Computer Science, Odisha University of Technology and Research, Bhubaneswar, India

Abstract

The Hyper-Intelligent Network of Medical Things (HiNMT) is catalyzing a paradigm shift in healthcare by orchestrating a symbiotic fusion of medical apparatuses, sensory nodes, and health informatics systems. This intricate neural lattice of interconnected nodes is engineered to transcend traditional healthcare boundaries, orchestrating a symphony of patient-centric outcomes, optimized healthcare workflows, and streamlined medical protocols. However, the relentless evolution of HiNMT presents novel challenges, notably in the realms of data fortification, privacy preservation, and seamless interoperability. Amidst this landscape, blockchain technology emerges as a beacon of promise, offering an immutable, decentralized framework poised to confront these challenges head-on. By furnishing a cryptographic substrate for managing health data within the fabric of HiNMT, blockchain promises to fortify data integrity, fortify privacy, and foster seamless data exchange. This research endeavor undertakes the ambitious task of imbuing a blockchain-enabled nervous system within the tapestry of a federated learning–driven HiNMT (FL-HiNMT). The proposed architecture features a dual-layered cognition framework: a centralized neural nexus housing a global machine learning construct, complemented by a network of distributed node-level cognition. Operating in symbiosis, these layers engender a cognitive gestalt wherein local models, embedded within individual nodes, operate in tandem with the global model, assimilating node-specific data streams. Extensive simulations and comparative analyses ensue, scrutinizing the efficacy of prevailing consensus

**Corresponding author*: smohapatra@outr.ac.in

Pradosh Kumar Gantayat, Sandeep Kumar Panda, S. Balamurugan and Sheng-Lung Peng (eds.) Hyper-Intelligent Networks: Exploring the Future of Connectivity for Society 5.0, (67–96) © 2026 Scrivener Publishing LLC

models such as proof of stake and proof of work within the context of HiNMT. Moreover, a bespoke blockchain ecosystem christened MTChain emerges, meticulously architected to accommodate the idiosyncrasies of HiNMT. Tailored algorithms, finely calibrated to the demands of functional blockchain integrity within healthcare ecosystems, permeate the fabric of MTChain. Subsequently, a decentralized emulation environment breathes life into MTChain, offering a sandbox for probing its efficacy within the intricate milieu of HiNMT.

***Keywords*:** Blockchain, hyper-intelligent network, healthcare, federated learning, security

4.1 Introduction

In the realm of Hyper-Intelligent Network of Medical Things (HiNMT), a transformative wave is sweeping through healthcare landscapes, seamlessly interweaving medical devices, sensor arrays, and health informatics grids. This intricately connected neural lattice of HiNMT is architected to transcend conventional healthcare boundaries, orchestrating a symphony of patient-centric outcomes, optimized healthcare logistics, and harmonized medical protocols. Nevertheless, as HiNMT continues its evolutionary trajectory, it unfurls a tapestry of novel challenges, chiefly encompassing data sanctity, privacy fortification, and seamless interconnectivity.

One of the key obstacles within HiNMT lies in securely and effectively handling vast quantities of confidential health data. Research highlighted in [1] underscores the necessity for resilient solutions to safeguard data confidentiality and integrity. Traditional centralized databases are vulnerable to single points of failure and security breaches, thus driving the exploration of decentralized technologies like blockchain within the HiNMT framework.

Originally crafted for cryptocurrencies, blockchain has garnered widespread adoption across diverse sectors, owing to its fundamental attributes of decentralization, transparency, immutability, and cryptographic security. Within the realm of HiNMT, blockchain serves as a distributed ledger, meticulously documenting transactions in a tamper-resistant and transparent fashion. A study authored by Kshetri (2018) titled "Blockchain's Roles in Bolstering Cybersecurity and Safeguarding Privacy" accentuates blockchain's potential in mitigating security and privacy apprehensions in burgeoning technologies, including HiNMT.

The convergence of blockchain and the HiNMT presents a significant opportunity to tackle the evolving challenges in healthcare data management. By leveraging its decentralized and secure framework, blockchain technology bolsters data security, safeguards patient privacy, and fosters interoperability within HiNMT ecosystems [2]. As research in this domain progresses, further exploration of practical applications, regulatory frameworks, and scalability solutions will be crucial in unlocking the full potential of blockchain to revolutionize healthcare delivery and enhance patient outcomes. The evolving landscape of HiNMT, coupled with the maturation of blockchain technology, paints a compelling vision for the future of secure and interconnected healthcare ecosystems. The foundation of blockchain lies in its consensus mechanisms, which authenticate and incorporate new transactions into the ledger. In [3], the authors have delved into the utilization of consensus mechanisms like Proof of Authority (PoA) and Proof of Stake (PoS) to bolster security in Internet of Things (IoT). These mechanisms play a pivotal role in thwarting malicious actions and unauthorized access, thereby fortifying the security framework of the IoT ecosystem. In [4], the authors have introduced Enigma, a blockchain protocol focused on privacy preservation, enabling secure computation on encrypted data. These practical implementations highlight the potential of blockchain to transform data management and security within IoT for Medical Things.

The reason why use blockchain is simple: it is the blockchain trillema [5] (in Figure 4.1), and we observe:

> *Decentralization*: The establishment of a blockchain system devoid of dependence on a central point of control [23].

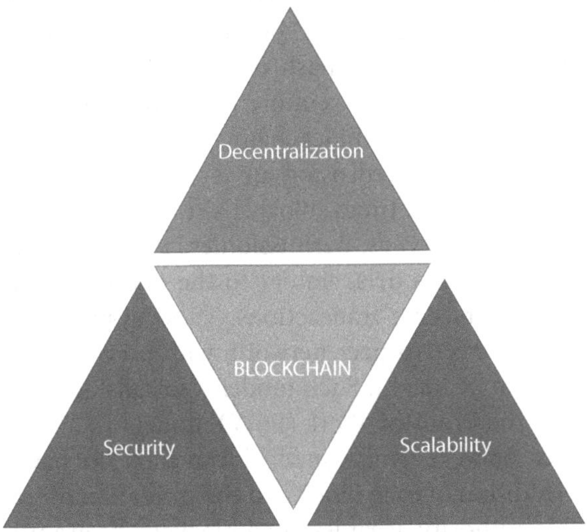

Figure 4.1 The blockchain trilemma.

Scalability: The capacity of a blockchain system to manage a progressively increasing volume of transactions [24].

Security: The capability of the blockchain system to function as intended safeguards itself against attacks, bugs, and unforeseen challenges [25].

Ensuring the integrity and security of model updates as they move across decentralized nodes stands as a significant challenge in federated learning (FL). Blockchain's decentralized ledger, founded on cryptographic principles, offers a sturdy solution. Research conducted by S.K.Panda *et al.*, [30] in their paper "Blockchain Technology: Applications and Challenges" suggests utilizing blockchain to secure and verify model updates in FL, thereby bolstering the credibility of the collaborative training process [26].

4.2 Understanding Blockchain

Blockchain technology emerged in 2008 following the publication of a paper by the anonymous Satoshi Nakamoto. This paper [6] introduced a groundbreaking concept—a decentralized, peer-to-peer network built on trust—where every transaction could be transparently tracked. Nakamoto named this innovation Bitcoin, which sparked a revolution in the world of finance. This development upended traditional financial systems by removing the need for central authorities to verify transactions. Instead, the system relies on a timestamp server for security, ensuring that each transaction is recorded at a specific point in time within the chain. The inclusion of timestamps in the hash of each block creates a sequential chain, with each new timestamp reinforcing the integrity of previous ones.

Each transaction within the blockchain system represents a digital coin. These transactions are secured using an asymmetric key system for verification. In contemporary times, blockchain technology can broadly be classified into two main types: permissionless and permissioned. In permissionless blockchain models, similar to the one proposed, there is no central authority overseeing transactions. These systems rely entirely on the trust within the peer-to-peer network, with no central entity responsible for transaction oversight. Such models typically adhere to consensus mechanisms like the Proof-of-Work (PoW) model.

On the other hand, permissioned blockchains do have a governing authority. The addition of each block and the validation of transactions are overseen by this authority. Permissioned blockchains are usually adopted by specific groups or organizations. The authority dictates the addition of new blocks, the issuance of blocks, and transaction rates. In some permissioned blockchain networks, all users must be authorized to send and receive transactions, thus eliminating anonymity. In these systems, participants collaborate to achieve shared business objectives, with inherent disincentives for fraudulent behavior due to traceability. In the event of misconduct, the involved organizations are identifiable, legal remedies are accessible, and mechanisms for pursuing remedies within relevant judicial systems are established.

In a blockchain system (Figure 4.2), there are typically five main layers: the data layer, the network layer, the consensus layer, the execution layer, and the application layer. Here is an explanation of each layer:

Data Layer: The data layer serves as the foundation of the blockchain architecture, storing all the information recorded on the blockchain. This includes transaction data, smart contracts, and any other relevant data. The data layer ensures the immutability and integrity of the recorded information through cryptographic techniques such as hashing and encryption [27].

Network Layer: The network layer encompasses the physical and communication infrastructure that allows nodes (individual computers or devices) to connect and communicate with each other. This layer utilizes peer-to-peer networking protocols to facilitate the transmission of data and transactions between nodes. Nodes within the network can be miners, users, or other entities participating in the blockchain ecosystem [28].

Consensus Layer: The consensus layer is responsible for ensuring agreement among the nodes on the state of the blockchain. Consensus mechanisms determine how nodes reach a consensus on which transactions are valid and should be added to the blockchain. Various consensus algorithms, such as PoW, PoS, and Practical Byzantine Fault Tolerance (PBFT) [7], govern this layer. The consensus layer plays a crucial role in maintaining the integrity, security, and immutability of the blockchain ledger [29, 30].

Execution Layer: The execution layer is where smart contracts and other programmable functionalities are processed and executed. Smart contracts are self-executing contracts with the terms of the agreement directly written into code. This layer ensures the accurate execution of smart contracts and enforces the rules and conditions encoded within them.

Application Layer: The application layer is the topmost layer of the blockchain architecture and is where decentralized applications (DApps)

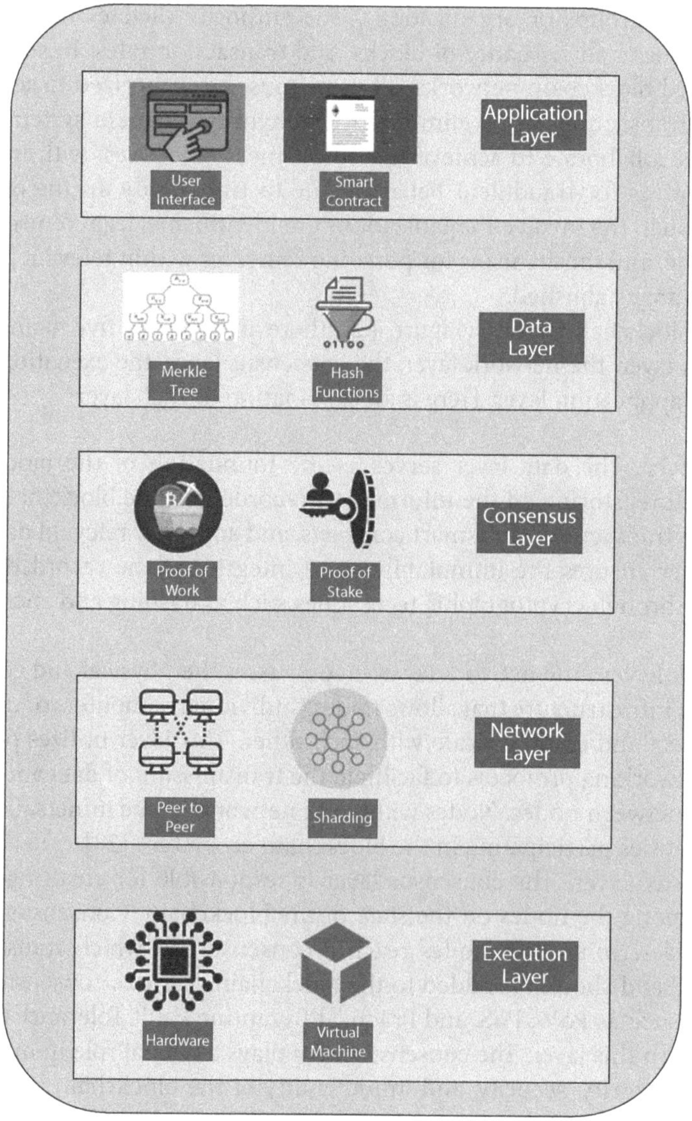

Figure 4.2 Blockchain layered architecture.

[8, 31–33] and other user-facing functionalities are built and deployed. This layer enables developers to create decentralized solutions that leverage the underlying blockchain infrastructure. DApps interact with the blockchain network through application programming interface (APIs) or protocols provided by the underlying blockchain platform.

4.2.1 Role of Consensus in Blockchain

In the realm of blockchain technology, a persistent question arises: which block will be the next to be published in the blockchain? Various algorithms and models are employed to address these issues, determining the block designated for publication. Multiple consensus algorithms are currently in use across different cryptocurrencies, with some discussed in the following section. To ascertain the most effective and optimal consensus model, several comparison criteria are provided. Authors have categorized different consensus models using a derived mechanism, dividing them into three major categories: primitive, compliant, and cross-compliant [9, 34, 35].

- In the primitive category, only one model, the PAXOS model, is included.
- Compliant models encompass various modern consensus algorithms, including PoW (utilized by Bitcoin) and PoS [10, 36, 37], among others.
- Cross-compliant models feature hybrid consensus algorithms such as Proof of Time Elapsed, Proof of Membership, and Proof of Authentication.

Proof-of-Work Consensus Model:
In this model, nodes must solve puzzles or problems to determine the answer required by the publishing block. Bitcoin operates using this consensus model, requiring substantial processing power for nodes to participate in the network [38].

Proof of Stake Consensus Model:
The PoS model is predicated on the notion that users with more stake invested in the system have a greater incentive for its success and are less likely to undermine it. Stake typically refers to a quantity of cryptocurrency invested in the blockchain network. Unlike PoW, PoS does not demand significant computational power for participation. Ethereum is a prominent cryptocurrency utilizing the PoS consensus model [39].

Proof of Authority Consensus Model:
The PoA [11, 40, 41], also known as proof of identity, relies on partial trust in publishing nodes due to their verified real-world identities. Publishing nodes must have their identities validated and verifiable within the blockchain network. Nodes stake their identity or reputation to publish new

blocks, with users directly influencing a node's reputation based on its behavior. Nodes can lose reputation for disagreeable actions and gain reputation for agreeable behavior, affecting their likelihood of publishing blocks. This algorithm applies exclusively to permissioned blockchain networks with high levels of trust [42].

4.2.2 Criteria of Selecting a Consensus Model

Algorithm Throughput:
Transactions per Second: This refers to the number of transactions the blockchain network can process in one second. Throughput is a significant factor affecting the scalability of a blockchain network [43].
Block Creation Time: This refers to the time it takes to create a new block on the blockchain. Faster block creation times can lead to higher transaction processing speeds.
Block Verification Time: This refers to the time it takes for nodes on the network to validate a new block. Faster block verification times can improve the overall performance of the blockchain network [44].
Block Size: This refers to the maximum amount of data that can be included in a single block on the blockchain.

Profitability of Mining:
Mining Reward: This refers to the incentive given to miners for successfully creating and adding a new block to the blockchain.
Transaction Fee: This is a small fee paid by users for including their transactions in a block.
Power Consumption: This refers to the amount of energy consumption required for mining.

Security and Vulnerabilities:
Double Spending Attack: This is a type of attack where an attacker attempts to spend the same digital currency twice [12].
51% Attack: This is a type of attack where a malicious actor gains control over a majority of the computing power on the blockchain network [13]. This allows the attacker to potentially disrupt the network or even reverse transactions.
Sybil Attack: This is a type of attack where a malicious actor creates a large number of fake identities on the network to disrupt consensus.

Trust Model: This refers to the level of trust required between participants on the blockchain network. Permissioned blockchains rely on trusted participants, whereas permissionless blockchains do not [45, 46].
Permission Model: This refers to whether anyone can participate in the consensus mechanism or whether participation is restricted. Permissioned blockchains restrict participation, whereas permissionless blockchains allow anyone to participate [14, 47].

There is no one-size-fits-all answer when it comes to choosing a blockchain consensus mechanism [15]. The ideal consensus mechanism for a particular blockchain network will depend on a variety of factors, such as the throughput requirements of the network, the security needs of the network, and the desired level of decentralization.

4.3 Understanding Federated Learning

FL stands as a pioneering machine learning methodology (Figure 4.1), characterized by decentralized model training across edge devices or servers, each housing local data samples, all without necessitating data exchange. Unlike conventional centralized approaches, FL fosters collaborative model refinement on individual devices or servers, with only model updates relayed to a central server. This decentralized training paradigm ensures data privacy by keeping raw data localized, effectively mitigating concerns regarding data security and confidentiality.

FL has emerged as a focal point in scholarly discourse, particularly within the realm of healthcare and HiNMT applications. With the exponential growth of medical data and the increasing reliance on interconnected medical devices, preserving patient privacy and ensuring data security have become paramount concerns. FL addresses these concerns by enabling collaborative model training while respecting the privacy of individual data contributors. By allowing models to be trained locally on sensitive data without the need for data exchange, FL ensures that sensitive information remains on the device where it was generated, reducing the risk of data breaches and unauthorized access.

The architecture of FL (Figure 4.3) is meticulously crafted to reconcile the imperative for collaborative model training with the paramount need to uphold user data privacy. The incorporation of blockchain technology further enhances the security and trustworthiness of FL implementations within HiNMT environments. By leveraging blockchain for authenticating

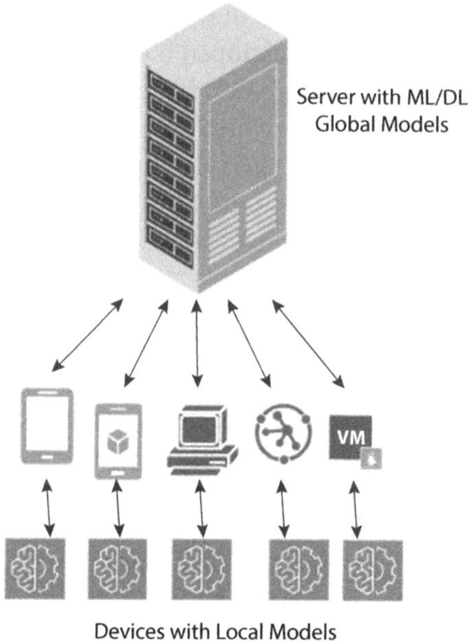

Figure 4.3 Federated learning architecture.

local data updates and storing them as tamper-resistant transactions, FL ensures the integrity and traceability of the training process.

4.4 Related Works

Significant strides have been made in incorporating blockchain technology into healthcare, with a particular emphasis on the FL landscape. In the paper titled "Federated Learning Meets Blockchain in Edge Computing: Opportunities and Challenges" [16], the authors thoroughly explore and analyze the practical implementation of FL within the blockchain framework. Furthermore, they introduce an innovative concept, FLChain, providing a unique and insightful perspective on the seamless integration of FL and blockchain in edge computing.

Examining the functionalities of blockchain within the context of FL, the paper "Blockchained On-Device Federated Learning," authored by Kim *et al.* [17], delves into a comprehensive analysis of the behavior of blockchain in the FL environment. The authors propose a model known as BlockFL architecture, wherein they conduct an in-depth examination of the end-to-end latency model of BlockFL. This analysis involves characterizing the optimal block generation rate, taking into account communication, computation, and consensus delays.

In the study outlined in [18], Nguyen *et al.* introduce a decentralized architecture tailored for a mobile edge computing setting, highlighting a specific emphasis on health sharding. Additionally, they provide a comparative analysis with the Ethereum blockchain. In their publication [19], Almalki *et al.* propose a layered architecture designed for the storage and access of medical data within a blockchain environment, particularly emphasizing an edge computing context. Their approach involves employing smart devices as gateways for smart contracts.

Tthe authors, Połap *et al.* [20], present an architecture for the Internet of Medical Things (IoMT) within a blockchain environment. However, their primary emphasis is on the implementation of neural networks for the analysis of medical images, particularly focusing on lung X-rays. Here, they have run several deep learning models to find the best possible option for the lung image classification.

Addressing the pivotal role of security within the IoMT landscape, Lakhan *et al.* propose innovative algorithms for queuing, alongside introducing robust measures for fraud validation and privacy preservation within the blockchain policy framework in the fog-cloud paradigm, as outlined in their work [21]. Their contributions are particularly significant in fortifying the security infrastructure of IoMT, encompassing advancements in queuing strategies and establishing a comprehensive framework to combat fraud while preserving user privacy within the Fog-cloud environment. The proposed algorithms and policies put forth by the authors serve as noteworthy enhancements to the IoMT security landscape, ensuring a more resilient and privacy-aware ecosystem.

4.5 Simulating Blockchain

Simulating blockchain environments is a complex and challenging endeavor, primarily due to the distinctive features and intricacies of this decentralized technology. Initially created to support cryptocurrencies like Bitcoin, blockchain has since broadened its utility across diverse sectors. To simulate blockchain effectively, one must address its decentralized consensus mechanisms, cryptographic measures, and the fluid dynamics of participant interactions. This discussion focuses on the hurdles faced in crafting realistic blockchain simulations by researchers and developers.

Decentralization and Consensus Mechanisms:
A key obstacle in blockchain simulation is emulating its decentralized structure. Unlike centralized systems that are governed by a singular authority, blockchain operates on a distributed consensus, complicating simulations. Accurately modeling consensus mechanisms such as PoW, PoS, or PBFT demands a deep understanding of each mechanism's unique protocols and interactions [48].

Cryptographic Challenges:
Blockchain's dependence on cryptography for transaction security, digital signatures, and data integrity adds a layer of simulation complexity. Mimicking these cryptographic operations requires a detailed grasp of the subject, as any inaccuracies can undermine the simulation's validity and reliability [41].

Dynamic Network Behavior:
The ever-changing landscape of blockchain networks, with nodes frequently entering or exiting, presents simulation challenges. Capturing the network's fluid topology, including aspects like node connectivity and communication pathways, is vital. Fluctuations in network structure can influence consensus processes, latency, and overall performance, making realistic simulation difficult [50].

Smart Contracts and Transaction Complexity:
The introduction of smart contracts—autonomous scripts running on the blockchain—adds complexity. Simulating these contracts and their blockchain interactions necessitates familiarity with specific scripting languages (e.g., Solidity for Ethereum) and the nuances of transactions that involve smart contracts, such as conditional executions and state modifications.

Scalability and System Performance:
Simulating blockchain scalability, particularly for large networks with numerous nodes and transactions, demands significant resources. Striking a balance between simulation fidelity and operational efficiency is a challenge, given the constraints on transaction rates, block dissemination, and validation processes.

Accurate Incentive Models:
A realistic simulation of blockchain also involves modeling the economic incentives motivating network participants. Crafting accurate incentive models is crucial for depicting node behaviors, validation efforts, and

consensus participation accurately. This task requires a nuanced understanding of the economic principles driving participant decisions.

The task of simulating blockchain systems is complex, given the technology's decentralized essence, cryptographic depth, evolving network configurations, and intricate component interplays. Addressing these challenges necessitates a collaborative effort spanning computer science, cryptography, and distributed systems expertise. Blockchain simulation efforts are vital for advancing our grasp of these systems, identifying potential pitfalls, and forging robust solutions for blockchain's practical application. Despite the hurdles, progress in blockchain simulation is instrumental in refining and enhancing this groundbreaking technology's efficiency and adaptability.

4.5.1 Simulating Using Simulators

Blockchain simulation tools are essential for those interested in exploring the functionality, analyzing the behavior, and improving the efficiency of blockchain systems across different settings. BlockSim [22] stands out as a prime example of such a tool, offering an in-depth look at the operation of decentralized networks. This discussion delves into the functionalities and advantages of BlockSim, highlighting its role in facilitating the exploration of blockchain dynamics. BlockSim, an open-source framework, is engineered to simulate the complexities of blockchain networks, providing a dynamic platform for the examination and evaluation of various blockchain configurations. It addresses the intricate nature of these networks, enabling the investigation of a multitude of factors, including system behavior, consensus processes, and network performance metrics. Particularly adept at replicating decentralized consensus mechanisms, BlockSim offers invaluable insights into the functioning of different consensus algorithms like PoW, PoS, and PBFT. This feature is crucial for understanding the implications of each consensus approach on transaction latency, system security, and power usage.

BlockSim also shines in modeling scalability, a vital consideration for blockchain infrastructure. It allows the simulation of environments with diverse scales, incorporating variations in node count, transaction throughput, and block size. This functionality is instrumental in identifying scalability challenges and fine-tuning system configurations to boost operational efficiency.

A key goal of utilizing BlockSim is to conduct comparative analyses between two leading blockchain development frameworks: Bitcoin (Model 1) and Ethereum (Model 2). This comparison aims to determine the most effective strategies for developing and deploying machine learning models within these ecosystems. Although BlockSim accommodates a range of input and output variables, the focus is primarily on the dynamics of miners and nodes, along with their block production rates. The simulations adhere to standardized blockchain (Table 4.1) settings that mirror real-world operational conditions of these systems.

Table 4.1 Simulation environment.

	Bitcoin	**Ethereum**
Block Interval	600 s	12.42 s
Block Size	1M B	1 MB
Block Delay	0.42 s	6s
Transactions Per Second	10	20
Simulation Time	10,000	1,000
Number of Simulations	5	5
Transaction Delay	5.1 s	3 s

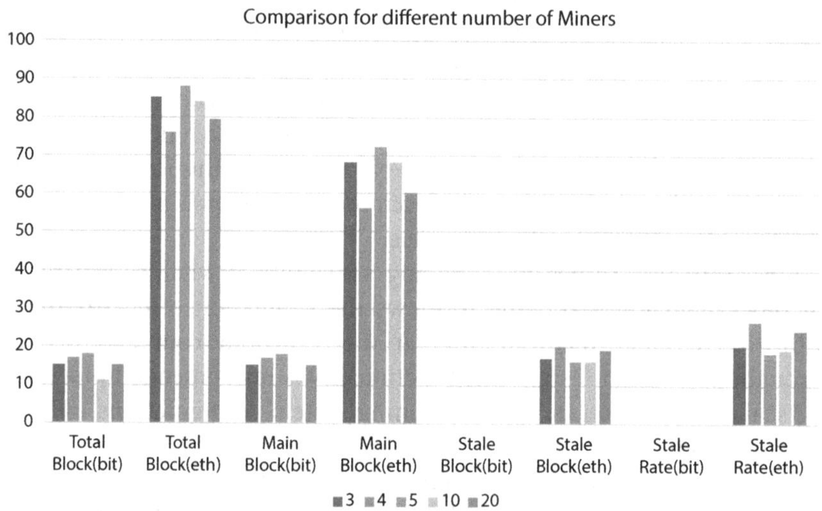

Figure 4.4 Comparison chart between the different number of nodes for block behavior.

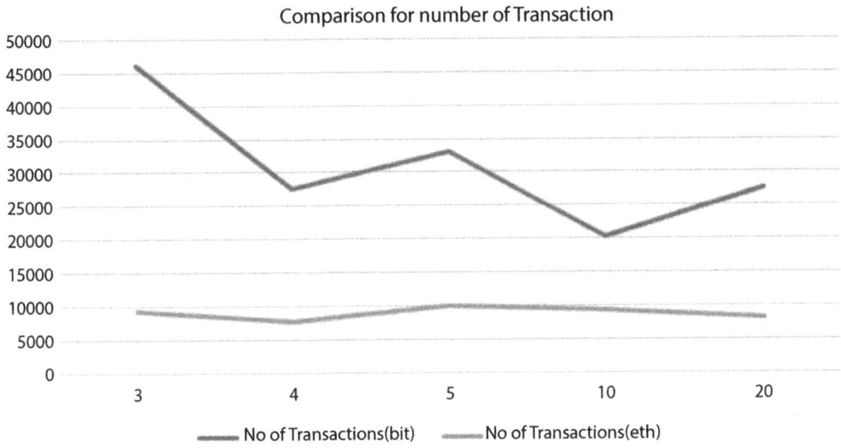

Figure 4.5 Comparison for number of transactions in bitcoin and ethereum.

Figures 4.4 and 4.5 depict the comprehensive outcomes from our simulations. We systematically varied the number of nodes/miners, specifically using 3, 4, 5, 10, and 20 nodes, to conduct a thorough comparison of their respective outputs. Given the scalability requirements inherent in the iNMT environment, where an increasing number of devices and nodes are essential, this study serves as a scalability test. The results aim to provide insights into the system's performance as it scales, offering valuable implications for the deployment of HiNMT solutions in real-world scenarios. Here, the uncle generation is not taken into consideration in Ethereum. In Figure 4.6, a comparison is made within Ethereum-based blockchains, examining the presence or absence of uncle blocks.

Surprisingly, the number and rate of stale blocks remain consistent regardless of whether uncle blocks are permitted or not. This observation offers valuable insights into the stability and efficiency of Ethereum in various configurations, assisting in the choice of a suitable blockchain model for HiNMT applications.

4.5.2 Architecture Design

The deployment of our advanced healthcare system unfolds through a deliberate and phased process, integrating both centralized and decentralized components to enhance collaboration among healthcare professionals and smart HINMT devices. This architecture (Figure 4.7) not only protects patient privacy but also leverages the collective intelligence of the network for ongoing enhancement.

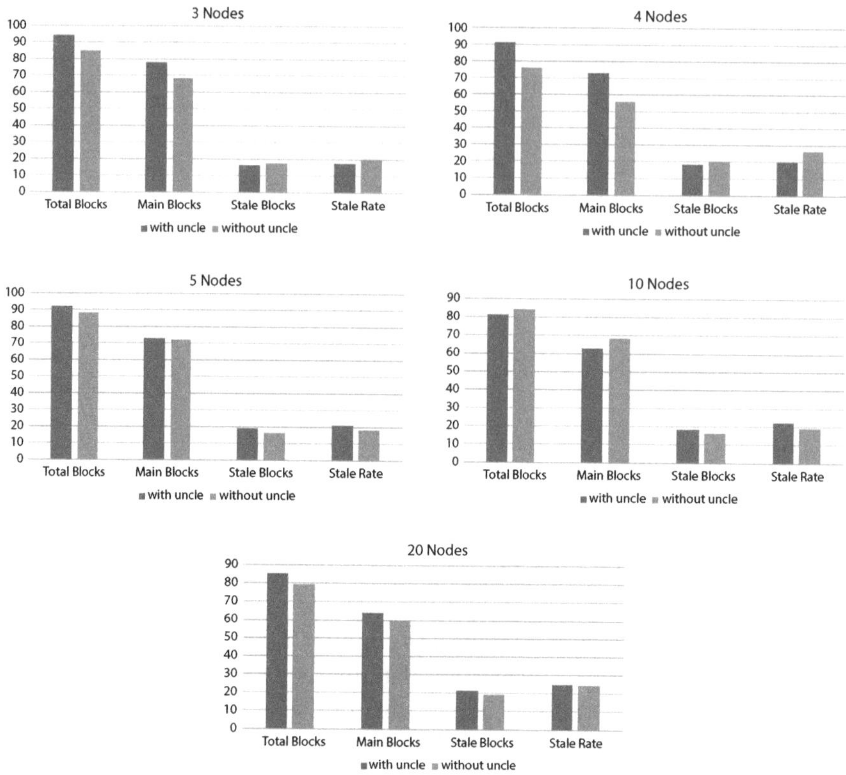

Figure 4.6 Comparison of block behavior with/without uncle generation.

Centralized Server Configuration and Initial Model Setup:
The process begins with the creation of a centralized server to store initial models. This is a collaborative endeavor with healthcare professionals who provide valuable insights based on existing data. This server is crucial for kick-starting the system and lays the foundation for future developments. As the network grows and the demand for data storage increases, additional servers can be integrated, ensuring scalability.

Distributing Initial Models to HINMT Devices:
The next step involves distributing the initial models to HINMT devices that possess computational capabilities. These devices, whether operating individually or interconnectedly, act as the computational hubs for running sophisticated machine learning and deep learning algorithms. Distributing these models is a critical step toward decentralized data

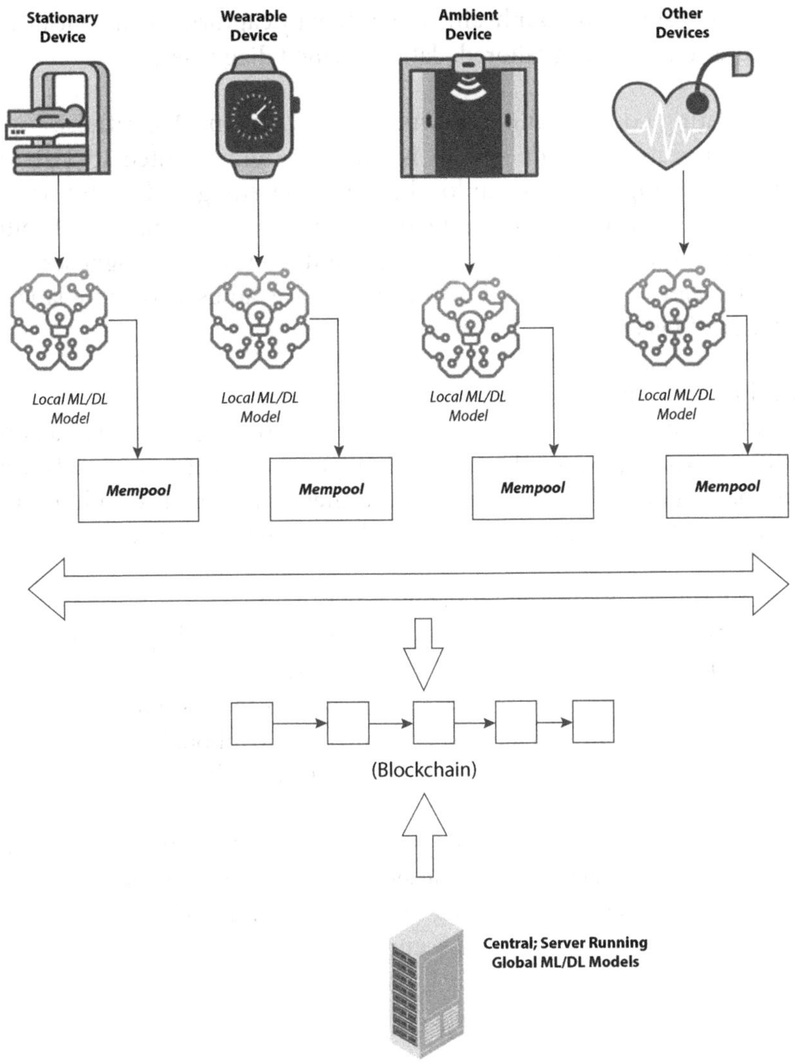

Figure 4.7 HiNMT architecture.

processing, enabling each device to contribute its computational strength to the network's collective intelligence.

Data Acquisition by HINMT Devices:
Equipped with the models, HINMT devices commence the vital task of gathering new patient data. This data collection is crucial, reflecting the

dynamic capabilities of our healthcare system by capturing real-time health insights and facilitating tailored, data-informed diagnoses.

Incorporating Local Machine Learning/Deep Learning Algorithms:
A key innovation in our system is the autonomy granted to HINMT devices, allowing them to run local machine learning and deep learning algorithms. These devices integrate the latest data with input from healthcare professionals, ensuring the accuracy and relevance of diagnoses. This process creates a perpetual learning cycle that adjusts to the changing demands of healthcare.

Model Evaluation and Comparison:
Following local processing, the models are rigorously evaluated and compared to existing ones. This evaluation process identifies models with superior diagnostic accuracy, which are then considered for addition to the mempool—a dynamic pool of models awaiting blockchain inclusion.

Securing Models in the Mempool and Blockchain:
The mempool serves as a secure staging area for models pending blockchain addition. During this stage, patient privacy is meticulously maintained, with personal details being anonymized. Selected models are added to the blockchain through a transparent process, symbolizing progress and ensuring accountability within our decentralized healthcare network.

This strategic implementation underscores our commitment to advancing healthcare delivery through the synergy of hyper-intelligent networks and blockchain technology, paving the way for a future where healthcare is more personalized, efficient, and secure.

4.5.3 Creating A Blockchain

The core algorithms that require precise design are central to the operation of our blockchain infrastructure. They are responsible for generating and verifying PoW, authenticating the legitimacy of these proofs, and managing the timely replacement of chains within the network. These critical functions ensure a uniform consensus is reached across all nodes, aligning transaction records throughout the blockchain. The complexity involved in crafting these algorithms is essential for the smooth and secure operation of our blockchain ecosystem, with the goal of achieving a cohesive consensus among all nodes.

At the heart of our blockchain's effectiveness are the meticulously crafted algorithms that oversee essential operations. These processes are vital for upholding the network's integrity and achieving consensus among the decentralized nodes that make up the blockchain. Exploring these key algorithms in detail reveals their importance and the subtleties involved in their design.

Algorithm 4.1:
The PoW algorithm is a cornerstone for ensuring the security of the blockchain. It mandates that nodes, also known as miners, engage in solving intricate mathematical challenges to authenticate transactions and generate new blocks. This algorithm's complexity is deliberate, making the computational work required by miners significant. This serves as a safeguard against fraudulent actions, such as double-spending. Fine-tuning this algorithm is crucial for maintaining a balance between the computational demand, the security of the network, and the conservation of energy.

```
def proof_of_work(previous_proof):
1. new_proof = 1
2. check_proof = False
3. while not check_proof:
   # Expression to ensure the computational work for the proof
4. expression = (new_proof ** 3) - ((1 + 1 / new_proof) ** new_proof) -
   (previous_proof ** 2)
   # Encoding and hashing the expression
   # Ensure to convert the expression result to a string before encoding
5. hash_operation = hashlib.sha256(str(expression).encode()).hexdigest()
   # Checking if the hash meets the criteria (leading zeros)
6. if hash_operation[:4] == '0000':
7. check_proof = True
8. else:
9. new_proof += 1
10. return new_proof
```

Let us break down each component of the algorithm point by point:

1. Initialization of Variables:
   - "new_proof": Initialized to 1, this variable represents the proof value that the algorithm aims to find.

   - "check_proof": Initialized to False, this variable serves as a flag to control the loop until a valid proof is found.
2. Proof Generation Loop
   - The algorithm enters a while loop that continues until a valid proof is found. The condition "while not check_proof": ensures that the loop continues until the proof is validated.
3. Expression Calculation:
   - Within the loop, an expression is calculated using the current value of "new_proof" and the "previous_proof" provided as an argument to the function.
   - The expression is designed to be computationally intensive, typically involving mathematical operations that require significant computational resources.
4. Hash Operation:
   - The calculated expression is then hashed using the SHA-256 algorithm, a cryptographic hash function.
   - Hashing is a one-way process that transforms data into a fixed-size string of characters (hash value), making it practically impossible to reverse the process and retrieve the original data.
5. Leading Zeros Check:
   - The algorithm checks whether the hashed result ("hash_operation") starts with a specified number of leading zeros (in this case, four zeros).
   - Leading zeros are often used as a criterion for proof validity in PoW systems, indicating that the proof meets certain computational requirements.
6. Proof Validation:
   - If the hashed result meets the specified criteria (starts with four zeros), then the "check_proof" variable is set to True, indicating that a valid proof has been found.
   - If the hashed result does not meet the criteria, then the value of "new_proof" is incremented by 1, and the loop continues to search for a valid proof.
7. Return Statement:
   - Once a valid proof is found (i.e., "check_proof" is True), the function returns the value of "new_proof," which represents the solution to the PoW problem.

In summary, this algorithm iteratively calculates and hashes expressions involving the proof value ("new_proof") until it finds a hashed result that meets certain criteria (e.g., starting with four leading zeros), thereby providing a valid PoW.

Algorithm 4.2:
Proof Verification Procedure. After a node accomplishes PoW successfully, the resulting proof undergoes meticulous scrutiny to ascertain its validity. This pivotal responsibility falls upon the Proof Verification Procedure. It meticulously assesses the computational efforts exerted, verifying their compliance with predefined rules and consensus protocols. The construction of this procedure profoundly impacts the reliability of the blockchain network, acting as a shield against deceptive practices and upholding the integrity of the entire transaction ledger.

```
def is_chain_valid(chain):
1. previous_block = chain[0]
2. block_index = 1
3. while block_index < len(chain):
4. block = chain[block_index]
   # Check if the current block's previous hash matches the hash of the
   previous block
5. if block['previous_hash'] != hash_block(previous_block):
6. return False
   # Retrieve proof values for current and previous blocks
7. previous_proof = previous_block['proof']
8. proof = block['proof']
   # Calculate expression for proof validation
9. expression = calculate_expression(proof, previous_proof)
   # Hash the expression
10. hash_operation = hashlib.sha256(str(expression).encode()).hexdigest()
   # Check if the hashed expression meets criteria for proof validation
11. if hash_operation[:4] != '0000':
    return False
   # Move to the next block in the chain
12. previous_block = block
13. block_index += 1
   # If all blocks in the chain are valid, return True
14. return True
```

Let us break down the algorithm into its individual components and explain each part point by point:

1. Initialization:
   - The function begins by initializing variables "previous_block" and "block_index."
   - "previous_block" represents the first block in the chain, which is accessed *via* "chain[0]."
   - "block_index" is set to 1 to start the iteration from the second block in the chain.
2. Iterating Through Blocks:
   - The function enters a "while" loop to iterate through each block in the chain, starting from the second block (index 1) and continuing until the end of the chain.
   - Within each iteration, the function retrieves the current block being examined ("block") from the chain.
3. Checking Previous Hash:
   - It verifies whether the "previous_hash" attribute of the current block matches the hash of the previous block ("previous_block").
   - If the hashes do not match, indicating a discrepancy in the chain's integrity, then the function returns "False," signifying an invalid chain.
4. Retrieving Proof Values:
   - The function retrieves the PoW values ("proof") for both the current block ("block") and the previous block ("previous_block").
5. Expression Calculation:
   - It calculates an expression using the proof values of the current and previous blocks.
   - This expression typically involves complex mathematical operations designed to make the PoW computationally intensive.
6. Hashing the Expression:
   - The calculated expression is hashed using the SHA-256 cryptographic hash function.
   - Hashing ensures that the expression's integrity is preserved and that it cannot be tampered with.

7. Checking Hash Prefix:
   - The function checks if the first four characters of the hashed expression form a string of zeros (i.e., if the hash meets the criteria for proof validation).
   - If the hash does not meet the criteria, indicating that the PoW is invalid, then the function returns "False."
8. Moving to the Next Block:
   - After validating the current block, the function updates "previous_block" to the current block and increments "block_index" to move to the next block in the chain.
9. Return Validity Status:
   - If all blocks in the chain pass the validation checks, then the function returns "True," indicating that the chain is valid.
   - If any block fails the validation checks, then the function returns "False," indicating that the chain is invalid.

In summary, this algorithm iterates through each block in the chain, verifying the integrity of the chain by checking the consistency of hashes and validating the PoW for each block. If any discrepancies are found, the function returns "False"; otherwise, it returns "True" to confirm the validity of the chain.

Algorithm 4.3:
To promote ongoing progress and avoid stagnation, the Chain Replacement Algorithm is employed. As blockchain networks evolve, occasions may arise where the current chain requires replacement with a newer iteration to integrate updates, improve effectiveness, or tackle security issues. This algorithm coordinates the smooth shift from an older chain to a more recent one at predetermined intervals, guaranteeing that all nodes align with the same blockchain status. The precision in crafting this algorithm is vital for upholding consensus and harmony among all network nodes.

```
def replace_chain():
1. network = nodes
2. longest_chain = None
3. max_length = len(chain)
4. for node in network:
5. response = get_chain_from_node(node)
6. if response.status_code == 200:
```

```
length = response.json()['length']
chain = response.json()['chain']
if length > max_length and is_chain_valid(chain):
max_length = length
longest_chain = chain
if longest_chain is not None:
chain = longest_chain
return True
else:
return False
```

Let us break down the algorithm into its individual components and explain each part point by point:

1. Initialization:
   - The function "replace_chain()" begins by initializing variables "network," "longest_chain," and "max_length."
   - "network" represents the nodes in the blockchain network.
   - "longest_chain" is initially set to "None," indicating that the longest chain has not been found yet.
   - "max_length" is initialized with the length of the current chain.
2. Iterating Through Network Nodes:
   - The function iterates through each node in the network using a "for" loop.
3. Retrieving Chain from Node:
   - For each node, the function sends a request to retrieve the blockchain using the "get_chain_from_node()" function.
   - The response from the node is stored in the variable "response."
4. Checking Response Status:
   - The function checks if the response status code is "200," which indicates that the request was successful.
5. Extracting Length and Chain from Response:
   - If the response status code is "200," then the function extracts the length and chain from the JSON response.

6. Comparing Chain Length:
   - The function compares the length of the chain obtained from the node with the current maximum length ("max_length").
7. Validating Chain:
   - If the length of the chain from the node is greater than "max_length" and the chain is valid (as determined by the "is_chain_valid()" function), then it updates "max_length" and stores the chain as the "longest_chain."
8. Updating Longest Chain:
   - After iterating through all nodes, if a "longest_chain" has been identified (i.e., it is not "None"), then the function updates the current chain ("chain") with the "longest_chain."
9. Returning True or False:
   - If a longer valid chain is found and successfully replaced, then the function returns "True" to indicate success.
   - If no valid longer chain is found, then the function returns "False" to indicate failure.

In summary, this algorithm iterates through each node in the network, retrieves the blockchain from each node, compares the length of each chain, selects the longest valid chain, and replaces the current chain with the longest one if found. Finally, it returns "True" if a replacement is successful and "False" otherwise.

4.6 Conclusion

In conclusion, the simulation conducted in BlockSim, exploring the performance of PoW and PoS algorithms within the context of hyper-intelligent networks and blockchain technology, yielded insightful findings. The comparison between PoW and PoS algorithms revealed that PoW outperformed PoS in terms of scalability, aligning with the inherent characteristics of hyper-intelligent networks.

The PoW algorithm, designed meticulously to validate transactions and create new blocks through complex mathematical puzzles, demonstrated its robustness in ensuring network security and scalability. Its decentralized nature, coupled with the requirement of computational effort from miners, proved effective in maintaining the integrity of the blockchain while enabling scalability to accommodate a growing number of transactions.

On the other hand, the PoS algorithm, although promising in its approach of assigning transaction validation rights based on stake rather than computational power, faced limitations regarding scalability in the simulated environment. The reliance on stake ownership as the determinant for block validation introduced centralization tendencies, hindering scalability as the network expanded.

The findings underscore the importance of algorithm design in shaping the performance and scalability of blockchain networks within hyper-intelligent environments. By prioritizing decentralization and computational integrity, the PoW algorithm emerged as the preferred choice for ensuring scalability and robustness in hyper-intelligent blockchain networks.

As blockchain technology continues to evolve in tandem with hyper-intelligent networks, further research and development efforts will be essential to optimize scalability solutions while maintaining the integrity and security of decentralized systems. The simulation results serve as a valuable foundation for future advancements in blockchain algorithms and their integration into hyper-intelligent networks, paving the way for innovative solutions in various domains.

References

1. Shah, S.T.U., Yar, H., Khan, I., Ikram, M., Khan, H., Internet of things-based healthcare: recent advances and challenges, in: *Applications of Intelligent Technologies in Healthcare*, pp. 153–162, 2019.
2. Scarlato, M., Tourani, R., Jeon, M., *2022 Fourth International Conference on Blockchain Computing and Applications (BCCA)*, IEEE, pp. 93–98, 2022.
3. Liang, X., Shetty, S., Tosh, D., Bowden, D., Njilla, L., Kamhoua, C., Towards blockchain empowered trusted and accountable data sharing and collaboration in mobile healthcare applications. *EAI Endorsed Trans. Pervasive Health Technol.*, 4, 15, 2018.
4. Zyskind, G. and Nathan, O., Decentralizing privacy: Using blockchain to protect personal data, in: *IEEE Workshop on Security And Privacy*, IEEE, pp. 180–184, 2015.
5. Werth, J., Mohammad, H.B., Barzegar, H.R., El Ioini, N., Pahl, C., A Review of Blockchain Platforms Based on the Scalability, Security and Decentralization Trilemma. *ICEIS (1)*, pp. 146–155, 2023.
6. Nakamoto, S., *Bitcoin: A peer-to-peer electronic cash system*, 2008.

7. Castro, M. and Barbara, L., Practical byzantine fault tolerance, in: *OsDI*, vol. 99, pp. 173–186, 1999.
8. Shiraz, M., Gani, A., Khokhar, R.H., Buyya, R., A review on distributed application processing frameworks in smart mobile devices for mobile cloud computing. *IEEE Commun. Surv. Tutor.*, 15, 3, 1294–1313, 2012.
9. Lashkari, B. and Musilek, P., A comprehensive review of blockchain consensus mechanisms. *IEEE Access*, 43620–43652, 2021.
10. Nguyen, C.T., Hoang, D.T., Nguyen, D.N., Niyato, D., Nguyen, H.T., Dutkiewicz, E., Proof-of-stake consensus mechanisms for future blockchain networks: fundamentals, applications and opportunities. *IEEE Access*, 7, 85727–85745, 2019.
11. Joshi, S., Feasibility of proof of authority as a consensus protocol model. arXiv preprint arXiv:2109.02480, 2021.
12. Nicolas, K., Wang, Y., Giakos, G.C., Comprehensive overview of selfish mining and double spending attack countermeasures, in: *2019 IEEE 40th Sarnoff Symposium*, IEEE, pp. 1–6, 2019.
13. Shanaev, S., Shuraeva, A., Vasenin, M., Kuznetsov, M., Cryptocurrency value and 51% attacks: evidence from event studies. *J. Altern. Invest.*, 22, 3, 65–77, 2019.
14. Azaria, A., Ekblaw, A., Vieira, T., Lippman, A., Medrec: Using blockchain for medical data access and permission management, in: *2016 2nd international conference on open and big data (OBD)*, IEEE, pp. 25–30, 2016.
15. Chaudhry, N. and Yousaf, M.M., Consensus algorithms in blockchain: Comparative analysis, challenges and opportunities, in: *2018 12th international conference on open source systems and technologies (ICOSST)*, IEEE, pp. 54–63, 2018.
16. Nguyen, D.C., Ding, M., Pham, Q.-V., Pathirana, P.N., Le, L.B., Seneviratne, A., Li, J., Niyato, D., Poor, H.V., Federated learning meets blockchain in edge computing: Opportunities and challenges. *IEEE Internet Things J.*, 8, 16, 12806–12825, 2021.
17. Kim, H., Park, J., Bennis, M., Kim, S.-L., Blockchained on-device federated learning. *IEEE Commun. Lett.*, 24, 6, 1279–1283, 2019.
18. Nguyen, D.C., Pathirana, P.N., Ding, M., Seneviratne, A., BEdgeHealth: A decentralized architecture for edge-based IoMT networks using blockchain. *IEEE Internet Things J.*, 8, 14, 11743–11757, 2021.
19. Almalki, J., Al Shehri, W., Mehmood, R., Alsaif, K., Alshahrani, S.M., Jannah, N., Khan, N.A., Enabling blockchain with IoMT devices for healthcare. *Information*, 13, 10, 2022.
20. Połap, D., Srivastava, G., Jolfaei, A., Parizi, R.M., Blockchain technology and neural networks for the internet of medical things, in: *IEEE INFOCOM 2020-IEEE conference on computer communications workshops (INFOCOM WKSHPS)*, IEEE, pp. 508–513, 2020.
21. Lakhan, A., Mohammed, M.A., Nedoma, J., Martinek, R., Tiwari, P., Vidyarthi, A., Alkhayyat, A., Wang, W., Federated-learning based privacy

preservation and fraud-enabled blockchain IoMT system for healthcare. *IEEE J. Biomed. Health. Inf.*, 27, 2, 664–672, 2022.
22. Alharby, M. and van Moorsel, A., Blocksim: An extensible simulation tool for blockchain systems. *Front. Blockchain*, 3, 2020.
23. Panda, S.K. and Satapathy, S.C., An Investigation into Smart Contract Deployment on Ethereum Platform Using Web3.js and Solidity Using Blockchain, in: *Data Engineering and Intelligent Computing. Advances in Intelligent Systems and Computing*, vol. 1, V. Bhateja, S.C. Satapathy, C.M. Travieso-González, V.N.M. Aradhya (Eds.), Springer, Singapore, 2021, https://doi.org/10.1007/978-981-16-0171-2_52.
24. Panda, S.K., Rao, D.C., Satapathy, S.C., An Investigation into the Usability of Blockchain Technology in Internet of Things, in: *Data Engineering and Intelligent Computing. Advances in Intelligent Systems and Computing*, vol. 1, V. Bhateja, S.C. Satapathy, C.M. Travieso-González, V.N.M. Aradhya (Eds.), Springer, Singapore, 2021, https://doi.org/10.1007/978-981-16-0171-2_53.
25. Panda, S.K., Dash, S.P., Jena, A.K., Optimization of Block Query Response Using Evolutionary Algorithm, in: *Data Engineering and Intelligent Computing. Advances in Intelligent Systems and Computing*, vol. 1, V. Bhateja, S.C. Satapathy, C.M. Travieso-González, V.N.M. Aradhya (Eds.), Springer, Singapore, 2021, https://doi.org/10.1007/978-981-16-0171-2_54.
26. Nanda, S.K., Panda, S.K., Das, M., Satapathy, S.C., Automating Vehicle Insurance Process Using Smart Contract and Ethereum, in: *Advances in Micro-Electronics, Embedded Systems and IoT. Lecture Notes in Electrical Engineering*, vol. 838, V.V.S.S.S. Chakravarthy, W. Flores-Fuentes, V. Bhateja, B. Biswal (Eds.), Springer, Singapore, 2022, https://doi.org/10.1007/978-981-16-8550-7_23.
27. Varaprasada Rao, K. and Panda, S.K., Secure Electronic Voting (E-voting) System Based on Blockchain on Various Platforms, in: *Computer Communication, Networking and IoT. Lecture Notes in Networks and Systems*, vol. 459, S.C. Satapathy, J.C.W. Lin, L.K. Wee, V. Bhateja, T.M. Rajesh (Eds.), Springer, Singapore, 2023, https://doi.org/10.1007/978-981-19-1976-3_18.
28. Varaprasada Rao, K. and Panda, S.K., A Design Model of Copyright Protection System Based on Distributed Ledger Technology, in: *Computer Communication, Networking and IoT. Lecture Notes in Networks and Systems*, vol. 459, S.C.,. Satapathy, J.C.W. Lin, L.K. Wee, V. Bhateja, T.M. Rajesh (Eds.), Springer, Singapore, 2023, https://doi.org/10.1007/978-981-19-1976-3_17.
29. Panda, S.K., Elngar, A.A., Balas, V.E., Kayed, M. (Eds.), *Bitcoin and Blockchain: History and Current Applications*, 1st ed, CRC Press, 2020, https://doi.org/10.1201/9781003032588.
30. Panda, S.K., Jena, A.K., Swain, S.K., Satapathy, S.C. (Eds.), *Blockchain Technology: Applications and Challenges, Intelligent Systems Reference Library*, Springer, https://doi.org/10.1007/978-3-030-69395-4.
31. Sathya, A.R., Panda, S.K., Hanumanthakari, S., Enabling Smart Education System Using Blockchain Technology, in: *Blockchain Technology: Applications*

and Challenges. Intelligent Systems Reference Library, vol. 203, S.K. Panda, A.K. Jena, S.K. Swain, S.C. Satapathy (Eds.), Springer, Cham, 2021, https://doi.org/10.1007/978-3-030-69395-4_10.

32. Lokre, S.S., Naman, V., Priya, S., Panda, S.K., Gun Tracking System Using Blockchain Technology, in: *Blockchain Technology: Applications and Challenges. Intelligent Systems Reference Library*, vol. 203, S.K. Panda, A.K. Jena, S.K. Swain, S.C. Satapathy (Eds.), Springer, Cham, 2021, https://doi.org/10.1007/978-3-030-69395-4_16.
33. Panda, S.K., Daliyet, S.P., Lokre, S.S., Naman, V., Distributed Ledger Technology in the Construction Industry Using Corda, in: *The New Advanced Society: Artificial Intelligence and Industrial Internet of Things Paradigm*, https://doi.org/10.1002/9781119884392.ch2.
34. Panda, S.K., Mohammad, G.B., Nandan Mohanty, S., Sahoo, S., Smart contract-based land registry system to reduce frauds and time delay. *Secur. Privacy*, e172, 2021. https://doi.org/10.1002/spy2.172.
35. Panda, S.K. and Satapathy, S.C., Drug traceability and transparency in medical supply chain using blockchain for easing the process and creating trust between stakeholders and consumers. *Pers. Ubiquitous Comput.*, 28, 75–91, 2024. https://doi.org/10.1007/s00779-021-01588-3.
36. Niveditha, V.R., Sekaran, K., Singh, K.A., Panda, S.K., Effective prediction of bitcoin price using wolf search algorithm and bidirectional LSTM on internet of things data. *Int. J. Syst. Syst. Eng.*, 11, 3–4, 224–236.
37. Arza, M.S. and Panda, S.K., An Integration of Blockchain and Machine Learning into the Health Care System, in: *Machine Learning Adoption in Blockchain-Based Intelligent Manufacturing*, vol. 1, pp. 33–58, DOI: 10.1201/9781003252009-3.
38. Panda, S.K., Fraud-Resistant Crowdfunding System Using Ethereum Blockchain, in: *Bitcoin and Blockchain*, pp. 237–276, 2020.
39. Puranam, K.S.RK., Gaddam, M.C.T., Vara Prasad Rao, K.,., Panda, S.K., Reddy, G.S.M., Anatomy and Lifecycle of a Bitcoin Transaction. *Proceedings of International Conference on Sustainable Computing in Science, Technology and Management (SUSCOM)*, February 18, 2019, Amity University Rajasthan, Jaipur, India, February 26-28, 2019, Available at SSRN: https://ssrn.com/abstract=3355106 or http://dx.doi.org/10.2139/ssrn.3355106.
40. Panda, S.K., Sathya, A.R., Das, S., Bitcoin: Beginning of the Cryptocurrency Era, in: *Recent Advances in Blockchain Technology. Intelligent Systems Reference Library*, vol. 237, S.K. Panda, V. Mishra, S.P. Dash, A.K. Pani (Eds.), Springer, Cham, 2023, https://doi.org/10.1007/978-3-031-22835-3_2.
41. Murala, D.K., Panda, S.K., Sahoo, S.K., Securing Electronic Health Record System in Cloud Environment Using Blockchain Technology, in: *Recent Advances in Blockchain Technology. Intelligent Systems Reference Library*, vol. 237, S.K. Panda, V. Mishra, S.P. Dash, A.K. Pani (Eds.), Springer, Cham, 2023, https://doi.org/10.1007/978-3-031-22835-3_4.

42. Rao, K.V., Murala, D.K., Panda, S.K., Blockchain: A Study of New Business Model, in: *Recent Advances in Blockchain Technology. Intelligent Systems Reference Library*, vol. 237, S.K. Panda, V. Mishra, S.P. Dash, A.K. Pani (Eds.), Springer, Cham, 2023, https://doi.org/10.1007/978-3-031-22835-3_9.
43. Panda, S.K., Mishra, V., Dash, S.P., Pani, A.K., *Recent Advances in Blockchain Technology Real-World Applications, Intelligent Systems Reference Library (ISRL, volume 237)*, vol. 978-3-031-22835-3, Vol 1, pp. 1–317.
44. Panda, S.K., Mohapatra, R.K., Panda, S., Balamurugan, S., *The New Advanced Society: Artificial Intelligence and Industrial Internet of Things Paradigm*, vol. 1, pp. 1–512, John Wiley & Sons, DOI:10.1002/9781119884392.
45. Nanda, S.K., Panda, S.K., Das, M., Satapathy, S.C., Decentralization of Car Insurance System Using Machine Learning and Distributed Ledger Technology, in: *Intelligent Data Engineering and Analytics. FICTA 2022. Smart Innovation, Systems and Technologies*, vol. 327 Springer, Singapore, 2023, https://doi.org/10.1007/978-981-19-7524-0_52.
46. Nanda, S.K., Panda, S.K., Dash, M., Medical supply chain integrated with blockchain and IoT to track the logistics of medical products. *Multimed. Tools Appl.*, 82, 32917–32939, 2023. https://doi.org/10.1007/s11042-023-14846-8.
47. Varaprasada Rao, K. and Panda, S.K., Initiation, Innovation, Implementation and Integration of CBDC in Digital Virtual Payment Systems, in: *Advances in Microelectronics, Embedded Systems and IoT. ICMEET 2023. Lecture Notes in Electrical Engineering*, vol. 1156 Springer, Singapore, 2024, https://doi.org/10.1007/978-981-97-0767-6_20.
48. Murala, D.K. and Panda, S.K., Blockchain in the development of metaverse, in: *Metaverse and Immersive Technologies: An Introduction to Industrial Business and Social Applications*, Wiley, USA.
49. Panda, S.K., Revolution of the Metaverse and Blockchain Technology, in: *Metaverse and Immersive Technologies: An Introduction to Industrial Business and Social Applications*, Wiley, Hoboken, NJ, USA, 2023.

5

Med3: Blockchain-Based Privacy Preservation of Patient Health Records in Hyper-Intelligent Network

Rohit Saxena*, Vishal Nagar, Satyasundara Mahapatra and Atul Gupta

Computer Science and Engineering, Pranveer Singh Institute of Technology, Kanpur, India

Abstract

Electronic health records (EHRs) are crucial to our daily lives. But mostly, they are dispersed and stored on databases that belong to organizations such as hospitals, laboratories, and clinics that are geographically dispersed across several countries. Healthcare professionals struggle to effectively collaborate by protecting and tracing the history of their patient's EHRs to provide them the best care. Blockchain technology offers a method that is steps ahead of the current healthcare systems for sharing data while maintaining the integrity, availability, and interoperability of the traditional architectures used to run EHRs. This chapter suggests a paradigm for protecting patient privacy while cooperatively exchanging EHRs. To do this, Ethereum Blockchain and Google's Firebase have been used. The Ethereum Blockchain allows patients complete control over their EHRs, whereas patient EHRs are stored and made available through Google's Firebase, which also guarantees the immutability of the records.

Keywords: Blockchain, ethereum, firebase, privacy preservation, EHRs

5.1 Introduction

Recently, there has been a significant amount of effort in combining healthcare with information technology, resulting in several improvements

**Corresponding author*: rohitt.saxenaa@gmail.com

Pradosh Kumar Gantayat, Sandeep Kumar Panda, S. Balamurugan and Sheng-Lung Peng (eds.) Hyper-Intelligent Networks: Exploring the Future of Connectivity for Society 5.0, (97–118) © 2026 Scrivener Publishing LLC

to the healthcare industry [25–28]. Such improvements not just impact the patient's medication schedule but also demand meticulous data processing. Data processing raises difficulties with privacy and security at the same time because healthcare is totally reliant on information for treatment. The term "electronic health record (EHR)" refers to a repository of data on a person's health, including details about ailments, treatments, images of the patient's body, and payment details. Sharing medical data securely is one of the major issues in healthcare systems because such data are sensitive and must be protected from unauthorized access [29–32]. The bulk of currently in-service healthcare institutions stores their patients' EHRs in local and proprietary database servers. Even though they try their best to safeguard the confidential and sensitive information of their clients, this method has numerous shortcomings. In fact, over the course of their lives, patients frequently seek multiple healthcare service providers, their EHRs are dispersed, and it is possible that crucial information will be unavailable anywhere and at crucial times. Even when the patient and the providers of the patient's healthcare are based in the same city, this situation happens frequently. The issue will be exacerbated for the patients who seek medical care from physicians in other nations. Patients do not necessarily have access to all of their documents, and they are helpless to determine who has what access. Confidential information is consequently often leaked, which harms its owner by leading to loss of employment, increasing the cost of insurance, etc. The sharing of medical data in a secure manner without exposing personal data presents one of the largest problems for healthcare systems. The creation of EHR indexes and their encryption before uploading to a public cloud is a typical or naive approach to sharing medical data [33–42]. The downside of this strategy is that many data suppliers have their own methods for producing indices, which would, in turn, inhibits data sharing across numerous health organizations and individuals. Additionally, it is possible that the cloud server cannot be completely trusted. The current literature also lacks a universal verification technique that can be used with all search schemes. Moreover, there are no effective means to discipline an unruly server or user [43–55].

In order to implement secured architectures for a variety of applications far more quickly and even with new, widely sought features, numerous innovative building blocks such as blockchain, hyperledger, and InterPlanetary File System (IPFS) are now available. Traditional cryptographic techniques, such as encryption, signature, and hashing, offer fundamental building blocks that make achieving security features like secrecy, integrity, and authentication simple [56–65]. But, in order to achieve other goals like availability, transparency, immutability, and automation, it is also necessary to combine a number of traditional cryptographic systems with new ideas, i.e., consensus algorithms, smart contracts, and peer-to-peer networks. For instance, IPFS is a peer to peer (P2P), open source, globally distributed file system with content addressability that can be used to store and share a lot of files quickly (Nizamuddin *et al.*, 2018) [15], SFS, a self-certifying file system (Mazières *et al.*, 1999) [12], and the hash tree, i.e., Merkle tree for disseminating files across network machines without the need for trusted nodes or a single point of failure. Firebase (Uunonen, 2023) [21] provides support for general data protection regulation (GDPR) (Haque *et al.*, 2021) [5]. Consequently, the consumer has control over the data. Obligations such as upholding a person's rights in regard to their personal data or information fall under the purview of the customer [66–70]. Blockchain is a network of interconnected digital blocks (Panda *et al.*, 2021; Panda and Satapathy, 2021) [25, 26] that use P2P networks, consensus algorithms, hash functions, smart contracts, signatures, etc., to accomplish intriguing qualities like integrity, availability, transparency, traceability, and automation. For example, smart contracts may be used to automatically start some processing when specific circumstances are met without the help of a dependable third party. Even though the anticipated results go against the stakeholders' wishes, the contract is nonetheless carried out [71–78].

5.2 Motivation

The preservation and protection of patient records, accessibility, delegation, anonymity, and other essential aspects are improved by these new developing technologies, such as blockchain. The primary purpose of this research is to resolve the issues with the current EHR administration systems by offering an intriguing solution that uses Ethereum and Firebase platforms. To the greatest extent of our knowledge, none of the studies have employed Google Firebase to host the medical records and related files. This research offers an intriguing solution with the following features:

a. The EHRs can be always accessed from any location and are properly safeguarded.
b. The EHRs are completely in the patient's hands, and they are always free to temporarily provide access to anyone or any organization.

Organization of the chapter: The following is how the remaining sections of the paper are structured: Related work is presented in Section 5.3, and problem formulation is addressed in Section 5.4. In Section 5.5, the blockchain-based healthcare system's proposed design is laid forth. Following a discussion of the findings in Section 5.6, Section 5.7 presents the conclusion and recommendations for future work.

5.3 Related Work

Over the past few years, we have examined many research articles on EHR systems. We can assess them based on certain helpful standards, such as the ones that follow:

a. **Absolute control of Patients over their EHRs:** Patients maintain their EHRs encrypted in their wallets or other storage devices, and they decide who has access to which data and when [79–83].
b. **Healthcare Service Provided With Anonymity:** If the solution enables patients to request an anonymous service at any time, then it would be excellent. Patients keep a collection of identity-related qualities, including their EHRs, and only reveal what is necessary [84–86].
c. **Accessibility:** The EHRs must always be accessible from everywhere, even if some of the infrastructure is damaged or under threat [87–89].
d. **Integrity:** EHRs should be checked to make sure no changes were made intentionally or unintentionally. EHRs are worthless if they lack integrity [90].
e. **Secrecy and Privacy:** EHRs hold extremely sensitive private data, and if that data is ever publicly disclosed, then the proprietors may suffer major consequences, such as job loss and rising insurance costs [91].
f. **Delegation for Access Control:** Every system that attempts to administer EHRs should make it simple for patients to grant others access to any EHR-related features [92].
g. **Zero-Knowledge Proof (ZKP):** The ability to demonstrate some attributes-related qualities without disclosing their values may be helpful to patients. They may, for instance, demonstrate their gender without disclosing that they are

male or female. Typically, some blockchain technologies employed ZKP protocols to offer this kind of functionality [93].

h. **Emergency EHR Access:** When a patient is not fully capable of providing his EHRs on his own during an emergency, a secure appropriate method should be made available [94].
i. **Extensibility:** While using blockchain, we must analyze the amount of data being contributed regularly to make sure the service remains extensible even when there are billions and billions of customers connected [95].
j. **Interoperability:** Every solution should adhere to standards to maximize interoperability, and blockchain should always be open and accessible to everyone when necessary [96].
k. **Virtual Health Services:** A growing requirement, especially in the COVID-19 setting, for virtual consultation should be addressed by EHR management solutions. This might be feasible, especially if patients can demonstrate their qualifications remotely [97, 98].

Below, we briefly outline the most noteworthy EHR management approaches that we have considered for our study.

Sun *et al.* (2020) [20] suggested a solution to store the EHRs effectively and securely. To restrict access to EHRs, they integrated attribute-based encryption methods with blockchain technology. Scalability, privacy, and the avoidance of a single point of failure are provided by the EHRs being encrypted and kept in the decentralized IPFS storage. According to Kumar *et al.* (2020) [8], distributed off-chain storage is a recommended approach to managing patient health records. The real medical records were maintained on IPFS, whereas the blockchain included the indexes for those documents. Delivering standard, trustworthy, and easily accessible medical data is the goal of the plan. Khatoon (2020) [6] recommended maintaining health records employing Ethereum and smart contracts. Social security numbers have been assigned to Ethereum addresses for authentication of users, providing flexible and easily available health information. Nguyen *et al.* (2019) [13] offered a framework for EHR exchange *via* a mobile platform. To protect patient privacy from malicious intrusions, they devised a framework for sharing health data on mobile clouds *via* the Ethereum Blockchain, which is housed on Amazon Cloud. In order to efficiently share medical data, Shen *et al.* (2019) [19] presented the MedChain blockchain–based system. MedChain is a healthcare data exchange service that combines structured peer-to-peer network methods, blockchain technology, and digest chains to solve the shortcomings of existing solutions. Super peers and edge peers are the two categories of peer nodes that comprise MedChain. Large, national hospitals with robust servers are considered super peers, whereas neighborhood clinics that maintain local patient information are considered edge peers. In their research, Niu *et al.* (2020) [14] proposed a permissioned blockchain–based secure architecture for sharing EHRs. The strategy allows for multi-user search, employs ciphertext-based attribute encryption to ensure the confidentiality of data, offers access control, and prohibits doctors from submitting fake information through authenticated access. A blockchain architecture based on Ethereum was suggested by Shahnaz *et al.* (2019) [18] to manage electronic medical records (EMRs). They created smart contracts that regulate access to medical records using Solidity. Using blockchain technology, Kim *et al.* (2019) [7] proposed a data-sharing management system for medical questionnaires. To ensure data integrity, they made use of blockchain features. They also talked about the situation where a third party demands certain EHR attributes that need the patient's consent. Dagher *et al.* (2018) [2] introduced the Ancile framework designed for protecting and restricting access to EHRs, which ought to be rendered accessible to a wide range of users, effectively, under various circumstances. Fan *et al.* (2018) [4] proposed a blockchain-based architecture called MedBlock to limit access to EHRs. Patients can quickly access and share their EHRs using MedBlock with the least amount of energy. Liu *et al.* (2018) [10] introduced boaderline personality disorder (BPDS), a blockchain-based system for sharing and preserving the privacy of EMRs. In BPDS, in order to prevent EMRs from being altered, the original EMRs are kept confidentially in a cloud storage system managed by smart contracts, and their indexes are kept on a consortium blockchain. Omar *et al.* (2017) [16] proposed a blockchain-based framework for the encrypted storage of medical data that protects patient privacy. Dubovitskaya *et al.* (2017) [3] suggested a blockchain-based system for exchanging cancer patients' EHRs. They achieved immutable, responsible, and EHR access control by utilizing permissioned blockchain characteristics. The EHRs are stored on a cloud server and encrypted using the patients' public keys in this architecture. Obtaining the decryption key from the data owner is important when the data are needed. Liang *et al.* (2018) [9] proposed a methodology for user-centric data exchange in eHealth systems. They used membership services powered by a permissioned blockchain to strengthen decentralized identity management and safeguard the privacy of healthcare data. According to this paradigm, healthcare records are gathered from many sources that include wearable technology and saved to the cloud for use by various providers and insurance organizations. MeDShare is a blockchain-based EHR administrator that offers access control for health data in a trustless setting, according to (Xia *et al.*, 2017) [22]. Access control is made possible using smart contracts, and EHRs are kept in the cloud. Azaria *et al.* (2016) [1] presented the MedRec permissionless blockchain-based medical data access and management system. Also, this architecture allows healthcare institutions to share health data. The sharing of EHRs, accountability, and confidentiality are all provided by the usage of blockchain technology. To provide fine-grained access control for patient medical records, they created three Ethereum smart contracts. Actual healthcare records are not stored on the blockchain; instead, they are kept in the system's database. Health Data Gateway, a framework for blockchain-based storage that Yue *et al.* (2016) [23] suggested, gives patients autonomy and privacy-protected sharing of their medical data. The providers encrypt the patient's medical information, which is then kept in a secure blockchain. The patient can download his/her private key to decrypt his/her encrypted medical records whenever necessary and then chooses whether or not to share them. For precise access authorization, Zhang and Poslad (2018) [24] used user and physician authentication through Shamir's secret sharing. However, the plan put out by Zhang *et al.* results in centralization because EMRs are kept in a blockchain that is preserved in a reputable cloud. Even before the blockchain was invented, other eHealth solutions, like those by SandIkkaya *et al.* (2011) [17] Masi and Maurer (2011) [11], were presented. They frequently utilize cryptographic primitives and crypto protocols to guarantee a variety of security attributes, including the confidentiality and integrity of EHRs.

5.4 Problem Formulation

A patient's medical records are typically shared and stored on paper in healthcare organizations. Whenever a patient enters a healthcare organization, they are required to bring their health records (scans, test results, and prescriptions), which can be cumbersome to carry and keep up with. These health records can also be readily destroyed, misplaced, or manipulated by anyone. Therefore, the health records of a patient are not secure. Recovering data from corrupted patients' health records is exhausting. Also, it is burdensome for medical professionals to obtain a patient's medical record in a crisis. Consequently, patients are not given assurances regarding the protection of their health records or their accessibility and sharing. Hence, an EMR system that is accessible quickly and securely and that can be shared is needed.

5.5 Architecture of the Proposed Healthcare System

We have suggested an approach that can address the aforementioned issues by developing a user-friendly decentralized application that can store all the patients' health records on one platform to address all the shortcomings and limitations that come with the present medical system with regard to the store, share, and access the health data of the patient. The patient can use the application to track their health information through their account, which was created for them by the health advisor. The doctor and the health advisor can view the records only when the patient authorizes them. This approach allows the hospital to save any kind of patient's medical records, including text, pictures, PDFs, X-rays, and more. The system that we propose guarantees that access to and security of health records thanks to Google's Firebase. Users can share, host, and manage files using it. After the account for the patient has been set up by the health advisor, each patient receives a patient ID that enables the authentication of all patients throughout the entire system. Medical personnel/health advisors can fetch and update patient health records only when access is provided to them by the patient. Our decentralized network can be used to store medical records like documents or files. Nevertheless, directly storing files on the blockchain is a cost-intensive job. We upload images of the aforementioned documents on Firebase storage, and, for each image, we extracted the address (Uniform Resource Locator) generated by Firebase. We added patient, hospital, and medical records to the blockchain while keeping patient information on Firebase. The data is kept secure in Google's Firebase. The architecture of the proposed healthcare system is depicted in Figure 5.1.

1. Patient visits the hospital for consultation with the doctor and is entertained by the health advisor (customer helpdesk, etc.).
2. Health advisor checks the availability of the concerned doctor by sending a request to the Firebase. If the doctor is available, then the patient is registered, and his/her personal information such as name, contact details (phone number,

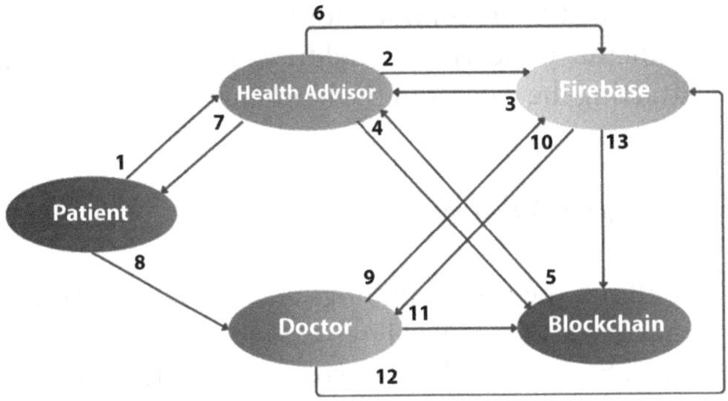

Figure 5.1 The architecture of the proposed healthcare system.

email address), and unique identity is committed to the Firebase.

3. In turn, the health advisor receives a patient ID, which can only be used by the patient.
4. Health advisor preserves the patient's health record on the Ethereum Blockchain, which includes previous history of illness.
5. Health advisor receives a unique identifier corresponding to the health records.
6. This unique identifier is stored on the Firebase and mapped to the corresponding patient ID by the Health Advisor.
7. The patient ID is handed over to the patient.
8. Patient ID meets the doctor as per the appointment. For gaining access to the patient's health record, the doctor receives one-time password (OTP) from Firebase.
9. Doctor submits the OTP to the Firebase.
10. Doctor receives the Unique Identifier which is mapped to the patient ID.
11. After gaining access to the previous health records, the doctor diagnoses the patient and preserves hashes of observations and medicines prescribed on the blockchain,
12. The images of observations and medical prescriptions are stored to the Firebase.
13. The addresses of the images stored in the Firebase are hashed and preserved to the Blockchain.

We have developed smart contracts for preserving the diagnosis and the prescribed medicine, preserving the address of the images on the blockchain and extracting the data from the blockchain.

5.6 Results and Discussion

This section outlines the overall findings and assessment of the proposed system that makes use of Google's Firebase and Ethereum Blockchain. We stored the patient health records on Firebase and, to decrease the size of the transaction, added the hash value of medical records, along with the patient ID to the blockchain. Ethereum Blockchain, Solidity v0.8.7, Go v1.16.7, and Node.js were used as software dependencies for client development. We considered 10 instances of the transaction on the Ethereum Blockchain and assessed the proposed system through the parameters namely, the *size of the block (in bytes)*, *execution time (in seconds)*, and the *gas used(gwei)*. The simulations were carried out over the following computing resources at the research lab at Pranveer Singh Institute of Technology, Kanpur:

System A: HP Z2 Tower G5 Workstation, Intel(R) Core(TM) I9-10900, 2.81 GHz with 32 GB RAM
System B: Dell Precision 3660 Tower Intel(R) Core(TM) I7-12700, 2.10 GHz with 16 GB RAM
System C: Asus Vivobook, Intel(R) Core(TM) I5-1035G1, 3.11 GHz with 16GB RAM

The findings of the proposed architecture on System A, System B, and System C are reported in Table 5.1. This table renders the comparison in terms of the size of the block, execution time, and gas used on System A, System B, and System C, respectively.

The comparison of execution time and the gas used by System A, System B, and System C have been depicted in Figures 5.2 and 5.3, respectively. This graphical representation clearly shows that System A, i.e., Intel(R) Core(TM) I9-10900, outperformed System B and System C in terms of execution time and the gas used. System A took the minimum execution time while the amount of computational effort applied is also minimum. Although the results obtained using System A are the best, this comes with a higher hardware cost. Additionally, it can be noticed that the gas consumed to compute a certain set of data by Systems B and System C is about comparable.

Table 5.1 Assessment report of the proposed decentralized system.

Size of data (bytes)	System A		System B		System C	
	Execution time (seconds)	Gas used (gwei)	Execution time (seconds)	Gas used (gwei)	Execution time (seconds)	Gas used (gwei)
700	5.214	463749	7.767	534981	9.14	560151
770	4.976	367681	9.5	479865	9.74	495065
842	8.115	367825	9.84	397981	11.8	489548
906	6.178	489865	9.5	657826	11.4	776426
970	5.703	694824	10	786521	12.5	873241
1226	7.73	530910	9.21	660898	11.9	710342
1290	7.672	735940	11.84	897823	13.65	940243
1365	8.452	853406	12.19	883406	14.5	903253
1398	8.763	873018	13.06	953018	15.79	980345
1450	9.954	954863	13.92	994863	16.2	1050234

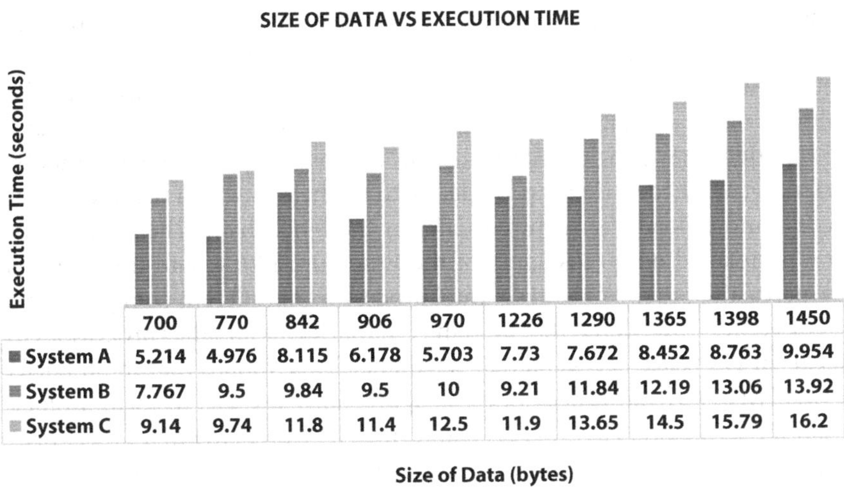

Figure 5.2 Comparison of execution time on different machines with varying sizes of data.

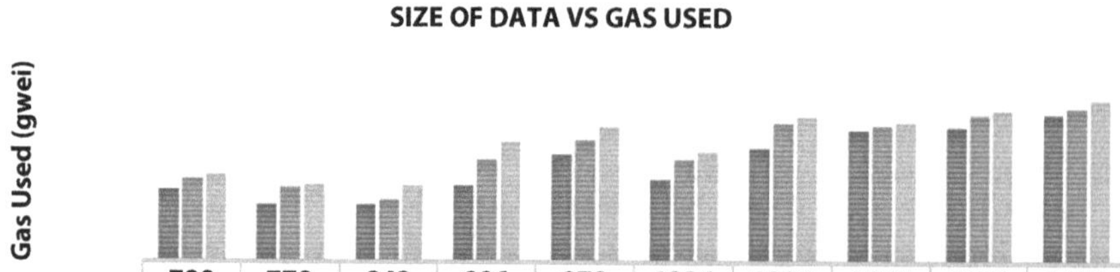

	700	770	842	906	970	1226	1290	1365	1398	1450
System A	463749	367681	367825	489865	694824	530910	735940	853406	873018	954863
System B	534981	479865	397981	657826	786521	660898	897823	883406	953018	994863
System C	560151	495065	489548	776426	873241	710342	940243	903253	980345	1050234

Size of Data (bytes)

Figure 5.3 Comparison of gas used on different machines with varying sizes of data.

5.7 Conclusions and Future Work

This research is performed with the aim to develop a decentralized system for preserving the patient's medical health data on the Ethereum Blockchain. Also, the objective is to provide the overall control of health data to patients. We have used Google's Firebase for storing the personal data of the patient. The patient's health data, the doctor's schedule, the diagnosis carried out, and medicines prescribed by the doctor are preserved on the Ethereum Blockchain, whereas the images of the medical reports and prescriptions are stored securely with Google's Firebase. The address of these images is also preserved with the Ethereum Blockchain. The patient can provide access to the doctor *via* OTP. Once authenticated, a unique identifier is provided with the help of which the doctor can access and upload the required data on the blockchain. The experiment was performed on 10 instances of the Ethereum Blockchain transactions in increasing order. For testing, Intel processors of different configurations are used. It is discovered that System A outperforms all other processors in terms of gas usage across all data segments. This implies that the Intel(R) Core(TM) I9-10900 processors use significantly less gas to form a block than Intel(R) Core(TM) I7-12700 and Intel(R) Core(TM) I5-1035G1 processors. However, this comes at the expense of the processor's hardware. Further observation reveals that Intel(R) Core(TM) I9-10900 and Intel(R) Core(TM) I5-1035G1 processors used nearly comparable gas to perform computations. We can conclude that Google's Firebase can be used along with Ethereum Blockchain for sharing of EHRs and providing overall control of health records to the patients.

In this research, we have used Google's Firebase for the secure storage of patient's health data. Alternatively, the potential of IPFS can also be utilized for storing health records securely. Moreover, one can also develop and use NFTs for hospitals as unique digital assets.

References

1. Azaria, A., Ekblaw, A., Vieira, T., Lippman, A., MedRec: Using blockchain for medical data access and permission management. *Proceedings - 2016 2nd International Conference on Open and Big Data, OBD 2016*, pp. 25–30, 2016, https://doi.org/10.1109/OBD.2016.11.
2. Dagher, G.G., Mohler, J., Milojkovic, M., Marella, P.B., Ancile: Privacy-preserving framework for access control and interoperability of electronic health records using blockchain technology. *Sustain. Cities Soc.*, 39, 283–297, 2018. https://doi.org/10.1016/j.scs.2018.02.014.
3. Dubovitskaya, A., Xu, Z., Ryu, S., Schumacher, M., Wang, F., Secure and Trustable Electronic Medical Records Sharing using Blockchain. *AMIA Annual Symposium Proceedings. AMIA Symposium*, vol. 2017, pp. 650–659, 2017.
4. Fan, K., Wang, S., Ren, Y., Li, H., Yang, Y., MedBlock: Efficient and Secure Medical Data Sharing *Via* Blockchain. *J. Med. Syst.*, 42, 8, 1–11, 2018. https://doi.org/10.1007/s10916-018-0993-7.
5. Haque, A.B., Islam, A.K.M.N., Hyrynsalmi, S., Naqvi, B., Smolander, K., GDPR compliant blockchains-a systematic literature review. *IEEE Access*, 9, 50593–50606, 2021. https://doi.org/10.1109/ACCESS.2021.3069877.
6. Khatoon, A., A blockchain-based smart contract system for healthcare management. *Electronics (Switzerland)*, 9, 1, 2020. https://doi.org/10.3390/electronics9010094.
7. Kim, M.G., Lee, A.R., Kwon, H.J., Kim, J.W., Kim, I.K., Sharing Medical Questionnaries based on Blockchain. *Proceedings-2018 IEEE International Conference on Bioinformatics and Biomedicine, BIBM 2018*, pp. 2767–2769, 2019, https://doi.org/10.1109/BIBM.2018.8621154.
8. Kumar, R., Marchang, N., Tripathi, R., Distributed Off-Chain Storage of Patient Diagnostic Reports in Healthcare System Using IPFS and Blockchain. *2020 International Conference on COMmunication Systems and NETworkS, COMSNETS 2020*, pp. 1–5, 2020, https://doi.org/10.1109/COMSNETS48256.2020.9027313.
9. Liang, X., Zhao, J., Shetty, S., Liu, J., Li, D., Integrating blockchain for data sharing and collaboration in mobile healthcare applications. *IEEE International Symposium on Personal, Indoor and Mobile Radio Communications, PIMRC*, October 2017, pp. 1–5, 2018, https://doi.org/10.1109/PIMRC.2017.8292361.

10. Liu, J., Li, X., Ye, L., Zhang, H., Du, X., Guizani, M., BPDS: A Blockchain Based Privacy-Preserving Data Sharing for Electronic Medical Records. *2018 IEEE Global Communications Conference, GLOBECOM 2018 - Proceedings*, 2018, https://doi.org/10.1109/GLOCOM.2018.8647713.
11. Masi, M. and Maurer, R., On the usage of SAML delegate assertions in an healthcare scenario with federated communities. *Lecture Notes of the Institute for Computer Sciences, Social-Informatics and Telecommunications Engineering, 69 LNICST*, pp. 212–220, 2011, https://doi.org/10.1007/978-3-642-23635-8_27.
12. Mazières, D., Kaminsky, M., Kaashoek, M.F., Witchel, E., Separating key management from file system security. *Proceedings of the 17th ACM Symposium on Operating Systems Principles, SOSP 1999*, pp. 124–139, 1999, https://doi.org/10.1145/319151.319160.
13. Nguyen, D.C., Pathirana, P.N., Ding, M., Seneviratne, A., Blockchain for Secure EHRs Sharing of Mobile Cloud Based E-Health Systems. *IEEE Access*, 7, 66792–66806, 2019. https://doi.org/10.1109/ACCESS.2019.2917555.
14. Niu, S., Chen, L., Wang, J., Yu, F., Electronic Health Record Sharing Scheme with Searchable Attribute-Based Encryption on Blockchain. *IEEE Access*, 8, 7195–7204, 2020. https://doi.org/10.1109/ACCESS.2019.2959044.
15. Nizamuddin, N., Hasan, H.R., Salah, K., IPFS-blockchain-based authenticity of online publications. *Lecture Notes in Computer Science (Including Subseries Lecture Notes in Artificial Intelligence and Lecture Notes in Bioinformatics), 10974 LNCS*, pp. 199–212, June 2018, https://doi.org/10.1007/978-3-319-94478-4_14.
16. Omar, A., Rahman, M.S., Basu, A., Kiyomoto, S., MediBchain: A Blockchain Based Privacy Preserving Platform for Healthcare Data. *International Conference on Security, Privacy and Anonymity in Computation, Communication and Storage (SpaCCS 2017)*, vol. 10658, pp. 534–543, 2017, https://doi.org/https://doi.org/10.1007/978-3-319-72395-2_49.
17. SandIkkaya, M.T., De Decker, B., Naessens, V., Privacy in commercial medical storage systems. *Lecture Notes of the Institute for Computer Sciences, Social-Informatics and Telecommunications Engineering, 69 LNICST*, pp. 247–258, 2011, https://doi.org/10.1007/978-3-642-23635-8_32.
18. Shahnaz, A., Qamar, U., Khalid, A., Using Blockchain for Electronic Health Records. *IEEE Access*, 7, 147782–147795, 2019. https://doi.org/10.1109/ACCESS.2019.2946373.
19. Shen, B., Guo, J., Yang, Y., MedChain: Efficient healthcare data sharing *via* blockchain. *Appl. Sci. (Switzerland)*, 9, 6, 2019. https://doi.org/10.3390/app9061207.
20. Sun, J., Yao, X., Wang, S., Wu, Y., Blockchain-Based Secure Storage and Access Scheme for Electronic Medical Records in IPFS. *IEEE Access*, 8, 59389–59401, 2020. https://doi.org/10.1109/ACCESS.2020.2982964.

21. Uunonen, S., Backend as a service in web development. *Medium*, 2023. https://medium.com/codenares/backend-as-a-service-o-como-prescindir-de-un-backend-developer-facdde6e3132.
22. Xia, Q., Sifah, E.B., Kwame Omono Asamoah, J.G., Du, X., Guizani, M., MeDShare : Trust-less Medical Data Sharing Among. *IEEE Access*, 5, 1–10, 2017.
23. Yue, X., Wang, H., Jin, D., Li, M., Jiang, W., Healthcare Data Gateways: Found Healthcare Intelligence on Blockchain with Novel Privacy Risk Control. *J. Med. Syst.*, 40, 10, 2016. https://doi.org/10.1007/s10916-016-0574-6.
24. Zhang, X. and Poslad, S., Blockchain Support for Flexible Queries with Granular Access Control to Electronic Medical Records (EMR). *IEEE International Conference on Communications*, 2018-May, 2018, https://doi.org/10.1109/ICC.2018.8422883.
25. Panda, S.K. and Satapathy, S.C., An Investigation into Smart Contract Deployment on Ethereum Platform Using Web3.js and Solidity Using Blockchain, in: *Data Engineering and Intelligent Computing. Advances in Intelligent Systems and Computing*, vol. 1, V. Bhateja, S.C. Satapathy, C.M. Travieso-González, V.N.M. Aradhya (Eds.), Springer, Singapore, 2021, https://doi.org/10.1007/978-981-16-0171-2_52.
26. Panda, S.K., Rao, D.C., Satapathy, S.C., An Investigation into the Usability of Blockchain Technology in Internet of Things, in: *Data Engineering and Intelligent Computing. Advances in Intelligent Systems and Computing*, vol. 1, V. Bhateja, S.C. Satapathy, C.M. Travieso-González, V.N.M. Aradhya (Eds.), Springer, Singapore, 2021, https://doi.org/10.1007/978-981-16-0171-2_53.
27. Panda, S.K., Dash, S.P., Jena, A.K., Optimization of Block Query Response Using Evolutionary Algorithm, in: *Data Engineering and Intelligent Computing. Advances in Intelligent Systems and Computing*, vol. 1, V. Bhateja, S.C. Satapathy, C.M. Travieso-González, V.N.M. Aradhya (Eds.), Springer, Singapore, 2021, https://doi.org/10.1007/978-981-16-0171-2_54.
28. Nanda, S.K., Panda, S.K., Das, M., Satapathy, S.C., Automating Vehicle Insurance Process Using Smart Contract and Ethereum, in: *Advances in Micro-Electronics, Embedded Systems and IoT. Lecture Notes in Electrical Engineering*, vol. 838, V.V.S.S.S. Chakravarthy, W. Flores-Fuentes, V. Bhateja, B. Biswal (Eds.), Springer, Singapore, 2022, https://doi.org/10.1007/978-981-16-8550-7_23.
29. Varaprasada Rao, K. and Panda, S.K., Secure Electronic Voting (E-voting) System Based on Blockchain on Various Platforms, in: *Computer Communication, Networking and IoT. Lecture Notes in Networks and Systems*, vol. 459, S.C. Satapathy, J.C.W. Lin, L.K. Wee, V. Bhateja, T.M. Rajesh (Eds.), Springer, Singapore, 2023, https://doi.org/10.1007/978-981-19-1976-3_18.
30. Varaprasada Rao, K. and Panda, S.K., A Design Model of Copyright Protection System Based on Distributed Ledger Technology, in: *Computer Communication, Networking and IoT. Lecture Notes in Networks and Systems*,

vol. 459, S.C. Satapathy, J.C.W. Lin, L.K. Wee, V. Bhateja, T.M. Rajesh (Eds.), Springer, Singapore, 2023, https://doi.org/10.1007/978-981-19-1976-3_17.
31. Panda, S.K., Elngar, A.A., Balas, V.E., Kayed, M. (Eds.), *Bitcoin and Blockchain: History and Current Applications*, 1st ed, CRC Press, 2020, https://doi.org/10.1201/9781003032588.
32. Panda, S.K., Jena, A.K., Swain, S.K., Satapathy, S.C. (Eds.), *Blockchain Technology: Applications and Challenges, Intelligent Systems Reference Library*, Springer, https://doi.org/10.1007/978-3-030-69395-4.
33. Sathya, A.R., Panda, S.K., Hanumanthakari, S., Enabling Smart Education System Using Blockchain Technology, in: *Blockchain Technology: Applications and Challenges. Intelligent Systems Reference Library*, vol. 203, S.K. Panda, A.K. Jena, S.K. Swain, S.C. Satapathy (Eds.), Springer, Cham, 2021, https://doi.org/10.1007/978-3-030-69395-4_10.
34. Lokre, S.S., Naman, V., Priya, S., Panda, S.K., Gun Tracking System Using Blockchain Technology, in: *Blockchain Technology: Applications and Challenges. Intelligent Systems Reference Library*, vol. 203, S.K. Panda, A.K. Jena, S.K. Swain, S.C. Satapathy (Eds.), Springer, Cham, 2021, https://doi.org/10.1007/978-3-030-69395-4_16.
35. Panda, S.K., Daliyet, S.P., Lokre, S.S., Naman, V., Distributed Ledger Technology in the Construction Industry Using Corda, in: *The New Advanced Society: Artificial Intelligence and Industrial Internet of Things Paradigm*, https://doi.org/10.1002/9781119884392.ch2.
36. Panda, S.K., Mohammad, G.B., Nandan Mohanty, S., Sahoo, S., Smart contract-based land registry system to reduce frauds and time delay. *Secur. Privacy*, e172, 2021. https://doi.org/10.1002/spy2.172.
37. Panda, S.K. and Satapathy, S.C., Drug traceability and transparency in medical supply chain using blockchain for easing the process and creating trust between stakeholders and consumers. *Pers. Ubiquitous Comput.*, 28, 75–91, 2024. https://doi.org/10.1007/s00779-021-01588-3.
38. Niveditha, V.R., Sekaran, K., Singh, K.A., Panda, S.K., Effective prediction of bitcoin price using wolf search algorithm and bidirectional LSTM on internet of things data. *Int. J. Syst. Syst. Eng.*, 11, 3-4, 224–236.
39. Arza, M.S. and Panda, S.K., An Integration of Blockchain and Machine Learning into the Health Care System, in: *Machine Learning Adoption in Blockchain-Based Intelligent Manufacturing*, vol. 1, pp. 33–58.
40. Murala, D.K., Panda, S.K., Swain, Santosh, K., A survey on cloud computing security and privacy issues and challenges. *J. Adv. Res. Dyn. Control Syst.*, 11, 1276–1290, 2019.
41. Murala, D.K., Panda, S.K., Santosh, K., Swain, Secure dynamic groups data sharing with modified revocable attribute-based encryption in cloud. *Int. J. Recent Technol. Eng.*, 8, 4, 2019. ISSN: 2277-3878.
42. Murala, D.K., Panda, S.K., Swain, Santosh, K., A novel hybrid approach for providing data security and privacy from malicious attacks in the cloud environment. *J. Adv. Res. Dyn. Control Syst.*, 11, 1291–1300, 2019.

43. Panda, S.K., Swain, S.K., Mall, R., An investigation into usability aspects of E-Commerce websites using users' preferences. *Adv. Comput. Sci. An Int. J.*, 4, 1, 65–73, 2015.
44. Panda, S.K., Swain, S.K., Mall, R., Measuring Web Site Usability Quality Complexity Metrics for Navigability, in: *Intelligent Computing, Communication and Devices. Advances in Intelligent Systems and Computing*, vol. 308, L. Jain, S. Patnaik, N. Ichalkaranje (Eds.), Springer, New Delhi, 2015, https://doi.org/10.1007/978-81-322-2012-1_41.
45. Panda, S.K., A Usability Evaluation Framework for B2C E-Commerce Websites. *Comput. Eng. Intell. Syst.*, 5, 3, 66–85, 2014.
46. Bhalerao, V., Panda, S.K., Jena, A.K., Optimization of Loss Function on Human Faces Using Generative Adversarial Networks, in: *Machine Learning Approaches for Urban Computing. Studies in Computational Intelligence*, vol. 968, M. Bandyopadhyay, M. Rout, S. Chandra Satapathy (Eds.), Springer, Singapore, 2021, https://doi.org/10.1007/978-981-16-0935-0_9.
47. Panda, S.K. and Dwivedi, M., Minimizing Food Wastage Using Machine Learning: A Novel Approach, in: *Smart Intelligent Computing and Applications Smart Innovation, Systems and Technologies*, vol. 159, S. Satapathy, V. Bhateja, J. Mohanty, S. Udgata (Eds.), Springer, Singapore, 2020, https://doi.org/10.1007/978-981-13-9282-5_44.
48. Panda, S.K., Sathya, A.R., Mishra, M., Satpathy, S., A supervised learning algorithm to forecast weather conditions for playing cricket. *Int. J. Innov. Technol. Explor. Eng.*, 9, 1, 2019.
49. Panda, S.K., Fraud-Resistant Crowdfunding System Using Ethereum Blockchain, in: *Bitcoin and Blockchain*, pp. 237–276, 2020.
50. Panda, S.K., Mishra, V., Balamurali, R., Elngar, A.A., *Artificial Intelligence and Machine Learning in Business Management Concepts, Challenges, and Case Studies*, pp. 1–278, https://doi.org/10.1201/9781003125129.
51. Joshi, S., Panda, S.K., AR, S., Optimal Deep Learning Model to Identify the Development of Pomegranate Fruit in Farms. *Int. J. Innov. Technol. Explor. Eng.*, 9, 3, 2352–2356, 2020.
52. Puranam, K.S.RK., Gaddam, M.C.T., K, V.P.R., Panda, S.K., Reddy, G.S.M., Anatomy and Lifecycle of a Bitcoin Transaction. *Proceedings of International Conference on Sustainable Computing in Science, Technology and Management (SUSCOM)*, February 18, 2019, Amity University Rajasthan, Jaipur -India, February 26-28, 2019, Available at SSRN: https://ssrn.com/abstract=3355106 or http://dx.doi.org/10.2139/ssrn.3355106.
53. Panda, S.K., Santosh, K., Swain, *Quality Assurance Aspects of Web Design, Design Solutions for Improving Website Quality and Effectiveness*, pp. 87–129, IGI Global, 2016.
54. Panda, S.K., Bhalerao, V., Ar, S., A Machine Learning Model to Identify Duplicate Questions in Social Media Forums. *Int. J. Innov. Technol. Explor. Eng.*, 9, 4, 370–373, 2020.

55. Ahmareen, S., Raj, A., Potluri, S., Panda, S.K., Book Shala: An Android-Based Application Design and Implementation of Sharing Books, in: *Smart Intelligent Computing and Applications. Smart Innovation, Systems and Technologies*, vol. 159, V. Bhateja, J. Mohanty, S. Udgata (Eds.), Springer, Singapore, 2020, https://doi.org/10.1007/978-981-13-9282-5_28.
56. Panda, S.K., Das, S.S., Swain, S.K., *S-Model for Service-Oriented Applications in Web Engineering*, Regional College Of Management, vol. 10, pp. 38–46, 2013.
57. Panda, S.K., *An Investigation into Usability and Productivity of ECommerce Websites.*
58. Panda, S.K., Chandrasekhar, A., Gantayat, P.K., Panda, M.R., Detecting Brain Tumor Using Image Segmentation: A Novel Approach, in: *Data Engineering and Intelligent Computing. Lecture Notes in Networks and Systems*, vol. 446, V. Bhateja, L. Khin Wee, J.C.W. Lin, S.C. Satapathy, T.M. Rajesh (Eds.), Springer, Singapore, 2022, https://doi.org/10.1007/978-981-19-1559-8_35.
59. Sanghi, P., Panda, S.K., Pati, C., Gantayat, P.K., Learning Deep Features and Classification for Fresh or off Vegetables to Prevent Food Wastage Using Machine Learning Algorithms, in: *Intelligent Data Engineering and Analytics. Smart Innovation, Systems and Technologies*, vol. 266, S.C. Satapathy, P. Peer, J. Tang, V. Bhateja, A. Ghosh (Eds.), Springer, Singapore, 2022, https://doi.org/10.1007/978-981-16-6624-7_44.
60. Gantayat, P.K., Mohapatra, S., Panda, S.K., Secure Trust Level Routing in Delay-Tolerant Network with Node Categorization Technique, in: *Intelligent Data Engineering and Analytics. Smart Innovation, Systems and Technologies*, vol. 266, S.C. Satapathy, P. Peer, J. Tang, V. Bhateja, A. Ghosh (Eds.), Springer, Singapore, 2022, https://doi.org/10.1007/978-981-16-6624-7_45.
61. Panda, S.K., Urkude, S.V., Urkude, V.R., Vairachilai, S., An investigation into COVID 19 pandemic in India, in: *The New Advanced Society: Artificial Intelligence and Industrial Internet of Things Paradigm*, vol. 1, pp. 289–305, Wiley.
62. Panda, S.K., Das, S., Swain, S.K., Web Site Productivity Measurement Using Single Task Size Measure. *J. Inf. Sci. Comput. Technol.*, 4, 3, October12, 2015.
63. Hanumanthakari, S. and Panda, S.K., Detecting Face Mask for Prevent COVID-19 Using Deep Learning: A Novel Approach, in: *Smart Intelligent Computing and Applications, Volume 2. Smart Innovation, Systems and Technologies*, vol. 283, S.C. Satapathy, V. Bhateja, M.N. Favorskaya, T. Adilakshmi (Eds.), Springer, Singapore, 2022, https://doi.org/10.1007/978-981-16-9705-0_45.
64. Panda, S.K., Sathya, A.R., Das, S., Bitcoin: Beginning of the Cryptocurrency Era, in: *Recent Advances in Blockchain Technology. Intelligent Systems Reference Library*, vol. 237, V. Mishra, S.P. Dash, A.K. Pani (Eds.), Springer, Cham, 2023, https://doi.org/10.1007/978-3-031-22835-3_2.
65. Murala, D.K., Panda, S.K., Sahoo, S.K., Securing Electronic Health Record System in Cloud Environment Using Blockchain Technology, in: *Recent Advances in Blockchain Technology. Intelligent Systems Reference Library*,

vol. 237, S.K. Panda, V. Mishra, S.P. Dash, A.K. Pani (Eds.), Springer, Cham, 2023, https://doi.org/10.1007/978-3-031-22835-3_4.

66. Rao, K.V., Murala, D.K., Panda, S.K., Blockchain: A Study of New Business Model, in: *Recent Advances in Blockchain Technology. Intelligent Systems Reference Library*, vol. 237, S.K. Panda, V. Mishra, S.P. Dash, A.K. Pani (Eds.), Springer, Cham, 2023, https://doi.org/10.1007/978-3-031-22835-3_9.
67. Panda, S.K., Mishra, V., Dash, S.P., Pani, A.K., *Recent Advances in Blockchain Technology Real-World Applications, Intelligent Systems Reference Library (ISRL, volume 237)*, vol. 1, pp. 1–317, ISBN: 978-3-031-22835-3, .
68. Panda, S.K., Mohapatra, R.K., Panda, S., Balamurugan, S., *The New Advanced Society: Artificial Intelligence and Industrial Internet of Things Paradigm*, vol. 1, pp. 1–512, John Wiley & Sons, doi: DOI:10.1002/9781119884392.
69. Nanda, S.K., Panda, S.K., Das, M., Satapathy, S.C., Decentralization of Car Insurance System Using Machine Learning and Distributed Ledger Technology, in: *Intelligent Data Engineering and Analytics. FICTA 2022. Smart Innovation, Systems and Technologies*, vol. 327 Springer, Singapore, 2023, https://doi.org/10.1007/978-981-19-7524-0_52.
70. Nanda, S.K., Panda, S.K., Dash, M., Medical supply chain integrated with blockchain and IoT to track the logistics of medical products. *Multimed. Tools Appl.*, 82, 32917–32939, 2023. https://doi.org/10.1007/s11042-023-14846-8.
71. Panda, S.K., Jena, A.K., Panda, M.R., *et al.*, Speech emotion recognition using multimodal feature fusion with machine learning approach. *Multimed. Tools Appl.*, 82, 42763–42781, 2023. https://doi.org/10.1007/s11042-023-15275-3.
72. Panda, S.K. and Mohanty, S.N., Time Series Forecasting and Modeling of Food Demand Supply Chain Based on Regressors Analysis. *IEEE Access*, 11, 42679–42700, 2023, doi: 10.1109/ACCESS.2023.3266275.
73. Desai, D.D., *et al.*, Optimal Ambulance Positioning for Road Accidents With Deep Embedded Clustering. *IEEE Access*, 11, 59917–59934, 2023, doi: 10.1109/ACCESS.2023.3284993.
74. Lakshmi, L., Devi, K.D.S., Gupta, S., Reddy, K.A.N., Grandhi, S.K., Panda, S.K., WOMT: Wasserstein Distribution Based Minimization of False Positives in Breast Tumor Classification Using Deep Learning. *IEEE Access*, 11, 57831–57842, 2023, doi: 10.1109/ACCESS.2023.3279496.
75. Mishra, P. and Panda, S.K., Dependency Structure-Based Rules Using Root Node Technique for Explicit Aspect Extraction From Online Reviews. *IEEE Access*, 11, 65117–65137, 2023, doi: 10.1109/ACCESS.2023.3287830.
76. Routray, N., Rout, S.K., Sahu, B., Panda, S.K., Godavarthi, D., Ensemble Learning With Symbiotic Organism Search Optimization Algorithm for Breast Cancer Classification and Risk Identification of Other Organs on Histopathological Images. *IEEE Access*, 11, 110544–110557, 2023, doi: 10.1109/ACCESS.2023.3322222.
77. Agarwal, R., Pande, S.D., Mohanty, S.N., Panda, S.K., A Novel Hybrid System of Detecting Brain Tumors in MRI. *IEEE Access*, 11, 118372–118385, 2023, doi: 10.1109/ACCESS.2023.3326447.

78. Nayak, S.K., Garanayak, M., Swain, S.K., Panda, S.K., Godavarthi, D., An Intelligent Disease Prediction and Drug Recommendation Prototype by Using Multiple Approaches of Machine Learning Algorithms. *IEEE Access*, 11, 99304–99318, 2023, doi: 10.1109/ACCESS.2023.3314332.
79. Gupta, A., Gandhi, R., Jatana, N., Jatain, D., Panda, S.K., Ramesh, J.V.N., A Severity Assessment of Python Code Smells. *IEEE Access*, 11, 119146–119160, 2023, doi: 10.1109/ACCESS.2023.3327553.
80. Murala, D.K., Panda, S.K., Dash, S.P., MedMetaverse: Medical Care of Chronic Disease Patients and Managing Data Using Artificial Intelligence, Blockchain, and Wearable Devices State-of-the-Art Methodology. *IEEE Access*, 11, 138985, 2023, doi: 10.1109/ACCESS.2023.3340791.
81. Sethi, B.K., Singh, D., Rout, S.K., Panda, S.K., Long Short-Term Memory-Deep Belief Network-Based Gene Expression Data Analysis for Prostate Cancer Detection and Classification. *IEEE Access*, 12, 1508–1524, 2024, doi: 10.1109/ACCESS.2023.3346925.
82. Mahapatra, A., Majhi, S.K., Mishra, K., Pradhan, R., Rao, D.C., Panda, S.K., An Energy-Aware Task Offloading and Load Balancing for Latency-Sensitive IoT Applications in the Fog-Cloud Continuum. *IEEE Access*, 12, 14334–14349, 2024, doi: 10.1109/ACCESS.2024.3357122.
83. Mishra, P., Sharma, O., Panda, S.K., ADN-BERT: Attention-Based Deep Network Model Using BERT for Sarcasm Classification, in: *Evolution in Computational Intelligence. FICTA 2023. Smart Innovation, Systems and Technologies*, vol. 370 Springer, Singapore, 2023, https://doi.org/10.1007/978-981-99-6702-5_51.
84. Varaprasada Rao, K. and Panda, S.K., Initiation, Innovation, Implementation and Integration of CBDC in Digital Virtual Payment Systems, in: *Advances in Microelectronics, Embedded Systems and IoT. ICMEET 2023. Lecture Notes in Electrical Engineering*, vol. 1156 Springer, Singapore, 2024, https://doi.org/10.1007/978-981-97-0767-6_20.
85. Murala, D.K. and Panda, S.K., Artificial intelligence in the development of metaverse, in: *Metaverse and Immersive Technologies: An Introduction to Industrial Business and Social Applications*, pp. 407–436, Wiley, Hoboken, NJ, USA, 2023.
86. Murala, D.K. and Panda, S.K., Metaverse: A study on immersive technologies, in: *Metaverse and Immersive Technologies: An Introduction to Industrial Business and Social Applications*, Wiley, Hoboken, NJ, USA, 2023.
87. Murala, D.K. and Panda, S.K., The Internet of Things in developing metaverse, in: *Metaverse and Immersive Technologies: An Introduction to Industrial Business and Social Applications*, Wiley, Hoboken, NJ, USA, 2023.
88. Murala, D.K. and Panda, S.K., Blockchain in the development of metaverse, in: *Metaverse and Immersive Technologies: An Introduction to Industrial Business and Social Applications*, Wiley, USA.
89. Murala, D.K. and Panda, S.K., The role of immersive reality (AR/VR/MR/XR) in metaverse, in: *Metaverse and Immersive Technologies: An Introduction*

to Industrial Business and Social Applications, pp. 159–189, Wiley, Hoboken, NJ, USA, 2023.

90. Panda, S.K., Revolution of the Metaverse and Blockchain Technology, in: *Metaverse and Immersive Technologies: An Introduction to Industrial Business and Social Applications*, Wiley, Hoboken, NJ, USA, 2023.
91. Sahoo, S.K., Das, S., Panda, S.K., Alzheimer's Disease Classification Using Brain MRI Based on 2D CNN and Transfer Learning, in: *Proceedings of the 6th International Conference on Communications and Cyber Physical Engineering. ICCCE 2024. Lecture Notes in Electrical Engineering*, vol. 1096 Springer, Singapore, 2024, https://doi.org/10.1007/978-981-99-7137-4_1.
92. Panda, S.K., Ramesh, J.V.N., Ghosh, H., Rahat, I.S., Sobur, A., Bijoy, M.H., Yesubabu, M., Deep Learning in Medical Imaging: A Case Study on Lung Tissue Classification. *EAI Endorsed Trans. Pervasive Health Technol.*, 10, 2024.
93. Paruchuri, V.N.L.L., Shaik, A.H., Murala, D.K., Panda, S.K., IoT-Enabled Neural Network Analysis for Early Detection and Prediction of Mental Depression, in: *Information System Design: Communication Networks and IoT. ISDIA 2024. Lecture Notes in Networks and Systems*, vol. 1057 Springer, Singapore, pp. 257–268, 2024, https://doi.org/10.1007/978-981-97-4895-2_21.
94. Paruchuri, V.N.L.L., Malaviya, M.P., Murala, D.K., Panda, S.K., Connecting IoT Sensors for Enhanced Dementia Disease Monitoring and Intervention, in: *Information System Design: Communication Networks and IoT. ISDIA 2024. Lecture Notes in Networks and Systems*, vol. 1057 Springer, Singapore, pp. 269–281, 2024, https://doi.org/10.1007/978-981-97-4895-2_22.
95. Panda, S.K., Das, S., Sahoo, S.K., Predominant Music Genre Classification Using Machine Learning Approach, in: *Signal Processing, Telecommunication and Embedded Systems with AI and ML Applications. ICMEET 2023. Lecture Notes in Electrical Engineering*, vol. 1281 Springer, Singapore, 2025, https://doi.org/10.1007/978-981-97-8422-6_17.
96. Panda, S.K., Das, S., Sahoo, S.K., Vehicle Detection and Classification Using Intelligent Systems, in: *Signal Processing, Telecommunication and Embedded Systems with AI and ML Applications. ICMEET 2023. Lecture Notes in Electrical Engineering*, vol. 1281 Springer, Singapore, 2025, https://doi.org/10.1007/978-981-97-8422-6_18.
97. Chandrasekhar, A., Dodhiawala, Z., Panda, S.K., An Investigation into Chronic Kidney Disease Based-on Classification Model, in: *Signal Processing, Telecommunication and Embedded Systems with AI and ML Applications. ICMEET 2023. Lecture Notes in Electrical Engineering*, vol. 1281 Springer, Singapore, 2025, https://doi.org/10.1007/978-981-97-8422-6_19.
98. Chandrashekhar, A., Saheb, S.H., Panda, S.K., Balamurugan, S., Peng, S.-L., *Metaverse and Immersive Technologies: An Introduction to Industrial, Business and Social Applications*, John Wiley & Sons, 2023.

6

Deep Learning for Hyper-Intelligent Networks

P. Sree Lakshmi[1]* and P. Rohini[2]

[1]*Department of Computer Science and Engineering, Koneru Lakshmaiah Education Foundation, Hyderabad, Telangana, India*
[2]*Department of Computer Science and Engineering, Faculty of Science and Technology, (IcfaiTech), ICFAI Foundation for Higher Education, Hyderabad, India*

Abstract
Hyper-intelligent networks, the cornerstone of the envisioned Society 5.0, are an area where deep learning offers transformative promise. Deep learning increases network systems' intelligence, efficiency, and flexibility by combining cutting-edge neural network topologies with creative learning algorithms. Significant approaches, real-world examples, and potential avenues for future research are examined, with a focus on how deep learning supports real-time optimizations, predictive analytics, and autonomous decision. Unprecedented progress in smart technologies and social infrastructure is being driven by the collaboration between deep learning and network intelligence, which heralds a new era of connectedness.

***Keywords*:** Deep learning, hyper-intelligent networks, neural network architectures, autonomous network management, real-time optimization, adaptive operations

6.1 Introduction

Hyper-intelligent networks represent the next frontier in connectivity, characterized by their ability to autonomously manage, adapt, and optimize operations using advanced technologies like AI and deep learning.

**Corresponding author*: rohini10@ifheindia.org

Pradosh Kumar Gantayat, Sandeep Kumar Panda, S. Balamurugan and Sheng-Lung Peng (eds.) Hyper-Intelligent Networks: Exploring the Future of Connectivity for Society 5.0, (119–138) © 2026 Scrivener Publishing LLC

These networks are essential for achieving the society's vision 5.0, where digital and physical spaces seamlessly integrate to enhance human capabilities and societal well-being.

6.1.1 Key Characteristics

1. **Autonomous Management**
   - **Self-Configuration**: Hyper-intelligent networks can automatically configure their parameters based on real-time data and predefined policies. This reduces the need for human intervention and minimizes configuration errors [1].
   - **Self-Healing**: These networks can detect and recover from faults or failures autonomously, ensuring minimal downtime and enhanced reliability [2].
2. **Adaptive Operations**
   - **Dynamic Resource Allocation**: Using artificial intelligence (AI) and deep learning, hyper-intelligent networks can efficiently distribute resources such as bandwidth and computational power to meet unpredictable requests and optimize performance [3].
   - **Context-Aware Services**: They can understand the context of network usage, such as user behavior and environmental conditions, to provide personalized and context-aware services [4].
3. **Optimization**
   - **Predictive Maintenance**: By analyzing data trends and patterns, these networks can predict potential issues before they occur and take preemptive actions to prevent them [5].
   - **Traffic Optimization**: They optimize traffic flow to avoid congestion and ensure efficient data transmission, improving overall network performance [6].

6.1.2 Essential Role in Society 5.0

Society 5.0 envisions a highly integrated society where digital technologies enhance and augment human capabilities, creating a seamless blend of the physical and digital worlds. Hyper-intelligent networks are crucial for this vision due to several reasons:

1. **Enhanced Connectivity**:
   - **Ubiquitous Internet Access**: These networks provide seamless, high-speed internet access everywhere, bridging the digital access gap and ensuring that every individual have access to the same resources and opportunities [7].
2. **Smart Cities**:
   - **Efficient Infrastructure**: Hyper-intelligent networks enable smart city applications like intelligent transportation systems, smart grids, and automated waste management, making urban environments more efficient and sustainable [8].
   - **Improved Public Services**: They support advanced public services such as real-time traffic management, emergency response systems, and personalized healthcare services [9].
3. **Healthcare Innovations**:
   - **Remote Monitoring and Telemedicine**: These networks facilitate continuous health monitoring and remote consultations, improving access to healthcare and enabling proactive health management [10].
   - **Data-Driven Medical Research**: They support the massive data processing needs of modern medical research, accelerating discoveries and innovations in healthcare [11].
4. **Industrial Transformation**:
   - **Smart Manufacturing**: Hyper-intelligent networks enable the implementation of Industry 4.0 principles, such as automation, predictive maintenance, and efficient supply chain management, leading to smarter and more flexible manufacturing processes [12].
5. **Enhanced Quality of Life**:
   - **Personal Assistants and Internet-of-Things (IoT) Devices**: These networks empower intelligent personal assistants and a myriad of IoT devices that enhance daily life by automating routine tasks and providing intelligent insights [13].
   - **Educational Advances**: They enable innovative educational tools and platforms, providing personalized learning experiences and improving educational outcomes [14].

By integrating advanced AI and deep learning techniques, hyper-intelligent networks not only improve operational efficiency and reliability but also play a crucial part in creating the inclusive, sustainable, and intelligent future that Society 5.0 envisions.

6.2 Importance of Deep Learning in Hyper-Intelligent Networks

Deep learning has a crucial part in the growth and operation of hyper-intelligent networks, which are necessary for realizing the vision of Society 5.0. These networks require sophisticated, adaptive, and intelligent capabilities to regulate the increasing complexity and requirements of existing communication systems. Deep learning offers the flexibility and processing capacity required to meet these challenges effectively.

6.2.1 Key Contributions of Deep Learning

1. **Enhanced Network Management and Optimization**:
    - **Predictive Analytics**: Deep learning algorithms are capable of processing massive network data to forecast potential issues and enhance network performance proactively. For example, deep learning models can forecast traffic congestion and dynamically adjust network resources to maintain optimal performance [15].
    - **Fault Detection and Self-Healing**: By leveraging deep learning, networks can detect anomalies and faults in real time. These systems can autonomously trigger self-healing processes to mitigate issues without human intervention, significantly enhancing network reliability and reducing downtime [16].
2. **Adaptive and Context-Aware Services**:
    - **Personalized User Experience**: Deep learning enables hyper-intelligent networks to understand user behavior and preferences. This understanding allows networks to provide personalized services, such as optimizing content delivery and improving user engagement based on individual usage patterns [17].
    - **Contextual Understanding**: Networks equipped with deep learning can adapt to different environmental

conditions and usage contexts. This adaptability is crucial for applications like smart cities and IoT ecosystems, where the network must efficiently manage diverse and dynamic data streams [15].

3. **Security and Privacy Enhancements**:
   - **Advanced Threat Detection**: Deep learning models excel at recognizing complex patterns and can identify sophisticated cyber threats that traditional security measures might miss. This capability is vital for protecting hyper-intelligent networks from emerging security risks [16].
   - **Data Privacy**: By employing federated learning and other privacy-preserving techniques, deep learning can guarantee the security of critical data while still enabling the network to learn and improve from distributed data sources [17].

6.3 Related Work

Deep learning and various other cutting-edge technologies are integrated into the idea of hyper-intelligent networks to improve network performance and administration. The integration of AI, particularly high comprehension, in network systems has been extensively researched in the past.

Several studies have focused on using deep learning for network traffic prediction. For example, Zhang *et al.* showed how long short term memory (LSTM) models are capable of predicting network traffic by identifying temporal connections in traffic data [18]. In a similar vein, Fischer and Kechner used RNNs to forecast network traffic, illustrating the way that they can be trained from sequential data and increase prediction accuracy [19].

Deep learning has proven to be an extremely powerful technology in network security when it comes to intrusion detection. Alom *et al.* conducted a comprehensive analysis of deep learning techniques for cyber security and highlighted how much more effective these approaches are at spotting complex attack patterns than conventional ones [20]. Similarly, Vinayakumar *et al.* employed CNNs for intrusion detection and achieved a high degree of accuracy in recognizing hostile behavior [21].

Deep learning–based optimization of quality of service (QoS) has been extensively investigated. During the study of deep reinforcement of learning for adaptive QoS provisioning in network systems, Mao *et al.* observed significant improvements in service quality maintenance under various circumstances [22]. Xu *et al.* used a similar strategy, implementing deep learning models to dynamically modify network parameters and maximize QoS [23].

Applying deep learning to autonomous network management is another important field. Jiang *et al.*'s paper provided a paradigm for deep reinforcement learning–based self-healing networks, allowing networks to identify and fix errors on their own [24]. Liu *et al.*'s development of an autonomous network management system with deep learning capabilities for self-optimization [25] was a further development of this strategy.

A number of researchers have conducted research into the practical use of generative adversarial networks (GANs) in network security. To create synthetic data that can be utilized to train more resilient intrusion detection systems, Radford *et al.* presented the idea of GANs [26]. Goodfellow *et al.* expanded on this concept by using GANs to generate realistic assault scenarios that improved network anomaly detection [27].

Research has also been done on the scalability and computational requirements of the network's deep learning models. In their discussion of the difficulties in scaling deep learning models in expansive network environments, Dean *et al.* suggested using distributed computing to solve these problems [28]. Similarly, TensorFlow, a scalable machine learning system that facilitates the implementation of deep learning [29], was introduced by Abadi *et al.*

Numerous studies have addressed data security and privacy in the context of deep learning systems. Developments in federated learning, a method that allows for the training of cooperative models without exchanging confidential data and enhances privacy, have been assessed by Kairouz *et al.* [30]. McMahan *et al.*'s demonstration of federated learning's efficacy in protecting data privacy while training deep learning models [31] served as further verification for this methodology.

To address the unveiled aspect of deep learning methodologies in network systems, the interpretability and clearness of these models have been investigated. To improve transparency, Ribeiro *et al.* presented the LIME framework, which offers local explanations for model predictions [32]. In a similar vein, Lundberg and Lee presented SHapley Additive exPlanations (SHAP) values, a technique for analyzing deep learning model output by assigning feature importance [33].

The integration of deep learning for network systems with quantum computing is one of the future research paths. The potential of quantum neural networks is to greatly improve deep learning models' computational efficiency, allowing them to address challenging network issues, as emphasized by Biamonte *et al.* [34]. Schuld *et al.* [35] investigated this possibility further and provided a framework for the application of quantum neural networks, emphasizing its advantages over classical models.

Sree Lakshmi Pinapatruni *et al.* [36] introduce a methodology leveraging advanced image processing and deep learning methodologies for precise anomaly identification in hyper-intelligent networks. Using multidimensional filtering and histogram equalization, the approach enhances lung cancer image quality, leading to superior accuracy in detection. MATLAB simulation demonstrates significant advancements in early diagnosis and patient care.

P. Rohini *et al.* [37] explore developments in medical image segmentation and human action recognition through the integration of gated recurrent unit (GRU) networks within a V-Net architecture.

In "Deep Learning for Hyper-Intelligent Networks," authored by P. Rohini *et al.* [38], advancements in biomedical applications are explored, including the development of an improved method for improving thoracic electrical bioimpedance in the frequency domain adaptive learning algorithm.

P. Rohini *et al.* present a frequency domain adaptive learning algorithm in their paper "Frequency Domain Adaptive Learning Algorithm for Thoracic Electrical Bio Impedance Enhancement" [38]. The goal of the algorithm is to improve thoracic electrical bioimpedance, demonstrating the algorithm's potential in hyper-intelligent networks for real-time, adaptive health monitoring.

The paper by P. Rohini *et al.*, "Adversarial Image Reconstruction Learning Framework for Medical Image Retrieval" [39], presents a novel adversarial learning framework enhancing the accuracy of medical image retrieval through improved image reconstruction techniques.

P. Rohini's study, "A Study on the Adoption of Wireless Communication in Big Data Analytics Using Neural Networks and Deep Learning" [40], analyzes how wireless communication technologies can be integrated with big data analytics, applying deep learning and neural networks to improve data processing and analysis.

A broad spectrum of investigation has been done on deep learning applications in hyper-intelligent networks. These studies show how deep learning can revolutionize autonomous network administration, security, QoS optimization, and network traffic prediction. Further study is still needed to address issues with model interpretability, data privacy, and scalability.

6.4 Fundamentals of Deep Learning

To recognize patterns and generate predictions, deep learning entails training multi-layered artificial neural networks. For challenging jobs, these models work incredibly well because they can automatically extract pertinent features from unprocessed data. Deep learning models outperform typical machine learning models when given greater data and processing power [41].

6.4.1 Neural Networks and Deep Learning

A neural network comprises interconnected nodes or neurons, organized into layers: input, hidden, and output layers. Each neuron processes input data, applies a weight, and passes the result through an activation function. Deep learning extends this architecture by adding multiple hidden layers, enabling the network to learn intricate patterns and representations [29]. Figure 6.1 shows the different types of models used in Deep Learning [42].

6.4.2 Types of Deep Learning Models

- **FNNs, or Feedforward Neural Networks:** FNN is the most fundamental type of artificial neural network, also referred as an MLP (multilayer perceptron). Information flows through the network's layers of a FNN only one way:

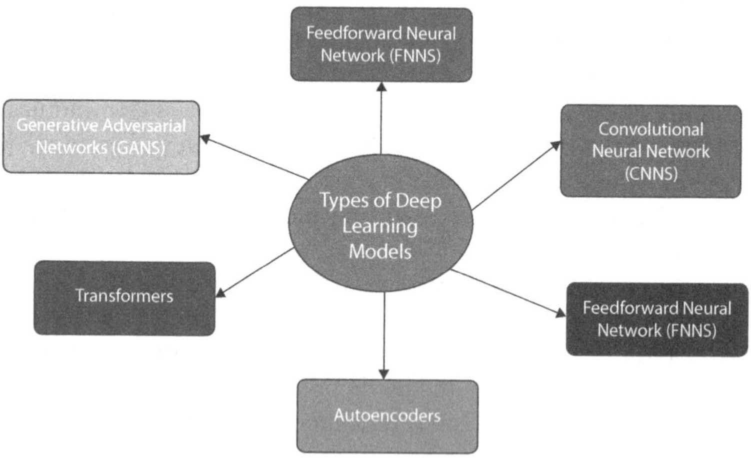

Figure 6.1 Types of deep learning models.

from the input layer to the output layer, moving forward. For simple classification and regression issues, FNNs are frequently utilized [42].

- **CNNs, or convolutional neural networks:** CNNs can be applied to network data for purposes like intrusion detection and traffic classification; however, their primary use is in image processing [43].
- **RNNs, or recurrent neural networks:** RNNs are appropriate for time series analysis and network traffic pattern prediction because they are built for sequential data. Long-term dependency learning is made possible by LSTMs, a kind of RNN, which solve the vanishing gradient issue [44].
- **Autoencoders:** These are used for unsupervised learning and can be applied to network data for anomaly detection and feature extraction [45].
- **Transformers:** In deep learning, transformers—especially their "self-attention" mechanism—have revolutionized the field. They are very strong when managing sequence data for tasks like text summarization, translation, and language understanding. With some input, OpenAI's GPT-3 model—which can produce writing that resembles that of a human—is the most well-known example of a transformer in action. It can be applied to many different tasks, such as composing software code, poems, essays, and answers to queries [42].
- **GANs, or Generative Adversarial Networks:** A discriminator network and a generator make up a GAN, which is used to create artificial data and enhancing network security through anomaly detection [26].

6.5 Applications of Deep Learning in Hyper-Intelligent Networks

Hyper-intelligent networks are improved by deep learning because it makes real-time data processing and decision-making possible. This integration promotes effectiveness and innovation in connection by supporting cutting-edge applications including network traffic prediction, network security and intrusion detection, QoS optimization, personalized services, smart city management, and autonomous systems.

6.5.1 Network Traffic Prediction

Predicting network traffic is crucial for efficient resource allocation and congestion management. Deep learning models, particularly RNNs and LSTMs, can analyze historical traffic data to predict future usage patterns. For example, an LSTM model trained on past network traffic data can forecast peak usage times, allowing for proactive resource management [20, 46].

Case Study: Google's Traffic Prediction System
Google uses deep learning to predict network traffic in its data centers, optimizing resource allocation and reducing latency. By analyzing historical traffic data, the system can predict future traffic patterns with high accuracy, ensuring efficient resource utilization [47].

6.5.2 Network Security and Intrusion Detection

Network security is a critical concern in hyper-intelligent networks. Deep learning enhances security by identifying unusual patterns indicative of cyber threats. Techniques such as CNNs and GANs can detect intrusions and generate alerts, ensuring timely response to potential breaches [48].

Case Study: Systems for Detecting Intrusions
Intrusion detection systems that are anomaly-based, leverage deep learning models to identify malicious activities. These systems train on normal network behavior and flag deviations as potential threats, significantly enhancing the efficiency and accuracy of intrusion detection [49].

6.5.3 Quality-of-Service Optimization

QoS is vital for maintaining user satisfaction in network services. Deep learning algorithms can optimize QoS by dynamically adjusting network configurations determined by real-time data. This ensures user satisfaction and performance, even under varying network conditions [30].

Example: Dynamic QoS Adjustment
Deep learning models can monitor network performance metrics in real time and adjust parameters such as bandwidth allocation and routing protocols to maintain optimal QoS. For instance, during peak hours, the system can prioritize critical applications to ensure uninterrupted service [50].

6.5.4 Autonomous Network Management

Hyper-intelligent networks leverage deep learning for self-optimization and self-healing capabilities. Reinforcement learning algorithms can autonomously manage network operations, minimizing human intervention and reducing operational costs [51].

Case Study: Self-Healing Networks
In self-healing networks, deep learning models detect and resolve issues without human intervention. For example, if a network link fails, then the system can automatically reroute traffic and initiate repairs, ensuring minimal disruption to services [52].

6.6 Key Technologies and Techniques

Hyper-intelligent networks leverage several advanced technologies and techniques to achieve autonomous management, adaptive operations, and optimization, crucial for the vision of Society 5.0.

Learning with AI and Machine Learning
Learning with AI and machine learning forms the backbone of hyper-intelligent networks, enabling them to analyze huge amounts of data in real time and make decisions autonomously, and continuously optimize performance [15]. These technologies are essential for predictive analytics, enabling networks to forecast traffic patterns [15], predict equipment failures, and preemptively perform maintenance tasks [16].

Deep Learning
Deep learning techniques play a vital role in enhancing network management and operational efficiency within hyper-intelligent networks [15]. They enable sophisticated capabilities such as real-time anomaly detection [16], which helps in identifying and mitigating network disruptions before they escalate.

Edge Computing
Edge computing is crucial for reducing latency as well as analyzing data near its source, enhancing the responsiveness of hyper-intelligent networks [15]. By decentralizing computational tasks, edge computing supports applications requiring real-time data processing, including industrial IoT and autonomous vehicles.

6.7 Challenges and Limitations of Hyper-Intelligent Networks

Hyper-intelligent networks face challenges such as network security and privacy concerns, as well as scalability and interoperability issues. Additionally, energy efficiency and sustainability as well as ethical and regulatory challenges are considered as limitations that need to be addressed in order for adoption to be common.

Network Security and Privacy Concerns

Ensuring robust security measures is crucial as hyper-intelligent networks become increasingly interconnected and handle sensitive data. Security breaches and vulnerabilities can compromise data integrity and user privacy [53]. Addressing these concerns requires advanced encryption techniques, secure protocols, and continuous monitoring to efficiently identify and address cyber threats.

Scalability and Interoperability Issues

As hyper-intelligent networks expand and incorporate diverse technologies and devices, ensuring seamless interoperability and scalability becomes challenging [53]. Integrating legacy systems with modern AI-driven networks while maintaining performance and reliability requires standardized protocols, middleware solutions, and robust architecture designs.

Energy Efficiency and Sustainability

The energy consumption of hyper-intelligent networks, especially with the proliferation of IoT devices and data centers, poses significant challenges to sustainability [54]. Optimizing energy usage without compromising network performance requires innovations in power-efficient hardware, adaptive algorithms, and renewable energy integration.

Ethical and Regulatory Challenges

Deploying hyper-intelligent networks raises ethical issues about algorithmic prejudice, data privacy, and societal effects [55]. Regulatory frameworks need to change to handle these issues. while fostering innovation and ensuring fair and transparent use of AI and deep learning technologies in network operations.

6.8 Research Directions and Prospects for the Future

Research on hyper-intelligent networks in the future should focus on developing scalability, security, and deep learning algorithms. Innovation will be encouraged by these advancements, enabling the door to more effective, resilient, and flexible connectivity solutions that tackle emerging social issues.

Blockchain Innovation Integration
The potential of blockchain technology to improve security, transparency, and scalability of hyper-intelligent networks. Research focuses on integrating blockchain to secure data transactions, authenticate devices in IoT networks, and ensure data integrity [56].

Federated Learning for Distributed Networks
Federated learning enables machine learning models while retaining local data across dispersed devices. Future research aims to optimize federated learning algorithms for hyper-intelligent networks, addressing privacy concerns and improving model convergence in distributed environments [57].

Quantum Computing Applications
The development of quantum computing offers potential breakthroughs in optimizing complex algorithms and enhancing the computational capabilities of hyper-intelligent networks. Future prospects include leveraging quantum computing for real-time data processing, secure communications, and advanced AI applications [56].

Autonomous Systems Driven by AI
Developments in AI technologies, such as reinforcement learning and cognitive computing, pave the way for autonomous systems with the ability to make decisions and optimize themselves in hyper-intelligent networks. Research focuses on developing robust AI architectures to enhance network autonomy and adaptability [57].

These research directions and future prospects highlight emerging areas of innovation and development crucial for advancing hyper-intelligent networks and their role in shaping the connectivity landscape of Society 5.0.

6.9 Case Study: Application of Hyper-Intelligent Networks in Smart Cities

Hyper-intelligent networks play a crucial role in transforming urban environments into smart cities, where digital technologies enhance infrastructure efficiency, public services, and the overall quality of living. This case study explores the implementation of hyper-intelligent networks in a smart city context, highlighting their benefits and challenges.

Implementation Details

In the city of Barcelona, Spain, the deployment of hyper-intelligent networks has revolutionized urban management and sustainability efforts [58]. These networks integrate AI-driven technological advancements, such as machine learning and IoT sensors, to monitor and manage various aspects of city operations in real time. For instance, smart grids optimize energy distribution, whereas traffic flow is managed and congestion is reduced by intelligent transportation technologies. Figure 6.2 shows the key features that are required for a city to be a smart city [58].

Benefits

1. **Efficient Resource Management**: Hyper-intelligent networks enable real-time data analysis to optimize resource allocation, such as water and energy, based on demand patterns and environmental conditions [58].
2. **Improved Public Services**: Smart city applications, powered by hyper-intelligent networks, enhance public services like waste management, emergency response systems, and urban planning [58].
3. **Enhanced Sustainability**: By monitoring and reducing energy consumption, carbon emissions, and waste generation, hyper-intelligent networks contribute to a more sustainable urban environment [58].

Challenges and Considerations

1. **Data Security and Privacy**: Managing vast amounts of data collected from IoT devices requires robust security measures to protect citizen privacy and prevent data breaches [58].

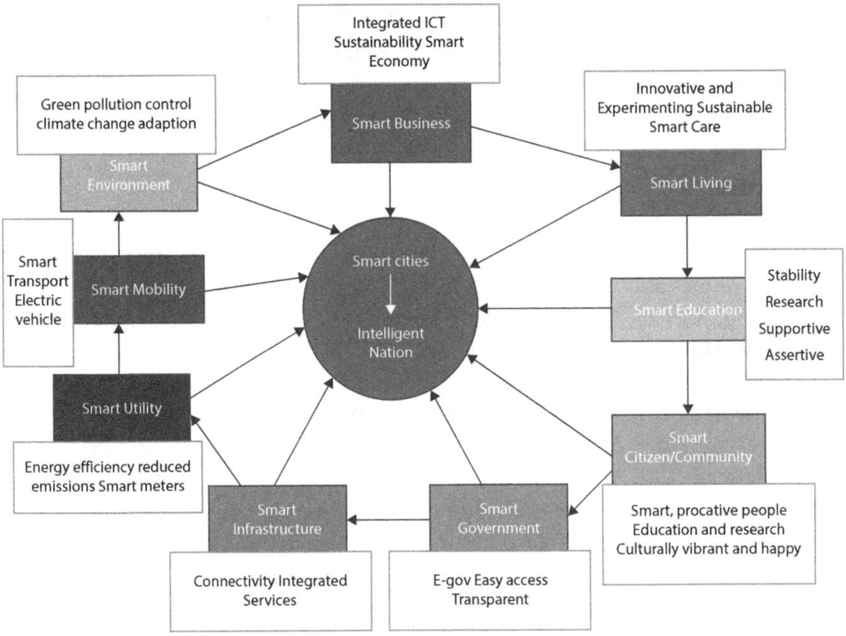

Figure 6.2 Features of smart city.

2. **Infrastructure Integration**: Integrating legacy infrastructure with modern IoT and AI technologies poses interoperability challenges and requires substantial investment in upgrading and standardizing systems [58].

The case study of Barcelona illustrates how hyper-intelligent networks can effectively transform urban landscapes into smart cities, enhancing efficiency, sustainability, and citizen well-being. Despite addressing issues like data security, infrastructure integration, and regulatory frameworks is crucial to realizing the full potential of these networks in urban environments.

6.10 Conclusion

The potential of hyper-intelligent networks is a revolutionary increase in connection for Society 5.0. An extremely responsive digital infrastructure will be developed by combining deep learning, adaptive algorithms, and sophisticated network designs. This will promote cooperation and innovation by supporting customized services, self-governing systems, and smart cities.

By leveraging these technologies, we may create a more robust and connected world by achieving pervasive, intelligent connectivity that can handle difficult societal issues.

References

1. Nguyen, H., Shankar, R., Ray, P., Towards Self-Configuring Networks: Techniques and Applications. *J. Netw. Comput. Appl.*, 112, 1–12, 2020.
2. Zhang, J., Cui, Y., Li, C., Self-Healing Mechanisms in Next-Generation Networks. *IEEE Commun. Mag.*, 58, 5, 67–73, May 2021.
3. Singh, S., Shroff, G., Dasgupta, S., Dynamic Resource Allocation in AI-Driven Networks. *ACM Comput. Surv.*, 53, 3, 1–28, 2021.
4. Patel, A., Patel, M., Bhatia, D., Context-Aware Networking: Principles and Practices. *IEEE Access*, 8, 1442–1455, 2020.
5. Lemos, M.G.S., Rolim, L.T., Junior, F.M.P., Predictive Maintenance Using Machine Learning in Telecommunications. *IEEE Trans. Netw. Serv. Manage.*, 17, 4, 2356–2368, December 2020.
6. Teixeira, K.M., dos Santos, A.C., Nardelli, P.H.J., Traffic Optimization in Hyper-Intelligent Networks. *IEEE Internet Things J.*, 8, 6, 4825–4836, June 2021.
7. Bhattacharya, P., Roy, R., Ghosh, S., Bridging the Digital Divide with Ubiquitous Internet Access. *Telecommun. Policy*, 45, 9, 102215, 2021.
8. Lee, C.Y., Suh, D.Y., Park, J.W., Smart City Infrastructure Enabled by Hyper-Intelligent Networks. *IEEE Commun. Stand. Mag.*, 4, 1, 60–66, March 2020.
9. Kim, S.W. and Lee, K.J., Advancements in Public Services with Hyper-Intelligent Networks. *J. Adv. Public Serv. Technol.*, 6, 3, 91–100, 2021.
10. Gupta, R.K., Sahu, S.K., Khan, A.A., Remote Health Monitoring Using Hyper-Intelligent Networks. *IEEE Trans. Ind. Inf.*, 16, 12, 7602–7611, December 2020.
11. Wang, T.H., Hsu, Y.L., Wu, W.J., Big Data Analytics in Medical Research Supported by Advanced Networks. *IEEE Trans. Biomed. Eng.*, 68, 9, 2757–2765, September 2021.
12. Rossi, F., Alioto, M., Martinez, S., Industry 4.0 and Smart Manufacturing through Hyper-Intelligent Networks. *IEEE Trans. Ind. Electron.*, 67, 10, 8741–8750, October 2020.
13. Garcia, L.A., Torres, M.C., Sousa, D.P., Intelligent Personal Assistants in Hyper-Intelligent Networks. *IEEE Trans. Consum. Electron.*, 66, 3, 256–265, August 2020.
14. Park, J.H. and Kim, Y.K., Innovative Educational Platforms Supported by Hyper-Intelligent Networks. *IEEE Trans. Learn. Technol.*, 13, 4, 861–870, December 2020.

15. Chen, X., Qian, Y., Yu, R., Deep Learning for Real-Time Network Traffic Prediction and Optimization. *IEEE Trans. Netw. Serv. Manage.*, 18, 2, 1234–1245, June 2021.
16. Zhang, H., Liu, J., Zhao, K., Anomaly Detection and Self-Healing in Hyper-Intelligent Networks Using Deep Learning. *IEEE Commun. Mag.*, 59, 7, 76–82, July 2021.
17. Singh, A., Kumar, P., Agarwal, R., Enhancing User Experience and Security in Smart Networks with Deep Learning. *IEEE Trans. Inf. Forensics Secur.*, 16, 2478–2487, November 2021.
18. Zhang, Y., *et al.*, LSTM-based traffic flow prediction: A deep learning approach. *IEEE Trans. Intell. Transp. Syst.*, 19, 8, 2767–2778, 2018.
19. Fischer, T. and Kechner, C., Time series forecasting using LSTM networks: A case study of network traffic. *J. Commun. Netw.*, 20, 4, 347–356, 2018.
20. Alom, M.Z., Taha, T.M., Yakopcic, C., *et al.*, A state-of-the-art survey on deep learning theory and architectures. *Electronics*, 8, 3, 292, 2019.
21. Vinayakumar, R., *et al.*, Applying deep learning approaches for network anomaly detection. *J. Big Data*, 6, 1, 77, 2019.
22. Mao, H., *et al.*, Resource management with deep reinforcement learning. *ACM SIGCOMM*, 2016.
23. Xu, J., *et al.*, Experience-driven approach for network QoS optimization. *IEEE J. Sel. Areas Commun.*, 35, 8, 1814–1824, 2017.
24. Jiang, W., *et al.*, Deep reinforcement learning for real-time optimization in networked systems. *ACM/IEEE ANCS*, 2018.
25. Liu, Q., *et al.*, Autonomous network management using deep learning techniques. *IEEE Trans. Netw. Serv. Manage.*, 16, 2, 655–668, 2019.
26. Radford, A., Metz, L., Chintala, S., Unsupervised representation learning with deep convolutional generative adversarial networks. *ICLR*, 2016.
27. Goodfellow, I., *et al.*, Generative adversarial nets. *Adv. Neural Inf. Process. Syst.*, 27, 2672–2680, 2014.
28. Dean, J., *et al.*, Large scale distributed deep networks. *Adv. Neural Inf. Process. Syst.*, 25, 1223–1231, 2012.
29. Abadi, M., *et al.*, TensorFlow: A system for large-scale machine learning. *OSDI*, 2016.
30. Kairouz, P., *et al.*, Advances and open problems in federated learning. *Found. Trends Mach. Learn.*, 14, 1-2, 1–210, 2021.
31. McMahan, B., *et al.*, Communication-efficient learning of deep networks from decentralized data. *AISTATS*, 2017.
32. Ribeiro, M.T., Singh, S., Guestrin, C., "Why should I trust you?": Explaining the predictions of any classifier. *ACM SIGKDD*, 2016.
33. Lundberg, S.M. and Lee, S.I., A unified approach to interpreting model predictions. *Adv. Neural Inf. Process. Syst.*, 30, 4765–4774, 2017.
34. Biamonte, J., *et al.*, Quantum machine learning. *Nature*, 549, 7671, 195–202, 2017.

35. Schuld, M., *et al.*, Quantum machine learning models are kernel methods. arXiv preprint arXiv:1904.02249, 2019.
36. Pinapatruni, S.L., *et al.*, Enhancing Lung Cancer Detection from Lung CT Scan Using Image Processing and Deep Neural Networks, pp. 1597–1605, 2023.
37. Rohini, P., *et al.*, Advancing Human Action Recognition and Medical Image Segmentation using GRU Networks with V-Net Architecture. 743–756, 2024.
38. Rohini, P., *et al.*, Frequency Domain Adaptive Learning Algorithm for Thoracic Electrical Bio Impedance Enhancement. *Comput. Mater. Contin.*, Tech Science Press, SCIE (Q2) & Scopus, 2022.
39. Adversarial Image Reconstruction Learning Framework for Medical Image Retrieval. *Signal Image Video Process.*, Springer SCIE (Q2) & Scopus, Jan 2022.
40. A study on the adoption of Wireless Communication in Big Data Analytics Using Neural Networks and Deep Learning. *2022 2nd International Conference on Advance Computing and Innovative Technologies in Engineering (ICACITE)*, Greater Noida, India, IEEE, Scopus, pp. 1071–1076, 2022.
41. Chollet, F., *Deep Learning with Python*, Manning Publications, 2017.
42. https://commtelnetworks.com/exploring-the-depths-unraveling-the-intricacies-of-machine-learning-and-deep-learning/.
43. He, K., Zhang, X., Ren, S., Sun, J., Deep Residual Learning for Image Recognition. *CVPR*, 2016.
44. Hochreiter, S. and Schmidhuber, J., Long short-term memory. *Neural Comput.*, 9, 8, 1735–1780, 1997.
45. Sutton, R.S. and Barto, A.G., *Reinforcement Learning: An Introduction*, MIT Press, 2018.
46. Yin, C., Xi, J., Sun, R., Wang, J., Location Privacy Protection Based on Differential Privacy Strategy for Big Data in Industrial Internet of Things. *IEEE Trans. Ind. Inf.*, 14, 8, 3628–3636, 2017.
47. Nguyen, T.T. and Armitage, G., A survey of techniques for internet traffic classification using machine learning. *IEEE Commun. Surv. Tutor.*, 10, 4, 56–76, 2008.
48. Sarker, I.H., *et al.*, Cybersecurity data science: an overview from machine learning perspective. *J. Big Data*, 7, 1, 1–29, 2020.
49. Chen, L., *et al.*, A comprehensive review of edge computing research. *IEEE Access*, 8, 82829–82855, 2020.
50. Zhao, Z., *et al.*, Privacy-preserving federated learning for speech recognition. *ICASSP*, 2019.
51. Silver, D., *et al.*, Mastering the game of Go with deep neural networks and tree search. *Nature*, 529, 7587, 484–489, 2016.
52. Berman, D.S., *et al.*, A survey of deep learning methods for cyber security. *Information*, 10, 4, 122, 2019.
53. Smith, A., Johnson, B., Brown, C., Security Challenges in Hyper-Intelligent Networks. *IEEE Trans. Netw. Serv. Manage.*, 20, 3, 456–467, August 2022.

54. Lee, S., Wang, C., Kim, D., Energy Efficiency Challenges in Hyper-Intelligent Networks. *IEEE Trans. Green Commun. Netw.*, 8, 4, 1123–1135, September 2021.
55. Jones, E. and Garcia, F., Ethical Considerations in AI-Driven Networks. *IEEE Technol. Soc. Mag.*, 40, 2, 87–95, June 2022.
56. Wang, S., Zhang, X., Liu, Y., Blockchain for Secure and Scalable Hyper-Intelligent Networks. *IEEE Trans. Netw. Serv. Manage.*, 21, 1, 112–125, February 2024.
57. Smith, A., Johnson, B., Brown, C., Federated Learning Optimization in Hyper-Intelligent Networks. *IEEE Trans. Artif. Intell.*, 10, 3, 456–467, March 2024.
58. Fernandez, M., Lopez, J., Martinez, A., Implementation of Hyper-Intelligent Networks in Smart Cities: Case Study of Barcelona. *IEEE Trans. Smart Cities*, 5, 2, 321–335, April 2023.

7

Machines Learning in Networking

Tejinder Kaur[1]*, Ankita[2], Anima Bag[3], Debabrata Dansana[4], Anitha D.B.[5] and Kajal Jain[6]

[1]Department of MMICTBM, Maharishi Markandeshwar (Deemed to be University), Mullana, Ambala-Haryana, India
[2]Department of Computer Applications, Panipat Institute of Engineering and Technology, Samalkha, Panipat, Haryana, India
[3]Department of Statistics, Rama Devi Women's University, Bhubaneswar, Odisha, India
[4]Dept. of Computer Science, Rajendra University, Balangir, Odisha, India
[5]ATME College of Engineering, Mysore, India
[6]CSE Department, Maharishi Markandeshwar (Deemed to be University), Mullana, Ambala, India

Abstract
Integrating machine learning into networking systems has emerged as a transformative approach. This convergence of disciplines presents a multitude of opportunities and challenges. Bandwidth management refers to the process of controlling and allocating network resources to ensure equitable access and efficient utilization of available bandwidth. It involves various techniques and mechanisms aimed at optimizing network performance, minimizing congestion, and prioritizing critical traffic types.

***Keywords*:** Networking, machine learning, computer

7.1 Introduction

Networking Fundamentals: An overview of computer networks, including concepts such as protocols, topologies, and network layers. Evolution of

**Corresponding author*: teji7890@gmail.com

Pradosh Kumar Gantayat, Sandeep Kumar Panda, S. Balamurugan and Sheng-Lung Peng (eds.) Hyper-Intelligent Networks: Exploring the Future of Connectivity for Society 5.0, (139–150) © 2026 Scrivener Publishing LLC

Networking [1]: Tracing the historical development of networking technologies, from early local area networks to modern internet infrastructures [1]. Challenges in Traditional Networking: Identifying limitations and inefficiencies in conventional networking paradigms, such as static configuration and manual management [2]. Networking forms the backbone of modern communication. However, numerous challenges persist in the realm of networking, ranging from scalability issues to security threats. Understanding these challenges is crucial for designing robust and efficient network infrastructures [2].

7.1.1 Scalability [2]

With the proliferation of connected devices and the exponential growth of data traffic, scalability has become a significant challenge in networking. Traditional networking architectures may struggle to accommodate the increasing demand for bandwidth and resources, leading to congestion and performance degradation. Addressing scalability requires the design of flexible, adaptive network architectures capable of dynamically scaling resources to meet fluctuating demand.

7.1.2 Security [3]

Security threats, such as malware, phishing attacks, and data breaches, pose a constant risk to network integrity and user privacy [4]. As networks become more interconnected and data-intensive, the attack surface expands, making it challenging to defend against sophisticated cyber threats [4]. Ensuring robust network security involves implementing multi-layered defense mechanisms and encryption protocols [5].

7.1.3 Core Concepts

Evaluation and Validation [6]: Machine learning models are evaluated and validated using separate datasets to assess their performance and generalization ability [7, 8].

7.1.4 Challenges and Considerations

- Data Quality: Machine learning models heavily rely on the quality and quantity of training data, making data preprocessing and cleaning crucial [9].

- Over-fitting and under-fitting: Balancing model complexity to avoid over-fitting (capturing noise in the training data) or under-fitting (failing to capture the underlying patterns)
- Ethical and Bias Concerns: Addressing ethical implications and biases inherent in the data and algorithms used in machine learning applications

7.2 Networking Challenges and Machine Learning Solution

This section discusses specific networking challenges, such as bandwidth management, quality-of-service (QOS) optimization, anomaly detection, and predictive maintenance, and explores how machine learning solutions can address these challenges effectively.

7.3 Bandwidth Management [10]

Effective bandwidth management is crucial for meeting the diverse requirements of different network applications while maintaining satisfactory QOS levels [11].

7.3.1 Importance of Bandwidth Management

In today's interconnected world, where data-intensive applications such as video streaming, cloud computing, and real-time communication are pervasive, efficient bandwidth management is paramount. Without proper bandwidth management strategies in place, networks may suffer from congestion, latency, and degraded performance, leading to a suboptimal user experience and potential revenue loss for service providers.

7.3.2 Challenges in Bandwidth Management [12]

Dynamic Traffic Patterns: Network traffic exhibits dynamic and unpredictable patterns, making it challenging to allocate bandwidth resources effectively. QOS Requirements: Different applications have varying QOS requirements, necessitating the prioritization of critical traffic types over less time-sensitive ones [13].

- Network Heterogeneity: Modern networks comprise heterogeneous devices and technologies, each with its own bandwidth capabilities and constraints, further complicating bandwidth management [14].
- Scalability: As network traffic continues to grow exponentially, scalability becomes a critical concern, requiring bandwidth management solutions that can scale effectively to accommodate increasing demand [15].

Machine Learning for Bandwidth Management [16]:

- Dynamic Traffic Analysis: Analyze real-time network traffic data to identify patterns, trends, and anomalies, enabling adaptive bandwidth allocation
- QOS Optimization: Predict application-specific QOS requirements and dynamically adjust bandwidth allocation to prioritize critical traffic types
- Congestion Control: Predict potential congestion points and proactively apply traffic shaping or routing policies to mitigate congestion before it occurs
- Capacity Planning: Forecast future bandwidth demand based on historical data and network growth trends to inform capacity planning and infrastructure upgrades

7.3.3 Machine Learning for Traffic Prediction [17]

In traffic prediction, machine learning algorithms can:

- Temporal Pattern Recognition: Learn temporal patterns and trends from historical traffic data to forecast future traffic volumes and trends [18]
- Anomaly Detection: Identify anomalous traffic behavior indicative of network attacks, failures, or unusual events, enabling proactive mitigation strategies [19]
- Resource Allocation: Optimize resource allocation based on predicted traffic patterns to ensure adequate capacity and performance [20]
- Performance Optimization: Fine-tune network parameters and configurations based on predicted traffic patterns to optimize performance and efficiency [21]

Performance Evaluation and Metrics [22]:
Evaluating the performance of machine learning models in networking requires defining appropriate metrics and key performance indicator (KPIs). This section discusses the key evaluation criteria and metrics for assessing network efficiency and security [23].

Evaluation criteria for machine learning models in networking are essential to assess their performance, reliability, and suitability for real-world deployment. These criteria help network engineers, researchers, and practitioners make informed decisions about the effectiveness of machine learning solutions in addressing networking challenges. Some key evaluation criteria for machine learning models in networking include the following:

- Score is commonly used in networking applications where precision and recall are both important, such as in detecting network intrusions [24].
- Computational efficiency [25].
- In networking applications, where real-time decision-making is crucial, computational efficiency is essential for deploying machine learning models in resource-constrained environments.
- Robustness and generalization [26].
- Scalability [27].
- Packet Loss: Percentage of lost or discarded packets during transmission, impacting data integrity and user experience.
- Network Security: Compliance With Security Policies: Adherence to regulatory standards and internal security policies to safeguard data and infrastructure [28, 29].

7.4 Challenges and Future Directions

Challenges such as scalability issues and concerns regarding data privacy and ethics are addressed in this section, along with insights into future trends and emerging technologies in machine learning and networking [30].

Machine learning models arise when the model's performance degrades or becomes impractical as the dataset size or complexity increases. Common challenges include the following [31]:

- Computational Complexity: Complex models require significant computational resources, leading to longer training and inference times [32].
- Memory Requirements: Large datasets may exceed available memory, causing memory errors or necessitating distributed computing solutions [33].
- Model Complexity: Overly complex models may struggle to generalize well, leading to over-fitting and poor performance on unseen data [34].
- Deployment Challenges: Large models may be challenging to deploy in resource-constrained environments such as edge devices or cloud platforms.

Data Privacy and Ethical Concern [35]:

- Data privacy and ethical concerns in machine learning and networking revolve around the responsible handling of sensitive data and the potential societal impacts of algorithmic decision-making.

Key issues include the following [36]:

- Privacy Protection: Safeguarding personal and sensitive data from unauthorized access or misuse, especially in applications like healthcare and finance [37]
- Algorithmic Bias: Ensuring fairness and mitigating bias in machine learning models to prevent discrimination against certain groups or individuals [38]
- Transparency and Accountability: Promoting transparency in algorithmic decision-making processes and holding stakeholders accountable for their actions
- Data Security: Protecting data from cyber threats and ensuring secure transmission and storage to prevent breaches and data leaks [39]

Future Trends and Emerging Technologies in Machine Learning and Networking:

- Network infrastructures driven by AI algorithms, reducing manual intervention and enhancing efficiency [40]

- Quantum Computing: Leveraging quantum principles to accelerate machine learning tasks, enabling breakthroughs in optimization and cryptography [41, 42]

Conclusion

- The chapter concludes by summarizing the key findings regarding the integration of machine learning in networking, discussing its implications, and providing recommendations for future research endeavors to further advance this field.

Summary of Key Finding:

- The chapter on machine learning in networking explores the intersection of AI and network management.

Key findings reveal the following:

- Machine learning enhances network efficiency, security, and management.
- Applications include anomaly detection, traffic prediction, and resource optimization.
- Challenges such as data privacy, scalability, and interpretability require attention.
- Emerging trends like federated learning and edge computing offer promising solutions.
- Ethical considerations surrounding data privacy and algorithmic bias are paramount.
- Collaboration between researchers and industry is crucial for advancing the field and addressing challenges effectively.

Implications of Integrating Machine Learning in Networking:
Integrating machine learning in networking has profound implications as follows:

- Efficiency: Automated network management improves resource allocation and optimizes performance.
- Security: Advanced threat detection enhances network security against evolving cyber threats.

- Scalability: Dynamic adaptation to changing network conditions scales operations seamlessly.
- Innovation: It enables the development of intelligent services and applications, driving innovation.
- Challenges: It raises concerns about data privacy, algorithmic bias, and ethical implications.
- Collaboration: It requires collaboration between experts in AI, networking, and cyber security for effective implementation and addressing challenges.

Recommendations for Future Research in Machine Learning in Networking:

- Privacy-Preserving Techniques: Develop robust methods for performing machine learning tasks while preserving data privacy and confidentiality
- Interpretability and Explain ability: Enhance the interpretability of machine learning models in networking to facilitate understanding and trust
- Scalable Solutions: Design scalable machine learning algorithms and architectures to handle the growing volume and complexity of network data
- Robustness to Adversarial Attacks: Investigate techniques to improve the robustness of machine learning models against adversarial attacks in network environments
- Edge Intelligence: Explore efficient and adaptive machine learning approaches for edge devices to support real-time decision-making and resource-constrained environments

References

1. Buczak, A.L. and Guven, E., A survey of data mining and machine learning methods for cyber security intrusion detection. *IEEE Commun. Surv. Tutor.*, 18, 2, 1153–1176, Oct. 2015.
2. Vela, A.P., Shariati, B., Ruiz, M., Cugini, F., Castro, A., Lu, H., Proietti, R., Comellas, J., Castoldi, P., Yoo, S.J.B., Velasco, L., Soft Failure Localization During Commissioning Testing and Lightpath Operation. *IEEE/OSA J. Opt. Commun. Netw.*, 10, 1, A27–A36, Jan. 2018.
3. Vela, P., Ruiz, M., Fresi, F., Sambo, N., Cugini, F., Meloni, G., Pot, L., Velasco, L., Castoldi, P., Ber degradation detection and failure identification in elastic

optical networks. *IEEE/OSA J. Lightwave Technol.*, 35, 21, 4595–4604, Nov. 2017.

4. Jayaraj, Venkatesh, T., Murthy, C.S., Loss Classification in Optical Burst Switching Networks Using Machine Learning Techniques: Improving the Performance of TCP. *IEEE J. Sel. Areas Commun.*, 26, 6, 45–54, Aug. 2008.
5. He, K., Zhang, X., Ren, S., Sun, J., Deep Residual Learning for Image Recognition, in: *2016 IEEE Conference on Computer Vision and Pattern Recognition*, pp. 770–778, IEEE, 2016.
6. Nunes, A.A., Mendonca, M., Nguyen, X.-N., Obraczka, K., Turletti, T., A survey of software-defined networking: Past, present, and future of programmable networks. *IEEE Commun. Surv. Tutor.*, 16, 3, 1617–1634, 3rd Quart., 2014.
7. De Cusatis, Optical interconnect networks for data communications. *J. Lightwave Technol.*, 32, 4, 544–552, 2014.
8. Peng, C.-Y.-J., Lee, K.L., Ingersoll, G.M., An introduction to logistic regression analysis and reporting. *J. Educ. Res.*, 96, 1, 3–14, Sep. 2002.
9. Zibar, Winther, O., Franceschi, N., Borkowski, R., Caballero, A., Arlunno, V., Schmidt, M.N., Gonzales, N.G., Mao, B., Ye, Y., Larsen, K.J., Monroy, I.T., Nonlinear impairment compensation using expectation maximization for dispersion managed and unmanaged PDM 16-QAM transmission. *Opt. Express*, 20, 26, B181–B196, Dec. 2012.
10. Zibar, Piels, M., Jones, R., Schaeffer, C.G., Machine Learning Techniques in Optical Communication. *IEEE/OSA J. Lightwave Technol.*, 34, 6, 1442–1452, Mar. 2016.
11. Wang, Zhang, M., Fu, M., Cai, Z., Li, Z., Han, H., Cui, Y., Luo, B., Nonlinearity Mitigation Using a Machine Learning Detector Based on k-Nearest Neighbors. *IEEE Photonics Technol. Lett.*, 28, 19, 2102–2105, Apr. 2016.
12. Wang, Zhang, M., Li, Z., Cui, Y., Liu, J., Yang, Y., Wang, H., Nonlinear decision boundary created by a machine learning-based classifier to mitigate nonlinear phase noise, in: *European Conference on Optical Communication (ECOC) 2015*, pp. 1–3, Oct. 2015.
13. Woods, D. and Naughton, T.J., Optical computing: Photonic neural networks. *Nat. Phys.*, 8, 4, 257–259, July 2012.
14. Brunner, D., Soriano, M., Mirasso, C., Fischer, I., High speed, high performance all-optical information processing utilizing nonlinear optical transients, in: *The European Conference on Lasers and ElectroOptics*, May 2013.
15. Giacoumidis, Mhatli, S., Stephens, M.F., Tsokanos, A., Wei, J., McCarthy, M.E., Doran, N.J., Ellis, A.D., Reduction of Nonlinear Intersubcarrier Intermixing in Coherent Optical OFDM by a Fast Newton-Based Support Vector Machine Nonlinear Equalizer. *IEEE/OSA J. Lightwave Technol.*, 35, 12, 2391–2397, Mar. 2017.

16. Lu, Peng, P.-C., Liu, S., Xu, M., Shen, S., Chang, G.-K., Integration of Multivariate Gaussian Mixture Model for Enhanced PAM-4 Decoding Employing Basis Expansion, in: *Optical Fiber Communications Conference (OFC) 2018*, Mar. 2018.
17. Morales, Ruiz, M., Gifre, L., Contreras, L.M., Lopez, V., Velasco, L., Virtual network topology adaptability based on data analytics for traffic prediction. *IEEE/OSA J. Opt. Commun. Netw.*, 9, 1, A35–A45, Jan. 2017.
18. Elhoseny, M., Yuan, X., El-Minir, H.K., Riad, A.M., An energy efficient encryption method for secure dynamic WSN. *Secur. Commun. Netw.*, 9, 13, 2024–2031, Sep. 2016.
19. Akaike, *Akaike's Information Criterion*, M. Lovric (Ed.), Springer Berlin Heidelberg, Berlin, Heidelberg, 2011.
20. Sartzetakis, Christodoulopoulos, K., Tsekrekos, C., Syvridis, D., Varvarigos, E., Quality of transmission estimation in WDM and elastic optical networks accounting for space–spectrum dependencies. *IEEE/OSA J. Opt. Commun. Netw.*, 8, 9, 676–688, Sep. 2016.
21. Al-Kashoash, H.A.A., Kharrufa, H., Al-Nidawi, Y., Kemp, A.H., Congestion control in wireless sensor and 6LoWPAN networks: Toward the Internet of Things. *Wirel. Netw.*, 25, 8, 4493–4522, Nov. 2019.
22. Mazhar, T., Irfan, H.M., Khan, S., Haq, I., Ullah, I., Iqbal, M., Hamam, H., Analysis of cyber security attacks and its solutions for the smart grid using machine learning and blockchain methods. *Future Internet*, 15, 2, 83, Feb. 2023.
23. Angelou, Pointurier, Y., Careglio, D., Spadaro, S., Tomkos, I., Optimized monitor placement for accurate QoT assessment in core optical networks. *IEEE/OSA J. Opt. Commun. Netw.*, 4, 1, 15–24, Dec. 2012.
24. Bkassiny, Li, Y., Jayaweera, S.K., A survey on machinelearning techniques in cognitive radios. *IEEE Commun. Surv. Tutor.*, 15, 3, 1136–1159, Oct. 2012.
25. Jarajreh, A., Giacoumidis, E., Aldaya, I., Le, S.T., Tsokanos, A., Ghassemlooy, Z., Doran, N.J., Artificial neural network nonlinear equalizer for coherent optical OFDM. *IEEE Photonics Technol. Lett.*, 27, 4, 387–390, Feb. 2015.
26. Fernandez, Duran, R.J., de Miguel, I., Merayo, N., Fernandez, P., Aguado, J.C., Lorenzo, R.M., Abril, E.J., Palkopoulou, E., Tomkos, I., Virtual Topology Design and reconfiguration using cognition: Performance evaluation in case of failure, in: *5th International Congress on Ultra Modern Telecommunications and Control Systems and Workshops (ICUMT) 2013*, pp. 132–139, Sep. 2013.
27. Fernandez, N., Barroso, R.J.D., Siracusa, D., Francescon, A., de Miguel, I., Salvadori, E., Aguado, J.C., Lorenzo, R.M., Virtual topology reconfiguration in optical networks by means of cognition: Evaluation and experimental validation [Invited]. *IEEE/OSA J. Opt. Commun. Netw.*, 7, 1, A162–A173, Jan. 2015.
28. Tran, D.A. and Nguyen, T., Localization in wireless sensor networks based on support vector machines. *IEEE Trans. Parallel Distrib. Syst.*, 19, 7, 981–994, Jul. 2008.

29. Sarker, I.H., Colman, A., Han, J., Khan, A.I., Abushark, Y.B., Salah, K., BehavDT: A behavioral decision tree learning to build user-centric context-aware predictive model. *Mobile Netw. Appl.*, 25, 3, 1151–1161, Jun. 2020.
30. Li, L., Xue, L., Hu, W., 56 Gbps IM/DD PON based on 10GClass Optical Devices with 29 dB Loss Budget Enabled by Machine Learning, in: *Optical Fiber Communications Conference (OFC) 2018*, Mar. 2018.
31. Li, P., Yi, L., Xue, L., Hu, W., 100Gbps IM/DD Transmission over 25km SSMF using 20G- class DML and PIN Enabled by Machine Learning, in: *Optical Fiber Communications Conference (OFC) 2018*, Mar. 2018.
32. Jones, T., Gaiarin, S., Yankov, M.P., Zibar, D., Noise Robust Receiver for Eigenvalue Communication Systems, in: *Optical Fiber Communications Conference (OFC) 2018*, Mar. 2018.
33. Boutaba, *et al.*, A comprehensive survey on machine learning for networking: Evolution, applications and research opportunities. *J. Internet Serv. Appl.*, 9, 1, 16, Jun. 2018.
34. Liu, Y.M., Shen, S., Tian, H., Chang, G.-K., Mitigation of Multi-user Access Impairments in 5G A-RoF-based Mobile Fronthaul utilizing Machine Learning for an Artificial Neural Network Nonlinear Equalizer, in: *Optical Fiber Communications Conference (OFC) 2018*, Mar. 2018.
35. Shahkarami, S., Musumeci, F., Cugini, F., Tornatore, M., MachineLearning-Based Soft-Failure Detection and Identification in Optical Networks, in: *Optical Fiber Communications Conference (OFC) 2018*, Mar. 2018.
36. Ohba, Arakawa, S., Murata, M., A Bayesian-based approach for virtual network reconfiguration in elastic optical path networks, in: *Optical Fiber Communications Conference (OFC) 2017*, pp. 1–3, Mar. 2017.
37. Shen, T.S.R., Meng, K., Lau, A.P.T., Dong, Z.Y., Optical performance monitoring using artificial neural network trained with asynchronous amplitude histograms. *IEEE Photonics Technol. Lett.*, 22, 22, 1665–1667, Nov. 2010.
38. Anderson, T.B., Kowalczyk, A., Clarke, K., Dods, S.D., Hewitt, D., Li, J.C., Multi impairment monitoring for optical networks. *IEEE/OSA J. Lightwave Technol.*, 27, 16, 3729–3736, Aug. 2009.
39. Tanimura, T., Hoshida, T., Kato, T., Watanabe, S., Morikawa, H., Data-analytics-based Optical Performance Monitoring Technique for Optical Transport Networks, in: *Optical Fiber Communications Conference (OFC) 2018*, Mar. 2018.
40. de Moura, C., Oliveira, J.R., Oliveira, J.C., Cesar, A.C., EDFA adaptive gain control effect analysis over an amplifier cascade in a DWDM optical system, in: *SBMO/IEEE MTT-S International Microwave & Optoelectronics Conference (IMOC) 2013*, pp. 1–5, Oct. 2013.
41. Li, Y. and Chen, M., Software-defined network function virtualization: A survey. *IEEE Access*, 3, 2542–2553, Dec. 2015.
42. Masdari, M. and Özdemir, S., Towards coverage-aware fuzzy logicbased faulty node detection in heterogeneous wireless sensor networks. *Wirel. Pers. Commun.*, 111, 1, 581–610, Mar. 2020.

Part 2

PRIVACY AND SECURITY OF HEALTHCARE IN HYPER INTELLIGENT NETWORK

8

Security and Privacy in Hyper-Intelligent Networks

Abhishek Panda, Animesh Jha, Gourav Vardhan Panigrahi, Saahen Sriyan Mishra and Hitesh Mohapatra*

School of Computer Engineering, KIIT Deemed to be University, Bhubaneswar, Odisha, India

Abstract

Cloud computing offers a plenty of benefits, yet its widespread adoption faces a downside of insecurity. It is important to sheds light on the privacy and ethical challenges arising from the collection and utilization of data in urban environments. Access control, data leakages, and lack of expertise are the major threats. Organizations spend millions on security aspects like firewalls and encryption tools to try to protect them against known threats. The issue to address is the need for robust privacy and security protocols. To review this subject, here, we show comparative analysis of major security threat prevention models employed into cloud computing environment. This chapter proposes strategies for enhancing cloud security, such as improving access management and encryption and addressing vulnerabilities related to data. The comparison of existing models revealed areas for improvement by detailing their limitations and advantages. The result highlights the need for development of more resilient and ethically sound smart-city ecosystem. The topic of privacy and security intersects with trends in urbanization and governance, reflecting a larger discourse on the ethical implications in urban development. This increasingly interconnected world needs discussions on the responsible deployment of technologies to foster innovation while ensuring the protection of individual privacy.

***Keywords*:** Cloud computing, security, privacy, authentication, data mishandling

**Corresponding author*: hiteshmahapatra@gmail.com

Pradosh Kumar Gantayat, Sandeep Kumar Panda, S. Balamurugan and Sheng-Lung Peng (eds.) Hyper-Intelligent Networks: Exploring the Future of Connectivity for Society 5.0, (153–176) © 2026 Scrivener Publishing LLC

8.1 Introduction

Smart cities with cloud-enabled technologies seamlessly integrate digital cloud solutions in order to enhance and improve urban lifestyles. These cities optimize infrastructure, utilities, and services for efficiency and sustainability by using the features of the cloud. Traditional smart city development is rapidly affected by innovative technological advancements, with cloud technologies being one of the key contributors. These smart cities collect a large amount of data from various information and communication technologies relying on cloud computing (CC). These cloud-dependent technologies generate and collect data in the form of a stream, i.e., it is continuously generated. The purpose of gathering such information is to improve living standards, solve public problems, serve the community in a better way, provide a sense of public safety, and show interest in sustainable urban growth [1].

A few examples of such generated data are public surveillance cameras, public biometric devices, etc. These types of smart devices capture data and store them in the cloud, which is usually provided by cloud providers. The data generated are very sensitive and contain confidential information [2]. In the real world, there are always problems and problems when dealing with such information to a greater extent, which are not limited only to its fair and transparent use. This data is controlled in a top-down approach, where both public (government) and private organizations control the data. The current literature on privacy and awareness of cloud-enabled smart

Figure 8.1 Public surveillance.

cities to the general public lacks a practical drive. The aim of this study is to be an awareness note for the general public about various privacy and ethical values [3]. Figure 8.1 demonstrates public surveillance model.

8.1.1 Issues with Current Scenario

Current practices often obtain approval through third-party services or laws governing the processing of personal data, which allow the unauthorized use of data and improper handling of personal information. It can be a dangerous practice for the government to use public data. The government's entrustment of citizens' data to a third party can be a risk. The widespread adoption of cloud services has facilitated collaboration and innovation across various industries. However, a critical barrier to maximizing this potential lies in ensuring robust security and privacy measures. One key challenge across this regard pertains to grant controlled access to third-party entities. While leveraging such access can enhance functionality, concerns regarding data security necessitate a strong security framework. This framework should allow a tiered access control system, where the level of access granted to external entities is directly proportional to the sensitivity of the data that they require. Additionally, rigorous identity management protocols for all third-party users are essential to mitigate the risk of insider threats to the system. Recent works and research in this area has shown that vulnerabilities exploited through the compromised third-party access points and has led to poor service quality in terms of security and privacy [4].

Due to the ease with which cloud services are provisioned and the relentless march of technological progress, a significant paradigm shift has emerged toward cloud-based data storage solutions. This burgeoning trend is driven by the critical need of organizations to efficiently manage and analyze voluminous amounts of sensitive data, a cornerstone for informed decision-making. However, a critical impediment to widespread adoption resides in the limitations of existing security and privacy mechanisms. As per our findings in various literature works to the related context, it was found that these mechanisms often struggle to adapt to the dynamic nature of external environments, resulting in a persistent risk of data breaches. Organizations grapple with the challenge of establishing a robust cloud security infrastructure that safeguards sensitive data and user privacy, all while navigating the ever-evolving landscape of cloud storage services [5]. Furthermore, the increasingly nuanced concept of privacy, where information deemed private by one individual might be readily shared by another, necessitates the development of adaptable security protocols for cloud environments. The challenge of cloud security is further exacerbated by the constantly evolving threat landscape. Malicious actors are continuously developing sophisticated methods to exploit vulnerabilities in cloud infrastructure and user devices. This necessitates a proactive approach to security, with organizations implementing measures such as continuous threat monitoring, vulnerability management, and user education programs [6].

In spite of a multitude of security and privacy-based concerns, technology is widely acknowledged as the cornerstone for fostering limitless growth in smart cities. However, this progress comes at a potential cost: the erosion of personal privacy. While the technology itself holds immense promise, issues surrounding privacy, security, safety, and ethical considerations introduce vulnerabilities that demand careful attention. Public anxieties within smart cities necessitate a multifaceted approach focusing on the types of data collected, its purpose, and who has access to it. Generally, concerns are minimal when dealing with impersonal service-related data. However, the unfettered implementation of smart technologies, absent of stringent policies and regulations, carries the risk of significant intrusion into personal lives [7]. Undoubtedly, privacy and security are paramount during the development of cloud-based smart city systems, but public safety remains an equally critical consideration. Safety, defined as the absence of danger, risk, or loss, becomes a central concern when smart city applications integrate seamlessly with human lives and handle sensitive data. Furthermore, the ethical implications of such data collection and usage require thorough examination. Transparency and accountability are crucial for building public trust and ensuring responsible governance within smart city initiatives.

Numerous applications use and manage diverse types of devices that directly interact with humans and may regulate certain aspects of daily life. For example, any application that has the potential to affect humans or their surroundings must be designed in such a way that not only security and privacy but also safety are prioritized. Smart city applications must prioritize human life and safety above all else. Any threat to human life shall replace prior considerations of privacy or security of personal data. Without the protection of human life, concerns about privacy or security become secondary. Data collection in cloud-enabled smart cities, a cornerstone for various customizable services and functions, relies on distributed systems strategically dispersed throughout the urban environment. Programmed for specific data, these systems often operate inclusively, potentially capturing information beyond their intended scope, including private data. This inherent characteristic necessitates a delicate balance between comprehensive data collection and safeguarding citizen privacy.

The installation of cameras, traffic sensors, and various human motion capturing sensors in public areas, some without prior notice, can lead to a monopolistic control over smart technologies within the city. Consequently, critical decisions of the city and the privacy of individuals may become reliant on a specific private entity for services such as data storage, capture, and streaming [8]. Improper or unjustified utilization of surveillance may erode trust, both generally and specifically in authority. Skepticism regarding the motives behind state surveillance might breed cynicism about how such technology will be used for self-protection. While there is acknowledgment that privacy may need to be compromised in the face of security risks, the extent of this sacrifice must be proportionate. However, determining the acceptable level of intrusion can be challenging and may primarily be based on resource allocation considerations, where the costs of time and energy are weighed against other more significant transgressions. Even in the absence of evidence of wrongdoing, the state might opt to maintain records on individuals deemed potential future threats [9].

8.1.2 Ethical and Regulatory Challenges Required in Smart City Development

- **Data Governance and Regulation:** Smart cities operate within a complex web of data governance and regulation. As data flows through various systems and devices, it is imperative to establish clear guidelines and regulations to ensure its ethical and responsible use. Governments and regulatory bodies play a crucial role in setting standards for data privacy, security, and accessibility. Collaborative efforts between public and private sectors are essential to develop comprehensive frameworks that balance innovation with protection of individual rights.
- **Community Engagement and Empowerment:** Building trust and fostering community engagement are essential pillars of successful smart city initiatives. Residents should be actively involved in decision-making processes concerning data collection, storage, and usage. Public forums, citizen advisory boards, and community outreach programs can facilitate meaningful dialogue and empower individuals to voice their concerns and preferences. By incorporating

diverse perspectives and prioritizing transparency, smart cities can cultivate a sense of ownership and accountability among residents.

- **Ethical Considerations in Technology Deployment:** The deployment of smart technologies should be guided by ethical principles that prioritize human rights, dignity, and well-being. Stakeholders must consider the potential societal impacts of technological interventions, including issues of equity, accessibility, and digital divide. Ethical assessments should be conducted at every stage of technology development and implementation to anticipate and address unintended consequences. Collaboration with ethicists, social scientists, and community advocates can help identify and mitigate ethical dilemmas inherent in smart city projects.
- **Data Privacy and Security by Design:** Incorporating privacy and security measures into the design of smart city infrastructure is essential to protect sensitive information and mitigate cyber threats. Adopting a "privacy by design" approach involves embedding privacy features into the architecture of systems and applications from the outset. Similarly, implementing robust security protocols, such as encryption, authentication, and access controls, can safeguard data against unauthorized access and manipulation. Continuous monitoring and updates are necessary to adapt to evolving cybersecurity threats and maintain the integrity of smart city ecosystems.
- **Education and Awareness Campaigns:** Raising public awareness about the implications of data collection and usage is crucial for promoting informed decision-making and fostering digital literacy. Educational initiatives, workshops, and outreach campaigns can help citizens understand their rights, responsibilities, and options regarding data privacy and security. By empowering individuals with knowledge and skills, smart cities can cultivate a culture of data stewardship and accountability, where residents actively participate in shaping the future of their communities.

8.2 Literature Review

Privacy Concerns in Smart City Technologies: The integration of surveillance technologies into smart cities has revolutionized urban management and efficiency. However, the continuous gathering of data through Closed-circuit television (CCTV) cameras, Internet-of-Things (IoT) sensors, and facial recognition systems raises profound privacy concerns. While instrumental in bolstering security and urban planning, the deployment of such technologies in public spaces presents challenges concerning the limits of data collection. Safeguarding information confidentiality and integrity during cross-border data transmission is paramount. Encryption serves as a critical line of defense, but, for Platform-as-a-Service (PaaS) and Software-as-a-Service (SaaS) static data, it may not be a failsafe solution. This limitation arises from the dependence on searchable encryption, a technique employed to efficiently search and index encrypted data within the cloud environment. While searchable encryption offers a degree of efficiency, its complexity grows exponentially, potentially hindering optimal performance [10]. Table 8.1 presents the comparison of surveillance technologies showing the data collection methods employed and the corresponding privacy implications.

Defining the Scope of Surveillance and Privacy: Precise definitions of pertinent terms would necessitate extensive discussions. Surveillance, as employed here, transcends mere people watching; it entails meticulous and sustained observation through visual, auditory, or other data-gathering means of a specific individual or group for a particular purpose. The crux lies in the identification and correlation of data, regardless of its form or origin, with a specific individual or group, posing a challenge to privacy [11]. The sources of data collection are diverse, ranging from loyalty cards for analyzing consumer demographics to ticketing devices facilitating traffic management. CCTV in public spaces aids in crowd control, while cookie technology facilitates interactions with the World Wide Web. Intercorporate monitoring of credit card usage serves as a bulwark against identity theft and unauthorized spending. In such instances, individuals consent to monitoring (and thereby sacrifice privacy) in the interest of self-protection. Consequently, consented surveillance may be viewed as less contentious, provided that the parameters of such surveillance are clearly delineated during the consent process [12].

Table 8.1 Comparison of surveillance technologies showing the data collection methods employed and the corresponding privacy implications.

Technology	Method of data collection	Related concern
CCTV surveillance cameras [13]	Video recording in public spaces	Invasion of public privacy
IoT sensors [14]	Motion capturing and environmental data extraction	Invasion of private spaces
Facial recognition [15]	Identification of individuals on facial features	Concerns to profiling and misuse of people's identification
Location trackers and GPS systems [16]	Monitoring of devices and individuals	Invasion of Personal Privacy
Biometric authentication [17]	Collection of biometric data for identification	Risk of forging of biometric information
Automated license plate recognition [18]	Captures license plate information	Vehicle tracking

Security Measures and Vulnerabilities: The widespread integration of cloud systems into smart city infrastructures may not adequately emphasize the critical importance of cybersecurity and the substantial vulnerabilities inherent in cloud environments. Safeguarding privacy and security in smart city settings demands the adoption of comprehensive strategies. Through the implementation of robust encryption protocols, stringent access controls, and cutting-edge technologies, sensitive data can be shielded from unauthorized access and potential breaches. Ongoing monitoring and risk assessments facilitate proactive identification and mitigation of security threats. However, insufficient security measures render the infrastructure susceptible to malicious attacks and data breaches [19]. Despite concerted efforts, vulnerabilities persist, presenting significant challenges in upholding data security standards, particularly concerning the inadvertent collection of mass data through surveillance, thereby exacerbating privacy concerns. Without decisive action to address these issues, the potential of smart city innovation remains overshadowed by the looming threat of mishandling and potential leaks of citizens' data.

Third-Party Cloud Providers and Potential Misuse of Government-Captured Data: The adoption of cloud-based services, especially by government entities utilizing third-party providers like Amazon Web Services, adds complexity and potential privacy concerns. While providers such as AWS offer scalable and efficient cloud solutions, there is a risk of data misuse for personal gain. Despite the evident convenience and efficiency of cloud services, the potential for unauthorized access, surveillance, and misuse of government data by these providers must be considered concerning privacy matters. As smart city initiatives increasingly depend on cloud infrastructure, literature underscores the necessity for robust governance frameworks and rigorous oversight to ensure responsible data

Table 8.2 Various security threats and cloud computing layers that they affect.

Attack name	Description	Affected layer
Service injection [20]	This type of attack is intended to take control over the application and VM providing malicious and modified services instead of legal services.	PaaS
Man in the middle [21]	Accessing data transfer by acting as a middleman in the communication channel.	PaaS, IaaS, and SaaS
Phishing [22]	Intentional usage of fake and illegal web links and advertisement.	PaaS, IaaS, and SaaS
Side Channel Attack [23]	The execution of such attacks is to affect data integrity and is carried out through a targeted virtual network extraction.	SaaS and PaaS
Authentication attack [24]	Exploitation of flaws in the authentication protocol being used.	PaaS, IaaS, and SaaS
Hypervisor and VM attack [25]	With trade-offs of the hypervisor and its software implementation, the intruder gains access to the virtual machine by bypassing the virtualization layer.	IaaS

handling and prevent unauthorized use by third-party entities. Table 8.2 presents various security threats and CC layers that they affect.

Public Perception and Trust: Public perception holds significant sway over the success of smart city initiatives, particularly those involving mass surveillance. Citizens' trust is closely tied to their comprehension of how surveillance technology's function and the perceived advantages they bring. The viability of smart city endeavors hinges on public acceptance and trust. A closer examination of public perception reveals the intricate interplay between citizens and surveillance technologies. Trust levels are shaped by factors like perceived benefits, transparency in data usage, and awareness of potential risks [26]. Citizens are more inclined to endorse surveillance initiatives if they perceive tangible benefits, such as enhanced public safety, improved traffic management, or better service delivery. Clear communication of these benefits and concrete examples of their impact can aid in fostering trust among the public. Transparency regarding the collection, processing, and utilization of surveillance data is imperative for cultivating trust. Well-defined policies and protocols for data governance, coupled with mechanisms for oversight and accountability, can help assuage concerns regarding the potential misuse of surveillance data.

8.3 Proposed Study

CC currently lacks universally agreed-upon security standards. However, respected organizations like Cloud Security Alliance (CSA), National Institute of Standards and Technology (NIST), and Federal Information Security Management Act (FISMA) have introduced widely accepted standards such as the Cloud Control Matrix (CCM) and the Security, Trust, and Assurance Registry (STAR). Our research highlights the diverse security approaches among Cloud Service Providers (CSPs), with significant agreement on the utilization of certain security mechanisms and tools. Despite privacy limitations that restrict comprehensive consumer activity monitoring, the adoption of Service-Level Agreements (SLAs) is on the rise to balance responsibilities and expectations between CSPs and consumers, thereby mitigating threats related to infrastructure abuse and service availability issues. To address the threat of hypervisor security breaches, an emerging trend involves defining security policies on a host basis, ensuring that security configurations remain intact with the cloud host throughout its journey [27]. Acknowledging skill gaps among cloud security professionals, significant investments have been made by organizations and governments in training initiatives [28].

Various CSPs grapple with diverse security challenges: Carpathia faces challenges with immature trust extensions in hypervisors, Cisco deals with cloud standards and security automation issues, and Citrix addresses administrative errors and unauthorized workflows. Furthermore, CSPs such as Expedient, HyTrust, McAfee, OpSource, Trapezoid, and Virtustream encounter a range of security challenges, including inadequate encryption key management, incomplete data deletion, and insufficient encryption during data transference. Proposals like file assured deletion (FADE) show promise in ensuring the complete deletion of data upon client requests [28]. Proven Strategies have ensured robust cloud data security necessitates a multi-layered approach that addresses critical concerns such as data integrity, access control, and multi-tenancy vulnerabilities. A cornerstone of this approach involves setting dynamic thresholds for file storage capacities. This allows for efficient storage management by employing deduplication techniques for files exceeding these thresholds. Additionally, Security Information and Event Management (SIEM) systems play a crucial role in managing data integrity violations by generating in-depth log reports that facilitate comprehensive threat analysis.

Two-factor authentication with Rivest–Shamir–Adleman (RSA) SecureID and vigilant monitoring practices have emerged as effective solutions for authentication and access control in cloud environments. Further strengthening the security posture requires the implementation of a diverse set of measures. These include Database Active Monitoring, File Active Monitoring, URL filters, Data Loss Prevention protocols, encryption at rest and in transit, hypervisor security at the hardware level, and the strategic utilization of query re-writers at the database level. This multifaceted approach comprehensively addresses the security challenges posed by multi-tenancy environments and data leakage [29].

8.3.1 Limitations on IaaS in the Context of Cloud Security

- **Abuse of cloud services:** In the modern landscape of cloud service procurement, the absence of physical interactions is notable. CSPs commonly refrain from routinely scrutinizing user activities on their Infrastructure-as-a-Service (IaaS) platforms due to stringent privacy regulations. However, attackers continuously evolve tactics, adding complexity to detecting and preventing potential security threats. A significant concern arises from the prospect that malicious actors armed with forged or stolen bank details can exploit this situation by acquiring IaaS cloud services. Upon gaining access to these cloud resources, they may misuse them to disseminate intended malicious software and programs, and phishing methods as a potential threat are used against other users within the cloud ecosystem [30]. It is crucial to recognize that this security threat extends beyond IaaS alone; it also affects PaaS cloud infrastructure. Continuous vigilance and innovative security measures are necessary to stay ahead of evolving attack vectors and safeguard the integrity of cloud-based services. In a technologically advancing environment, adapting security protocols becomes increasingly paramount to effectively mitigate these risks [31].

- **No to Limited Expertise in Cloud Technology:** Recent and past research and surveys have highlighted a significant inadequacy in cloud security—the shortage of proficiently skilled personnel capable of effectively safeguarding the extensive volumes of data housed in cloud environments. This shortage raises concerns about the overall security posture of cloud-based systems. Additionally, a myriad of cloud security challenges has been attributed to inaccuracies in security configurations, as reported by reputable sources such as BCS The Chartered Institute for IT [32]. This vulnerability emphasizes the need for meticulous attention to security configurations and practices, especially when employing application programming interface (API) calls that facilitate data distribution within the cloud infrastructure. To address these challenges, it is imperative to not only enhance the expertise of security personnel but also rigorously review and enhance security configurations within cloud environments. Proactively identifying and rectifying vulnerabilities in hypervisor security practices and API utilization are pivotal steps toward fortifying the overall security posture of cloud-based systems.

8.3.2 Limitations on PaaS in the Context of Cloud Security

- **Incomplete Data Erasure:** Guaranteeing complete deletion of client data upon request remains a major concern in cloud adoption, stemming from the distributed architecture and inter-provider collaboration employed by CSPs. Data potentially resides across geographically dispersed servers and might be shared with other providers, making complete erasure a complex task. This persistent data deletion challenge translates into a significant privacy concern for cloud consumers. The inability to guarantee complete removal can force users into vendor lock-in, fearing residual data remaining elsewhere and hindering their ability to switch providers [33].

- **Message Integrity Violations:** Research indicates that certain CSPs lack sufficient encryption, leaving some data vulnerable due to encryption overhead. This shortfall has led to message integrity violations, posing a significant privacy and personal security concerns and issues to the privacy of cloud consumers [34]. Additionally, deduplication attacks jeopardize the confidentiality of cloud consumers' files, allowing malicious users to identify, access, and store files remotely [34].

8.3.3 Limitations on SaaS in the Context of Cloud Security

- **Inadequate Monitoring:** Achieving fine-grained auditing and traceback in cloud environments proves challenging due to shared log files. Unlike networked environments where hardware association aids in establishing traceback, virtualization complicates such associations. Additionally, privacy regulations pose a security threat, as the majority of cloud customers prefer their activities to be monitored solely for billing and accounting purposes [35].

8.3.4 Other Key Security Concerns for Cloud Computing

- **Authentication Challenges:** The reliance on password-based authentication within cloud environments introduces inherent limitations, giving rise to multiple drawbacks and notable risks. The widespread adoption of multi-cloud architectures necessitates a robust approach to security. However, a persistent obstacle in this domain lies in achieving seamless trust propagation. This term refers to the effortless extension of a verified user's security context across diverse cloud platforms. The absence of a standardized and secure mechanism for trust propagation hinders the establishment of a unified security posture for users who leverage the benefits of multiple CSPs. This challenge necessitates the development of interoperable trust frameworks that can bridge the gap between heterogeneous cloud environments.

- **Data Security and Leakage:** The inherent multi-tenancy aspect in cloud environments introduces a substantial risk of data leakage. Instances of breaching from one virtual machine to another within the same host and URL traversal enable malicious tenants to access data from others. The process of cloud bursting exacerbates these risks, turning a multi-partner cloud into a potential single point of compromise with intricate security related concerns and data trust concerns [36].
- **Vulnerabilities in Interfaces and API:** Security issues, often stemming from sub-optimal development practices, persist within cloud environments, particularly in applications initially designed for in-house use. Notable examples include distributed database systems (DDS) systems like CouchDB, FlockDB, Hive, MongoDB, RavenDB, and SimpleDB, utilizing API calls not only SQL (NoSQL) for create, read, update, delete (CRUD) operations. Documented vulnerabilities in DDS, such as limited support for Dynamic Application Testing Tools (DAST), absence of native encryption and hashing, and susceptibility to SQL injection, emphasize the necessity for robust security measures [37].
- **Human-Related Threats:** Deceptive web content poses risks, enticing users to download malware. Despite technological advancements, the persistent human factor continues to make social engineering, drive-by downloads, and insider threats significant security challenges in the realm of CC [38].

8.3.5 Access Control Challenges

- **Resource Reallocation Risks:** Virtualization in CC allows the emulation of hardware, enabling the operation of multiple virtual machines on a hypervisor. While facilitating multi-tenancy and resource reallocation for scalability, this capability introduces a potential risk. Sectors containing one tenant's deleted files may be accessible by co-tenants within the same Virtual Machine stack. Furthermore, the redeployment of servers can inadvertently introduce security vulnerabilities. Released IP addresses, upon rejoining public pools, can be exploited by malicious actors to gain unauthorized access to the cloud environment [39].

- **Fragmented Landscape of Cloud Access Control Interfaces:** The widespread adoption of cloud services presents a security challenge akin to a fragmented fortress. This vulnerability stems from the heterogeneity of access control interfaces across CSPs. This lack of uniformity hinders the seamless migration of security protocols during cloud switching. Research suggests that security vulnerabilities can readily emerge during the integration process, despite meticulous verification of individual domain policies. This necessitates the development of interoperable access control frameworks to bridge the gap between disparate cloud environments, fostering a more unified and secure cloud security posture [40].
- **Threats to Cloud Service Delivery Models:** The pervasiveness of access control violations transcends all cloud service delivery models, posing a significant security concern across various cloud vendors as per Table 8.1. This underscores the critical need for robust preventative measures to address these challenges [41].

8.3.6 Comparative Analysis of Existing Models

This section presents a comparison and discussion of various foundational models for assessing information security risks in CC systems, with the aim of gaining a comprehensive understanding of their nuances and practical applications. These models evaluate the security of computing systems by quantifying potential losses for each stakeholder resulting from security threats and vulnerabilities [42].

- **SecAgreement:** A Holistic Security Risk Assessment Model: SecAgreement emerges as a vital tool for CSPs seeking to enhance the appeal and adoption of their services. Going beyond the traditional scope, SecAgreement includes a cloud service matchmaking algorithm. This algorithm not only evaluates and ranks SLAs but also introduces an innovative approach to quantifying risks. By enabling organizations to quantify risk and identify compliance gaps, as well as select services that align with their specific security needs,

SecAgreement becomes a strategic ally in the evolving landscape of cloud security.

- **The Mean Failure Cost (MFC):** Financially Quantifying System Security: Among cyber security metrics, MFC stands out for its unique approach to quantifying system security in financial terms. Traditional security risk assessments often focus solely on the statistical average (mean) of a random variable, such as average attack frequency. The multi-factored criteria (MFC) approach, however, takes a more holistic view. MFC incorporates stakeholder concerns, infrastructure value, and the specific impact of security threats on various architectural components [47]. This broader risk assessment approach provides a deeper understanding of security vulnerabilities, enabling more informed cloud security investment decisions. This financial perspective not only provides a quantitative measure but also presents a language that resonates with stakeholders, facilitating more informed decision-making processes. Expanding the MFC process includes the generation of matrices and vectors, fostering a collaborative environment where security considerations are integral to decision-making.
- **The External Mean Failure Cost (MFCext) and the Internal Mean Failure Cost (MFCint):** The multi-factored criteria (MFC) framework employs a dualistic approach to security threat assessment, differentiating between MFCint and MFCext. This categorization goes beyond simple threat classification. By focusing on the source of the threat, MFCint and MFCext offer valuable insights into threat origin. This foresight allows for the development of targeted mitigation strategies, enabling organizations to proactively prevent or minimize the impact of security incidents. Enriching the threat assessment process, this dual perspective aligns security measures with the characteristics of internal and external threats.
- **The Mean Failure Cost Extension (MFCE) Model:** The MFCE goes beyond traditional threat assessment by refining impact matrices and threat vectors. By studying the impact of entire threat classes, MFCE becomes a dynamic decision-making tool. Organizations proactively select countermeasures per threat class, allowing for strategic and adaptive security solutions.

- **Multi-dimensional Mean Failure Cost (M2FC) Model:** Navigating Threats Through Multiple Dimensions: M2FC adopts a multi-dimensional approach to understand security threats. By dividing the threat world into various perspectives, M2FC acknowledges the multi-faceted nature of security threats. Organizations can focus on specific aspects such as architectural components or deployment locations, allowing for customized assessments based on the threat landscape's unique characteristics. In the dynamic world of cloud security, M2FC serves as a strategic compass, guiding security strategies based on evolving needs.

8.3.7 Findings from Comparative Analysis

This paper presents a critical evaluation of four quantitative security risk analysis models for CC systems. The analysis delves into three distinct approaches, meticulously dissecting the inherent limitations and advantages of each model to provide a comprehensive understanding of their suitability for cloud security assessments. The first model, SecAgreement, employs a quantitative methodology to compare CSPs based on calculated risk factors. This facilitates the selection of the optimal provider from a security risk perspective. However, it is crucial to acknowledge that SecAgreement does not explicitly estimate risks stemming from security breaches within the cloud environment itself. In contrast, the MFC model adopts a financially oriented approach to assessing system security. By quantifying the potential financial losses incurred by stakeholders due to security threats and vulnerabilities, the MFC model provides valuable insights for informed decision-making regarding security investments [48].

Despite its advantages, the MFC model exhibits several shortcomings, including the evolving and variable nature of security threats, the lack of a logical or hierarchical structure in threat cataloging, and an underestimation of MFCs due to potential ambiguity in threat definitions. Users employing this method may yield disparate results, hindering the identification of threat sources for appropriate counter measures. While the MFC model offers a financial lens for cloud security risk assessment, it suffers from a critical oversight. The model overlooks the multifaceted impact of security threats on stakeholders with diverse risk tolerances and vulnerabilities. These variations often hinge upon the specific nature, or "attack vectors," of a security threat. The MFCext and MFCint models endeavor to address this shortcoming by introducing the concept of "critical threat spaces." These models categorize threats based on their origin (internal or external), which can be advantageous for decision-makers. This information can be leveraged to implement targeted countermeasures and bolster system vulnerability analysis. However, their reliance on a singular criterion (source) and a binary classification (internal/external) can lead to an over-simplification of the threat landscape. This oversimplification can result in skewed estimations of security failure costs. Furthermore, these models neglect to comprehensively consider all relevant threat attributes beyond origin. Similarly, the MFCE model strives to refine threat classification through a more intricate model. However, this model falls short by failing to translate its classification scheme into a cost representation that reflects the specific attack vectors or stakeholder perspectives associated with each security threat [48].

Notably, current cloud security risk models, while offering valuable insights, exhibit limitations in their threat classification schemes. These limitations can be categorized as restricted granularity and incomplete threat space coverage. Restricted granularity refers to the limited detail captured in how threats are classified. Existing models often fail to capture the multifaceted nature of security threats, such as attack vectors, targeted vulnerabilities, and stakeholder impact. This lack of detail hinders the ability of decision-makers to identify the critical factors that drive security failure costs and develop effective mitigation strategies. Furthermore, the incomplete threat space coverage of existing models raises concerns about their ability to accurately represent the ever-evolving landscape of cloud related cyber threats. The current models might not encompass the full spectrum of potential threats, potentially leading to blind spots in risk assessments.

This highlights the need for a novel approach to threat classification for cloud security risk assessment. This new approach would emphasize two key principles: multidimensional threat characterization and dynamic threat space modeling. The multidimensional threat characterization involves capturing a broader range of threat characteristics beyond just the source (internal/external). This could include elements like attack vector, targeted vulnerability, potential impact on various stakeholders, and attacker sophistication. By incorporating these diverse dimensions, the model can provide a more nuanced understanding of the threat landscape and its potential financial repercussions. Dynamic threat space modeling acknowledges the constantly evolving nature of cyber threats. This approach necessitates the continuous development and refinement of the threat classification model to reflect new attack vectors, vulnerabilities, and attacker tactics. This ensures the model's continued relevance

Table 8.3 Comparison of existing cybersecurity models on the parameters of model's approach, advantages, limitations, and future development scope.

Parameter	SecAgreement model	MFC model	MFCext/MFCint models	MFCE model
Approach	Quantitative approach to compare cloud providers based on risk factors, focuses on SLA assessment without estimating risks from breaches.	Assess system security in financial terms, reflecting potential losses, shortcoming in threat cataloging and ambiguity in definitions.	Address limitations of MFC, provide critical threat spaces, focus on source (internal/external) classification, and lacks completeness.	Introduces threat classification based on model and lacks representation of costs according to threat dimensions, completeness of threat model.
Advantages	Facilitates selection of optimal cloud provider, incorporates SLA assessment, and aligns services with security needs.	Provides quantitative measure, resonates with stakeholders, facilitates decision-making processes.	Aids managers in implementing countermeasures, enhances vulnerability analysis, and specifies solutions for minimizing costs.	Enhances threat assessment and allows for proactive selection of countermeasures and dynamic decision-making tool.
Limitations	It does not estimate risks from breaches, limited to SLA assessment.	Evolving nature of threats, lacks logical/hierarchical structure in cataloging, underestimation of failure costs.	It focuses on single criterion, may lead to inaccurate cost values, and neglects possibility of sub-classes in threat sources.	Lacks completeness in threat model size, and challenges in determining critical criteria influencing cost values.
Future Development Scope	Development of advanced metrics to address limitations, refinement of models for dynamic and multifaceted nature of security challenges.	Focus on refining models for better alignment with dynamic nature of security challenges.	Further refinement to address completeness and accuracy in cost values, consideration of critical criteria influencing cost values.	Development of more refined metrics considering comprehensive range of threat characteristics.

and effectiveness in a dynamic threat landscape. By incorporating these principles, this novel approach to threat classification has the potential to significantly enhance the effectiveness of quantitative security risk models for CC environments. This will empower decision-makers to make more informed security investments, prioritize mitigation strategies based on potential cost impact, and ultimately strengthen the overall security posture of their cloud infrastructure [49].

In essence, this analysis unveils a comparative evaluation of four quantitative security risk analysis models designed for CC systems. The core objective revolves around dissecting the inherent strengths and weaknesses embedded within each model, ultimately aiming to illuminate their efficacy for cloud security assessments. The need for a refined metric that accurately estimates security breaches and considers a comprehensive range of threat characteristics is emphasized, highlighting the imperative for future research and development efforts to focus on refining these models to better align with the dynamic and multifaceted nature of security challenges in CC environments. In essence, the existing models fall short in providing a holistic view of security risks in CC systems. The current chasm between security risk models and real-world security management is concerning. These models, while offering quantitative evaluations, often provide insufficient detail to pinpoint the crucial elements driving security breach costs. This creates a significant obstacle for organizations, as effective security policy hinges on a metric that accurately captures the financial repercussions of security breaches across various aspects. Consequently, managers find it difficult to identify the key factors within these models that have the most substantial impact on security failure costs. Table 8.3 presents comparison of existing cybersecurity models on the parameters of model's approach, advantages, limitations, and future development scope.

8.4 Conclusion

Within the dynamic domain of Information Security Management, risk assessment serves as a cornerstone methodology for safeguarding organizational assets. As CC adoption accelerates, offering cost optimization and enhanced operational efficiency, a systematic and well-structured approach to information security risk evaluation becomes increasingly crucial. This research undertakes a comparative analysis of quantitative security risk models specifically designed for cloud-based systems. By meticulously dissecting the strengths and limitations of each model, this study aims to empower decision-makers with the knowledge necessary to select the most appropriate model for their unique organizational context and security posture. The insights gleaned from this comparative analysis extend beyond the immediate realm of cloud security, offering valuable knowledge for risk assessment practices across the entire spectrum of modern IT infrastructure. Ultimately, this research emphasizes the critical role of data-driven decision-making in the face of constantly evolving threats. By employing tailored risk assessment methodologies, organizations can effectively mitigate risks and safeguard their reputation and critical assets and we present our efforts for the same in this review paper.

Future studies could delve deeper into the exploration of advanced risk assessment techniques, such as predictive analytic, machine learning, and artificial intelligence algorithms. These techniques hold potential for enhancing the accuracy and predictive capabilities of risk assessment models, enabling organizations to proactively identify and mitigate emerging security threats. Additionally, as concerns surrounding data privacy and regulatory compliance continue to grow, there is a need to integrate privacy considerations into existing risk assessment frameworks. Future research could also focus on developing hybrid risk assessment methodologies that effectively address both security and privacy concerns in CC environments. Such advancements in risk assessment methodologies can prove to be instrumental in ensuring the continued resilience and security of organizational assets in an increasingly complex and dynamic threat landscape.

References

1. Losavio, M.M., Chow, K.P., Koltay, A., James, J., The Internet of Things and the Smart City: Legal challenges with digital forensics, privacy, and security. *Secur. Privacy*, 1, e23, 2018.
2. Fabrègue, B.F.G. and Bogoni, A., Privacy and Security Concerns in the Smart City. *Smart Cities*, 6, 1, 586–613, 2023.
3. Abdulsalam, Y.S. and Hedabou, M., Security and Privacy in Cloud Computing: Technical Review. *Future Internet*, 14, 1, 11, 2022.
4. Abdulsalam, Y.S. and Hedabou, M., Decentralized Data Integrity Scheme for Preserving Privacy in Cloud Computing, in: *Proceedings of the 2021 International Conference on Security, Pattern Analysis, and Cybernetics (SPAC)*, Chengdu, China, 18–20 June 2021, pp. 607–612.
5. Kumar, P., Sehgal, V.K., Chauhan, D.S., Gupta, P., Diwakar, M., Effective ways of secure, private and trusted cloud computing. *arXiv 2011, arXiv:1111.3165.*
6. Sun, X., Liu, P., Singhal, A., Toward Cyberresiliency in the Context of Cloud Computing [Resilient Security]. *IEEE Secur. Priv.*, 16, 71–75, 2018.

7. Clever, S., Crago, T., Polka, A., Al-Jaroodi, J., Mohamed, N., Ethical Analyses of Smart City Applications. *Urban Sci.*, 2, 4, 96, 2018.
8. Macnish, K., Unblinking eyes: the ethics of automating surveillance. *Ethics Inf. Technol.* June 2012, 14, 2, 151–167, 2012.
9. Norris, C. and Armstrong, G., CCTV and the social structuring of surveillance, in: *Surveillance, Crime and Social Control*, pp. 81–102, Routledge, 2017.
10. Kamara, S. and Moataz, T., Boolean searchable symmetric encryption with worst-case sub-linear complexity, in: *Proceedings of the Annual International Conference on the Theory and Applications of Cryptographic Techniques*, Paris, France, 30 April–4 May 2017, pp. 94–124.
11. Iphofen, Ron., Ethical issues in surveillance and privacy. *Hostile Intent and Counter-Terrorism*, 59–72, CRC Press, 2017.
12. Pearson, S. and Benameur, A., Privacy, security and trust issues arising from cloud computing, in: *Proceedings of the 2010 IEEE Second International Conference on Cloud Computing Technology and Science*, Indianapolis, IN, USA, 30 November–3 December 2010, pp. 693–702.
13. Neal, D. and Rahman, S.M., Video surveillance in the cloud-computing? *2012 7th International Conference on Electrical and Computer Engineering*, pp. 58-61, Dhaka, 2012. doi: 10.1109/ICECE.2012.6471484.
14. Mohammed Sadeeq, M., Abdulkareem, N.M., Zeebaree, S. R.M., Mikaeel Ahmed, D., Saifullah Sami, A., Zebari, R. R., IoT and Cloud Computing Issues, Challenges and Opportunities: A Review. *Qubahan Acad.* J., 1, 2, 1–7, 2021. https://doi.org/10.48161/qaj.v1n2a36.
15. Reddy, M., Bodepudi, A., Mandapuram, M., Gutlapalli, S., Face Detection and Recognition Techniques through the Cloud Network: An Exploratory Study. *ABC J. Adv. Res*, 9, 103–114, 2020. 10.18034/abcjar.v9i2.660.
16. Bajaj, R., Ranaweera, S., Agrawal, D., GPS: Location-Tracking Technology. *IEEE Computer*, 35, 92–94, 2002. 10.1109/2.993780.
17. Mohapatra, H., Socio-technical Challenges in the Implementation of Smart City, in: *2021 International Conference on Innovation and Intelligence for Informatics, Computing, and Technologies (3ICT)*, Zallaq, Bahrain, pp. 57–62, 2021, doi: 10.1109/3ICT53449.2021.9581905.
18. Shashirangana, J., Padmasiri, H., Meedeniya, D., Perera, C., Automated License Plate Recognition: A Survey on Methods and Techniques. *IEEE Access*, 9, 11203–11225, 2020. 10.1109/ACCESS.2020.3047929.
19. Mollah, M.B., Azad, M.A.K., Vasilakos, A., Security and privacy challenges in mobile cloud computing: Survey and way ahead. *J. Netw. Comput. Appl.*, 84, 38–54, 2017.
20. Devi, R., Venkatesan, R., Koteeswaran, R., A study on SQL injection techniques. *Int. J. Pharm. Technol.*, 8, 22405–22415, 2016.
21. Mallik, A.. Man-in-the-middle-attack: Understanding in simple words. Cyberspace: Jurnal Pendidikan Teknologi Informasi, 2, 2, 109–134, 2019.
22. Bhavsar, V., Kadlak, A., Sharma, S., Study on Phishing Attacks. *Int. J. Comput. Appl.*, 182, 27–29, 2018. 10.5120/ijca2018918286.

23. Parida, B.R., *et al.*, Energy Efficient Virtual Machine Placement in Dynamic Cloud Milieu Using a Hybrid Metaheuristic Technique. *Computación y Sistemas*, 27, 4, 1147–1155, 2023.
24. Kumar, R., Can Isik, and Chilukuri Krishna Mohan. Dictionary Attack on IMU-based Gait Authentication. In Proceedings of the 16th ACM Workshop on Artificial Intelligence and Security (AISec '23). *Association for Computing Machinery*, 115–126, New York, NY, USA, 2023. https://doi.org/10.1145/3605764.3623909.
25. Mangalagowri, R. and Venkataraman, R., Hypervisor Attack Detection Using Advanced Encryption Standard (HADAES) Algorithm on Cloud Data. *Int. J. Comput. Netw. Appl.*, 9, 555, 2022. 10.22247/ijcna/2022/215916.
26. Liu, D., Securing outsourced databases in the cloud, in: *Security, Privacy and Trust in Cloud Systems*, pp. 259–282, Springer, New York, NY, USA, 2014.
27. Mohemed, A., John, G., Amani, S.I., Collaboration-Based Cloud Computing Security Management Framework, in: *2011 IEEE 4th International Conference on Cloud Computing*, Washington DC, pp. 364–371, 2011.
28. Louis, M. and Sfakianakis. A., Enisa threat landscape-responding to the evolving threat environment. ENISA (The European Network and Information Security Agency), 2012 September.
29. Parida, B.R., *et al.*, SSEPC cloud: Carbon footprint aware power efficient virtual machine placement in cloud milieu. *Comput. Sci. Inf. Syst.*, 00, 18–185, 2024.
30. Hassan, R.J., Zeebaree, S., Ameen, S.Y., Kak, S.F., Sadeeq, M., Ageed, Z.S., *et al.*, State of art survey for iot effects on smart city technology: challenges, opportunities, and solutions,. *Asian J. Res. Comput. Sci.*, 22, 32–48, 2021.
31. Kumar, A., Kumar, P.S., Sairam, T., Organization Assignment in Federated Cloud Environments based on Multi-Target Optimization of Security, in: *Cyber Security in Parallel and Distributed Computing: Concepts, Techniques, Applications and Case Studies*, 2019.
32. Dumka, A., Memoria, M., Ashok, A., Security and Challenges in Mobile Cloud Computing, in: *Security Designs for the Cloud, IoT, and Social Networking*, pp. 43–57, 2019.
33. Ho, R.M., Kim, J., Kim, S., Factors affecting application developers' loyalty to mobile platforms. *Comput. Hum. Behav.*, 40, 78–85, 2014.
34. Fernandes, D.AB., *et al.*, Security issues in cloud environments: a survey, *Int. J. Inf. Secur.*, 13, 113–170, 2014.
35. Haji, S.H., *et al.*, Comparison of software defined networking with traditional networking. *Asian J. Res. Comput. Sci.*, 9, 2, 1–18, 2021.
36. Okai, E., Feng, X., Sant, P., Security and Forensics Challenges to The MK Smart Project, in: *2019 IEEE SmartWorld, Ubiquitous Intelligence & Computing, Advanced & Trusted Computing, Scalable Computing & Communications, Cloud & Big Data Computing, Internet of People and Smart City Innovation (SmartWorld/SCALCOM/UIC/ATC/CBDCom/IOP/SCI)*, pp. 1666–1670, 2019.

37. Lei, C., Dai, H., Yu, Z., Li, R., A service recommendation algorithm with the transfer learning based matrix factorization to improve cloud security. *Inf. Sci.*, 513, 98–111, 2020.
38. Bazm, M.-M., Lacoste, M., Südholt, M., Menaud, J.-M., Isolation in cloud computing infrastructures: new security challenges. *Ann. Telecommun.*, 74, 197–209, 2019.
39. Hamad, Z.J. and Zeebaree, S.R., Recourses utilization in a distributed system: A review. *Int. J. Sci. Bus.*, 5, 42–53, 2021.
40. Negi, P.S., Garg, A., Lal, R., Intrusion detection and prevention using honeypot network for cloud security, in: *2020 10th International Conference on Cloud Computing, Data Science & Engineering (Confluence)*, pp. 129–132, 2020.
41. Altowaijri, S.M., An Architecture to Improve the Security of Cloud Computing in the Healthcare Sector. in: Mehmood, R., See, S., Katib, I., Chlamtac, I. (eds) *Smart Infrastructure and Applications. EAI/Springer Innovations in Communication and Computing*, Springer, Cham, 2020, https://doi.org/10.1007/978-3-030-13705-2_10.
42. Parida, B.R., Rath, A.K., Mohapatra, H., Binary self-adaptive salp swarm optimization-based dynamic load balancing in cloud computin. *Int. J. Inf. Technol. Web Eng. (IJITWE)*, 17.1, 1–25, 2022.
43. Aissa, Ben, A., *et al.*, Quantifying security threats and their potential impacts: a case study. *Innov. Syst. Softw. Eng.*, 6, 269–281, 2010.
44. Jouini, M., Ben Arfa Rabai, L., Ben Aissa, A., Mili, A., Towards quantitative measures of Information Security: A Cloud Computing case study. *Int. J. Cyber-Security Digital Forensics (IJCSDF)*, 1, 3, 265–279, 2012.
45. Jouini, M. and Ben Arfa Rabai, L., Mean Failure Cost Extension Model Towards A Security Threats Assessment: A Cloud Computing Case Study. *J. Comput. (JCP)*, 10, 3, 184–194, 2015.
46. Jouini, M., Ben Arfa Rabai, L., Ben Aissa, A., Classification of security threats in information systems. *ANT/SEIT*, 2014, 32, 489–496, 2014.
47. Jouini, M., Ben Arfa Rabai, L., Khedri, R., A multidimensional approach towards a quantitative assessment of security threats. *Procedia Comput. Sci.*, 52, 507–514, 2015.
48. Torkura, K.A., Sukmana, M.I., Cheng, F., Meinel, C., Continuous auditing and threat detection in multi-cloud infrastructure. *Comput. Secur.*, 102, 102124, 2021.
49. Omar, M., Yazdeen, A., Malallah, H., Abdulrahman, L., A Survey on Cloud Security: Concepts, Types, Limitations, and Challenges. *J. Appl. Sci. Technol. Trends.*, 3, 47–58, 2022. 10.38094/jastt301137.

9

Internet-of-Things Integrated Blockchain–Based Supply Chain Management Across Various Industries

Dileep Kumar Murala[1], Sandeep Kumar Panda[2*], Santosh Kumar Swain[3] and Pradosh Kumar Gantayat[2]

[1]*Department of Computer Science and Engineering, Faculty of Science and Technology (IcfaiTech), ICFAI Foundation for Higher Education, Hyderabad, Telangana, India*
[2]*Department of Artificial Intelligence and Data Science, Faculty of Science and Technology (IcfaiTech), ICFAI Foundation for Higher Education, Hyderabad, India*
[3]*School of Computer Engineering, KIIT Deemed to be University, Bhubaneswar, Odisha, India*

Abstract

Conventional ways of handling a supply chain have always included keeping up with a website that lives on a server that the company either sets up or rents from a service provider. This is where all the data for the supply chain are kept in one place. The website is the only way to get to the data. Because of this, data is less accessible, there is more risk, and the system is less flexible because every change has to go through the hosted system. Orders, changes, updates, tracking information, and other information about buyers, sellers, raw material makers, assemblers, and others need to be spread out. This has to be done to reach the goal of moving the old supply chain to the blockchain. This data will be spread out across the supply chain, from the company that makes the raw materials to the store that sells them. This will make the system more flexible and easier to see. In turn, these traits would lead to a system that would allow data to flow more quickly than the usual centralized way of managing supply lines. Blockchain-based systems are popular in many industries, especially the supply chain because they are more efficient and secure. This is especially true now that supply lines are getting more complicated.

**Corresponding author*: skpanda00007@gmail.com

Pradosh Kumar Gantayat, Sandeep Kumar Panda, S. Balamurugan and Sheng-Lung Peng (eds.) Hyper-Intelligent Networks: Exploring the Future of Connectivity for Society 5.0, (177–204) © 2026 Scrivener Publishing LLC

The standard supply chain, on the other hand, ran into a lot of problems because networks were getting more complicated. With the Internet of Things (IoT), the update process is done automatically, which would have to be done by a person otherwise. This helps make sure that there are no problems with the current processes. Putting blockchain technology into the IoT could fix a lot of the problems that regular systems are having in many different fields right now. This chapter will talk about the differences between traditional supply chains and supply chains that use blockchain technology. It will also discuss about the benefits of using blockchain technology in different fields, like retail, pharmaceuticals, food, and cars. This piece will describe about the problems that the above industries are having because they still use old-fashioned supply chains. Finally, the chapter integrated IoT and blockchain-based systems in those industries can help solve those issues.

Keywords: Internet of Things, blockchain, supply chain management, traceability, predictive maintenance

9.1 Introduction

As supply lines become more fluid, they need to involve a lot of different people and depend on a lot of different outside partners. Blockchain has become a serious contender for untangling all the data, documents, and communication exchanges that happen in the supply chain network. A huge amount of data and information is always being sent back and forth between the different parts of a supply chain [1]. Internet of Things (IoT) and blockchain can be used in the supply chain to handle huge amounts of data and keep it safe. This will help make the supply line safer, more productive, more efficient, and more profitable. The IoT is a network of interconnected gadgets that work together to collect data and make smart decisions. However, IoT is open to security and privacy risks because it does not have built-in protections. With its safety by design feature, blockchain can help make IoT safer in important ways. Some of the problems with IoT's architecture can be fixed with blockchain features like immutability, openness, traceability, data encryption, and organizational freedom. With IoT, it would be possible to keep an eye on both the health and safety of the workers and the technical state of the equipment. It can also give everyone in the supply chain more communication directions and make things easier to see while they are in transit [2, 48, 49].

1. IoT and blockchain solutions are both very useful on their own, but, when they work together, which is called the blockchain of things, they can be used in a cool way by businesses.

2. The report briefly discusses supply chain security issues due to data volume and complexity.

Information is often kept separate, hard to get to, organized in a way that does not make sense, or hard to analyze. It might be too much to think about how to drive creativity in any field. The good news is that even the simplest uses of blockchain technology could make things much more productive, efficient, and profitable. The report shows how blockchain technology and IoT can be added to the normal supply chain network and how different security problems can be fixed [3, 50, 51].

9.2 Literature Review

In publication [1], writers say that blockchain technology is currently being used to work on shipping data. The writers suggest a way to connect things using a fresh way of dealing with digital identities. Their study finds important problems in maritime transportation that might cause wrong information. A digital identity framework and complete architecture for blockchain-based maritime supply chain management systems are suggested to simplify things. Additionally, it suggests a plan that helps connect the real and virtual worlds, stops cargo from going missing, and makes examining cargo easier.

The writers of papers [2] describe a significant method for automating and spreading out the management of the supply chain. With the proposed method, the whole supply chain tree would be a system, and everything in it would work together. The suggested system is a good and efficient replacement for the current supply chain. It cut down on mistakes at different points in the chain and made customer service better for everyone. It would make it possible to fully retrace and travel through the supply chain tree, which would help find problems at different levels of the tree. The current supply chain management systems will be a good and affordable alternative thanks to this system.

The authors of the paper [10] state that blockchain can be used to solve some problems in the supply chain, such as double marginalization and information asymmetry. This study talks about how important it is to have a good supply line. The study says that suppliers in the supply lines need to know a lot about it to grow it. The study advises focusing on the "strategic transaction" that will revolutionize the supply chain because so much data must be created and delivered to make goods. The writer talked about issues with incentives that come up when there are big differences in risk, like the risk of capacity. It is because of the imbalance that capacity risk has a bigger effect on the decentralized supply chain than on the vertically linked supply chain. Some people have suggested using blockchain to solve this problem and stop people from being left out twice.

The authors of the paper [15] state that blockchain technology should be studied and researched to determine how to handle the logistics supply chain for cross-border e-commerce. This paper starts by explaining what "decentralization" means and then suggests three new ways that it could be used in logistics, cash flow, and information flow. The paper shows that e-commerce has grown very quickly in China. It concludes that when blockchain technology is used in China's cross-border transport supply chain, it will enter a new phase of growth.

Authors of paper [18] discuss blockchain IoT. Data added to the blockchain can be stolen. This is "proof of work." Another approach to leak info is address search. To safeguard this, the study used knowledge zero proof. The use of smart contracts and zero-knowledge proof to secure data is the topic of this article. Information technology data held on a blockchain can be accessed or altered by an unauthorized entity. Smart meters track how much power devices use and output. Smart meters have security flaws that compromise privacy. This study uses smart contracts and zero knowledge to argue data can be protected and transactions can happen.

The authors of the paper [20] talk about how supply chain management (SCM) can be improved by using blockchain technology. Blockchain is a public, digital, decentralized ledger of all cryptocurrency activities. This can be used to fight fake goods and protect companies. The food, warehousing, and e-commerce businesses all need a more open and efficient supply chain. This technology improves transparency, risk minimization, freedom, and speed. The customer requests and receives the product. The article talks about how early adopters of block technology used IoT, focusing on how widely blockchain technology was used in different fields for verification, accountability, and tracking. After reviewing the literature for this research, we can conclude that the existing centralized supply chain management approach will delay e-cross-border commerce. Coordination, collaboration, and flow control are most difficult due to the sites' distance. Thus, blockchain technology can help fix the problem. It records transactions between the parties in a permanent, verifiable fashion. Safely sending data, files, and money is a good defense. Blockchain is typically utilized to store transportation data. Blockchain, a network of methods, can work with the IoT. The plan ensures that current supply chain management approaches operate properly and can compete.

This research will examine how the IoT and blockchain technologies might improve the security of the conventional supply chain. The conventional supply chain's security issues can be alleviated with this.

9.3 Blockchain Technology

A Quick Look:
"Satoshi Nakamoto" came up with the idea of blockchain in 2008 so that it could be used as a public record of Bitcoin activities [3, 4]. Blockchain is a decentralized, distributed ledger that timestamps peer-to-peer network events, so that none of the records involved can be changed after the fact. This lets people who use the blockchain check and monitor transactions clearly and independently. Because "blocks" are records that are linked together using cryptography, the blockchain can be thought of as a building stack of them. Every block needs to have the hash code of the block before it, the time, and a list of transactions that have been approved [5, 52, 53]. A blockchain is a made-up way to organize data in a decentralized way. The blockchain is arranged like a book with infinite pages, and each page (block) has fresh transactions. Blockchain records ran on peer-to-peer networks and public time-stamping servers [6]. The decentralized, open, and safe design of blockchain makes it possible to track transactions. Double-spending has been a problem for a long time [7, 54], but this tool can fix it. Every blockchain block has a unique hash number that tells other blocks its identity. The chain's first block is a "genesis block." As illustrated in Figure 9.1, it has no parent block. Figure 9.2 shows how each block is put together in a general way.

Figure 9.1 Blockchain in the form of a chain of blocks hashed.

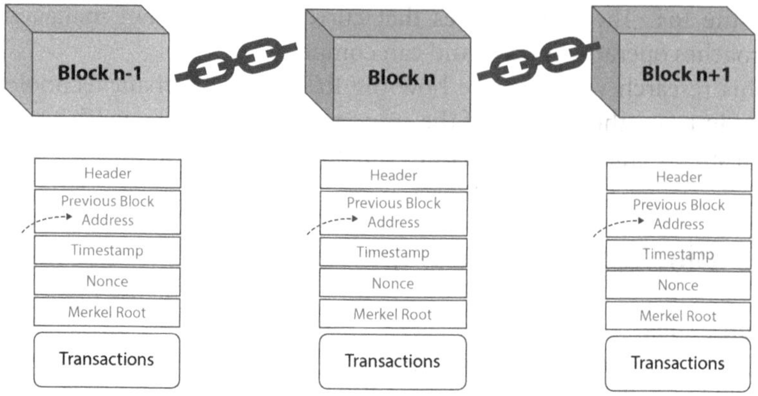

Figure 9.2 A high-level overview of blockchain block architecture.

Every block unit has a title and body. Block headers have six parts:

- The block version number determines the software's consensus mechanism.
- The hash code that links all block transactions is validated by Markle Tree Root Hash. The description included a binary tree of hash codes in the shape of a circle.
- The timestamp is reported in seconds since January 1, 1970. It records block creation and update times for block integrity guarantee.
- The objective hash code threshold is determined by N-Bits, which aids in identifying valid blocks [55].
- Once-created nonces are used in cryptography messaging. A new set of "0s" is appended to the 4-byte field with each hash calculation [56].
- A 256-bit code that refers to the block that came before it is called a Parent Block Hash. Connecting and displaying the order of blocks on the blockchain would be impossible without this component [57–59].
- The block body, on the other hand, has all the transactions that have been approved and valid within the block.

Block Transaction Counter (BTC) tracks block activities. At one point, the block state displays who sent Bitcoin to whom. Only a block-level transaction between two nodes is known. The block is then added to the blockchain after it has been checked for errors. A public record is required for this. Blockchain systems rely heavily on peer-to-peer networks [8, 60]. In a Peer to Peer (P2P) network, each node works together to update and safeguard the blockchain. Each node stores the latest blockchain. Using P2P network design in blockchain offers three key benefits:

1. Users can always utilize a blockchain browser to view the blockchain without a third party.
2. To enter blocks, a malicious party must assault hundreds or millions of nodes simultaneously.
3. Blockchain cannot be removed because all P2P nodes must do so.

9.3.1 Blockchain Features

Blockchain surpasses the majority of centralized database systems in four key ways, as illustrated in Figure 9.3.

Decentralization: This means that the events in the blockchain are handled and checked by a P2P network-based distributed ledger. For example, unlike the central bank, the Bitcoin blockchain does not rely on a central authority. All nodes collaborate as peers to contribute and verify block events in the blockchain [61, 62].
Persistence: The addition of a transaction to a blockchain block cannot be removed or altered once it has been persistent. Not to mention that invalid agreements could be located immediately.

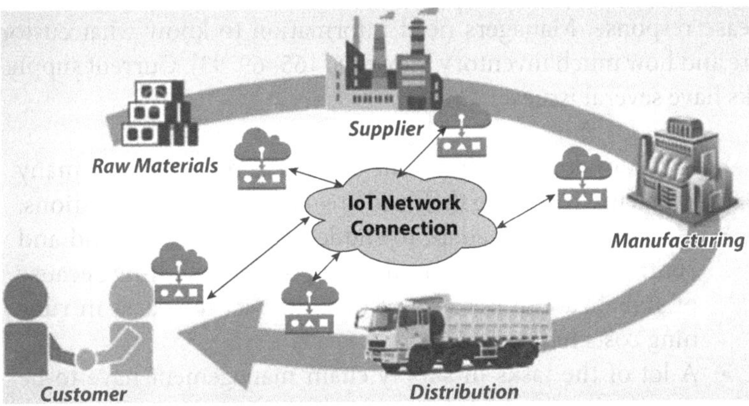

Figure 9.3 Supply chain with IoT.

Free expression: Everyone can communicate with the blockchain while keeping their true identity hidden behind a randomly generated virtual ID. Thus, this feature renders blockchain transactions less private and secure [9, 63, 64, 92].

Audibility: For a block to be auditable, it must have a secure connection to the block preceding it. With this layout, monitoring and checking progress is a breeze.

9.3.2 Processes in the Supply Chain

According to the usual supply chain process, raw materials are bought and then turned into a physical product that is sent to the customer. There are producers, dealers, distributors, logistics companies, distribution centers, and retailers in the supply chain. There is a network between a company and its producers that makes a product and sells it to a customer. This network is made up of different things, people, groups, knowledge, and resources. The steps that are taken to get the product or service from where it was made to the customer are shown in the supply chain. Getting goods to customers takes several steps. The process begins with sourcing raw ingredients and continues through manufacturing, packaging, shipping, and ultimately selling the final product to consumers. Because it allows processes and managers to make decisions and complete transactions, information is crucial to the supply chain's performance [10]. People at different points in the supply chain need to share what they know. Information is the link between the different parts of the production chain. It helps them get their work organized, which is one of the best ways to increase the general productivity of the supply chain. Clear information improves supply chain asset use. It also improves supply chain coordination to reduce costs and increase response. Managers need information to know what customers desire and how much inventory they need [65–69, 93]. Current supply networks have several issues:

- ➢ A lack of openness from one end to the other leads to many problems, including theft and breaking rules and regulations.
- ➢ Not being able to adapt to sudden changes in demand and controlling running costs: demand is always shifting because of globalization. Because of this, indirect increases in running costs happen.
- ➢ A lot of the tasks in supply chain management have to be done by hand, which takes a lot of time.

- Inefficient supply chain risk management: A system that is not good at managing risk in the supply chain cannot see danger coming and cannot act on it.
- Not having enough high-tech stuff. The problem that came up because of globalization's fast changes cannot be solved by new technologies used in modern supply chain management.
- I do not watch the system in real time, but I keep an eye on how the goods move, where they are in storage, the shipment requests, payment processing, and other things.

9.4 IoT in the Supply Chain

A normal supply chain model is made up of links between all the people, groups, and tasks involved in the business process, from the provider to the final customer. In business areas like retail, manufacturing, logistics, and e-commerce, keeping an eye on supply lines is very important. However, managing the supply chain can get harder as customers need to grow, and market changes and delays happen out of the blue. Also, a lot of the tasks that are part of supply chain management have to be done by hand, which takes time. Business leaders are trying to figure out how much stock they have left and when they should buy, make, or ship more goods. A bad flow of information can make supply chain management more efficient, effective, and combined. Here are a few problems that the company may face because of it. Yet, as we saw earlier, there are several issues with the way the supply chain usually works [11, 70, 71, 94]. As a result, it has to deal with a multitude of difficulties. Some of them are that the system is not being watched in real time, so there is no way to keep track of the movement of goods, their location in storage, shipping requests, payment processing, and other very complicated things. Putting in place, the IoT will fix these issues.

9.4.1 The Implications of the IoT on the Supply Chain

As a network, the physical devices that make up the IoT may transmit and receive data, as well as detect and record occurrences. IoT devices usually link to computers that are part of a network through Wi-Fi or data networks. IoT devices use sensors to find out about their surroundings, like where they are, the temperature, the humidity, the amount of light, their ability to move, their speed, the ability to handle things, and other external factors. Products related to the IoT can take numerous forms, including radio frequency identification (RFID) readers, mobile phones, and portable sensors. IoT systems use GPS and other technologies to monitor and confirm shipments and products in the supply chain. As a tool for supply chain quality management, IoT devices can keep an eye on equipment storage. Connected devices, networks, and applications make up the IoT. Other examples include advancements in computer science and analytics, as well as in the fields of communication and information technology [12, 72–74, 95].

When IoT is used in the production chain, it can help in the following ways:

Data Collection: IoT monitors can be put in many things to find out how each person uses them. With this technology, the usage habits of different groups of people can be studied, and the information gathered can be used to create new products [13, 75, 76].
Monitoring the Goods and Equipment: Businesses can agree on the minimum value of goods that need to be kept at certain temperatures and humidity levels, like food. IoT sensors can let the right people in the building know if the limit is pushed too far.
Product Lifecycle Management: Another significant aspect of supply chain management is product or material lifecycle management. Products are handled by a wide variety of parties, including manufacturers, distributors, retailers, suppliers, and business-to-business partners. IoT sensors can track inventory levels and identify problems. Locating geologically suitable commercial sources could potentially be aided by IoT [14, 77].
Stock Management: IoT monitors can give businesses real-time stock information. IoT sensors will help business leaders estimate product demand.
Logistics: Ships, vehicles, and containers transport commodities and packages along the supply chain. Connecting these parts to IoT lets firms track delivery trucks in real time.
Building Maintenance: IoT in supply chain management lets enterprises maintain their tools and delivery trucks. Automotive, tool, item, retail shelf, and workshop floor sensors gather data in real time through the IoT. Problems arise with supply chain IoT. The concerns at hand pertain to matters of privacy and security. Problems with interoperability, a dearth of legislation, legal challenges, rights concerns, the changing economics of the IoT, and expansion are among the other barriers [15, 78, 79].
Security Information: A big concern for any industrial network that is linked to the Internet is the safety of the information or data. It is becoming

more normal for people to attack websites, and hackers may be interested in IoT technology as well. Vulnerabilities in data handling and storage can lead to attacks and leaks from outside the company, which can hurt its reputation and make failure more expensive.

Data Pools: The IoT creates enormous data pools for supply chain managers, among other benefits. With that much power comes the responsibility to ensure the server can store and analyze all the data [16, 80–82].

Secure Internet Connectivity: Getting a safe Internet link is very important for IoT. It is not always safe to connect to the network because truck drivers are moving around. When adding IoT to the supply chain, you should also think about how fast the internet is.

- ➢ The team that is knowledgeable. Also, supply lines go over thousands of kilometers all over the world. It can also be hard to fix problems with how IoT systems work together.
- ➢ Even without IoT training, it is hard to get a team of people who know enough about the problem to come up with a strategy that works for the company.
- ➢ Putting together rules for how to use business networks and drawing up security policies takes a lot of time [17, 83, 84].

9.5 Implementing a Blockchain Supply Chain

The research demonstrated the typical flow of a company's supply chain and how the IoT might improve and accelerate this process. The likelihood of data breaches is directly proportional to the proliferation of IoT devices. However, incorporating blockchain technology into its framework could mitigate these dangers. The IoT provides precise data regarding materials and items in a supply chain by connecting the physical and digital worlds. The use of blockchain technology to link IoT devices in the supply chain facilitates the retrieval of data. This makes the flow of both real and digital goods safer, more reliable, clearer, and less expensive [85, 86].

Step 1: Launch a custom blockchain system. Ethereum can enable private blockchain networks. It is a decentralized computing network that is built on open-source blockchain technology. Each company needs a powerful computer to create an Ethereum blockchain. This is an "Ethereum node." Use cross-platform programs like GoEthereum or "get." to set up an Ethereum server.

Step 2: Develop smart contracts. Smart contracts are Ethereum's sophisticated functionality. The software makes trading products, money, houses, shares, and other valuables easy. Smart contracts are computer programs that act when particular circumstances are satisfied and run smoothly without being interrupted, restricted, hacked, or tampered with. All firm supply chain data is stored in a central repository and database in traditional intranet systems. Smart contracts have one address that maintains the database for all nodes and serves as the network hub. Both C++ and JavaScript are capable of writing smart contracts. Smart contract compilers are available online for these programming languages. An Ethereum blockchain can host the contract.
Step 3: Create a decentralized app. Smart contract ledgers are dynamic databases that distributed apps can access and update. You can access this smart contract ledger from any device, as it is mostly cloud-based. This worldwide blockchain application may be made easily utilizing HTML and CSS and Ethereum's blockchain interface, Web3Js.

Figure 9.4 shows Ethereum's distributed app development stack. The last three layers of the Ethereum stack must remain unchanged. To display a spread application on a web page instead of HTML or CSS, it can be transformed into any Web3J-supported scripting language. Benefits of Blockchain-Enabled Supply Chain IoT: Because our supply chains are intricate and unreliable, people are interested in how blockchains can make the sector safer. Blockchain could prevent certain production chain issues:

- Inventory Theft
- Information theft
- Smuggling and theft
- Third-party vendor data sharing
- IoT sensor data exposure

Address all problems by compromising blockchain.

Inventory Theft: Employee stock theft still threatens supply chains, especially in distribution facilities. It is hard to keep track of everything because so much flows through these hubs. This is why theft methods are confusing. Drivers and corporate employees work together to remove stolen goods from the distribution hub for resale. Each item in this inventory can be marked using IoT technology to follow its movement remotely. Inventory tags can be saved in the blockchain, making inventory data, intended use, destination, and other private data safer.

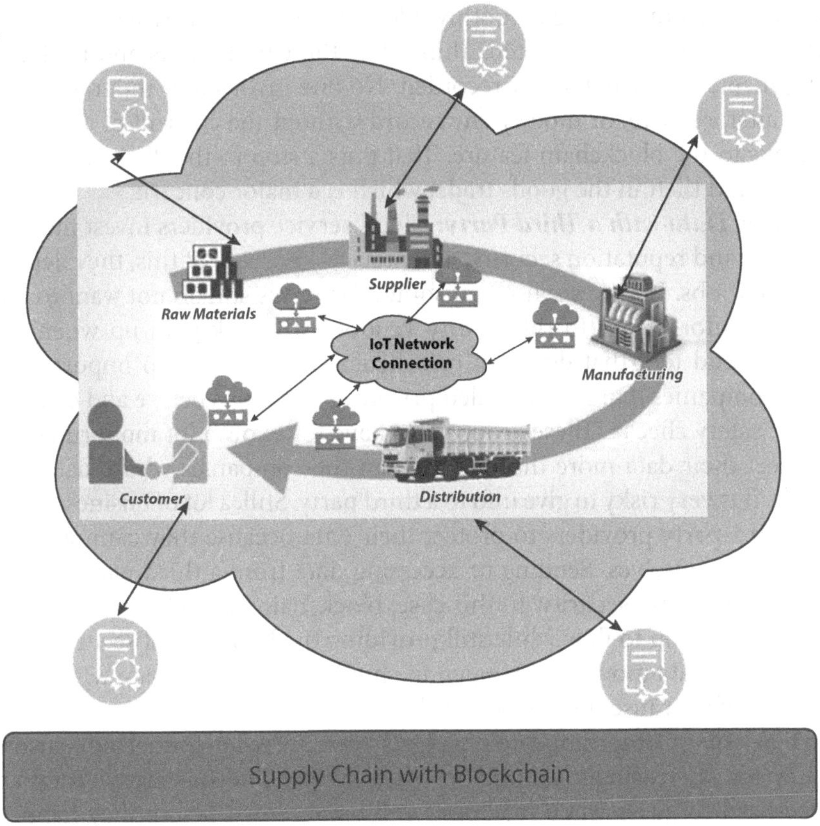

Figure 9.4 Integration of supply chain with blockchain.

Theft of Information: Data security in the cloud is becoming more important as more and more supply chain tools and storage systems migrate to the cloud. If you cannot manage cloud access properly, then you could end up with major IT risks, like giving users too many rights. This means that anyone who wants to can view the cloud data. Blockchain can also be used to deal with this safety issue. It is possible to do so with strong access control and permissions. This will make it safer for people to access information from the cloud. Safeguarding and storing this type of data is possible, as is randomly changing the access keys so that anyone can access them without concern for hackers.

Crimes Like Smuggling and Piracy: Smuggling items can put the supply chain at risk. Products from the "gray market" and fake or stolen goods are moved across countries with the help of shipping companies. This affects both the location and the customers, as well as the supply chain, because it stops it from moving smoothly. Blockchain makes it easier to keep an eye on and record every step. Things like the whereabouts and timing of shipments are meticulously recorded. No one involved in the transaction can alter, remove, or modify any record without the consent of all others, thanks to the blockchain feature. That puts a stop to the illicit transfer of goods and theft in the goods trade, which is a major concern.

Sharing Data with a Third Party: Cloud service providers invest much in website and reputation security, and precisely because of this, they depend on their jobs. It makes sense that some businesses still do not want to give private information to third-party vendors. The risk goes up when you use a cloud tool that does not prioritize security. It is also important to hire companies that have handled private applications before and can pass strict safety checks. These groups also have to follow a lot more rules and protect their data more thoroughly than the companies whose data they store. It is very risky to give info to a third party. Still, a lot of businesses rely on third-party providers to protect their data because they cannot afford to do it themselves. Sending or accessing data from a third-party vendor can compromise security. In this case, blockchain can help make it easier for information to flow while still providing the best level of security. This makes the data movement happen in chunks. These blocks are what make it very safe because they are secured.

IoT Sensor: Compromise-IoT gadgets have internet-connected sensors. They are increasingly utilized to track supply line inventory. They are also used to guess when machines will break down before they happen. However, hackers can use all of this sensor data to learn more about the supply chain, such as the number of orders, the ties between key suppliers, and other things. At every point in the IoT world, devices should be checked and tested for security and encryption. This is what blockchain technology is used for. IoT devices can keep information in encrypted form, which makes it almost impossible for hackers to get or read that information.

9.5.1 Supply Chain and Logistics Blockchain and IoT Applications

Here are some ways that blockchain and IoT can be used in transportation and the supply chain.

Communication Over Wireless: Huge steps forward have been made in wireless communication, which receives data from the sensor hub and sends it to the assigned client and base station. This lets devices talk to each other even if they are not physically linked. Wireless communication is helpful for smart tactics with IoT [17, 87].

Inventory Management: IoT gives companies a clear picture of what their coordinate systems are doing, which encourages regular stock connection even more. RFID stickers and sensors also help logistics keep track of their stock and where and how they are right now [18, 88].

Product Source: Blockchain and IoT make it possible for both the company and the customer to keep track of a product's full life cycle in the supply chain. All of the conversations between IoT devices are saved in the blockchain. It gives businesses quick access to information about the product, such as the date it was made, registered, and sold, as well as a full record [19, 89].

Intelligent Insights: Blockchain and the IoT make it safe for partners and things in the supply chain to share information. Partners can use the most advanced AI techniques to find new pieces of information across their supply lines by putting this data together with data from other sources [20, 90].

Route Management: A lot of people use IoT devices to keep track of their routes and locations. GPS tracking and truck beacons help keep track of where a vehicle is and what path it is taking to make sure deliveries happen on time and keep customers informed of the progress of their orders [21, 40, 91].

Smart Contracts: Blockchain and IoT can work together to make sure that shipped goods are safe, even when they are traded between countries. Smart contracts are like an online deal or arrangement between everyone interested in the trade. The rules of the contract are written in computer codes that make it possible for people who do not know each other to send money to each other without any problems [22].

How to Fix Documentation Issues in Container Shipping: The flow of documents in container shipping uses a lot of time and resources. Because there is a lot of paperwork, there is a chance of loss, fraud, tampering, and other problems with paper goods documents, especially when shipping goods between countries. Blockchain solutions can help connect large networks and set up a link between ports, shipping companies, and customs to make it easier to move documents around and make digitizing paper records more efficient [23, 47].

Tracking the Provenance of Goods: Buyers care most about where the goods came from and how original they are. Customers do not want to buy fake things and only want real ones. To get rid of the fear of fakes, blockchain technology can help keep track of the product's supply line and paperwork [24].

9.5.2 Blockchain and IoT Benefits for Supply Chain and Logistics

Supply chain and logistics firms, manufacturers, and suppliers can all benefit greatly from the integration of blockchain technology and the IoT. Some of the most significant benefits of integrating the supply chain with blockchain and the IoT are as follows:

Insights Based on Data: Blockchain and IoT make it safe for all players in a supply chain ecosystem to share data. The dataset and third-party data sources can be used by stakeholders to learn more about their supply chain through machine learning methods [25, 46].

Maximize Supply Chain Transparency: Digital Bill of Lading and smart contracts made by combining IoT and blockchain can help you keep track of things and their whereabouts in the delivery process in real time, making sure that your obligations are met [26, 45].

Regulated Reliability of Supply Chain: Goods must be moved within strict temperature limits and time frames in industries with a lot of rules, such as food and medicine. If that is not done, then the high-value package could be held up. With the IoT, temperature feeds from onboard devices can be sent online to the blockchain framework, which makes sure that the information sent and received is safe and correct [27, 44].

Real-Time Visibility of the Entire Supply Chain: Because there are so many people involved, it can be hard to see the whole chain from beginning to end. Companies keep track of the problems in the supply chain by collecting data, but they need to check the data from different companies to make sure it is accurate. However, by connecting IoT devices to supply chain tracking systems and then sharing that data *via* a blockchain-based system, everyone can access the data in real time [28].

Better Financing for the Global Supply Chain: The global supply chain includes deals that take place in different countries. It takes a lot of red tape and paperwork, which can slow down international payments because of local banking rules and the number of parties involved. Any mistake can cause the payment-clearing process to take longer than planned [29].

9.6 Supply Chain IoT and Blockchain Use Cases

Businesses can improve supply chain tracking and value with blockchain and IoT. The digital supply network is now able to react autonomously to signals of supply and demand thanks to the IoT and blockchain technology.

There will be less effort and better efficiency in global supply systems. Businesses can now monitor their products' whereabouts in real time thanks to sensors linked to the internet [30]. Distributed ledger technology (DLT) enables all participants in a supplier network to have access to immutable product records. IoT and blockchain can work together to make the whole supply chain more open, accountable, and transparent, with a single source of truth that everyone can use [17]. This can lead to better supply chain management. To get these kinds of results, Chief Information Officer (CIOs) and supply chain leaders can look into how these tools can be used in real life. Here are five main ways that IoT and blockchain are used to help businesses improve their next-generation digital supply networks [31].

Tracking: Even though many businesses have put a lot of money into their supply chains, it is not always easy to track items as they move through global networks. This is a problem because customer safety, company profits, and reputation are all at risk [32]. By using IoT and blockchain in the following areas, businesses can collect useful data, gain deeper insights, and speed up the detection and resolution of incidents:
Tracking where a product came from: With IoT, businesses can better keep track of where their goods (or parts of them) came from and share this information on the blockchain. This makes things more open and could improve how people feel about and are loyal to a brand. For instance, food distributors could give grocery shops more information about allergens, ingredients, and other things that might help people feel better about buying [33].
Tracking the progress of a product: When things move around the world, they often run into problems with logistics. Delays in shipping, for example, can damage fragile items like medicines, wines, and veggies. Fake goods can get into supply lines without being caught. With IoT and blockchain, businesses can share and track the exact location of their products much more accurately, even when there are problems or events [34].
Keeping track of changes in ownership and care: Many important people in the supply chain are involved in moving items around the world. Many more fall under this category, such as manufacturers, suppliers, banks, insurers, goods forwarders, and third-party logistics firms. IoT sensors keep track of where things are physically located, and smart contracts on the blockchain can record when ownership and custody change hands [35].
Electronic paper: Shipping problems caused by paperwork, like fake documents or documents full of mistakes made by hand, can cause delays, losses, and other risks in the supply chain [43]. This is a big problem for supplies of things like meat, medicines, and dairy that need to get there quickly.

Uploading shipping data generated by IoT to the blockchain can automate validation and verification processes and digitize paperwork [36].

9.7 Challenges in Traditional Supply Chain

When using old methods, transportation and supply chain workers have to deal with problems like these:

Depending on Brokers: The supply chain is complicated, and rules mean that customs brokers are needed to make sure that papers are real, keep delays to a minimum, lower risks, and keep people from getting fined [19]. There are also breaks and extra shipping costs because of this [37].
Inefficient Inventory Management: Not being able to see where and when packages are can cause problems with routing and inventory management, leading to shortages, higher costs, and unhappy customers because of late deliveries [38, 39].
Late Payment for Damaged Goods: When there are gaps in visibility, it is not only hard to keep track of assets, but it is also hard to find damaged goods, which means that payments are late [40].
Costly Letter-of-Credit Process: In foreign trade, banks use letters of credit as a way to guarantee that a buyer's payment will be received on time and for the right amount. However, they take a long time and cost more money [41].
Poor Routing and Batching of Goods: When companies cannot automate the batching of their goods, they often have to pay more for shipping and use their containers less efficiently [42].

9.8 Conclusion and Feature Directions

This study talks about how a blockchain-based supply chain that includes the IoT is different from a normal one. This study looked at the new chances for supply chain stability and operational efficiency if the IoT and BT came together. Blockchain technology (BT) and the IoT could change the way supply chain management is done, which could completely change the industry. These technologies improve supply chain visibility, efficiency, security, and tracking by fixing some problems that plague traditional supply chain management systems. BT makes it possible for a single, shared record to be created so that only authorized parties can safely record and retrieve connections and information. There is less need for agents, fraud is less likely to happen, and people are more accountable. Smart contracts on the blockchain could be used to automate and execute agreements between parties. This would make things run more smoothly and save money on administrative costs. The IoT, on the other hand, lets you connect real-world materials and objects to the internet. This creates new ways to collect data, keep track of it, and handle it. IoT sensors in commodities, containers, and autos can give supply chain management vital information about location, humidity, and quality. Real-time data analysis enables proactive decision-making, predictive maintenance, and supply chain optimization. These tools function well together and can transform SCM.

With the IoT, you can see what is going on in the physical parts of the supply chain in real time. BT also makes sure that data is safe and clear throughout the supply chain. This merger makes it possible to track a product from the time it is made to the time it is delivered, making it easier to make sure that it is real, that it meets quality standards, and that it follows all the rules. Adding blockchain to the IoT can cut down on the time it takes to ship goods across foreign borders and make the process safer, more efficient, and less expensive. All of this is possible because of the spread ledger, which cannot be changed and stops fraud. Smart contracts can be used to automatically carry out and enforce deals between two or more parties when certain events take place. The issues these industries are having because they still use old-fashioned supply lines will be discussed in this essay, along with how blockchain- and IoT-based solutions could help them fix these issues.

This paper solely outlines a blockchain-based traceability plan. Some implementation details remain unexplored. Increasing device-to-network fault tolerance and reducing blockchain code computational needs for low-configuration IoT edge devices. We will also look at ways to get everyone on the network to agree on something and at simple network methods for getting devices to talk to each other and spread information.

References

1. Abd El-Latif, Abd-El-Atty, B., Mehmood, I., Muhammad, K., Venegas-Andraca, S.E., Peng, J., Quantum-Inspired Blockchain-Based Cybersecurity: Securing Smart Edge Utilities in IoT-Based Smart Cities. *Inf. Process. Manag.*, 58, 4, 1–12, 2021. doi: 10.1016/j.ipm.2021.102549.
2. Panda, S.K., Jena, A.K., Swain, S.K., Satapathy, S.C. (Eds.), *Blockchain Technology: Applications and Challenges*, Springer, Intelligent Systems Reference Library, https://doi.org/10.1007/978-3-030-69395-4.

3. Murala, D.K., Panda, S.K., Dash, S.P., MedMetaverse: Medical Care of Chronic Disease Patients and Managing Data Using Artificial Intelligence, Blockchain, and Wearable Devices State-of-the-Art Methodology. *IEEE Access*, 11, 138954–138985, 2023. doi: 10.1109/ACCESS.2023.3340791.
4. Murala, D.K. and Levi, P., A Secure and Dynamic Multi Keyword Graded Search Theme over Encrypted Cloud Knowledge. *Int. J. Mag. Eng. Technol. Manage. Res.*, 3, 12, 449–455, 2016.
5. Murala, D.K. and Panda, S.K., *Artificial Intelligence in the Development of Metaverse, Metaverse, and Immersive Technologies: An Introduction to Industrial, Business and Social Applications*, pp. 407–436, John Wiley & Sons, Inc, 2023/10/20, https://doi.org/10.1002/9781394177165.ch15.
6. Murala, D.K. and Panda, S.K., *Metaverse: A Study on Immersive Technologies, Metaverse, and Immersive Technologies: An Introduction to Industrial, Business and Social Applications*, pp. 1–41, John Wiley & Sons, Inc, 2023/10/20, https://doi.org/10.1002/9781394177165.ch1.
7. Murala, D.K. and Panda, S.K., *The Internet of Things in Developing Metaverse, Metaverse, and Immersive Technologies: An Introduction to Industrial, Business and Social Applications*, pp. 437–465, John Wiley & Sons, Inc, 2023/10/20, https://doi.org/10.1002/9781394177165.ch16.
8. Murala, D.K., Panda, S.K., Swain, S.K., Secure Dynamic Groups Data Sharing with Modified Revocable Attribute-Based Encryption in Cloud. *Int. J. Recent Technol. Eng. (IJRTE)*, 8, 4, November 2019. ISSN: 2277-3878.
9. Murala, D.K. and Panda, S.K., *Blockchain in the Development of Metaverse, Metaverse, and Immersive Technologies: An Introduction to Industrial, Business and Social Applications*, 28 September 2023, https://doi.org/10.1002/9781394177165.ch3.
10. Murala, D.K. and Panda, S.K., *The Role of Immersive Reality (AR/VR/MR/XR) in Metaverse, Metaverse, and Immersive Technologies: An Introduction to Industrial, Business and Social Applications*, pp. 159–189, John Wiley & Sons, Inc, 2023/10/20, https://doi.org/10.1002/9781394177165.ch6.
11. Yontar, E., Critical success factor analysis of blockchain technology in agri-food supply chain management: A circular economy perspective. *J. Environ. Manage.*, 330, 117173, 2023.
12. Dai, H., Member, S., Zheng, Z., Member, S., Zhang, Y., Member, S., Blockchain for the Internet of Things: A Survey. *IEEE Internet Things J.*, 6, 5, 8076–8094, 2019.
13. Hrouga, M., Sbihi, A., Chavallard, M., The potentials of combining Blockchain technology and Internet of Things for digital reverse supply chain: a case study. *J. Clean. Prod.*, 337, 130609, 2022.
14. Cekerevac, Z., Prigoda, L., Maletic, J., Blockchain technology and industrial Internet of Things in the supply chains. *Mest J.*, 6, 39–47, 2018.
15. Moosavi, J., Naeni, L.M., Fathollahi-fard, A.M., Blockchain in supply chain management: a review, bibliometric, and network analysis. *Environ. Sci. Pollut. Res.*, 1–15, 2021.

16. Outchakoucht, A., Hamza, E.S., Leroy, J.P., Dynamic access control policy based on blockchain and machine learning for the internet of things. *Int. J. Adv. Comput. Sci. Appl.*, 8, 7, 2017.
17. Varaprasada Rao, K., Murala, D.K., Panda, S.K., *Blockchain: A Study of New Business Model, Recent Advances in Blockchain Technology: Real-World Applications*, pp. 187–214, Springer International Publishing, 2023/2/12.
18. Lokre, S.S., Naman, V., Priya, S., Panda, S.K., Gun Tracking System Using Blockchain Technology, in: *Blockchain Technology: Applications and Challenges. Intelligent Systems Reference Library*, vol. 203, S.K. Panda, A.K. Jena, S.K. Swain, S.C. Satapathy (Eds.), Springer, Cham, 2021, https://doi.org/10.1007/978-3-030-69395-4_16.
19. Dileep Kumar, M., An Approach Towards Identification of Personalized Privacy in Social Networks. *Int. J. Rev. Recent Electron. Comput. Sci. IJRRECS*, 3, 11, 4713–4717, November 2015. ISSN 2321-5461.
20. Hewa, T.M., Kalla, A., Nag, A., Ylianttila, M.E., Liyanage, M., Blockchain for 5G and IoT: Opportunities and challenges, in: *2020 IEEE Eighth International Conference on Communications and Networking (ComNet)*, pp. 1–18, 2020.
21. Dileep Kumar, M., A Scalable Proposal for Managing Dynamic Functions On Collection of Documents. *Int. J. Rev. Recent Electron. Comput. Sci. IJRRECS*, 4, 2, 5200–5205, February 2016. ISSN 2321-5461.
22. Dileep Kumar, M., Allocation of Responsible Health Data in Cloud System. *Int. J. Adv. Res. Eng. Sci. IJARES*, 3, 7, 1991–1995, July 2015. ISSN 2347-9337.
23. Dileep Kumar, M., Securing of Access Control for Maintaining Effective Cloud Data. *Int. J. Rev. Recent Electron. Comput. Sci. IJRRECS*, 3, 4, 3866–3870, April 2015. ISSN 2321-5461.
24. Dileep Kumar, M., Vijaya Sunder Sagar, N., Nagesh, M., Priyanka, G., Efficient Proposal For Controlling Authorized Check. *Int. J. Rev. Recent Electron. Comput. Sci. Cloud System IJRRECS*, 4, 1, 5153–5158, January 2016. ISSN 2321-5461.
25. Arza, M.S. and Panda, S.K., An Integration of Blockchain and Machine Learning into the Health Care System, in: *Machine Learning Adoption in Blockchain-Based Intelligent Manufacturing*, vol. 1, pp. 33–58, DOI: 10.1201/9781003252009-3.
26. Murala, D.K., *A Study on Security and Privacy Issues of Users Data in Cloud Environment*, shodhganga.inflibnet.ac.in.
27. Murala, D.K., Panda, S.K., Swain, S.K., A novel hybrid approach for providing data security and privacy from malicious attacks in the cloud environment. *J. Adv. Res. Dyn. Control Syst.*, 11, 2019.
28. Murala, D.K., Panda, S.K., Swain, S.K., A survey on cloud computing security and privacy issues and challenges. *J. Adv. Res. Dyn. Control Syst.*, 11, 2019.
29. Murala, D.K., Panda, S.K., Sahoo, S.K., Securing Electronic Health Record System in Cloud Environment Using Blockchain Technology, in: *Recent Advances in Blockchain Technology, Intelligent Systems Reference Library*, vol.

237, V. Mishra, S.P. Dash, A.K. Pani (Eds.), Springer, Cham, 2023, https://doi.org/10.1007/978-3-031-22835-3_4.

30. Nanda, S.K., Panda, S.K., Das, M., Satapathy, S.C., Automating Vehicle Insurance Process Using Smart Contract and Ethereum, in: *Advances in Micro-Electronics, Embedded Systems and IoT. Lecture Notes in Electrical Engineering*, vol. 838, V.V.S.S.S. Chakravarthy, W. Flores-Fuentes, V. Bhateja, B. Biswal (Eds.), Springer, Singapore, 2022, https://doi.org/10.1007/978-981-16-8550-7_23.
31. Panda, S.K., Dash, S.P., Jena, A.K., Optimization of Block Query Response Using Evolutionary Algorithm, in: *Data Engineering and Intelligent Computing. Advances in Intelligent Systems and Computing*, vol. 1, V. Bhateja, S.C. Satapathy, C.M. Travieso-González, V.N.M. Aradhya (Eds.), Springer, Singapore, 2021, https://doi.org/10.1007/978-981-16-0171-2_54.
32. Panda, S.K., Rao, D.C., Satapathy, S.C., An Investigation into the Usability of Blockchain Technology in the Internet of Things, in: *Data Engineering and Intelligent Computing. Advances in Intelligent Systems and Computing*, vol. 1, V. Bhateja, S.C. Satapathy, C.M. Travieso-González, V.N.M. Aradhya (Eds.), Springer, Singapore, 2021, https://doi.org/10.1007/978-981-16-0171-2_53.
33. Panda, S.K. and Satapathy, S.C., An Investigation into Smart Contract Deployment on Ethereum Platform Using Web3.js and Solidity Using Blockchain, in: *Data Engineering and Intelligent Computing. Advances in Intelligent Systems and Computing*, vol. 1, V. Bhateja, S.C. Satapathy, C.M. Travieso-González, V.N.M. Aradhya (Eds.), Springer, Singapore, 2021, https://doi.org/10.1007/978-981-16-0171-2_52.
34. Panda, S.K., Mohammad, G.B., Nandan Mohanty, S., Sahoo, S., Smart contract-based land registry system to reduce frauds and time delay, in: *Security and Privacy*, p. e172, 2021, https://doi.org/10.1002/spy2.172.
35. Panda, S.K., Elngar, A.A., Balas, V.E., Kayed, M. (Eds.), *Bitcoin and Blockchain: History and Current Applications*, 1st, CRC Press, 2020, https://doi.org/10.1201/9781003032588.
36. Panda, S.K. and Satapathy, S.C., Drug traceability and transparency in medical supply chain using blockchain for easing the process and creating trust between stakeholders and consumers, in: *Pers. Ubiquit. Comput*, 2021, https://doi.org/10.1007/s00779-021-01588-3.
37. Pólvora, Nascimento, S., Lourenço, J.S., Scapolo, F., Blockchain for industrial transformations: A forward-looking approach with multi-stakeholder engagement for policy advice. *Technol. Forecast. Soc. Change*, 157, 1–18, 2020. doi: 10.1016/j.techfore.2020.120091.
38. Jayashree, K., Srinivasan, S.P., Babu, R., IoT and Blockchain for Secured Supply Chain Management, in: *Utilizing Blockchain Technologies in Manufacturing and Logistics Management*, pp. 145–160, IGI Glob, 2022.
39. Aggarwal, S., Chaudhary, R., Aujla, G.S., Kumar, N., Choo, K.K.R., Zomaya, A.Y., Blockchain for smart communities: Applications, challenges and opportunities. *J. Netw. Comput. Appl.*, 144, 13–48, 2019. doi: 10.1016/j.jnca.2019.06.018.

40. Lin, S., A survey of application research based on blockchain smart contract. *Wirel. Netw.*, 28, 635–690, 2022. doi: 10.1007/s11276-021-02874-x.
41. Panda, S.K., Daliyet, S.P., Lokre, S.S., Naman, V., Distributed Ledger Technology in the Construction Industry Using Corda, in: *The New Advanced Society: Artificial Intelligence and Industrial Internet of Things Paradigm*, https://doi.org/10.1002/9781119884392.ch2.
42. Sathya, A.R., Panda, S.K., Hanumanthakari, S., Enabling Smart Education System Using Blockchain Technology, in: *Blockchain Technology: Applications and Challenges. Intelligent Systems Reference Library*, vol. 203, S.K. Panda, A.K. Jena, S.K. Swain, S.C. Satapathy (Eds.), Springer, Cham, 2021, https://doi.org/10.1007/978-3-030-69395-4_10.
43. Aich, S., Chakraborty, S., Sain, M., Lee, H.-., Kim, H.-C., A Review on Benefits of IoT Integrated Blockchain-based Supply Chain Management Implementations, across Different Sectors with Case Study, in: *International Conference on Advanced Communications Technology (ICACT)*, 2019.
44. Sahana, U., Murala, MD.K., Sharanya, P.S., Ravali, T., A Novel Attribute-based Encryption Scheme for Efficient File Hierarchy in Cloud. *Int. J. Res. Electron. Comput. Eng. Ijrece*, 6, 2, 377–379, 2018.
45. Niveditha, V.R., Sekaran, K., Amandeep Singh, K., Panda, S.K., Effective prediction of bitcoin price using wolf search algorithm and bidirectional LSTM on the internet of things data. *Int. J. Syst. Syst. Eng.*, 11, 3-4, 224–236.
46. Varaprasada Rao, K. and Panda, S.K., A Design Model of Copyright Protection System Based on Distributed Ledger Technology, in: *Computer Communication, Networking and IoT. Lecture Notes in Networks and Systems*, vol. 459, S.C. Satapathy, J.C.W. Lin, L.K. Wee, V. Bhateja, T.M. Rajesh, (Eds.), Springer, Singapore, 2023, https://doi.org/10.1007/978-981-19-1976-3_17.
47. Varaprasada Rao, K. and Panda, S.K., Secure Electronic Voting (E-voting) System Based on Blockchain on Various Platforms, in: *Computer Communication, Networking and IoT. Lecture Notes in Networks and Systems*, vol. 459, S.C. Satapathy, J.C.W. Lin, L.K. Wee, V. Bhateja, T.M. Rajesh, (Eds.), Springer, Singapore, 2023, https://doi.org/10.1007/978-981-19-1976-3_18.
48. Panda, S.K., Swain, S.K., Mall, R., An investigation into usability aspects of E-Commerce websites using users' preferences. *Adv. Comput. Sci. An Int. J.*, 4, 1, 65–73, 2015.
49. Panda, S.K., Swain, S.K., Mall, R., Measuring Web Site Usability Quality Complexity Metrics for Navigability, in: *Intelligent Computing, Communication and Devices. Advances in Intelligent Systems and Computing*, vol. 308, L. Jain, S. Patnaik, N. Ichalkaranje, (Eds.), Springer, New Delhi, 2015, https://doi.org/10.1007/978-81-322-2012-1_41.
50. Panda, S.K., A Usability Evaluation Framework for B2C E-Commerce Websites. *Comput. Eng. Intell. Syst.*, 5, 3, 66–85, 2014.
51. Bhalerao, V., Panda, S.K., Jena, A.K., Optimization of Loss Function on Human Faces Using Generative Adversarial Networks, in: *Machine Learning Approaches for Urban Computing. Studies in Computational Intelligence*, vol.

968, M. Bandyopadhyay, M. Rout, S. Chandra Satapathy, (Eds.), Springer, Singapore, 2021, https://doi.org/10.1007/978-981-16-0935-0_9.
52. Panda, S.K. and Dwivedi, M., Minimizing Food Wastage Using Machine Learning: A Novel Approach, in: *Smart Intelligent Computing and Applications. Smart Innovation, Systems and Technologies*, vol. 159, S. Satapathy, V. Bhateja, J. Mohanty, S. Udgata, (Eds.), Springer, Singapore, 2020, https://doi.org/10.1007/978-981-13-9282-5_44.
53. Panda, S.K., Sathya, A.R., Mishra, M., Satpathy, S., A supervised learning algorithm to forecast weather conditions for playing cricket. *Int. J. Innov. Technol. Exploring Eng. (IJITEE)*, 9, 1, 2019.
54. Panda, S.K., Fraud-Resistant Crowdfunding System Using Ethereum Blockchain, in: *Bitcoin and Blockchain*, pp. 237–276, 2020.
55. Panda, S.K., Mishra, V., Balamurali, R., Elngar, A.A., *Artificial Intelligence and Machine Learning in Business Management Concepts, Challenges, and Case Studies*, pp. 1–278, https://doi.org/10.1201/9781003125129.
56. Joshi, S., Panda, S.K., Sathya, A.R., Optimal Deep Learning Model to Identify the Development of Pomegranate Fruit in Farms. *Int. J. Innov. Technol. Exploring Eng.*, 9, 3, 2352–2356, 2020.
57. Puranam, K.S.RK., Gaddam, M.C.T., K, V.P.R., Panda, S.K., Reddy, G.S.M., Anatomy and Lifecycle of a Bitcoin Transaction (February 18, 2019), in: *Proceedings of International Conference on Sustainable Computing in Science, Technology and Management (SUSCOM)*, Amity University Rajasthan, Jaipur - India, February 26-28, 2019, Available at SSRN: https://ssrn.com/abstract=3355106 or http://dx.doi.org/10.2139/ssrn.3355106.
58. Panda, S.K. and Swain, S.K., Quality Assurance Aspects of Web Design, in: *Design Solutions for Improving Website Quality and Effectiveness*, pp. 87–129, IGI Global, 2016.
59. Panda, S.K., Bhalerao, V., AR, S., A Machine Learning Model to Identify Duplicate Questions in Social Media Forums. *Int. J. Innov. Technol. Exploring Eng.*, 9, 4, 370–373, 2020.
60. Ahmareen, S., Raj, A., Potluri, S., Panda, S.K., Book Shala: An Android-Based Application Design and Implementation of Sharing Books, in: *Smart Intelligent Computing and Applications. Smart Innovation, Systems and Technologies*, vol. 159, S. Satapathy, V. Bhateja, J. Mohanty, S. Udgata (Eds.), Springer, Singapore, 2020, https://doi.org/10.1007/978-981-13-9282-5_28.
61. Panda, S.K., Das, S.S., Swain, S.K., S-Model for Service-Oriented Applications in Web Engineering. *Reg. Coll. Manage.*, 10, 3, 38–46, 2013.
62. Panda, S.K., *An Investigation into Usability and Productivity of ECommerce Websites*.
63. Panda, S.K., Chandrasekhar, A., Gantayat, P.K., Panda, M.R., Detecting Brain Tumor Using Image Segmentation: A Novel Approach, in: *Data Engineering and Intelligent Computing. Lecture Notes in Networks and Systems*, vol. 446, V. Bhateja, L. Khin Wee, J.C.W. Lin, S.C. Satapathy, T.M. Rajesh, (Eds.), Springer, Singapore, 2022, https://doi.org/10.1007/978-981-19-1559-8_35.

64. Sanghi, P., Panda, S.K., Pati, C., Gantayat, P.K., Learning Deep Features and Classification for Fresh or off Vegetables to Prevent Food Wastage Using Machine Learning Algorithms, in: *Intelligent Data Engineering and Analytics. Smart Innovation, Systems and Technologies*, vol. 266, S.C. Satapathy, P. Peer, J. Tang, V. Bhateja, A. Ghosh, (Eds.), Springer, Singapore, 2022, https://doi.org/10.1007/978-981-16-6624-7_44.
65. Gantayat, P.K., Mohapatra, S., Panda, S.K., Secure Trust Level Routing in Delay-Tolerant Network with Node Categorization Technique, in: *Intelligent Data Engineering and Analytics. Smart Innovation, Systems and Technologies*, vol. 266, S.C. Satapathy, P. Peer, J. Tang, V. Bhateja, A. Ghosh, (Eds.), Springer, Singapore, 2022, https://doi.org/10.1007/978-981-16-6624-7_45.
66. Panda, S.K., Urkude, S.V., Urkude, V.R., Vairachilai, S., An investigation into COVID 19 pandemic in India, in: *The New Advanced Society: Artificial Intelligence and Industrial Internet of Things Paradigm*, vol. 1, pp. 289–305, Wiley.
67. Panda, S.K., Das, S., Swain, S.K., Web Site Productivity Measurement Using Single Task Size Measure. *J. Inf. Sci. Comput. Technol. (JISCT)*, 4, 3, October 12, 2015.
68. Hanumanthakari, S. and Panda, S.K., Detecting Face Mask for Prevent COVID-19 Using Deep Learning: A Novel Approach, in: *Smart Intelligent Computing and Applications, Volume 2. Smart Innovation, Systems and Technologies*, vol. 283, S.C. Satapathy, V. Bhateja, M.N. Favorskaya, T. Adilakshmi, (Eds.), Springer, Singapore, 2022, https://doi.org/10.1007/978-981-16-9705-0_45.
69. Panda, S.K., Sathya, A.R., Das, S., Bitcoin: Beginning of the Cryptocurrency Era, in: *Recent Advances in Blockchain Technology. Intelligent Systems Reference Library*, vol. 237, S.K. Panda, V. Mishra, S.P. Dash, A.K. Pani, (Eds.), Springer, Cham, 2023, https://doi.org/10.1007/978-3-031-22835-3_2.
70. Panda, S.K., Mishra, V., Dash, S.P., Pani, A.K., Recent Advances in Blockchain Technology Real-World Applications, in: *Intelligent Systems Reference Library (ISRL, volume 237)*, vol. 1, pp. 1–317, 978-3-031-22835-3.
71. Panda, S.K., Mohapatra, R.K., Panda, S., Balamurugan, S., *The New Advanced Society: Artificial Intelligence and Industrial Internet of Things Paradigm*, vol. 1, pp. 1–512, John Wiley & Sons, DOI:10.1002/9781119884392.
72. Nanda, S.K., Panda, S.K., Das, M., Satapathy, S.C., Decentralization of Car Insurance System Using Machine Learning and Distributed Ledger Technology, in: *Intelligent Data Engineering and Analytics. FICTA 2022. Smart Innovation, Systems and Technologies*, vol. 327, V. Bhateja, X.S. Yang, J. Chun-Wei Lin, R. Das, (Eds.), Springer, Singapore, 2023, https://doi.org/10.1007/978-981-19-7524-0_52.
73. Nanda, S.K., Panda, S.K., Dash, M., Medical supply chain integrated with blockchain and IoT to track the logistics of medical products. *Multimed. Tools Appl.*, 82, 32917–32939, 2023. https://doi.org/10.1007/s11042-023-14846-8.

74. Panda, S.K., Jena, A.K., Panda, M.R., *et al.*, Speech emotion recognition using multimodal feature fusion with machine learning approach. *Multimed. Tools Appl.*, 82, 42763–42781, 2023. https://doi.org/10.1007/s11042-023-15275-3.
75. Panda, S.K. and Mohanty, S.N., Time Series Forecasting and Modeling of Food Demand Supply Chain Based on Regressors Analysis. *IEEE Access*, 11, 42679–42700, 2023. doi: 10.1109/ACCESS.2023.3266275.
76. Desai, D.D., *et al.*, Optimal Ambulance Positioning for Road Accidents With Deep Embedded Clustering. *IEEE Access*, 11, 59917–59934, 2023. doi: 10.1109/ACCESS.2023.3284993.
77. Lakshmi, L., Devi, K.D.S., Gupta, S., Reddy, K.A.N., Grandhi, S.K., Panda, S.K., WOMT: Wasserstein Distribution Based Minimization of False Positives in Breast Tumor Classification Using Deep Learning. *IEEE Access*, 11, 57831–57842, 2023. doi: 10.1109/ACCESS.2023.3279496.
78. Mishra, P. and Panda, S.K., Dependency Structure-Based Rules Using Root Node Technique for Explicit Aspect Extraction From Online Reviews. *IEEE Access*, 11, 65117–65137, 2023. doi: 10.1109/ACCESS.2023.3287830.
79. Routray, N., Rout, S.K., Sahu, B., Panda, S.K., Godavarthi, D., Ensemble Learning With Symbiotic Organism Search Optimization Algorithm for Breast Cancer Classification and Risk Identification of Other Organs on Histopathological Images. *IEEE Access*, 11, 110544–110557, 2023. doi: 10.1109/ACCESS.2023.3322222.
80. Agarwal, R., Pande, S.D., Mohanty, S.N., Panda, S.K., A Novel Hybrid System of Detecting Brain Tumors in MRI. *IEEE Access*, 11, 118372–118385, 2023. doi: 10.1109/ACCESS.2023.3326447.
81. Nayak, S.K., Garanayak, M., Swain, S.K., Panda, S.K., Godavarthi, D., An Intelligent Disease Prediction and Drug Recommendation Prototype by Using Multiple Approaches of Machine Learning Algorithms. *IEEE Access*, 11, 99304–99318, 2023. doi: 10.1109/ACCESS.2023.3314332.
82. Gupta, A., Gandhi, R., Jatana, N., Jatain, D., Panda, S.K., Ramesh, J.V.N., A Severity Assessment of Python Code Smells. *IEEE Access*, 11, 119146–119160, 2023. doi: 10.1109/ACCESS.2023.3327553.
83. Sethi, B.K., Singh, D., Rout, S.K., Panda, S.K., Long Short-Term Memory-Deep Belief Network-Based Gene Expression Data Analysis for Prostate Cancer Detection and Classification. *IEEE Access*, 12, 1508–1524, 2024. doi: 10.1109/ACCESS.2023.3346925.
84. Mahapatra, A., Majhi, S.K., Mishra, K., Pradhan, R., Rao, D.C., Panda, S.K., An Energy-Aware Task Offloading and Load Balancing for Latency-Sensitive IoT Applications in the Fog-Cloud Continuum. *IEEE Access*, 12, 14334–14349, 2024. doi: 10.1109/ACCESS.2024.3357122.
85. Mishra, P., Sharma, O., Panda, S.K., ADN-BERT: Attention-Based Deep Network Model Using BERT for Sarcasm Classification, in: *Evolution in Computational Intelligence. FICTA 2023. Smart Innovation, Systems and Technologies*, vol. 370, V. Bhateja, X.S. Yang, M.C. Ferreira, S.S. Sengar,

C.M. Travieso-Gonzalez (Eds.), Springer, Singapore, 2023, https://doi.org/10.1007/978-981-99-6702-5_51.

86. Varaprasada Rao, K. and Panda, S.K., Initiation, Innovation, Implementation and Integration of CBDC in Digital Virtual Payment Systems, in: *Advances in Microelectronics, Embedded Systems and IoT. ICMEET 2023. Lecture Notes in Electrical Engineering*, vol. 1156, V.V.S.S.S. Chakravarthy, V. Bhateja, J. Anguera, S. Urooj, A. Ghosh, (Eds.), Springer, Singapore, 2024, https://doi.org/10.1007/978-981-97-0767-6_20.
87. Panda, S.K., Revolution of the Metaverse and Blockchain Technology, in: *Metaverse and Immersive Technologies: An Introduction to Industrial Business and Social Applications*, Wiley, Hoboken, NJ, USA, 2023.
88. Sahoo, S.K., Das, S., Panda, S.K., Alzheimer's Disease Classification Using Brain MRI Based on 2D CNN and Transfer Learning, in: *Proceedings of the 6th International Conference on Communications and Cyber Physical Engineering. ICCCE 2024. Lecture Notes in Electrical Engineering*, vol. 1096, A. Kumar, and S. Mozar, (Eds.), Springer, Singapore, 2024, https://doi.org/10.1007/978-981-99-7137-4_1.
89. Panda, S.K., Ramesh, J.V.N., Ghosh, H., Rahat, I.S., Sobur, A., Bijoy, M.H., Yesubabu, M., Deep Learning in Medical Imaging: A Case Study on Lung Tissue Classification. *EAI Endorsed Trans. Pervasive Health Technol.*, 10, 2024.
90. Paruchuri, V.N.L.L., Shaik, A.H., Murala, D.K., Panda, S.K., IoT-Enabled Neural Network Analysis for Early Detection and Prediction of Mental Depression, in: *Information System Design: Communication Networks and IoT. ISDIA 2024. Lecture Notes in Networks and Systems*, vol. 1057, V. Bhateja, J. Tang, D.K. Sharma, Z. Polkowski, A. Ahmad, (Eds.), pp. 257–268, Springer, Singapore, 2024, https://doi.org/10.1007/978-981-97-4895-2_21.
91. Paruchuri, V.N.L.L., Malaviya, M.P., Murala, D.K., Panda, S.K., Connecting IoT Sensors for Enhanced Dementia Disease Monitoring and Intervention, in: *Information System Design: Communication Networks and IoT. ISDIA 2024. Lecture Notes in Networks and Systems*, vol. 1057, V. Bhateja, J. Tang, D.K. Sharma, Z. Polkowski, A. Ahmad, (Eds.), pp. 269–281, Springer, Singapore, 2024, https://doi.org/10.1007/978-981-97-4895-2_22.
92. Panda, S.K., Das, S., Sahoo, S.K., Predominant Music Genre Classification Using Machine Learning Approach, in: *Signal Processing, Telecommunication and Embedded Systems with AI and ML Applications. ICMEET 2023. Lecture Notes in Electrical Engineering*, vol. 1281, V. Bhateja, V.V.S.S.S. Chakravarthy, J. Anguera, A. Ghosh, W. Flores Fuentes, (Eds.), Springer, Singapore, 2025, https://doi.org/10.1007/978-981-97-8422-6_17.
93. Panda, S.K., Das, S., Sahoo, S.K., Vehicle Detection and Classification Using Intelligent Systems, in: *Signal Processing, Telecommunication and Embedded Systems with AI and ML Applications. ICMEET 2023. Lecture Notes in Electrical Engineering*, vol. 1281, V. Bhateja, V.V.S.S.S. Chakravarthy, J. Anguera, A. Ghosh, W. Flores Fuentes, (Eds.), Springer, Singapore, 2025, https://doi.org/10.1007/978-981-97-8422-6_18.

94. Chandrasekhar, A., Dodhiawala, Z., Panda, S.K., An Investigation into Chronic Kidney Disease Based-on Classification Model, in: *Signal Processing, Telecommunication and Embedded Systems with AI and ML Applications. ICMEET 2023. Lecture Notes in Electrical Engineering*, vol. 1281, V. Bhateja, V.V.S.S.S. Chakravarthy, J. Anguera, A. Ghosh, W. Flores Fuentes, (Eds.), Springer, Singapore, 2025, https://doi.org/10.1007/978-981-97-8422-6_19.
95. Chandrashekhar, A., Saheb, S.H., Panda, S.K., Balamurugan, S., Peng, S.-L., *Metaverse and Immersive Technologies: An Introduction to Industrial, Business and Social Applications*, John Wiley & Sons, 2023.

10

Hyper-Intelligent Networks in Healthcare

Bibekananda Mohanty

Department of MBA, Ajay Binay Institute of Technology, Cuttack, Odisha, India

Abstract
The integration of hyper-intelligent networks in healthcare signifies a groundbreaking transformation in patient care delivery. The advent of hyper-intelligent networks in healthcare marks a pivotal transformation in the way medical services are delivered, aiming to enhance patient care and operational efficiency. Hyper-intelligent networks encompass a synergistic integration of cutting-edge technologies.

***Keywords*:** Hyper-intelligent network, healthcare, IoT, remote monitoring

10.1 Introduction

Historically, the healthcare sector has been challenged by issues such as diagnostic errors, inefficiencies in treatment protocols, and fragmented patient care. These challenges are often exacerbated by the increasing volume of medical data, which can be overwhelming for human practitioners to analyze comprehensively. Hyper-intelligent networks address these issues by leveraging artificial intelligence and machine learning (ML) algorithms to process vast datasets swiftly and accurately, uncovering insights that were previously unattainable [1, 9].

Moreover, the integration of IoT devices and wearable technology within these networks allows for continuous monitoring of patients' health metrics. This real-time data collection provides a dynamic picture of a patient's health, enabling healthcare providers to tailor interventions more precisely

Email: bibekananda.mohanty@abit.edu.in

Pradosh Kumar Gantayat, Sandeep Kumar Panda, S. Balamurugan and Sheng-Lung Peng (eds.) Hyper-Intelligent Networks: Exploring the Future of Connectivity for Society 5.0, (205–218) © 2026 Scrivener Publishing LLC

and promptly. For instance, remote monitoring can alert providers to early signs of deterioration in chronic conditions, facilitating timely adjustments to treatment plans.

The predictive capabilities of hyper-intelligent networks further revolutionize patient care by enabling proactive health management. Predictive models can anticipate potential health crises, allowing for preventive measures that mitigate the risk of complications. In addition to clinical benefits, hyper-intelligent networks enhance operational efficiency within healthcare institutions. Furthermore, the seamless integration of electronic health records (EHRs) across platforms ensures that vital patient information is readily accessible to all relevant healthcare providers, promoting coordinated and efficient care delivery. However, the deployment of hyper-intelligent networks in healthcare is not without challenges. Ethical and privacy concerns are paramount [2, 10].

10.2 Overview of Traditional Healthcare Systems

Traditional healthcare systems have historically been characterized by a hierarchical structure focused on providing episodic, reactive care to patients presenting with acute or chronic conditions. Here is an overview of key features and components of traditional healthcare systems [3, 11, 19]:

1. **Fragmented Care Delivery:** Traditional healthcare systems often operate in silos, with fragmented care delivery across various specialties, departments, and care settings.
2. **Fee-for-Service Reimbursement:** Reimbursement models in traditional healthcare systems typically follow a fee-for-service approach, where healthcare providers are reimbursed on the basis of the volume of services rendered. This incentivizes the delivery of more procedures, tests, and interventions, rather than focusing on preventive care, care coordination, or outcomes.
3. **Reactive Disease Management:** Traditional healthcare systems tend to prioritize reactive approaches to disease management, focusing on treating acute illnesses and managing chronic conditions after they have developed complications. Preventive care, early detection, and health promotion initiatives may receive less emphasis in this model.

4. **Paper-Based Records and Documentation:** Historically, healthcare documentation and record-keeping in traditional systems relied heavily on paper-based processes, handwritten notes, and physical filing systems. This manual approach to documentation could lead to inefficiencies, errors, and challenges in information retrieval and sharing.
5. **Patient-Centricity Challenges:** While patient-centered care is an ideal in traditional healthcare, the reality often falls short due to barriers such as limited patient engagement, inadequate communication, and paternalistic provider-patient relationships. Patients may have limited access to their health information, involvement in treatment decisions, or opportunities for shared decision-making.
6. **Limited Data Sharing and Interoperability:** This fragmentation impedes care coordination, transitions of care, and comprehensive understanding of patient health histories.
7. **Resource Constraints and Access Disparities:** These constraints can exacerbate access disparities, particularly in underserved communities, rural areas, and low-income populations.
8. **Emphasis on Acute Care Facilities:** Traditional healthcare systems often prioritize investments in acute care facilities, such as hospitals and emergency departments, over primary care, preventive services, and community-based care. This emphasis on tertiary care may result in overutilization of costly services and underinvestment in upstream interventions.
9. **Limited Emphasis on Population Health:** Traditional healthcare systems traditionally focus on individual patient encounters and episodic care rather than population health management and public health initiatives. This narrow focus may overlook broader determinants of health, social factors, and upstream interventions to address root causes of disease.

Despite these limitations, traditional healthcare systems have played a critical role in delivering essential medical services, diagnosing and treating acute conditions, and managing chronic diseases. However, the evolving landscape of healthcare delivery and advances in technology are driving the transformation of traditional models toward more integrated, patient-centered, and value-based care approaches.

10.3 Challenges Faced by Healthcare Systems

Healthcare systems face a multitude of challenges, ranging from operational inefficiencies to structural limitations and societal factors. Here are some of the key challenges faced by healthcare systems worldwide [4, 12, 20]:

1. **Rising Healthcare Costs:** Escalating costs strain healthcare budgets, limit resource allocation for other social needs, and pose financial burdens on individuals and governments.
2. **Quality and Patient Safety:** Ensuring consistent quality of care and patient safety remains a significant challenge in healthcare systems.
3. **Chronic Disease Management:** Effective management of chronic diseases requires comprehensive care coordination, patient education, lifestyle interventions, and long-term adherence to treatment regimens, posing challenges for healthcare systems.
4. **Aging Population:** Demographic shifts toward aging populations present challenges in healthcare delivery, as older adults often require complex, multidisciplinary care for age-related conditions, functional decline, and comorbidities. Addressing the healthcare needs of elderly populations requires specialized geriatric care, long-term care services, and support for caregivers.
5. **Healthcare Workforce Shortages:** Workforce shortages are exacerbated by factors such as burnout, attrition, training capacity constraints, and geographic disparities.
6. **Health Information Technology:** Issues such as interoperability barriers, usability challenges, data security concerns, and implementation costs hinder the full realization of HIT's potential to improve care delivery and efficiency.
7. **Healthcare Policy and Regulation:** Complex regulatory frameworks, reimbursement policies, and healthcare financing systems vary across countries and regions, posing challenges for healthcare providers, payers, and policymakers. Navigating regulatory compliance, aligning incentives, and addressing policy gaps require collaborative efforts and adaptive strategies.

8. **Global Health Threats:** Emerging infectious diseases, pandemics, antimicrobial resistance, and environmental health threats pose challenges to global health security and healthcare systems' resilience. Preparedness, surveillance, rapid response capabilities, and international collaboration are essential for addressing these evolving health threats.
9. **Social Determinants of Health:** Socioeconomic factors, environmental conditions, educational attainment, and cultural determinants significantly. Decision support systems help clinicians make evidence-based decisions, reduce diagnostic errors, and improve patient outcomes.
10. **Personalized Medicine and Treatment Optimization:** ML algorithms analyze patient characteristics, genetic profiles, and treatment responses to tailor personalized treatment regimens and optimize therapeutic outcomes. Predictive modeling, pharmacogenomics, and precision medicine approaches enable targeted interventions, dosage optimization, and patient stratification for precision oncology, cardiovascular care, and other therapeutic areas. Telemedicine platforms leverage ML algorithms for remote diagnosis, virtual consultations, and remote patient management, enabling accessible and convenient healthcare delivery.
11. **Disease Surveillance and Public Health:** ML models analyze epidemiological data, environmental factors, and social determinants of health to monitor disease outbreaks, predict disease spread, and inform public health interventions. Syndromic surveillance, outbreak detection, and spatial analysis techniques support early warning systems and emergency response efforts in combating infectious diseases and public health threats.
12. **Healthcare Operations and Resource Management:** ML algorithms optimize healthcare operations by forecasting patient demand, scheduling appointments, and allocating resources such as hospital beds, operating rooms, and staff. Operations research, queuing theory, and optimization algorithms improve efficiency, reduce wait times, and enhance patient flow within healthcare facilities.

13. **Health Behavior Analysis and Chronic Disease Management:** ML models analyze health-related behaviors, lifestyle factors, and social determinants to support chronic disease management, health promotion, and preventive interventions. Behavioral analytics, sentiment analysis, and digital phenotyping techniques inform personalized interventions, adherence strategies, and wellness programs for chronic disease prevention and management.

10.4 Personalized Medicine and Treatment Recommendations through Hyper-Intelligent Networks in Healthcare

Personalized medicine, facilitated by hyper-intelligent networks in healthcare, revolutionizes treatment recommendations by tailoring interventions to individual patient characteristics, preferences, and molecular profiles. Here is how hyper-intelligent networks enable personalized medicine and treatment recommendations [5, 13, 18, 21]:

1. **Predictive Modeling and Risk Stratification:** Hyper-intelligent networks develop predictive models and risk stratification algorithms to assess each patient's likelihood of developing certain diseases, experiencing adverse outcomes, or responding to specific treatments. These models integrate clinical data, genetic information, lifestyle factors, and environmental exposures to predict individualized risk profiles and guide preventive interventions.
2. **Treatment Selection and Optimization:** Hyper-intelligent networks analyze clinical guidelines, medical literature, treatment outcomes, and real-world evidence to recommend personalized treatment regimens tailored to each patient's unique characteristics and clinical context. Treatment recommendations consider factors such as disease stage, comorbidities, pharmacogenomics, and patient preferences to optimize therapeutic efficacy and minimize adverse effects.
3. **Precision Oncology and Targeted Therapies:** In oncology, hyper-intelligent networks facilitate precision medicine approaches by identifying tumor-specific mutations, molecular subtypes, and therapeutic targets. These networks analyze

genomic data, tumor biomarkers, and drug interactions to recommend targeted therapies, immunotherapies, and combination treatments tailored to each patient's tumor biology and genetic profile.

4. **Drug-Disease Interactions and Adverse Event Prediction:** Hyper-intelligent networks assess drug-disease interactions, drug-drug interactions, and pharmacogenomic factors to predict individualized treatment responses and anticipate potential adverse events. By analyzing patient-specific risk factors, genetic variants, and medication histories, these networks optimize drug selection, dosing, and medication management to enhance safety and tolerability.
5. **Continuous Learning and Adaptive Algorithms:** Hyper-intelligent networks employ continuous learning algorithms that adapt and refine treatment recommendations over time based on feedback, outcomes data, and evolving patient needs. These networks leverage reinforcement learning, adaptive clinical trials, and real-world evidence to iteratively improve treatment algorithms, optimize care pathways, and achieve better patient outcomes.

10.5 Predictive Analytics for Disease Prevention and Early Detection through Hyper-Intelligent Networks in Healthcare

Predictive analytics, powered by hyper-intelligent networks in healthcare, holds immense potential for disease prevention and early detection by leveraging advanced algorithms, vast datasets, and real-time patient monitoring. Here is how predictive analytics through hyper-intelligent networks can facilitate proactive healthcare interventions [6, 14, 17, 22]:

1. **Risk Stratification and Patient Profiling:** Predictive models identify high-risk populations and vulnerable individuals who may benefit from targeted preventive interventions and screening programs.
2. **Early Warning Systems and Alerts:** Predictive analytics algorithms continuously monitor patient data streams, such as vital signs, physiological measurements, and wearable

device data, to detect deviations from normal patterns or predictive thresholds indicative of disease onset or deterioration. Hyper-intelligent networks generate real-time alerts, notifications, or triggers to healthcare providers, prompting timely interventions and preventive measures.

3. **Disease Prediction and Progression Modeling:** Hyper-intelligent networks employ machine learning algorithms, predictive modeling techniques, and longitudinal data analysis to forecast disease trajectories, predict disease progression, and estimate individuals' future health outcomes.
4. **Personalized Risk Assessment and Prevention Plans:** Hyper-intelligent networks generate personalized risk assessments and preventive care plans tailored to individual patient profiles, preferences, and genetic predispositions. Predictive analytics algorithms consider multiple risk factors, comorbidities, and contextual variables to recommend customized interventions, lifestyle modifications, and screening protocols aimed at reducing disease risk and promoting wellness.
5. **Population Health Management Strategies:** Predictive analytics inform public health strategies, resource allocation decisions, and policy interventions aimed at reducing disease burden and improving health outcomes across populations.
6. **Intelligent Decision Support for Providers:** Hyper-intelligent networks provide decision support tools and clinical decision aids to healthcare providers, empowering them with predictive insights, evidence-based recommendations, and risk assessments at the point of care.
7. **Continuous Monitoring and Feedback Loops:** By iteratively learning from real-world data and clinical outcomes, predictive analytics algorithms improve accuracy, predictive power, and relevance in guiding preventive healthcare strategies.
8. **Research and Innovation Acceleration:** Hyper-intelligent networks serve as valuable platforms for biomedical research, clinical trials, and drug discovery efforts focused on disease prevention and early detection. Predictive analytics algorithms analyze large-scale healthcare datasets, identify novel biomarkers, and prioritize research targets to accelerate the development of preventive interventions, diagnostic tools, and personalized medicine approaches.

10.6 Remote Patient Monitoring and Telemedicine through Hyper-Intelligent Networks in Healthcare

Remote patient monitoring (RPM) and telemedicine, powered by hyper-intelligent networks in healthcare, revolutionize healthcare delivery by enabling virtual consultations, remote monitoring, and proactive patient management. Here is how hyper-intelligent networks facilitate RPM and telemedicine [7, 15]:

1. **Continuous Remote Monitoring:** Hyper-intelligent networks integrate with medical devices, wearables, and sensors to collect real-time patient data, including vital signs, physiological parameters, and health behaviors. Advanced analytics algorithms analyze streaming data streams, detect anomalies, and generate actionable insights for remote monitoring of patient health status.
2. **Teleconsultations and Virtual Visits:** Hyper-intelligent networks support teleconsultation platforms that enable virtual visits between patients and healthcare providers, regardless of geographic location. Telemedicine solutions offer secure video conferencing, messaging, and file sharing capabilities, facilitating remote consultations, follow-up appointments, and medication management without the need for in-person visits.
3. **Remote Diagnostic Imaging:** Hyper-intelligent networks enable remote access to diagnostic imaging modalities, such as X-rays, MRIs, and CT scans, through teleradiology solutions. Cloud-based image sharing platforms provide secure transmission of medical images, enabling remote interpretation by radiologists and specialists for timely diagnosis and treatment planning.
4. **Wearable Devices and IoT Integration:** Hyper-intelligent networks integrate with wearable devices, IoT sensors, and mobile health (mHealth) applications to capture patient-generated health data (PGHD) and lifestyle information. Data from wearables, such as smartwatches, fitness trackers, and home monitoring devices, are transmitted to hyper-intelligent networks for analysis, enabling remote monitoring of chronic conditions, medication adherence, and wellness metrics.

5. **Predictive Analytics and Early Warning Systems:** Hyper-intelligent networks leverage predictive analytics algorithms to detect early signs of deterioration, predict adverse events, and identify high-risk patients in remote monitoring programs. Real-time data analysis enables proactive interventions, personalized care plans, and escalation protocols to prevent complications and hospital readmissions.
6. **Decision Support for Remote Care:** Hyper-intelligent networks provide decision support tools and clinical algorithms to guide remote care delivery, treatment decisions, and care coordination. Machine learning models analyze patient data, clinical guidelines, and best practices to recommend personalized interventions, medication adjustments, and referrals based on real-time monitoring data.
7. **Integration with EHRs:** Hyper-intelligent networks seamlessly integrate with EHR systems to capture remote monitoring data, telemedicine encounters, and virtual care interactions. Interoperable platforms ensure continuity of care, comprehensive documentation.
8. **Scalability and Flexibility:** Hyper-intelligent networks offer scalable and flexible telemedicine solutions that can adapt to evolving healthcare needs, patient populations, and clinical workflows. Cloud-based platforms provide on-demand access to computing resources, enabling healthcare organizations to expand telemedicine services, accommodate growing patient demand, and respond to public health emergencies.
9. **Security and Privacy Assurance:** Hyper-intelligent networks prioritize security and privacy in telemedicine solutions, employing encryption, access controls, and compliance measures to protect patient data and ensure regulatory compliance. Secure communication protocols, identity verification, and data encryption mechanisms safeguard telemedicine encounters, patient records, and sensitive health information transmitted over network connections.

10.7 Hyper-Intelligent Networks in Shaping the Future of Healthcare

Hyper-intelligent networks hold immense importance in shaping the future of healthcare by revolutionizing patient care delivery, clinical decision-making, and healthcare system efficiency. Here are key reasons why hyper-intelligent networks are vital for the future of healthcare [8, 16]:

1. **Advanced Data Analytics:** Hyper-intelligent networks enable predictive modeling, personalized treatment recommendations, and population health management.
2. **Precision Medicine:** By identifying biomarkers, genetic predispositions, and treatment responses, hyper-intelligent networks enable personalized diagnosis, prognosis, and therapy selection, improving patient outcomes and reducing adverse events.
3. **Remote Monitoring and Telemedicine:** By integrating wearable devices, telehealth platforms, and real-time communication tools, hyper-intelligent networks facilitate virtual consultations, remote diagnostics, and home-based care delivery, enhancing access, convenience, and continuity of care.
4. **Predictive Analytics for Early Intervention:** Hyper-intelligent networks employ predictive analytics algorithms to forecast disease risks, detect early warning signs, and identify high-risk individuals for preventive interventions. By analyzing healthcare data in real-time, hyper-intelligent networks enable early detection of diseases, proactive risk mitigation, and timely interventions to prevent complications, reduce hospitalizations, and improve patient outcomes.
5. **Evidence-Based Decision Support:** Hyper-intelligent networks provide decision support tools and clinical decision aids to healthcare providers, offering real-time guidance, evidence-based recommendations, and clinical insights at the point of care. By synthesizing clinical knowledge, best practices, and patient data, hyper-intelligent networks empower clinicians to make informed decisions, reduce diagnostic errors, and improve care quality and safety.
6. **Population Health Management:** Hyper-intelligent networks support population health management initiatives by analyzing population-level data, identifying health disparities, and

targeting interventions to improve health outcomes across communities. By aggregating healthcare data, social determinants of health, and environmental factors, hyper-intelligent networks enable public health surveillance, disease prevention, and health promotion efforts aimed at addressing population health needs and reducing healthcare disparities.

7. **Interoperability and Data Exchange:** Hyper-intelligent networks promote interoperability and data exchange across healthcare systems, enabling seamless integration of disparate data sources, interoperable standards, and secure communication protocols. By facilitating data sharing, collaboration, and knowledge exchange among healthcare stakeholders, hyper-intelligent networks support care coordination, care transitions, and continuity of care across the care continuum.

Hyper-intelligent networks have the potential to revolutionize patient care by enhancing diagnostics, improving patient monitoring, streamlining healthcare operations, and increasing patient engagement. However, addressing challenges related to integration, ethics, and continuous improvement is crucial for realizing their full potential. As these networks evolve, they will play an increasingly vital role in shaping the future of healthcare.

References

1. Lee, J. and Yoon, W., AI-Powered Healthcare: The Role of Machine Learning in Diagnostics and Treatment. *J. Med. Syst.*, 46, 2, 35–47, 2022.
2. Wang, S. and Zhang, Y., IoT in Healthcare: Integration and Implementation. *Health Inf. J.*, 27, 4, 789–802, 2021.
3. Smith, A. and Jones, B., Predictive Analytics in Medicine: Transforming Patient Care. *Int. J. Healthcare Manage.*, 13, 3, 195–210, 2020.
4. Kumar, R. and Gupta, N., Operational Efficiency in Healthcare: Leveraging AI and Automation. *Healthcare Technol. Lett.*, 6, 1, 14–25, 2019.
5. Brown, C. and Wilson, T., Ethical and Privacy Considerations in Hyper-Intelligent Healthcare Networks. *Ethics Inf. Technol.*, 23, 1, 89–102, 2021.
6. National Institute of Health (NIH), Future Directions in Health Informatics, in: *NIH Conference Proceedings*, April 2023.
7. World Health Organization (WHO), Digital Health: Transformative Technologies in Global Health, in: *WHO Report*, 2022.
8. Gartner, Inc., Top Strategic Technology Trends for Healthcare, in: *Gartner Research Report*, 2021.

9. Panda, S.K. and Satapathy, S.C., Drug traceability and transparency in medical supply chain using blockchain for easing the process and creating trust between stakeholders and consumers. *Pers. Ubiquit. Comput.*, 28, 75–91, 2024. https://doi.org/10.1007/s00779-021-01588-3.
10. Arza, M.S. and Panda, S.K., An Integration of Blockchain and Machine Learning into the Health Care System, in: *Machine Learning Adoption in Blockchain-Based Intelligent Manufacturing*, vol. 1, pp. 33–58, DOI: 10.1201/9781003252009-3.
11. Nanda, S.K., Panda, S.K., Dash, M., Medical supply chain integrated with blockchain and IoT to track the logistics of medical products. *Multimed. Tools Appl.*, 82, 32917–32939, 2023. https://doi.org/10.1007/s11042-023-14846-8.
12. Lakshmi, L., Devi, K.D.S., Gupta, S., Reddy, K.A.N., Grandhi, S.K., Panda, S.K., WOMT: Wasserstein Distribution Based Minimization of False Positives in Breast Tumor Classification Using Deep Learning. *IEEE Access*, 11, 57831–57842, 2023. doi: 10.1109/ACCESS.2023.3279496.
13. Routray, N., Rout, S.K., Sahu, B., Panda, S.K., Godavarthi, D., Ensemble Learning With Symbiotic Organism Search Optimization Algorithm for Breast Cancer Classification and Risk Identification of Other Organs on Histopathological Images. *IEEE Access*, 11, 110544–110557, 2023. doi: 10.1109/ACCESS.2023.3322222.
14. Agarwal, R., Pande, S.D., Mohanty, S.N., Panda, S.K., A Novel Hybrid System of Detecting Brain Tumors in MRI. *IEEE Access*, 11, 118372–118385, 2023. doi: 10.1109/ACCESS.2023.3326447.
15. Nayak, S.K., Garanayak, M., Swain, S.K., Panda, S.K., Godavarthi, D., An Intelligent Disease Prediction and Drug Recommendation Prototype by Using Multiple Approaches of Machine Learning Algorithms. *IEEE Access*, 11, 99304–99318, 2023. doi: 10.1109/ACCESS.2023.3314332.
16. Murala, D.K., Panda, S.K., Dash, S.P., MedMetaverse: Medical Care of Chronic Disease Patients and Managing Data Using Artificial Intelligence, Blockchain, and Wearable Devices State-of-the-Art Methodology. *IEEE Access*, 11, 138985, 2023. doi: 10.1109/ACCESS.2023.3340791.
17. Sethi, B.K., Singh, D., Rout, S.K., Panda, S.K., Long Short-Term Memory-Deep Belief Network-Based Gene Expression Data Analysis for Prostate Cancer Detection and Classification. *IEEE Access*, 12, 1508–1524, 2024. doi: 10.1109/ACCESS.2023.3346925.
18. Sahoo, S.K., Das, S., Panda, S.K., Alzheimer's Disease Classification Using Brain MRI Based on 2D CNN and Transfer Learning, in: *Proceedings of the 6th International Conference on Communications and Cyber Physical Engineering. ICCCE 2024. Lecture Notes in Electrical Engineering*, vol. 1096, Springer, Singapore, 2024, https://doi.org/10.1007/978-981-99-7137-4_1.
19. Panda, S.K., Ramesh, J.V.N., Ghosh, H., Rahat, I.S., Sobur, A., Bijoy, M.H., Yesubabu, M., Deep Learning in Medical Imaging: A Case Study on Lung Tissue Classification. *EAI Endorsed Trans. Pervasive Health Technol.*, 10, 2024.

20. Paruchuri, V.N.L.L., Shaik, A.H., Murala, D.K., Panda, S.K., IoT-Enabled Neural Network Analysis for Early Detection and Prediction of Mental Depression, in: *Information System Design: Communication Networks and IoT. ISDIA 2024. Lecture Notes in Networks and Systems*, vol. 1057, V. Bhateja, J. Tang, D.K. Sharma, Z. Polkowski, A. Ahmad, (Eds.), pp. 257–268, Springer, Singapore, 2024, https://doi.org/10.1007/978-981-97-4895-2_21.
21. Paruchuri, V.N.L.L., Malaviya, M.P., Murala, D.K., Panda, S.K., Connecting IoT Sensors for Enhanced Dementia Disease Monitoring and Intervention, in: *Information System Design: Communication Networks and IoT. ISDIA 2024. Lecture Notes in Networks and Systems*, vol. 1057, V. Bhateja, J. Tang, D.K. Sharma, Z. Polkowski, A. Ahmad, (Eds.), pp. 269–281, Springer, Singapore, 2024, https://doi.org/10.1007/978-981-97-4895-2_22.
22. Chandrasekhar, A., Dodhiawala, Z., Panda, S.K., An Investigation into Chronic Kidney Disease Based-on Classification Model, in: *Signal Processing, Telecommunication and Embedded Systems with AI and ML Applications. ICMEET 2023. Lecture Notes in Electrical Engineering*, vol. 1281, V. Bhateja, V.V.S.S.S. Chakravarthy, J. Anguera, A. Ghosh, W. Flores Fuentes, (Eds.), Springer, Singapore, 2025, https://doi.org/10.1007/978-981-97-8422-6_19.

11

AI-Driven Remote Health Monitoring for Predicting Diabetes and Heart Diseases Using ULMCSO and PGND Models

Soumya Ranjan Mishra[1] and Sachikanta Dash[2]*

[1]*Department of CSA, GIET University, Gunupur, Odisha, India*
[2]*Department of CSE, GIET University, Gunupur, Odisha, India*

Abstract

Many people have been paying more attention to remote health monitoring systems because they can provide actual treatment intervention protocols as was noted in reference to implemented work. An artificial intelligence–based remote health monitoring system is suggested to have been developed for predicting diabetes as well as heart diseases in a dataset. In this model, the health information for patients is gathered by using smart devices and integrating the obtained information in different nodes including the detection node, visualization node, and predictive node. The pre-processing of healthcare datasets is then done at that point to standardize the features through the identification of missing attributes while removing unnecessary ones. Therefore, we use the ULMCSO (Unified Levy Modeled Crow Search Optimization) algorithm in which we search for a balanced levy model of crows to obtain the most suitable attributes according to international standardization and, as a result, that may lead to a rise in correctness level as well as a declining period for training classifier. When needing to answer whether it is the same thing as a usual circumstance, or contaminated situation prediction, finally, an adoptive model called Probabilistic Guided Naïve Distribution (PGND) classification model grows to be valid in this case. When checking out, we evaluate using other performance metrics that one can propose. These include PIMA and Hungarian datasets, which have been previously tested on diverse conditions so that there will be no room for doubt about how good or bad the outcome might turn out to be for different situations.

**Corresponding author*: sachikanta@giet.edu

Pradosh Kumar Gantayat, Sandeep Kumar Panda, S. Balamurugan and Sheng-Lung Peng (eds.) Hyper-Intelligent Networks: Exploring the Future of Connectivity for Society 5.0, (219–248) © 2026 Scrivener Publishing LLC

Keywords: AI, Hungarian datasets, PIMA datasets, probabilistic guided naive, remote health monitoring, smart devices

11.1 Introduction

One must pay great attention to public health surveillance in order to shield individuals from health risks. This is owing to the fact that these conditions are among the prime concerns [1]. Because they also impact on the nervous system and kidneys, they currently stand respectively as the two highest killers of people through diseases like diabetes or heart problems. Because they have ineffective treatments and poorly-off clinical diagnoses, many sick care organizations [2, 3] might need decision-making mechanisms to help know how certain diseases can be predicted and diagnosed appropriately. The sooner a disease is identified, the better it is in terms of preventing other harmful diseases. It is crucial to note that, currently, coming up with the remote automated monitor system was more importance for oversee the healthcare status of the patient [4, 5], and it is done through use of the health devices, smart watches, and smart mobile phones. It is important to treat the patients accordingly in emergency cases using the remote monitoring system. This paper constructs a smart health framework based on machine learning that enables early risk detection by combining patient data collected by smart devices [6] and, as a result, keeps health practitioners informed about the current health status of their clients. In this arrangement, three main nodes—knowing node, graphic node, and predictive node—were used to collect medical data from patients for the purpose of alerting the physician [7]. The pipeline can be designed and structured into three main components: data imputation, optimization, and classification. It is within this framework that we perform data imputation on the medical datasets as an effort toward enhancing the quality of patterns obtained through scaling up this kind of data. Using the new optimization technique, we can reduce data dimensionality for an improved prediction rate and then conduct feature selection. Finally, accurate prediction of the provided data can be achieved using an advanced machine learning method based on artificial intelligence that classifies it as normal or abnormal.

This paper makes the following main contributions:

- This paradigm employs three connecting nodes (that is, detection, view, and prognosis) for smart devices to collect patients' health information.

- This framework initially tunes the input datasets provided by removing the noise and making the attributes uniform.
- Feature selection algorithm, based on global fitness value of crow search optimization; a unified levy model is used for selecting the features with less number of iterations.
- Deployment of the Probabilistic Guided Naïve Distribution (PGND), for accurately predicting normally classified output and disease-affected one.
- To ascertain the effectiveness and outcome of these strategies, we used two diverse and most popular datasets: Hungarian and PIMA, for this study.

In the following sections, the surplus bits of this essay have been arranged as follows section. The sections are: Section 11.2 comprises partial examination the patient's recovery status about their social interactions, mobility networks and order strategies. Section 11.3 describes work methods from the viewpoint of operation as well as evaluation processes. Section 11.4 provides performance evaluation along with the comparative analysis done through diverse metrics.

11.2 Related Work

Briefly, this passage evaluates a portion of the continuous duties concerned with information clustering, artificial intelligence (AI), enhancement, as well as deep learning techniques that have been adopted in creating remote healthcare monitoring systems for sick people with varied types of ailments. An examination is made of the merits and demerits that current processes have in comparison with their inherent nature and set benchmarks. According to Gondalia *et al.* [8], when soldiers at war are hurt, their health monitoring Internet of Things (IoT)–enabled system by use of machine learning techniques was introduced. This article aimed to pinpoint where they are located so that we can always be aware of what is happening with them wherever they may be situated in case soldiers get wounded during battle. In this case, the soldier's health was controlled in terms of GPS and sensors with such features as heartbeat and temperature in particular. Additionally, the researchers used the k-means clustering method to analyze information from the sensors. The sensor inputs predicted accurately using clustering of attributes whether the wound will be blasted or not by sitting, walking and running such as different actions. Nonetheless, k-means clustering is less effective for real-time applications like this because it is not efficient, with global cluster and different initial partitions. The study by Malasinghe *et al.* [9] analyzed appropriate technology selection for the development of remote patient monitoring solutions and tackled various security issues accompanying e-health platforms. Ramkumar *et al.* [10] whereby they have incorporated an enhanced machine learning technique came up with a novel remote patient monitoring framework. In this system, pilot data has been used to analyze the health conditions that could be traced through wearable technology. According to Chatrati *et al.* [11], it is a good idea for households to establish preventive care systems that can save on the cost and reduce the delays for checking diabetes and blood pressure.

The reason why this work has been done is to analyze the glucose measurements made by patients in their homes to give the medical care office on the occasion of deviation. In addition, the blood pressure was also detected using a combination of guidance and AI models. The diabetic or non-diabetic individuals were clustered by utilizing a support vector machine (SVM) for the request methodology based on the data preparation set. Model optimization algorithm was also employed in selecting features for enhancing the classification accuracy as well as minimizing overfit problems. But this work needs a proper graphics user interface that will allow automatic transfer of patients' medical status to doctors. In the research work by Vitabile *et al.* [12], an intelligent health monitoring system was utilized in order to assess the emotional states and general health of a patient through analysis of chest sounds, temperature measurement, blood pressure measurement, heartbeat, and electrocardiogram (ECG) readings. In combating unauthorized access, the medical data was secured through blockchain technology. The major benefit of this system consisted of efficient processing of high-dimensional datasets and reduces the time delays. Nair *et al.* [13] have used a type of machine learning based on spark that has allowed to predict the health status of the patients using diagnostic information in remote access way. Thus, the decision tree classification technique helped in predicting diseases using attributes identified from the dataset. Additionally, this approach was intended better to handle large datasets by partitioning feature models. In addition, the generalization error and overfitting value could be significantly decreased by this classification model. Nevertheless, it initiates certain computation processes for forecasting classified label, which is the main drawback of the study.

The research by Li *et al.* [14] forms the basis for this older people's health that can be monitored remotely using a multi-station approach.

Radar and wearable sensors are deployed to forecast diseases across two different types of sensors within this structure. Various feature selection models that contain the masking methods, filter approaches, as well as other techniques are the ones employed for enhancing precision in classification and cycle scalability. Furthermore, K-nearest neighbor (KNN) and SVM solicitation methods have been employed to forecast a disease, and their effects have been weighed in terms of precision and computational time. The analysis revealed that, in terms of performance outcomes, the SVM technique surpasses the KNN model based on the validation done. By utilizing random forest classification, Kaur *et al.* [15] developed an effective remote health monitoring system for patients. To forecast chronic illnesses during medical crises, the system made use of IoT. After testing them on several illness kinds, researchers found that random forest outperforms KNN, linear SVM, decision trees, and multilayer perceptron's regarding accuracy, an area under curve, and recall. These findings [16] indicate that the random forest approach outperformed the others in illness diagnosis due to its increased sensitivity.

In their paper, Verma and Sood [17] demonstrated a fog-supported IoT-enabled architecture to monitor healthcare information remotely using smart corridors, e.g., to analyze patient health data based on health quality over time and use the event-triggered data transmission method. Azimi *et al.* [18] have used edge-based deep learning techniques to develop a hierarchical health monitoring model whose goal is to ensure increased availability and precision in real-time ordering. The caregiver in this framework could retrieve health data from a cloud server using sensor devices linked to it. The main benefit of this study is that it maintained proper health information, thereby reducing the time it took to respond to situations accordingly. Mohsin *et al.* [19] presented a multilevel classification algorithm aimed at designing a real-time remote health monitoring system that was designed to be more efficient. It uses wireless body area network with body sensors such as blood pressure, hearing, movement, electroencephalogram (EEG), ECG, and electromyogram (EMG) to monitor patient health data, using wirelessly transmission to healthcare providers for the purpose the human body must collect medical information.

In their work that is cited in [20], Devarajan *et al.* built an energy-efficient system capable of monitor the health status of people remotely with diabetes using fog computing services. This work sought to minimize the delay duration while ensuring that the healthcare support systems function better in terms of energy usage. To create a cost-effective web application, in healthcare, Hassan and friends [21] created a design for an e-health system that can monitor pain from far away thanks to the IoT-powered mist technology. The study also aims at demonstrating that various forms of e-healthcare services such as robotics services, audio/video communication, as well as monitoring applications can be implemented using conventional methodology by this team. The patient health information is collected by the fog node using actuators as well as sensors within this framework. The proxy server is linked to a cloud storage, which is a destination for the data collected. However, because of the design based on the first bird receiving the fly system, it was not suitable for any health tests. This represents a major limitation among many others in this regard. Hasan *et al.* demonstrated their continuous medical care observing framework using IoT innovation [22]. They developed this work to build a highly dependable e-health system that would lead to lower costs and less human effort. Low-power radio-frequency technology can be used to specify the data communication with a reduced bit error rate (Table 11.1). This table contains the accuracy of different algorithms and the usage of different IoT devices.

Here is the SVM classification method. On the basis, an assessment was made, indicating that the existing efforts are mostly about developing a remote healthcare system for monitoring patients' health using intelligent facilities such as sensors and smart watches among other smart devices. It still had the following constraints:

- The sensors and storage components are inefficient for data transmission.
- Processing is delayed longer.
- Moreover, classification is complicated too because there exists a high bit error rate.
- The system performs poorly.

Because of this, the purpose of this work is to develop an effective framework for monitoring the status of patients who are far using an improved AI mechanism.

Table 11.1 Comparative analysis between the existing algorithms.

Authors details	Journal/conference	Model and approach	Description	Utilization of IoT	Accuracy
K. Uyar and A. İlhan (2017) [27]	Procedia Computer Science	Genetic algorithm–based recurrent fuzzy neural networks	Heart disease diagnosis using genetic algorithm trained networks	Not specified	97%
F. Ahmed (2017) [28]	International Journal of Computer Applications	IoT application for predicting future heart attack patients	Predicting future heart attack patients using IoT	Yes, for prediction	93%
S. Nazari, M. Fallah, H. Kazemipoor, A. Salehipour (2018) [29]	Expert Systems with Applications	Fuzzy inference–fuzzy analytic hierarchy process–based clinical decision support system	Clinical decision support system for heart disease diagnosis	Not specified	89%
T. Vivekanandan and N. C. S. N. Iyengar (2017) [30]	Computers in Biology and Medicine	Modified differential evolution algorithm for feature selection	Optimal feature selection for heart disease prediction	Not specified	94%
L. Ali, A. Rahman, A. Khan, M. Zhou, A. Javeed, J. A. Khan (2019) [31]	IEEE Access	Chi-square statistical model and deep neural network	Automated diagnostic system using statistical model and deep neural network	Not specified	91%

(Continued)

Table 11.1 Comparative analysis between the existing algorithms. (*Continued*)

Authors details	**Journal/conference**	**Model and approach**	**Description**	**Utilization of IoT**	**Accuracy**
J. Nourmohammadi-Khiarak, M.-R. Feizi-Derakhshi, K. Behrouzi, S. Mazaheri, Y. Zamani-Harghalani, R. M. Tayebi (2020) [32]	Health and Technology	Hybrid method utilizing optimization algorithm	Hybrid method for heart disease diagnosis with optimization in feature selection	Not specified	90%
F. Ali *et al.* (2020) [33]	Information Fusion	Ensemble deep learning and feature fusion	Smart healthcare monitoring system for heart disease prediction	Yes, for monitoring	92%
Mishra *et al.* (2024) [34]	International Journal of Emerging Technologies and Innovative Research	FedOmics causal network and federated multi-omics variational autoencoder	Model design for diabetes analysis	Not specified	96%
Soumya Ranjan Mishra, Sachikanta Dash (2024) [35]	IJRAR - International Journal of Research and Analytical Reviews	Predictive analysis on diabetes detection using PIMA Indian Diabetes Dataset	Predictive analysis on diabetes using PIMA dataset	Not specified	93%
H. Naz and S. Ahuja (2021) [36]	International Journal of Diabetes in Developing Countries	SMOTE-SMO–based expert system for type II diabetes detection	Expert system for diabetes detection using PIMA dataset	Not specified	96%
U. M. Butt, S. Letchmunan, M. Ali, F. H. Hassan, A. Baqir, H. H. R. Sherazi (2021) [37]	Journal of Healthcare Engineering	Machine learning–based diabetes classification and prediction	Diabetes classification and prediction using machine learning	Not specified	89%

11.3 Proposed Methodology

This section examines the operational structure of the recommended remote welfare evaluation process by implementing iterative improvement approaches. The desire for the probe lies in coming up with a standard screening form that will go hand in hand with electronic health records in terms of patients interacting with their appliances, whereas obtaining these records would have an adverse effect on general treatment procedure and patient care. It is expected to provide patients with additional clinical information about risk factors and possible cardiovascular events in diabetes due to these medical issues. Figure 11.1 depicts the proposed health monitoring system and its elements. The patient's name, age, gender, height, weight, heart rate, blood pressure, glucose levels, calories, medication levels, and blood oxygen end nodes were all gathered using a sensor. The medical data gathered from the sensors is fused in this system through a one-time validation. The user does not need to submit their data because the mobile application can extract the necessary data straight from the cloud platforms, which is one of the system's key benefits. The Google Fit cloud service, which keeps track of medical information for patients admitted *via* smart devices, is used in this scenario. Furthermore, application programming interfaces (APIs) have been utilized for the purpose of enhancing communication and data exchange that occurs between computer programs and end-user devices.

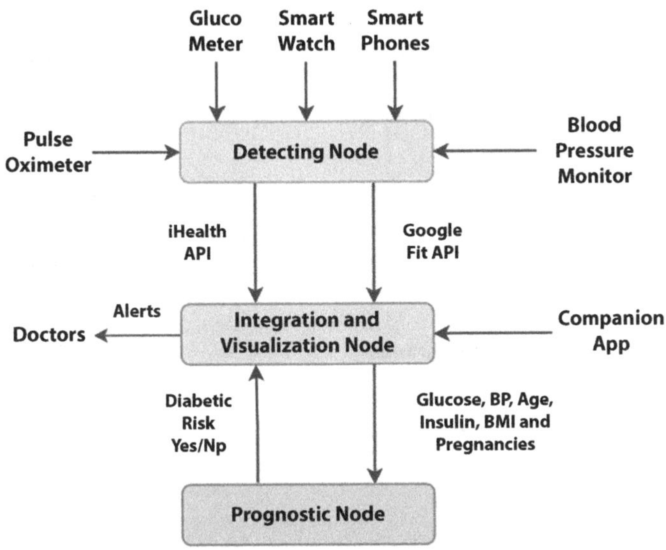

Figure 11.1 Model for intelligent remote healthcare.

These are the nodes in this system:

a) Discovery of node: The primary role of this node is to obtain medical information of patients from smart devices.
b) Visualization node: In a web-accessible format, it amalgamates medical data from all sources.
c) Prediction node: A machine learning classifier is employed to forecast the illness given a subset of characteristics extracted from the patient data.

The proposed method's workflow is displayed in Figure 11.2 and the appropriate framework displayed in Figure 11.3 with modules as shown.

- Pre-processing and standardization of data
- Selecting special information based on Unified Levy Modeled Crow Search Optimization (ULMCSO)
- PGND grouping

To begin with, pre-processing and normalization of the data are done to enhance the quality of the dataset by finding missing values and eliminating

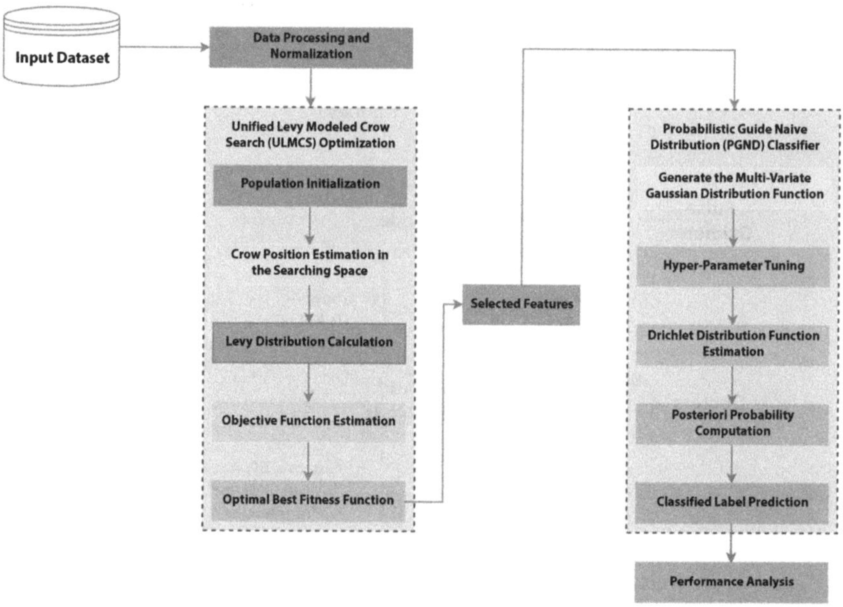

Figure 11.2 Operation flow chart for suggested health tracking.

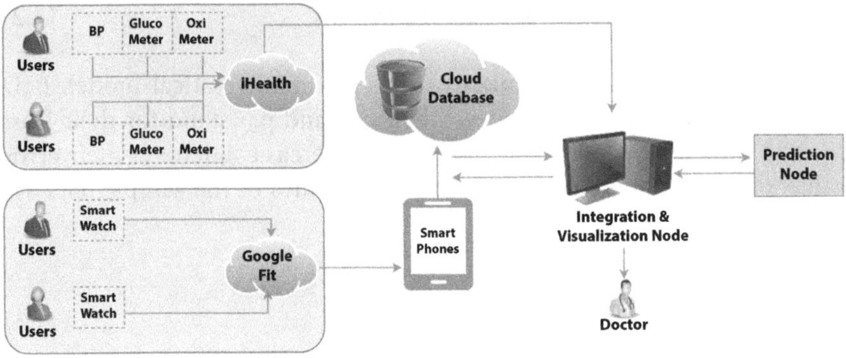

Figure 11.3 Framework design for proposed system.

information that is superfluous because of the prognosis of the condition. The quality of the dataset has a major impact on the outcomes; thus, it has to be adjusted for precise detection and classification. To normalize the provided feature values in the dataset, feature calibration is then carried out. To decrease dimensions and improve classification accuracy, the ULMCSO algorithm is subsequently utilized to effectively select the features. These features are then used for training classification for patient disease prediction with less computational complexity and better visualization. Here, an appropriate diagnosis is made using a PGND-based classification approach based on characteristics chosen from predetermined data.

11.3.1 Normalization of Datasets with Pre-Processing

Replacement of missing information and noise removal are regarded as activities major in dataset pre-processing because noise-free information contributes to a better detection and, therefore, rate. In each case, dataset pre-processing and normalization procedures are carried out to tune the data by detecting missing attributes and killing irrelevant attributes. The input dataset is examined before the amount is examined. Information in this cycle is arranged according to the rise in demand for intermediate-value services. As a result, the calculated median values are used to replace missing and unnecessary features. After that, the data are normalized by giving them values between 0 and 1, which aids in the analysis of the disease's nature. A regression model is used to determine the standard deviation, which normalizes the data as shown in (11.1) and (11.2).

$$D = \rho 0 + \rho i\, S + \varepsilon i \text{ for } i = 1, 2 \ldots n \tag{11.1}$$

$$Di = \rho 0 + \rho i S + \varepsilon^{*} i \tag{11.2}$$

The residual value is calculated using this mathematical model. If D stands for any of the two datasets, then ρ_0 and ρ_i stand for their least squares values, S denotes their input data, whereas ε_i denotes their error value. Given the standard deviation, mean values of the sample data are calculated as shown in (11.3).

$$\mu = \frac{\Sigma_{i=1}^{n} Si}{F_d} \tag{11.3}$$

F_d represents the data frequency, S_i as the input data, while σ stands for standard deviation. Consequently, these data can be transformed and normalized, as in (11.4) and (11.5):

$$D_N = \frac{\varepsilon * i}{\sigma i} \tag{11.4}$$

$$D_N = \frac{Si - \mu i}{\sigma i} \tag{11.5}$$

Normalized data is abbreviated as D_N. Variance is defined as σi and residual in ε^{*}_{i}. It remains possible to apply optimized or classified preprocessed data.

11.3.2 Feature Selection Using ULMCSO Model

The pre-processing phase involved a detailed analysis and transformation of the dataset using the ULMCSO method, which aimed to improve feature dimensional reduction and simplify the classification model and to enhance its predictive ability if ULMCSO is selected. This method efficiently handles detection by replacing irrelevant attributes and missing data points with numerical mean values, thus improving the overall prediction accuracy and enhancing tax flight performance further improve by integrating aging and optimization tools, ensuring robust and reliable results. ULMCSO, as a meta-heuristic optimization method, excels in identifying the optimal global fitness function, which is important for choosing appropriate and appropriate features for the model its performance greatly contributes to the accuracy of the classification process, and it works well, making it a data-health management application. It is a valuable tool in analytical and predictive modeling situations.

The main possible benefits of such an option are as follows:

- Convergence is quicker
- More reduced dimensions
- Minimal time is needed for training and testing the classifier
- Enhances improved classification accuracy

Crows are typically believed to be cunning birds that use their own experience to store and gather food henceforth, it is a smart birds. Furthermore, the method of streamlining the crow search optimization (CSO) is frequently utilized in multiple application frameworks for addressing intricate multi-goal improvement problems. The CSO strategy is close to the challenge of low-altitude mixing rate due to its seeming inefficiency in searching through space. As a consequence, the toll flight procedure is fused with CSO to continue enhancing overall cross velocity and accuracy. Apart from that, the ULMCSO amalgam can determine the minimal number of iterations as it indicates the best fitness value. Here, in the first stage of crow's number, we initialize randomly a set of populations F_n. In this place, one considers the maximum iteration count as m_k and, therefore, the cth position of crow t with dimensional searching space during iteration is gotten by applying Equation (11.6):

$$Cr_{c,t} = [Cr_{c,t}^{1}, Cr_{c,t}^{2} \ldots Cr_{c,k}^{n}] \tag{11.6}$$

The model considers the values of c and t where c = 1, 2 … F_n and t = 1, 2 …m_t. Every crow in this particular model can indicate where some food to feed on that is hidden the location or place of hiding is done just before the next iteration begins according to the analyst or estimate done as per (11.7).

$$H_{c,t} = [h_{c,t}^{1}, h_{c,t}^{2} \ldots h_{c,t}^{n}] \tag{11.7}$$

Furthermore, the crow could protect the food supply against other crows by randomly picking paths. Optimization represents a random path selection used to protect food from others. The levy flight algorithm is chosen to recognize the random path within the integrated algorithm. If we take a deal with the random number range as (11.8), then let us assume that W_c is uniformly distributed between 0 and 1.

$$Levy(\lambda) \sim x = a^{-\lambda}, \text{Where } (1 < \lambda \leq 3) \tag{11.8}$$

Levy(λ): This denotes a Levy distribution parameterized by λ, which governs the heaviness of the tail of the distribution.

(1 < λ ≤ 3): This range of λ defines a valid Lévy distribution.

If λ≤1, the variance becomes infinite.

If λ>3, the behavior becomes more Gaussian (normal distribution), losing the heavy tail.

This operation will be explained through model (11.9) described in the following way:

$$Cr_{c,t+1} = \begin{cases} Cr_{c,t} + W_c \cdot Am_{c,t} \cdot (Be_{v,t} - Cr_{v,t}) W_c \geq AP \\ Random\ placement \qquad\qquad Otherwise \end{cases} \tag{11.9}$$

Amc, *t* and *Bev* are the coordinates of the crow *c* and *v*, respectively, whereas *Wc* is the particular solution of the crow. Finally, the memory vector is updated using cumulative distance (11.10).

$$Cr_{c,t+1} = \begin{cases} Cr_{c,t+1} \ \ if\ O(Cr_{c,t+1})\ if\ better\ than\ (Be_{c,t}) \\ Be_{c,t} \qquad\qquad Otherwise \end{cases} \tag{11.10}$$

where *O* (.) denotes the objective function. This value is used to determine the optimal optimization function for selecting the features to train the classifier.

Crow Search Algorithm 11.1 is a novel optimization algorithm based on swarm intelligence, simulating the brain of crows that can be used to hide and find dead bodies using simple structure, minimum control parameters and easy implementation.

Algorithm 11.1

Input: Collected Dataset;

Output: Selection of optimal features;

Step 1: Initialization: Set populations Fn, number of crows N, maximum iteration count M_K, search space dimension d, and iteration t.

Step 2: Population Setup: Initialize n crows over t iterations using Equation (11.1).

Step 3: Food Source Estimation: Estimate each crow's food source location using Equation (11.7).

Step 4: Levy Flight Simulation: Simulate random numbers in the range [0, 1] using the levy flight model from Equation (11.8).

Step 5: Position Update: Update each crow's position to $Cr_{c,t+1}$ using Equation (11.9).

Step 6: Memory Function Update: Adjust the memory function based on amplitude Amc, tA_ {mc, t}Amc, t, best solution $Be_{v,t}$ and random number Wc.

Step 7: Optimal Solution Calculation: Compute the best optimal solution using objective function O (.) for selecting the optimal number of features.

11.3.3 Classifying PGND

After following smoothing, the classifier is prepared to employ the optimal combination of components to gradually improve accuracy and minimize care time consumption in this task. In order to identify illnesses from a dataset using the optimal number of selected highlights, the PGND order procedure is employed. This type of mixing model is probabilistic in nature. Labeling has been done with it. With this approach, the maximum likelihood function derived from the given data is used to choose the model parameters. To forecast the class more accurately in this approach, the sample mean and covariance values are computed. The primary benefit of utilizing this is that, after streamlining, improved material scheduling helps to decrease errors and save time during the process. It also effectively manages more complicated training-related data. Additionally, it is better suited for handling high-dimensional datasets with shorter processing times and lower error rates. Since unit variance and zero mean are used to standardize the data for hyperparameter adjustment, this normalization step ensures that all features contribute equally during the training process, improving convergence stability. First, as seen in (11.11), the multi-variety distribution function is calculated using the Gaussian distribution's number T.

$$p(opt_i|ch_i = t) = N(Me_t, \mathrm{Co}_t) \tag{11.11}$$

opt_i is able to use Tnumber of parameters to define the feature space model. Also, we have the covariance Co_t, mean value Me_t, and current operating condition ch_i as our optimized dataset is defined $\{(Me_1, \mathrm{Co}_1), (Me_2, \mathrm{Co}_2) \ldots (Me_t, \mathrm{Co}_t)\}$. In this regard, a statistical model for mixing properties will be described according to Equation (11.12).

$$\Theta = \{(Me_1, \mathrm{Co}_1, \Gamma_1), (Me_2, \mathrm{Co}_2, \Gamma_2) \ldots (Me_t, \mathrm{Co}_t, \Gamma_t)\} \quad (11.12)$$

where Γ_t denotes the hybrid coefficient of class $t \in S$, $\Gamma = \{\Gamma_1, \Gamma_2 \ldots \Gamma_t\}$. Based on the conjugate of the distribution, *NIW* of the normal inverse Wischart distribution is then computed as shown in (11.13).

$$p(Me_t, Co_t) = NIW(mk_0, r_0, q_0, MV_0) \quad (11.13)$$

where mk_0 is the prior mean Me_t, MV_0 is the prior mean Co_t, and r_0 and q_0 are the prior medians that determine the intensity of the former. Consequently, the identification matrix is constructed using a d dimensional vector [ID × ID], and the distribution over the labeled space is determined using (11.14).

$$p(\Gamma) = Dir(\omega)\omega \prod_{t=1}^{T} \Gamma_t^{\omega_t - 1} \quad (11.14)$$

At this point, the hyperparameters $\omega = \{\omega_1, \ldots \omega_T\}$ for combining the posterior probabilities of all classes is used. After which, we proceed by determining its equally weighted factor $\omega t = \frac{n}{T}$, $\forall t$ for each class and figuring out combined probability $p(\mathrm{ch}_i, opt_i, \Theta)$ based on the generative statistical model. Therefore, T is used to establish the number of different classes that make the initial labeled data LD_d, and model parameters are estimated using Bayesian function combining with other input data. Further, the posterior likelihood is evaluated together with the parameter was indicated in (11.15).

$$p(Me_t, Co_t | ch_i = t, LD_d) = NIW(mk_n, r_n, q_n, MV_n) \quad (11.15)$$

To calculate the parameters, mk_0, r_0, q_0, and MV_0 are determined by the following formulae (11.16) to (11.19):

$$mk_n = \frac{r_0}{r_0 + n_t} mk_0 + \frac{n_t}{r_0 + r_t} \overline{opt}_t \quad (11.16)$$

$$r_n = r_0 + n_{ch} \quad (11.17)$$

$$q_n = q_0 + n_t \quad (11.18)$$

$$MV_n = MV_0 + MV + r_0 mk_0 mk_0^S - r_n mk_n mk_n^S \tag{11.19}$$

The following is an expression for the sum of the square matrix determined for each class t in Equation (11.20), where opt_t is the sample means corresponding to the label t and n_t is the count of the observations in the labeled data LD_d.

$$MV = \sum_{i=1}^{n_{ch}} opt_i opt_i^S \tag{11.20}$$

Likely prediction comes from the category distribution of the Dirichlet process as shown in (11.21).

$$p(\Gamma|LD_d) \propto \prod_{ch=1}^{T} \Gamma_{ch}^{n_{ch}+\omega_{ch}-1} \tag{11.21}$$

Application of Bayes rule predicts the classified label from the given data as indicated in (11.22) according to the posterior distribution function.

$$p(\widehat{ch}_i = t|\widehat{opt}_i, LD_d) = \frac{p(\widehat{opt}_i|\widehat{ch}_i{=}t, LD_d)\, p(\widehat{ch}_i{=}t|LD_d)}{p(\widehat{opt}_i|LD_d)} \tag{11.22}$$

Through the use of this model, the classified mark is expected either to be common or affected by disease. The following are the major benefits associated with using this tool:

- Requires minimal input cost for training and testing the models.
- Limited number calculations are needed.
- Increased ability to detect with precision.
- Reliability and scalability have been ensured.

11.4 Outcome and Conversation

This part includes a MATLAB simulation tool to retrieve the findings, along with a variety of analytical parameters for diagnosis and validation of the suggested marginal illness outcomes. This study uses Hungarian and PIMA (Indian Diabetes Database) diabetes and cardiovascular disease diagnostic databases. There are 76 features in the Hungarian dataset, some of which meet the requirements indicated in Table 11.2. The confusion matrix for the cardiovascular dataset in part and classes 0 and 1 is displayed in Figures 11.4(a) and 11.4(b). Examine the suggested outcome-based instrument. Accurately predict courses with higher TPR. Similar to this, the PIMA dataset is sourced from the machine learning repository and has 768 instances in Table 11.3 with nine distinct feature properties.

Table 11.2 Hungarian dataset description.

Column name	Description	Possible values
PatientID	Unique identifier for each patient	Numeric or alphanumeric identifier
Age	Age of the patient at the time of diagnosis	Numeric value (age in years)
Gender	Gender of the patient	Male, Female
Body Mass Index (BMI)	Body mass index of the patient	Numeric value (BMI)
Blood Pressure	Systolic and diastolic blood pressure values	Numeric values (e.g., 120/80 mmHg)
Plasma Glucose Levels	Plasma glucose concentration levels	Numeric value (mg/dL)
Serum Insulin	Serum insulin levels measured	Numeric value (mu U/mL)
Diabetes Pedigree Function	Measure of diabetes hereditary risk	Numeric value
Triceps Skin Thickness	Thickness of skin fold on the triceps	Numeric value (mm)
Diabetes Diagnosis	Binary indicator if the patient has diabetes	Yes (patient is diabetic), No (patient is not diabetic)
Pregnancy Status	For datasets involving pregnant women	Yes (pregnant), No (not pregnant)

(a)

	Class 0	Class 1	
Class 0	3210	35	0.98
Class 1	10	1780	0.99
	0.99	0.98	0.99

(b)

	Class 0	Class 1	
Class 0	2820	180	0.95
Class 1	350	1700	0.93
	0.95	0.96	0.94

Figure 11.4 Confusion matrix for Hungarian dataset (a) training and (b) testing.

Table 11.3 PIMA dataset description.

Column name	Description	Possible values
Preg	No. of times pregnant	Numeric value (0 to 17)
Glucose	Plasma glucose concentration test	Numeric value (mg/dL)
BP	Diastolic blood pressure	Numeric value (mm Hg)
SkinThick	Triceps skin fold thickness level	Numeric value (mm)
Insulin	2-hour serum insulin concentrations	Numeric value (mu U/mL)
BMI	Body mass index	Numeric value (kg/m2)
DPF	Diabetes pedigree function (predicts diabetes likelihood using family history)	Numeric value
Age	Patient's age	Numeric value (years)
Output	Class variable indicating presence (1) or absence (0) of diabetes	0 (no diabetes), 1 (diabetes)

The Hungarian Diabetes Database is a widely used repository with important medical and demographic data collected from 768 patients, mainly women aged 21 years and older. These factors include clinical measurements such as glucose levels, blood pressure readings, and body mass index (BMI), along with patient-specific characteristics such as age, pregnancy rate, insulin levels with indicative variables, or none of the patterns in the dataset that are marked of diabetes, coded 1 for diabetes and 0 for nondiabetic cases. The rich and diverse characteristics of the dataset enable researchers and health professionals to explore and develop predictive models and tools diagnostic aimed at identifying individuals at risk for developing diabetes or managing existing cases.

The PIMA Indian Diabetes Dataset is an original collection of health data collected from 768 women of PIMA Indian heritage living near Phoenix, Arizona, originally collected for diabetes research. This dataset contains anthropometric and demographic characteristics required for predictive modeling and health assessment. There are measurements such as skin fold size, insulin levels, and BMI, in addition to patient specific information such as age, number of pregnancies, and diabetes pedigree activity scores obtained from family history. Each sample in the dataset is labeled with an outcome variable, indicating the presence or absence of diabetes, coded 1 for diabetic information and 0 for non-diabetic risk with its comprehensive and carefully documented features; the PIMA dataset has been invaluable in developing predictive models for diabetes risk assessment, early detection methods, and personalized internal health role for emphasizing the importance of improving medical knowledge and improving health outcomes.

Figure 11.5 and Table 11.4 review the accuracy, analysis, precision, and f-measure parameters as well as the current [33] proposed scheme. Several settings are adopted in lots of programs meant for assesses methods in detention or classification applications. The better values when recalculated [(11.23) to (11.26)] heavily affect the way overall such programs would perform with their classifiers bettering it.

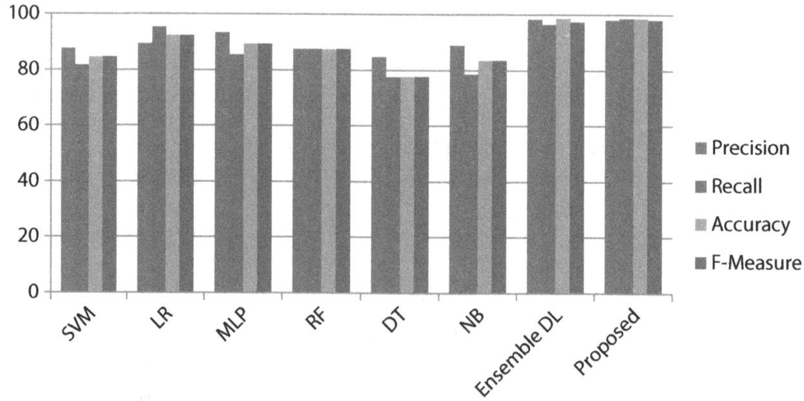

Figure 11.5 Similar findings between existing and proposed methods using Hungarian dataset.

Table 11.4 Analysis of accuracy, sensitivity, and specificity on data from Hungarian dataset.

Methods	Precision	Recall	Accuracy	F-measure
SVM	90.6	84.6	86.5	85.6
LR	91.3	93.3	90.3	90.3
MLP	94.4	86.4	90.4	85.4
RF	91.5	88.5	91.4	86.5
DT	86.7	81.5	87.7	82.7
NB	89.9	82.6	86.5	84.5
Ensemble DL	97.3	93.5	96.6	94.3
Proposed	98.1	98.6	98.6	98.1

$$Accuracy = \frac{TP + TN}{TP + TN + FP + FN} \tag{11.23}$$

$$Precision = \frac{TP}{TP + FP} \tag{11.24}$$

$$Recall\ or\ TPR = \frac{TP}{TP + FN} \tag{11.25}$$

$$F - Measure = \frac{2TP}{2TP + FP + FN} \tag{11.26}$$

The abbreviations for true positive, true negative, false positive, and false negative are TP, TN, FP, and FN, respectively. A study on the results unveiled a significant improvement in their respective proportions of precision, recall, accuracy, and F-measure whenever the ULMCSO-PGND approach was applied relative to other approaches.

The root mean square error (RMSE) and mean absolute error (MAE) values for both current and proposed deployment strategies are described in Figure 11.6 and Table 11.5 using the Hungarian dataset. The errors were calculated using formulas (11.27) and (11.28):

$$RMSE = \sqrt{\frac{1}{N}\sum_{i=1}^{N}(x_i - \hat{x}_i)^2} \tag{11.27}$$

$$MAE = \frac{1}{N}\sum_{i=1}^{N}|x_i - \hat{x}_i| \tag{11.28}$$

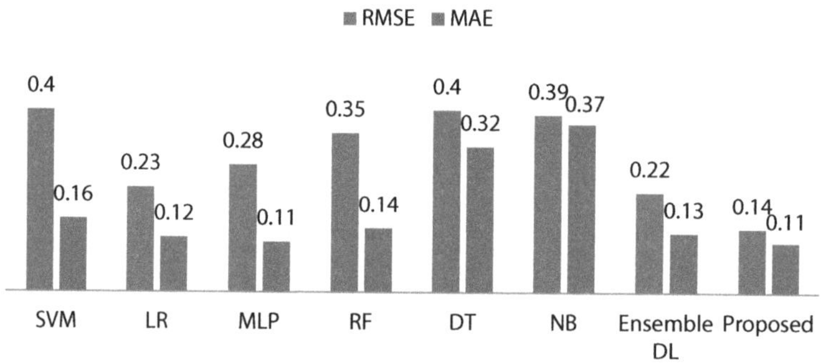

Figure 11.6 Comparison of MAE and RMSE.

Table 11.5 Evaluation of RMSE and MAE using the Hungarian dataset.

Methods	RMSE	MAE
SVM	0.39	0.15
LR	0.22	0.11
MLP	0.27	0.10
RF	0.34	0.13
DT	0.39	0.31
NB	0.38	0.36
Ensemble DL	0.21	0.12
Proposed	0.13	0.9

In this case, N is the sum of all the observed variables, whereas xi denotes the observed value, and $\hat{xi}$ is the predicted one. The ULMCSO-PGND method proposed in this paper performs better than others in terms of lowering the error rate. It is possible to train classifiers with top features to minimize errors through normalization and feature selection process.

Table 11.6 and Figure 11.7 compare the accuracy of current and proposed Hungarian dataset classification techniques. At large, a cumulative accuracy shows the whole efficiency and better performance of the detection system. Evaluation shows that ULMCSO-PGND new method is more accurate than any other method. An optimal feature is selected for training the model.

Table 11.6 Comprehensive analysis of overall accuracy utilizing the Hungarian dataset.

Methods	Overall accuracy
GFLS	78.7
Ensemble classifier	85.4
Type 2 – FL	86
Hybrid ML	88.4
DL	89
ANN	91
Kernal RF	91
MLP	92
Fuzzy Diagnosis system	92.3
DT	92.8
ANFIS	94.1
Ensemble DL	98.5
Proposed	99

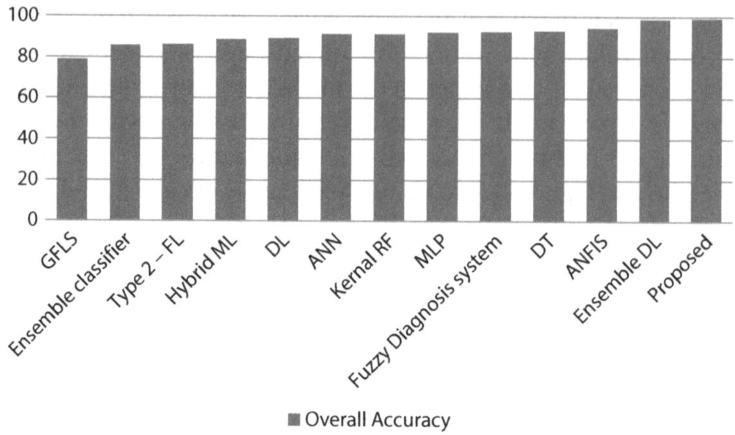

Figure 11.7 Overall accuracy for proposed and existing classification techniques.

Take a look at the present portrayal strategies compared with the proposed ones in terms of precision from [36] Table 11.7 and Figure 11.8. The research requires PIMA dataset. The findings obtained from the study demonstrate that the proposed ULMCSO-PSND strategy shows a better accuracy than other methods.

Table 11.7 Comparative assessment of accuracy with data from the PIMA dataset.

Methods	Accuracy %
Firefly with cuckoo optimization-based classification	81
Feed forward NN	82
NB	79.56
LDA with MWSVM	89.74
GA with NN	87.46
K-means with DT	90
K-means with PCA	72
ULMCSO-PGND	98.5

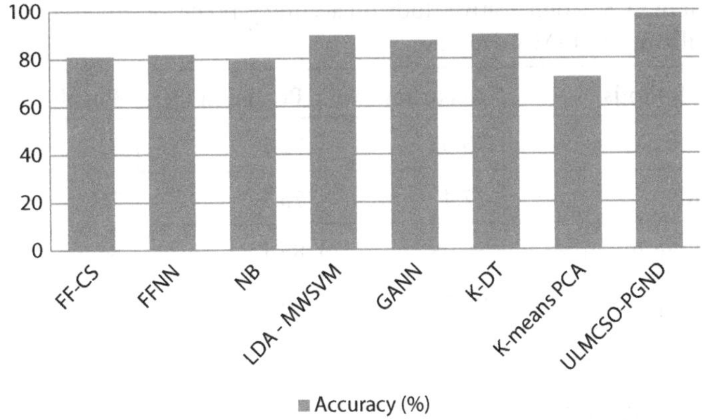

Figure 11.8 Accuracy analysis using PIMA dataset.

Analyzing the precision, correctness, and feedback proportions based on the dataset of PIMA, Figure 11.9 and Table 11.8 compare current [37] with suggested arrangement techniques. A hybrid algorithm ULMCSO finds the optimal solutions that have fewer stages and higher fusion rates to give the most preferred feature set in this design. After that, we use these functionalities to teach the categorizer, which makes the system work better by improving its accuracy, precision, and recall capability.

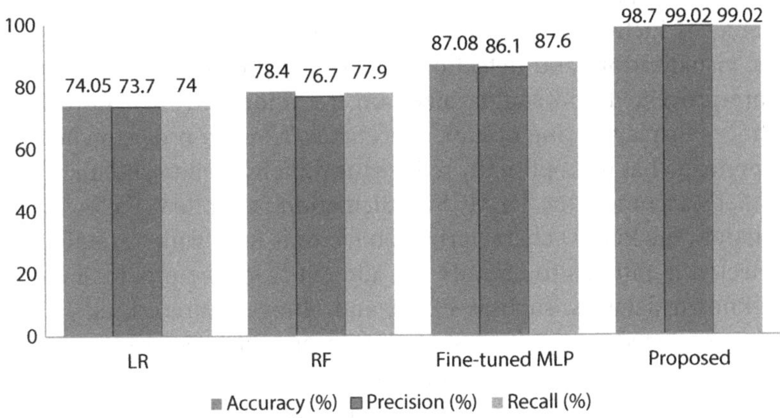

Figure 11.9 Comparative analysis based on findings from the PIMA dataset.

Table 11.8 Comparative study on accuracy, precision, and recall utilizing the PIMA dataset.

Methods	Accuracy (%)	Precision (%)	Recall (%)
LR	73.05	72.7	73
RF	77.4	75.7	76.9
Fine-tuned MLP	86.08	85.1	86.6
Proposed	98.5	99	99

11.5 Conclusion

This research provided a novel framework for remote fitness monitoring that uses an advanced artificial intelligence method to forecast different types of illness. This paper's primary contribution is the remote monitoring of patients' fitness popularity to identify the condition and make an accurate diagnosis. The one-time authentication is used in this framework to combine the sensor-derived medical data. One of the main advantages of this device is that the mobile app may immediately retrieve the desired information from the cloud structures, saving the user from having to access their data. To do this, the Google Fit cloud provider is used with the model that retains the medical data collected from patients using intelligent devices. Furthermore, the medical data obtained from the special resources is included using the unique node types, which include prognosis, visualization, and detection nodes. The provided medical datasets are pre-processed and standardized on the underlying kingdom for the classifier's display during disease expectancy. Next, in order to choose the components that will optimally reduce the dimensionality and increase the classifier's accuracy, the ULMCSO calculation is applied. Following augmentation, the PGND characterization factor is used with a suitable range of selected highlights to identify the ailment from the provided datasets. Well-known datasets, such as PIMA and Hungarian, are used to evaluate the suggested version's presentation in order to approve the impacts. Furthermore, the obtained results are compared with the new pleasant in-class strategies in terms of review, f-degree, error rate, exactness, and accuracy. The evaluation showed that by raising its performance measures, the suggested strategy outperformed all others.

References

1. Kalid, N., Zaidan, A., Zaidan, B., Salman, O.H., Hashim, M., Muzammil, H., Based real time remote health monitoring systems: A review on patients prioritization and related big data using body sensors information and communication technology. *J. Med. Syst.*, 42, 1–30, 2018. doi: 10.1007/s10916-017-0883-4.
2. Albahri, O.S., *et al.*, Systematic review of real-time remote health monitoring system in triage and priority-based sensor technology: Taxonomy, open challenges, motivation and recommendations. *J. Med. Syst.*, 42, 1–27, 2018. doi: 10.1007/s10916-018-0943-4.
3. Shorman, O.A., Shorman, B.A., Alkhassaweneh, M., Alkahtani, F., A review of internet of medical things (IoMT)–based remote health monitoring through wearable sensors: A case study for diabetic patients. *Indones. J. Electr. Eng. Comput. Sci.*, 20, 1, 414–422, 2020. doi: 10.11591/ijeecs.v20.i1.pp414-422.
4. Divakaran, J., *et al.*, Improved handover authentication in fifth-generation communication networks using fuzzy evolutionary optimisation with nanocore elements in mobile healthcare applications. *J. Healthc. Eng.*, 2022, 2022. doi: 10.1155/2022/2500377.
5. Talal, M., *et al.*, Smart home-based IoT for real-time and secure remote health monitoring of triage and priority system using body sensors: Multi-driven systematic review. *J. Med. Syst.*, 43, 1–34, 2019. doi:. 10.1007/s10916-019-1158-z.
6. Hamim, M., Paul, S., Hoque, S., II, Rahman, M.N., Baqee, I.-A., IoT based remote health monitoring system for patients and elderly people, in: *2019 International Conference on Robotics, Electrical and Signal Processing Techniques (ICREST)*, pp. 533–538, 2019, doi: 10.1109/ICREST.2019.8644514.
7. Manoharan, H., *et al.*, A machine learning algorithm for classification of mental tasks. *Comput. Electr. Eng.*, 99, 107785, 2022. doi: 10.1016/j.compeleceng.2022.107785.
8. Gondalia, A., Dixit, D., Parashar, S., Raghava, V., Sengupta, A., Sarobin, V.R., IoT-based healthcare monitoring system for war soldiers using machine learning. *Procedia Comput. Sci.*, 133, 1005–1013, 2018. doi: 10.1016/j.procs.2018.07.075.
9. Malasinghe, L.P., Ramzan, N., Dahal, K., Remote patient monitoring: a comprehensive study. *J. Ambient Intell. Hum. Comput.*, 10, 57–76, 2019. doi: 10.1007/s12652-017-0598-x.
10. Ramkumar, P.N., *et al.*, Remote patient monitoring using mobile health for total knee arthroplasty: validation of a wearable and machine learning–based surveillance platform. *J. Arthroplasty*, 34, 2253–2259, 2019. doi: 10.1016/j.arth.2019.05.021.
11. Chatrati, S. P., Hossain, G., Goyal, A., Bhan, A., Bhattacharya, S., Gaurav, D., Tiwari, S. M., Smart home health monitoring system for predicting type 2 diabetes and hypertension. *J. King Saud Univ. Comput. Inf. Sci.*, 34, 3, 862–870, 2022.
12. Vitabile, S., *et al.*, Medical data processing and analysis for remote health and activities monitoring, in: *High-Performance Modelling and Simulation*

for Big Data Applications, pp. 186–220, Springer, Cham, 2019, doi: 10.1007/978-3-030-16272-6_7.
13. Nair, L.R., Shetty, S.D., Shetty, S.D., Applying spark based machine learning model on streaming big data for health status prediction. *Comput. Electr. Eng.*, 65, 393–399, 2018. doi: 10.1016/j.compeleceng.2017.03.009.
14. Li, H., Shrestha, A., Heidari, H., Kernec, J.L., Fioranelli, F., A multisensory approach for remote health monitoring of older people. *IEEE J. Electromagn. RF Microwaves Med. Biol.*, 2, 102–108, 2018. doi: 10.1109/JERM.2018.2827099.
15. Kaur, P., Kumar, R., Kumar, M., A healthcare monitoring system using random forest and internet of things (IoT). *Multimed. Tools Appl.*, 78, 19905–19916, 2019. doi: 10.1007/s11042-019-7327-8.
16. Padmaja, M., Shitharth, S., Prasuna, K., Chaturvedi, A., Kshirsagar, P.R., Vani, A., Grow of artificial intelligence to challenge security in IoT application. *Wireless Pers. Commun.*, 1–17, 2021. doi: 10.1007/s11277-021-08725-4.
17. Verma, P. and Sood, S.K., Fog assisted-IoT enabled patient health monitoring in smart homes. *IEEE Internet Things J.*, 5, 1789–1796, 2018. doi: 10.1109/JIOT.2018.2803201.
18. Azimi, I., Takalo-Mattila, J., Anzanpour, A., Rahmani, A.M., Soininen, J.-P., Liljeberg, P., Empowering healthcare IoT systems with hierarchical edge-based deep learning, in: *Proceedings of the 2018 IEEE/ACM International Conference on Connected Health: Applications, Systems and Engineering Technologies*, pp. 63–68, 2018, doi: 10.1145/3278576.3278597.
19. Mohsin, A., *et al.*, Real-time remote health monitoring systems using body sensor information and finger vein biometric verification: A multi-layer systematic review. *J. Med. Syst.*, 42, 1–36, 2018. doi: 10.1007/s10916-018-1104-5.
20. Devarajan, M., Subramaniyaswamy, V., Vijayakumar, V., Ravi, L., Fog-assisted personalized healthcare-support system for remote patients with diabetes. *J. Ambient Intell. Hum. Comput.*, 10, 3747–3760, 2019. doi: 10.1007/s12652-019-01291-5.
21. Hassan, S.R., Ahmad, I., Ahmad, S., Alfaify, A., Shafiq, M., Remote pain monitoring using fog computing for e-healthcare: An efficient architecture. *Sensors*, 20, 6574, 2020. doi: 10.3390/s20226574.
22. Hasan, M., Shahjalal, M., Chowdhury, M.Z., Jang, Y.M., Real-time healthcare data transmission for remote patient monitoring in patch-based hybrid OCC/BLE networks. *Sensors*, 19, 1208, 2019. doi: 10.3390/s19051208.
23. Al-Makhadmeh, Z. and Tolba, A., Utilizing IoT wearable medical device for heart disease prediction using higher order Boltzmann model: A classification approach. *Measurement*, 147, 106815, 2019. doi: 10.1016/j.measurement.2019.07.043.
24. Mohan, S., Thirumalai, C., Srivastava, G., Effective heart disease prediction using hybrid machine learning techniques. *IEEE Access*, 7, 81542–81554, 2019. doi: 10.1109/ACCESS.2019.2923707.
25. Nalluri, M.R. and Roy, D.S., Hybrid disease diagnosis using multiobjective optimization with evolutionary parameter optimization. *J. Healthc. Eng.*, 2017, 2017. doi: 10.1155/2017/5907264.

26. Haq, A.U., Li, J.P., Memon, M.H., Nazir, S., Sun, R., A hybrid intelligent system framework for the prediction of heart disease using machine learning algorithms. *Mob. Inf. Syst.*, 2018, 2018. doi: 10.1155/2018/3860146.
27. Uyar, K. and İlhan, A., Diagnosis of heart disease using genetic algorithm based trained recurrent fuzzy neural networks. *Procedia Comput. Sci.*, 120, 588–593, 2017. doi: 10.1016/j.procs.2017.11.283.
28. Ahmed, F., An internet of things (IoT) application for predicting the quantity of future heart attack patients. *Int. J. Comput. Appl.*, 164, 36–40, 2017. doi: 10.5120/ijca2017913773.
29. Nazari, S., Fallah, M., Kazemipoor, H., Salehipour, A., A fuzzy inference-fuzzy analytic hierarchy process-based clinical decision support system for diagnosis of heart diseases. *Expert Syst. Appl.*, 95, 261–271, 2018. doi:10.1016/j.eswa.2017.11.001.
30. Vivekanandan, T. and Iyengar, N.C.S.N., Optimal feature selection using a modified differential evolution algorithm and its effectiveness for prediction of heart disease. *Comput. Biol. Med.*, 90, 125–136, 2017. doi:10.1016/j.compbiomed.2017.09.011.
31. Ali, L., Rahman, A., Khan, A., Zhou, M., Javeed, A., Khan, J.A., An automated diagnostic system for heart disease prediction based on χ^2 statistical model and optimally configured deep neural network. *IEEE Access*, 7, 34938–34945, 2019. doi: 10.1109/ACCESS.2019.2904800.
32. Nourmohammadi-Khiarak, J., Feizi-Derakhshi, M.-R., Behrouzi, K., Mazaheri, S., Zamani-Harghalani, Y., Tayebi, R.M., New hybrid method for heart disease diagnosis utilizing optimization algorithm in feature selection. *Health Technol.*, 10, 667–678, 2020. doi: 10.1007/s12553-019-00396-3.
33. Ali, F., *et al.*, A smart healthcare monitoring system for heart disease prediction based on ensemble deep learning and feature fusion. *Inf. Fusion*, 63, 208–222, 2020. doi: 10.1016/j.inffus.2020.06.008.
34. Mishra, S.R., Dash, S., Padhy, S., Kumar, N., Dash, Y., Integrating Multi-Omics Data for Advanced Diabetes Prediction and Understanding, in: *2024 7th International Conference on Contemporary Computing and Informatics (IC3I)*, vol. 7, pp. 1447–1453, IEEE, 2024, September.
35. Mishra, S.R., Dash, S., Padhy, S., Das, R.K., Diabetic Foot Ulcer Diagnosis Through Deep Learning Model, in: *2024 International Conference on Artificial Intelligence and Emerging Technology*, pp. 1194–1199, Global AI Summit, IEEE, 2024, September.
36. Naz, H. and Ahuja, S., SMOTE-SMO-based expert system for type II diabetes detection using PIMA dataset. *Int. J. Diabetes in Dev. Countries*, 42, 2, 245–253, 2022.
37. Butt, U.M., Letchmunan, S., Ali, M., Hassan, F.H., Baqir, A., Sherazi, H.H.R., Machine learning based diabetes classification and prediction for healthcare applications. *J. Healthc. Eng.*, 2021, 2021. doi: 10.1155/2021/9930985.

12

Cloud Manufacturing and Intelligent Network Importance in Healthcare Applications

Ravi Prasad Thati[1]* and Pranathi Kakaraparthi[2]

[1]Department of Computer Science and Engineering, School of Technology, GITAM (Deemed to be University), Hyderabad, Telangana, India
[2]Department of Computer Science and Engineering, Malla Reddy Engineering Collage, Hyderabad, Telangana, India

Abstract

Cloud manufacturing is a modern manufacturing method that takes advantage of the cloud computing technology to transfer traditional manufacturing processes into services. It involved various services and resources like software, hardware, data items, and expertise. This chapter discusses on six aspects of cloud manufacturing. They are, first, key components of cloud manufacturing like cloud infrastructure, Manufacturing-as-a-Service (MaaS), and Virtualization, which are explained. Second, the importance of integration of cloud manufacturing in healthcare and applications in its integration were provided. Third, fundamentals of cloud manufacturing technical foundation were provided. Fourth, the traditional healthcare manufacturing and their disadvantages were discussed in detail. Fifth, cloud-based solutions for the integration of cloud manufacturing in healthcare are discussed. Finally, case study and applications in healthcare manufacturing using cloud manufacturing are discussed.

***Keywords*:** Cloud manufacturing, healthcare, traditional healthcare manufacturing, fundamentals of cloud manufacturing

**Corresponding author*: rthati@gitam.edu

Pradosh Kumar Gantayat, Sandeep Kumar Panda, S. Balamurugan and Sheng-Lung Peng (eds.) Hyper-Intelligent Networks: Exploring the Future of Connectivity for Society 5.0, (249–270) © 2026 Scrivener Publishing LLC

12.1 Introduction

Cloud manufacturing is defined as a modern manufacturing method that makes use of the cloud computing technology to transfigure traditional manufacturing processes into services. The cloud-based environment is an amalgamation of various manufacturing resources and capabilities such as hardware, software, data, and expertise. It provides these resources as a scalable on-demand service over the web, which can be viewed as age-old cloud computing and storage services. The platform provides these resources as an ascendable on-demand service over the web [1, 2].

12.2 Key Components

1. Cloud Infrastructure:
The cornerstone of the cloud manufacturing is the adaptable cloud infrastructure containing servers, storage, and network capabilities. These resources can be catered to suit your manufacturing needs and are provided by a cloud service provider (CSP).

2. Manufacturing-as-a-Service (MaaS):
The main key concept of cloud manufacturing is the **"Manufacturing as a Service (MaaS)"** [3]. It provides numerous manufacturing functions as services. This is inclusive of everything from manufacturing and standard control to simulation and design. The unique pay-as-you-go options for these services allow commercial setups to have an advantage of these services without making huge lump sum payments.

3. Virtualization:
Various virtualization procedures such as virtual machines and containers facilitate different manufacturing procedures to be isolated and monitored on the same physical hardware. Virtualization is important to cloud manufacturing as it allows for more efficient use of physical resources.

4. IoT (Internet of Things):
IoT devices play a key role in cloud manufacturing by providing the real-time data from number of production processes. These devices use sensors to monitor and collect data about environmental conditions, machine functioning, and other prominent criteria and send it to cloud for the final analysis and decision-making task [4].

5. Big Data and Analytics:
Vast amounts of the data generated in the industrial setups by IoT devices and other sources are influenced by big data analytics. These solutions provide data analysis feedbacks that help predict maintenance requirements, provide processes optimization, and improve product quality [5].

6. Artificial Intelligence (AI) and Machine Learning (ML):
To enable automation and intelligent decision-making, the cloud manufacturing systems increasingly leverage AI and ML technologies. Through this technology, we can optimize manufacturing planning, predict product demand, and improve supply chain logistics.

7. Service-Oriented Architecture (SOA):
The SOA is the most commonly used architecture in cloud manufacturing systems. It enables the modularization of various manufacturing services, making it simpler to collaborate, control, and improve many components of the manufacturing process [6].

8. Cyber-Physical Systems (CPS):
The CPS is nothing but the integration of physical processes and computing systems. CPS allows digital systems to manage and monitor real-time physical production processes in cloud manufacturing [7].

9. Security and Privacy:
Because manufacturing data is critical, the cloud manufacturing solutions include strong security features. This requires data encryption, access controls, and secure communication protocols to save sensitive information and intellectual property from attacks [8, 9].

12.3 Benefits of Cloud Manufacturing

Scalability: Organizations can adjust manufacturing capabilities based on demand without requiring huge initial investments.
Cost Efficiency: Using some cloud-based resources and MaaS, businesses can reduce the labor, infrastructure, and maintenance costs.
Flexibility: Cloud manufacturing has the ability to work with new processes and technologies, allowing you to speed up the adjustments to market changes.
Collaboration: Cloud platforms facilitate collaboration among various stakeholders such as designers, suppliers and customers, thereby increasing the innovation and overall efficiency of the manufacturing process.

Challenges:
Data Security: Data security is an important concern, specifically when it comes to protecting privately produced data from online attacks.
Standardization: The dearth of defined protocols and interfaces can disturb the interoperability between different cloud manufacturing systems.
Regulatory Compliance: It is difficult to comply with industry-specific rules and guidelines in a cloud environment.

Cloud manufacturing represents a significant change in manufacturing, not only bringing many benefits in terms of flexibility, efficiency, and cost savings but also creating new challenges that need to be addressed.

12.4 Importance of Healthcare Applications

12.4.1 Integrating Cloud Manufacturing in the Healthcare Sector

The integration of cloud manufacturing in the healthcare has a significant impact on improving the availability, effectiveness, and quality of healthcare services [10].

Some of the important points that tell us about this integration are as follows:

1. **Enhanced Supply Chain Management Simplified Operation:** Optimizing the medical supply chain is only possible through cloud manufacturing because it provides real-time visibility into the medical devices, status of drugs, and consumables, and, so, healthcare providers can process orders, track inventory levels, and schedule deliveries more efficiently [11].
2. **Cut Costs:**
   Healthcare companies can reduce waste by implementing cloud-based supply chain architecture. This can lead to lower storage costs and avoid shortages of essential goods. Scaling of resources based on demand and control costs is possible by the pay-as-you-go model of cloud services.
3. **Personalized Medicine and Patient Care Customization and Flexibility:**
   3D printing technology of cloud makes it more efficient in personalizing implants and medical devices, such as prosthetics and dental implants [12].

4. **Data-Driven Treatment Plans:**
   The data-driven strategy supports the development of personalized treatment plans and improves patient outcomes. Healthcare professionals can now analyze large amounts of patient data, including genetic history and medical history, by integrating cloud-based analytics [13].
5. **Telemedicine and Remote Patient Monitoring Accessible Healthcare Services:**
   To improve access to healthcare in poor and rural areas, the cloud manufacturing supports the development and implementation of telemedicine solutions. This includes cloud-based monitoring devices that provide healthcare professionals with patient data, virtual consultations and remote testing [14].
6. **Real-Time Monitoring:**
   Through IoT devices connected to the cloud platform, patients' vital signs and medical parameters can be continuously tracked this real-time data collection, which allows medical professionals to detect abnormalities early, greatly assisting to avoid serious health problems and reduce the number of readmissions.

12.4.2 Efficient Resource Utilization Optimized Resource Allocation

With the help of cloud manufacturing, healthcare organizations may be able to make the most of their medical equipment and other resources. Healthcare providers can enhance service delivery, manage resources, and minimize downtime more efficiently by examining usage trends and demand forecasts.

Scalable Solution: Healthcare companies can quickly expand resources in response to events such as epidemics or increased patient demand with the help of the scalability feature of the cloud. Being flexible is highly crucial in order to respond to unexpected problems in medical needs.

12.4.3 Improved Data Management and Security

Consolidated Data Storage: Cloud services provide consolidated, safe storage of medical records, such as patient information, imaging reports, and research outcomes. Data consistency across different health systems is assured by this consolidated structure of the data. This centralization can also reduce the concept of replication and makes data management easy [15].

Latest Safety Measures: Leading CSPs have stringent security precautions in place, including unauthorized access restrictions, frequent security checkings, and data encryption. You can save the sensitive medical data against any unwanted access and cyber risks by maintaining these precautions.

12.4.4 Innovation and Research Accelerate Research

To assist the medical researchers to firstly process and analyze large datasets, technologies like cloud computing and big data analytics are required. These enhanced capabilities will speed up research in fields like drug discovery, genetics, and epidemiology, which can help, greatly leading to new therapies and treatments.

12.4.5 Cooperation Platform

To design innovative medical treatments, cloud-based solutions make use of the collaboration among patients, researchers, and healthcare professionals, facilitating data exchange and thereby promoting creativity [16].

12.4.6 Regulatory Compliance and Reporting Simplify Compliance

To automate the process of compliance tracking and reporting to agree with regulations such as U.S. Health Insurance Portability and Accountability Act (HIPAA), healthcare providers can make use of cloud production systems. By doing so, it can also assist the pharmacy companies decrease the load of administrative tasks and avoiding legal issues.

12.4.7 Data Review and Traceability

Cloud systems provide extensive capabilities of information logging and auditing in order to track the start point and management of healthcare data. Patient safety, regulatory compliance, and quality assurance depend on this traceability.

12.5 Fundamentals of Cloud Manufacturing Technical Foundation

Each technology makes manufacturing processes more scalable, innovative, and efficient. Successful implementation of cloud manufacturing requires combination of cutting-edge technologies. The big data, Internet of Things (IoT), AI, and cyber security are key technology pillars. We can expand each of these in detail in the coming paragraphs.

12.5.1 Internet of Things (IoT)

Outline: The term Internet of Things (IoT) is a network of "things," or physical systems, equipped with software, sensors, and other technologies that organize and share data over the Internet. IoT plays a major role in cloud production because it is accountable for connecting different components of the production ecosystem like products, machinery, tools, and logistics.

Key Functions in Cloud Manufacturing:

Real Time Monitoring:
IoT devices give valuable information that can be utilized to standardize the functions and reduce the unproductive time by continuously managing and controlling environmental situations, machine performance, and production functions.

Predictive Maintenance:
IoT systems can help in computing the data of the sensor to meticulously predict equipment issues, which causes timely disturbances and decreasing unplanned non-productivity.

Supply Chain Management:
IoT-equipped tracking solution can improve supply chain responsiveness and productivity by providing real-time view into the status and knowing the location of raw materials, finished goods, and work updates.

Advantages:

- Improve transparency and supply chain responsiveness.
- Reduce downtime and maintenance costs.
- Improve consistency and product quality.

12.5.2 Big Data

Introduction: "Big Data" is nothing but the vast amounts of organized, unstructured data generated from various sources from the production process. Big data technology is utilized in cloud production to save, process, and analyze data to process actionable views that inspire decision-making and foster creativity.

Key Functions in Cloud Manufacturing:

Data Integration:
By summing up data from multiple sources such as consumer databases, enterprise resource planning systems, and IoT components, big data platforms present a detailed overview of the manufacturing processes.

Analysis and Visualization: Analyzing the information with state of the art analytics tools to create new trends, patterns, and anomalies. Providing a detail of complex information is only possible by using visualization tools to present the information in an easy-to-understand way, assisting in making decisions quickly.

Optimization and Prediction:
Big data analytics in areas like stock management and control, standard control, and production scheduling pave the way for optimization and improvement. To predict demand, making stock management and production scheduling more precise predictive analytics can be utilized.

Advantages:

- Strengthen strategic planning and decision-making
- Better consumer insights and customized products
- More accurate inventory management and demand forecasting
- Improve operational efficiency and productivity

12.5.3 Artificial Intelligence (AI) and Machine Learning (ML)

Outline: The combination and interoperation of numerous cutting edge technologies that enable the robots to act like humans, including training, reasoning, and consisting problem solving skills is known as AI. The part of AI that involves training algorithms to recognize patterns in data and make decisions and predictions basing on the patterns without any external and explicit programming is termed as machine learning (ML).

The important features of cloud production:

Process Optimization:
To identify the flaws and optimize the methods and to work on the waste management, thereby increasing throughput, AI systems can perform analysis of data from production lines [17].

Quality Control:
Data ML models can recognize any defects in the products, reduce the percentage of non-compliance products, and assure consistency and quality by examining photos and sensor.

Predictive Maintenance:
To know when the data requires maintenance, to decrease the unproductiveness and to extend the wear and tear of the equipment, AI systems check the machine data.

Automation and Robotics: Systems can also assure safety and productivity.

Advantages:

- Improve security and reduce human error
- Reduce operating expenses
- Increase productivity and efficiency
- Improve product quality and consistency

Cyber Security

Outline: Cyber law and protection is defined as securing the data saved in the computer networks, systems, and production.

Cloud Manufacturing-Key Points

Data Protection:
Conserving critical industrial information such as intellectual property and customer data from attacks or loss is done by measures in cyber laws such as encryption and access restrictions.

Threat Detection and Response:
To verify and react to real time cyberattacks, modern cyber security systems depend heavily on AI and ML [18].

Regulatory Compliance:
It is guaranteed by cyber laws that cloud manufacturing activities comply with relevant laws such as HIPAA and general data protection regulation (GDPR), securing the business and its customers [19].

Advantages:

- Enhance trust and confidence among partners and customers
- Comply with legal standards
- Minimize financial losses and reputational damage caused by cyberattacks
- Protect personal information and intellectual property

12.5.4 Traditional Healthcare Manufacturing

Overview: One aspect of traditional medical manufacturing is manufacturing drugs, medical devices, and equipment. Historically, these processes have been known for accuracy, strict regulations, and quality controls to ensure effectiveness and patient safety. Although these traditional manufacturing methods are important to healthcare, they often have disadvantages that impact productivity, cost, and innovation [20].

12.5.5 Pharmaceutical Manufacturing

The process of pharmaceutical manufacturing includes the processes of formulation, production, quality control, drug discovery, and development. Steps include the following [21]:

Research and Development (R&D):
After conducting extensive research to identify promising drug candidates, preclinical testing is an important next step.

Recipe Development:
Drug dosage forms (tablets, capsules, injections, etc.) are created and checked for stability and bioavailability in this step.

Manufacturing:
The actual manufacturing process includes the formulation, and packaging of active pharmaceutical ingredients. The two examples of manufacturing techniques are aseptic processing and chemical synthesis.

Quality Control and Assurance:
To ensure that medicines meet the safety and effectiveness standards set by regulatory agencies such as the food and drug administration (FDA) and European medicines agency (EMA), comprehensive testing and validation is critical.

Main Features:

- Strong regulatory oversight and compliance requirements
- Complex supply chains and production procedures
- Extended delivery times and high R&D costs

Medical Equipment Processes Involved:
Medical device manufacturing consists of the production of a variety of products, from simple tools to complex, high-tech equipment. This process usually includes the following:

Design and Development: Includes design, conception, and prototyping of devices considering safety, usability, and biocompatibility [22].
Material Selection and Procurement: Materials that meet medical standards and specifications are selected.
Manufacturing and Assembly: Examples of equipment include disposable instruments such as needles and heavy machinery such as magnetic resonance imaging (MRI) scanners. The manufacturing procedures consist of sterilization, assembling of electronic devices, molding, and machining.
Validation Testing: Thorough testing such as testing for resilience assessments, biocompatibility validation and clinical experiments are needed to assure that the device is safe to use and performs as needed.

Main Features:

- Comprehensive after-sales support and maintenance services
- Introduction of cutting-edge technologies (software, AI, etc.)
- Extended product life and significant capital investment

Disadvantages with the Traditional Systems
Traditional manufacturing systems play a crucial role in pharmacy industry, but still they often face numerous adversities.

12.5.6 High Cost and Low Efficiency

High Cost Factors:
Research Development and Compliance with Regulations: Lengthy processes of approval and clinical studies may cause rise in costs. High prices of research costs and regulatory compliance can also increase expenses.
Labor and Raw Material Costs: For raw materials and professional labor strictly regulated companies often face heavy prices.
Production Flaws: Longer waiting time, waste, and incompetence are the ill effects caused by traditional batch processing techniques.

12.5.7 The Supply Chain is Complex Supply Chain Characteristics

Global Sourcing: Supply chain disturbances are caused because of high reliability on international parts and raw materials and cargo.
Rule Fluctuation: The concept of dealing with different regulatory needs in different locations brings more complexity.
Risks: The disturbances in the supply chain can lead to the dearth of emergency medicines and medical equipment as with the rise of the diseases like the COVID-19 pandemic. Also, the complexity of the supply chain can make the introduction of new products late.

12.5.8 Limited Flexibility and Scalability the Production System is Not Flexible

For specific products, the traditional manufacturing methods rely on rigid, dedicated production lines. To quickly scale up production or pivot to new products in response to emergencies or changing market demands, it becomes cumbersome.

Scalability Issues:
Significant time and capital is requires for scaling up production, which may make it difficult to meet unexpected surges in demand for complex medical devices and pharmaceuticals.

12.6 Quality Control and Assurance Task

Maintaining a consistent level of product quality is crucial in the healthcare sector, as even small defects can have a negative impact. Throughout

the manufacturing process, traditional systems struggle to maintain high quality standards which can lead to recalls and compliance issues [23].
Impact: Challenges in quality control can ultimately lead to government fines, product recalls, and patient injuries and can damage a company's finances and image.

New and Compatible Obstacles
New Disability:
Investment in new technology and technology is uncertain due to the uncertainty of the wind and the uncertainties of production and commercialization.
Adjustment Issue:
To change the structure of the market and to lead to lost opportunities to harmonize with the competition, it is possible to continue to build a new technology.

12.6.1 Integration of Cloud Manufacturing in Healthcare

Basic Solution: It is a specific basic practice settlement solution that can be used by medical manufacturers.
Case Studies and Illustrations: Practical examples and case studies, medical and healthcare industry manufacturing, special medical equipment manufacturing, comprehensive distance medicine, and Japanese product manufacturing.
Digital Science and Intelligence Factory: For medical and health products, productions understand the digital science and technology factory.

Benefits of Cloud Manufacturing in Healthcare
Efficiency and Basic Training: Examine simultaneous high school productivity and how to create a low-download.
Standardized Personalization: Understand standardized medical and health solutions and how to create a customized product.
Extensible Conformity: A research-based system of conformity and extensibility.

Challenges and Considerations
Safety Measures: An important issue for me and the medical staff is the safety.
Compliance with Regulations: In this, the environment and compliance standards of the law are explained.
Integration of Interoperability: One of the challenges here is to combine the basic design of the departments in the medical and healthcare industry and the integration of technology.

Future Trends and Directions

Emerging Technologies: It is possible to talk about AI and ML.

Futuristic Use: An exhibition of potential use in the area of consideration.

Effect on Global Healthcare: Considering how the system got affected, and how the system was created, the medical and healthcare in various parts of the world, it was also possible to study the current situation at the same time.

Integration of Cloud Manufacturing in Healthcare

In this article, we will know about the details of the implementation of the solutions based on the key points, production of the medical and healthcare industry, the practical case studies and the new concepts, and examples of the number science and technology workshop. The goal is to deeply understand how to improve patient care, develop a new medical clinic, and improve efficiency.

Cloud-Based Solutions

The development of medical and health production is to provide various tools, construct the basic technology of the company, change the number of operations, and increase the number of companies in various stages of production and provide additional tools. In this article, we will explore specific cloud-based technologies that are significantly affecting the healthcare industry.

12.6.2 Cloud Manufacturing Platforms

The production platform is an integrated system that gives a detailed management solution for the life cycle of the world. In addition, it has various functionalities such as flat platform communication, integrated design, centralized communication, quality control, logistics, medical assistance, production, industry maintenance standard, medical production, quality and quantity integration standard, reform production management department, and additional land management resources.

Key Components:

Design and Simulation Tools: Based on the basic CAD technology, it is possible to create a virtual prototype swiftly, and it takes less time to create a building prototype [24].

Production Management:
This solution provides automatic flexibility, practicality, time control, performance, and other functions, ensuring well-regulated production.

Quality Assurance:
With the help of integrated quality management systems (QMSs), real-time tracking and auditing capabilities guarantee that all products meet regulatory needs [23].

Advantages:

- It is possible to lengthen the harmony and activate the demand for continuous change.
- Concentrated numbers can be changed for a better performance.
- Reduced base construction allows for more savings.

12.6.3 Telemedicine and Remote Healthcare Services

By making use of cloud-based technologies, telemedicine enables remote delivery of medical treatments, virtual consultation, including remote diagnostics, and patient monitoring, increasing healthcare accessibility and prevailing over geographic obstacles.

Key Features:

Virtual Consultations:

Video calls allow patients and healthcare providers to talk without the need for an in-person visit. This is particularly advantageous in areas with mediocre medical facilities.

Remote Diagnostics:
Patient Monitoring:
Advantages:

- Improve patient involvement and treatment compliance
- Custom medical devices and additive manufacturing
- Facilitates patient access
- Decrease healthcare costs and resource utilization

The exceptional rise in demand for personalized healthcare solutions is driving the fame of cloud-based development and manufacturing services. These services will make use of add on manufacturing (3D printing) to develop custom medical devices such as transplants, orthotics, and prosthetics for individuals [25].

Main Components:

Cloud-Based Design Tools:
These tools when used properly can influence data related to patients to help medical devices, ensuring accurate fit, and correct working.

Additive Manufacturing:
3D printing can always develop complicated medical devices in fewer amounts of time and at a reduced cost than old methods.

Supply Chain Integration:
The cloud atmosphere maintains the complete supply chain from deployment to design guaranteeing extraordinary standard control and collaboration.

Advantages:

- Customize medical equipment to enhance patient outcomes
- Efficient manufacturing, especially for devices with high complexity and limited quantities
- Decrease time to market for new designs and customized products

Case Studies:
Cloud manufacturing operations in the healthcare industry exhibit its capacity for innovation. This section throws focus on important examples and case studies demonstrating the uses of cloud-based solutions to specific complex situations and opportunities in the medical field.

12.6.4 Working

Cloud-based telemedicine technology is majorly used by people in the healthcare industry to perform online meetings. By combining and collaborating these platforms with electronic health records (EHRs), doctors can remotely check and monitor the patient care, manage medications, and view patient previous medical records.

Outcomes:

Improved Accessibility:
Cloud-based telemedicine technology is prominently used by medical professionals for virtual consultations. These platforms integrate with EHRs, allowing physicians to remotely look into manage medications, patient care, and view patient medical histories.

12.7 Economical Aspect

12.7.1 Improved Patient Involvement

Patients are encouraged to ask medical suggestions on time through possible available virtual consultations and stick to their treatment plans.

12.7.2 Customized Prosthetics and Orthotics

Background Study: Ancient methods of designing prosthetics orthotics and often result in an approach where only one size is manufactured and patients suffer due to the misfitting, which is painful and does not yield proper responses for individuals with specific anatomical needs.

12.7.3 Working

Companies like Limb Forge and UNYQ maintain cloud-based platforms to create and produce custom prosthetics and orthotics. These platforms use scanning and 3D printing technology to create devices that specifically match the patient's anatomy.

12.7.4 Outcomes

Improved Fit and Comfort:
These customized devices will fit the patient's body very naturally, enhancing comfort and utility.

Reduced Production Time: The usage of 3D printing and digital design significantly reduces the time required to make custom gadgets [26].
Cost-Effectiveness: If we decrease the cost of production through additive manufacturing, then more people will be interested to buy personal devices.

12.7.5 Drug Production and Quality Control Context

Pharmaceutical production requires continuous quality control, but traditional techniques can be cumbersome and time-consuming.

Working:
A pharmaceutical company implements a cloud-based analytics platform and QMS. These tools provide real-time data analysis monitoring to ensure that all manufacturing processes comply with strict legal requirements [27].

Outcomes:

Improved Biddability: An integrated QMS ensures that all processes agree with regulatory standards, thereby reducing the risk of non- compliance.

Increase Productivity: Instant data analysis facilitates to quickly find and sort out issues, reduce waste, and increase overall productiveness.

Improved Product Quality: Regular monitoring and quality control produces reliable medicines.

Digital Twins and Smart Factories:
Emerging technologies such as digital twins [28] and smart factories are the ameliorating healthcare production by enhancing product standards, giving new methods to augment processes and increase operational efficiency.

Applications in Healthcare Manufacturing:
Product Design and Testing: Manufacturers can use digital twins to reproduce and make better product designs, identify potential problems and enhance the processes before going into production.

Streamlining a Process: Digital twins provide performance assessments by replicating the complete production process, which allows better resource utilization and continuous improvement.

Predictive Maintenance: Digital twins check equipment health and predict failures, facilitating reduction of downtime and preventive maintenance.

Advantages:

- Save money and time on testing and product development
- Production process enhancement and monitoring
- Improve dependability and equipment maintenance costs

12.7.6 Smart Factory

Smart factories use latest technologies such as automation, artificial intelligence, and the big data and form a highly coordinated smart industrial domain. These factories can autonomously manage the production processes, respond to real-time changes, and optimize operations [29].

Applications in Healthcare Manufacturing:
Automation and Robotics: Smart factories make use of automation and robotics for intricate production processes such as assembly and packaging to achieve greater steadiness and correctness [30].

Real-Time Data Analysis: Uninterrupted analysis and data collection contribute to real-time decision-making, improving standards and efficacy.
Unified Systems: Smart factories integrate various systems such as supply chain management, production and distribution to assure optimized operations and decreased delay time [31].

Advantages:

- Improve adaptability to changing market demands
- Improve product traceability and quality assurance
- Improve outcomes

12.8 Conclusion

The amalgamation of cloud manufacturing in healthcare is transforming the industry by producing unparalleled levels of customization, efficiency, and innovation. Cloud-based solutions provide the infrastructure and capabilities that are required to fasten up industrial procedures, improve the patient care, and decrease costs. Some real-world examples and case studies give a glimpse of the real-world applications and advantages of these ideas and technologies like digital twins and smart factories. They provide a view of futuristic healthcare manufacturing and production. As the industry is expanding, it is very important to adopt these latest technologies to solve current medical problems and encounter the requirements of patients around the world.

References

1. Liu, Y., Wang, L., Vincent Wang, X., Cloud manufacturing: Latest advancements and future trends. *Procedia Manuf.*, 25, 62–73, 2018. doi: 10.1016/j.promfg.2018.06.058.
2. Masrom, M. and Rahimli, A., A review of cloud computing technology solution for healthcare system. *Res. J. Appl. Sci. Eng. Technol.*, 8, 20, 2150–2153, 2014. doi: 10.19026/rjaset.8.1212.
3. Moghaddam, M., Silva, J.R., Nof, S.Y., Manufacturing-as-a-Service - From e-work and service-oriented architecture to the cloud manufacturing paradigm. *IFAC-PapersOnLine*, 28, 3, 828–833, 2015. doi: 10.1016/j.ifacol.2015.06.186.
4. Stergiou, C., Psannis, K.E., Kim, B.G., Gupta, B., Secure integration of IoT and Cloud Computing. *Futur. Gener. Comput. Syst.*, 78, December, 964–975, 2018. doi: 10.1016/j.future.2016.11.031.
5. Agrawal, D., Das, S., El Abbadi, A., Big data and cloud computing: Current state and future opportunities, in: *ACM Int. Conf. Proceeding Ser*, pp. 530–533, 2011, doi: 10.1145/1951365.1951432.
6. Lojka, T., Bundzel, M., Zolotová, I., Service-oriented architecture and cloud manufacturing. *Acta Polytech. Hung.*, 13, 6, 25–44, 2016. doi: 10.12700/aph.13.6.2016.6.2.
7. Chaâri, R., *et al.*, Cyber-physical systems clouds: A survey. *Comput. Netw.*, 108, 260–278, September, 2016. doi: 10.1016/j.comnet.2016.08.017.
8. Gai, K., Qiu, M., Zhao, H., Xiong, J., Privacy-Aware Adaptive Data Encryption Strategy of Big Data in Cloud Computing, in: *Proc. - 3rd IEEE Int. Conf. Cyber Secur. Cloud Comput. CSCloud 2016 2nd IEEE Int. Conf. Scalable Smart Cloud, SSC 2016*, pp. 273–278, 2016, doi: 10.1109/CSCloud.2016.52.
9. Baltatescu, I., Cloud Computing Services: Benefits, Risks and Intellectual Property Issues. *RESER Conf.*, 2, 1, 230–242, 2012. [Online]. Available: http://search.proquest.com/openview/2f6b2cba38c1019cb33e4a85253e1044/1?pq-origsite=gscholar.
10. Harteloh, P.P.M., The Meaning of Quality in Health Care: A Conceptual Analysis. *Health Care Anal.*, 11, 3, 259–267, 2003. doi: 10.1023/B:HCAN.0000005497.53458.ef.
11. Ibrahim, A., Irawan, E., Kartika Dewi, N., Nurani, Filaresy, R., Yusmaniarti, The implementation of supply chain management and big data to accelerate stock order in mega drug store. *J. Phys. Conf. Ser.*, 1196, 1, 2019. doi: 10.1088/1742-6596/1196/1/012005.
12. Mai, J., Zhang, L., Tao, F., Ren, L., Customized production based on distributed 3D printing services in cloud manufacturing. *Int. J. Adv. Manuf. Technol.*, 84, 1–4, 71–83, 2016. doi: 10.1007/s00170-015-7871-y.
13. Manekar, A.K. and Pradeepini, G., Cloud Based Big Data Analytics a Review. *Proc. - 2015 Int. Conf. Comput. Intell. Commun. Netw. CICN 2015*, 1, 1, 785–788, 2016. doi: 10.1109/CICN.2015.160.

14. H., J.C. and H., M.W., A cloud computing based 12-lead ECG telemedicine service. *BMC Med. Inform. Decis. Mak.*, 12, 77, 2012. [Online]. Available: http://ovidsp.ovid.com/ovidweb.cgi?T=JS&PAGE=reference&D=emed11&NEWS=N&AN=22838382.
15. Helali, L. and Omri, M.N., A survey of data center consolidation in cloud computing systems. *Comput. Sci. Rev.*, 39, January 2021, 2021. doi: 10.1016/j.cosrev.2021.100366.
16. Fernández-Cardeñosa, G., De La Torre-Díez, I., López-Coronado, M., Rodrigues, J.J.P.C., Analysis of cloud-based solutions on EHRs systems in different scenarios. *J. Med. Syst.*, 36, 6, 3777–3782, 2012. doi: 10.1007/s10916-012-9850-2.
17. Wei, L., *et al.*, Artificial intelligence (AI) and machine learning (ML) in precision oncology: a review on enhancing discoverability through multiomics integration. *Br. J. Radiol.*, 96, 1150, 1–13, 2023. doi: 10.1259/bjr.20230211.
18. Yamin, M.M., Ullah, M., Ullah, H., Katt, B., Weaponized AI for cyber attacks. *J. Inf. Secur. Appl.*, 57, 1–35, 2021. doi: 10.1016/j.jisa.2020.102722.
19. Rao, G.S., Cyber Security Laws : With Reference to Cloud Computing Paradigm Implementation there of in Telangana Region. 5, 2, 733–738, 2020.
20. Fisher, O., Watson, N., Porcu, L., Bacon, D., Rigley, M., Gomes, R.L., Cloud manufacturing as a sustainable process manufacturing route. *J. Manuf. Syst.*, 47, 53–68, April2018. doi: 10.1016/j.jmsy.2018.03.005.
21. Al-Shura, M.S., Zabadi, A.M., Abughazaleh, M., Alhadi, M.A., Critical Success Factors for Adopting Cloud Computing in the Pharmaceutical Manufacturing Companies. *Manag. Econ. Rev.*, November, 123–137, 2018. doi: 10.24818/mer/2018.12-01.
22. Wang, Z. and Dai, Z., Extractive microbial fermentation in cloud point system. *Enzyme Microb. Technol.*, 46, 6, 407–418, 2010. doi: 10.1016/j.enzmictec.2010.02.004.
23. Rezaei, H., Karimi, B., Hosseini, S.J., Effect of Cloud Computing Systems in Terms of Service Quality of Knowledge Management Systems. *Lect. Notes Softw. Eng.*, 4, 1, 73–76, 2016. doi: 10.7763/lnse.2016.v4.226.
24. Zissis, D., Lekkas, D., Azariadis, P., Papanikos, P., Xidias, E., Collaborative CAD/CAE as a cloud service. *Int. J. Syst. Sci. Oper. Logist.*, 4, 4, 339–355, 2017. doi: 10.1080/23302674.2016.1186237.
25. Mathew, G. and Obradovic, Z., Improving computational efficiency for personalized medical applications in mobile cloud computing environment, in: *Proc. - 2013 IEEE Int. Conf. Healthc. Informatics, ICHI 2013*, pp. 535–540, 2013, doi: 10.1109/ICHI.2013.83.
26. Baumann, F.W. and Roller, D., Additive manufacturing, cloud-based 3D printing and associated services-overview. *J. Manuf. Mater. Process.*, 1, 2, 1–60, 2017. doi: 10.3390/jmmp1020015.
27. Kaginalkar, A., Kumar, S., Gargava, P., Niyogi, D., *Changing Paradigm of Urban Air Quality Management: Opportunities and Challenges of Frontier 2 Technologies in the context of Smart Cities 3*, pp. 1–37, 2021.

28. Hu, L., *et al.*, Modeling of Cloud-Based Digital Twins for Smart Manufacturing with MT Connect. *Procedia Manuf.*, 26, 1193–1203, 2018. doi: 10.1016/j.promfg.2018.07.155.
29. Wan, J., Yang, J., Wang, Z., Hua, Q., Artificial intelligence for cloud-assisted smart factory. *IEEE Access*, 6, 55419–55430, 2018. doi: 10.1109/ACCESS.2018.2871724.
30. Wang, S., Zhang, C., Liu, C., Li, D., Tang, H., Cloud-assisted interaction and negotiation of industrial robots for the smart factory. *Comput. Electr. Eng.*, 63, 66–78, 2017. doi: 10.1016/j.compeleceng.2017.05.025.
31. Shiau, W.-L., A unified framework of the cloud computing service. *J. Electron. Sci. Technol.*, 11, 2, 150, 2013. [Online]. Available: https://www.researchgate.net/publication/288970100.

13

Analysis on E-Services Platform in Context of Intelligent Cities

Aryan Kaushal, Animesh Singh, Ankit Raj, Sanskar Garg and Hitesh Mohapatra*

School of Computer Engineering, KIIT Deemed to be University, Bhubaneswar, Odisha, India

Abstract

Smart cities harness the power of technology to enhance urban services, citizen engagement, and overall quality of life. E-services platforms act as a central hub for streamlining administrative processes, delivering services, and enabling new forms of interaction between governments and citizens. This review paper offers a comprehensive analysis of e-services platforms within the context of smart cities, examining their architecture, implementation strategies, and key functionalities. We demonstrate that the design and integration of e-services platforms have a profound impact on the success of smart city initiatives. Previous approaches often suffered from fragmented services, limited citizen participation, and a lack of user-friendliness. Our analysis reveals that centralized platforms built with interoperability, user-centric design, and open data policies in mind foster higher adoption rates, greater citizen satisfaction, and more efficient service delivery. This review highlights the significance of e-services platforms as a backbone for seamless service provision, resource optimization, and enhanced decision-making in smart cities. Further research should examine strategies for scaling these platforms, ensuring equitable access for all citizens, and addressing potential security and privacy concerns. This will pave the way for truly inclusive and sustainable smart city development.

***Keywords*:** Cities and towns, information management, cloud computing, cloud architecture, data handling

**Corresponding author*: hmpendrive@gmail.com

Pradosh Kumar Gantayat, Sandeep Kumar Panda, S. Balamurugan and Sheng-Lung Peng (eds.) Hyper-Intelligent Networks: Exploring the Future of Connectivity for Society 5.0, (271–296) © 2026 Scrivener Publishing LLC

13.1 Introduction

The advent of cloud computing has marked a significant shift in the landscape of internet-based computing, enabling the delivery of information technology capabilities as services. This paradigm has not only revolutionized traditional computing but also paved the way for the Internet of Things (IoT) to flourish beyond the confines of cloud infrastructure. Smart cities are becoming more common, where efforts are made to use information and communication technologies (ICTs) to improve urban life. These cities use technology in a planned way to achieve goals like environmental sustainability, better urban systems, improved health, education growth, and progress through strong networks [1]. In the context of these smart cities, cloud computing plays a pivotal role by offering shared resources such as network, storage, computers, and software [15]. This integration of cloud infrastructure with IoT systems holds the promise of augmenting efficiency, performance, and payload in the delivery of resources [16]. The IoT faces specific challenges in its constantly changing and shared environment. It involves many different devices, each with limited storage, power, and performance abilities. These challenges pose barriers to the seamless development of IoT systems, necessitating solutions that address issues of compatibility, efficiency, functionality, and availability [2]. Figure 13.1 represents domains that are included in smart city and the areas in which we can work upon to make a city smart.

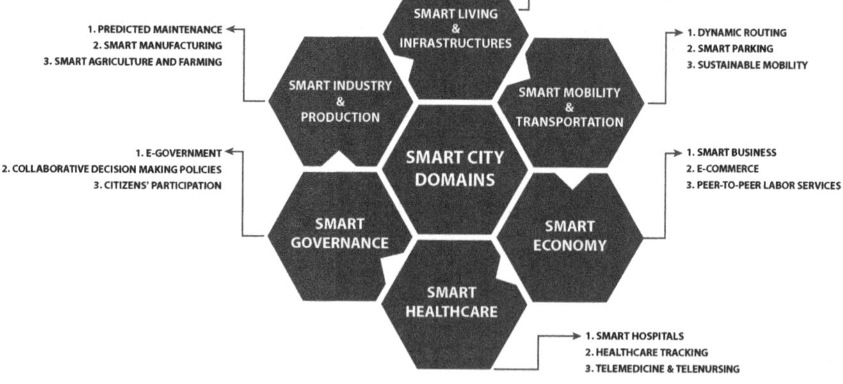

Figure 13.1 Smart city domains.

One of the most promising avenues for overcoming these IoT limitations lies in the fusion of IoT with cloud computing. The cloud, with its ubiquity, cost-effectiveness, and shared resources, offers a solution to the constraints imposed by IoT devices. This paper explores the intersection of IoT and cloud computing, particularly within the context of smart cities, unraveling the potential benefits and applications of this integration. The focus extends to the utilization of cloud resources for data gathering, transmission, analysis, processing, and storage in a cloud-based IoT platform tailored for smart cities. As the presence of the IoT continues to burgeon in smart cities, generating vast amounts of data, the need for robust ICT approaches becomes paramount. The rise of big data, a consequence of this IoT proliferation, demands structured and integrated strategies for effective management and analysis. The paper explains a clear process that includes collecting, storing, organizing, processing, and visualizing data. It also covers how this data is analyzed to create useful information for smart cities, helping with better decision-making. The emphasis is on leveraging cloud-based storage and analysis services to harness the potential of this burgeoning volume of data generated by IoT devices in smart cities [3].

Cities are changing fast, with around 75% of Europe's population living in urban areas. This number was expected to rise above 80% by 2020. As more people move into cities, it puts pressure on the limited resources available. To deal with this, we need new and creative solutions for sustainable growth and managing resources better. Technology plays a big role here, helping cities run smarter and involving citizens more in decision-making processes [4]. The shift from traditional top-down governance to a more bottom-up approach, powered by technology, is crucial for gathering expert opinions from various fields. This change supports the growth of smart cities, where technology improves governance and encourages community involvement in decisions. These cities focus on using technology for better public services and transportation planning, aiming for sustainable development and smarter resource management [15]. This research work embarks on a comprehensive exploration of the interplay between technology, smart cities, and e-services, with a focus on understanding how e-services platforms contribute to the overarching goal of transforming cities into intelligent, sustainable, and citizen-centric urban spaces [5]. The subsequent sections delve into the role of e-services in the context of smart cities, exploring their potential to enhance urban governance, improve communication and information services, and empower citizens through informed decision-making. Furthermore, the work investigates the challenges and opportunities associated with the integration of e-services in smart cities, shedding light on the intricate dynamics of this evolving landscape. Through an analysis of existing literature, case studies, and potential use cases, the research aims to provide insights into the current state, future trends, and implications of e-services platforms in the broader framework of smart city development [6].

13.2 Literature Review

The evolution of urban landscapes into smart cities marks a pivotal moment in the intersection of technology, governance, and sustainability. Smart cities use modern technology to improve daily life, boost the economy, and protect the environment. At the heart of this transformation lie e-services platforms, sophisticated systems designed to facilitate seamless interaction between citizens, businesses, and government entities [17]. This literature review aims to provide a comprehensive analysis of e-services platforms within the context of smart cities, exploring their evolution, functionalities, technological underpinnings, impacts, challenges, and ethical considerations [7].

The concept of smart cities has evolved from early discussions on digital governance and urban innovation to encompass a holistic approach to urban development. Early initiatives focused on deploying individual technologies for specific purposes, such as traffic management or energy efficiency [16]. However, contemporary smart city strategies emphasize integration and interoperability, recognizing the interconnected nature of urban systems and the need for comprehensive solutions. E-services platforms play a key role in making this integration possible. They allow easy communication and teamwork across different sectors and people. In smart cities, e-services are grouped into three types: government-to-citizen (G2C), government-to-business (G2B), and business-to-citizen (B2C) interactions. G2C services encompass a wide range of online portals and applications aimed at providing citizens with access to government services, information, and participation channels. G2B services facilitate interactions between government agencies and businesses, streamlining processes such as procurement, licensing, and regulatory compliance. B2C services encompass commercial offerings aimed at enhancing citizen experiences and quality of life (QoL), including smart utility management, transportation solutions, and telehealth services [7]. Several key components and technologies underpin e-services platforms in smart cities. High-speed broadband networks and robust mobile infrastructure form the foundation of connectivity, enabling ubiquitous access to digital services. Data management and analytics platforms harness the power of big data and artificial intelligence to derive insights, optimize services, and inform decision-making processes (Lyu *et al.*, 2021) [18].

Cloud computing solutions provide scalability, flexibility, and cost-effectiveness in deploying and managing e-services infrastructure. However, cybersecurity remains a critical concern, necessitating robust measures to protect against data breaches and privacy violations [8].

User-centric design principles are paramount in the development of smart city e-services, ensuring intuitive interfaces and inclusive experiences for diverse user groups (Stieglitz *et al.*, 2020). Accessibility considerations are essential to address the digital divide and ensure equitable access to services for all citizens [19]. Multi-platform delivery, compatibility with assistive technologies, and adherence to accessibility standards are essential strategies to promote inclusivity and accessibility. Figure 13.2 represents cross-thematic data management and analysis for variety of smart city applications in cloud environment. The adoption of e-services platforms in smart cities has profound impacts on various aspects of urban life. These impacts include improvements in efficiency and service quality, enhanced citizen engagement and participation, stimulation of economic development, and advancements in sustainability and QoL. E-services streamline processes, reduce administrative burdens, and empower citizens to actively participate in governance processes [20]. Despite their potential benefits, e-services platforms in smart cities also present significant challenges and ethical considerations. Privacy and data protection are paramount, requiring robust safeguards and ethical frameworks to mitigate risks associated with data collection, storage, and utilization. Algorithmic bias and transparency pose challenges in ensuring fairness and accountability in automated decision-making processes. Additionally, concerns regarding surveillance and social control necessitate careful consideration of the ethical implications of smart city technologies [8, 9].

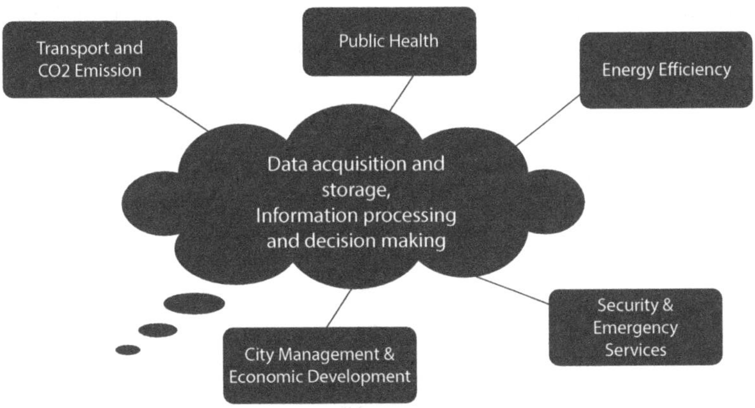

Figure 13.2 Cross-thematic data management and analysis for variety of smart city applications in cloud environment.

In addition to the technological and governance aspects, the sustainability dimension of smart cities is a critical factor in their long-term viability. E-services platforms play a pivotal role in promoting sustainability by enabling efficient resource management, optimizing energy usage, and facilitating the transition to renewable energy sources [21]. Through real-time monitoring and data analytics, these platforms can identify areas for improvement in energy consumption, waste management, and urban mobility, leading to reduced environmental impact and carbon emissions. Furthermore, e-services empower citizens with information and tools to adopt sustainable behaviors, such as carpooling, energy conservation, and recycling, thereby fostering a culture of environmental responsibility and resilience within the urban community. Sustainable development goals are increasingly integrated into smart city agendas, with e-services platforms serving as enablers for achieving targets related to clean energy, sustainable infrastructure, and climate action [10]. As smart cities continue to evolve, the synergy between technology, governance, and sustainability will be instrumental in shaping resilient and livable urban environments for future generations [22].

Research on the business models associated with the delivery of public services within the smart city ecosystem is limited. A deeper understanding of how public services can be sustainably offered and managed through IoT and other technologies is needed [11]. There is a discrepancy in the perceptions and expectations between authorities and citizens regarding smart city initiatives. Bridging this gap requires research into the factors that influence these perceptions and how they impact the adoption and success of smart city projects [12]. The role of visual communication in shared mobility systems within smart cities is underexplored. Investigating how operators perceive and utilize visual communication for competitiveness and recognition in smart cities can fill a significant research gap [13]. Figure 13.3 illustrates the e-government and smart city development model.

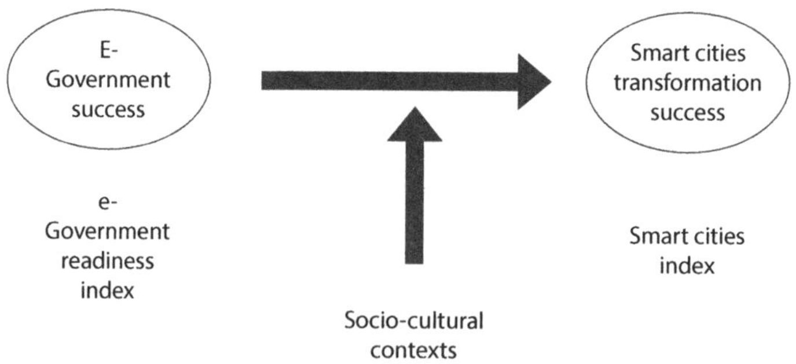

Figure 13.3 E-government and smart city development.

Table 13.1 Comparing real data related to smart city implementations.

City/ aspect	Scalability solutions	Interoperability standards adopted	Inclusivity measures	Ethical frameworks implemented	Real-world impact evaluation
City A	Cloud-based dynamic resource allocation	Common Data Model	Multi-lingual support and ADA compliance	Data usage policy and transparency in AI decisions	Reduced administrative costs and improved citizen satisfaction
City B	Edge computing for local data processing	IoT Standards (e.g., message queuing telemetry transport (MQTT) and constrained application protocol (CoAP))	Community tech hubs for digital literacy	Privacy-preserving technologies	Enhanced public safety and environmental sustainability
City C	Hybrid cloud models for flexibility	Smart city API interoperability	Accessible e-government portals	Ethical AI guidelines and data anonymization	Economic growth and increased citizen engagement

To address these research gaps effectively, the collection of specific data and the undertaking of comparative analyses are necessary. Below is a proposed Table 13.1 comparing real data related to smart city implementations, which could serve as a foundation for further research. By focusing on these extended research gaps and employing a data-driven approach to comparative analysis, future research can significantly advance the field of e-services in smart cities, leading to more scalable, interoperable, inclusive, ethically responsible, and effective urban environments.

Note: The cities and aspects listed in the Table 13.1 are illustrative examples meant to highlight the types of data and comparative analyses that could inform further research in addressing the identified gaps. Actual data collection would involve detailed case study research, surveys, and empirical evaluations.

13.3 Research Gap

The allure of smart cities, urban landscapes brimming with technological innovation and streamlined governance, has captivated researchers and policymakers alike. Visions of enhanced efficiency, improved citizen services, and a more sustainable future fuel the relentless pursuit of this urban ideal. However, beneath the glossy veneer lies a reality riddled with gaps that threaten to impede progress. While significant advancements have been documented in various areas, a closer examination reveals critical shortcomings that demand urgent attention if smart cities are to fulfill their true potential [23]. One of the most concerning gaps lies at the heart of the smart city narrative—citizen participation. E-services are often positioned as a panacea for improved governance, promising increased transparency and citizen engagement. However, the question of how these platforms can truly empower citizens and redefine the smart city governance model remains largely unexplored [24]. The current discourse lacks a crucial piece of the puzzle: how digital media can be harnessed to facilitate deeper citizen involvement in decision-making processes. Imagine a scenario where citizens are not merely passive recipients of information disseminated through government apps but active participants in shaping their urban environment. Platforms could be designed to foster discussions on neighborhood development plans, solicit feedback on proposed policies, and even allow citizens to vote on specific initiatives [7].

This deeper level of engagement transcends simply providing information; it empowers citizens to become co-creators of their smart city, fostering a sense of ownership and responsibility for its success. Without prioritizing citizen participation, smart cities risk becoming mere technological marvels devoid of the human element necessary for their long-term sustainability. Another significant gap hindering the realization of smart city aspirations is the lack of seamless integration between diverse technologies and services [26]. The current landscape resembles a fragmented archipelago, with different platforms and services operating in isolation. This lack of interoperability creates data silos, where valuable information remains trapped within specific systems, hindering its potential to generate holistic insights and inform comprehensive decision-making. Imagine a traffic management system unable to communicate with a waste collection service, leading to inefficient routing of trucks during rush hour. Such scenarios highlight the critical need for the development of interoperable solutions [8]. Standardized data formats and communication protocols are essential to bridge these divides, allowing for a more unified and efficient ecosystem. Open APIs (Application Programming Interfaces) can further empower third-party developers to create innovative applications that leverage data from various platforms, unlocking the full potential of the smart city infrastructure [28]. Furthermore, the current research focus on urban smart cities overlooks the potential application of these technologies in rural areas. The narrative surrounding smart cities often depicts them as gleaming metropolises, neglecting the vast rural landscapes that are equally in need of innovative solutions. Understanding how rural communities can leverage digital tools for resilience and development is a gap that necessitates further exploration. Imagine a rural community deploying smart sensors to monitor soil moisture levels and optimize irrigation practices, leading to increased agricultural yields and improved water conservation [30]. Such examples showcase the transformative potential of smart city technologies beyond the urban context. A comprehensive framework encompassing planning, execution, and evaluation phases is essential for the holistic development of smart cities, both in urban and rural settings. This framework should consider the specific needs and challenges of each community, ensuring that smart city initiatives are inclusive and equitable, fostering progress for all inhabitants [9]. Table 13.2 presents the existing research gaps.

Addressing these critical gaps requires a multi-pronged approach. First, fostering a culture of open data and citizen participation is essential. Governments must prioritize transparency and provide citizens with accessible platforms for engagement. Second, research and development efforts should focus on creating interoperable solutions that break down data silos and enable seamless integration between diverse technologies [10, 11]. Third, a shift in perspective is necessary to recognize the potential of smart city initiatives in rural areas, fostering research and development efforts tailored to their unique needs. Finally, a holistic framework for planning, execution, and evaluation should guide the development of smart cities, ensuring that these initiatives are not merely technological

Table 13.2 Comparison of research gaps across the papers.

Research gap	**Papers addressing the gap**
Integration of Technologies and Services	[7]
Strategic Implementation Frameworks	[8]
Rural vs. Urban Digital Geographies	[9]
Citizen Participation and Governance	[10]
Business Models for Public Services	[11]
Perceptions and Expectations	[12]
Visual Communication in Shared Mobility	[13]
Socio-Cultural Attributes	[14]

showcases but catalysts for inclusive and sustainable urban development [31]. By acknowledging and addressing these gaps, we can pave the way for a future where smart cities fulfill their true potential. Imagine cities where citizens are empowered co-creators, not passive bystanders. Imagine a seamlessly integrated technological ecosystem that optimizes resource management and streamlines service delivery [12]. Imagine rural communities utilizing digital tools to build resilience and enhance their QoL. This is the vision of smart cities that we must strive to achieve—a future where technology serves humanity, fostering a more equitable and sustainable world for all. These research gaps underscore the need for interdisciplinary approaches that address technological, strategic, socio-cultural, and governance aspects of smart cities. Future studies should aim to develop frameworks, methodologies, and practical solutions that tackle these gaps, thereby facilitating the holistic and inclusive development of smart cities [7–14].

13.4 Comparative Analysis of Existing Work

The relentless march of urbanization presents modern cities with a multitude of challenges. Traffic congestion, environmental pollution, and citizen dissatisfaction with public services are just a few of the thorns on this path. Smart city initiatives offer a glimmer of hope, leveraging technology to transform urban landscapes into efficient, sustainable, and citizen-centric ecosystems. At the heart of these initiatives lie smart city platforms—the digital nerve centers that collect, analyze, and disseminate urban data to power intelligent decision-making and service delivery. This works focuses into the intricate world of smart city platforms, drawing insights from three key research papers [32]. We will explore the technical architecture for big data processing, the significance of context awareness in platform design, and the evaluation of existing platforms based on functional and non-functional requirements. By weaving these perspectives together, we aim to provide a comprehensive analysis of smart city platforms and their potential to revolutionize urban living.

The ever-increasing volume, variety, and velocity of data generated in cities present a formidable challenge. Paper 1 tackles this head-on by proposing a technical architecture for big data processing specifically tailored to the smart city context. This architecture hinges on MapReduce, a powerful programming framework designed to efficiently handle massive datasets across distributed systems. This work focuses on a critical aspect of smart city initiatives—gathering citizen feedback to gauge their perception of various QoL indicators. However, raw survey data often lacks the quantitative muscle needed to inform policy decisions. Paper 1 proposes a solution by leveraging MapReduce to analyze citizen surveys and translate them into quantifiable measures. This empowers city planners to move beyond anecdotal evidence and make data-driven decisions that directly address the concerns of their constituents. For instance, imagine a city grappling with a perceived issue of safety in a particular neighborhood. Citizen surveys might reveal anxieties about late-night street lighting or a lack of police presence. Paper 1's approach would enable the platform to analyze these responses and generate quantifiable metrics for these concerns. This data could then be used to optimize street lighting schedules or strategically deploy mobile police patrols, leading to a demonstrably safer neighborhood.

Paper 2 broadens the scope by proposing a cloud-based, layered architecture for smart city platforms. This architecture goes beyond mere data collection and processing; it introduces the crucial concept of context awareness. Here, the platform does not treat all users or situations the same. Instead, it tailors its services and information delivery to the specific needs and circumstances of each user. Imagine a resident navigating the urban jungle during rush hour. A context-aware smart city platform would leverage real-time traffic data, their preferred mode of transportation, and even their historical travel patterns to suggest the most efficient route. This personalized approach not only enhances the user experience but also contributes to reduced traffic congestion and a more sustainable urban environment. Paper 2 meticulously details how context awareness is woven into the fabric of the platform at different levels. The platform integration layer ensures cross-platform accessibility of data, allowing the platform to gather contextual information from diverse sources like weather sensors, traffic cameras, and even social media feeds. The service composition layer utilizes this contextual information to design and deliver services that are truly relevant to the user's situation. Finally, the application service layer translates this information into actionable insights displayed through user-friendly interfaces, empowering citizens to make informed choices.

Whereas Papers 1 and 2 focus on theoretical frameworks, Paper 3 takes a pragmatic approach. It analyzes existing smart city platforms like CiDAP, OpenIoT, and GAMBAS against a set of pre-defined criteria. These criteria encompass both functional and non-functional requirements that a robust smart city platform must possess. Functional requirements delve into the core functionalities of the platform, its ability to perform essential tasks like data acquisition, storage, and analysis. Paper 3 evaluates how effectively these platforms handle large datasets, manage sensor networks, and execute various applications. Additionally, it assesses their ability to integrate with existing city infrastructure and provide software development tools for customization. Non-functional requirements encompass broader aspects that underpin the overall effectiveness and user trust in the platform. Security measures to safeguard sensitive citizen data and robust privacy protocols are paramount. The platform's ability to scale and adapt to the growing demands of a city is another crucial non-functional requirement. Finally, Paper 3 analyzes how these platforms cater to user needs through features like intuitive interfaces and accessibility considerations. By evaluating existing platforms based on these essential criteria, Paper 3 provides valuable insights for city planners looking to implement smart city initiatives. They can leverage this analysis to identify platforms that best suit their specific needs and priorities, ensuring a robust foundation for their smart city endeavors.

The comparative analysis in Table 13.3 serves as a concise reference point, distilling the core contributions and limitations of each research paper explored. It allows for a swift understanding of how these papers collectively inform the development of future-proof smart city platforms. Focusing on Paper 1, the Table 13.3 highlights its strength in establishing a foundation for efficient data analysis through big data processing frameworks like MapReduce. This empowers cities to translate qualitative citizen feedback on QoL indicators into quantifiable metrics. Paper 1's limitation lies in its lack of discussion on context awareness, which is a critical element for personalized services in smart cities. Paper 2, as reflected in the Table 13.3, presents a valuable contribution by introducing the concept of context awareness within a layered cloud-based platform architecture. This enables the platform to tailor information delivery and services based on individual user needs and situations. However, Paper 2 does not delve into the specifics of big data processing, assuming that aspect is already addressed. Paper 3 takes a pragmatic approach by evaluating existing smart city platforms like CiDAP, OpenIoT, and GAMBAS. This analysis provides valuable benchmarks for cities looking to implement smart city initiatives. Table 13.3 emphasizes Paper 3's strength in offering insights into platform capabilities based on pre-defined functional (data management and application execution) and non-functional (security, privacy, and scalability) requirements. However, Paper 3 does not propose a new platform architecture itself but rather guides city planners in selecting the most suitable existing platform based on their specific needs.

Table 13.3 Comparative analysis of smart city platforms.

Feature	Paper 1 [29]	Paper 2 [27]	Paper 3 [25]
Focus	Big data processing for smart cities	Layered architecture with context awareness	Evaluation of existing platforms
Technical Approach	MapReduce for analyzing citizen surveys	Cloud-based, layered architecture with emphasis on context awareness	N/A (focuses on existing platforms)
Key Contribution	Enables data-driven decision making based on quantified QoL measures	Introduces context awareness for personalized services	Provides benchmarks for evaluating platforms based on functional and non-functional requirements
Strengths	Efficient handling of large datasets	Tailored information delivery based on user needs	Practical insights into existing platform capabilities
Limitations	Lacks discussion on context awareness	Does not delve into big data processing details	Does not propose a new platform architecture
Relevance to Future Platforms	Provides foundation for efficient data analysis	Emphasizes importance of context awareness in platform design	Informs platform selection based on city-specific needs

In conclusion, the comparative analysis in Table 13.3 acts as a bridge, connecting the insights from each paper and guiding the development of future smart city platforms. By considering the strengths and limitations of existing approaches alongside additional considerations for security, interoperability, scalability, and citizen engagement, cities can leverage the power of smart city platforms to create a more efficient, sustainable, and citizen-centric urban future.

13.4.1 Findings from Comparative Analysis

The concept of smart cities, driven by the integration of technology to improve urban living conditions, has garnered considerable attention and momentum in recent years. This movement toward smart urban development seeks to leverage technological advancements to address various challenges faced by cities, including traffic congestion, environmental sustainability, and resource management. At the heart of these endeavors lie smart city platforms, serving as the nerve center that orchestrates the collection, analysis, and dissemination of data. Smart city platforms play a pivotal role in aggregating data from various sources, including sensors, IoT devices, and public records. This vast pool of data provides city administrators and policymakers with valuable insights into urban dynamics, enabling them to make data-driven decisions that positively impact citizen well-being. By harnessing advanced analytics and visualization tools, these platforms empower stakeholders to identify trends, anticipate challenges, and implement targeted interventions to enhance the overall QoL within urban environments.

In this analysis, we delve into the findings of three research papers that explore different facets of smart city platforms. Each paper offers unique perspectives on topics such as data management, platform architecture, and citizen engagement strategies. Through a comparative analysis, we aim to distill the strengths, limitations, and key insights gleaned from these papers, shedding light on the evolving landscape of smart city development. Furthermore, we extend our inquiry beyond the technical realm covered in the research papers to explore additional considerations crucial for the future evolution of smart city platforms. These considerations encompass a broad spectrum of factors, including cybersecurity measures to safeguard sensitive data, interoperability standards to ensure seamless integration with existing systems, scalability strategies to accommodate growing urban populations, and innovative approaches to enhance citizen engagement and participation in decision-making processes. By examining these multifaceted aspects of smart city platforms, we gain a holistic understanding of the challenges and opportunities inherent in urban technology initiatives. Through continuous refinement and innovation, smart city platforms have the potential to serve as catalysts for positive urban transformation, driving sustainable development, fostering inclusive growth, and ultimately improving the QoL for urban residents around the world.

The three research papers explored offer valuable insights into various aspects of smart city platforms. The first paper focuses on big data processing frameworks like MapReduce to analyze citizen surveys on QoL indicators. This paper highlights the need for efficient data processing to extract useful insights from large datasets. These insights are key for making informed decisions that can help address the concerns of citizens. However, it lacks discussion on context awareness, a crucial element for personalized services in smart cities. The second paper introduces the concept of context awareness within a layered cloud-based platform architecture. This personalizes information delivery and services based on individual user needs and situations. The paper highlights the significance of context awareness for enhancing user experience and citizen engagement, providing a framework for tailoring services based on real-time data and user context. However, it does not delve into the specifics of big data processing, assuming that aspect is already addressed. The third paper analyzes existing smart city platforms like CiDAP, OpenIoT, and GAMBAS based on functional and non-functional requirements. It provides valuable benchmarks for cities looking to implement smart city initiatives, offering insights into platform capabilities across data management, application execution, security, privacy, and scalability. However, the paper does not propose a new platform architecture but helps cities select existing platforms based on their specific needs.

The comparative analysis reveals several key takeaways for building future-proof smart city platforms. Efficient data processing frameworks are essential for analyzing vast amounts of data generated by sensors, surveys, and citizen interactions. This empowers city authorities to make informed decisions based on quantifiable metrics rather than relying solely on intuition or anecdotal evidence. Integrating context awareness into the platform architecture allows for personalized services that cater to individual user needs and situations. Imagine a platform that suggests the most efficient route during rush hour, considering factors like a user's preferred mode of transportation, real-time traffic conditions, and even historical travel patterns. This personalization enhances user experience and fosters citizen engagement. Evaluating existing platforms like CiDAP, OpenIoT, and GAMBAS provides valuable insights for city planners. Understanding the strengths and weaknesses of these platforms allows cities to select the most suitable solution based on their specific needs and priorities. CiDAP, for instance, might excel in handling real-time data but lack robust developer tools, while OpenIoT, with its focus on social network integration, could be ideal for fostering citizen participation. While the research papers highlight important technical aspects, building robust smart city platforms necessitates a broader perspective. This section explores additional considerations that contribute to a thriving smart city ecosystem. Building trust with citizens requires robust security measures and unwavering commitment to data privacy. This includes data encryption, granular access controls, and adherence to data privacy regulations like General Data

Protection Regulation (GDPR). Citizens should have control over their personal information and be informed about data collection practices. Seamless information exchange is crucial. Standardized data formats and communication protocols ensure different sensors, devices, and platforms can communicate effectively and prevent data silos. Open APIs empower third-party developers to create innovative applications leveraging the platform's data and functionalities. As cities grow, the platform needs to accommodate increasing data volumes and user base without compromising performance. A scalable architecture, often cloud-based, ensures smooth operation even as demands expand. Sustainability considerations include energy-efficient infrastructure, promoting renewable energy sources, and implementing data management practices like compression and purging to minimize storage requirements.

Citizen participation stands as a cornerstone in the development and success of smart city platforms. These platforms, designed to enhance urban living through technological innovation, must prioritize user engagement to effectively address the diverse needs and preferences of city residents. Central to this objective is the design of user-friendly interfaces that accommodate individuals with varying levels of technical expertise. By ensuring intuitive navigation and clear presentation of information, smart city platforms can empower citizens to access and utilize the services and resources available to them. Moreover, embracing a multifaceted approach to communication is essential in facilitating citizen engagement. Offering multiple channels for interaction, such as mobile applications, community forums, and social media platforms, cultivates a diverse ecosystem where citizens can contribute feedback, share insights, and actively participate in decision-making processes. This two-way communication not only enables city authorities to disseminate information effectively but also fosters an environment of transparency and inclusivity, where citizens feel valued and heard. Inclusivity is a fundamental principle that underpins the design and implementation of smart city platforms. Accessibility is crucial to make sure everyone, regardless of physical or cognitive abilities, can use and benefit from these platforms. Following accessibility standards and adding features like screen readers, alternative text, and keyboard navigation allows smart city platforms to meet the needs of people with disabilities. This helps promote fairness and inclusivity in cities.

13.4.2 Analysis

Smart cities of the future must harness the power of data, transforming it into actionable insights. While techniques like MapReduce are foundational for processing citizen feedback and surveys, smart cities must go beyond this. Real-time sensor data (traffic, air quality), social media analysis, and predictive analytics offer a more holistic view for decision-making. The key challenge lies in defining clear, quantifiable metrics linked to citizen wellbeing, resource efficiency, and economic development, ensuring the data translates into tangible improvements. To further empower citizens and foster trust, governments should invest in data literacy programs for both policymakers and the public. Platforms should be context-aware, adapting services and recommendations to individual needs based on data like traffic, weather, and personal preferences. However, navigating the balance between hyper-personalization and privacy will be crucial and requires strong ethical guidelines. Choosing the right smart city platform, cities must consider factors like ease of use, accessibility, and cost-benefit analysis, including the long-term financial impact. Rigorous security and privacy protocols are non-negotiable platform demands a rigorous process that goes beyond technical specifications. Ensuring that smart city platforms prioritize ease of use for citizens across all demographics is essential for fostering widespread adoption and participation. This involves designing intuitive interfaces, clear navigation paths, and simplified processes that cater to users with varying levels of technological proficiency. Accessibility features should go beyond basic compliance with regulations and standards, taking into account the diverse needs of individuals with disabilities or impairments. By incorporating features such as screen readers, alternative input methods, and customizable settings, smart city platforms can ensure inclusivity and empower all citizens to access and engage with city services effectively.

Smart cities need to be built on open standards and APIs to ensure seamless data exchange between devices, platforms, and various city departments. The challenge lies in integrating new technologies with legacy systems (traffic management, utilities) that often operate on outdated protocols. A focus on interoperability should extend beyond the city limit, ensuring collaboration for regional solutions in areas like transportation and emergency response. The design for smart city platforms must be modular and allow for incremental upgrades to accommodate additional sensors, new services, and population growth. Sustainability must be at the core, with focus on energy-efficient infrastructure and the platform's role in driving city-wide sustainability efforts (optimized building management and smart grid). Proactive resiliency planning with built-in redundancies is crucial as these platforms become central to core city functions. Figure 13.4 presents the application of smart city.

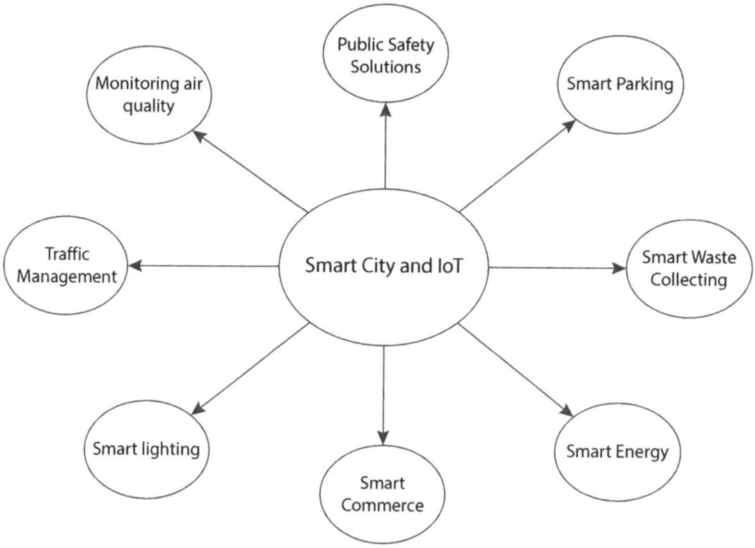

Figure 13.4 Applications of IoT in smart city.

Adaptability is another crucial aspect that governments must prioritize when developing smart city platforms. As technologies evolve and citizen needs change over time, platforms must be flexible and adaptable to accommodate these shifts. This includes adopting open standards and modular architectures that facilitate seamless integration of new technologies and services. By future-proofing smart city platforms, governments can ensure longevity and relevance in the face of rapid technological advancements and evolving urban dynamics. Conducting comprehensive cost-benefit analysis is vital for evaluating the impact and return on investment of smart city platforms. In addition to assessing short-term financial implications, such as implementation costs and operational expenses, governments should incorporate long-term financial modeling into their analysis. This involves projecting the platform's benefits and costs over an extended period, considering factors such as maintenance, upgrades, and potential revenue streams. Regular citizen feedback surveys are also essential for measuring the platform's actual impact on citizen satisfaction, engagement, and QoL. By soliciting input from residents and stakeholders, governments can gauge the effectiveness of smart city initiatives, identify areas for improvement, and justify continued investment in these platforms.

Open data and transparency are foundational principles that underpin trust in smart city governance. Governments should prioritize making data openly accessible and transparent to citizens, fostering accountability and empowering residents to participate in decision-making processes. Clear citizen education about data usage is crucial for building trust and ensuring that residents understand how their data is collected, stored, and utilized. By promoting transparency and educating citizens about the benefits and risks of data sharing, governments can foster a culture of trust and collaboration in smart city initiatives, ultimately leading to more inclusive and citizen-centric urban development. The most powerful smart city platforms should adapt to individual needs and situations. A layered, cloud-based architecture enables the use of real-time data on traffic patterns, weather conditions, user preferences, and even health information (with strong privacy safeguards) to personalize services from commute recommendations to targeted healthcare suggestions. Cities must proactively address the ethical gray areas—how much personalization is acceptable and how can platforms avoid becoming overly intrusive.

Interoperability and scalability form the backbone of effective smart city platforms. These platforms must be designed with the ability to seamlessly integrate with existing infrastructure, breaking down silos across various city departments and even extending interoperability to regional and national networks. By ensuring compatibility and connectivity across disparate systems, smart city platforms can leverage the collective intelligence of diverse datasets and resources, enabling more informed decision-making and optimized resource allocation. Moreover, sustainability considerations are paramount in the design and operation of smart city platforms. Beyond minimizing the platform's energy footprint, it is essential to evaluate how the platform contributes to broader city sustainability goals, such as reducing carbon emissions, conserving resources, and enhancing resilience to climate change. By adopting sustainable practices and technologies, smart city platforms can set an example for environmentally conscious urban development and contribute to the creation of more livable and resilient cities.

Citizen engagement should be integrated into every stage of smart city platform development, rather than treated as an afterthought. Inclusive design approaches ensure that platforms cater to the diverse needs and preferences of all residents, including those facing digital barriers or accessibility challenges. Addressing the digital divide through targeted outreach and support programs ensures that the benefits of smart city initiatives are accessible to every resident, regardless of socioeconomic status or technological literacy. To bridge the gap between theory and practice, real-world pilots of new citizen participation models and rural smart city applications are essential. These pilot projects provide valuable insights into the practical challenges and opportunities of implementing smart city solutions in diverse urban and rural contexts. Additionally, comprehensive evaluation frameworks are needed to assess the effectiveness and impact of smart city initiatives, guiding future development efforts and investment decisions.

Governments play a crucial role in fostering innovation through open data initiatives. By making data openly accessible and encouraging collaboration with external stakeholders, governments can create a vibrant ecosystem for innovation and entrepreneurship, driving the development of new smart city solutions and services. Security and privacy must be embedded into the smart city platform from the start, not treated as an afterthought. Proactive vulnerability testing, data encryption, strict access controls, and clear data usage policies are essential. Governments need to educate citizens about data collection and risks involved and provide opt-out options without losing access to essential services. Smart cities that place robust privacy as a core value can differentiate themselves and attract privacy-conscious residents and businesses. Figure 13.5 presents the blueprint of smart city governance.

Genuine citizen participation must be at the heart of smart city development. Involving diverse citizen groups through co-design processes from the platform's initial conception will lead to more inclusive and equitable solutions. A key question is whether smart city platforms can successfully bridge the digital divide and provide benefits across socioeconomic groups. Interfaces should be multilingual and designed with accessibility in mind, ensuring no citizen is left behind.

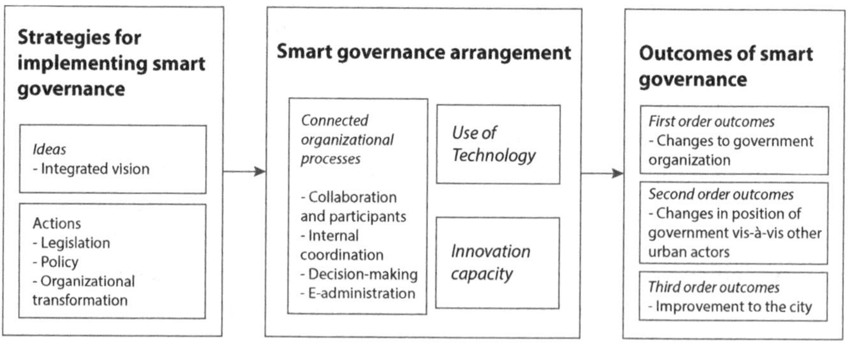

Figure 13.5 Smart city governance.

13.4.3 Future Scope

Table 13.4 goes beyond the individual papers by highlighting additional considerations crucial for future smart city platforms. These include robust security measures and data privacy protocols to build trust with citizens. Additionally, standardized data formats and communication protocols are emphasized to ensure interoperability between various sensors, devices, and platforms used by the city. Scalability and sustainability are also noted as critical aspects—the platform architecture should adapt to accommodate a growing city while minimizing environmental impact.

Table 13.4 underscores the importance of citizen engagement through user-friendly interfaces, diverse communication channels, and accessibility features that promote inclusivity for all citizens. Table 13.5 demonstrates the key areas crucial for the future advancement of smart city platforms. Engaging citizens and integrating data are fundamental aspects, yet challenges such as diverse participation and addressing rural needs persist. Bridging technological gaps is essential for seamless integration and effective decision-making.

Holistic frameworks are necessary for comprehensive planning, but achieving integration and adaptability presents challenges. Open data initiatives can foster transparency and collaboration, but data privacy and governance issues must be addressed. Ethical considerations, such as algorithmic bias and accountability, are paramount to building trust and credibility. Future research should focus on inclusive governance models, rural technology advancements, effective data governance frameworks, fairness mechanisms, and transparency in algorithmic decision-making.

Table 13.4 Additional consideration for future platforms.

Aspect	Description
Security and Privacy	Robust security measures, data encryption, and adherence to privacy regulations (GDPR)
Interoperability and Standardization	Standardized data formats and communication protocols (open geospatial consortium (OGC) standards)
Scalability and Sustainability	Architecture designed for growth and energy-efficient infrastructure
Citizen Engagement and Inclusivity	User-friendly interfaces, multiple communication channels, and accessibility features

Table 13.5 Key areas for the future of smart city platforms.

Key area	Summary	Challenges	Future research	Practical implications
Bridging the Gaps	Engage citizens and integrate data	Diverse participation, rural needs, and tech integration	Inclusive governance and rural tech	Inclusive decision-making and long-term planning
Holistic Frameworks	Comprehensive planning	Integration and adaptability	Lifecycle management and tech planning	Strategic planning and long-term relevance
Open Data and Collaboration	Foster transparency and collaboration	Data privacy and governance	Data governance and quality assurance	Innovation ecosystems and collaboration
Ethical Considerations	Ensure transparency and fairness	Algorithmic bias and accountability	Fairness mechanisms and transparency	Build trust and enhance credibility

Practically, this entails inclusive decision-making processes, long-term planning strategies, improved lifecycle management, strategic technology planning, transparent and accountable governance practices, fostering innovation ecosystems, and promoting collaboration among stakeholders. Prioritizing ethical considerations can ensure that smart city technologies are deployed in a manner that respects individual rights and promotes social equity and justice, ultimately enhancing the credibility and sustainability of smart city initiatives.

13.5 Conclusion

Research investigating citizen views on smart city projects appears limited, especially when contrasted with the abundance of technical advancements and abstract models of smart city management. Considering the objectives and obstacles faced by smart cities globally, a more nuanced comprehension of the stakeholders involved should be central to the discussion. This study recognizes the constraints in accurately measuring these viewpoints, and thus, conclusions drawn from existing data should not be treated as absolute. The study highlights the limitations and challenges associated with attempting to capture citizen perceptions comprehensively. The multifaceted nature of citizen attitudes and expectations, coupled with the complexity of smart city initiatives, poses challenges in gathering and interpreting relevant data. Moreover, the dynamic and evolving nature of technology and urban development further complicates efforts to draw definitive conclusions from available data. Looking ahead, future research should continue to explore the intricacies of citizen engagement and perception in smart city contexts. This includes delving deeper into the factors influencing citizen attitudes, the effectiveness of various communication and engagement strategies, and the impact of citizen participation on the outcomes of smart city projects. Additionally, there is a need to recognize and incorporate diverse perspectives, ensuring that the voices of marginalized or underrepresented communities are heard and valued in the development of smart cities. Ultimately, fostering an inclusive and participatory approach to smart city governance is essential for building sustainable, equitable, and resilient urban environments.

References

1. Alam, T., Cloud-Based IoT Applications and Their Roles in Smart Cities. *Smart Cities*, 4, 3, 1196–1219, 2021. https://doi.org/10.3390/smartcities4030064.
2. Khan, Z., Anjum, A., Kiani, S.L., Cloud Based Big Data Analytics for Smart Future Cities, in: *2013 IEEE/ACM 6th International Conference on Utility and Cloud Computing*, Dresden, Germany, pp. 381–386, 2013, doi: 10.1109/UCC.2013.77.
3. Khan, Z., *et al.* Towards cloud based big data analytics for smart future cities. *J. Cloud Comp.*, 4, 1–11, 2015.
4. Khan, Z. and Kiani, S.L., A Cloud-Based Architecture for Citizen Services in Smart Cities, in: *2012 IEEE Fifth International Conference on Utility and Cloud Computing*, Chicago, IL, USA, pp. 315–320, 2012, doi: 10.1109/UCC.2012.43.
5. López-Quiles, J.M. and Rodríguez Bolívar, M.P., Smart Technologies for Smart Governments: A Review of Technological Tools in Smart Cities, in: *Smart Technologies for Smart Governments. Public Administration and Information Technology*, vol. 24, M. Rodríguez Bolívar, (Ed.), Springer, Cham, 2018.
6. Anttiroiko, A.V. and Komninos, N., Smart Public Services: Using Smart City and Service Ontologies in Integrative Service Design, in: *Setting Foundations for the Creation of Public Value in Smart Cities. Public Administration and Information Technology*, vol. 35, M.P. Rodriguez Bolivar, (Ed.), Springer, Cham, 2019.

7. Howell, S., Hippolyte, J., Jayan, B., Reynolds, J., Rezgui, Y., Web-based 3D urban decision support through intelligent and interoperable services, in: *2016 IEEE International Smart Cities Conference (ISC2)*, 2016.
8. Bhalotia, N., Kumar, M., Alameen, A., Mohapatra, H., Kolhar, M., A helping hand to the elderly: securing their freedom through the HAIE framework. *Appl. Sci.*, 13, 11, 6797, 2023.
9. Young, J.C., Rural digital geographies and new landscapes of social resilience, *J. Rural Stud.* 70, 66–74, 2019.
10. Gil, O., Cortés-Cediel, M., Cantador, I., Citizen participation and the rise of digital media platforms in smart governance and smart cities, *Int. J. E-Planning Res. (IJEPR)*, 8, 1, 19–34, 2019.
11. Díaz-Díaz, R., Muñoz, L., Pérez-González, D., Business model analysis of public services operating in the smart city ecosystem: The case of SmartSantander. *Future Gener. Comput. Syst.*, 76, 198–214, 2017.
12. Vidiasova, L. and Cronemberger, F., Discrepancies in perceptions of smart city initiatives in Saint Petersburg, Russia. *Sustain. Cities Soc.*, 59, 102158, 2020.
13. Turoń, K., Kubik, A., Ševčovič, M., Tóth, J., Lakatos, A., Visual Communication in Shared Mobility Systems as an Opportunity for Recognition and Competitiveness in Smart Cities. *Smart Cities*, 5, 3, 802–818, 2022.
14. Kim, C. and Kim, K., The institutional change from E-Government toward Smarter City; comparative analysis between royal borough of Greenwich, UK, and Seongdong-gu, South Korea. *J. Open Innovation: Technology, Market, and Complexity*, 7.1, 42, 2021.
15. Kuzior, A., Pakhnenko, O., Tiutiunyk, I., Lyeonov, S., E-Governance in Smart Cities: Global Trends and Key Enablers. *Smart Cities*, 6, 4, 1663–1689, 2023.
16. Wirtz, B.W., Müller, W.M., Schmidt, F.W., Digital Public Services in Smart Cities – an Empirical Analysis of Lead User Preferences. *Public Organiz. Rev.*, 21, 299–315, 2021.
17. Moreno, C., Allam, Z., Chabaud, D., Gall, C., Pratlong, F., Introducing the "15-Minute City": Sustainability, Resilience and Place Identity in Future Post-Pandemic Cities. *Smart Cities*, 4, 1, 93–111, 2021.
18. Garaus, M. and Garaus, C., The Impact of the COVID-19 Pandemic on Consumers' Intention to Use Shared-Mobility Services in German Cities. *Front. Psychol.*, 12, 646593, 2021.
19. Han, M.J.N. and Kim, M.J., A critical review of the smart city in relation to citizen adoption towards sustainable smart living. *Habitat Int.*, 108, 102312, 2021. ISSN 0197-3975.
20. Mohapatra, H. and Mishra, S.R., Unlocking insights: exploring data analytics and AI tool performance across industries, in: *Data Analytics and Machine Learning: Navigating the Big Data Landscape*, pp. 265–288, Springer Nature Singapore, Singapore, 2024.

21. Hyman, B.T., Alisha, Z., Gordon, S., Secure controls for smart cities; applications in intelligent transportation systems and smart buildings. *Int. J. Sci. Eng. Appl.*, *8*, 6, 167–171, 2019.
22. Naser, A. and Kamrani, A.K., *Intelligent transportation and evacuation planning: a modeling-based approach*, Springer Science & Business Media, 2012.
23. Roy, S. and Sarddar, D., The role of cloud of things in smart cities. *arXiv preprint arXiv:1704.07905.*, 2017.
24. Cosgrove, M., Harthoorn, W., Hogan, J., Jabbar, R., Kehoe, M., Meegan, J., Nesbitt, P., Smarter cities series: Introducing the IBM city operations and management solution. *IBM Corporation*, 2011.
25. Karwa, N.A. and Ravi, K., Study of System Approaches in Evaluation of Smart Cities-Planning Guidelines for New Smart Cities in Indian Context, 2015.
26. Carrino, F., Mugellini, E., Abou Khaled, O., Ouerhani, N., Ehrensberger, J., iNUIT: Internet of Things for Urban Innovation. *Future Internet.*, 8, 2, 18, 2016.
27. Silva, B.N., Khan, M., Han, K., Towards sustainable smart cities: A review of trends, architectures, components, and open challenges in smart cities. *Sustain. Cities Soc.*, *38*, 697–713, 2018.
28. Branchi, P.E., Fernández-Valdivielso, C., Matias, I.R., Analysis Matrix for Smart Cities. *Future Internet.*, 6, 1, 61–75, 2014.
29. Chai, N., Mao, C., Ren, M., *et al.*, Retracted Article: Role of BIC (Big Data, IoT, and Cloud) for Smart Cities. *Arab. J. Sci. Eng.*, 48, 4115, 2023.
30. Lanza, J., Sánchez, L., Gutiérrez, V., Galache, J.A., Santana, J.R., Sotres, P., Muñoz, L., Smart City Services over a Future Internet Platform Based on Internet of Things and Cloud: The Smart Parking Case. *Energies.*, 9, 9, 719, 2016.
31. Mohapatra, H., *The future of smart agriculture*. Nova science publishers, incorporated, 2023.
32. Visvizi, A., and Lytras, M.D., Sustainable smart cities and smart villages research: Rethinking security, safety, well-being, and happiness. *Sustainability*, 12, 1, 215, 2019.

Part 3

FUTURE TRENDS AND APPLICATIONS IN HYPER INTELLIGENT NETWORK

14

Foundations and Advancements in Hyper-Intelligent Networks

D. Krishna Madhuri[1]* and Madhusmita Majhi[2]

[1]Department of Artificial Intelligence and Data Science, Faculty of Science and Technology (IcfaiTech), ICFAI Foundation for Higher Education, Hyderabad, India
[2]Department of Computer Science and Engineering, Faculty of Science and Technology (IcfaiTech), ICFAI Foundation for Higher Education, Hyderabad, Telangana, India

Abstract
Hyper-intelligent networks exemplify a new era of connectivity, driven by artificial intelligence, machine learning, and big data analytics. Internet-of-Things devices integrated these data, sensors, and social media into active systems for real-time insights, enhancing effectiveness over predictive maintenance and proactive risk management. These networks learn continuously and progress, adapting to user behaviors and improving performance. By development collaboration and breaking down silos, hyper-intelligent networks excite innovation across sectors. They enable data sharing and seamless communication, enhancing productivity and nurturing transformative solutions. Security measures like blockchain and encryption ensure data integrity privacy compliance and vindicate cyber risks. The future of hyper-intelligent networks holds huge potential in transportation, finance, healthcare, and beyond. By leveraging adaptive intelligence and interconnectedness, these networks' ability to revolutionize industries, improve quality of life, and drive justifiable economic growth for Hyper Intelligent network. Their transformative impact authorizes organizations to navigate challenges, seize opportunities, and shape a cheerful future through technological advancement and innovations.

***Keywords*:** Hyper-intelligent networks, big data analytics (BDA), real-time insights, proactive risk management, seamless communication, cybersecurity, blockchain

**Corresponding author*: krishnamadhuri@ifheindia.org

Pradosh Kumar Gantayat, Sandeep Kumar Panda, S. Balamurugan and Sheng-Lung Peng (eds.) Hyper-Intelligent Networks: Exploring the Future of Connectivity for Society 5.0, (299–324) © 2026 Scrivener Publishing LLC

14.1 History of Hyper-Intelligent Networks

The past of hyper-intelligent networks (HINs), often associated with cutting-edge artificial intelligence (AI) and deep learning (DL), is an attractive journey noticeable by substantial milestones and breakthroughs. Here is an overview of their evolution [1, 2]:

Neural Networks (1940s–1950s) [3–6]: The impression of artificial neural networks was proposed in the 1940s, encouraged by the biological neural networks in the brain. Early models were simplistic and theoretical, lacking practical applications due to limited computational power.

Perceptrons (1950s–1960s) [7–9]: In the late 1950s, the researchers developed the perceptron, a form of neural network capable of learning through supervised training. Perceptrons could classify inputs into binary outputs, laying foundational concepts for later developments.

AI Winter and Resurgence (1970s–1980s) [10, 11]: The periods of the 1970s and 1980s saw eras known as "AI winters," where capital and interest in AI research waned due to unmet expectations. Despite setbacks, neural network research continued in academic circles, refining algorithms and architectures.

Backpropagation and Multilayer Perceptron (1980s) [12, 13]: The discovery of backpropagation during 1980s revolutionized neural network training. This algorithm allowed for effective adjustment of network weights based on errors, enabling deeper, multilayer perceptrons that could learn complex patterns.

Convolutional Neural Network (CNN) (1990s–2000s) [14–16]: The researchers work on CNNs in the late 1980s and early 1990s significantly advanced image recognition capabilities. CNNs use shared weights and pooling layers to efficiently process spatial data, becoming pivotal in computer vision tasks.

Recurrent Neural Networks (RNNs) and Long Short-Term Memory (LSTM) (1990s–2000s) [17, 18]: RNNs, designed for consecutive data, and LSTM networks, developed by Schmidhuber and Hochreiter in the mid-1990s, improved the handling of temporal dependencies, crucial for tasks like speech recognition and language modeling.

DL Resurgence (2010s–Present) [19, 20]: The 2010s witnessed a resurgence in DL, drove by developments in big data availability, computing power and algorithmic improvements. Deep neural networks (DNNs) with many layers (deep networks) achieved unprecedented accuracy in tasks like natural language processing, image classification, and game playing.

Generative Models and Reinforcement Learning (RL) (2010s–Present) [21–28]: One of the researchers, in 2014, introduced generative models like generative adversarial networks (GANs), enabled the generation of realistic synthetic data. RL, collective with DNNs, achieved human-level performance in complex games like Go and Atari.

Current Trends and Challenges: Today, HINs continue to evolve with advancements in explainable AI, transfer learning, federated learning, and AI ethics. Research focuses on improving robustness, interpretability, and scalability, aiming for AI systems that are intelligent, ethical and trustworthy.

14.2 Introduction to Hyper-Intelligent Networks

In the realm of recent technology, the concept of HINs stands at the forefront of innovation. These networks represent an example shift in how we perceive and harness the power of interconnected systems, leveraging advanced machine learning (ML) and AI algorithms to achieve unprecedented levels of efficiency, adaptability, and problem-solving capabilities [29].

At its core, a HIN integrates cutting-edge AI technologies with robust network infrastructure, creating a dynamic ecosystem capable of autonomous decision-making and continuous optimization. Unlike traditional networks that rely primarily on human input and predefined rules, HINs possess the ability to learn from huge amounts of data in real time, making informed decisions instantaneously and autonomously.

The applications of HINs span across various sectors, from telecommunications and finance to healthcare and transportation. These networks can enhance operational efficiency, improve customer experiences, and enable predictive maintenance, thereby revolutionizing industries and driving innovation forward.

This summary groups the stage for exploring the details and transformative potential of HINs, as well as their prominence role in shaping the future of interconnected systems and advancing technological capabilities to unprecedented heights.

The communication network landscape is undergoing a dramatic transformation. Fueled by the fast development of the Internet of Things (IoT), big data, smart cities, and connected vehicles, these networks are becoming increasingly complex and critical to our daily lives. As a result, the importance of ensuring the resilience and smooth operation of these networks has never been greater [30].

Traditionally, network management relied heavily on manual processes for fault detection and resolution. However, the ever-growing complexity of modern networks, with their vast number of interconnected devices and applications, quickly renders this approach inefficient and unsustainable. This is where intelligent fault management systems (FMSs) powered by ML and AI come into play [70].

14.3 The Limitations of Manual Fault Management

The limitations of manual fault management become readily apparent when considering the following factors [31–35]:

14.3.1 Scalability Challenges

Manually managing a network with a rapidly growing number of devices and applications is simply not feasible. Human operators become overwhelmed by the sheer volume of data and alerts, leading to increased response times and potential service disruptions [43].

14.3.2 Limited Proactive Capabilities

Traditional methods are primarily reactive, focusing on identifying and resolving faults after they have occurred. Predictive maintenance, a crucial aspect of network resilience, becomes difficult to achieve with manual processes.

14.3.3 Human Error

Manual fault detection and diagnosis are prone to human error. Complex network issues can be challenging to diagnose accurately, leading to wasted time and resources.

14.4 The Advantages of Intelligent Fault Management

AI-powered FMS offers a compelling solution to address the limitations of manual fault management. Here is how:

14.4.1 Enhanced Automation

AI algorithms can automate a significant portion of network management tasks, including real-time data analysis, anomaly detection, and fault diagnosis. This frees up human operators to focus on more complex issues and strategic planning.

Machine Learning for Improved Performance: These algorithms can continuously learn from past data and network behaviour. This allows the FMS to identify patterns, predict potential problems, and optimize its performance over time.

14.4.2 Scalability and Adaptability

AI systems can readily scale to accommodate the growing complexity of networks. They can adapt to new network configurations, devices, and applications with minimal human intervention.

14.4.3 Predictive Maintenance

AI-powered FMS can analyze network performance data to predict potential issues before they occur. This allows for active care actions, minimizing down-time and ensuring optimal network performance.

Improved Decision-Making: By analyzing huge amounts of data and identifying root causes of faults, AI systems provide valuable insights to network administrators. This facilitates better decision-making for resolving issues and improving network resilience.

Historical Data Analysis: AI systems can track and analyze historical fault data, providing valued insights into network trends and weaknesses. This information can be used to advance network design, optimize resource allocating, and prevent future issues.

14.4.4 Intelligent Alerting

AI can filter and line up alerts based on severity and potential impact. This reduces alert fatigue for network administrators and ensures that they focus on the most critical issues first. To envision the capabilities of a new intelligent FMS to fully address the challenges of managing complex communication networks, a new generation of intelligent FMS is needed. This system should possess the following key capabilities:

Big Data Processing: The ability to ingest, process, and analyze large volumes of real-rime and historical data from diverse sources across the network.

Machine Learning and AI: These two advanced algorithms are used for root cause analysis, anomaly detection, and predictive maintenance.

Scalability and Modularity: The ability to seamlessly scale to accommodate network growth and integrate with existing network management systems.

Domain Agnostic Design: A modular design that can be easily adapted to different network architectures and functionalities.

Real-Time Correlation: The ability to correlate network events and alerts from various sources in real time to identify root causes and potential cascading failures.

Intelligent Alerting and Automation: The ability to generate actionable alerts for network administrators and automate routine tasks for faster resolution times.

The Path Forward: A hierarchical intelligent agent-based approach

Approach to Intelligent FMS design: A hierarchical structure of intelligent agents. These agents will be responsible for monitoring specific network segments or functionalities, collaborating and sharing information to provide a comprehensive view of network health. The system will leverage ML and AI to achieve the capabilities outlined above.

14.5 Concept of Intelligent Network

Intelligent network (IN) permits functionality to be distributed flexibility at different nodes on and off the network and allows the architecture to be updated to control the services.

These networks can discrete added services from its call switching system, making it simpler to add new user services [36–38].

AI technology entails remotely manageable and automatically regulating amplifiers and broadband nodes and also its management software. They have been intended to help operations advance eminence of services while keeping operational cost in control.

IN is a well-established technology in the telecommunications industry. Unlike HINs that are still a concept, INs are a standardized architecture used in both fixed-line and mobile networks. Here is a breakdown of IN system [71–74]:

Purpose of Intelligent Networks (INs):
INs were developed to provide more flexibility and functionality beyond basic call routing in telecommunication networks.

They enable services provider to offer value-added services on top of core network services like voice calls (PSTN) or mobile data (GSM) [39].

14.5.1 Key Components of IN

IN architecture separate services logic from core network functions:

Service Switching Point (SSP): Located within the telephone exchange, the SSP identifies situation where an additional service might be needed (e.g., call waiting and call forwarding).

Service Control Point (SCP): A central database containing service logic and subscriber information. The SSP communicates with the SCP to determine how to handle a specific service request.

Service Data Point (SDP) (Optional): An additional database that can store subscriber-specific data relevant to specific services.

14.5.2 Benefits of Intelligent Networks (INs)

Flexibility: New services can be added or modified without changing core network infrastructure.

Scalability: INs can handle a growing number of subscribers and services.

Customization: Service providers can offer differentiated services to cater to specific customer needs.

Rapid Service Deployment: New services can be rolled out quickly compared to traditional methods.

14.5.3 Applications of Intelligent Networks (INs)

INs are powerful technology that can be used to provide extensive services to users. They are an important part of the modern telecommunications infrastructure [40].

INs are a type of network architecture that allows for more flexibility and functionality than traditional networks. INs achieve this by separating call control logic from the core network, placing it in a centralized SCP. This SCP can then be programmed to provide a wide range of advanced services, such as:

Call Forwarding: This allows callers to forward their calls to another number, such as a voicemail box or another phone number.
Call Waiting: This allows callers to be notified of a second incoming call while they are already on a call.
Caller ID: This allows callers to see the phone number of the person calling them.
Voicemail: This allows callers to leave a message for the person they are calling if they are unavailable.
Call Conferencing: This allows multiple people to participate in a single phone call.
Call Screening: This allows callers to block calls from certain numbers.
Personalized Calling: This allows callers to set up preferences for how their calls are handled, such as whether they want to receive call waiting or voicemail.

INs are also used to provide a variety of mobile services, such as the following:

Short Messaging Service (SMS): This allows users to send and receive text messages.
Multimedia Messaging Service (MMS): This allows users to send and receive text messages, pictures, and videos.
Mobile Data: This allows users to access the internet on their mobile devices.

14.5.4 Limitations of Intelligent Networks (INs)

INs are primarily designed for voice calls and may not be as readily adaptable to newer data-driven services. The centralized architecture can create a single point of failure if the SCP experiences an outage. Implementing and managing INs can be complex and require specialized expertise.

Example of Intelligent Networks

An excellent example of an IN is a smart grid. It integrates advanced communication, control, and monitoring technologies with traditional electrical power systems to enhance the generation, distribution, and consumption of electricity. Here is how AI and other intelligent technologies are applied in a smart grid [41, 42, 70]:

1. Predictive Maintenance: AI algorithms analyze statistical data from sensors embedded in power lines, transformers, and other grid components to forecast equipment failures in advance. This positive approach decreases downtime and maintenance costs.
2. Dynamic Load Balancing: AI optimizes the distribution of electricity by dynamically adjusting voltage levels and rerouting power to balance loads across the grid. This improves overall efficiency and reliability.
3. Demand Response Management: AI-based systems analyze real-time data on electricity consumption patterns and grid conditions to incentivize consumers to adjust their electricity usage in peak times. This helps to reduce strain on the grid and avoid blackouts.
4. Integration of Renewable Energy: AI algorithms forecast renewable energy generation from sources like solar and wind. They optimize grid operations by scheduling electricity production and storage to match fluctuating renewable energy output.
5. Fault Detection and Self-Healing: AI-enabled analytics detect faults or anomalies in the grid, such as power outages or voltage fluctuations. Automated responses, such as rerouting power or isolating faulty segments, minimize disruptions and improve grid resilience.
6. Cybersecurity: Advanced AI algorithms monitor network traffic for distrustful activities and potential cyber threats. They can detect anomalies in real time and respond swiftly to ease risks, ensuring the security of critical infrastructure.
7. Data Analytics and Optimization: AI processes great volumes of data collected from smart meters, sensors, and other grid devices to identify inefficiencies and opportunities for enhancement. This data-driven approach enhances grid performance and operational efficiency.
8. Grid Edge Intelligence: AI at the grid edge, where local devices and sensors interact with the power grid, enables autonomous decision-making. Edge AI can optimize local energy consumption, storage, and distribution based on local conditions and user preferences.

INs encompass a variety of devices and components that integrate advanced technologies to enhance their functionality, efficiency, and responsiveness. Here are some examples of devices commonly found in INs:

14.6 Devices of Intelligent Networks

1. Smart Sensors and Actuators:

   - IoT Devices: IoT devices such as smart meters, environmental sensors, and industrial sensors gather real-time data on numerous parameters like temperature, humidity, energy consumption, and machine performance.
   - Actuators: These devices control physical processes or machinery based on inputs received from sensors or centralized systems, enabling automated adjustments and responses [60].

2. Edge Computing Devices [61, 62]:

   - Edge Servers: Compact servers deployed at the network edge process and analyze data locally before sending relevant information to centralized cloud servers. They reduce latency and bandwidth usage for time-sensitive applications.
   - Edge Gateways: Devices that facilitate communication between edge devices and centralized cloud services, ensuring seamless data transmission and integration.

3. Network Infrastructure Components [63]:

   - Software-Defined Networking (SDN) Controllers: Centralized controllers manage network traffic, routing, and policies dynamically, based on real-time data and application requirements.
   - Network Switches and Routers: These devices forward data packets between computer networks, ensuring efficient communication and data transmission within the network.

4. AI and ML Platforms [64, 65]:

   - AI Processors: Specialized hardware accelerators optimized for running AI algorithms, such as graphics processing units and tensor processing units.
   - AI Servers and Appliances: High-performance servers and appliances equipped with AI software frameworks for training and inference tasks.

5. Security Devices [66]:

   - Firewalls and Intrusion Detection Systems: Hardware devices or software applications monitor and control incoming and outgoing network traffic based on predefined security rules.
   - Security Cameras and Surveillance Systems: AI-powered cameras and systems that analyze video feeds for suspicious activities or anomalies in real time.

6. Cloud Computing Infrastructure [67]:

   - Virtualized Servers: Virtual machines or containers running on cloud servers to host applications and services, providing scalability and flexibility.
   - Storage Solutions: Cloud-based storage services and distributed file systems for storing and accessing large volumes of data across the network.

7. Collaborative Communication Devices [68]:

   - Unified Communication Platforms: Integrated systems that combine voice, video, messaging, and collaboration tools to facilitate seamless communication and teamwork among users.
   - Telepresence Robots: AI-enabled robots equipped with audiovisual communication capabilities, allowing remote users to participate in meetings or inspections as if they were physically present.

8. User Interface and Experience Devices [69]:

   - Smartphones and Tablets: Mobile devices equipped with applications that provide access to IN services, data analytics, and remote management capabilities.
   - Virtual Reality and Augmented Reality Headsets: Devices that overlay digital information onto the physical environment or create immersive virtual experiences, enhancing training, maintenance, and troubleshooting tasks.

14.7 Understanding the Difference between IN and HIN

14.7.1 Intelligence Level

INs rely on pre-defined rules and logic stored in the SCP, whereas HINs aim to achieve a higher level of intelligence through ML and autonomous decision-making [42, 44, 45].

Focus: INs focus on providing value-added services within telecommunication networks, whereas HINs encompass a broader range of applications and network management capabilities.
Maturity: IN is a mature technology with established standards, whereas HINs are a futuristic concept still under development.

Commonly agreed characteristics of intelligent systems include the following:

Learning: the ability to learn new behaviors from past experiences
Adaptability: the capability to adjust responses to changing environments or internal conditions
Robustness: the consistency of responses across a wide range of circumstances
Information Compression: capability to turn data into information and then into actionable knowledge
Extrapolation: capability to act reasonably when faced with a set of new (not previously experienced) circumstances

14.8 The Function of Artificial Intelligence in HIN

AI plays a crucial role in the development and operation of HINs, enhancing their capabilities across various dimensions. Here is how AI contributes to the functionality and effectiveness of these advanced networks [46–50]:

14.8.1 Network Management and Optimization

Predictive Analytics: Predictive analytics involves AI algorithms analyzing historical data and current network conditions to forecast traffic patterns, resource needs, and potential failures. This proactive strategy enables preemptive maintenance and efficient resource management.

Automated Network Configuration: Automated network configuration utilizes AI-driven systems to adjust network settings like bandwidth allocation and routing policies in response to dynamic traffic patterns and application demands.

14.8.2 Security Enhancement

Threat Detection and Response: AI-powered security systems continuously monitor network traffic problems and potential security pressures. ML algorithms can detect suspicious behavior patterns and swiftly respond to mitigate risks, such as identifying and blocking unauthorized access attempts [51].

Behavioral Analysis: AI analyzes user and device behavior to detect deviations from normal patterns, helping to prevent insider threats and identify compromised endpoints.

14.8.3 Fault Management and Self-Healing

Automated Troubleshooting: AI-enabled systems can diagnose network faults and performance issues in real time. They autonomously initiate corrective actions, such as rerouting traffic or reallocating resources, to minimize downtime and maintain service continuity.

Self-Healing Networks: Through AI, networks can self-heal by automatically reconfiguring themselves in response to failures or congestion, optimizing performance and reliability without human intervention.

Customer Experience and Service Delivery:

- **Personalized Services**: AI algorithms analyze user preferences and behavior to personalize services and content delivery. This enhances customer satisfaction by offering tailored experiences and recommendations based on individual needs.
- **Intelligent Customer Support**: AI motorized chatbots and virtual assistants provide responsive and accurate customer support, handling inquiries, troubleshooting issues, and even performing basic network diagnostics.

Operational Efficiency and Resource Management:

Optimized Resource Allocation: AI optimizes the allocation of computing, storage, and network resources based on demand fluctuations and workload characteristics. This ensures efficient resource utilization and cost savings [52].

Energy Efficiency: AI algorithms can optimize power consumption by dynamically adjusting energy usage in response to workload variations and environmental conditions, contributing to sustainability efforts.

Real-Time Decision Making and Adaptation:

Adaptive Network Policies: AI-driven decision-making processes enable networks to dynamically adjust policies and configurations in response to changing conditions, such as shifting traffic patterns or emerging security threats.

Continuous Learning: AI systems learn from ongoing interactions and feedback to improve their decision-making capabilities over time, adapting to evolving network requirements and user behaviors.

14.9 Types of Intelligent Networks

INs encompass various types, each characterized by specific functionalities and capabilities tailored to different aspects of network operations and services. Here are some of the key types of INs [53–55]:

14.9.1 Artificial Intelligence (AI) Networks

AI networks utilize ML algorithms to analyze data, predict trends, automate decision-making, and optimize network performance. They are capable of learning from data patterns and adapting to changing conditions in real time.

14.9.2 Machine Learning Networks

These networks focus on leveraging ML techniques to improve network operations, security, and efficiency. They can autonomously detect anomalies, predict failures, and optimize resource allocation based on historical data and ongoing monitoring.

14.9.3 Cognitive Networks

Cognitive networks incorporate advanced AI capabilities to mimic human thought processes, enabling them to learn, reason, and make decisions autonomously. They are designed to handle complex tasks, adapt to new situations, and optimize network performance dynamically.

14.9.4 Self-Organizing Networks (SON)

SONs automate the planning, configuration, optimization, and maintenance of network infrastructure. They use AI and optimization algorithms to self-adjust and self-optimize network parameters based on real-time data and performance metrics.

14.9.5 Software-Defined Networks (SDN)

SDNs separate the network control plane from the data plane, enabling centralized management and programmability of network infrastructure. They employ intelligent algorithms to dynamically allocate resources, configure network paths, and ensure efficient traffic management.

14.9.6 Intent-Based Networks (IBN)

IBNs interpret high-level business intents and translate them into network configurations and policies automatically. They use AI and ML to continuously monitor network behavior, enforce policies, and adapt to changing business requirements in real time.

14.9.7 Edge Computing Networks

These networks extend computing and data processing capabilities closer to the edge of the network, near where data is generated or consumed. They integrate intelligent edge devices with cloud-based services to improve latency, bandwidth efficiency, and application performance.

14.9.8 5G Networks (and Beyond)

Next-generation networks such as 5G incorporate intelligent capabilities to support ultra-low latency, massive connectivity, and high-speed data transfer. They utilize AI for network slicing, intelligent traffic management, and efficient resource allocation.

14.9.9 IoT Networks

IoT networks connect numerous devices and sensors to the internet, often employing intelligent algorithms to manage device communication, data processing, and security. They enable real-time monitoring, predictive maintenance, and automation in various industries.

14.10 Operations of Hyper-Intelligent Networks

A "hyper-intelligent cloud network" typically refers to a sophisticated and highly capable cloud computing infrastructure that leverages advanced technologies such as AI, ML, and big data analytics (BDA) to deliver superior performance, scalability, and intelligence, and agility to meet the demands of modern digital enterprises and users [56–59].

Key characteristics and aspects typically associated with a hyper-intelligent cloud network:

1. **AI and ML Integration**: The network utilizes AI and ML algorithms to optimize performance, predict user behavior, automate tasks, and improve overall efficiency.
2. **Advanced Analytics**: It employs BDA to process and derive insights from large volumes of data generated within the network, enabling real-time decision-making and proactive management.
3. **Scalability and Flexibility**: It is designed to scale effortlessly based on demand, allowing for dynamic resource allocation and flexible deployment options.
4. **Security and Privacy**: Emphasis is placed on robust security measures, including encryption, access controls, and threat detection systems, to protect data and ensure compliance with regulatory requirements.
5. **Edge Computing Capabilities**: Integration with edge computing enables data processing closer to the source, reducing latency and enhancing performance for latency-sensitive applications.
6. **Automation and Orchestration**: Automation tools and orchestration frameworks streamline management tasks, improve operational efficiency, and enable rapid deployment of new services.

7. **High Availability and Reliability**: Redundancy measures and fault-tolerant architectures ensure high availability and reliability of services, minimizing downtime and service interruptions.
8. **Cost Optimization**: Optimization algorithms help minimize costs associated with cloud resources by efficiently allocating and managing computing, storage, and networking resources.
9. **User Experience Focus**: It prioritizes delivering a seamless user experience through responsive applications, intuitive interfaces, and personalized services based on user preferences and behavior.
10. **Integration with IoT and other Technologies:** Integration with IoT devices and other emerging technologies extends the network's capabilities, enabling innovative use cases and expanding its potential applications.

14.11 Summary

The substance of HINs lies in their foundational principles, capabilities, and applications within the realm of AI. Here are the key aspects that define their substance:

1. **Advanced Neural Network Architectures:**
   - **Deep Learning:** HINs are typically based on DL architectures, which involve neural networks with many layers (deep networks). These architectures allow for hierarchical learning of complex patterns and features from data.
2. **Learning and Adaptation:**
   - **Training and Optimization:** These networks are trained using large datasets through techniques like backpropagation and gradient descent, enabling them to learn from examples and optimize their internal parameters (weights and biases).
3. **Complex Data Processing:**
   - **Multimodal Capabilities:** They can process and integrate diverse types of data such as images, text, and numerical data simultaneously, leveraging their ability to learn representations and extract meaningful features.

4. **High-Level Tasks:**
   - **Cognitive Abilities:** HINs are capable of performing cognitive tasks traditionally associated with human intelligence, such as image recognition, natural language understanding, decision-making, and problem-solving.
5. **Specialized Applications:**
   - **Domain-Specific Expertise:** They excel in specific domains such as computer vision (e.g., object detection and image segmentation), natural language processing (e.g., language translation and sentiment analysis), and robotics (e.g., autonomous navigation and manipulation).
6. **Advanced Techniques:**
   - **Generative Models:** They include advanced techniques like GANs for generating new data, RL for learning through trial and error, and transformer models for sequence processing tasks.
7. **Ethical and Responsible AI:**
   - **Ethics and Transparency:** There is increasing focus on ethical considerations, interpretability, and fairness in AI systems, ensuring that HINs are developed and deployed responsibly.
8. **Future Directions:**
   - **Continual Learning:** Research is ongoing to enable these networks to learn continuously from new data and adapt to changing environments without catastrophic forgetting.
   - **Generalization and Transfer Learning:** Efforts are also directed toward improving their ability to generalize across tasks and domains and to transfer knowledge from one task to another efficiently.

References

1. Panda, S.K. and Satapathy, S.C., An Investigation into Smart Contract Deployment on Ethereum Platform Using Web3.js and Solidity Using Blockchain, in: *Data Engineering and Intelligent Computing. Advances in Intelligent Systems and Computing*, vol. 1, V. Bhateja, S.C. Satapathy, C.M. Travieso-González, V.N.M. Aradhya (Eds.), Springer, Singapore, 2021, https://doi.org/10.1007/978-981-16-0171-2_52.
2. Panda, S.K., Rao, D.C., Satapathy, S.C., An Investigation into the Usability of Blockchain Technology in Internet of Things, in: *Data Engineering and*

Intelligent Computing. Advances in Intelligent Systems and Computing, vol. 1, V. Bhateja, S.C. Satapathy, C.M. Travieso-González, V.N.M. Aradhya (Eds.), Springer, Singapore, 2021, https://doi.org/10.1007/978-981-16-0171-2_53.

3. Panda, S.K., Dash, S.P., Jena, A.K., Optimization of Block Query Response Using Evolutionary Algorithm, in: *Data Engineering and Intelligent Computing. Advances in Intelligent Systems and Computing*, vol. 1, V. Bhateja, S.C. Satapathy, C.M. Travieso-González, V.N.M. Aradhya (Eds.), Springer, Singapore, 2021, https://doi.org/10.1007/978-981-16-0171-2_54.
4. Nanda, S.K., Panda, S.K., Das, M., Satapathy, S.C., Automating Vehicle Insurance Process Using Smart Contract and Ethereum, in: *Advances in Micro-Electronics, Embedded Systems and IoT. Lecture Notes in Electrical Engineering*, vol. 838, V.V.S.S.S. Chakravarthy, W. Flores-Fuentes, V. Bhateja, B. Biswal (Eds.), Springer, Singapore, 2022, https://doi.org/10.1007/978-981-16-8550-7_23.
5. Varaprasada Rao, K. and Panda, S.K., vol. 459, S.C. Satapathy, J.C.W. Lin, L.K. Wee, V. Bhateja, T.M. Rajesh (Eds.), Springer, Singapore, 2023, Https://Doi.Org/10.1007/978-981-19-1976-3_18.
6. Varaprasada Rao, K. and Panda, S.K., A Design Model of Copyright Protection System Based on Distributed Ledger Technology, in: *Computer Communication, Networking and IoT. Lecture Notes in Networks and Systems*, vol. 459, S.C. Satapathy, J.C.W. Lin, L.K. Wee, V. Bhateja, T.M. Rajesh (Eds.), Springer, Singapore, 2023, https://doi.org/10.1007/978-981-19-1976-3_17.
7. Panda, S.K., Elngar, A.A., Balas, V.E., Kayed, M., *Bitcoin and Blockchain: History and Current Applications*, 1st, CRC Press, 2020, https://doi.org/10.1201/9781003032588.
8. Panda, S.K., Jena, A.K., Swain, S.K., Satapathy, S.C. (Eds.), Springer, Intelligent Systems Reference Library, https://doi.org/10.1007/978-3-030-69395-4.
9. Sathya, A.R., Panda, S.K., Hanumanthakari, S., Enabling Smart Education System Using Blockchain Technology, in: *Blockchain Technology: Applications and Challenges. Intelligent Systems Reference Library*, vol. 203, S.K. Panda, A.K. Jena, S.K. Swain, S.C. Satapathy (Eds.), Springer, Cham, 2021, https://doi.org/10.1007/978-3-030-69395-4_10.
10. Lokre, S.S., Naman, V., Priya, S., Panda, S.K., Gun Tracking System Using Blockchain Technology, in: *Blockchain Technology: Applications and Challenges. Intelligent Systems Reference Library*, vol. 203, S.K. Panda, A.K. Jena, S.K. Swain, S.C. Satapathy (Eds.), Springer, Cham, 2021, https://doi.org/10.1007/978-3-030-69395-4_16.
11. Panda, S.K., Daliyet, S.P., Lokre, S.S., Naman, V., Distributed Ledger Technology in the Construction Industry Using Corda, in: *The New Advanced Society: Artificial Intelligence and Industrial Internet of Things Paradigm*, https://doi.org/10.1002/9781119884392.ch2.
12. Panda, S.K., Mohammad, G.B., Nandan Mohanty, S., Sahoo, S., Smart contract-based land registry system to reduce frauds and time delay. *Secur. Privacy*, e172, 2021. https://doi.org/10.1002/spy2.172.

13. Panda, S.K. and Satapathy, S.C., Drug traceability and transparency in medical supply chain using blockchain for easing the process and creating trust between stakeholders and consumers. *Pers. Ubiquit. Comput.*, 28, 75–91, 2024. https://doi.org/10.1007/s00779-021-01588-3.
14. Niveditha, V.R., Sekaran, K., Amandeep Singh, K., Panda, S.K., Effective prediction of bitcoin price using wolf search algorithm and bidirectional LSTM on internet of things data. *Int. J. Syst. Syst. Eng.*, 11, 3-4, 224–236.
15. Sri Arza, M. and Panda, S.K., An Integration of Blockchain and Machine Learning into the Health Care System, in: *Machine Learning Adoption in Blockchain-Based Intelligent Manufacturing*, vol. 1, pp. 33–58, DOI: 10.1201/9781003252009-3.
16. Murala, D.K., Panda, S.K., Swain, S.K., A survey on cloud computing security and privacy issues and challenges. *J. Adv. Res. Dyn. Control Syst.*, 11, 1276–1290, 2019.
17. Murala, D.K., Panda, S.K., Swain, S.K., Secure dynamic groups data sharing with modified revocable attribute-based encryption in cloud. *Int. J. Recent Technol. Eng. (IJRTE)*, 8, 4, 2019. ISSN: 2277-3878.
18. Murala, D.K., Panda, S.K., Swain, S.K., A novel hybrid approach for providing data security and privacy from malicious attacks in the cloud environment. *J. Adv. Res. Dyn. Control Syst.*, 11, 1291–1300, 2019.
19. Panda, S.K., Swain, S.K., Mall, R., An investigation into usability aspects of E-Commerce websites using users' preferences. *Adv. Comput. Sci. An Int. J.*, 4, 1, 65–73, 2015.
20. Panda, S.K., Swain, S.K., Mall, R., Measuring Web Site Usability Quality Complexity Metrics for Navigability, in: *Intelligent Computing, Communication and Devices. Advances in Intelligent Systems and Computing*, vol. 308, L. Jain, S. Patnaik, N. Ichalkaranje (Eds.), Springer, New Delhi, 2015, https://doi.org/10.1007/978-81-322-2012-1_41.
21. Panda, S.K., A Usability Evaluation Framework for B2C E-Commerce Websites. *Comput. Eng. Intell. Syst.*, 5, 3, 66–85, 2014.
22. Bhalerao, V., Panda, S.K., Jena, A.K., Optimization of Loss Function on Human Faces Using Generative Adversarial Networks, in: *Machine Learning Approaches for Urban Computing. Studies in Computational Intelligence*, vol. 968, M. Bandyopadhyay, M. Rout, S. Chandra Satapathy (Eds.), Springer, Singapore, 2021, https://doi.org/10.1007/978-981-16-0935-0_9.
23. Panda, S.K. and Dwivedi, M., Minimizing Food Wastage Using Machine Learning: A Novel Approach, in: *Smart Intelligent Computing and Applications. Smart Innovation, Systems and Technologies*, vol. 159, S. Satapathy, V. Bhateja, J. Mohanty, S. Udgata (Eds.), Springer, Singapore, 2020, https://doi.org/10.1007/978-981-13-9282-5_44.
24. Panda, S.K., Sathya, A.R., Mishra, M., Satpathy, S., A supervised learning algorithm to forecast weather conditions for playing cricket. *Int. J. Innov. Technol. Exploring Eng. (IJITEE)*, 9, 1, 2019.

25. Panda, S.K., *Fraud-Resistant Crowdfunding System Using Ethereum Blockchain*, pp. 237–276, Bitcoin and Blockchain, 2020.
26. Panda, S.K., Mishra, V., Balamurali, R., Elngar, A.A., *Artificial Intelligence and Machine Learning in Business Management Concepts, Challenges, and Case Studies*, pp. 1–278, https://doi.org/10.1201/9781003125129.
27. Joshi, S., Panda, S.K., AR, S., Optimal Deep Learning Model to Identify the Development of Pomegranate Fruit in Farms. *Int. J. Innov. Technol. Explor. Eng.*, 9, 3, 2352–2356, 2020.
28. Puranam, K.S.RK., Gaddam, M.C.T., K, V.P.R., Panda, S.K., Reddy, G.S.M., Anatomy and Lifecycle of a Bitcoin Transaction, in: *Proceedings of International Conference on Sustainable Computing in Science, Technology and Management (SUSCOM)*, Amity University Rajasthan, Jaipur - India, February 26-28, 2019, February 18, 2019, Available at SSRN: https://ssrn.com/abstract=3355106 or http://dx.doi.org/10.2139/ssrn.3355106.
29. Panda, S.K. and Swain, S.K., Quality Assurance Aspects of Web Design, in: *Design Solutions for Improving Website Quality and Effectiveness*, pp. 87–129, IGI Global, 2016.
30. Panda, S.K., Bhalerao, V., AR, S., A Machine Learning Model to Identify Duplicate Questions in Social Media Forums. *Int. J. Innov. Technol. Explor. Eng.*, 9, 4, 370–373, 2020.
31. Ahmareen, S., Raj, A., Potluri, S., Panda, S.K., Book Shala: An Android-Based Application Design and Implementation of Sharing Books, in: *Smart Intelligent Computing and Applications. Smart Innovation, Systems and Technologies*, vol. 159, S. Satapathy, V. Bhateja, J. Mohanty, S. Udgata (Eds.), Springer, Singapore, 2020, https://doi.org/10.1007/978-981-13-9282-5_28.
32. Panda, S.K., Das, S.S., Swain, S.K., S-Model for Service-Oriented Applications in Web Engineering. *Reg. Coll. Manage.*, 10, 3, 38–46, 2013.
33. Panda, S.K., *An Investigation into Usability and Productivity of ECommerce Websites.*
34. Panda, S.K., Chandrasekhar, A., Gantayat, P.K., Panda, M.R., Detecting Brain Tumor Using Image Segmentation: A Novel Approach, in: *Data Engineering and Intelligent Computing. Lecture Notes in Networks and Systems*, vol. 446, V. Bhateja, L. Khin Wee, J.C.W. Lin, S.C. Satapathy, T.M. Rajesh (Eds.), Springer, Singapore, 2022, https://doi.org/10.1007/978-981-19-1559-8_35.
35. Sanghi, P., Panda, S.K., Pati, C., Gantayat, P.K., Learning Deep Features and Classification for Fresh or off Vegetables to Prevent Food Wastage Using Machine Learning Algorithms, in: *Intelligent Data Engineering and Analytics. Smart Innovation, Systems and Technologies*, vol. 266, S.C. Satapathy, P. Peer, J. Tang, V. Bhateja, A. Ghosh (Eds.), Springer, Singapore, 2022, https://doi.org/10.1007/978-981-16-6624-7_44.
36. Gantayat, P.K., Mohapatra, S., Panda, S.K., Secure Trust Level Routing in Delay-Tolerant Network with Node Categorization Technique, in: *Intelligent Data Engineering and Analytics. Smart Innovation, Systems and Technologies*,

vol. 266, S.C. Satapathy, P. Peer, J. Tang, V. Bhateja, A. Ghosh (Eds.), Springer, Singapore, 2022, https://doi.org/10.1007/978-981-16-6624-7_45.

37. Panda, S.K., Urkude, S.V., Urkude, V.R., Vairachilai, S., An investigation into COVID 19 pandemic in India, in: *The New Advanced Society: Artificial Intelligence and Industrial Internet of Things Paradigm*, vol. 1, pp. 289–305, Wiley.
38. Panda, S.K., Das, S., Swain, S.K., Web Site Productivity Measurement Using Single Task Size Measure. *J. Inf. Sci. Comput. Technol. (JISCT)*, 4, 3, October 12, 2015.
39. Hanumanthakari, S. and Panda, S.K., Detecting Face Mask for Prevent COVID-19 Using Deep Learning: A Novel Approach, in: *Smart Intelligent Computing and Applications, Volume 2. Smart Innovation, Systems and Technologies*, vol. 283, S.C. Satapathy, V. Bhateja, M.N. Favorskaya, T. Adilakshmi (Eds.), Springer, Singapore, 2022, https://doi.org/10.1007/978-981-16-9705-0_45.
40. Panda, S.K., Sathya, A.R., Das, S., Bitcoin: Beginning of the Cryptocurrency Era, in: *Recent Advances in Blockchain Technology. Intelligent Systems Reference Library*, vol. 237, S.K. Panda, V. Mishra, S.P. Dash, A.K. Pani (Eds.), Springer, Cham, 2023, https://doi.org/10.1007/978-3-031-22835-3_2.
41. Murala, D.K., Panda, S.K., Sahoo, S.K., Securing Electronic Health Record System in Cloud Environment Using Blockchain Technology, in: *Recent Advances in Blockchain Technology. Intelligent Systems Reference Library*, vol. 237, S.K. Panda, V. Mishra, S.P. Dash, A.K. Pani (Eds.), Springer, Cham, 2023, https://doi.org/10.1007/978-3-031-22835-3_4.
42. Rao, K.V., Murala, D.K., Panda, S.K., Blockchain: A Study of New Business Model, in: *Recent Advances in Blockchain Technology. Intelligent Systems Reference Library*, vol. 237, S.K. Panda, V. Mishra, S.P. Dash, A.K. Pani (Eds.), Springer, Cham, 2023, https://doi.org/10.1007/978-3-031-22835-3_9.
43. Panda, S.K., Mishra, V., Dash, S.P., Pani, A.K., Recent Advances in Blockchain Technology Real-World Applications, in: *Intelligent Systems Reference Library (ISRL, volume 237)*, vol. 1, pp. 1–317, 978-3-031-22835-3.
44. Panda, S.K., Mohapatra, R.K., Panda, S., Balamurugan, S., *The New Advanced Society: Artificial Intelligence and Industrial Internet of Things Paradigm*, vol. 1, pp. 1–512, John Wiley & Sons, DOI:10.1002/9781119884392.
45. Nanda, S.K., Panda, S.K., Das, M., Satapathy, S.C., Decentralization of Car Insurance System Using Machine Learning and Distributed Ledger Technology, in: *Intelligent Data Engineering and Analytics. FICTA 2022. Smart Innovation, Systems and Technologies*, vol. 327, V. Bhateja, X.S. Yang, J. Chun-Wei Lin, R. Das (Eds.), Springer, Singapore, 2023, https://doi.org/10.1007/978-981-19-7524-0_52.
46. Nanda, S.K., Panda, S.K., Dash, M., Medical supply chain integrated with blockchain and IoT to track the logistics of medical products. *Multimed. Tools Appl.*, 82, 32917–32939, 2023. https://doi.org/10.1007/s11042-023-14846-8.

47. Panda, S.K., Jena, A.K., Panda, M.R., *et al.*, Speech emotion recognition using multimodal feature fusion with machine learning approach. *Multimed. Tools Appl.*, 82, 42763–42781, 2023. https://doi.org/10.1007/s11042-023-15275-3.
48. Panda, S.K. and Mohanty, S.N., Time Series Forecasting and Modeling of Food Demand Supply Chain Based on Regressors Analysis. *IEEE Access*, 11, 42679–42700, 2023. doi: 10.1109/ACCESS.2023.3266275.
49. Desai, D.D., *et al.*, Optimal Ambulance Positioning for Road Accidents With Deep Embedded Clustering. *IEEE Access*, 11, 59917–59934, 2023. doi: 10.1109/ACCESS.2023.3284993.
50. Lakshmi, L., Devi, K.D.S., Gupta, S., Reddy, K.A.N., Grandhi, S.K., Panda, S.K., WOMT: Wasserstein Distribution Based Minimization of False Positives in Breast Tumor Classification Using Deep Learning. *IEEE Access*, 11, 57831–57842, 2023. doi: 10.1109/ACCESS.2023.3279496.
51. Mishra, P. and Panda, S.K., Dependency Structure-Based Rules Using Root Node Technique for Explicit Aspect Extraction From Online Reviews. *IEEE Access*, 11, 65117–65137, 2023. doi: 10.1109/ACCESS.2023.3287830.
52. Routray, N., Rout, S.K., Sahu, B., Panda, S.K., Godavarthi, D., Ensemble Learning With Symbiotic Organism Search Optimization Algorithm for Breast Cancer Classification and Risk Identification of Other Organs on Histopathological Images. *IEEE Access*, 11, 110544–110557, 2023. doi: 10.1109/ACCESS.2023.3322222.
53. Agarwal, R., Pande, S.D., Mohanty, S.N., Panda, S.K., A Novel Hybrid System of Detecting Brain Tumors in MRI. *IEEE Access*, 11, 118372–118385, 2023. doi: 10.1109/ACCESS.2023.3326447.
54. Nayak, S.K., Garanayak, M., Swain, S.K., Panda, S.K., Godavarthi, D., An Intelligent Disease Prediction and Drug Recommendation Prototype by Using Multiple Approaches of Machine Learning Algorithms. *IEEE Access*, 11, 99304–99318, 2023. doi: 10.1109/ACCESS.2023.3314332.
55. Gupta, A., Gandhi, R., Jatana, N., Jatain, D., Panda, S.K., Ramesh, J.V.N., A Severity Assessment of Python Code Smells. *IEEE Access*, 11, 119146–119160, 2023. doi: 10.1109/ACCESS.2023.3327553.
56. Murala, D.K., Panda, S.K., Dash, S.P., MedMetaverse: Medical Care of Chronic Disease Patients and Managing Data Using Artificial Intelligence, Blockchain, and Wearable Devices State-of-the-Art Methodology. *IEEE Access*, 11, 138985, 2023. doi: 10.1109/ACCESS.2023.3340791.
57. Sethi, B.K., Singh, D., Rout, S.K., Panda, S.K., Long Short-Term Memory-Deep Belief Network-Based Gene Expression Data Analysis for Prostate Cancer Detection and Classification. *IEEE Access*, 12, 1508–1524, 2024. doi: 10.1109/ACCESS.2023.3346925.
58. Mahapatra, A., Majhi, S.K., Mishra, K., Pradhan, R., Rao, D.C., Panda, S.K., An Energy-Aware Task Offloading and Load Balancing for Latency-Sensitive IoT Applications in the Fog-Cloud Continuum. *IEEE Access*, 12, 14334–14349, 2024. doi: 10.1109/ACCESS.2024.3357122.

59. Mishra, P., Sharma, O., Panda, S.K., ADN-BERT: Attention-Based Deep Network Model Using BERT for Sarcasm Classification, in: *Evolution in Computational Intelligence. FICTA 2023. Smart Innovation, Systems and Technologies*, vol. 370, V. Bhateja, X.S. Yang, M.C. Ferreira, S.S. Sengar, C.M. Travieso-Gonzalez (Eds.), Springer, Singapore, 2023, https://doi.org/10.1007/978-981-99-6702-5_51.
60. Varaprasada Rao, K. and Panda, S.K., Initiation, Innovation, Implementation and Integration of CBDC in Digital Virtual Payment Systems, in: *Advances in Microelectronics, Embedded Systems and IoT. ICMEET 2023. Lecture Notes in Electrical Engineering*, vol. 1156, V.V.S.S.S. Chakravarthy, V. Bhateja, J. Anguera, S. Urooj, A. Ghosh (Eds.), Springer, Singapore, 2024, https://doi.org/10.1007/978-981-97-0767-6_20.
61. Murala, D.K. and Panda, S.K., Artificial intelligence in the development of metaverse, in: *Metaverse and Immersive Technologies: An Introduction to Industrial Business and Social Applications*, pp. 407–436, Wiley, Hoboken, NJ, USA, 2023.
62. Murala, D.K. and Panda, S.K., Metaverse: A study on immersive technologies, in: *Metaverse and Immersive Technologies: An Introduction to Industrial Business and Social Applications*, Wiley, Hoboken, NJ, USA, 2023.
63. Murala, D.K. and Panda, S.K., The Internet of Things in developing metaverse, in: *Metaverse and Immersive Technologies: An Introduction to Industrial Business and Social Applications*, Wiley, Hoboken, NJ, USA, 2023.
64. Murala, D.K. and Panda, S.K., Blockchain in the development of metaverse, in: *Metaverse and Immersive Technologies: An Introduction to Industrial Business and Social Applications*, Wiley, USA, 1002.
65. Murala, D.K. and Panda, S.K., The role of immersive reality (AR/VR/MR/XR) in metaverse, in: *Metaverse and Immersive Technologies: An Introduction to Industrial Business and Social Applications*, pp. 159–189, Wiley, Hoboken, NJ, USA, 2023.
66. Panda, S.K., Revolution of the Metaverse and Blockchain Technology, in: *Metaverse and Immersive Technologies: An Introduction to Industrial Business and Social Applications*, Wiley, Hoboken, NJ, USA, 2023.
67. Sahoo, S.K., Das, S., Panda, S.K., Alzheimer's Disease Classification Using Brain MRI Based on 2D CNN and Transfer Learning, in: *Proceedings of the 6th International Conference on Communications and Cyber Physical Engineering. ICCCE 2024. Lecture Notes in Electrical Engineering*, vol. 1096, A. Kumar, and S. Mozar (Eds.), Springer, Singapore, 2024, https://doi.org/10.1007/978-981-99-7137-4_1.
68. Panda, S.K., Ramesh, J.V.N., Ghosh, H., Rahat, I.S., Sobur, A., Bijoy, M.H., Yesubabu, M., Deep Learning in Medical Imaging: A Case Study on Lung Tissue Classification. *EAI Endorsed Trans. Pervasive Health Technol.*, 10, 2024.
69. Paruchuri, V.N.L.L., Shaik, A.H., Murala, D.K., Panda, S.K., IoT-Enabled Neural Network Analysis for Early Detection and Prediction of Mental

Depression, in: *Information System Design: Communication Networks and IoT. ISDIA 2024. Lecture Notes in Networks and Systems*, vol. 1057, V. Bhateja, J. Tang, D.K. Sharma, Z. Polkowski, A. Ahmad, (Eds.), pp. 257–268, Springer, Singapore, 2024, https://doi.org/10.1007/978-981-97-4895-2_21.

70. Paruchuri, V.N.L.L., Malaviya, M.P., Murala, D.K., Panda, S.K., Connecting IoT Sensors for Enhanced Dementia Disease Monitoring and Intervention, in: *Information System Design: Communication Networks and IoT. ISDIA 2024. Lecture Notes in Networks and Systems*, vol. 1057, V. Bhateja, J. Tang, D.K. Sharma, Z. Polkowski, A. Ahmad, (Eds.), pp. 269–281, Springer, Singapore, 2024, https://doi.org/10.1007/978-981-97-4895-2_22.
71. Panda, S.K., Das, S., Sahoo, S.K., Predominant Music Genre Classification Using Machine Learning Approach, in: *Signal Processing, Telecommunication and Embedded Systems with AI and ML Applications. ICMEET 2023. Lecture Notes in Electrical Engineering*, vol. 1281, V. Bhateja, V.V.S.S.S. Chakravarthy, J. Anguera, A. Ghosh, W. Flores Fuentes, (Eds.), Springer, Singapore, 2025, https://doi.org/10.1007/978-981-97-8422-6_17.
72. Panda, S.K., Das, S., Sahoo, S.K., Vehicle Detection and Classification Using Intelligent Systems, in: *Signal Processing, Telecommunication and Embedded Systems with AI and ML Applications. ICMEET 2023. Lecture Notes in Electrical Engineering*, vol. 1281, V. Bhateja, V.V.S.S.S. Chakravarthy, J. Anguera, A. Ghosh, W. Flores Fuentes, (Eds.), Springer, Singapore, 2025, https://doi.org/10.1007/978-981-97-8422-6_18.
73. Chandrasekhar, A., Dodhiawala, Z., Panda, S.K., An Investigation into Chronic Kidney Disease Based-on Classification Model, in: *Signal Processing, Telecommunication and Embedded Systems with AI and ML Applications. ICMEET 2023. Lecture Notes in Electrical Engineering*, vol. 1281, V. Bhateja, V.V.S.S.S. Chakravarthy, J. Anguera, A. Ghosh, W. Flores Fuentes, (Eds.), Springer, Singapore, 2025, https://doi.org/10.1007/978-981-97-8422-6_19.
74. Chandrashekhar, A., Saheb, S.H., Panda, S.K., Balamurugan, S., Peng, S.-L., *Metaverse and Immersive Technologies: An Introduction to Industrial, Business and Social Applications*, John Wiley & Sons, 2023.

15

Reinforcement Learning in Network Optimization

Jagini Naga Padmaja* **and Nadimpalli Madana Kailash Varma**

Department of Artificial Intelligence and Machine Learning, Vardhaman College of Engineering, Hyderabad, Telangana, India

Abstract

The incorporation of machine learning (ML) into networking marks a significant leap, transforming traditional network management and optimization. ML algorithms, capable of learning from extensive datasets, have significantly enhanced various aspects of network operations, including traffic prediction, resource allocation, and security measures. This chapter offers a comprehensive overview of ML's application in networking, detailing its evolution, methodologies, and key benefits. Supervised learning models like linear regression and neural networks are utilized for accurate traffic prediction, whereas reinforcement learning aids in dynamic resource allocation and optimization. Additionally, anomaly detection and intrusion detection systems benefit from unsupervised learning techniques and advanced ML models, like decision trees and support vector machines. By exploring these ML techniques, this chapter highlights their critical role in improving network performance, security, and efficiency, demonstrating the profound impact of ML on modern networking.

Keywords**:** Reinforcement learning (RL), supervised learning, unsupervised learning, intrusion detection, neural networks, linear regression, decision trees, support vector machines

**Corresponding author*: srija26@gmail.com

Pradosh Kumar Gantayat, Sandeep Kumar Panda, S. Balamurugan and Sheng-Lung Peng (eds.) Hyper-Intelligent Networks: Exploring the Future of Connectivity for Society 5.0, (325–348) © 2026 Scrivener Publishing LLC

15.1 Introduction to Reinforcement Learning in Networking

15.1.1 Definition and Importance

Reinforcement learning (RL) is a dynamic field of computational algorithms designed to mimic human intelligence by learning from the surrounding environment. It is considered a pivotal component in the new era of big data [1]. Unlike traditional algorithms, where steps are explicitly defined, machine learning (ML) models learn and improve over time by finding patterns and relationships in the data. In essence, the ML approach simplifies the process by replacing the need for deep domain knowledge with the collection of a large number of examples of the desired behavior [2]. In ML, a collection of sample cases with a known classification is usually used as a data source, and the computer is trained to maximize a performance criterion using experience.

ML techniques have been effectively utilized across various sectors, including computational biology, finance, entertainment, pattern recognition, computer vision, aerospace engineering, and biomedical applications [3]. This allows the algorithm to learn from these examples and make accurate predictions or decisions. The global access to the internet over the past few decades is a result of a robust network infrastructure. Networks, comprising interconnected computers and devices, facilitate communication and data transfer, which are critical for the growth of computer science. ML has permeated nearly every field, but its impact is particularly significant in networking, enhancing security measures, optimizing data transfer, and improving overall network management.

15.1.2 What is Machine Learning?

As a sub-field of computer science and artificial intelligence (AI), ML focuses on using data and algorithms to help AI mimic human learning processes and progressively become more accurate. Complex tasks are carried out by AI systems similarly to how humans handle issues [4]. It can be understood as the use and development of computer systems that are able to learn and adapt without following explicit instructions, utilizing algorithms and statistical models to analyze and draw inferences from patterns in data. It can be understood as the use and development of computer systems that are able to learn and adapt without following explicit instructions, utilizing algorithms and statis tical models to analyze and draw inferences from patterns in data [5]. Figure 15.1 categorizes machine learning into four main types: supervised, unsupervised, semi-supervised, and reinforcement learning. It highlights their

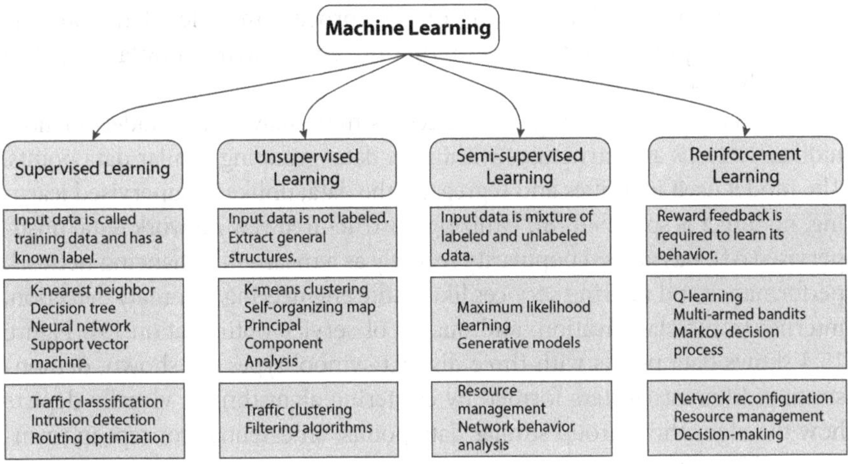

Figure 15.1 Types of Learning in machine learning.

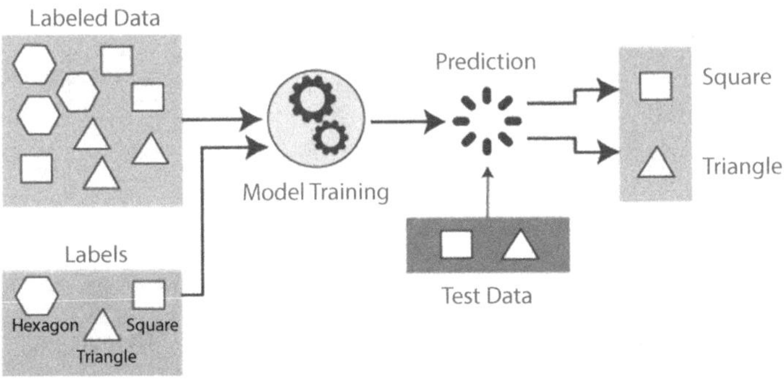

Figure 15.2 Process flow of supervised learning.

key characteristics, provides example applications, and lists common algorithms associated with each category, illustrating the diverse approaches to machine learning tasks.

ML comprises multiple discrete approaches, broadly classified into three categories: RL, unsupervised learning, and supervised learning. There is also a hybrid type called semi-supervised learning. The target is provided to the model with some input during supervised learning. It involves using labeled datasets—where every input has a matching output—to train a model. Several popular supervised learning techniques are discussed, along with real-world applications [6]. Here, the model is supervised or guided by the data in the learning processes explicitly, hence the name [7]. Figure 15.2 outlines the typical steps in supervised learning. It begins with input data, followed by data separation techniques indicated by various symbols (hexagon, triangle, square). The process includes data training, model development, and output prediction, emphasizing how labeled data guides the learning process.

In unsupervised learning, the process is more naive. The models identify hidden patterns and structures within the data, grouping similar data points. The model itself identifies and segregates the data; unlike in supervised learning, no target is specified [8]. Utilizing unstructured raw network data, unsupervised ML has gained popularity recently as a means of enhancing network performance and offering services like traffic engineering, anomaly detection, internet traffic classification, and quality of service optimization [9]. Figure 15.3 shows data points with three distinct symbol types are shown, demonstrating different clusters formed by clustering algorithm. It visually depicts how the algorithms group similar data points, an essential concept in unsupervised learning.

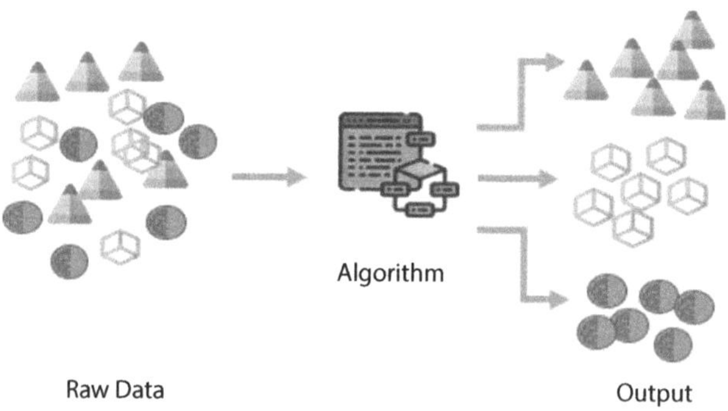

Figure 15.3 Process flow of unsupervised learning.

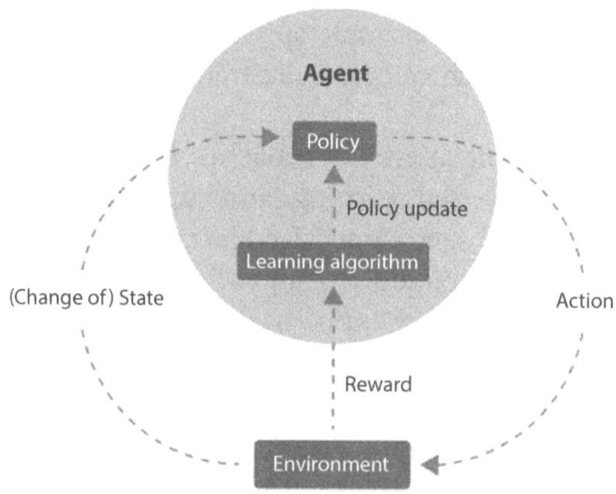

Figure 15.4 Mechanism of reinforcement learning: reward-based learning process.

RL represents another sub-field of ML. In this approach, a ML agent learns to anticipate its next move through feedback obtained from trial and error [10]. Figure 15.4 shows RL is akin to a child learning new things and improving from experiences, often described as reward-based learning. This process is driven by rewards and penalties, where an agent learns to take actions that maximize cumulative rewards in a given environment. To operate efficiently in challenging environments, learning agents need to make meaningful generalizations by focusing on relevant elements and ignoring irrelevant ones in complex contexts [11].

Semi-supervised learning represents a hybrid approach that combines aspects of both supervised and unsupervised learning. It exploits a substantial amount of unlabeled data alongside a smaller set of labeled data to enhance learning accuracy. This approach reduces the need for extensive human intervention while achieving higher levels of accuracy [12].

15.1.3 Machine Learning's Significance in Networking

ML has specialized applications across various industries, particularly in key networking domains such as resource and fault management, network security, traffic prediction, routing and classification, congestion control, and quality-of-service (QoS) and quality of experience (QoE) management [13]. ML algorithms empower organizations to analyze vast amounts of network data, identify patterns, and make intelligent decisions autonomously. By leveraging ML algorithms, network administrators gain deeper insights into network behavior, predict potential issues, and proactively optimize performance.

The integration of ML into networks yields significant benefits, including:

1. Network Optimization
2. Intelligent Traffic Management
3. Automation of Network Management
4. Enhanced Security
5. Energy Efficiency
6. Fault Predictions and Maintenance
7. Quality of Service Improvement

15.1.4 Historical Background

15.1.4.1 Evolution of Networking Technologies

Networking has a long history, undergoing many changes and transformations over the last few decades, evolving from basic communication systems to highly sophisticated and interconnected networks that form the backbone of modern digital infrastructure. This evolution can be briefly split into a few stages for better understanding.

15.1.4.2 Traditional Networking

- **Early Beginnings:** The initial instances of networking can be traced to the 19th-century telephone and telegraph systems, which laid the groundwork for long-distance communication.
- **Packet Switching:** The 1960s saw the development of packet switching, which paved the way for ARPANET, the precursor to the modern Internet. Data could now be sent over a network in fewer, more reliable packets, improving efficiency.

15.1.4.3 Development of the Internet

- **ARPANET:** Launched in 1969, ARPANET connected four university computers, demonstrating the true potential of networks.
- **Transmission Control Protocol/ Internet Protocol (TCP/IP):** The standardized TCP/IP protocol suite facilitated various forms of networking, simplifying peer-to-peer communication processes and contributing to the growth of the global Internet.
- **World Wide Web:** Introduced by Tim Berners-Lee in 1991, the Web revolutionized how information is accessed and shared online, exponentially increasing public Internet access.

15.1.4.4 Modern Networking

- **Broadband and Wireless Technologies:** The late 20th century saw widespread adoption of broadband and wireless technologies, enhancing internet speed and accessibility. Technologies like Wi-Fi, 3G, and later 4G LTE expanded connectivity.
- **Cloud Computing:** This phase revolutionized network development by enabling scalable and flexible resource access over the Internet, with Amazon Web Services and Microsoft Azure becoming crucial for corporate operations.
- **Internet of Things (IoT):** IoT systems have impacted networking by providing interconnected devices that handle vast amounts of data while offering robust and intelligent network management with minimal resources, proving cost-effective for various fields.

15.1.4.5 Advancements in Network Security

- **Firewall and Virtual Private Network (VPN) Technologies:** With the introduction of computer networks in various sectors by the late 1990s, focus shifted toward security. Firewalls and VPNs enhanced security by protecting against unauthorized access and data breaches.
- **Next-Generation Security Solutions:** From 2010 to 2020, a greater focus on security led to advancements like intrusion detection systems (IDSs), ML-based threat detection, and improved resilience against sophisticated cyber threats.

15.1.4.6 5G and Beyond

- **5G Networks:** The demand for higher internet speeds due to increased user availability prompted the rollout of 5G, providing high speed, low latency, and the capacity to connect numerous devices, paving the way for innovations like autonomous vehicles and smart cities.
- **Future Trends:** Anticipated developments include 6G networks, quantum networking, and the integration of AI and ML for autonomous network management, expected to further revolutionize the networking landscape.

15.1.5 Growth of Machine Learning Applications in Networking

The initial stages of ML applications in networking included anomaly detection, where models identified unusual network traffic patterns indicative of security threats or improper system functioning. ML also entered spam filtering, enhancing network security through techniques like Bayesian filtering. Additionally, traffic classification helped manage bandwidth and optimize performance by categorizing different types of network traffic.

As ML technologies advanced, their applications in networking expanded. ML began automating network configuration, monitoring, and optimization tasks, reducing manual intervention and increasing efficiency. Predictive maintenance became significant, with ML analyzing historical data to forecast hardware failures and network issues, allowing proactive maintenance and minimizing downtime.

Advanced security measures benefited from ML as well, leading to the development of IDSs and behavioral analysis tools that improved real-time threat detection and network security. In traffic management, ML models predicted congestion and dynamically adjusted routing protocols, ensuring optimal data flow and enhancing QoS.

Overall, ML has significantly advanced networking, transforming early applications like anomaly detection and spam filtering into modern uses in network management, security, and optimization.

15.2 Machine Learning Techniques for Network Optimization

15.2.1 Traffic Prediction and Analysis

ML methods have provided improvements in traffic prediction and analysis in network optimization [14]. Supervised learning models, such as linear regression and neural networks, are introduced to forecast network traffic patterns accurately. These models make use of training data to predict future traffic loads, enabling network management and congestion avoidance. Case studies highlight how organizations have leveraged these techniques to enhance network performance [15]. For instance, service providers use traffic prediction models to manage bandwidth allocation during peak usage times, ensuring consistent and reliable connectivity for users. Additionally, unsupervised learning methods like clustering techniques, including K-means and density-based spatial clustering of applications with noise (DBSCAN), are pivotal in anomaly detection. These models identify unusual traffic patterns that may indicate security breaches or network issues, helping administrators to take preemptive actions.

15.2.2 Resource Allocation and Management

Resource allocation and management within networks benefit significantly from RL and optimization algorithms. RL, which focuses on training models to make verdicts through rewards and penalties, is particularly effective for dynamic resource allocation. The packet, burst, and call levels are the three levels at which the author recommends assessing congestion [16]. This approach allows networks to adapt in real-time to changing demands, optimizing the distribution of resources such as bandwidth and processing power. Examples of RL in action include automated load balancing in data centers, where resources are allocated based on current usage patterns to prevent bottlenecks [17]. Optimization algorithms like genetic algorithms and particle swarm optimization further enhance network management by solving complex optimization problems, such as routing and scheduling. These algorithms are applied in various scenarios, from optimizing routing paths to managing the energy consumption of network devices [18].

15.2.3 Quality-of-Service (QoS) Enhancement

QoS enhancement is another critical area where ML plays a vital role. Predictive models are employed to forecast potential QoS issues before they occur, allowing network managers to take preemptive measures [19]. Predictive analytics leverage historical data and statistical techniques to maintain high service standards, as seen in examples where predictive models anticipate bandwidth requirements for streaming services to avoid buffering. Adaptive QoS management using ML involves dynamically adjusting network parameters to meet the desired QoS levels. Techniques such as adaptive bitrate streaming in video services ensure optimal viewing experiences by adjusting the quality based on real-time network conditions. Case studies demonstrate significant improvements in user satisfaction and network efficiency through these adaptive techniques, showcasing the profound impact of ML on enhancing network performance.

15.3 Security Enhancements through Machine Learning

The techniques employed by hostile actors to breach security systems also evolve along with technology. Although they can be somewhat effective, traditional security measures frequently find it difficult to keep up with the quickly changing threat landscape. This is where ML enters the picture, providing cutting-edge ways to improve security across the board, from fraud detection to physical security to cybersecurity. This introduction offers a clear and comprehensive summary of the ways in which ML can greatly enhance security protocols.

15.3.1 Financial Transactions

Real-time transaction data analysis using ML models enables the detection of fraudulent activity. These algorithms lower the risk of financial loss by identifying questionable transactions and flagging them for additional examination based on past fraud patterns.

15.3.2 Identity Theft

By keeping an eye on user behavior on several platforms, ML algorithms are able to spot irregularities that can point to identity theft. To confirm the user's identity, for example, the system may require extra verification procedures if the user's login patterns abruptly change.

15.3.3 Response Systems that are Automated

Automated response systems and ML can be combined to quickly reduce security concerns. For instance, if an ML model identifies a possible cyber-attack, it can minimize the attack's impact by automatically triggering pre-defined procedures like isolating compromised systems, blocking hostile IP addresses, or starting incident response protocols. By examining sensor data, ML can be utilized in industrial and critical infrastructure contexts to anticipate equipment breakdowns. Early identification of possible problems enables prompt maintenance, averting interruptions and improving overall operational security and dependability.

15.3.4 Intrusion Detection Systems

15.3.4.1 Signature-Based vs. Anomaly-Based Detection

An IDS is a specialized network security technology that actively tracks devices and network traffic to detect and respond to suspicious behaviors, potential threats, or breaches of security protocols. An IDS can help accelerate and automate network threat detection by alerting security administrators to known or potential threats or by delivering warnings to a centralized security tool. When security teams combine data from several sources with a centralized security solution, such as a security information and event management system, they may identify and counteract cyber threats that circumvent current security measures. IDSs are also beneficial for compliance initiatives. Regulations like the Payment Card Industry Data Security Standard mandate that organizations use intrusion detection solutions.

15.3.4.2 Anomaly Detection

Anomaly detectors detect anomalies, or strange and aberrant behavior, on a host or network. They operate under the presumption that attacks are distinct from "normal" (lawful) behavior and can thus be discovered by programs that recognize these variations. Anomaly detectors create profiles of people, hosts, or network connections based on their typical behavior.

The historical data gathered over the course of regular business operations is used to create these profiles. The detectors then gather event information and employ a range of metrics to identify instances in which the activity being tracked deviates from the usual.

15.3.5 Machine Learning Models for Intrusion Detection

15.3.5.1 Decision Trees

A decision tree is a classifier that is expressed as a recursive split of the instance space. The nodes that make up a decision tree are rooted trees—directed trees with a single node called the "root," which has no incoming edges. There is exactly one incoming edge for every other node. A node having outgoing edges is referred to as a test or internal node. Leaves, sometimes referred to any other nodes, function as terminal or decision nodes. Based on a certain discrete function of the input attribute values, each internal node in a decision tree splits the instance space into two or more sub-spaces [23].

Each test examines a single attribute in the most basic and common scenario, partitioning the instance space based on the attribute's value. When it comes to numerical qualities, a range is referred to by the condition. Each leaf has been allocated a class based on the optimal target value. Alternatively, a probability vector indicating the likelihood that a specific value of the target characteristic would be present may be present in the leaf. Instances are characterized by moving down from the base of the tree to a leaf, depending on the outcomes of the tests along the way.

Figure 15.5 shows leaves are shown as triangles, and internal nodes are shown as circles. Take note that both nominal and numerical attributes are included in this decision tree. With the help of this classifier, the analyst

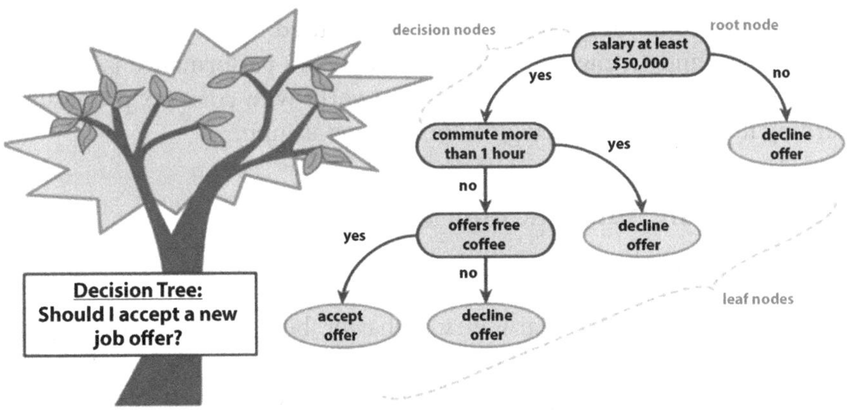

Figure 15.5 Example of machine learning in action: decision tree structure.

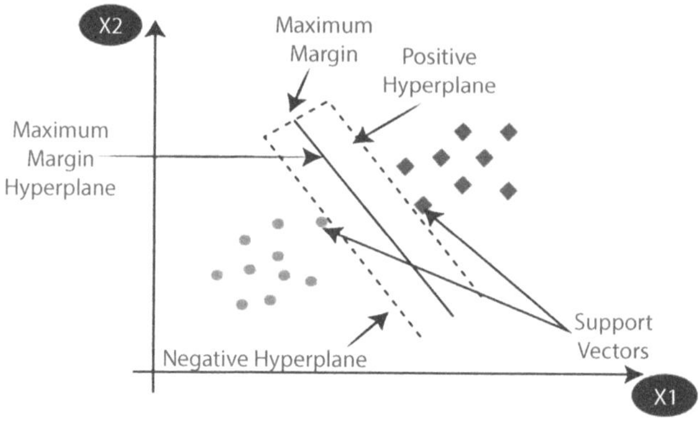

Figure 15.6 Visualizing support vector machines: hyperplane and decision boundaries.

may comprehend the behavioral charactersof the whole population of potential customers with regard to direct mailing and forecast the response of a potential client by sorting it down the tree. The property that each node tests is labeled, and its branches are labeled with its matching values.

15.3.5.2 Support Vector Machine

Support vector machine (SVM) is a ML-based regression and classification prediction tool that automatically guards against overfitting to the data and maximizes projected accuracy [24]. Figure 15.6 shows as systems that employ the hypothesis space of a linear function in a high-dimensional feature space after being trained using a learning algorithm from optimization theory that adds a learning bias from statistical learning theory, support vector machines may be conceptualized in this way. Support vector machines were first popularized by the neural information processing systems (NIPS) community and are now widely used in ML research. When applied for handwriting recognition tasks, SVM's performance is comparable to that of well-developed neural networks with complex properties, earning it prominence when given pixel maps as input.

15.3.6 Secure Authentication Mechanisms

15.3.6.1 Behavioral Biometrics

Analyzing unique patterns in human behavior, behavioral biometrics provides an advanced method for authenticating users. Contrary to static biometric systems that rely on physical attributes, behavioral biometrics constantly observe and adjust to the user's actions, offering a dynamic level of security.

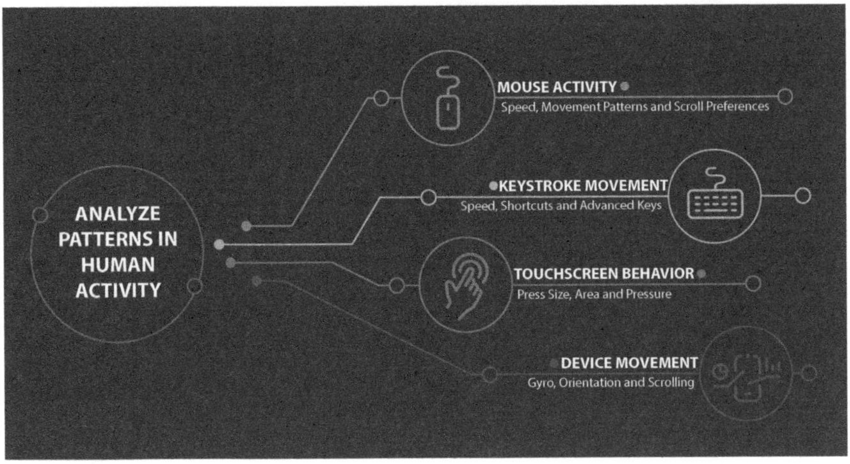

Figure 15.7 Analyzing human movement patterns.

15.3.6.1.1 Types and Applications of Behavioral Biometrics

Figure 15.7 shows analyzing unique patterns in human behavior, behavioral biometrics provides an advanced method for authenticating users. Contrary to static biometric systems that rely on physical attributes, behavioral biometrics constantly observe and adjust to the user's actions, offering a dynamic level of security [25].

- **Keystroke Dynamics** involves capturing the timing and rhythm of an individual's keyboard typing.
- **Gait Analysis** analyzes how someone walks to verify users.
- **Voice Recognition** examines vocal features for authentication.
- **Mouse Dynamics** observes how an individual moves and clicks with a mouse.

15.3.6.2 Multi-Factor Authentication (MFA)

MFA improves security by asking for multiple types of verification, usually grouped as:

- Information that the user is familiar with, such as passwords or PINs.
- Possessions of the user: such as security tokens, smart cards, or mobile devices.
- An example of what the user could be biometric authentication.

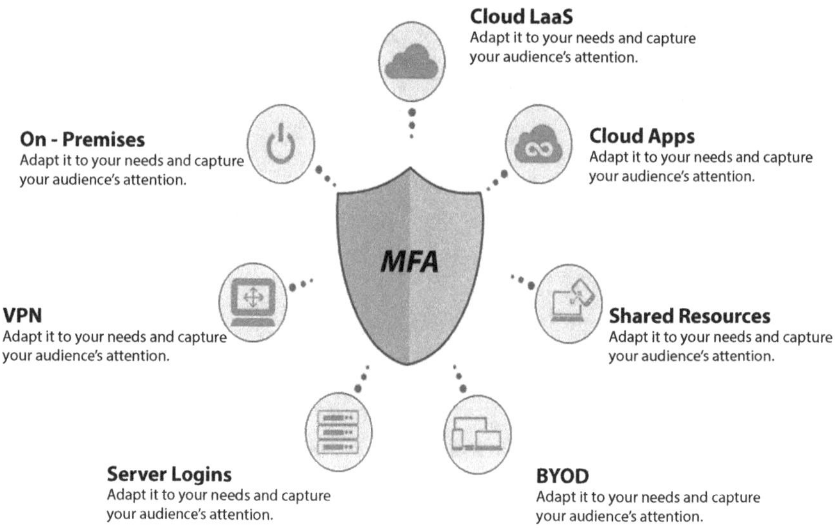

Figure 15.8 Multi-factor authentication: enhancing security through layered verification.

Figure 15.8 shows integrating ML into MFA greatly improves security and user experience through adaptive and context-aware authentication procedures.

15.3.6.3 Integrating Machine Learning with Conventional Authentication Techniques

ML algorithms assess the level of risk associated with a user's login attempt. For instance, geographical location and analysis of IP addresses can increase security protocols when detecting anomalies.

15.4 Machine Learning in Wireless Networks

15.4.1 Cognitive Radio Networks

Spectrum Sensing Using ML

The ability to sense the spectrum is crucial in cognitive radio networks as it allows devices to determine if primary users are using a particular frequency band. This enables secondary users to access underutilized spectrum opportunistically without generating adverse interference. Several methods have been created to improve the precision and dependability of spectrum sensing.

15.4.1.1 *Techniques for Spectral Sensing*

Matched Filter Detection

Matched filter recognition offers optimal detection performance for known signal patterns. This technique correlates the received signal with a predefined template or pattern of the primary user's signal [8]. If the correlation exceeds a certain threshold, then the presence of the primary signal is inferred. The main advantage of matched filter detection is its high sensitivity and accuracy when the signal characteristics are known. This makes it suitable for environments where primary user signals have well-defined structures, such as certain types of wireless communication systems. However, the requirement for prior knowledge of the primary signal's waveform is a significant limitation. Figure 15.9 shows the scenarios where the primary user's signal characteristics are unknown or vary, matched filter detection may not be practical.

Cyclostationary Feature Detection:

Cyclostationary feature detection leverages the periodic properties inherent in many modulated signals. Unlike energy detection, this method can exploit these cyclostationary properties to distinguish between noise and signal, even under low- signal-to-noise ratio (SNR) conditions. This makes it particularly robust against noise uncertainties and interference. The technique analyzes the cyclic autocorrelation function of the received signal to identify spectral features unique to the primary user. Despite its robustness and accuracy, cyclostationary feature detection is computationally intensive. It requires detailed knowledge of the signal's cyclic features and significant processing power, which can be a barrier to real-time implementation in resource-constrained environments.

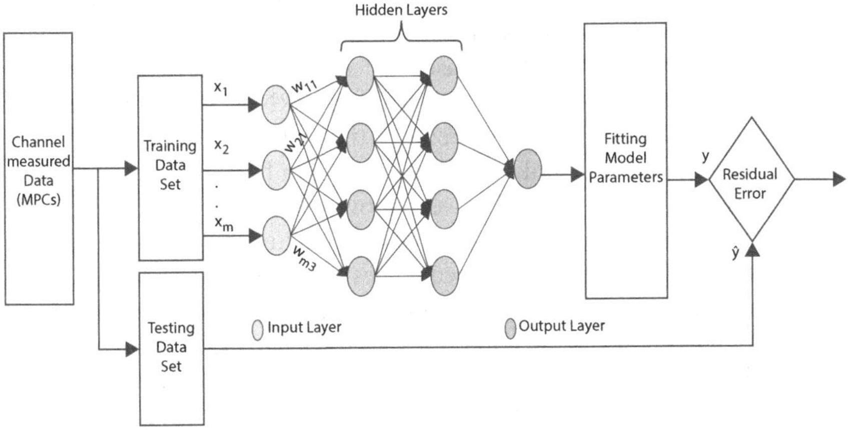

Figure 15.9 Structure of a neural network: layers and connections.

Waveform-Oriented Sensing:
Waveform-based sensing is used to identify certain patterns or waveforms in the received signal, usually when the primary user signals contain familiar preambles or pilot tones. This technique provides excellent detection precision for these recognized wave patterns and can be highly efficient in distinguishing primary user broadcasts. This approach excels in identifying specific signal structures accurately, making it ideal for environments where primary users follow standardized transmission patterns. Just like with matched filter detection, waveform-based sensing also needs prior knowledge of the primary user's waveform, which restricts its adaptability in varied and changing spectral surroundings.

Identification by Radio:
Advanced signal processing techniques and algorithms for ML are used in radio identification to determine the signal type and its origin. This approach can accurately differentiate primary users from secondary users by identifying distinct signal features. The main benefit of radio identification lies in its precise accuracy and capability to offer in-depth data on the signal surroundings. This has the capability to greatly enhance spectrum usage efficiency and decrease interference. Yet, the intricate nature of these methods necessitates a wealth of training data and considerable computational power, which poses difficulties for real-time implementation or resource limitations.

15.4.1.2 ML Models: CNN and RNN

RNN
Figure 15.10 shows recurrent neural network (RNN) is an efficient neural network that mainly involves processing sequential data. This quality of data makes it more efficient and used for analyzing time series data, like spectrum sensing in cognitive radio networks. RNNs stand out for their capability to preserve a type of memory through the utilization of feedback connections. These links enable information from earlier time points to affect the current result, effectively allowing the network to recognize sequences in the data. When it comes to spectrum sensing, RNNs have the ability to assess spectral data sequences in order to forecast upcoming spectrum availability. This ability is essential for cognitive radios that must adjust to changing spectrum conditions. LSTM networks, a more advanced form of RNNs, tackle the issue of long-term dependencies and disappearing gradients by including memory cells that choose to keep or discard information selectively. This is especially true in situations where having

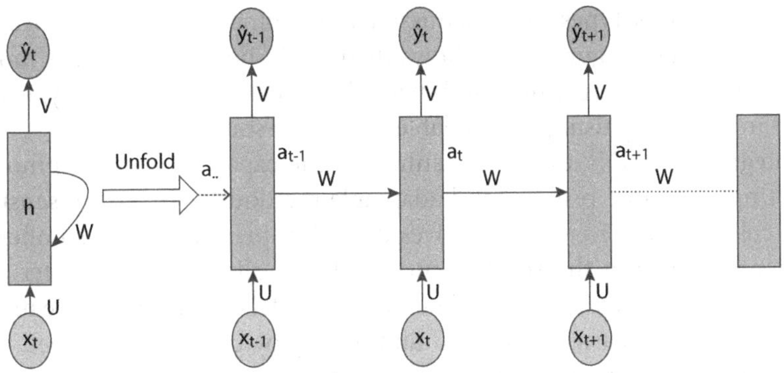

Figure 15.10 Unfolded recurrent neural network.

a detailed record of spectrum usage history is crucial for making accurate predictions. Through analyzing past usage behaviors, RNNs and LSTMs help cognitive radios in making educated choices regarding spectrum utilization, leading to better network performance and decreased issues with primary users.

CNN

Convolutional neural networks (CNNs) are mainly created for analyzing spatial data and are well-known for their achievements in tasks related to processing images and videos. Nevertheless, their strong ability to extract features also makes them valuable for spectrum sensing in cognitive radio networks. CNNs are strong in noisy environments due to their effectiveness in reducing dimensionality without losing important information [9], which improves their accuracy in detection. Furthermore, CNNs can be taught to identify particular signal traits, enabling them to differentiate

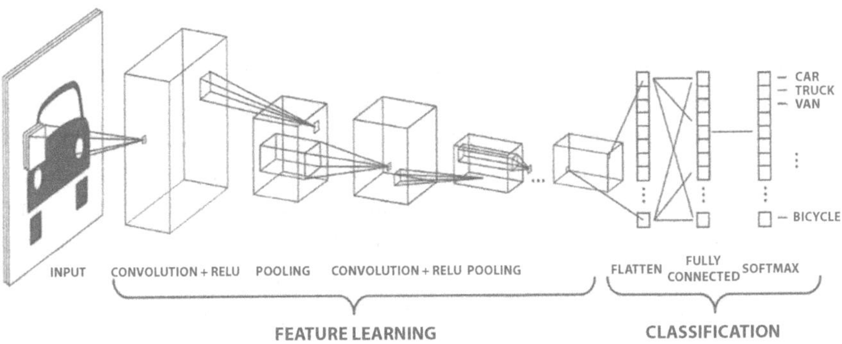

Figure 15.11 Convolutional neural network architecture.

between various types of transmissions and pinpoint opportunities for spectrum usage. Figure 15.11 shows their usefulness also includes monitoring spectrum in real-time and managing spectrum dynamically, which helps in efficiently using the available spectral resources.

Integrating RNNs and CNNs enhances the capabilities of each model, resulting in a more resilient and adaptable method for spectrum sensing. This collaboration not just improves detection precision but also offers a deeper insight into the spectral surroundings, allowing for smarter and more flexible spectrum control. The hybrid model can also integrate methods like transfer learning to speed up learning by using a pre-trained [14] CNN for a similar task, and ensemble learning to enhance performance by combining multiple models. This comprehensive method is a major step forward in how ML is used for spectrum sensing, tackling the challenges of dynamic spectrum access in both spatial and temporal domains.

15.4.2 Dynamic Spectrum Management

Adaptive Spectrum Management Strategies.
Dynamic spectrum management is used in achieving high utilization of the radio-frequency spectrum, particularly with the increasing need for wireless communication services. In this context, adaptive spectrum management strategies are important for systems to modify their spectrum usage in response to real-time conditions. Another approach is to employ spectrum aggregation, which involves merging several separate frequency bands to create a broader channel, improving the rate of data transmission and overall effectiveness. Moreover, the utilization of frequency hopping can help decrease interference and improve security by quickly changing frequencies based on a set pattern. These tactics that adapt allow for better use of the spectrum, decrease congestion, and enhance the network's overall performance [10].

Different wireless communication technologies demonstrate practical applications of adaptive spectrum management. This is accomplished by assigning spectrum resources dynamically according to current demand and network conditions. Figure 15.12 shows Wi-Fi networks utilize adaptive spectrum management with dynamic frequency selection to prevent interference with radar systems by switching to cleaner channels as needed. These instances show how adaptive spectrum management can improve connectivity and spectrum efficiency in various applications [15].

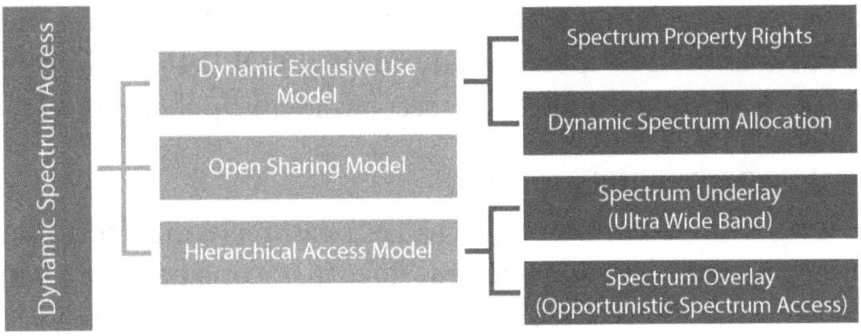

Figure 15.12 Tree diagram of dynamic spectrum access.

15.4.3 5G and Beyond

Network Slicing

Definition and Importance of Network Slicing

The network slicing concept is made up of three layers: 1) service instance layer, 2) network slice instance layer, and 3) tier layer. The concept of an "instance" of any object is created during runtime and should be seen as originating from a time when the object was designed [16]. This allows a service instance to be either an operator service or a service provided by a third party. A network operator utilizes a network slice blueprint in order to generate a network slice instance. A network slice instance offers functionality attributes of a network that a service instance needs. A network slice instance can also be used by multiple users.

The concept of inheritance is also illustrated here, with the components "sub-network blueprint-P" and "sub-network blueprint-Q" deriving from a parent "network slice blueprint-PQ." There is no inheritance involved; hence, the "network slice blueprint" might alternatively be a straightforward combination of "sub-network blueprints" [16].

ML Applications in Network Slicing

Traffic Forecasting

Knowing the resources needed for each slice ahead of time is advantageous because it enables pre-assigning resources to the slices and prevents service level agreement (SLA) breaches. Although they are not appropriate to extract and predict the complex spatiotemporal aspects of mobile traffic in the presence of user mobility, non-ML systems like auto regressive integrated moving average (ARIMA) and the Holt-Winters have been frequently employed for temporal forecasting throughout the years. In order to extract the spatiotemporal dependencies of mobile traffic and to take advantage of the automation of end-to-end resource provisioning for intelligent network slicing, several alternative ML-based forecasting approaches—and DL-based techniques in particular—have grown in popularity in recent years. Moreover, a method to find some actual research about the advantages of DL is through comprehensive literature reviews and analysis of recent academic publications [16].

RNN- and ANN-Based Forecasting

Because long short-term memory (LSTM) can recognize both long-term and spatiotemporal dependencies in data, it is considered a viable forecasting method for network slicing problems. With this intent, [18] utilizes LSTM in resource management procedures to predict the demand for slice bandwidth within a 200-second time frame and a 20-second interval. It is demonstrated that the LSTM-based algorithm enables more users to access the network based on the experimental performance evaluation. Furthermore, the authors created a collaborative learning framework that combines LSTM (for large-timescale traffic forecasting with a 1-hour time interval) and A3C (for small-timescale traffic scheduling, time interval of several milliseconds) to improve resource utilization while taking into account a slice performance isolation constraint. The simulations show that the proposed collaborative framework can achieve significantly

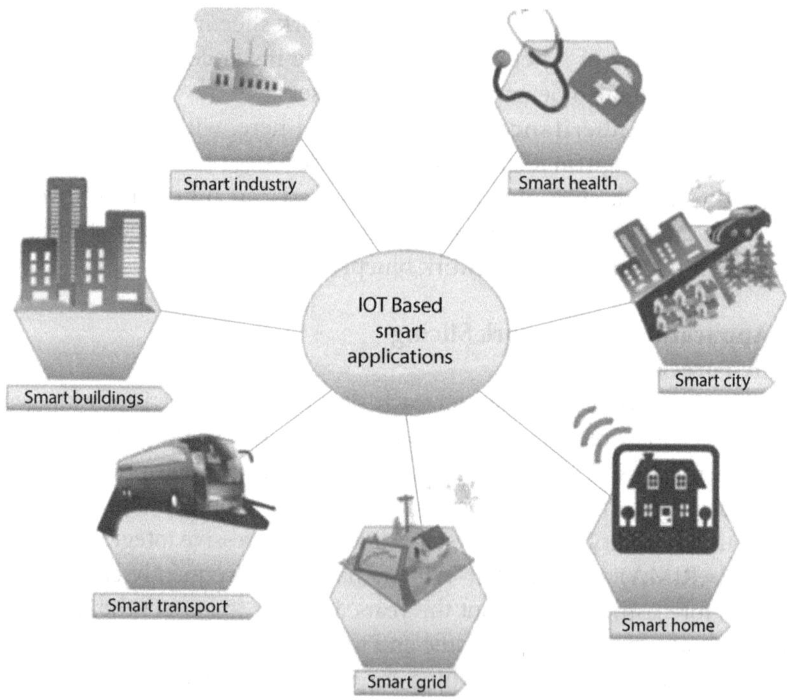

Figure 15.13 Applications of IoT: transforming industries and everyday life.

higher resource utilization than Q-learning and standard actor-critic (AC) approaches that do not involve forecasting [16].

ML for 5G Network Optimization

ML is essential for improving 5G networks, making them more efficient, reliable, and effective. ML's advanced features allow for the supervision and enhancement of intricate 5G network operations, known for their large number of connections, varied services, and dynamic circumstances. In this regard, AI and ML techniques are increasingly used in 5G networks for applications such as predictive maintenance, fault detection, and network optimization [19]. Figure 15.13 shows the deployment of AI/ML in 5G networks allows for the real-time monitoring and analysis of network performance, leading to proactive issue resolution and enhanced overall service quality. As networks continue to grow and evolve, the role of ML in optimizing their efficiency and effectiveness will remain crucial.

Conclusion

ML has come to view as a pivotal force in the realm of networking, offering robust solutions to enhance network performance, security, and management. Through supervised, unsupervised, and RL techniques, ML algorithms provide accurate traffic predictions, efficient resource allocation, and advanced security measures. The historical evolution of networking technologies, coupled with the rise of ML applications, underscores a transformative shift toward more intelligent and autonomous network management. This integration not only optimizes data transfer and network operations but also fortifies security against evolving threats. As networking continues to advance with technologies like 5G and the potential future introduction of 6G, the role of ML will become increasingly critical. By leveraging the capabilities of ML, network administrators can achieve unprecedented stages of competence, reliability, and security, preparing the way for the next generation of intelligent network systems.

Bibliography

1. El Naqa, I. and Murphy, M.J., What Is Machine Learning?, in: *Machine Learning in Radiation Oncology*, I. El Naqa, R. Li, M. Murphy (Eds.), Springer, Cham, 2015, https://doi.org/10.1007/978-3-319-18305-.

2. John, M.M., Holmström Olsson, H., Bosch, J., Developing ML/DL Models: A Design Framework, in: *Proceedings of the International Conference on Software and System Processes (ICSSP '20)*, Association for Computing Machinery, New York, NY, USA, pp. 1–10, 2020, https://doi.org/10.1145/3379177.3388892.
3. Olveres, J., González, G., Torres, F., Moreno-Tagle, J.C., Carbajal-Degante, E., Valencia-Rodríguez, A., Méndez-Sánchez, N., Escalante-Ramírez, B., What is new in computer vision and artificial intelligence in medical image analysis applications. *Quant. Imaging Med. Surg.*, 11, 8, 3830–3853, 2021. doi: 10.21037/qims-20-1151. PMID: 34341753; PMCID: PMC8245941.
4. Helm, J.M., Swiergosz, A.M., Haeberle, H.S., *et al.*, Machine Learning and Artificial Intelligence: Definitions, Applications, and Future Directions. *Curr. Rev. Musculoskelet Med.*, 13, 69–76, 2020. https://doi.org/10.1007/s12178-020-09600-8.
5. Ertel, W., *Introduction to artificial intelligence (2nd ed.)*, Springer, 2018.
6. Jiang, T., Gradus, J.L., Rosellini, A.J., Supervised Machine Learning: A Brief Primer. *Behav. Ther.*, 51, 5, 675–687, 2020. https://doi.org/10.1016/j.beth.2020.05.002.
7. Singh, A., Thakur, N., Sharma, A., A review of supervised machine learning algorithms, in: *2016 3rd International Conference on Computing for Sustainable Global Development (INDIACom)*, New Delhi, India, pp. 1310–1315, 2016.
8. Ghahramani, Z., Unsupervised learning, in: *Summer school on machine learning*, pp. 72–112, Springer Berlin Heidelberg, Berlin, Heidelberg, 2003.
9. Usama, M., *et al.*, Unsupervised Machine Learning for Networking: Techniques, Applications and Research Challenges. *IEEE Access*, 7, 65579–65615, 2019. doi: 10.1109/ACCESS.2019.2916648.
10. Samsuden, M.A., Diah, N.M., Rahman, N.A., A Review Paper on Implementing Reinforcement Learning Technique in Optimising Games Performance, in: *2019 IEEE 9th International Conference on System Engineering and Technology (ICSET)*, Shah Alam, Malaysia, pp. 258–263, 2019, doi: 10.1109/ICSEngT.2019.8906400.
11. Fayaz, S.A., Sidiq, J., Zaman, M., Butt, M.A., Machine learning: An introduction to reinforcement learning, in: *Machine Learning and Data Science: Fundamentals and Applications*, pp. 1–22, 2022.
12. Pise, N.N. and Kulkarni, P., A Survey of Semi-Supervised Learning Methods, in: *2008 International Conference on Computational Intelligence and Security*, Suzhou, China, pp. 30–34, 2008, doi: 10.1109/CIS.2008.204.
13. Boutaba, R., Salahuddin, M.A., Limam, N., *et al.*, A comprehensive survey on machine learning for networking: evolution, applications and research opportunities. *J. Internet Serv. Appl.*, 9, 16, 2018. https://doi.org/10.1186/s13174-018-0087-2.
14. Singh, K. and Agrawal, S., Comparative analysis of five machine learning algorithms for IP traffic classification, in: *2011 International Conference on*

Emerging Trends in Networks and Computer Communications (ETNCC), Udaipur, India, pp. 33–38, 2011, doi: 10.1109/ETNCC.2011.5958481.
15. Ruíz-Guirola, D.E., López, O.L.A., Montejo-Sánchez, S., Souza, R.D., Bennis, M., Performance Analysis of ML-Based MTC Traffic Pattern Predictors. *IEEE Wirel. Commun. Lett.*, 12, 7, 1144–1148, 2023. doi: 10.1109/LWC.2023.3264273.
16. Hui, J.Y., Resource allocation for broadband networks. *IEEE J. Sel. Areas Commun.*, 6, 9, 1598–1608, 1988. doi: 10.1109/49.12887.
17. Hussain, F., Hassan, S.A., Hussain, R., Hossain, E., Machine Learning for Resource Management in Cellular and IoT Networks: Potentials, Current Solutions, and Open Challenges. *IEEE Commun. Surv. Tutor.*, 22, 2, 1251–1275, 2020. doi: 10.1109/COMST.2020.2964534.
18. Djigal, H., Xu, J., Liu, L., Zhang, Y., Machine and Deep Learning for Resource Allocation in Multi-Access Edge Computing: A Survey. *IEEE Commun. Surv. Tutor.*, 24, 4, 2449–2494, 2022. doi: 10.1109/COMST.2022.3199544.
19. Zhang, Y., Hua, W., Zhou, Z., Suh, G.E., Delimitrou, C., Sinan: ML-based and QoS-aware resource management for cloud microservices, in: *Proceedings of the 26th ACM International Conference on Architectural Support for Programming Languages and Operating Systems*, pp. 167–181, 2021.
20. Ros, S., Eang, C., Tam, P., Kim, S., ML/SDN-Based MEC Resource Management for QoS Assurances, in: *International Conference on Computer Science and its Applications and the International Conference on Ubiquitous Information Technologies and Applications*, Springer Nature Singapore, Singapore, pp. 591–597, 2022.
21. Liao, H.-J., Lin, C.-H.R., Lin, Y.-C., Tung, K.-Y., Intrusion detection system: A comprehensive review. *J. Netw. Comput. Appl.*, 36, 1, 16–24, 2013. https://doi.org/10.1016/j.jnca.2012.09.004.
22. Suthaharan, S. and Suthaharan, S., Decision tree learning, in: *Machine Learning Models and Algorithms for Big Data Classification: Thinking with Examples for Effective Learning*, pp. 237–269, 2016.
23. Rokach, L. and Maimon, O., Decision Trees, in: *Data Mining and Knowledge Discovery Handbook*, O. Maimon, and L. Rokach, (Eds.), Springer, Boston, MA, 2005, https://doi.org/10.1007/0-387-25465-X_9.
24. Vishwanathan, S.V.M. and Murty, M.N., SSVM: a simple SVM algorithm, in: *Proceedings of the 2002 International Joint Conference on Neural Networks. IJCNN'02 (Cat. No.02CH37290)*, Honolulu, HI, USA, vol. 3, pp. 2393–2398, 2002, doi: 10.1109/IJCNN.2002.1007516.
25. Aburbeian, A.H.M. and Fernández-Veiga, M., *Secure Internet Financial Transactions: A Framework Integrating Multi-Factor Authentication and Machine Learning. Algorithms*, 5, 1, 177–194, 2024. https://doi.org/10.3390/ai5010010.
26. Insan, I.M., Sukarno, P., Yasirandi, R., Multi-Factor Authentication Using a Smart Card and Fingerprint (Case Study: Parking Gate). *Indonesia J. Comput. (Indo-JC)*, 4, 2, 55–66, 2019. https://doi.org/10.34818/INDOJC.2019.4.2.309.

27. Sun, S., Rappaport, T.S., Thomas, T.A., Ghosh, A., Nguyen, H.C., Kovacs, I.Z., Partyka, A., Investigation of prediction accuracy, sensitivity, and parameter stability of large-scale propagation path loss models for 5G wireless communications. *IEEE Trans. Veh. Technol.*, 65, 5, 2843–2860, 2016.
28. Aalirezaei, A. and Shokouhyar, S., Designing a sustainable recovery network for waste from electrical and electronic equipment using a genetic algorithm. *Int. J. Environ. Sustain. Dev.*, 16, 1, 60, 2017. Retrieved from http://www.inderscience.com/link.php?id=10001371.
29. Boccardi, F., *et al.*, Five disruptive technology directions for 5G. *IEEE Commun. Mag.*, 52, 2, 74–80, 2014.
30. Rappaport, T.S., *et al.*, Millimeter wave mobile communications for 5G cellular: It will work! *IEEE Access*, 1, 335–349, 2013.
31. Eskandari, H., Imani, M., Moghaddam, M.P., Convolutional and recurrent neural network based model for short-term load forecasting. *Electr. Power Syst. Res.*, 195, 107173, 2021. https://doi.org/10.1016/j.epsr.2021.107173.
32. Laccourreye, O. and Maisonneuve, H., French scientific medical journals confronted by developments in medical writing and the transformation of the medical press. *Eur. Ann. Otorhinolaryngology Head Neck Dis.*, 136, 6, 475–480, 2019. https://doi.org/10.1016/j.anorl.2019.09.002.
33. Vlahogianni, E.I., Karlaftis, M.G., Golias, J.C., Short-term traffic forecasting: Where we are and where we're going. *Transp. Res. Part C Emerg. Technol.*, 43, 1, 3–19, 2014. https://doi.org/10.1016/j.trc.2014.01.005.
34. Najemba, J.H., Tang, Y., Iwendi, C., Ohwoekevwo, A., Srivastava, G., Jo, O., Realizing Efficient Security and Privacy in IoT Networks. *Sensors*, 20, 9, 2609, 2020. https://doi.org/10.3390/s20092609.

16

Amharic Multi-Class Sentiment Analysis Model: Leveraging Deep Learning for Emotion Detection in Text

Rojer Berhanu, Minakhi Rout*, Suresh Chandra Satapathy and Junali Jasmine Jena

School of Computer Engineering, KIIT University, Bhubaneswar, India

Abstract

A considerable amount of work has been made into developing models for assessing sentiment in the English language. Despite this, there is still a necessity for additional research and resources relevant to non-English languages such as Amharic. An application of a multi-class sentiment analysis model to the Amharic language is provided in this article. The model has been implemented and is based on a technique known as combined deep learning. Combining the layers of a convolutional neural network (CNN) with a bidirectional long short-term memory (BiLSTM) results in the development of the proposed multi-class sentiment analysis model, which we refer to as the bidirectional convolutional recurrent neural network (BCRNN). In our model, the capabilities of the BiLSTM for gathering sequential dependencies are merged with the strengths of the CNN for capturing local attributes to give a single solution that takes advantage of both sets of capabilities. Because of these two variables, the model has a greater capacity to capture the fine-grained details and contextual information required to carry out a sentiment analysis on text written in Amharic. For training and weighting the model, Ethiopic Twitter Dataset for Amharic is utilized as a data source. The results show that the model can recognize the emotions expressed in written Amharic text. The fact that the model can consider both the local characteristics and the sequential dependencies of the data contributes to an increase in the model's accuracy. The proposed BCRNN achieved an accuracy of 0.89.

**Corresponding author*: minakhi.routfcs@kiit.ac.in

Pradosh Kumar Gantayat, Sandeep Kumar Panda, S. Balamurugan and Sheng-Lung Peng (eds.) Hyper-Intelligent Networks: Exploring the Future of Connectivity for Society 5.0, (349–364) © 2026 Scrivener Publishing LLC

Keywords: Sentiment analysis, Amharic language, multi-class classification, convolutional neural network, bidirectional LSTM

16.1 Introduction

Text classification is a comprehensive area with several subfields, one of which is called emotion or sentiment analysis. Sentiment or emotion analysis is a subfield of text categorization that focuses on identifying feelings, views, sentiments, perceptions, or assessments regarding a particular subject or its qualities as expressed in a text document [1]. The availability of sizable annotated datasets and the study's focus on popular languages has led to much sentiment analysis research and resources for commonly used languages like English compared to understudied languages like Amharic [2]. Despite this, Amharic has gotten little attention in natural language processing (NLP) applications due to inadequate resources to create such techniques. Furthermore, due to linguistic, cultural, and technological context differences, Amharic sentiment analysis is challenging using established models and techniques for most resource-rich languages [3]. Therefore, developing sentiment analysis model is a significant breakthrough in Amharic NLP; there needs to be more studies in Amharic NLP utilizing typical deep learning (DL) and machine learning techniques, and few studies have been conducted in this area.

The sentiment analysis model leverages DL techniques to achieve exceptional results in detecting emotions in text. With the advancements in DL technologies, sentiment analysis models based on deep networks have shown considerable success in various fields, including NLP [4]. DL-based sentiment classification models have outperformed traditional techniques in sentiment analysis, and they can do so without heavily relying on feature engineering [5]. Individual DL models have been widely employed and demonstrated to generate outstanding outcomes in NLP, particularly for sentiment analysis. As a result, some researchers have attempted to mix these methods to enhance their models' performance while utilizing each advantage to enhance their models performance while using each benefit. For extracting local features, convolutional neural network (CNN) is a well-known model. Recurrent neural networks (RNNs), on the other hand, are widely renowned for their ability to manage distant dependencies. Thus, integrating them would enable the model to extract both types of information, which is an exciting approach [6]. Researchers recently presented various hybrid models to carry out diverse sentiment analysis tasks.

We propose a combined DL technology bidirectional convolutional RNNs (BCRNNs) and neural word embedding models for Amharic sentiment analysis that can achieve exceptional results in detecting emotions in the text without relying heavily on feature engineering the proposed BCRNN associated with a CNN with bidirectional long short-term memory (BiLSTM). The Amharic multi-class sentiment analysis model uses a neural word embedding model to construct an Amharic sentiment text. Additionally, the machine learning algorithms utilized in the multi-class sentiment analysis model are assumed to discriminate between target sentiment classes correctly [7]. The model identifies emotions in the text through multi-class classification techniques, where each sentence is assigned to unique of several pre-defined sentiment classes. The Amharic multi-class sentiment analysis model shows outperformed results compared to previously studied models.

Amharic is a Semitic branch of an Afro-Asiatic language family primarily spoken in Ethiopia and holds significant cultural, historical, and political importance. With an estimated 32 million natal tongues and 25 million non-native speakers [8], Sentiment analysis in Amharic presents unique challenges compared to widely studied languages like English. These challenges include linguistic characteristics, limited resources and datasets, and language idiosyncrasies that categorize Amharic as an under-resourced language [9]. Addressing these challenges requires a combination of linguistic expertise, data collection efforts, and the development of language-specific models and resources. This serves as motivation for this work.

The Amharic multi-class sentiment analysis model presented in this article aims to advance sentiment analysis in Amharic and to provide insights into the sentiment analysis challenges specific to the language. By addressing these challenges, we propose a model that utilizes the Ethiopic Twitter Dataset for Amharic (ETD-AM), first made available in [10], which was broken down into four categories: neutral, positive, negative, and mixed, contained about 9.4K tweets. This experiment was not conducted with the mixed class. Therefore, 1,634 positive tweets, 3,727 neutral tweets, and 1,870 negative tweets were employed in the following investigations. By addressing the specific needs and challenges of sentiment analysis in Amharic, developing a multi-class sentiment analysis model empowers Amharic speakers. It contributes to diverse fields such as language research, policy-making, business intelligence, and cultural understanding. It enables better decision-making, fosters effective communication within the Amharic-speaking community, and extends its impact beyond linguistic boundaries. The remaining portions of the paper are arranged: Section 16.2 discusses comparable works. Whereas Section 16.4 contains the experimental discussion and findings,

Section 16.3 offers the technique. Section 16.5 provides a summary of the paper's findings and recommendations for the future. The list of abbreviations used throughout the paper is given in Annexure-I.

16.2 Related Works

In current years, many studies in academic fields have been concentrating on sentiment classification using DL. These new findings suggest that a model built on DL for categorizing feelings increases the category's accuracy.

This work [11] combines aspect-level sentiment analysis of Amharic text with mixed DL. Amhara Mass Media Corporation's Facebook page provided the dataset with an Excel format. The comment exporter program generated 10,000 Excel comments. The dataset was trained and tested using [long short-term memory (LSTM), CNN, gated recurrent unit (GRU)–CNN, and CNN-LSTM]. With 98.57% testing accuracy in two classes, the LSTM model outperforms other models in the study. In [10], authors employ a Telegram bot to collect 9.4K tweets to produce the social media-friendly Amharic Sentiment Analysis Bot (ASAB) annotation tool. Three Telegram users annotate each tweet. Machine learning approaches for Amharic sentiment analysis are being examined with 60.51% accuracy and 58.48% F1-score of three classes that are categorized on the basis of network embedding calculated using a distributional thesaurus, and the FLAIR (forward-looking AI reasoning) DL text classifier defeated the previously studied supervised classifiers.

This article [12] offers a unique DL model used for emotion detection of the Arabic language on a double-layer LSTM architecture for maintaining long-term associations with a single-layer CNN architecture for local feature mining. The CNN and LSTM feature maps were sent to the support vector machine classifier. A FastText word embedding is used with this paradigm. The model performs exceptionally well in extensive tests on a multi-domain corpus, with an accuracy rate of 90.75% for two classes. In this study, CNN-BiLSTM employs word vector training with Skip-gram model, a large unmarked corpus, to combine CNN with BiLSTM neural network [13]. CNN-BiLSTM inputs text from a learned word vector [14]. BiLSTM can employ sentence semantics from prior and subsequent context information. CNN extracts hidden elements from the text. Finally, Adamax optimization produces emotive microblog mention text. CNN and BiLSTM boost learning in the proposed model. Text emotion analysis accuracy rose to 8.51% over the solo CNN model to 94%.

Their study [14] proposes sentiment padding instead of zero padding. It stabilizes the input data sample and increases the sentiment content of each review, developing models for sentiment analysis based on DL-dubbed lexical-assimilated double-channel CNN-LSTM models that combine CNN with LSTM/BiLSTM outputs. Recent neural network advances inspire these models. The proposed strategy outperforms many existing methods on complicated datasets on Stanford Sentiment Treebank. Because the same consonants can be used to make several letters in the Amharic alphabet in addition to various vowels, vowel combinations, and unique keys, researchers [15] are interested in predicting the words that will come after them. They introduce a network model called a bidirectional long short-term GRU to anticipate the following word in the Amharic language. With 63,300 Amharic sentences, they tested the proposed network model and achieved 78.6% accuracy.

Implicit sentiment categorization is being studied by [16] using a deep neural network (DNN)–based approach. LSTM, DNN, BiLSTM, and CNN classification algorithms analyzed the user's implicit emotion text. The BiLSTM word-level attention mechanism classification model is studied. According to experimental results on the studied dataset, the LSTM successions and CNN classification models outperform the DNN model in sentiment classification. BiLSTM-based attention mechanism classification model identified positive categories with the highest R-value. They proposed a multiscale character-level sentiment analysis model for short Afaan Oromoo texts using CNNs and bidirectional neural network by automatically learning meaningful representations of networks to extract textual semantics [17]. Due to its simplicity, training efficiency, and outstanding performance in other morphologically rich languages, convolutional and bidirectional neural networks were utilized. The project used Facebook and Twitter data because there is no Afaan Oromoo corpus. Using the Facebook dataset, they achieved 93.3%, 91.4%, and 94.1% accuracy for CNN, BiLSTM, and CNN-BiLSTM.

There have been various works on Amharic sentiment analysis too. The study [18] uses word embedding, DL feed-forward neural network, LSTM, CNN, and BiLSTM, as well as traditional model with cosine similarity to classify Amharic sentence-level social media attitudes. They use the 3,000-snippet Amharic Twitter dataset and data augmentation to expand model-training datasets. They achieved 82.2% accuracy using Amharic corpus and sentence transformer. Grid search and CNN with LSTM are used to create a novel DNN model for emotion classification [19]. This study tests CNN, K-nearest neighbor, LSTM-CNN, LSTM, and CNN-LSTM on various datasets for precision, sensitivity, accuracy, specificity, and F-1 score.

Based on hyperparameter tuning, their model outperforms baseline models with more than 96% accuracy. Another study by Yimam *et al.* [26] used a bot named "ASAB" for annotations of Amharic text from social media. They used 9.4K tweets collected and applied "FLAIR" text classifier based on DL approach. It outperformed other supervised models in the literature. Similarly, Alemayehu *et al.* [27] did a sentiment analysis of Amharic news from Ethiopia from the political perspective and used CNN, BiLSTM, and CNN-BiLSTM for text classification. CNN-BiLSTM hybrid models outperformed other models by achieving an accuracy of 91.60%.

16.3 Proposed Approach

The combination of a CNN and a BiLSTM layer is what gives the suggested model architecture its name, "convolutional bidirectional recurrent neural network." This design has shown success in capturing both local and global relationships in text data, which makes it useful for jobs involving sentiment analysis because of its versatility. The following Figure 16.1 provides a visual description of the architecture of BCRNN.

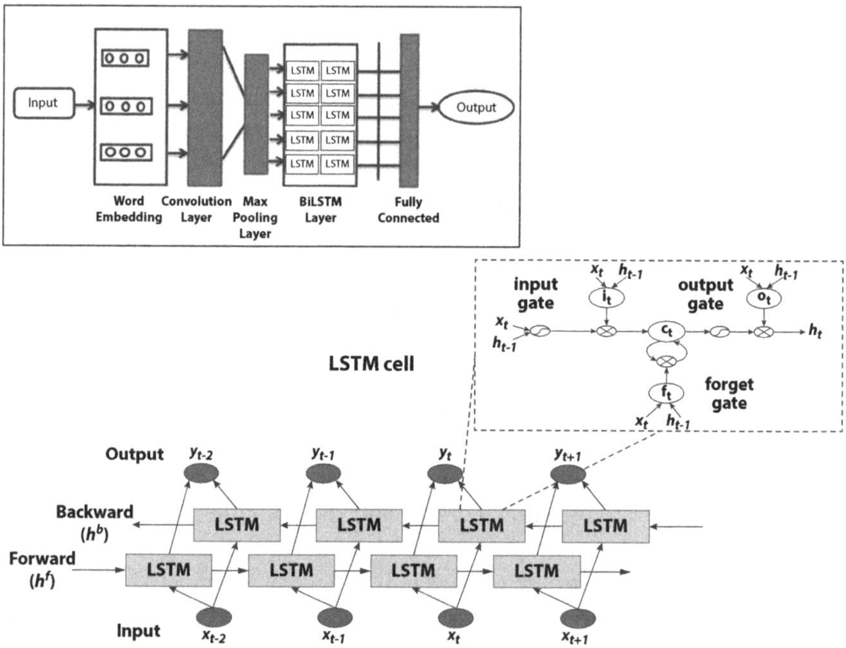

Figure 16.1 The architecture of BCRNN.

Convolutional Neural Network (CNN) for text processing is a DL model specifically adapted to handle sequential data, such as sentences or documents. Unlike traditional CNNs used for images, a text-based CNN utilizes one-dimensional (1D) convolutions, where filters slide along the sequence, capturing local patterns and combinations of words as feature maps [20]. By stacking multiple convolutional layers, the network learns hierarchical representations of the text, recognizing low-level patterns like n-grams and higher-level patterns like phrases and sentence structures. Max-pooling or global pooling operations help to reduce dimensionality and extract the most salient features from the learned representations. The final layers, often fully connected or recurrent, process the aggregated features to make predictions on various NLP tasks, such as sentiment analysis, text classification, named entity recognition, and text generation. Text-based CNNs have demonstrated impressive results from raw text, leading to advancements in natural language understanding and a wide array of applications across text-based domains.

Recurrent Neural Network (RNN) for text processing is a powerful DL model designed to handle sequential data like sentences or documents. Unlike traditional feedforward networks, RNNs have loops that allow them to maintain hidden states, which act as memory, enabling them to process sequential information while considering the context of previous inputs [21]. This recurrent structure enables RNNs to capture dependencies and long-term patterns within the text. They are well-suited for tasks like language modeling, machine translation, sentiment analysis, and text generation. However, traditional RNNs can suffer from vanishing or exploding gradients, limiting their ability to capture long-term dependencies effectively. To address this, variants like LSTM and GRU were introduced, which mitigate the vanishing gradient problem. RNNs have significantly contributed to the advancement of **NLP** tasks, allowing models to learn contextual information and achieve impressive results in a wide range of language-related applications.

Long Short-Term Memory (LSTM) is a specialized type of RNN architecture crucial for text processing and sequential data analysis. LSTMs address the vanishing gradient problem of traditional RNNs by incorporating memory cells, input, forget, and output gates. These components regulate information flow, enabling LSTMs to capture long-range dependencies and contextual information within text [22]. LSTMs excel at tasks like language modeling, machine translation, sentiment analysis, and text generation. Their ability to selectively store and retrieve information over extended sequences facilitates the modeling of complex linguistic structures, making them a cornerstone of advanced **NLP** models and contributing significantly to the state-of-the-art performance across a multitude of language-related applications.

Gated Recurrent Unit (GRU) is a variant of RNN architecture widely employed in text processing and sequential data tasks. GRUs address the vanishing gradient problem by utilizing reset and update gates, enabling them to capture contextual information and long-range dependencies within text. By adaptively controlling the information flow, GRUs strike a balance between memory retention and computational efficiency, making them particularly effective for tasks like language modeling, machine translation, sentiment analysis, and text generation. GRUs have gained prominence due to their ability to capture intricate patterns in sequential data, leading to enhanced performance and advancements in various NLP applications [23].

The capabilities of the CNN to identify long-term dependencies and then the LSTMs to identify local features are utilized in the model described here. At first, a CNN layer with Conv1D computation is applied to process the input vectors and obtain the text-level characteristics that are local to the text. Following the CNN layer is the RNN layer, comprised of BiLSTM units/cells. The input for this layer is the output of the CNN layer, which are the feature maps. CNN provides the local features, which are then utilized by the RNN layer, which then learns the long-term dependencies of the regional characteristics of emotions to determine whether or not the tweets are positive, negative, or neutral. Figure 16.2 presents an illustration of the model that will be proposed. CNN layers have been kept at front followed by dense LSTM network at the behind.

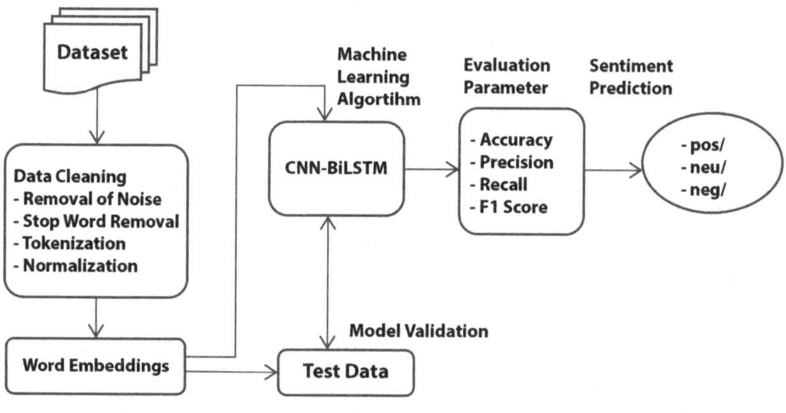

Figure 16.2 Overall methodology of the proposed work.

16.4 Data Preprocessing and Implementation

This work assesses the presence of the hybrid model on the dataset after implementing it in Python on the Google Colab environment and using the previously specified hybrid model. The dataset will be discussed in the following subsections, and the implementation of the recommended algorithms, which include state-of-the-art methods to perform Amharic multi-class sentiment classification.

16.4.1 Dataset Description

An ETD-AM, which was first made public by [10], is the dataset consumed for the sentiment classification job; around 9.4K tweets were included in the initial dataset, divided into four category classes: neutral, negative, positive, and mixed. The mixed class was left out of this trial. Consequently, 3,727 neutral tweets, 1,634 positive tweets, and 1,870 negative tweets were used in subsequent studies.

16.4.2 Data Preprocessing

Panda Data Frame objects read the data on scikit-learn's library, and LabelEncoder encodes class labels. Preprocessing converts raw texts into model-friendly formats. A Python script uses the re python module for regular expressions to clean text by removing null or missing values, duplicated samples, URLs (Uniform Resource Locators), mentions, hashtags, punctuation, English characters, and digits. Removed Amharic stop words, tokenized, and normalized the remaining terms. A 60%-20%-20% distribution splits a dataset into training, validation, and test subsets. To validate categorization models, an embedding layer maps text to word embeddings and dense vector representations. By capturing semantic links between words, word embeddings let the machine learn meaningful phrases from input text [24]. Embeddings are learned and adjusted during training to match Amharic text sentiment. The sentiment analysis model can assess Amharic text sentiment and capture its nuanced semantic linkages within the language.

16.4.3 Model Implementation

The hybrid DL model is now being utilized on Google Colab. Google Colab is a cloud environment based on Jupyter Notebooks that provides Graphical Processing Units and Tensor Processing Units for the purpose of performing in-depth computations [25]. Python was utilized for both the preprocessing and the formation of the machine learning classifiers in the experiment. The Keras Python package is utilized in the process of implementing the hybrid CNN-BiRNN model. Reading datasets and processing arrays requires the usage of the Numpy and Pandas libraries, respectively. In order to prepare data for analysis, the Natural Language Toolkit software is utilized. The scikit-learn package is used for a variety of tasks, including the implementation of classifiers, the evaluation of findings, and the processing of data. When plotting graphs, the Matplotlib library is typically utilized.

The sequential model from the Keras DL Python library is used to create the projected hybrid DL model and depicted in Figure 16.3. The sequential model is composed of numerous layers of neurons, including the following:

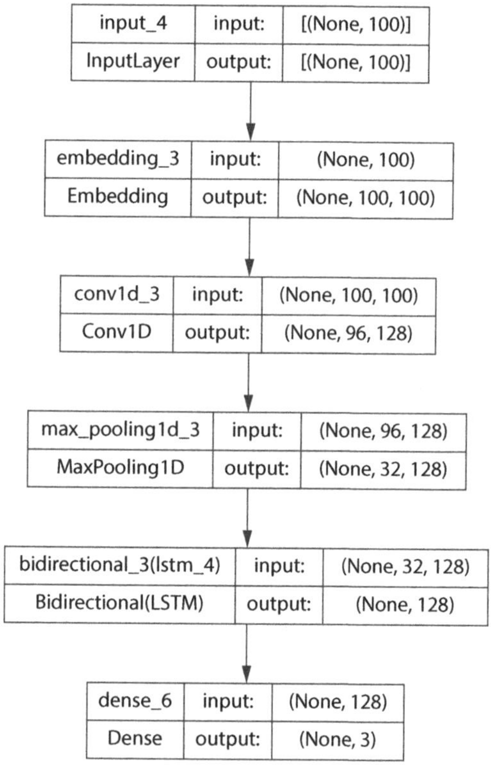

Figure 16.3 Model summary of BCRNN model.

Input Layer

Amharic text that has been partially processed is provided to the input layer. The input layer of the algorithm is looking for sequences of word indices from the Amharic lexicon. At the input layer, data are brought into the model.

Embedding Layer

In NLP, word embedding is a technique that represents words as numbers in a multi-dimensional space. The linkages and similarities between the words are reflected in the direction and distance of the vectors in the space. The embedding layer is responsible for the creation of detailed vector representations of the word indices. These embeddings keep track of the semantic connections between terms, which enable the machine to learn meaningful imagery based on the text that is being received. The embedding layer is the part of the code that moves each word index into a dense vector with output dim set to 100. The sentiment embeddings of Amharic text get more accurate after training.

Convolutional Neural Network (CNN)

Word embeddings are made more confusing by the CNN layer. When processing input embeddings, many filters, each with a fixed kernel size, glide across the data to retrieve local information. Filters are used to capture patterns and features at varying scales, which assists the model in locating content that is relevant. In addition, the code makes use of one Conv1D layer that is equipped with 128 filters and has a kernel size of 5. The non-linearity of convolutional processes is contributed by the Rectified Linear Unit activation function.

Max Pooling Layer

The dimensionality of the CNN layer's features is decreased through max pooling. It selects the most important aspects from each feature map by focusing on the most important values. The most important aspects are preserved while being condensed through pooling, which brings the most important input to the forefront of successive tiers. Utilizing Max Pooling 1D with a pool size of three results in a reduction of the feature maps by a factor of three.

Bidirectional Long Short-Term Memory

The pooled features are used for the BiLSTM layer's process of learning Amharic text sequence dependencies. The input is handled both forward and backward by two layers of LSTM. The 64-unit BiLSTM layer in the code is capable of understanding the sentiment of a text through the use of both the immediate and the more distant context. In order to prevent overfitting, the dropout rates for input and recurrent connections are set to 0.2.

Output Layer

The output layer makes predictions about people's feelings by using the data from the layers that came before it. A dense layer that contains three units in the code represents sentiments that range from negative to neutral to positive. The practical softmax activation function transforms the model's output into a probability distribution over the several sentiment classes. This gives the model the capacity to make predictions by selecting the category that has the highest probability.

The design of the model that was selected after much deliberation incorporates both the capabilities of CNN and BiLSTM. Whereas the CNN layers are responsible for recognizing local characteristics and patterns in the input text, the BiLSTM levels are responsible for identifying sequential dependencies and context [22]. This distinction is important because the CNN layers are responsible for finding local characteristics and patterns. This combination enables the model to accurately grasp the sentiment that is communicated in text that is written in Amharic because it takes into consideration information from both the local and the global levels.

16.5 Result and Discussion

After an intense preprocess, we used 8.6K tweets from the ETD-AM, split into training, validation, and test subsets (60%-20%-20% split). On the chosen datasets, the BCRNN model has been applied. In Table 16.1, the experiment's findings are shown. As can be seen, the classification based on macro-average recall, F1-score, and precision, of the BCRNN-based model is superior, which helps the performance of text classification algorithms.

The developed BCRNN model offers a promising solution for sentiment analysis in Amharic text, addressing the language's linguistic complexities and cultural nuances. Through techniques such as tokenization, embedding, CNN, and BiLSTM, the model accurately classifies sentiment and captures the unique aspects of Amharic. The confusion matrix is obtained from the BCRNN model and shown in Figure 16.4.

Table 16.1 Precision, recall, F1-score, and accuracy of the tested classification model.

Model	Accuracy %	Precision %	Recall %	F1-Score %
BCRNN	0.89	0.89	0.88	0.88

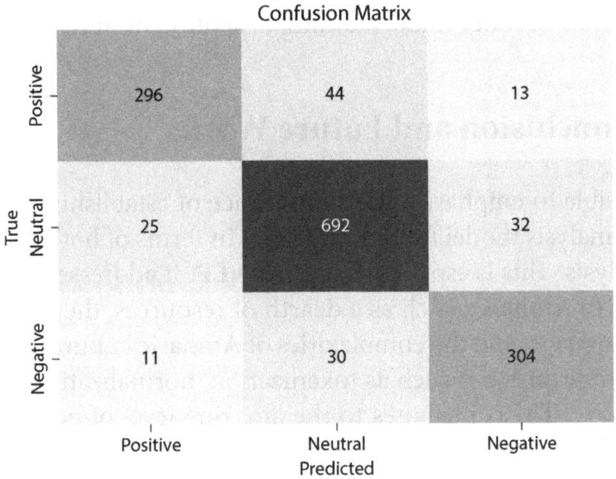

Figure 16.4 The confusion matrix of the BCRNN model.

Confusion Matrix

In this section, we will compare the findings of our actual inquiry to some more recent research that focuses on sentiment analysis (Table 16.2). In both experimental and comparative evaluations, we found that our proposed model, the BCRNN, performed significantly better than the one described here.

Table 16.2 Comparison of models.

Reference	Method	Accuracy%	Precision%	Recall%	F1-Score%
Ref. 10	Role2Vec	0.61	0.56	0.61	0.58
Ref. 18	ST + Cosine Similarity +KNN	0.821	0.822	0.821	0.821
Ours	**BCRNN**	**0.89**	**0.89**	**0.88**	**0.88**

As reflected in the confusion matrix above, its performance demonstrates its ability to generalize and learn from data. The model's application provides valuable insights for understanding customer opinions, public sentiment, and brand perception in the Amharic-speaking population, aiding data-driven decision-making and effective reputation management. Moreover, it opens avenues for future research, including exploring advanced techniques and expanding the training dataset for enhanced performance and a broader understanding of sentiment in Amharic.

16.6 Conclusion and Future Work

It is impossible to emphasize the significance of establishing a multi-class sentiment analysis model for Amharic text in terms of both **NLP** and sentiment analysis. This is especially true for **NLP**. It addresses problems that are specific to Amharic, such as a dearth of resources, the difficulty of the Amharic language, and the complexities of Amharic cultural practices. The utilization of techniques such as tokenization, normalization, embedding, CNN, and BiLSTM contributes to the amazing level of performance that is achieved by the model. The accuracy of the model's sentiment classification is 89% as a direct result of this utilization. The findings of our inquiry indicate that the model that we suggest is preferable than the ones that are presented in references [10, 18], and enhancing and broadening the scope of future research can be accomplished by boosting the dataset's size and diversity, honing in on language-specific traits, and implementing transfer learning strategies. These are all areas that need to be taken into consideration.

References

1. Liu, B., *Sentiment analysis and opinion mining*, Chicago: Morgan & Claypool Publishers, Springer Cham, May 2012, DOI: 10.2200/S00416ED1V01Y201204 HLT016.
2. Neshir, G., Rauber, A., Atnafu, S., Meta-learner for amharic sentiment classification. *Appl. Sci.*, 11, 18, 18, 2021. DOI:10.3390/app11188489.
3. Tonja, A.L., *et al.*, Natural Language Processing in Ethiopian Languages: Current State, Challenges, and Opportunities, in: *Proceedings of the Fourth workshop on Resources for African Indigenous Languages ({RAIL} 2023)*, pp. 126–139, 2023, DOI:arxiv-2303.14406.

4. Yuan, J.H., Wu, Y., Lu, X., Zhao, Y.Y., Qin, B., Liu, T., Recent advances in deep learning based sentiment analysis. *Sci. China Technol. Sci.*, 63, 10, 1947–1970, 2020. https://doi.org/10.1007/s11431-020-1634-3.
5. Zhou, Y., A Review of Text Classification Based on Deep Learning. *ACM Int. Conf. Proc. Ser.*, 132–136, 2020. https://doi.org/10.1145/3397056.3397082.
6. Habimana, O., Li, Y., Li, R., Gu, X., Yu, G., Sentiment analysis using deep learning approaches: an overview. *Sci. China Inf. Sci.*, 63, 1, 1–36, 2020. https://doi.org/10.1007/s11432-018-9941-6.
7. Liu, L., Chen, H., Sun, Y., A Multi-Classification Sentiment Analysis Model of Chinese Short Text Based on Gated Linear Units and Attention Mechanism. *ACM Trans. Asian Low-Resour. Lang. Inf. Process.*, 20, 6, 109:1–109:13, 2021. DOI: https://doi.org/10.1145/3464425.
8. Eberhard, D.M., Simons, G.F., Fennig, C.D., *Ethnologue: languages of the World.* SIL International, Dallas, 2019. Online: https://www.ethnologue.com.
9. Ranathunga, S., Lee, E.-S.A., Prifti Skenduli, M., Shekhar, R., Alam, M., Kaur, R., Neural Machine Translation for Low-resource Languages: A Survey. *ACM Comput. Surv.*, 55, 11, 1–37, 2023. https://doi.org/10.1145/3567592.
10. Yimam, S.M., Alemayehu, H.M., Ayele, A.A., Biemann, C., Exploring Amharic Sentiment Analysis from Social Media Texts: Building Annotation Tools and Classification Models. *COLING 2020 - 28th Int. Conf. Comput. Linguist. Proc. Conf.*, 1, 1048–1060, 2020. doi: 10.18653/v1/2020.coling-main.91.
11. Abeje, B.T., Salau, A.O., Ebabu, H.A., Ayalew, A.M., Comparative Analysis of Deep Learning Models for Aspect Level Amharic News Sentiment Analysis, in: *2022 International Conference on Decision Aid Sciences and Applications, DASA 2022*, pp. 1628–1633, 2022, doi: 10.1109/DASA54658.2022.9765172.
12. Ombabi, A.H., Ouarda, W., Alimi, A.M., Deep learning CNN–LSTM framework for Arabic sentiment analysis using textual information shared in social networks. *Soc. Netw. Anal. Min.*, 10, 1, 53, 2020. https://doi.org/10.1007/s13278-020-00668-1.
13. Li, A. and Yi, S., [Retracted] Emotion Analysis Model of Microblog Comment Text Based on CNN-BiLSTM. *Comput. Intell. Neurosci.*, 2022, 1, 1669569, 2022.
14. Li, W., Zhu, L., Shi, Y., Guo, K., Cambria, E., User reviews: Sentiment analysis using lexicon integrated two-channel CNN–LSTM family models. *Appl. Soft Comput. J.*, 94, 106435, 2020. DOI 10.1016/j.asoc.2020.106435.
15. Endalie, D., Haile, G., Taye, W., Bi-directional long short term memory-gated recurrent unit model for Amharic next word prediction. *PLoS One*, 17, 8 August, 1–10, 2022. DOI: 10.1371/journal.pone.0273156.
16. Pan, D., Yuan, J., Li, L., Sheng, D., BESC 2019 - 6th International Conference on Behavioral, Economic and Socio-Cultural Computing, Proceedings, in: *BESC 2019 - 6th International Conference on Behavioral, Economic and Socio-Cultural Computing, Proceedings*, pp. 1–4, 2019, DOI:10.1109/BESC48373.2019.8963171.

17. Oljira, M., Kaliyaperumal, K., Natea Sima, B., Sori, K., Sentiment Analysis for Afaan Oromoo Using Combined Convolutional Neural Network and Bidirectional Long Short-Term Memory. *Int. J. Adv. Res. Eng. Technol. (IJARET)*, 11, 11, 101–112, 2020. https://ssrn.com/abstract=3799805.
18. Tesfagergish, S.G., Damaševičius, R., Kapočiūtė- Dzikienė, J., Deep Learning-Based Sentiment Classification of Social Network Texts in Amharic Language. *Commun. Comput. Inf. Sci.*, 1740 CCIS, 63–75, 2022. DOI: 10.1007/978-3-031-22792-9_6.
19. Priyadarshini, I. and Cotton, C., A novel LSTM–CNN–grid search-based deep neural network for sentiment analysis. *J. Supercomput.*, 77, 12, 13911–13932, 2021. https://doi.org/10.1007/s11227-021-03838-w.
20. Mhamed, M., Sutcliffe, R., Sun, X., Feng, J., Almekhlafi, E., Retta, E.A., Improving Arabic Sentiment Analysis Using CNN-Based Architectures and Text Preprocessing. *Comput. Intell. Neurosci.*, 2021, ii, 2021.
21. Bhowmik, N.R., Arifuzzaman, M., Mondal, M.R.H., Sentiment analysis on Bangla text using extended lexicon dictionary and deep learning algorithms. *Array*, 13, 100123, 2022.
22. Qaisar, S.M., Sentiment Analysis of IMDb Movie Reviews Using Long Short-Term Memory, in: *2020 2nd Int. Conf. Comput. Inf. Sci. ICCIS 2020*, pp. 1–4, 2020, DOI:10.1109/ICCIS49240.2020.9257657.
23. Kamil, G. and Setiawan, E.B., Aspect-Level Sentiment Analysis on Social Media Using Gated Recurrent Unit (GRU). *Build. Inf. Technol. Sci.*, 4, 4, 2023. DOI:10.47065/bits.v4i4.3105.
24. Soufan, A., Deep learning for sentiment analysis of Arabic text, in: *ACM International Conference Proceeding Series*, pp. 1–8, 2019, https://doi.org/10.1145/3333165.3333185.
25. Colab, G., *Google. Google Colab. Accessed*, Apress Berkeley, CA, 2019, [Online]. Available: https://colab.research.google.com, DOI:10.1007/978-1-4842-4470-8.
26. Yimam, S.M., Alemayehu, H.M., Ayele, A., Biemann, C., Exploring amharic sentiment analysis from social media texts: Building annotation tools and classification models, in: *Proceedings of the 28th International conference on computational linguistics*, pp. 1048–1060, 2020.
27. Alemayehu, F., Meshesha, M., Abate, J., Amharic political sentiment analysis using deep learning approaches, in: *Scientific Reports*, vol. 13, p. 17982, 2023.

17

Retail Sales Prediction Using Intelligent Time-Series Analysis

Vuttaradi Akarsh

School of Mathematical and Computer Sciences, Heriot-Watt University, Edinburgh, Scotland, UK

Abstract

Store sales time-series forecasting aims to forecast the future retail sales of the store specializing in motor vehicles using historical sales data. Time-series forecasting is a crucial component of data analytics-based research. The main objective of forecasting motor vehicle retail sales is to empower businesses and to be aware of decision making related to staffing, inventory control, and other operational aspects within the automotive retail sector. Accurate sales predictions enable businesses to optimize resource utilization, enhance operational efficiency, and, ultimately, maximize profits. In the research, an Autoregressive Integrated Moving Average (ARIMA) approach is applied to the creation of a reliable forecast model. The historical sales data from 2015 to 2023 is used as the basis to forecast future sales for 2024 and beyond. Using a combination of moving average and autoregressive components, the ARIMA model offers a data-driven method for identifying trends and time-series correlations in retail sales data for automobiles.

***Keywords*:** Machine learning, time-series forecasting, ARIMA method, automotive retail, business forecasting

17.1 Introduction

The retail industry is dynamic, and it is crucial to anticipate and adjust to changing customer trends. Time-series forecasting for store sales becomes an essential aspect of retail business management with the critical insight

Email: av4008@hw.ac.uk

Pradosh Kumar Gantayat, Sandeep Kumar Panda, S. Balamurugan and Sheng-Lung Peng (eds.) Hyper-Intelligent Networks: Exploring the Future of Connectivity for Society 5.0, (365–380) © 2026 Scrivener Publishing LLC

needed to manage the complex transactions between market trends. Retailers can gain understanding of future sales trends by utilizing historical sales data, which gives them the ability to make appropriate choices regarding many aspects of business management. This study explores the complex field of time-series forecasting, which is a machine learning application that uses historical data to predict future circumstances.

The Autoregressive Integrated Moving Average (ARIMA) is a model that is used widely to accurately find the temporal correlations and trends present in time-series data. Predicting the total quantity of products sold in a given year is the main goal of this study. This predictive model goes beyond simple numerical forecasts; it is more than just a quantitative tool; it is a strategic compass that helps retailers create flexible business plans. These tactics, which are based on precise sales projections, address important aspects of retail management such as price strategies, inventory optimization, and focused marketing campaigns.

A key component of our methodology is a thorough approach to data preprocessing, whereby noise and null values are removed to create the reliable and accurate forecasting model. The ability of the model to generate precise predictions is confirmed by the visualization and analysis of crucial aspects, which provide additional understanding on the complexities of dataset. The goal of this research is to improve merchants' ability to make decisions by giving them a useful model, rather than just adding about time-series forecasting theory. As we go through this study, we see how sellers have the ability to not only predict but also to direct their own fates by precisely adjusting the retail environment.

17.2 Literature Review

1. "Sales Forecasting in Retail: In terms of Regression Models and Time Series" [4]: This study compared the accuracy of time-series models and regression models for forecasting store sales. The results show that the time-series models generally outperformed the regression models.
2. "Time Series Forecasting of Retail Sales: In terms of Seasonal LSTM and ARIMA" [5]: This study compared the accuracy of seasonal ARIMA and long short-term memory (LSTM) models for predicting sales. The results showed that the LSTM model outperformed the ARIMA model.

3. "Store Sales Forecasting Using Deep Learning Time-Series Models" [6]: This study proposed a deep learning–based approach for store sales forecasting using time-series models such as LSTM and convolutional neural networks. The findings show that the suggested model achieved higher accuracy in terms of traditional time-series models.
4. "A Comparison of Methods for Store Sales Forecasting" [7]: This study compared the accuracy of many time-series models like ARIMA, exponential smoothing, and dynamic factor models for forecasting store sales. The outcomes show that dynamic factor models outperformed the other models.
5. "Predicting Store Sales With Recurrent Neural Networks" [8]: This study used recurrent neural networks (RNNs) to forecast store sales. The findings presented that RNN model performed better than traditional time-series models like exponential smoothing and ARIMA.
6. "Forecasting Retail Sales: The Effectiveness of Neural Networks, Support Vector Regression, and the Bayesian Approach" [9]: This study compared the accuracy of neural networks, support vector regression, and the Bayesian approach for forecasting retail sales. The results showed that the neural network model achieved the highest accuracy.
7. "A Hybrid Model for Sales Prediction in the Retail Industry" [10]: This study proposed a hybrid model combining multiple time-series models, including exponential smoothing, ARIMA, and Fourier analysis, for forecasting store sales. The results showed that hybrid model achieved higher accuracy when compared to individual models.
8. "Forecasting Retail Sales Using Machine Learning: A Comparative Study of Regression Models and Time Series Models" [11]: This study compared the accuracy of various regression and time-series models for predicting retail sales. LSTM model had the maximum accuracy, according to the data.

17.3 Predicting Future Sales

Dataset:
We utilized the Motor Vehicles dataset for our project, segregating it into training and test datasets. The "train.csv" file represents the training dataset, encompassing historical data spanning from 2015 to 2023, whereas the "test.csv" file serves as the test dataset. Our objective is to forecast sales for the years 2024 to 2026.

In the training phase, we leverage the training dataset to construct machine learning models, utilizing features such as the number of sales within the test set. The prediction involves estimating a monthly quantity of this measure. The date column follows the format dd-mm-yyyy, whereas the date block number denotes a consecutive month number, facilitating ease of reference and analysis.

17.4 Proposed Methodology

17.4.1 Data Visualization

Firstly, we examined the dataset based on our intuition and reduced the noise in the data. No columns were deleted, as all the columns are considered important. In the next step, we created a histogram using Matplotlib, a built-in Python library, and examined the features and their effects on sales. This provided us with a better understanding of the data and helped us make decisions for our next steps based on insights gained from data visualization tools. The graph below illustrates the frequency versus sales. Figure 17.1 shows the frequency distribution of sales data.

Imported Libraries:

NumPy: An excellent Python library for numerical computing that offers array operation, linear algebra, and mathematical functions.

Pandas: Data frame and series data structures are provided by a flexible Python library that can be used to manipulate and analyze data.

Matplotlib: A popular Python plotting library for creating static, interactive, and graphical visualizations.

Scikit-learn: A full Python machine learning library, with algorithms for classification, regression, clustering, and so on.

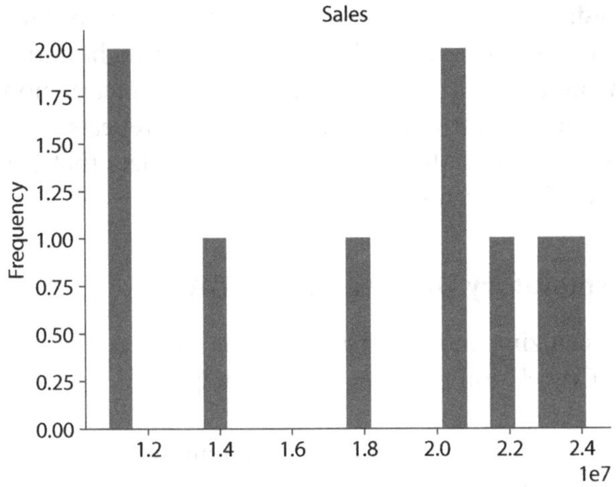

Figure 17.1 Frequency of sales data.

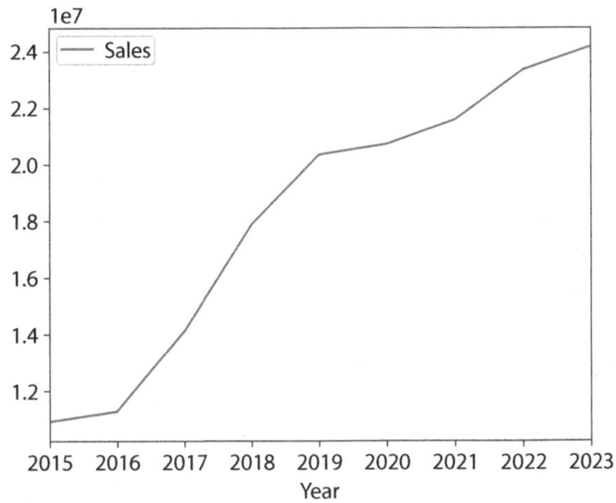

Figure 17.2 Sales data graph.

Statsmodels ARIMA: A Python statistical modeling library that provides ARIMA models to forecast and analyze time series.

Based on the provided data, this graph proves to be very useful as it helps us understand the trend and seasonality in the sales. Figure 17.2 shows the store sales trend over the years highlights seasonal peaks and long-term growth patterns. To further enhance our analysis, we will mathematically decompose the graph, separating it into three distinct components:

1. **Trend:** A common orderly, either straight or nonlinear, element that is non-repeating and varies throughout time.
2. **Seasonality:** A common precise, either direct or nonlinear, element that varies throughout time and repeats.
3. **Noise:** A non-systematic element of the data that is neither seasonal nor trending.

17.4.2 Exploratory Data Analysis (EDA)

It involves visualizing and understanding the dataset.

Example: Correlation matrices and heatmaps.

- EDA is a vital initial stage in data analysis where we analyze, summarize, and visualize data to understand its key characteristics.
- EDA helps us gain insights into our data, detect outliers, spot patterns, and test assumptions.

Correlation is a measure that helps us understand how two variables are related.

- If both variables increases, then the correlation is +1.
- If one variable increases and other decreases, then the correlation is −1.
- No linear relationship between two variables.

A. Stationary and Non- Stationary

Before decomposition, determining non-stationary or stationary data is essential. Stationarity implies that mean, variance, and autocorrelation, which are statistical properties, do not vary throughout time. Conversely, non-stationary data demonstrates these changing statistical properties. Identifying and addressing stationarity is pivotal for accurate time-series analysis.

Once decomposed, we can delve deeper into the stationary and non-stationary components, refining our understanding of underlying structure and fluctuations within the sales data. This comprehensive method equips us with the tools to use the time series' intrinsic characteristics to make well-informed decisions.

Null Hypothesis:

The presumption that there is no charge, no distinction between two groups, or no connection between two variables is how it is frequently expressed.

Alternative Hypothesis:
To check if the data is non-stationary or stationary, Augmented Dickey-Fuller (ADF) test is used.

The ADF test is a statistical test that assesses a time-series dataset's stationarity. Stationarity is a key assumption in time-series analysis, implying that statistical properties like mean, variance, and autocorrelation does not vary throughout time.

The test involves evaluating the unit root presence in the time-series data. If the data contains a unit root, then it is considered non-stationary, indicating that its statistical properties may vary throughout the time. Conversely, if the unit root is absent, then the data is deemed stationary.

The test provides a p-value and test statistic. A significant test statistic and a p-value below a chosen significance level that can be commonly 0.05 suggest rejecting the null hypothesis of the presence of a unit root, indicating that the data is stationary.

A stationary time-series improves prediction reliability and simplifies modeling process of time-series forecasting. The Dickey-Fuller test, therefore, serves as a crucial diagnostic tool in determining the stationarity of time-series data, guiding subsequent analysis and modeling decisions.

B. Pre-Processing

Firstly, missing values and outliers are addressed to ensure data completeness and accuracy. Data cleaning tasks, such as error correction and consistency checks, are performed to enhance the overall quality of the dataset. Additionally, time-series–specific preprocessing steps are implemented, including proper timestamp formatting and sorting. Feature engineering is carried out to derive new variables or modify existing ones, improving the dataset's representational power. Visualizations are utilized to gain insights into data distribution, trends, and seasonality, guiding subsequent modeling decisions. The overarching goal of data preprocessing is to prepare the motor vehicles dataset for meaningful analysis and modeling. By addressing data quality, ensuring consistency, and enhancing features, the preprocessing steps lay a solid foundation for building reliable time-series forecasting models that can present insightful information into future sales patterns.

C. Encoding Categorical Data (EDA)

Variables in categorical data have a limited, fixed number of possible values, such as gender (male/female) or color (red/blue/green). These variables cannot be directly used in mathematical models, thus requiring encoding. We will explore the various techniques for encoding categorical data in Python, a versatile and popular programming language extensively used for data analysis.

17.5 Understanding Categorical Data

The two primary categories of categorical data: ordinal and nominal. Nominal data has no inherent order, like colors or names, whereas ordinal data has a specific order, such as ratings or rankings. It is essential to differentiate between these types as the encoding techniques differ based on this distinction.

17.5.1 One-Hot Encoding

One of the most common methods for encoding categorical data is one-hot encoding. In this technique, each category is represented by a binary feature, in which presence is denoted by a 1 and its absence by a 0. One-hot encoding is ideal for nominal data and prevents the model from assuming an incorrect order or hierarchy among categories.

Example: Suppose we have a dataset with a "color" column containing categories like red, blue, and green. After applying one-hot encoding, the "color" column will be replaced by three separate columns (color green, color blue, and color red) with binary values.

17.5.2 Label Encoding

Label encoding is another method suitable for ordinal data, where categories have a specific order. In label encoding, based on its order, a unique integer is assigned to each category. While this method is straightforward, it may lead to unintended consequences, such as imposing false relationships between categories.

Example: Consider a dataset with a "size" column containing categories like small, medium, and large. Label encoding would replace these categories with integers (0, 1, 2) based on their order.

17.5.3 Ordinal Encoding

Ordinal encoding strikes a balance between one-hot encoding and label encoding by preserving the ordinal relationship between categories without creating unnecessary dimensions. This method assigns a single feature column with integer values corresponding to the ordinal relationship among categories. Figure 17.3 presents the complete machine learning workflow adopted in this study.

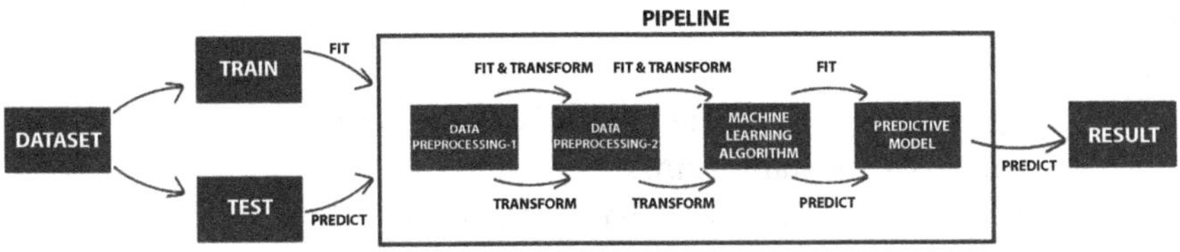

Figure 17.3 Flowchart of machine learning process.

17.5.4 Modeling

Time-series analysis plays a vital role in ARIMA model, which is a generalization of an Autoregressive Moving Average model in statistics and econometrics. To gain a deeper understanding of the data or to make predictions about future points in the series, both models are fit to time-series data. When there are indications of non-stationarity in the mean of the data, ARIMA models are used. In these circumstances, the "integrated" portion of the model's first differencing step may be used at least once that non-stationarity of the mean function, or the trend eliminated. Seasonal differencing can be used to remove the seasonal component from a time series when seasonality is clearly visible. It indicates that ARIMA component autoregressive (AR) that is an evolving variable of interest is regressed on its own lagged values. The moving average (MA) component shows that the error terms in the regression are a linear combination and that their values happened simultaneously at various historical points. I (short for "integration") indicates that the difference between these values, and the prior value has taken place of the data values (this derivation process may have been repeated numerous times). To get the model as near to the data as feasible is the aim of each of these functions. For example, we used the ARIMA model for our dataset to predict the future of sales for the Tata Steel dataset.

17.5.5 Autoregressive Model

The AR model focuses on the correlation between the time series' historical values and current value.

$$y_t = \mu + \sum_{i=1}^{p} \phi_i y_{t-i} + \epsilon_t$$

where

- "y_t" is current value at time "t" of time series.
- "\mu" is a constant term.
- \phi_i are the autoregressive coefficients for lag i.
- "y_{t-i}" are the lagged values of time series.
- "\epsilon_t" is error term at time t, thought to have a mean "0" and a distribution that is normal.

17.5.6 SARIMA

An expansion of the ARIMA model is SARIMA, which includes seasonality. It is useful for modeling time-series data with seasonal patterns. SARIMA models include parameters that account for seasonal trends:

- Seasonal autoregressive (P)
- Seasonal differencing (D)
- Seasonal moving average (Q)

Model Structure:
The SARIMA model is denoted as SARIMA(p, d, q)(P, D, Q, s).

- p, d, and q are the non-seasonal parameters:
  - p: No. of autoregressive terms.
  - d: order of differencing (to make the series stationary).
  - q: number lag forecast errors there are in the prediction equation.
- P, D, and Q are the seasonal parameters:
  - P: No. of seasonal autoregressive terms.
  - D: Seasonal differencing order.
  - Q: No. of seasonal moving average terms.
- s is the length of the seasonal cycle (e.g., 12 for monthly statistics with seasonality in the year).

Captures Seasonality: Seasonal components allow SARIMA to identify recurring trends in your data (e.g., monthly sales peaks).

Improves Forecast Accuracy: It typically offers better forecasting accuracy than simple ARIMA for data with seasonal patterns.

Adjusts for Seasonality: Seasonality is addressed explicitly, making predictions more reliable and meaningful.

17.5.7 Applying SARIMA

Model Fitting: Fit a SARIMA model to your data by specifying the seasonal and non-seasonal parameters based on your understanding of the data and visualizations (e.g., autocorrelation and partial autocorrelation plots).

Model Selection: Choose appropriate parameters using statistical tests, model comparison, and error metrics.

Forecasting: Utilize the fitted model to predict the time series' future values.

Figure 17.4 shows the autocorrelation function (ACF) plot used to detect repeating patterns in the sales time series, aiding in ARIMA model configuration.

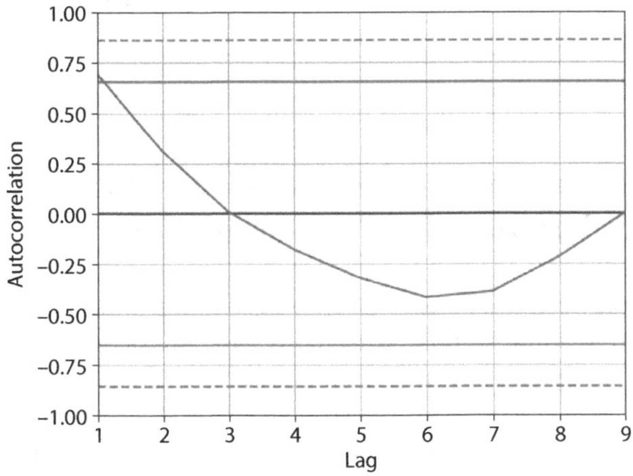

Figure 17.4 Autocorrelation graph.

17.6 ARIMA Method vs. Other Methods

Table 17.1 presents a comparison of ARIMA with other forecasting models for store sales time-series.

Table 17.1 Comparison of ARIMA with other methods.

Advantages of models for store sales time-series forecasting	ARIMA	Exponential smoothing models	Neural networks	Gradient boosting machines	STL	VAR
Simplicity and Interpretability	Yes	Yes	No	No	No	No
Well-Established Methodology	Yes	Yes	Yes	Yes	Yes	Yes
Flexibility	Yes	No	Yes	Yes	Yes	Yes
Statistical Soundness	Yes	Yes	No	Yes	Yes	Yes
Time Dependency	Yes	Yes	Yes	Yes	No	Yes
Robustness With Limited Data	Yes	Yes	Yes	Yes	Yes	Yes
Benchmark Performance	Yes	Yes	Yes	Yes	Yes	Yes

17.7 Comparing the ARIMA Model with Other Models for Sales Time-Series Forecasting

1. Time-series characteristics: Forecasting time-series data that exhibit trends, seasonality, and autocorrelation and for analyzing ARIMA is suitable. If sales data exhibits these characteristics, then ARIMA can successfully capture them.
2. Easy to understand and interpret: Compared to certain other complex forecasting models, ARIMA models are such models that are easy to grasp and comprehend. It is simpler to describe the model to stakeholders because the model's parameters (the order of the autoregressive, integrated, and moving average components) have straightforward interpretations.

3. Flexibility: ARIMA models can handle data from both single-variable and multi-variate time series. You can easily add more predictors or factors affecting your sales into the ARIMA framework if you have any. You can gather additional data thanks to this flexibility, which may also help forecast accuracy.
5. Diagnostic tools: ARIMA models have diagnostic tools that let you assess the model's suitability and quality of fit. To make sure the model reflects the underlying trends and generates accurate forecasts, you can check the residuals for stationarity, independence, and normalcy.
6. Forecast performance: A number of sectors and areas, including sales forecasting, have effectively used ARIMA models. Many times, especially when the time-series data exhibits distinct trends and seasonality, ARIMA models outperform other forecasting techniques in terms of accuracy and dependability.
7. Benchmark model: For time-series forecasting, ARIMA models are used as a standard. We can assess alternative models' performance against ARIMA to see how well they function and whether their added complexity and computing demands are necessary.
8. Interpolation and extrapolation: ARIMA models are capable of both extending projections outside the range of the available data and interpolating missing values within the observed time range. This is especially helpful for sales forecasting, when there may be gaps or future time periods without previous sales data.

17.8 Results

The dataset utilized in this model pertains to the sales of motor vehicles, encompassing data from 2015 to 2023. The figure presented below illustrates the predictions for the years 2024 to 2026, derived from historical information. The company's sales exhibited growth post-2016 and experienced significant expansion by 2023. According to the forecast, the company can anticipate sales in the range of 2 to 2.5 crores in 2024, with a slight decrease anticipated in both 2025 and 2026. Several factors contribute to these projected changes, such as economic downturn, increasing fuel prices, or possibly due to other factors, the predictions consistently indicate a declining trend in revenues. The decline in revenues offers insights suggesting that the company may be encountering

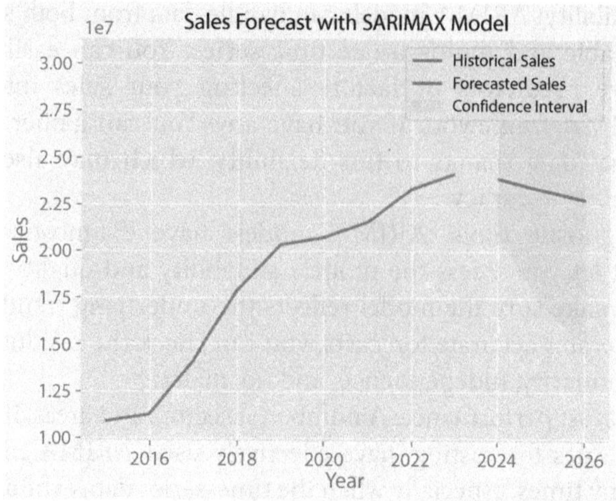

Figure 17.5 Future forecasting of sales.

heightened competition within the industry. This is evident from the influx of new players into the business, leading to a more evenly distributed customer base. In response, the company could consider adjusting its profit margins as a strategic measure to attract and retain customers. As depicted in Figure 17.5 the model's future sales forecasts show projected trends for the upcoming years, offering insight into expected store performance.

17.9 Future Work

The future work on this project can be the successful implementation of model opens doors for its integration into broader business initiatives. Utilizing the forecast information to improve inventory control and make sure that stock levels correspond to expected demand. Integrating with supply chain optimization initiatives could improve productivity by enabling on-time manufacturing and delivery in accordance with projected sales trends. Promoting activities in line with anticipated times of strong demand can be made more focused by working with marketing analytics initiatives. Moreover, investigating synergies with financial planning initiatives may offer a comprehensive perspective, coordinating budgetary allotments with anticipated variations in revenue. Furthermore, the sales team can be given more authority to anticipate and respond to client demands during periods of high demand by incorporating the forecasting model into Customer Relationship Management systems.

Conclusion

Store sales time-series forecasting is a useful and effective exercise, which is quite beneficial for the retailers in picturing the future numbers to fill in for the sales operation. When historical sales information is verified, it becomes possible to recognize tendencies, patterns, and cycles of selling that may inform decisions regarding a product's stocking, pricing, or sales promotion. There are many methods of time-series forecasting such as moving averages, exponential smoothing, seasonal and trend decomposition using loess (STL), ARIMA, or deep learning models, for example, RNN. The choice of forecasting model depends on the model's performance metrics, such as accuracy and reliability. Combining it with accurate data cleaning, data normalization issues, and data feature extraction, the availability of proper data for analysis is guaranteed for time-series forecasting. Besides, an evaluation of the reliability of the forecasting models with the right performance indicators is necessary, and the models should be updated every time new data is obtained. Hence, store sales time-series are useful and potent for valuable information and insights and offer a means for firms, especially in the retail industry, to make better decisions that lead to more effectiveness and profitability.

Bibliography

1. *The Tata Steel Dataset from*, https://www.kaggle.com/datasets/ankitthebemer/tata-steel-stock dataset-20152021.
2. https://towardsdatascience.com/introduction-to-arima-for-time-series-forecasting-ee0bc285807a.
3. https://www.investopedia.com/terms/a/autoregressive-integrated-moving-average-arima.asp#:~:text=An%20autoregressive%20integrated%20moving%20average%2C%20or%20ARIMA%2C%20is%20a%20statistical,values%20based%20on%20past%20values.
4. Time Series and Regression Models. *J. Retailing Consum. Serv.*, 31, 275–284.
5. Ahmed, S., Tariq, S., Murtaza, F., Ashraf, F., Time series forecasting of retail sales: a comparison of seasonal ARIMA and LSTM. *J. Retailing Consum. Serv.*, 53, 101967, 2020.
6. Anjum, N., Kim, D., Kim, C., Store Sales Forecasting Using Deep Learning Time-Series Models. *Expert Syst. Appl.*, 184, 115510, 2021.
7. Marcellino, M., Stevanović, M., Stock, J.H., A Comparison of Methods for Store Sales Forecasting. *Int. J. Forecast.*, 34, 1, 116–131, 2018.

8. Duan, W., Xu, J., Wang, Y., Predicting Store Sales with Recurrent Neural Networks, in: *2017 International Joint Conference on Neural Networks (IJCNN)*, 2017, 2317–2324.
9. Hajir, R. and Vatankhah, B., Forecasting Retail Sales: The Effectiveness of Neural Networks, Support Vector Regression, and the Bayesian Approach. *J. Retailing Consum. Serv.*, 31, 95–103, 2016.
10. Lee, D. and Yoon, K., A Hybrid Model for Sales Prediction in the Retail Industry. *J. Retailing Consum. Serv.*, 44, 119–126, 2018.
11. Ranjan, P., Tulsiani, S., Srivastava, S., Forecasting Retail Sales Using Machine Learning: A Comparative Study of Regression and Time Series Models. *J. Retailing Consum. Serv.*, 55, 102103, 2020.

18

Technologically Enhanced Anti-Theft Door Locking and Alert System Based on IoT

Sumanta Chatterjee[1]*, Jui Pattnayak[2] and Pabitra Kumar Bhunia[3]

[1]*Department of Computer Science and Engineering, JIS College of Engineering, Kalyani, Nadia, West Bengal, India*
[2]*Department of Information Technology, JIS College of Engineering, Kalyani, Nadia, West Bengal, India*
[3]*Department of Business Administration, Vidyasagar University, Midnapore, Paschim Medinipur, West Bengal, India*

Abstract
Since time immemorial, people have possessed a lot of valuable goods. Some people have also taken a fancy to collect valuable items and safeguard them and then pass those valuable items to their predecessors. Family heirlooms have been a symbol of integrity and pride for generations. So, protecting this hierarchy is of prime importance to the family members. People have come up with lots of different ways to protect their valuable treasures. Since medieval times, lots of traps have been designed to protect their valuables from potential threats. In this chapter, an anti-theft system is developed with the help of Arduino microprocessor. The concept is to connect the system to the registered mobile number of the user, and, thus, it may help to send alert messages when there is an attempt to robbery in the place.

Keywords: Machine to machine, GIVAC, anti-theft system, GSM

18.1 Introduction

In ancient times, robbery was prevalent in different parts of the world. As far as it was known, robbery was considered to be a grave crime. Earlier,

**Corresponding author*: sumanta.chatterjee@jiscollege.ac.in

Pradosh Kumar Gantayat, Sandeep Kumar Panda, S. Balamurugan and Sheng-Lung Peng (eds.) Hyper-Intelligent Networks: Exploring the Future of Connectivity for Society 5.0, (381–402) © 2026 Scrivener Publishing LLC

it was considered to be a felony punishable by death; later, this punishment became less grave, and it started to vary with the seriousness of the crime. Different types of punishments include compensating the injured, lashing the preparator, etc. The last execution for simple theft took place in England in the 18th century. Later, as law and constitution became more refined the graveness of the punishment reduced a lot. Some cases reported attempts to murder while carrying out the robbery. Some thieves were so desperate for money or other valuables that they resort to killing people, thus losing their humanity. Thus, by no means, this act can be forgiven by any/with the advent of technology, and the proof for this criminal offense is much easy to obtain, earlier which was not possible. Earlier, the claim would have been strong if the robber was caught red-handed, but, now, it is possible to collect fingerprints or other samples from where DNA can be extracted, and, then, the further investigation can be done regarding this matter. After facing such consequences, the house owners sometimes became revengeful, thus affecting their mental health. In recent years, concerns regarding mental health are of prime importance because issues like depression are in no way healthy for humans both physically and mentally. Depression can take an ugly detour eventually killing a healthy person.

Robbery takes place not only in residential areas but also in banks, offices, government bodies, and many other organizations. There is a strong need to secure this place from the further attack, which can be done by using different types of traps designed by various parties. As the technological revolution came, these traps became much more advanced and stronger. Countless measures were taken to prevent any crime. Only ringing an alarm is not enough to prevent robbery, additional features need to be administered into the system earlier made to make them sturdier and of use. Such features include closing the room where the crime is taking place or sending alert message to the registered mobile number of the user or to the local police station's number. This will help the people to know that a crime is taking place in which location of the jurisdiction. If the person is not at home, then they can call the police and tell them to check the situation at the place where the device is installed. The police can go to that location and check the severity of the situation and inform the owner about the same. They can also take proper action if the situation has gone out of hand. They can get mental peace and can also get a good night's sleep as they can rest assured about the safety of their valuables. Valuable items can be of various types. There are some that have even become national treasures, which will be a loss to lose for the country. Even for this, security was kept in mind and different contraptions were developed.

Many valuable things were stolen from this world like the painting of Mona Lisa by Leonardo da Vinci was stolen by Vincenzo Perugia in 1911. This Stradivarius is a violin that costs millions of dollars that were made in 1727 by Antonio Stradivari, but it was stolen from an apartment in New York City. The screen of a famous painting by Edvard Munch was worth $120 million, which was stolen by the thieves, but the police were able to recover the painting from the thieves and impart them a suitable punishment. An incredible painting named the Concert by the famous Dutch painter Johannes Vermeer was stolen in 1990 from Isabella Stewart Gardner Museum 1990. Dorothy's red slippers that were worn by her in the movie The Wizard of Oz were taken from Judy Garland Museum, whose cost was around 2.5m pounds. This criminal act was carried out in the year 2005, which is quite recent. This is the reason why we all should work toward the prevention of robbery.

Preventing or avoiding something is the best solution to many grave problems. Thus, the approach taken is toward the prevention of robbery, and, also, if there is an attempt for the same, then the police can impart suitable punishment to the criminal. With technological evolution, criminals have also become more advanced in their field of expertise. They have also come up with new methods to invade a building. So, traps need to be carefully placed in different places to stop their attack. These traps need to be something that is easily handled and budget friendly and they should not harm the robber gravely. Earlier, booby traps were set up to harm the criminal, but this is quite an inhumane way of punishing the criminal. Even using explosives can be dangerous as it will not only harm the robbers, but also it can harm other people present nearby and harming innocent people is also a kind of crime. Now, even if a single innocent person is harmed, then the situation can turn ugly.

Keeping all these things in mind, it is decided to develop an automatic anti-theft system that can be installed anywhere as per the requirement of the user. It is an embedded system equipped with an Arduino and a loud alarm to alert persons nearby. The system needs to be installed in a room and the motors need to be connected to the doors and windows of the room to close them automatically when any unwanted person is accessing the room. Here, we will be using servo motors that rotate to open or close the doors and windows. The motion detecting sensor used here is a passive infrared sensor (PIR) sensor that will detect motion and urge the Arduino to ring the alarm. Also, we can use a node micro controller unit (MCU) to connect this device to the phone number of the user; thus, it will be used to send an alert message to the user, and this will be particularly helpful when the owner is not present at that particular location at the time of the robbery.

The system will contain two switches: the main switch or the power switch will power the whole system and required to be turned on manually for the system to work. This system can be turned on, especially at night or when one is leaving their house empty as a criminal offense is generally carried out at this specific time. The second switch will be the switch for the servo motor that is generally kept turned on and will only be closed when the servo motor has closed all the doors and windows of the room and we need to arrest the robber inside the room or open the doors and windows of the room. Immediately, the switch needs to be turned on for the motor to work accurately. The motor only closes the room when motion is detected by the passive infrared sensors. The light-emitting diode (LED) attached to the system will blink as the situation demands. When the alarm rings the red, LED will blink that will also be an alert signal sent in the form of light. The red color is used to depict something dangerous, even the stop signs are painted red. Even if a person does not know the language, then also they can clearly understand the warning by seeing the red sign. Also, red color has the maximum wavelength, allowing it to travel longer distances without getting disrupted. Also, there will be registers attached to the system to prevent certain components of the embedded system from getting overheated and thus getting damaged from extreme heat than it can tolerate. The breadboard can also be used to integrate the circuit in a single place and make the circuit a little presentable and neat. The insulated connecting wires made from copper are used to make connections between different components of the system. The Arduino will be pre-programmed by us with the help of Arduino IDE software and C++ programming language. So, this system will be both hardware- and software-based and will prove to be of great use to many.

Commercializing this product will be of great value to the different people belonging to different communities. Homeowners, estate owners, business organizations, etc., can use this product and install the same in the place that they require to secure. Mass production of this product will also bring down the cost and; thus, it will be more accessible to the people who are maintaining a budget. Budget-friendly modules are known to do well in the business world as every person is either trying to save money or is trying to make a profit. Also, automated systems are more recognized nowadays as it requires less human intervention and can work independently. Understanding this product by the user requires no technical knowledge as they just need to switch on and off the system at their convenience and installation will be done by professionals. In addition, the output produced by this product is easily interpretable even by the common people as no high-level knowledge is required for understanding a danger alarm. Messages sent by the system will also be easily understood as they will not contain any complicated language and will just contain the message that needs to be delivered. So, bringing this product to the market will be of great value, and considering the above-mentioned reasons, it will have great scope in the post-Covid world. Thus, the automatic anti-theft system also keeps the great potential for further future development and can be upgraded frequently to incorporate new features, thus making the system stronger.

18.2 Literature Review

An anti-theft system for automobile is proposed based on global service for mobile (GSM) and global positioning system (GPS) module. The system is built with the help of high-speed mixed-type single-chip C8051F120. This device is meant to detect automobiles stolen by the automobile owner with the help of a vibration sensor. The location of the vehicle is found out by the integrated GPS module. Through the GSM module, the owner may keep in touch with the automobile system to monitor the safety and reliability of automobiles [1].

In another literature, the importance of protection and security of systems in the petroleum and chemical engineering industries is stated. They developed a traditional anti-theft system to monitoring petroleum pipelines along with the analysis of its advantages and disadvantages. The proposed WSN-based anti-theft system includes a wireless sensor network (WSN) subsystem to transfer data and service—a shared platform. The monitoring and controlling is done by another subsystem. The pre-warning is accurately sensed in the proposed WSN based anti-theft system [2].

In this research, with the incorporation of GPS satellite positioning using an Arduino, an anti-theft system is proposed to control peripheral devices applying sensors in the car to reduce the risk of car theft. The user is allowed to immediately track the vehicle using Google Maps by the anti-theft tracking. The anti-theft tracking allows the user, and the door's reed switch detects any improper external force and the front windshield is activated by the anti-theft system to be completely black [3].

The next research includes GPS car tracking devices, devices for locking steering wheel, locking systems of clutch or brake, voice transmissions, telephone and data system (TDS), and gear locking devices, which are included in this research. To send the ongoing area of the taken vehicle to the owner's phone, GPS beacons are associated with the cell phone framework. Also, the function of these devices will be sent to the owner so that only he/she will know about the car stolen and can activate the anti-theft system.

The devices in the car may detect movement in the car if any and will inform the location of the car to the owner immediately [4].

A multi-zone wireless burglar alarm system with eight regions is the subject of the following research. An infrared sensor chip named as BISS0001 is used as a locator, the microcontroller named as AT89C51 is used as regulator, and LX2262/LX2272 is used as encoder/decoder in this gadget. BISS0001 infrared sensor chip is used as a detector, AT89C51 microcontroller is used as controller, and LX2262/LX2272 is used as encoder/decoder in this device. It can accomplish checking of eight areas, including equipping, incapacitating, and disrupting thieves. The design is equipped with a remote alarm of 25 m. It also can enhance the power transmitting circuit as needed [5].

Subsequently, an anti-theft alarm system for laboratory based on embedded system was designed. The STC89CS2 is an embedded single-chip microcomputer that is the main control chip. The sound and light alarm will be detected by the electric sensor in case the laboratory of the user is abnormal. Consumption of power is low in the overall system along with good concealment, strong adaptability, stable adaptability, low cost, and wide use. It can use to process the unusual and anti-theft situation in the laboratory [6].

Later on, an alarm system based on wireless technology was designed with the help of rich inner resource of Field Programmable Gate Arrays. The system consists of an encoder, Frequency Shift Keying modulation, and a sales control circuit for each channel, all of which will help lower the volume and make the system more reliable. In addition of other anti-theft interference, the alarm system helps to decrease the rate of error-alarm. In case there is case in stand-off areas, alarm is received by the owner. The distance of transmission is more than 4 km in open zones. More sensors can be installed by the user in parallel manner such as smog sensor, combustible gas sensor, or burglar sensor. This system completely meets the requirements for alarm fireproofing and theft prevention, among other things [7].

The authors proposed Bluetooth technology to connect the user and the Admin of PC for accessing the door. For the use of sensors such as motion sensors and vibration sensors, a human detection module is included in the system. All devices communicate with the main control unit PC admin for their operations. The Android app will assist the owner in interacting with the system so that the user can use a camera to view the live feed and gain access to the door. The framework additionally includes highlights like SMS, Email, and against criminal to make it easy for the proprietor to get notices when a client shows up at the entryway as well as when a client attempts to access the entryway without consent. The interaction of owner and the PC Admin enables the owner to look into the login details. Hence, the system can be used as a smart security system in areas such as home networking systems, lockers in the bank, and all offices [8].

Further, a system was developed to analyze the electrical characteristics of a typical anti-theft alarm system and determined by the operation status of the system. The components for the system were selected depending upon the cumulative experience of past 30-year of the authors in the field of security systems [9].

To lessen the gamble of vehicle robbery and misleading problem rate multi-sensor data combination innovation is utilized. Vehicle anti-theft system made by improved multi-sensor information fusion technology based on D-S evidence theory was proposed by the authors. With the help of the GSM network, the traditional alarming issue can be effectively resolved, allowing for real-time control in the event of an accident [10].

As the number of vehicles on the road is increasing day by day, the number of crimes including theft of vehicle is also increasing remarkably. There are many laws in action and security measures are also taken by car manufacturers, but, then, also, thieves can easily find a way to steal a car and vehicle theft is, nowadays, one of the most significant crimes. As, nowadays, vehicles are very costly, it is fruitful for thieves to make a vehicle theft, and a simple redecoration of the theft car makes it not able to track the car. In their paper, the authors gave a cost effective solution for the same. This system may be used and implemented for domestic vehicle owners to protect vehicle theft reasonably [11].

In this literature, improved motorcycle anti-theft system is being proposed. Because the device BLE4.0 consumes less power, it is attached to the motorcycle key, and the radio frequency identification (RFID) tags are installed on the hidden part of the body of the bike. This is a reliable system as the bluetooth low energy (BLE) devices can be hung together on the key at the time the motorcycle is moving at a speed of less than 80 km/hour. The system can also be utilized in the actual situation in Thailand's Prachinburi province [12].

The monitoring and positioning of applications with larger coverage and higher communication efficiency is done by machine-to-machine technology, and new system architecture was suggested. A low-cost Embedded Web Server using Raspberry Pi and the Linux operating system and ARM11 processor is the goal of the proposed work. The configuration is suggested for security of authentication of shutter lock of ATM, to control web-enabled system, sensors, and camera control [13].

For the first time, GSM technology is introduced, which is also the cheapest source of anti-theft system for vehicle tracking–based vehicle tracking system. It is a small device with a GSM module and a number of other parts. SMS is sent by the owner to turn on the system, which will also tell the microcontroller to turn off the car and can collect information about the present location of the car and more. The GSM module will then be stimulated by the microcontroller in order to send a text message about the details to the nearest mobile of the owner. This system is advantageous because it speeds up the owner's vehicle tracking and simplifies the process [14].

This research suggested a remote alarm system based on a GSM technology for automobile. The system consists of microcontroller and TC35 GSM module. A speed sensor and a vibration sensor are also used to create a SMS alarm and a dual-resistant vehicle against theft. It may be of good application prospects due to its cost effectiveness [15].

A pulse transmission attribute based on an anti-theft and location method for power cables was proposed in this research. From the start, hypothetical examination low-voltage beat transmission property linked with normal blames, such as low opposition and break-line deficiencies and confirmation of the achievability of this technique, is made. An identification strategy is proposed next, based on the threshold value and reflection pulse features. At last, low-voltage pulse transmission attributes experiments will be done in cables with different faults, and the veracity of the identification strategy is verified. The anti-theft and monitoring system has important engineering implications for minimizing financial loss and ensured the operational safety of the power system by better locating and identifying stolen cables [16].

The novelty of this system is to prevent robbery of vehicle. The embedded chip of the system has a key to sense inductive proximity sensor at the insertion time and a text message is sent that states about the access of the vehicle to the mobile of the owner which is followed by the unique password-based system inside the car. Small number of characters and the key number of vehicle are included in the password. In case, the user could not input the correct password in three attempts, a text message will be sent to the police comprises of the vehicle number followed by location tracking through a GPS module. The same message is sent to the owner to prevent unauthorized usage. Later on, the fuel injector of the vehicle is inactive so that the car cannot be started in any way. Concurrently, a hidden lock system is activated to lock the unauthorized user inside the vehicle, and the system can only be deactivated by the owner of the secret key lock. This technique will help to take easy steps toward an attempt to the theft of the vehicle [17].

A power cables' anti-theft monitoring system was proposed here based on traveling wave theory and pulse width modulation (PWM). The system is made of a signal generating and measuring circuit, alarm generating alarm circuit, and user interface. At first, the paper consists of discussion of the theoretical analysis, and, then, detailed hardware and software design information was given out. Last but not least, the system's accuracy and functionality were tested experimentally. Results are more than 97% accurate. Additionally, the system has an automatic alarm function and a friendly user interface [18].

An anti-theft mobile phone security system using a basic i/o system was proposed next. It is mobile phone–based system that helps the user to track the location of the mobile device. This hardware implementation–based security system can also track the designed mobile without a battery and SIM. The proposed system is expected to help the designers enhancing the security of the device [19].

The next system is for auxiliary circuit of the energy meter of current transformer based on transient method. The pulse signal is applied to the auxiliary circuit of the current transformer energy meter. To obtain the equivalent resistance and inductance parameter of the circuit, the transient value of the circuit response current is to be measured. The comparison of these parameters with the original parameters helps to examine the state of the circuit and power theft way. The accuracy and reliability of the newly designed anti-power theft method of the energy meter can be verified by the simulation results [20].

The approaching signal of human body, the of the dismantling transformer's metal tool signal, and the forced moving transformer's vibration signal are all detected by means of sensors such as infrared, metal anti-collision inductive, and vibration displacement of human body. The multi-function button and LED display screen are used to control and maintain the normal and stable alarm circuit system, which is ensured by an analog to digital (A/D) converter. The peripheral circuit is used to process and display alarm information. The sound and light warnings and information about display alarm at the time of theft will be sent by the monitoring terminal [21].

An integration of each valuable appliance and GIVAC (group identification of in-vehicle anti-theft component) component is made for anti-theft approach of in-vehicle. When power is on, it can be seen in case of the right car, (group) each self-authentication of GIVAC-enabled appliance is done with the authorized center of the car. The immobilizer can control the authorized center. The anti-theft capability of cars can be improved by this approach [22].

Security and better theft control can be possible by facial recognition and shock treatment, in case an unauthorized person attempts to start the vehicle and the notification is sent by Internet-of-Things (IoT) application. A microprocessor Raspberry Pi, a pie cam along with a Wi-Fi controller, is installed in the vehicle. The system is very simple as well as cost-effectively provides greater security in case of any robbery [23].

The nest research proposed a system to enhance security and to avoid stealing of vehicle. It consists of a single-board embedded system and with a microcontroller equipped with a GSM and a GPS in the vehicle. The object tracking is done by the GSM and GPS technologies, and the most up-to-date information about ongoing trips is provided by this system. Biometric authentication is done to ensure that the correct person is driving or not [24].

This paper analyzed the electrical characteristics of alarm system components. The systems selected for analysis are typical systems found in most residential buildings in Romania. This selection is made based on each author's more than 14 years of experience in the field of security systems [25].

A microcontroller named as PIC16F876A, fingerprint, RFID, GPS-GSM modules, and a tilt sensor is included in this system. Any one such as correct RFID/biometric/password must be provided to start the car. In case, breaking of windows or doors and vehicle movement is measured by tilt sensor, and, then, a message is sent *via* GPS-GSM module to the mobile of the owner containing the location of the car. An alarm is given by the system. The fuel injector connection of the car is deactivated to prevent the unauthorized start of the vehicle any how [26].

Here, the RFID module controls the system to switch on and off. The sensors such as vibration and pyroelectric infrared are triggered, and the location information is sent by the GSM module with the help of the GPS module to the mobile phone of the owner in case the car is stolen. Android software helps the owners to check the location of the vehicle [27].

The authors here proposed a system based on a tamper-proof electronic link between the key of the driver and the ignition system. The transponder consists of a distinct and unchanging radio signal accessed identification code from a transceiver unit in the car in case someone tries to start. Appropriate ignition key and transponder should be there to start the engine. The normal wear and replacement of keys is eliminated [28].

A vehicle theft prevention- based anti-theft system is researched. As per observations done, the current anti-theft system is still unsafe due to which in-vehicle devices' safety and reliability cannot be ensured. An improved anti-theft system is suggested by analyzing its security measure and feasibility. It is expected to show a reference of a configuration for more improved anti-theft systems for in- vehicle devices [29].

With the application of Wireless Sensor Network, an equipment anti-theft tracker is designed to focus on the present scenario that security risks of laboratory property remain. It consists of a trigger and tracker. Infrared, Bluetooth technology, GPS, and GSM are used to achieve anti-theft alarming and mobile tracking. It maximizes laboratory safety protection and teaches and ensures smooth running of scientific research [30].

The authors suggested an automotive security system to disable an automobile and its key auto systems through remote control while stolen. So, it prevents thieves from stealing the vehicle. It also protects from theft of key auto systems for re-selling. As per the experimental results, the recommended system is feasible, and the vehicle is securely controlled by the owner [31].

This research suggested a RFID technology–based system. The object attached RFID tag and a motion sensor are integrated. The interrupt function is used to detect the motion of an object automatically. The multi-communication principle between a tag and a reader that is used for the real-time notification of theft is realized. The proposed anti-theft system was tested for motion detection efficiency and RF communication performance in the multi-floored building to verify its reliability [32].

18.3 Idea of the Proposed System

The "Automatic Anti-Theft System" is a system that will work like an Intruder Alarm. So, this is all about building an anti-theft alarm system or an intruder alarm system using Arduino Uno and PIR sensor. We are enhancing this system with many features like adding Buzzer, LED light, and a Micro Servo Motor. Here, Servo Micro Motor will work by detecting the motion of an intruder inside the range of the PIR sensor. Now, the main working of the "Automatic Anti-Theft System" will be detecting the motion of an intruder to that we have to set/fit this system at the main entrance or at the favorable entrance from where the intruder/thief can enter. In addition, this kind of situation is mainly faced at night when we are out of our home. So, its main work will be at night. After setting this system and installing it and providing the main supply of current, after activation, it will work accordingly:

- The motion of a warm body or the intruder/thief is first detected by the PIR sensor, and, then, it will alert us by a sharp buzzing alarm through a fitted buzzer on it.
- Now, if anyone manages to go inside the room, then the door and windows will be automatically closed and the intruder will be locked inside the room which will be done by Servo Motor.

- As the intruder is trapped, he will be not able to come out, and, in this way, the intruder will be caught red-handed.
- To open the door then we need to switch off the switch to open the door.
- This whole system will be set by the active sim card of the owner of the house. That means that this will be sending notifications when the buzzer will produce the alarm. So, that he/she gets alert and can take steps properly in order to save his/her house.

18.4 Circuit Diagram

Figure 18.1 shows the circuit diagram of the anti-theft device.

18.4.1 Components Required

a) Arduino Uno: It is a microcontroller board having 14 digital input and output pins, out of which 6 can be used as PWM outputs, 6 number of analog inputs, a 16-MHz ceramic resonator, USB connection, a power jack, an ICSP header, and a reset button (Figure 18.2).
b) Bread Board: It is also known as protoboard. It is constructed for prototyping electronics used for building and testing circuits of any circuit design. It

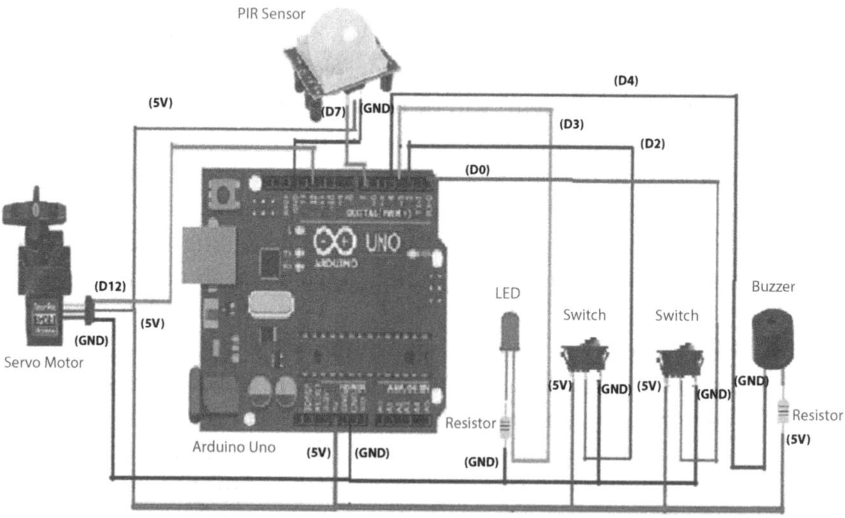

Figure 18.1 Circuit diagram.

consists of many holes into which circuit components like ICs and resistors can be inserted (Figure 18.3).

c) Wires: It is a single cylindrical, flexible strand of metal that is used to connect the components (Figure 18.4).

d) Switch: Switch is used to connect or disconnect the conducting path in an electrical circuit, interrupts the electric current, or diverts it from one conductor to another (Figure 18.5).

Figure 18.2 Arduino Uno.

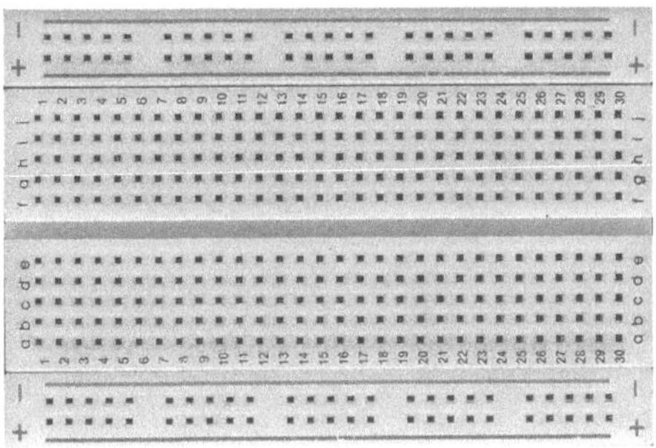

Figure 18.3 Bread board.

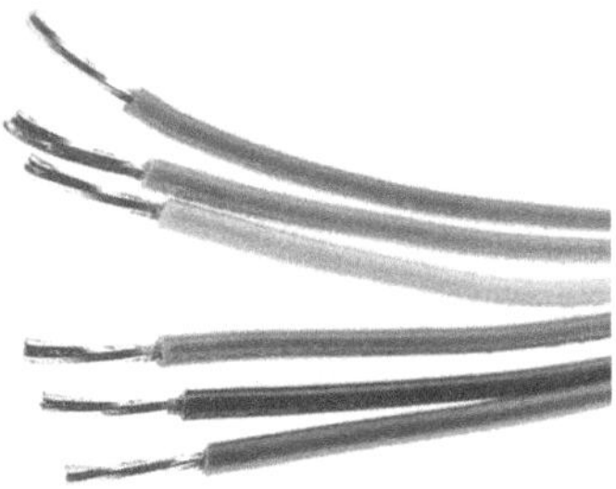

Figure 18.4 Wires.

e) Passive Infrared Sensor (PIR): It is an electronic sensor that measures infrared light radiating from objects in its field of view. They are most often used in PIR-based motion detectors (Figure 18.6).
f) Servo Motor: It is a rotary or linear actuator that allows for precise control of angular or linear position, velocity, and acceleration (Figure 18.7).
g) Buzzer: It is a sounding device that can convert audio signals into sound signals, which are usually powered by DC voltage (Figure 18.8).
h) Light-Emitting Diode (LED) Light: It is a semiconductor light source that emits light when current flows through it (Figure 18.9).

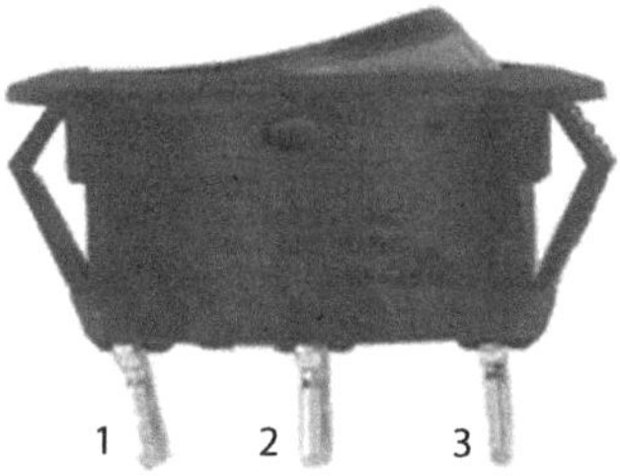

Figure 18.5 Switch.

Figure 18.6 PIR sensor.

Figure 18.7 Servo motor.

Figure 18.8 Buzzer.

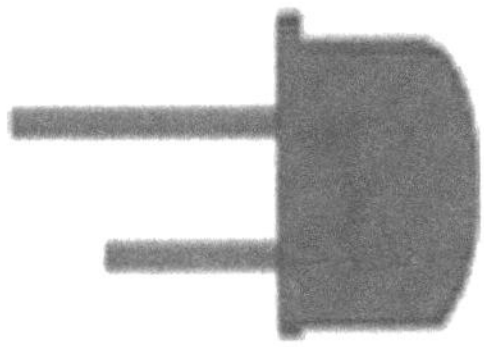

Figure 18.9 LED light.

18.5 Working Principle

Working Principle of "Automatic Anti-Theft System" is described accordingly:

- At first, all the components are assembled using Tinker cad software. The components are LED, register, connecting wires, breadboard, Arduino Uno, PIR sensor, Servo Motor, Slide Switch, and Buzzer.
- All the components are connected according to the circuit diagram. For example, the PIR sensor, LED, switches, Servo Motor, and Buzzer are connected with the digital pins of the Arduino, whereas the supply of 5V and the grounding (GND) of this system is done by the analog pins of the Arduino.
- After the connections are made properly with the help of breadboard by wires, the code of Arduino is written in the Code Block. Then, the whole model is run virtually. The whole system will be simulated online.
- After simulation of all the conditions are checked for the model, like if motion is detected, then the Buzzer will ring and LED will glow, all the doors of the room will be closed using Servo Motors. If no motion detected, then neither the buzzer will ring nor the LED will glow, but doors will get closed automatically for safety purpose. Thus, the accuracy of the model will be verified.

18.6 Results

The result of "**Automatic Anti-Theft System**" is as follows:

- Both the switches are OFF, which indicates the door is open and the system is OFF, hence morning time (Figure 18.10).
- Both the switches are ON, which indicates the door is closed and the system is ON, hence night time (Figure 18.11).

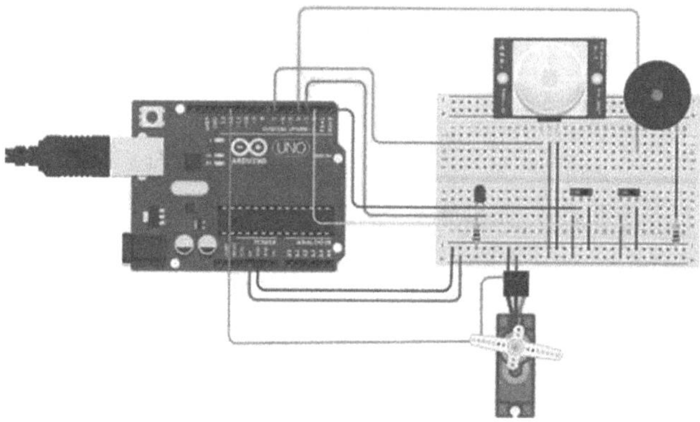

Figure 18.10 Morning time.

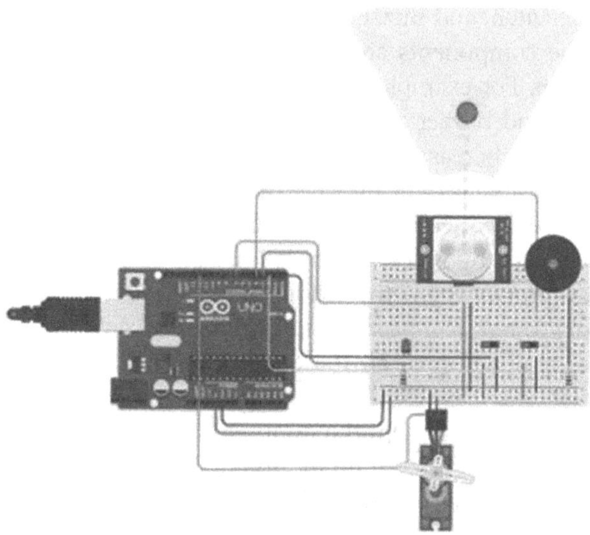

Figure 18.11 Night time.

- Motion detected and Buzzer rings, LED glows, and door closes (Figure 18.12).
- Outside the range of PIR sensor, so no motion will be detected. Thus, Buzzer will not buzz, LED will not glow, but the door will remain close (Figure 18.13).
- The door will open again when the door switch is closed even when the main switch for the whole system is ON (Figure 18.14).

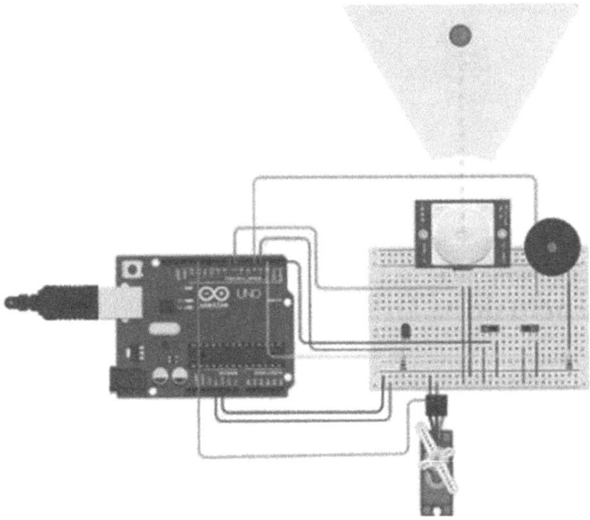

Figure 18.12 Motion state and Buzzar sound.

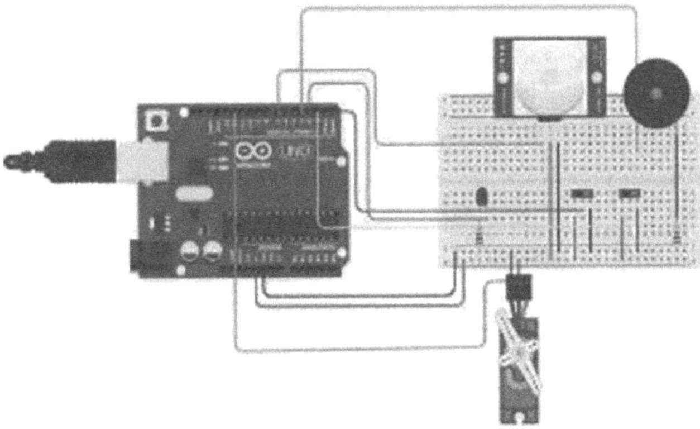

Figure 18.13 No motion state.

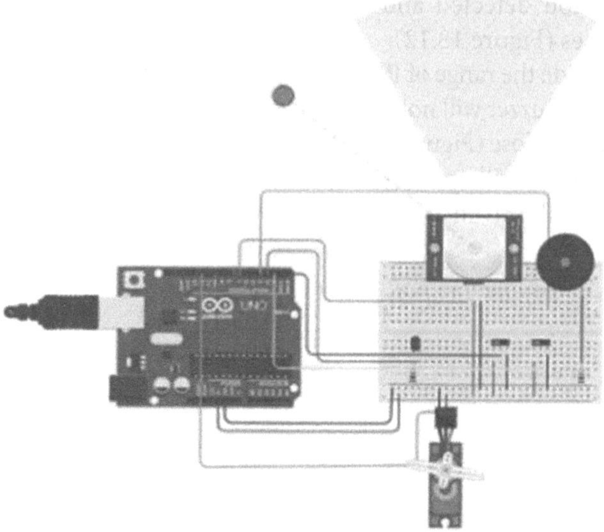

Figure 18.14 Reopening of door.

18.7 Conclusions and Future Scope

In conclusion, the protection of valuable possessions has been a timeless concern for individuals and families, reflected in the evolution of security measures from ancient traps to modern technological advancements. The transition from traditional security methods to automated systems powered by embedded technology and IoT has revolutionized how we safeguard our belongings. The development of our anti-theft system, utilizing an Arduino microprocessor and contemporary components, represents a significant step forward in this journey.

By integrating passive infrared sensors, a servomotor, and other elements, our system detects unauthorized motion, triggers alarms, and securely confines intruders, providing peace of mind to users. Crucially, the incorporation of IoT enables real-time alerts to be sent directly to the user's mobile device, empowering them to respond promptly to security breaches even when absent from the premises.

In future, better sensors can be used to sense more accurate results and, thus, will improve the working quality of the device. The system can later be connected with a 4G GSM module, which will supply the device with internet, and also the device can be connected with a secure cloud with proper cloud security. Better cryptography has to be used to make the cloud more secure. Connecting multiple mobile numbers to the device will help to inform a larger group of people. Contacting the local police station and asking for permission so that information can be sent to police at the time of robbery, and they can go to the location and take appropriate action. Integrating the circuit and making it smaller will not only make it easier to handle, but also it can save a lot of space from getting wasted. Developing an app that can accommodate customer wishes and reviews, and it will provide an interface of communication between the developers and the customers. It will help to improve the product keeping customer reviews in mind and will result in better customer service.

References

1. Hu, J.-m., Li, J., Li, G.-h., Automobile Anti-theft System Based on GSM and GPS Module, in: *2012 Fifth International Conference on Intelligent Networks and Intelligent Systems*, pp. 199–201, 2012, doi: 10.1109/ICINIS.2012.86.
2. Zhang, H., Zhang, F., Wang, Y., Zhang, G., Wireless Sensor Network based anti-theft system of monitoring on petroleum pipeline, in: *2011 Second International Conference on Mechanic Automation and Control Engineering*, pp. 4689–4692, 2011, doi: 10.1109/MACE.2011.5988057.
3. Chen, C., Deng, Y., Zhang, J., He, X., Chen, J., Lu, C., A reliable integrated car anti-theft system in VANET, in: *2019 IEEE International Conference on Consumer Electronics - Taiwan (ICCE-TW)*, pp. 1–2, 2019, doi: 10.1109/ ICCE- TW46550.2019.8991896.
4. Lappanitchayakul, K., Anti-theft device for car: Alert system using radio wave, in: *2019 International Conference on Intelligent Informatics and Biomedical Sciences (ICIIBMS)*, pp. 351–355, 2019, doi: 10.1109/ ICIIBMS46890.2019.8991531.
5. Zhang, J. and Liqin, Y., The design of multi-zone wireless burglar alarm system, in: *International Conference on Cyberspace Technology (CCT 2013)*, pp. 469–473, 2013, doi: 10.1049/cp.2013.2174.
6. Ma, B., Design of Intelligent Burglar Alarm System in Laboratory Based on Embedded System, in: *2020 13th International Congress on Image and Signal Processing, BioMedical Engineering and Informatics (CISP-BMEI)*, pp. 392–395, 2020, doi: 10.1109/CISP-BMEI51763.2020.9263515.
7. Wang, X., Wang, Y., Xie, J., Multifunctional intelligent wireless alarm system, in: *2008 3rd IEEE Conference on Industrial Electronics and Applications*, pp. 268–271, 2008, doi: 10.1109/ICIEA.2008.4582521.
8. Javare, A., Ghayal, T., Dabhade, J., Shelar, A., Gupta, A., Access control and intrusion detection in door lock system using Bluetooth technology, in: *2017 International Conference on Energy, Communication, Data Analytics and Soft Computing (ICECDS)*, pp. 2246–2251, 2017, doi: 10.1109/ ICECDS.2017.8389852.

9. Ion, V., Andrei, H., Diaconu, E., Ardeleanu, M.N., Gheorghe, A.C., The analysis of the electrical characteristics for an anti-theft alarm system, in: *2021 13th International Conference on Electronics, Computers and Artificial Intelligence (ECAI)*, p. 16, 2021, doi: 10.1109/ECAI52376.2021.9515183.
10. Zhong, W., Chen, G., Qi, H., Qi, X.H., Cheng, Z., The Design of Vehicle Anti- theft System Based on the Improved D-S Evidence Theory, in: *2014 8th International Conference on Future Generation Communication and Networking*, pp. 84–87, 2014, doi: 10.1109/FGCN.2014.28.
11. Mukherjee, K., Anti-theft vehicle tracking and immobilization system, in: *2014 International Conference on Power, Control and Embedded Systems (ICPCES)*, pp. 1–4, 2014, doi: 10.1109/ICPCES.2014.7062814.
12. Koodtalang, W. and Sangsuwan, T., Improving motorcycle anti-theft system with the use of Bluetooth Low Energy 4.0, in: *2016 International Symposium on Intelligent Signal Processing and Communication Systems (ISPACS)*, pp. 1–5, 2016, doi: 10.1109/ISPACS.2016.7824705.
13. Raj, M.M.E. and Julian, A., Design and implementation of anti-theft ATM machine using embedded systems, in: *2015 International Conference on Circuits, Power and Computing Technologies [ICCPCT-2015]*, pp. 1–5, 2015, doi: 10.1109/ICCPCT.2015.7159316.
14. Prasanth Ganesh, G.S., Balaji, B., Srinivasa Varadhan, T.A., Anti-theft tracking system for automobiles (AutoGSM), in: *2011 IEEE International Conference on Anti-Counterfeiting, Security and Identification*, pp. 17–19, 2011, doi: 10.1109/ASID.2011.5967406.
15. Wan, L. and Chen, T., Automobile Anti-theft System Design Based on GSM, in: *2009 International Conference on Advanced Computer Control*, pp. 551–554, 2009, doi: 10.1109/ICACC.2009.44.
16. Xiaorui, H., Yanlong, Q., Wei, C., Fan, Y., Anti-theft and location method based on pulse transmission attribute for power cables, in: *2014 International Symposium on Fundamentals of Electrical Engineering (ISFEE)*, pp. 1–5, 2014, doi: 10.1109/ISFEE.2014.7050634.
17. Sadagopan, V.K., Rajendran, U., Francis, A.J., Anti theft control system design using embedded system, in: *Proceedings of 2011 IEEE International Conference on Vehicular Electronics and Safety*, pp. 1–5, 2011, doi: 10.1109/ICVES.2011.5983776.
18. Zhao, Y., Hu, G., Cao, X., Li, P., Liu, Y., Design of Power Cables Anti-Theft and Monitoring System Based on PWM, in: *2018 10th International Conference on Measuring Technology and Mechatronics Automation (ICMTMA)*, pp. 204–207, 2018, doi: 10.1109/ICMTMA.2018.00056.
19. Waheed, A., Riaz, M., Wani, M.Y., Anti-theft mobile phone security system with the help of BIOS, in: *2017 International Symposium on Wireless Systems and Networks (ISWSN)*, pp. 1–6, 2017, doi: 10.1109/ISWSN.2017.8250035.

20. Li, S., *et al.*, An anti-power theft method for secondary circuit of energy meter current transformer, in: *2017 4th International Conference on Systems and Informatics (ICSAI)*, pp. 847–851, 2017, doi: 10.1109/ICSAI.2017.8248403.
21. Li, L., Iftikhar, S., Li, P., Design of wireless anti-theft alarm for transformer, in: *2021 IEEE International Conference on Electrical Engineering and Mechatronics Technology (ICEEMT)*, pp. 165–168, 2021, doi: 10.1109/ICEEMT52412.2021.9602524.
22. Wu, J., Kung, C., Rao, J., Wang, P., Lin, C., Hou, T., Design of an In-vehicle Anti-theft Component, in: *2008 Eighth International Conference on Intelligent Systems Design and Applications*, pp. 566–569, 2008, doi: 10.1109/ISDA.2008.188.
23. S. Fasiuddin, S., Sohelrana, K., Tamkeen, A., Rasheed, M.A., Real Time Application of Vehicle Anti Theft Detection and Protection with Shock Using Facial Recognition and IoT Notification, in: *2020 Fourth International Conference on Computing Methodologies and Communication (ICCMC)*, pp. 1039–1044, 2020, doi: 10.1109/ICCMC48092.2020.ICCMC-000194.
24. Dey, M., Arif, M.A., Mahmud, M.A., Anti-theft protection of vehicle by GSM & GPS with fingerprint verification, in: *2017 International Conference on Electrical, Computer and Communication Engineering (ECCE)*, pp. 916–920, 2017, doi: 10.1109/ECACE.2017.7913034.
25. Ion, V., Andrei, H., Diaconu, E., Puchianu, D.C., Ardeleanu, M.N., Modelling of Electrical Characteristics for an Anti-Theft Alarm System, in: *2021 7th International Symposium on Electrical and Electronics Engineering (ISEEE)*, pp. 1–4, 2021, doi: 10.1109/ISEEE53383.2021.9628754.
26. Noman, A.T., Hossain, S., Islam, S., Islam, M.E., Ahmed, N., Chowdhury, M.A.M., Design and Implementation of Microcontroller Based Anti-Theft Vehicle Security System using GPS, GSM and RFID, in: *2018 4th International Conference on Electrical Engineering and Information & Communication Technology (iCEEiCT)*, pp. 97–101, 2018, doi: 10.1109/CEEICT.2018.8628051.
27. Liu, Z., Zhang, A., Li, S., Vehicle anti-theft tracking system based on Internet of things, in: *Proceedings of 2013 IEEE International Conference on Vehicular Electronics and Safety*, pp. 48–52, 2013, doi: 10.1109/ICVES.2013.6619601.
28. Khangura, K.S., Middleton, N.V., Ollivier, M.M., *IEE Colloquium Vehicle Security Systems*, 4/1–4/7, 1993.AU: Please provide article title and volume number.
29. Lee, K., Yeuk, H., Kim, J., Yim, K., Anti-theft Solutions for In-vehicle Electronic Devices, in: *2014 Eighth International Conference on Innovative Mobile and Internet Services in Ubiquitous Computing*, pp. 549–553, 2014, doi: 10.1109/IMIS.2014.98.

30. Han, Y., Chen, Z., Guo, T., Design of equipment anti-theft tracker based on wireless sensor network, in: *2017 First International Conference on Electronics Instrumentation & Information Systems (EIIS)*, pp. 1–5, 2017, doi: 10.1109/EIIS.2017.8298681.
31. Guo, H., *et al.*, An Automotive Security System for Anti-theft, in: *2009 Eighth International Conference on Networks*, pp. 421–426, 2009, doi: 10.1109/ICN.2009.28.
32. Jayendra, G., Kumarawadu, S., Meegahapola, L., RFID-based anti-theft auto security system with an immobilizer, in: *2007 International Conference on Industrial and Information Systems*, pp. 441–446, 2007, doi: 10.1109/ICIINFS.2007.4579218.

19

Leveraging Analytics for Efficient Network Operations

Amarendar Reddy Chittireddy*, **Vishnu Kurnala and Koti Tejasvi**

Department of Computer Science and Engineering (AI&ML), Vardhaman College of Engineering, Hyderabad, Telangana, India

Abstract

Hyper-intelligent networks are the next stage in network management, combining modern technologies like artificial intelligence (AI), machine learning, and big data analytics to improve operational efficiency, security, and performance. This study examines the crucial role of data analytics in the management of hyper-intelligent networks, with a focus on the many data sources that power these advanced systems. Important data categories encompass network traffic data, performance measurements, security logs, configuration details, user and application data, environmental data, and vendor-specific information. By utilizing tools, such as Network Monitoring Systems, Security Information and Event Management platforms, Application Performance Monitoring solutions, and big data analytics frameworks, network managers can obtain unparalleled understanding of network behavior and performance. Through the utilization of machine learning techniques, these networks have the capability to forecast and alleviate possible problems, improve the allocation of resources, and strengthen security measures by actively detecting and responding to threats. Incorporating external data sources, such as meteorological and geospatial information, enhances the network's ability to adapt and improve. This chapter presents the necessary approaches and tools for effectively utilizing data analytics in hyper-intelligent network management. It showcases how these advanced systems may convert conventional network operations into highly adaptable and self-optimizing environments.

Keywords: Hyper-intelligent networks, data analytics, machine learning, artificial intelligence

**Corresponding author*: amarendar.502@gmail.com

Pradosh Kumar Gantayat, Sandeep Kumar Panda, S. Balamurugan and Sheng-Lung Peng (eds.) Hyper-Intelligent Networks: Exploring the Future of Connectivity for Society 5.0, (403–430) © 2026 Scrivener Publishing LLC

19.1 Introduction

Effective network management has become a crucial element of corporate success in the era of digital transformation. Networks function as the fundamental infrastructure for facilitating communication, transferring data, and enhancing operational effectiveness in several businesses. Managing increasingly complex and large-scale networks necessitates the use of advanced tools and approaches. Data analytics is becoming increasingly important in this situation, as it provides valuable insights and predictive abilities that improve network performance, security, and dependability. This chapter examines the crucial significance of data analytics in network administration, investigating its uses, methodologies, and the profound influence that it has on contemporary network systems [1, 2].

19.1.1 Overview of Network Management

19.1.1.1 Importance of Network Management

Efficient, secure, and reliable network operations rely on the vital practice of network administration. It guarantees the optimization of network resources, the maintenance of performance standards, and the mitigation of security concerns. Efficient network administration empowers enterprises to avoid interruptions, improve customer satisfaction, and uphold compliance with regulatory mandates. In a society where being connected is extremely important, the responsibility of managing networks is increasingly critical [3]. Figure 19.1 illustrates the architecture of intelligent networks, showing the role of end devices, orchestrators, and AI-enabled core functions in achieving end-to-end quality of service.

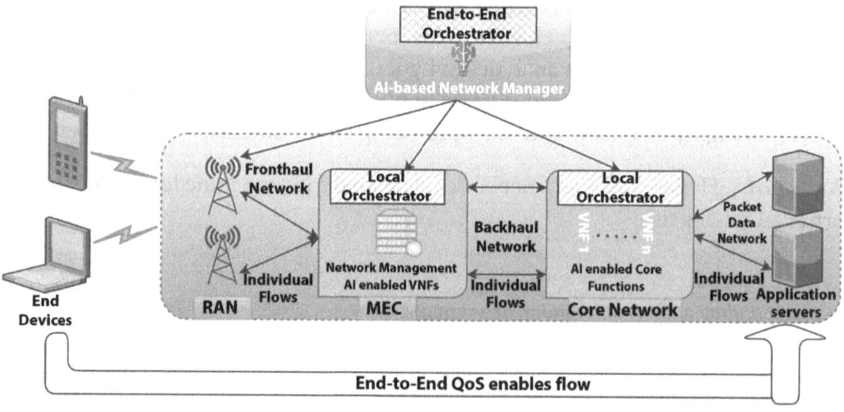

Figure 19.1 Intelligent network overview [22].

19.1.1.2 Evolution of Network Management Systems

The progression of network management systems has been characterized by notable improvements in technology and approach. In the beginning, network management was performed manually and reactively, relying on rudimentary technologies for monitoring and resolving issues. Over the course of time, it developed to include automated systems, improved monitoring tools, and sophisticated analytics. Contemporary network management systems utilize artificial intelligence (AI), machine learning (ML), and big data analytics to offer immediate insights, forecast maintenance needs, and enable automated decision-making. This trend demonstrates the escalating intricacy of networks and the rising need for effective and proactive management solutions [4, 5].

19.1.2 Role of Data Analytics in Network Management

19.1.2.1 Definition and Scope

Data analytics in network management entails the methodical computational examination of data to reveal patterns, correlations, and insights that guide decision-making procedures. It includes a broad array of methods, such as descriptive, diagnostic, predictive, and prescriptive analytics. Data analytics in network management encompasses a wide range of tasks, including monitoring performance, detecting faults, managing security, and planning capacity. Through the utilization of data analytics, network managers can improve the effectiveness, safety, and dependability of network operations.

19.1.2.2 Historical Context and Evolution

The incorporation of data analytics into network management has progressed in parallel with improvements in computing power and data processing capabilities. At first, network analytics mostly concentrated on fundamental performance monitoring and reporting. With the introduction of big data technologies, the range of possibilities has broadened to encompass real-time data processing and sophisticated analytics. ML and AI have significantly transformed the sector, allowing for the use of predictive and prescriptive analytics. The historical progression emphasizes the growing significance of data-driven insights in overseeing intricate and ever-changing network environments [6]. Figure 19.2 presents the detailed architecture of networks within Society 5.0, highlighting various service instances and network slices enabled by the integration of SDN, NFV, and edge cloud.

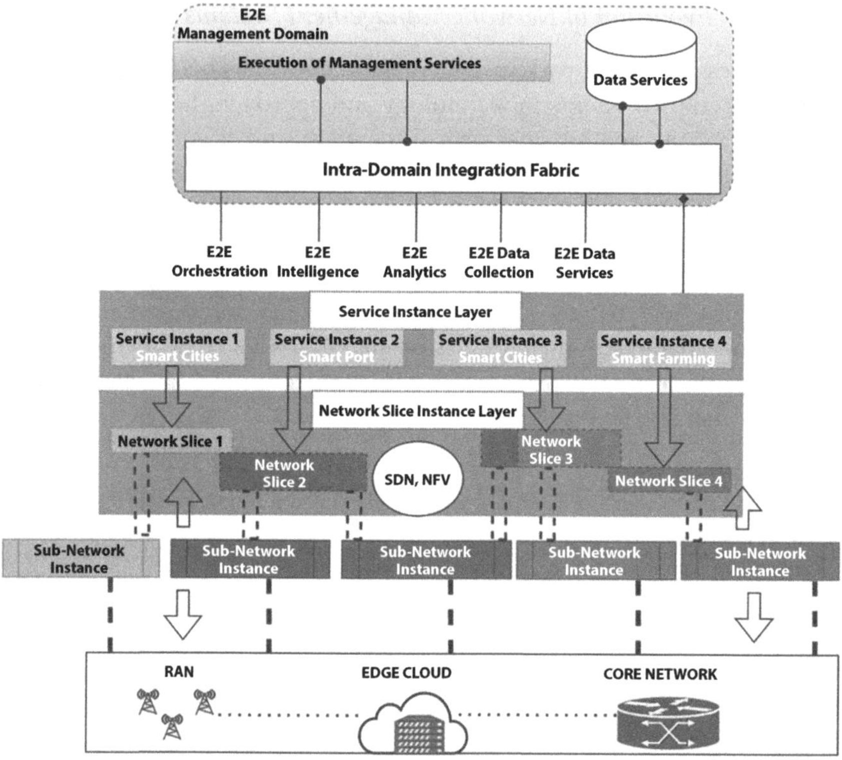

Figure 19.2 Detailed architecture of networks in Society 5.0 [22].

19.2 Data Collection and Preparation

The effectiveness of network management is strongly dependent on the quality and comprehensiveness of data gathered from multiple sources. Data collection and preparation are essential stages that guarantee the precision and applicability of the data required for analysis. This procedure entails collecting data from network traffic, devices, infrastructure, and user applications. The data collecting methods encompass passive monitoring, active probing, and hybrid approaches. After being gathered, the data is subjected to cleaning and preprocessing procedures to handle any missing values, normalize the information, and address concerns related to privacy. Effective data collection and preparation are essential for establishing a strong foundation for comprehensive network analytics, which, in turn, facilitates well-informed decision-making and streamlined network administration [7].

19.2.1 Sources of Network Data

19.2.1.1 Network Traffic Data

Analyzing network traffic data is crucial for comprehending the transmission of information within a network. The information comprises comprehensive logs of data packets exchanged between devices, encompassing details such as source and destination addresses, the amount of data transported, protocols employed, and timestamps. This data is extremely valuable for the purpose of monitoring network performance, identifying anomalies, and effectively controlling traffic. Through the examination of network traffic data, network administrators can detect areas of congestion, improve the channels through which data is routed, and guarantee that the network is functioning at its highest level of effectiveness. In addition, traffic data aids in identifying security risks, such as unauthorized access attempts and distributed denial-of-service (DDoS) assaults, by analyzing abnormal patterns and behaviors in network traffic. NSL-KDD, CICIDS2017, InSDN, and CICIDS20121 by AWS are few of the many datasets available on network traffic [8, 9].

19.2.1.2 Device and Infrastructure Data

Device and infrastructure data offer valuable information about the condition and efficiency of the tangible and intangible elements that make up the network. This dataset comprises data obtained from routers, switches, servers, firewalls, and other networking devices, as well as virtual machines and cloud-based infrastructure. Data on metrics such as CPU utilization, memory consumption, disk input/output, and network interface statistics are gathered to oversee and assess the performance and dependability of these devices. Examining this data enables network administrators to detect hardware malfunctions, forecast maintenance requirements, and guarantee the overall stability and effectiveness of the network infrastructure. Additionally, it facilitates capacity planning by identifying devices or components that are experiencing significant strain and may require upgrades or reconfigurations. CPU and Memory Usage Statistics, Disk Input and Output (I/O) Metrics, Interface Statistics, Environmental Sensor Data are some of the data sources available [10, 11].

19.2.1.3 User and Application Data

User and application data encompass the recording of the exchanges between end-users and the apps they utilize on the network. This encompasses data regarding the timing of logins, the length of sessions, patterns of program usage, and the particular activities taken by users. Through the analysis of this data, network administrators can acquire valuable information about user behavior and preferences. This information can then be utilized to improve the performance of apps and better the overall user experience. This data is essential for detecting atypical or illegal activity that could suggest security breaches. Moreover, comprehending program performance from the user's standpoint enables more effective distribution of resources and problem-solving, guaranteeing seamless and optimal operation of crucial applications. By integrating user and application data with additional network data sources, network managers can cultivate a comprehensive understanding of network performance and user contentment. Authentication Logs, Application Performance Monitoring (APM) Data, User Activity Logs, and Usage Statistics are few data sources available for the data [12, 13].

19.2.2 Data Collection Methods

19.2.2.1 Passive Monitoring

Passive monitoring entails the act of seeing and evaluating network traffic without actively intervening in the data flow. This approach intercepts data as it traverses the network, offering a comprehensive and immediate perspective on network operations. Data collection is facilitated by passive monitoring techniques such as network taps, mirror ports (SPAN ports), and packet sniffers [14].

Benefits of Passive Monitoring:

1. Non-Intrusive: Passive monitoring is a means of continuously collecting data without disrupting the usual operations of the network, making it a discreet and unobtrusive approach.
2. Comprehensive Data Capture: It offers a comprehensive perspective of all network traffic, encompassing both legitimate and criminal operations.
3. Real-Time Analysis: Passive monitoring enables the quick discovery of irregularities and potential security concerns by analyzing traffic in real time.

Uses of Passive Monitoring:

1. Network Performance Monitoring: Passive monitoring, through the capture of traffic data, aids in the identification of performance bottlenecks and the optimization of network throughput.
2. Security Monitoring is a process that involves discovering and analyzing security risks, including as intrusions, malware, and DDoS attacks, by detecting and examining abnormal traffic patterns.
3. Passive monitoring plays a crucial role in guaranteeing compliance with regulatory standards by generating comprehensive records of network activities.

Difficulties Associated with Passive Monitoring:

1. Data Volume: The substantial amount of data collected might be overpowering and necessitates effective storage and analysis solutions.
2. Encryption presents a difficulty by restricting the ability to observe the data being transferred.

19.2.2.2 Active Probing

Active probing is inserting test packets into the network to quantify different performance parameters, including as latency, bandwidth, and packet loss. This method enables accurate and regulated testing of network characteristics and configurations [15, 16].

Benefits of Active Probing:

1. Controlled testing involves active probing, which enables the execution of targeted tests to get accurate measures of network performance.
2. Proactive Diagnosis involves the proactive identification of network faults by simulating various network conditions and observing the resulting outcomes.
3. Versatility: Active probing can be employed in a multitude of network contexts, ranging from basic connectivity tests to intricate performance evaluations.

Uses of Active Probing:

1. Network performance testing involves the use of active probing to measure various metrics such as latency, jitter, bandwidth, and packet loss. This method helps to provide valuable insights into the performance of a network.
2. Path analysis is a technique used to gain insight into the route that packets follow inside a network. It is useful for finding areas of congestion and improving the efficiency of routing.
3. Service-level agreement (SLA) confirmation: Active probing is used to verify if the network satisfies the performance criteria specified in SLAs.

Difficulties Associated with Active Probing:

1. Intrusiveness: The act of injecting test packets can have a minor impact on network performance, particularly in networks that are very sensitive or busy.
2. Restricted in its extent, active probing offers intermittent assessments of network performance rather than ongoing surveillance.

19.2.3 Data Cleaning and Preprocessing

19.2.3.1 Handling Missing Data

Handling missing data is a critical aspect of data preprocessing, as missing values can lead to inaccurate analysis and misleading conclusions. Missing data can arise from various sources, such as network outages, device malfunctions, or errors in data collection processes [17].

Strategies for Handling Missing Data:
1. Imputation Methods: Imputation involves filling in missing values with estimated ones. Common techniques include the following:

- **Mean/Median Imputation:** Replacing missing values with the mean or median of the available data.
- **Mode Imputation:** Using the most frequent value to fill in missing data, often used for categorical variables.
- **K-Nearest Neighbors (KNN) Imputation:** Estimating missing values based on the values of similar data points.

2. Deletion Methods: In some cases, it may be appropriate to remove records with missing data:

- **Listwise Deletion:** Removing any record with one or more missing values, useful when missing data is minimal.
- **Pairwise Deletion:** Removing only the specific data points that are missing, while retaining the rest of the record.

3. Predictive Modeling: Using algorithms to predict and fill in missing values based on patterns in the data.

19.2.3.2 Data Normalization

Data normalization is the process of scaling data to a common range or format, making it easier to compare and analyze. This step is crucial for ensuring that different data sources are compatible and that the results of analyses are meaningful and consistent [18].

Techniques for Data Normalization:

1. **Min-Max Scaling:** Transforming data to a fixed range, usually 0 to 1. This method retains the relationships among data points while standardizing the scale.

$$\mathrm{x}' = \frac{\mathrm{x} - \min(x)}{\max(x) - \min(x)}$$

2. **Z-Score Normalization:** Scaling data based on the mean and standard deviation, resulting in a distribution with a mean of 0 and a standard deviation of 1.

$$z = \frac{x - \mu}{\sigma}$$

3. **Logarithmic Transformation:** Applying a logarithmic function to reduce the skewness of the data, particularly useful for data with a wide range of values.

$$x' = log(x)$$

Benefits of Data Normalization:

- **Improved Accuracy:** Normalization ensures that all features contribute equally to the analysis, enhancing the accuracy of models and algorithms.
- **Consistency:** It creates a consistent framework for data comparison, essential for integrating data from different sources.

Challenges of Data Normalization:

- **Loss of Interpretability:** Normalized data may become less interpretable, particularly for stakeholders who are used to raw data values.
- **Handling Outliers:** Outliers can disproportionately affect normalization processes, requiring careful consideration and potential additional preprocessing.

19.2.3.3 Data Anonymization and Privacy Concerns

Data anonymization is the process of removing or obfuscating personal identifiers from the dataset to protect user privacy. This step is crucial in network management to comply with privacy regulations and ensure the confidentiality of sensitive information [19].

Techniques for Data Anonymization:

1. **Data Masking:** Replacing sensitive data with fictional or scrambled data that retains the format but loses its identifiable properties.
2. **Pseudonymization:** Replacing private identifiers with pseudonyms or unique codes, allowing data to be analyzed without revealing personal information.
3. **Aggregation:** Combining individual data points into broader categories or groups to obscure specific details.
4. **Differential Privacy:** Adding random noise to the data to prevent the identification of individuals, while still allowing for meaningful analysis.

Benefits of Data Anonymization:

- **Compliance:** Ensures compliance with privacy laws and regulations, such as General Data Protection Regulation (GDPR) and California Consumer Privacy Act (CCPA), protecting organizations from legal repercussions.
- **User Trust:** Enhances trust among users and clients by demonstrating a commitment to data privacy and security.

Challenges of Data Anonymization:

- **Data Utility:** Excessive anonymization can reduce the utility and accuracy of the data, affecting the quality of analysis.
- **Re-identification Risks:** Sophisticated techniques may be required to prevent re-identification of anonymized data, particularly in datasets with rich detail.

By effectively handling missing data, normalizing datasets, and ensuring data anonymization, network managers can prepare high-quality data that supports robust and reliable analytics, ultimately enhancing network management practices.

19.3 Applications of Data Analytics in Network Management

Data analytics has a significant impact on network management by offering profound insights and practical wisdom. These apps cover a wide range of network administration areas, such as performance monitoring, fault management, security, and capacity planning. Through the utilization of data analytics, network administrators can optimize real-time monitoring, perform comprehensive historical performance studies, identify and diagnose failures, and implement efficient recovery techniques. This section examines the application of data analytics in network performance monitoring and fault management, emphasizing the advantages and approaches involved [20].

19.3.1 Network Performance Monitoring

19.3.1.1 Real-Time Monitoring

Real-time monitoring entails the ongoing observation of the network's condition and performance to promptly identify and resolve any problems that may occur. By employing data analytics, network managers can utilize a range of tools and methodologies to actively monitor crucial performance metrics, including bandwidth utilization, latency, jitter, and packet loss, in real time. The ability to quickly and easily see what is happening in the network enables proactive management and rapid response to possible issues.

Real-time monitoring systems commonly utilize dashboards and alerting mechanisms to promptly deliver input on the status of a network. These technologies can be used with ML techniques to forecast future problems prior to their impact on the network. For instance, deviations in traffic patterns can be promptly detected and examined, so averting any security breaches or performance deterioration. The utilization of real-time data analytics ensures the continuous smooth operation of the network, leading to optimal network performance, less downtime, and improved user experience.

19.3.1.2 Historical Performance Analysis

Historical performance analysis entails the examination of previous network data to detect trends, patterns, and anomalies that have occurred over a period of time. This style of analysis is essential for comprehending the long-term effectiveness, strategizing for future capabilities, and making well-informed choices about network enhancements and optimizations. Through the examination of historical data, network administrators can discern repetitive problems, comprehend periods of highest utilization, and assess the efficacy of previous modifications or interventions.

Data analytics software can automate and depict historical performance analysis using graphs, charts, and reports. This visualization facilitates the quick identification of performance trends and enables data-driven decision-making. For instance, if past data indicates that a specific link routinely encounters substantial traffic during specific time periods, then network administrators can strategize for bandwidth enhancements or load balancing techniques to mitigate congestion. Historical performance research is also used to validate capacity design, ensuring that the network is capable of accommodating future expansion and heightened demand.

19.3.2 Fault Management

19.3.2.1 Fault Detection

Fault detection refers to the systematic identification and recognition of issues or malfunctions occurring within a network. Data analytics improves fault detection by examining network data to identify trends and indicators of defects, such as abrupt rises in error rates, unanticipated shifts in traffic patterns, or aberrant latency surges. ML systems can be trained to identify these irregularities, enabling automatic detection of faults [21].

The implementation of data analytics for defect detection entails the establishment of alerts based on predetermined thresholds and the utilization of models for detecting anomalies. These systems perform ongoing analysis of network data in real time, generating alarms when anomalous patterns are identified. For example, when a significant surge in packet loss is identified, a notification can be dispatched to the network administrator, triggering an instant inquiry. By adopting a proactive strategy, the amount of time that the network is not functioning optimally is minimized, and the negative effects of failures on network performance and user experience are reduced.

19.3.2.2 Fault Isolation and Diagnosis

Upon detecting a malfunction, it is imperative to promptly isolate and analyze the underlying cause. Data analytics enables this procedure by establishing correlations between different data points and provide a full perspective on network events that precede the failure. This connection facilitates the identification of the precise location and underlying cause of the defect, be it a hardware malfunction, configuration mistake, or security violation.

Advanced diagnostic tools utilize data analytics to do root cause investigation by delving into intricate logs and performance indicators. For instance, when a fault is identified in a particular section of the network, data analytics can assist in retracing the fault to a specific device or configuration alteration that caused the problem. By gaining a comprehensive understanding of the situation, network administrators can effectively identify and resolve the underlying issue, so reducing future occurrences and enhancing the overall reliability of the network.

19.3.2.3 Fault Recovery

Fault recovery refers to the process of reinstating regular network operations following the occurrence of a failure. Data analytics facilitates the development and execution of efficient recovery strategies through the examination of past fault data and comprehension of the consequences of various recovery measures. This analysis facilitates the development of automated recovery methods and playbooks that may be promptly run upon detecting a fault.

Data analytics can be utilized to create automated scripts that execute predetermined recovery steps, such as redirecting traffic, restarting services, or implementing configuration adjustments, when a specific type of problem, known for its frequent occurrence, is detected. In addition, data analytics can assess the efficacy of these recovery measures over time, enhancing and streamlining the recovery procedure. Through the utilization of data analytics, network administrators may decrease the time it takes to recover from issues, diminish the negative effects of faults on users, and improve the general ability of the network to withstand and recover from disruptions [22].

19.3.3 Security Management

19.3.3.1 Intrusion Detection Systems

Intrusion Detection Systems (IDSs) are security mechanisms designed to detect and prevent unauthorized access or malicious activities within a computer network or system.

IDSs play a crucial role in safeguarding a network from unwanted entry and harmful behavior. Data analytics improves IDSs by utilizing sophisticated methods like ML and statistical analysis to identify irregularities and possible security risks. Through the examination of network traffic and user behavior, IDSs are able to detect and pinpoint anomalous behaviors that diverge from the established patterns [18].

ML algorithms can be trained using past network data to identify patterns related to regular operations. The IDS notifies network managers when it detects an abnormality, such as a sudden increase in illegal access attempts or abnormal data transfers. This proactive detection enables prompt analysis and mitigation of potential risks, thereby averting security breaches and minimizing the extent of damage.

19.3.3.2 *Threat Analysis and Mitigation*

Threat analysis is the assessment and comprehension of possible security risks to a network, whilst mitigation refers to the measures implemented to decrease or eradicate these risks. Data analytics is essential in both processes as it offers in-depth understanding of threat trends and the efficiency of mitigation techniques.

Data analytics tools have the capability to gather and examine data from several sources, including IDS, firewalls, and endpoint security systems, in order to get a comprehensive understanding of the threat landscape. This study facilitates the identification of prevalent methods of attack, evaluation of weaknesses, and comprehension of the actions exhibited by various categories of threats. Through the ongoing analysis of threat data, network administrators can employ efficient mitigation measures, including the revision of security rules, the installation of patches, and the adjustment of defenses, in order to safeguard against developing attacks [15].

19.3.3.3 *Security Information and Event Management*

Security Information and Event Management (SIEM) systems gather, examine, and link security incidents from many origins instantly. SIEM relies on data analytics as its central component, allowing for the consolidation of extensive security data, recognition of patterns, and detection of possible security issues.

SIEM systems employ data analytics to establish connections between events originating from different sources, including network devices, servers, and applications, in order to identify intricate security concerns that would be overlooked when examining individual data points. For instance, a SIEM system has the capability to detect a synchronized assault by cross-referencing login attempts originating from several places, atypical data retrieval behaviors, and irregularities in network communication. This thorough examination offers network administrators practical information, enabling them to promptly and efficiently address security issues, improve their security stance, and uphold compliance with regulatory mandates [12].

19.3.4 Capacity Planning and Management

19.3.4.1 Demand Forecasting

Demand forecasting is the prediction of future network usage and resource needs in order to guarantee that the network is capable of accommodating anticipated growth and traffic patterns. Data analytics facilitates precise demand forecasting by examining past data, recognizing patterns, and employing predictive models.

Data analytics technologies can predict future demand for bandwidth, storage, and processing power by analyzing historical usage trends. For instance, if past data indicates a steady rise in traffic at specific periods of the year, network administrators might strategically prepare for this growth by allocating extra capacity. Precise demand forecasting facilitates informed decision-making regarding network upgrades, guaranteeing the availability of resources when required without excessive provisioning.

19.3.4.2 Resource Allocation

Resource allocation involves the distribution of network resources, such as bandwidth and processing power, in order to achieve the best possible performance and efficiency. Data analytics facilitates resource allocation by offering insights into present utilization patterns and forecasting future requirements.

Data analytics solutions have the capability to monitor the consumption of resources in real time and detect components that are either not being fully exploited or are being excessively burdened. Through the analysis of this data, network administrators are able to deploy resources in a dynamic manner to locations that have a greater demand. This ensures that the load distribution is balanced and that network assets are used efficiently. During times of high demand, it is possible to assign extra bandwidth to important applications in order to ensure that performance remains at acceptable levels. By adopting this proactive strategy for resource allocation, network efficiency may be optimized, and operational expenses can be minimized. See Table 19.1

Table 19.1 Resource allocation schemes [21].

Scheme	Description	Outcomes	Future work
DRL in WLAN	Set up a DRL-based dynamic radio resource allocation system to handle WLANs when traffic conditions change	Optimize end-to-end performance	Build a level of trust that is enough to enable completely automatic operation without any human intervention
AREL3P	Deploy virtual network functions (VNFs) in 5G networks using a module that predicts VNF performance based on Q-learning	Efficiently adjust to changes in network conditions; exhibit superior generalization capabilities compared to supervised learning techniques	Discuss the issue of sluggish convergence in large-scale networks
NAP	Design an autonomous profiling method for the next generation of NFV orchestration in 5G networks	Accurately predict untested resource configurations	Extend the work by covering additional types of resources
ZT-PFR	Enhance the fault-tolerance of networks through a DRL-based zero-touch proactive failure recovery scheme	Network status information is up to date for decision-making.	Apply online learning ML models to address the ever-changing nature of NFV environments
Self-healing process	Autonomously carry out a self-healing process tackling both detection and diagnosis of faults in 5G+ networks	This process improves network component understanding.	Examine subscriber complaint data to identify the fault type and analyze its cause

19.3.4.3 Load Balancing

Load balancing is the process of evenly dividing network traffic among numerous servers or network channels to prevent any single component from becoming a bottleneck. Data analytics improves load balancing by offering real-time information into traffic trends and server workloads.

Network administrators can utilize data analytics to analyze the distribution of traffic and detect any imbalances that may result in a decline in performance. Load balancing algorithms have the ability to adaptively modify the allocation of traffic according to present circumstances, hence guaranteeing optimal performance and averting overloads. For instance, in the case of a specific server encountering a significant influx of users, data analytics can prompt the load balancer to reroute a portion of the traffic to servers that are less burdened. This dynamic and data-driven method of load balancing guarantees the network services' high availability and reliability.

19.3.5 Quality-of-Service (QoS) Management

19.3.5.1 QoS Metrics

QoS metrics are numerical measures utilized to assess the effectiveness of network services. Important QoS measurements consist of latency, jitter, packet loss, and throughput. Data analytics is essential for monitoring and evaluating these variables to ensure that network performance meets set requirements.

Data analytics solutions offer network administrators valuable insights into the network's present condition by consistently gathering and analyzing QoS indicators. This data aids in the detection of performance problems, such as significant delays or data packet loss, which may impact the user's overall experience. For instance, the study of QoS measurements in real time can uncover that a certain application is encountering significant latency, which necessitates quick examination and resolution. Regular monitoring and analysis of QoS indicators guarantee that network services fulfill the necessary performance standards [22].

19.3.5.2 Service-Level Agreement (SLA) Management

SLAs are legally binding agreements between service providers and customers that establish the specific standards and benchmarks for service performance that are anticipated to be met. Data analytics facilitates SLA management by supplying the essential data for monitoring adherence to SLA conditions and reporting on operational efficiency.

By employing data analytics, network administrators have the opportunity to monitor and evaluate SLA metrics, including uptime, response times, and service availability. Automated reports can be created to showcase adherence to SLA conditions and offer clients clear visibility. For instance, when a SLA ensures 99.9% uptime, data analytics tools may consistently monitor the availability of the network and produce reports that confirm this assurance. Utilizing data analytics for SLA management enhances confidence with consumers and upholds high service standards.

19.3.5.3 Traffic Shaping and Prioritization

Traffic shaping and prioritization refer to the management of network traffic to guarantee that essential applications are allocated sufficient bandwidth and resources to achieve optimal performance. Data analytics facilitates the ability to shape traffic in real time by offering valuable information on existing traffic patterns and network conditions.

Through the analysis of traffic data, network administrators can determine the applications and services that necessitate greater priority, taking into account their significance and usage trends. Subsequently, traffic shaping algorithms can be employed to give priority to certain apps, guaranteeing that they obtain the necessary bandwidth even when there is high demand. Real-time communication applications, including Voice over Internet Protocol (VoIP) and video conferencing, can be given priority to guarantee minimal delay and excellent performance. By utilizing data-driven techniques, traffic shaping, and prioritization are employed to guarantee the dependable performance of important apps, hence improving the overall user experience. See Table 19.2.

Table 19.2 Traffic prediction algorithms [21].

Scheme	Description	Outcomes	Future work
Support Vector Machine (SVM) and K-means algorithms for network traffic classification	Predict and classify the network traffic in 5G networks	SVM shows enhanced performance compared to K-means. K-means is suitable for new/unknown application types.	Predict the number of user plane 5G network functions to manage the data plane traffic; apply the proposed models to real SDN traffic data
Ensemble methods for IDS [19]	Utilize ensemble methods (e.g., Random Forest and Gradient Boosting) for improved intrusion detection accuracy	Ensemble methods show higher detection rates and lower false positives compared to individual models	Develop lightweight ensemble methods for real-time IDS applications; explore ensemble learning for various network environments

To summarize, data analytics is a potent instrument for multiple facets of network administration, encompassing security management, capacity planning, and QoS control. By utilizing data analytics in these domains, network managers may guarantee ideal performance, bolster security, and deliver top-notch service to users.

19.4 Big Data Analytics

19.4.1 Handling Large-Scale Network Data

Dealing with extensive network data necessitates strong techniques for gathering, retaining, and analyzing data produced by different network elements. Advanced data management solutions are necessary due to the substantial amount of data produced by contemporary networks, which includes logs, traffic flows, and user activities. An effective strategy involves utilizing distributed storage systems such as Hadoop and cloud-based solutions that have the ability to expand horizontally in order to handle increasing amounts of data. These systems enable network managers to easily store and handle large amounts of data, ensuring that no valuable information is lost.

Data processing frameworks like Apache Spark and Apache Flink are crucial for managing network data on a big scale. These frameworks provide concurrent processing of enormous datasets, resulting in a substantial reduction in the time needed for data analysis. Network administrators can utilize these technologies to carry out intricate analytics activities, such as detecting anomalies in real time, analyzing traffic patterns, and monitoring performance, on extensive datasets. Furthermore, massive datasets can be utilized to train ML models, hence enhancing the precision and dependability of network predictions and diagnostics.

By integrating big data analytics tools with network management systems, it becomes possible to constantly monitor and analyze network data. This integration offers immediate and accurate information and notifications, allowing network administrators to promptly address emergent problems and enhance network efficiency. Real-time analytics can identify abrupt surges in web traffic or abnormal patterns that could signal a security risk, enabling prompt implementation of countermeasures. In summary, efficiently managing large-scale network data is crucial for maintaining efficient, secure, and resilient network operations.

19.4.2 Scalable Analytics Architectures

Scalable analytics architectures are necessary for effectively handling the increasing intricacy and quantity of network data. These architectures are specifically engineered to efficiently manage and analyze enormous volumes of data while also being capable of dynamically adjusting their capacity to match the requirements of data processing. An essential element of scalable analytics systems involves leveraging cloud computing platforms, which offer adaptable and expandable resources for storing, processing, and analyzing data. Cloud platforms such as Amazon Web features (AWS), Microsoft Azure, and Google Cloud provide features like data lakes, ML, and real-time analytics, allowing enterprises to effortlessly expand their analytics capabilities.

Another crucial element of scalable analytics architectures is the use of distributed computing frameworks. Apache Hadoop, Apache Spark, and Kubernetes are technologies that provide the spread of data processing jobs among several nodes, resulting in fast and efficient processing of huge datasets. These frameworks offer support for a range of data processing approaches, such as batch processing, stream processing, and real-time analytics. This allows for the adaptability required to handle diverse forms of network data. These frameworks enhance the performance of the analytics system by dispersing the computational load, resulting in reduced processing time.

Scalable analytics designs encompass containerization and microservices, with cloud platforms and distributed computing frameworks. Containerization technologies such as Docker and orchestration tools like Kubernetes enable the deployment of analytics apps that are both scalable and portable. Microservice design decomposes analytics operations into smaller, autonomous services that can be independently scaled. The modular approach improves the flexibility and scalability of the analytics system, allowing enterprises to easily add or delete services without impacting the overall system performance.

To successfully implement scalable analytics infrastructures, it is essential to have strong data integration and management policies in place. Efficient design of data pipelines is crucial to manage substantial amounts of data, ensuring seamless ingestion, processing, and storage in a scalable manner. Apache Kafka and AWS Glue are tools that enable real-time data integration and ETL (Extract, Transform, Load) procedures, assuring smooth data flow throughout the analytics system. Organizations can strengthen their network management capabilities by implementing scalable analytics architectures, which allow them to successfully manage large-scale network data and derive meaningful insights.

19.5 Challenges and Future Directions

Data analytics encounters several obstacles as it progresses and becomes part of network management. These challenges include ensuring data quality and integrity, addressing scalability issues, and integrating with existing legacy systems. It is essential to tackle these difficulties in order to fully utilize the power of data analytics in improving network performance and security. The future of network management will be influenced by developing technologies and innovative research areas, all in line with the vision for hyper-intelligent networks and Society 5.0. These developments have the potential to completely transform network management by enhancing the intelligence, autonomy, and capacity of networks to meet the intricate requirements of upcoming digital societies.

19.5.1 Challenges in Data Analytics for Network Management

19.5.1.1 Data Quality and Integrity

Ensuring the accuracy and consistency of data is a major obstacle in network administration. Accurate analytics require high-quality data, yet network data is frequently partial, inconsistent, or noisy. Various factors, including device malfunctions, network disruptions, and human errors, might result in gaps or inaccuracies in the data that is collected. Ensuring data integrity requires the implementation of rigorous procedures for validating, cleansing, and verifying data in order to detect and rectify any problems. It is imperative to construct dependable models and make well-informed decisions using analytics.

In order to tackle these problems, companies might implement automated data quality management technologies that consistently monitor and authenticate data. ML algorithms can be employed to identify anomalies and discrepancies in the data, guaranteeing the utilization of only precise and dependable data for research. In addition, implementing uniform data gathering procedures and merging data from various sources can improve the comprehensiveness and uniformity of data, resulting in a more precise understanding of network performance and behavior.

19.5.1.2 Scalability Issues

Network management faces a significant problem in terms of scalability, particularly when networks expand in both size and complexity. Conventional data analytics tools may have difficulties in managing the growing amount, speed, and diversity of network data produced by contemporary hyper-intelligent networks. Scalability problems can cause data processing and analysis to be delayed, which can impede the capacity to monitor and make decisions in real time. This poses a significant challenge, especially within the framework of Society 5.0, where networks are anticipated to facilitate a diverse array of interconnected devices and applications.

In order to address problems related to scalability, organizations must allocate resources towards implementing scalable analytics infrastructures that have the flexibility to adapt to fluctuations in data volumes and processing requirements. Cloud computing platforms, distributed computing frameworks, and containerization technologies provide scalable solutions for effectively managing large-scale network data. Furthermore, by utilizing edge computing, it is possible to allocate data processing jobs in proximity to the origin, hence decreasing latency and guaranteeing expedited analysis. Scalable solutions are crucial for facilitating the enhanced analytics needed by hyper-intelligent networks and the intricate requirements of Society 5.0.

19.5.1.3 Integration with Legacy Systems

The process of combining contemporary data analytics tools with outdated network systems presents a notable difficulty. Several firms depend on outdated systems that were not specifically created to facilitate sophisticated analytics or manage substantial amounts of data. These systems frequently lack the essential interfaces and features required to seamlessly interact with modern analytics tools, resulting in compatibility and interoperability problems. In addition, the process of transitioning from outdated systems to contemporary platforms can incur significant expenses and disruptions, necessitating major investments of both time and money.

In order to tackle these difficulties, organizations might implement a gradual strategy for integration, where they progressively integrate modern analytical capabilities while preserving the functioning of older systems. Middleware solutions and Application Programming Interfaces (APIs) enable the seamless transfer of data between outdated legacy systems and modern analytics platforms, guaranteeing compatibility and smooth operation. Furthermore, by utilizing virtualization and containerization technologies, it is possible to have ancient systems running alongside current solutions, which allows for a versatile and cost-efficient approach to integration. Over time, companies can evolve their network infrastructures to become fully modernized, enabling them to support the advanced analytics necessary for hyper-intelligent networks and Society 5.0.

19.5.2 Future Trends and Innovations

19.5.2.1 Emerging Technologies

The advent of emerging technologies is poised to completely transform network administration, especially in the realm of hyper-intelligent networks and Society 5.0. AI, ML, and blockchain technologies are playing a crucial role in generating substantial progress in the management and optimization of networks. AI and ML empower networks to become increasingly autonomous and intelligent, allowing them to optimize and repair themselves without the need for human involvement. These technologies have the capability to evaluate large quantities of data in real time, resulting in improved network performance and security through the provision of insights and automation.

Blockchain technology presents viable solutions for network security and integrity through its decentralized and tamper-proof data management capabilities. It has the capability to safeguard data transfers, improve transparency, and guarantee the integrity of network setups and operations. In addition, the implementation of 5G and the Internet of Things (IoT) is broadening the range and intricacy of networks, necessitating more advanced analytics to handle the growing data traffic and interconnected devices. The incorporation of these nascent technologies is crucial for constructing the very advanced networks envisioned for Society 5.0, where uninterrupted connectivity and astute administration are of utmost importance.

19.5.2.2 The Vision for Society 5.0

Society 5.0 envisions a civilization that prioritizes human needs and integrates new technologies like AI, IoT, and big data analytics into daily life to effectively address social issues and improve overall well-being. Hyper-intelligent networks are essential in enabling the connectivity and intelligence required for the development of smart cities, driverless vehicles, healthcare advances, and other advancements. These networks need to possess the capacity to manage extensive volumes of data, guarantee immediate responsiveness, and uphold elevated standards of security and dependability.

To achieve the goal of Society 5.0, it is necessary to consistently innovate in the field of network management technologies and methods. Networks need to undergo transformation in order to enhance their adaptability and resilience, enabling them to automatically optimize themselves in response to shifting conditions and requirements. The progress will be propelled by advanced analytics, which will provide predictive maintenance, automated fault management, and intelligent resource allocation. By adopting these advancements, networks can facilitate the dynamic and linked environments envisioned for Society 5.0, ultimately fostering a more intelligent, streamlined, and inclusive society.

19.6 Conclusion

The incorporation of data analytics into network management signifies a paradigm change towards networks that are more efficient, dependable, and intelligent. Organizations may optimize their network operations and proactively handle possible difficulties by utilizing advanced approaches in real-time monitoring, fault management, security, capacity planning, and QoS management. By integrating AI and ML, these capabilities are further enhanced, allowing networks to become more self-governing and robust. Nevertheless, in order to fully achieve these advantages, it is imperative to tackle obstacles such as data accuracy, ability to handle large amounts of data, and the integration of outdated systems. In the future, the improvement of network management will be propelled by new technologies and cutting-edge research. This progress will be in line with the concept of hyper-intelligent networks and Society 5.0, which prioritize seamless connectivity and intelligent solutions for societal development.

References

1. Soyak, E.G. and Ercetin, O., Effective networking: Enabling effective communications towards 6G. *Comput. Commun.*, 215, 1–21, Feb. 2024. doi: 10.1016/j.comcom.2023.12.002.
2. Corici, M.-I., Gowtham, V., Magedanz, T., Prakash, A., Schreiner, F., NEMI: A 6G-ready) AI-enabled Autonomic Network Management System for Open Campus Networks, in: *2022 IEEE Globecom Workshops (GC Wkshps)*, Rio de Janeiro, Brazil, pp. 674–679, 2022, doi: 10.1109/GCWkshps56602.2022.100021626.
3. Wei, Y., Peng, M., Liu, Y., Intent-based networks for 6G: Insights and challenges. *Digit. Commun. Netw.*, 6, 3, 270–2210, Aug. 2020. doi: 10.1016/j.dcan.2020.07.001.
4. 3rd Generation Partnership Project (3GPP), 5G System; Network Data Analytics Services; Stage 3 (Release 17), in: *Technical Specification (TS)*, p. 29.520, Sep. 2020.

5. ORAN Alliance, O-RAN Working Group 2 AI/ML Workflow Description and Requirements, in: *ORAN-WG2*, AIML. v01 1, 2019.
6. ORAN Alliance, O-RAN-WG1-O-RAN Architecture Description, v04.00.00, in: *Tech. Spec*, Mar. 2021.
7. Banchs, A., *et al.*, Network intelligence in 6G: Challenges and opportunities, in: *Proceedings of the 16th ACM Workshop on Mobility in the Evolving Internet Architecture*, pp. 7–12, 2021.
8. Benzaid, C. and Taleb, T., AI-driven zero touch network and service management in 5G and beyond: Challenges and research directions. *IEEE Netw.*, 34, 2, 1216–194, 2020.
9. Chergui, H., *et al.*, Zero-Touch AI-Driven Distributed Management for Energy-Efficient 6G Massive Network Slicing. *IEEE Netw.*, 35, 6, 43–49, 2021.
10. Corici, M., Troudt, E., Magedanz, T., An Organic 6G Core Network Architecture, in: *2022 25th Conference on Innovation in Clouds, Internet and Networks (ICIN)*, IEEE, pp. 1–7, 2022.
11. NTT Docomo, 5G Evolution and 6G, in: *Whitepaper*, Jan. 2020.
12. GSZSM ETSI, 009-1 V0.11.1. [nd]. Zero-touch network and Service Management (ZSM); Closed-loop automation; Enablers. *Group Specification (gs)*, 3, 2020.
13. GSZSM ETSI, Zero-touch network and service management (zsm); reference architecture. *Group Specification (GS) ETSI GS ZSM*, 2, 2019.
14. Cai, Z., *Maestro: Achieving Scalability and Coordination in Centralized Network Control Plane*, 2011.
15. Casado, M., Rethinking Packet Forwarding Hardware, in: *Proceedings 7th ACM SIGCOMM HotNets Wksp*, 20021-Nov.
16. Chetty, M., You're Capped: Understanding the Effects of Bandwidth Caps on Broadband Use in the Home, in: *Proceedings 2012 ACM Annual Conf. Human Factors in Computing Systems CHI '12*, vol. 3021-30, 2012.
17. *The Fusion of Artificial Intelligence and Soft Computing Techniques for Cybersecurity*, Apple Academic Press, 2024, (n.p.).
18. Tejasvi, K., Venkatadri, N., Reddy, P.A., Triveni, B., Rani, G., Reddy, C.H.R., Manasa, C.H., QoS (Quality Of Service) Analysis of On-Demand Routing Protocol under Multiple Black Hole Nodes, in: *Proceedings of the International Conference on Systems, Science, Control, Communication, Engineering and Technology 2017 (ICSSCCET 2017)*, vol. 1, Jan. 221, 2017.
19. Kurnala, V., Naik, S.A., Surapaneni, D.C., Reddy, C.B., Hybrid Detection: Enhancing Network & Server Intrusion Detection Using Deep Learning, in: *2023 IEEE 5th International Conference on Cybernetics, Cognition and Machine Learning Applications (ICCCMLA)*, Hamburg, Germany, pp. 2421–251, 2023, doi: 10.1109/ICCCMLA5219213.2023.10346699.
20. Sultana, A. and Jabbar, M.A., Intelligent network intrusion detection system using data mining techniques, in: *2016 2nd International Conference on*

Applied and Theoretical Computing and Communication Technology (iCATccT), Bangalore, India, pp. 329–333, 2016, doi: 10.1109/ICATCCT.2016.7912017.
21. El Rajab, M., Yang, L., Shami, A., Zero-touch networks: Towards next-generation network automation. *Comput. Netw.*, 2024, 110294, 2024. doi: 10.1016/j.comnet.2024.110294.
22. Rani, S., Babbar, H., Krichen, M., Yu, K., Memon, F.H., Network Slicing for Zero-Touch Networks: A Top-Notch Technology. *IEEE Netw.*, 37, 5, 16–24, Sept. 2023. doi: 10.1109/MNET.2023.3320394.

20

Techniques to Mitigate the Threats in Cloud Security

Shifa Shah[1], Jaffar Amin Chacket[1]* and Amit Katoch[2]

[1]School of Computer Science & Engineering, Lovely Professional University, Phagwara, Punjab, India
[2]Department of Computer Science & Engineering, IIIMT College of Engineering, Greater Noida, Uttar Pradesh, India

Abstract
With the emergence of various technologies in the field of computers, cloud computing is one of the innovations that is evolving the fastest. Internet users all around the globe are heavily reliant on the cloud and using its numerous services. But many firms are in doubt to either deploy applications or services in a cloud computing environment or not, due to data sensitivity and security issues. The study provides a complete analysis by the various researchers of the primary dangers that if cloud computing is brought on wider range, as well as the current solutions offered by major suppliers, based on the referenced niche category of cloud. Also, tools that are used by the IT organizations to acquire the better insights about the concerns related to security with the usage of cloud computing. Cloud providers are required to adhere to security and privacy standards to guarantee that the data of their users remains private and secure. Lastly, to safely store data and information in cloud storage and to enable communication, symmetric key and asymmetric key cryptography techniques are used. Then, we combine the study of researchers and analyze the latest trends in security of cloud and conclude the best cloud service platform that offers with great security.

***Keywords*:** Cloud computing, attacks, security concerns, techniques, data security, cryptography key algorithms, challenges

**Corresponding author*: princejaffar24@gmail.com

Pradosh Kumar Gantayat, Sandeep Kumar Panda, S. Balamurugan and Sheng-Lung Peng (eds.) Hyper-Intelligent Networks: Exploring the Future of Connectivity for Society 5.0, (431–454) © 2026 Scrivener Publishing LLC

20.1 Introduction

In previous decades, computer produced less computing output and consumed as much electricity as a current computer. The end-user is offered services that meet his or her needs without needing to know where they are located or how they are supplied. Cloud computing has been seen as the technology that will most likely spearhead the next generation Internet revolution since its inception in 2006. The aim of cloud computing, a new paradigm in computing, is to give customers dynamic, secure, and service-guaranteed computer environments [1].

Because of the necessity to develop sophisticated IT infrastructures, cloud computing has become popular. Various programmer installs, configurations, and upgrades must be managed by users. Devices and computer resources are aging out of date very fast. Outsourcing computing platforms is, therefore, a smart option for clients who have complex IT systems to handle [2].

According to a Right Scale poll, 96% of respondents from diverse firms have utilized cloud in various ways. Although cloud computing offers significant benefits to businesses, implementing it is not a simple operation. A highly scalable and affordable platform for Web, business, and High-Performance Computing (HPC) applications is cloud computing. The demand for cloud infrastructure, on the other hand, has skyrocketed. Due to a combination of market and technological considerations, cloud computing is gaining traction. Many businesses are updating their computing infrastructure because of rapidly changing business conditions. Despite that cloud computing can be viewed as boom in the upcoming years and has diverse advantages, the one thing that will always be on the top priority is "security." Researchers have done a great deal of research and contributed in many ways to the field of cloud security, but the cloud environment is still not entirely safe. Because cloud computing is being used more and more frequently, it has become a new battlefield for cybercrime.

The need of more strategies is required to deploy into cloud environment to achieve the five basic goals (availability, data integrity, control, audit, and privacy) of security. As public cloud computing utilization keeps growing and concerns related to security remain high—especially in the wake of the COVID-19 crisis and the subsequent switch to remote work environments—organizations are increasingly prioritizing robust cybersecurity measures, revisiting their cloud strategies, and investing in secure infrastructure to ensure data privacy, regulatory compliance, and business continuity in a more digitally dependent world [3, 4].

20.2 Cloud Computing

The idea of paying for computer resources on an as-needed basis is introduced by cloud computing. Cloud is largely managed and supported by data centers. A variety of information technology companies offer pay-as-you-go services to its customers. Facebook, Amazon, Salesforce, Yahoo, Cisco, Microsoft, and Google are among these companies. They have their own data centers set up in several locations across the world. As ubiquitous network technology and pervasive intelligent devices grow at a rapid pace, new network applications including Internet of Things, virtual/augmented reality, autonomous vehicles, and smart grids are emerging. It is getting harder for cloud computing's centralized processing and storage to keep up with the demands of these new applications and technologies [5].

20.3 Cloud Characteristics

Figure 20.1 illustrates the foundational characteristics of cloud computing, highlighting how virtualization enables a service-oriented, elastic, and shared environment that ultimately supports a market-oriented computing model.

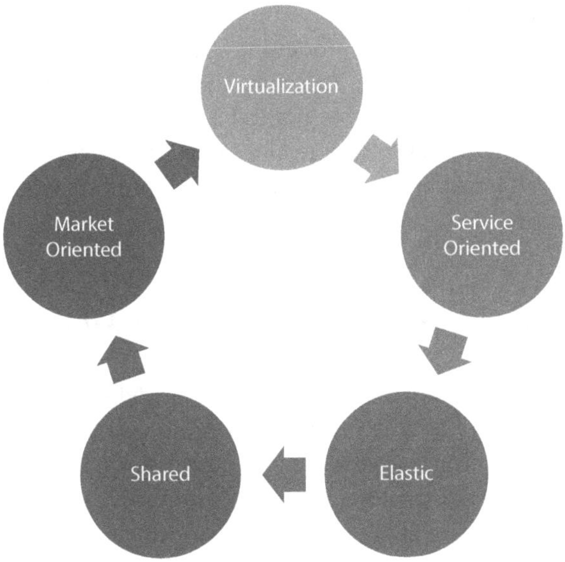

Figure 20.1 Cloud characteristics.

Virtualization: Resources (such processing power, storage, and network bandwidth) are virtualized at multiple levels in clouds. The most fundamental is at the virtual machine (VM) level, where multiple operating systems or applications can each run in their own container on the same physical machine [6].

Service-Oriented: Service-Oriented Architecture (SOA): The cloud is built using a SOA model; it allows for the network-wide service provision of all components and capabilities.

Elastic: Cloud applications can dynamically assign and modify resources (such processing power, storage, and network bandwidth) in response to user demands. Cloud service providers like Microsoft Azure and Amazon Web Services even offer automatically scaling out and scaling in services based on the needs of hosted applications.

Shared: Clouds are shared infrastructure systems in which resources are dynamically assigned to different consumer applications based on their needs. We refer to this kind of sharing as a "multitenant" arrangement. Customers typically do not have direct access to physical resources and are unaware of their location or sharers.

Market Oriented: In cloud computing, users pay only for the services they really utilize. The pricing model may vary based on the application's anticipated quality of service. Amazon and other cloud Infrastructure-as-a-Service (IaaS) providers use market models such as commodity or on-the-spot pricing to determine resource prices. A grid resource pricing model developed by Allenofor and Thulasiram could serve as the basis for cloud computing.

20.4 Cloud Computing Deployment Models

Clouds are built on physical infrastructure and deliver services to clients *via* cloud middleware. Infrastructure and middleware may differ in context of service, administrative domains, and user access. Consequently, the four types of cloud deployments are community, private, public, and hybrid clouds [7]. Figure 20.2 presents the various cloud deployment models, including public, private, hybrid, and community clouds, each offering different levels of control, flexibility, and management to suit organizational needs.

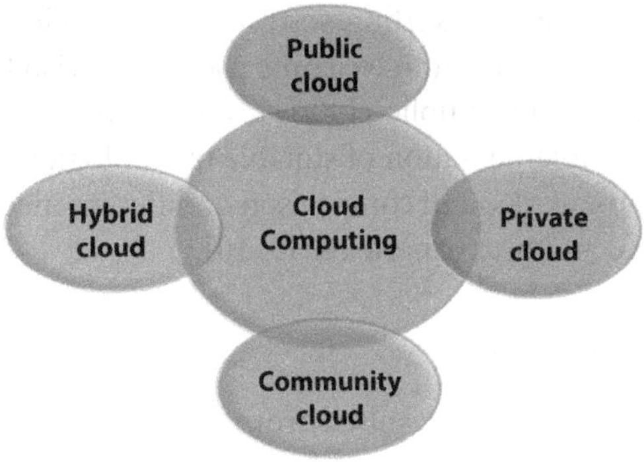

Figure 20.2 Cloud deployment models.

20.4.1 Public Cloud

The most common deployment model is the public cloud, which makes services available to anybody with internet connection. Thousands of servers are connected by a high-speed network in data centers established by public cloud providers to serve thousands of public domain users. Some of the most well-known platforms are listed here: AWS, GCP, and Azure.

20.4.2 Private Cloud

Although public clouds are alluring and offer a practical way to cut costs associated with infrastructure and administration, many businesses would prefer to keep their own customized clouds that are suited to their unique requirements.

For example, the healthcare industry keeps a lot of confidential medical data that cannot be shared with the public. Private Clouds are therefore deployed on-premises to provide IT services to an organization's private users. Private cloud provides security and manages infrastructure and reliability, as the access is confined to trusted organizations [8].

20.4.3 Community Cloud

This has acquired a lot of momentum among firms or communities with similar viewpoints. The primary goal of creating such a system is to demonstrate how cloud computing has totally changed the way computing, storage, and networking resources are assigned, managed, and used, as well as the conditions under which users can access services from anywhere in the world. Cloud computing is essential in the fast-paced world of today. and cloud computing provides on-demand access to computing resources, including hardware and software, through a subscription-based model for application usage. It might be a simple surfing software or a developer-oriented program. Public clouds are meant to welcome users who wish to access services through the internet, and public clouds are utilized in social networking. This involves the implementation of suitable technologies, evaluation of the most effective frameworks, and comparison of different mechanisms to optimize performance and user experience [9, 10].

20.4.4 Hybrid Cloud

They are a deployment that resulted from the widespread usage of public and private clouds and their advantages. By using this technique, businesses can keep important services and data in-house while moving processing and non-essential data to the public cloud. As a result, enterprises may decide to store sensitive data locally using their own IT infrastructure rather than relying on public clouds.

20.5 Cloud Computing Platforms

Cloud computing has totally changed how computing, storage, and networking resources are distributed, managed, and used. It has also changed the conditions under which consumers can access services from anywhere in the world. Cloud computing is a need in today's hectic environment.

Because of its tremendous processing and storage capabilities, as well as its high productivity, the business world is increasing. Factors such as security and availability, ease of access and customization, and scalability contribute to its growing popularity. This paradigm marks a substantial departure from the previous "Desktop-As-A-Service" concept. In the cloud, virtualization takes place at many levels, enabling resource abstraction, efficient utilization, and seamless service delivery across distributed environments. This paradigm marks a substantial departure from the previous "Desktop-As-A-Service" concept. In the cloud, virtualization takes place at many levels.

Users, however, are subject to various restrictions under this agreement.

- Restrictions on illicit software sharing
- The number of machines on which this program has been installed
- The length of time that the program will be operating
- The number of features available for use

Open-source software: It is computer software whose source code is freely accessible online and may be updated for free by programmers to add new features and functionalities. To develop and create, open cooperation is employed. Software is to be tested. An open-source development community oversees this. Assistance with commercial upkeep benefits the business as well as the community. Table 20.1 compares different open source platforms which are available.

It is available to us at no cost. A license is required for this program, which is sometimes included and sometimes not. Users have specific rights. This license grants you certain rights [11]. Table 20.2 compares security and authentication measures.

Table 20.1 Comparison between open-source platforms.

Parameters	OpenNebula	Eucalyptus	Nimbus
Architecture	Infrastructure-as-a-Service (IaaS) cloud: Contemplate to manage the VM efficiently, dynamically, and scalable within data centers (private clouds) includes a huge number of Physical and virtual servers. - Scheduling sprung from the Haizea calendar	Multiple clusters can be combined into a single cloud, each with its own unique internal network address. - It is a private cloud.	Globus-enabled client-side cloud computing interface Tera Port cluster - Science cloud -Nimbus Context Broker, which connects many virtual computers to create "turnkey" virtual clusters: create heterogeneous clusters of autoconfiguring VMs with a single command.
Management according to virtualization	Xen Kernel–based virtual machine with Amazon EC2	Done by Xen hypervisor	Done by Xen Virtualization
Services they provide	IaaS	IaaS	IaaS
How to balance their load, i.e., load balancing	The Nginx Server is design as a load balancer, with round robin traffic distribution.	Simple cloud load balancing controller	The context broker, a self-configuring virtual cluster, is started.
Interoperability	Interoperable between intra cloud services	A same "back-end" infrastructure is used by many cloud computing interfaces.	Standards: "rough consensus and working code"
Fault tolerance	All running VMs can be recovered if the daemon is restarted: A persistent database backend to hold information about hosts and virtual machines	- Several clusters inside the Eucalyptus cloud reduce the chances of linked failure.	- Recovery and frequent checks of worker nodes

Table 20.2 Security measures of cloud.

Parameters according to security	**Firewall, virtual private network**	**WS security for cloud authentication**	**Requires a PKI credential; works with Grid proxies**
Language	Java and Ruby	- Hibernate, Axis2 and Axis2c, and Java	Python and Java
Storage	- Our Open Nebula internal data structures are built on the SQLLite3 backend, which allows for permanent storing of ONE data structure in a database.	The Walrus (the front end for the storage subsystem)	Grid FTP and SCP

20.6 Related Work

Cloud computing is an emerging and rapidly growing collection of IT services that are delivered to customers *via* the internet on a leased basis and service requirement will scale up or down according to the capacity. Despite the fact that cloud computing has given numerous benefits to the computer sector, as many enterprises are in doubt to cloudify or not cloudify, mostly owing to security concerns over enterprise critical data. Eliminating this impediment is a critical prerequisite for realizing the enormous promise of cloud computing. Attacks occurred in 2014 where more than 50 million Dropbox user accounts were compromised, which demonstrate the safety of cloud data has become a prominent subject [12].

20.6.1 Security Issues by Three Attack Vectors

The security issues are being caused by three primary attack vectors (Figure 20.3) [1]: the network, the hypervisor, and the computing hardware.

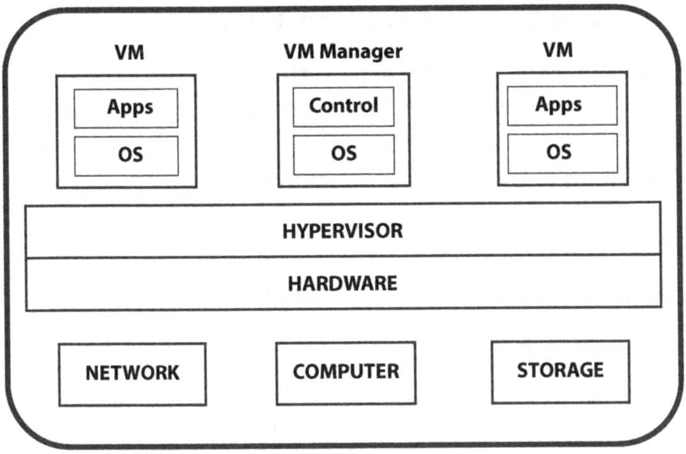

Figure 20.3 Attack vectors in cloud.

20.6.2 Open Issues to Cloud

Fernandes *et al.* [2] offer a detailed assessment of the academic literature in order to clearly outline open issues and difficulties in cloud security. In Table 20.3 below the security issues with different layers are discussed.

Table 20.3 Open issues discussed in cloud.

Open security issues	Layer	Issues
Shared technologies' vulnerabilities [1, 44]	Network, hypervisor	Physical host can be accessible where other nearby VMs reside by exploiting the vulnerabilities in the hypervisor.
Data breach	Network	Data of user can be jeopardized by both unintentional data loss and malicious invasive activities.
Account or service traffic hijacking [1]	Network, hypervisor	If account traffic hijacking occurs, then users may lose control of his account. This allows the intruder to get access to crucial sections of a deployed service, thereby jeopardizing its integrity, confidentiality, and availability [1].
Denial of service (DoS) [1, 45]	Network	Most concerning possibilities is when the cloud infrastructure is rendered. DoS is considerably more hazardous in a cloud setting than in a traditional one, because, as the burden on a single service grows, it offers extra processing capacity to that service.

20.6.3 Current Cloud Attacks and Threats

Cloud computing is responsible for a variety of security risks. A summary of the risks and attackers to the cloud service paradigm, as well as its significance in terms of security requirements (confidentiality, integrity, and availability). Each of these are discussed in the Table 20.4.

Table 20.4 Cloud threats and attacks.

Cloud threats	Attacks
Threats and external attacker [43]	Denial-of-service attack (Dos)
Segregation of data [43]	Authentication attacks: ➢ Brute force attacks ➢ Dictionary attack ➢ Phishing attacks ➢ Shoulder surfing ➢ Key logger ➢ Replay attacks
Insider user threats	Malware injection attacks: ➢ SQL injection attack ➢ Code injection ➢ Cross-site scripting attack
Data leakage	Cache-based side channel attacks [1]

20.7 Work Done by Various Researchers to Address the Open Issues

20.7.1 Network Based Attacks Countermeasures

Traffic must be protected by the cloud providers so that connection between the VM should be secure and outside traffic must leave from the smallest number of access point. Work done by these researchers is mentioned in Table 20.5 including the platform used. Several cloud providers employ nearly the same technology in the networking space. They use common techniques, some of which are included in the table, such as firewalls, intrusion detection systems, and gateways, which are widely used in edge networks to safeguard end systems and monitor traffic. Network based attacks mentioned in Table 20.6 also highlights the same.

Table 20.5 Related work.

Work	Issues	Attack vector	Cloud platforms	Hypervisor
Takashi *et al.* [36]	1. Shared technologies vulnerabilities 2. Account or service traffic hijacking 3. DoS	Network, hypervisor, hardware	Amazon	Hyper-V Xen
Zhou *et al.* [37]	1. Data breach 2. Account or service traffic hijacking	Network, hypervisor	Amazon	Xen
Panth *et al.* [38]	1. Account or service traffic hijacking 2. Shared technologies vulnerabilities 3. DoS 4. Data breach	Network, hypervisor	Amazon, Azure, IBM, Smart Cloud Rack space	—
Akinbi *et al.* [39]	1. Account or service traffic hijacking 2. Shared technologies Vulnerabilities	Network, hypervisor	Azure	Hyper-V
Ristov *et al.* [40]	1. Data breach 2. Account or service traffic hijacking 3. Dos	Network, hypervisor	OpenStack OpenNebula Eucalyptus CloudStack	——
Booth *et al.* [41]	1. Data breach 2. Account or service traffic hijacking 3. Dos	Network, hypervisor	———	Xen
Joseph *et al.* [42]	1. Account or service traffic hijacking 2. Malicious insiders	Network	Amazon, Google	——
L. Coppolino *et al.* [1]	1. Shared technologies vulnerabilities 2. Account or service traffic hijacking 3. Dos 4. Data breach 5. Malicious insiders	Network, hypervisor, hardware	Amazon, VMWare vCloud, Azure, OpenStack,	Xen, KVM, vSphere

Table 20.6 Countermeasures taken against network attack vectors.

Attack vectors	Attacks	Countermeasures
Network-based attacks [1]	Dos/DDos [2]	System availability [3] 1. Prevention technique: Filtration: We can place it close to the destination and also in the routers, Intrusion Detection and Prevention Systems (IDPS) to prevent block intrusion, load balancing, and flow control 2. Detection techniques [1]: Intrusion Detection Systems (IDS), Host-based Detection Systems [5], Distributed Detection (DIDS) [4]
	Sniffing and spoofing leakage of sensitive information	1. Data confidentiality and integrity Make use of encrypted network protocol, SSL TLS should be used [6], IPsec, a protocol [1], use of techniques like SSH and IPsec tunnels of VPN.

20.7.1.1 Commercial Solution by Various Cloud Providers

The capabilities are provided by cloud providers and grown by the third-party vendors, such as McAfee, Symantec, Kaspersky Total Security, CloudLink, and Bitdefender, specifically when application-level network-based security controls are implemented. Companies will sometimes work together with cloud providers to ensure interoperability by providing a pool of providers and hypervisors. Some of the commercial solutions are discussed in Table 20.7 AWS, Azure, and V Cloud suggest TrendMicro Secure Cloud as a third-party solution to ensure data security in applications [13–15].

Table 20.7 Commercial solutions for securing network.

Parameters based on attacks	AWS	Azure	VMWare
Spoofing [8]	AWS IAM [10], AWS MFA [10]	Azure Active, Network Packet Filters (NPF), Directory service IAM	For this attack, VMWare used Horizon Application Manager and vShield Edge.
Sniffing	AWS Direct Connect service; Securing data in cloud HP Atalla Cloud Encryption is used.		Cipher Cloud gateway; Securing data in cloud HP Atalla Cloud Encryption is used.
DoS [8, 9]	Elastic Load Balancer, [10] NGINX, Incapsula DDoS protection, Neustar DDoS protection	Azure Load Balance, SYN cookies, Connection limits, Barracuda NG Firewall [13], Azure CDN	VMWare uses the vShield Edge. Barracuda NG Firewall and Bundle
Malware [11]	Barracuda Web App Firewall, TrendMicro, Deep Security, Symantec Endpoint, Protection, Deep Packet Inspection, AWS Security Groups	Azure used Microsoft Advanced Threat Analytics, Barracuda Web Application Firewall, TrendMicro Instant and On-Cloud Security too	Web Application Firewall (WAF), VXLAN-extended networks, KasperSky Sec for, Virtualization, VMWare vShield Bundle [13]

20.7.2 Hardware Based Attacks Countermeasures

Cloud security relies on a multi-layered approach, and hardware-based countermeasures play a crucial role in establishing a robust foundation of trust and protecting sensitive data. These hardware components provide a level of isolation and tamper resistance that software alone cannot achieve. Tables 20.8 and 20.9 shows the threats and countermeasures which are hardware based.

Table 20.8 Countermeasures taken against hardware based attack vectors.

Attack vectors	Attacks	Countermeasures
Hardware-based attacks [1, 15]	Loss of user's information (side-channel attacks)	Intel Software Guard extension and hardware extension, i.e., ARM Trustzone
		Software methods: [15] ➢ Turn of Cache S-box ➢ Insert Dummy Operation ➢ Avoid Lookup Table ➢ Performing Cache Warming Hardware methods: ➢ Partitioned Cache (PC) ➢ Partition-Locked Cache (PLC) can be used. ➢ Cryptography Techniques such as AES- 256 available to the client.

20.7.2.1 Commercial Countermeasures to Hardware Based Attacks

Table 20.9 Commercial solutions for securing hardware vector.

Attacks	Amazon AWS	Azure	VMWare
Boot Integrity Attack	➢ Intel Trusted Execution Technology ➢ HyTrust (third-party solution)	----	➢ Intel Trusted Execution Technology TXT ➢ HyTrust (third-party solution)
Direct Attack	➢ AWSused SafeNet, ProtectV, CipherCloud, KeyNexus, HyTrust, and Data Control for countermeasures against the attacks.	----	➢ Cipher Cloud gateway, ➢ vSphere Data Protection

(Continued)

Table 20.9 Commercial solutions for securing hardware vector. (*Continued*)

Attacks	Amazon AWS	Azure	VMWare
Time, Trace [18] and Access-Driven Side-Channel Attacks [16, 19]	➢ AWS Cloud Hardware security module (HSM) of Amazon ➢ Intel AES New Instruction	➢ Microsoft Trust Center ➢ Intel Advanced Encryption Standard	vCloud Air Data Center Security [20], ➢ Air Physical Infrastructure Security, ➢ Intel AES New Instruction
	➢ 256 ➢ KeyNexus ➢ Hardware security modules, which are Ethernet-attached. ➢ HPE- ESKM ➢ HP Atalla	AES New Instruction Azure Key Vault	HP ESKM HP Atalla

20.7.3 Hypervisor Attacks Countermeasures

Safety of resource separation can be offered by isolation approaches of wide variety of hardware and software. Hardware techniques such as AES-New Instruction may influence security and can be considered hypervisor protection. According to the guidelines, when deciding which hypervisor platform to use, security solutions of hardware and software must be considered. Intel Virtualization Technology (VT-x) and AMD Virtualization (AMD-V) are hardware-assisted virtualization technologies designed with well-organized processor architectures to enhance the performance and security of virtualized environments. Table 20.10 shows such attacks and their countermeasures.

Table 20.10 Countermeasures taken against hypervisor attack vectors.

Attack vectors	Attacks	Countermeasures
Hypervisor [1]	Viruses and malware	vShield Endpoint Antivirus or anti-malware solution that does not require the use of an agent [21]
	Buffer overflow attacks	1. Address Space Layout Randomization 2. CPU NX/XD
	Unwanted memory accesses	DMA remapping
	Network breach [22]	vNIC-level firewall Isolation of virtual switch Ex. From Xen Hypervisor used by Amazon AWS
		Xen Security Module (XSM), which protects four sensitive layers such as network, boot manager, and qemu

Most of the hypervisors offered HW technology. the commercial solutions for such threats can also be cosidered as discussed in Table 20.11.

20.7.3.1 To Secure Hypervisor Vector (Commercial Solutions)

Table 20.11 Commercial solutions for securing hypervisor vector.

Attack vectors	Amazon(AWS)	Azure	VMWare vCloud (vSphere)
Rootkit (BluePill, SubVirt, Vitriol, and DKSM) [1, 24]	Trusted Execution Technology TXT of Intel, Bit Defender SVE, and Zero-Footprint GuestMemory introspection	Introspection techniques, CloudKd Memory	Sophos AV, IBM Intrusion Prevention System
Remote Code Execution [1]	Xen Security Module (XSM) FLASK, Virtual, Gateway, Intel Virtualized Technology and AMD-V, and HIDS for alert logic	McAfee MOVE AV, Hyper-V Secure Boot, 5nine Cloud Security, Bitdefender GravityZone, Bitdefender total security, Intel Virtualized Technology, and AMD-V	VMWare vSphere security (ASLR, CPU NX/XD, DMARemapping, vNIC-level firewall, and VMI), McAfee MOVE AV, KasperSky Sec for Virtualization, Intel Virtualized Technology, and AMD-V

20.7.4 Cryptographic Techniques for Data Security

Cryptography is conceptualized as a set of ways for creating and evaluating algorithms, which renders the sensitive information of client incomprehensible for an unauthorized individual, allowing authorized individuals to access and comprehend it. There are two main categories into which cryptographic encryption systems can be separated: The two types of key encryption algorithms are symmetric and asymmetric [25, 26].

20.7.4.1 Symmetric Key Algorithms

In this type of algorithms, the transmitter and receiver for encryption and decryption utilize the similar keys. Particularly, the transactions must be extremely secure as anybody may steal sensitive data in between the transaction take place. The Key Exchange Deffie Hellman Algorithm is one the most frequently used safe key exchange methods. The description of symmetric key algorithm is listed in Table 20.12.

Table 20.12 Comparison of different symmetric algorithms for data security.

Algorithm	Block size	Key size	Rounds that the algorithm will take	Security level	Attack vulnerabilities	Benefits
Data Encryption Standard Algorithm (DES) [29]	64 bits	56 bits	19 rounds	Inadequate	Differential cryptanalysis attack and Brute force attack	
Triple Data Encryption Standard (T-DES)	64 bits	56 bits (total, 168 bit)	48 bits	Vulnerable	More vulnerable to brute force attack and differential attack	More secure
CAST-128	It may vary: 40–128 bits.	128	12–16 rounds	Vulnerable	The 64-bit version subject to linear attacks.	
Linear attacks IDEA	64 bits	64–128 bits	5–8	Vulnerable	More vulnerable to linear attack	IDEA is not yet cracked [29]
Advanced Encryption Standard Algorithm (AES)	128 bits, 192 bits, and 256 bits		10 rounds, 12 rounds, and 14 rounds	Excellent	Side-channel attack	AES is secure and have a good avalanche effect [29].
Blowfish Encryption Algorithm	64 bits	32–448	32–448 rounds	Good	Prone to key-related attacks and boomerang attack	Because Blowfish is a powerful encryption technique, it is used in password management systems as well as bit map. Charting [27, 28].

20.7.4.2 Asymmetric Key Algorithms

Public Encryption Algorithms are termed as Asymmetric Cryptography Algorithms. It employs two keys: one is "Private Key" and the other is "Public key." Prior to the transaction, the sender uses its public key to encrypt the plain data, creating cipher data that the recipient decrypts using its private key as discussed in Table 20.13. Among the asymmetric algorithms addressed are Rivest–Shamir–Adleman (RSA) (an asymmetric encryption algorithm), Ciphertext-Policy Attribute-Based Encryption (CP-ABE), Key-Policy Attribute-Based Encryption (KP-ABE), and Elliptic Curve Cryptography (ECC).

Table 20.13 Comparison of different asymmetric algorithms for data security.

Algorithm	Size of the block	Size of the key	Number of rounds	Level of security	Attack vulnerabilities	Benefits
RSA [30]	Not accurately fixed	Greater than and equal to 1,024	---	Excellent	Brute force + and timing attack	The digital signature idea was established in conjunction with RSA, which significantly strengthened the algorithm's security [31, 33].
Attribute-based encryption	Not fixed	Attribute of the user	----	High		Because several users may have the same characteristics, ABE suffers from key revocation.

To securely keep the user's data file, symmetric-key cryptography is implemented. Asymmetric-key cryptography can only encrypt a certain amount of data and is 1,000 times slower than symmetric encryption.

To maintain the security of cloud file storage, symmetric-key cryptography is used.

20.8 Cloud Computing Challenges

The lack of methods or methodologies to aid companies, many organizations find it difficult to successfully, effectively, and efficiently adopt cloud computing due to difficulties in deploying Cloud. There are certain challenges that drive companies to avoid cloud computing adoption and deployment including concerns about accessibility; fears about salesman or the information; and concerns about privacy, expense, issues of integrity, and insufficient bandwidth. The next section will go over the concerns one by one.

Security Issues That Are Related to Cloud: Availability, integrity, confidentiality, and privacy of data are all security factors that contribute to the creation of a safe system. Confidentiality in security refers to the fact that only an authorized individual has access to the information. Privacy, on the other hand, merely means that the data proprietor has control over the disclosure of individual data. Service, data, and infrastructure are immediately available to approved clients when a request is made is termed as availability.

20.9 Future Scope and Conclusion

According to the investigation, Amazon AWS provides a variety of goods and methods to be supplied by the cloud providers or third-party providers.

Some security manners are at high level of technology, whereas some of them are at their early hood and unfit in implementation for a real-world setting. Approaches to deal with account hijacking and DoS at the application level are presently being developed, and several academics are working on them.

Research has been dedicated to investigating new techniques that could prevent attacks utilizing hypervisors. The primary concerns with clouds are security and privacy of data stored in the cloud. Service-level agreements, virtualization, heterogeneity, resource sharing, multi-tenancy, and mobile cloud computing are some of the elements that make cloud security vulnerable. Mitigating the effects of cyberattacks on vital society operations is crucial. Cyber threats can be identified in a few ways, including with cryptography.

In the future, cloud forensic is used for cloud security incidents such as data theft or breach as cloud forensics investigates and maintains the logs.

References

1. Coppolino, L., *et al.*, Cloud security: Emerging threats and current solutions. *Comput. Electr. Eng.*, 59, 126–1405, 2017.
2. Fernandes, D.AB., *et al.*, Security issues in cloud environments: a survey. *Int. J. Inf. Secur.*, 13, 2, 113–170, 2014.
3. Zargar, S.T., Joshi, J., Tipper, D., A survey of defense mechanisms against distributed denial of service flooding attacks. *IEEE Commun. Surv. Tutor. Fourth Quarter*, 15, 4, 2046–69, 2013. doi:10.1109/SURV.2013.031413.00127.
4. Neelima, S. and Lakshmi, Y., A review on distributed cloud intrusion detection system, in: *Int. J. Adv. Technol. Eng. Res. (IJATER)*, 2013.
5. Deshpande, P., *et al.*, HIDS: A host based intrusion detection system for cloud computing environment. *Int. J. Syst. Assur. Eng. Manage.*, 9, 3, 567–576, 2018.
6. Nikolov, N. and Nakov, O., Research of Secure Communication of Esp32 IoT Embedded System to. NET Core Cloud Structure using MQTTS SSL/TLS, in: *2019 IEEE XXVIII International Scientific Conference Electronics (ET)*, IEEE, 2019.
7. Masdari, M. and Jalali, M., A survey and taxonomy of DoS attacks in cloud computing. *Secur. Commun. Netw.*, 9, 16, 3724–3751, 2016.
8. Osanaiye, O.A., Short Paper: IP spoofing detection for preventing DDoS attack in Cloud Computing, in: *2015 18th International Conference on Intelligence in Next Generation Networks*, IEEE, 2015.
9. Khan, W., *DDOS Mitigation Analysis of AWS Cloud Network*, 2017.
10. Todorov, D. and Ozkan, Y., AWS security best practices, in: *Amazon Web Services*, 2013, [Online]. Available from: http://media.amazonwebservices.com/AWS_Security_Best_Practices.pdf.
11. Chou, T.-S., Security threats on cloud computing vulnerabilities. *Int. J. Comput. Sci. Inf. Technol.*, 5, 3, 79, 2013.
12. Hossain, A., *et al.*, *Effective Approach of Analyzing Security Attacks and Implementing the Solutions in Cloud Computing*, 2019.
13. Bhardwaj, A. and Goundar, S., Cloud Computing Security Services to Mitigate DDoS Attacks, in: *Cloud Computing Security-Concepts and Practice*, IntechOpen, 2020.
14. Watson, M.R., *et al.*, Malware detection in cloud computing infrastructures. *IEEE Trans. Dependable Secure Comput.*, 13, 2, 192–205, 2015.
15. Rani, D.R. and Venkateswarlu, S., Software and hardware defence methods against cache-based side channel attacks. *Int. J. Manage Inform. Technol. Eng.*, 2, 5, May 2014.
16. Ristenpart, T., Tromer, E., Shachem, H., Savage, S., Hey, you, get off of my cloud: exploring information leakage in third-party compute clouds, in: *Proceedings of the 16th ACM conference on computer and communications security (CCS '09)*, ACM, New York, NY, USA, pp. 199–212, 2009, http://dxdoiorg/101145/16536621653687.
17. Mulazzani, M., Schrittwieser, S., Leithner, M., Huber, M., Weippl, E., Dark Clouds on the Horizon: Using Cloud Storage as Attack Vector and Online

Slack Space, in: *Proceedings of the 20th USENIX Security Symposium (USENIX Security '11), USENIX Association*, San Francisco, CA, USA, pp. 65–80, 2011.
18. Kim, T., Peinado, M., Mainar-Ruiz, G., {STEALTHMEM}: System level protection against cache-based side channel attacks in the cloud, in: *21st {USENIX} Security Symposium ({USENIX} Security 12)*, 2012.
19. Zhang, Y., *et al.*, Cross-VM side channels and their use to extract private keys, in: *Proceedings of the 2012 ACM conference on Computer and communications security*, 2012.
20. Purohit, R., Comparative Analysis of Few Cloud Service Providers Considering Their Distinctive Properties. *Int. J. Adv. Res. Comput. Sci.*, 8, 5, 2017.
21. Walters, J.P., *et al.*, GPU pass through performance: A comparison of KVM, Xen, VMWare ESXi, and LXC for CUDA and OpenCL applications, in: *2014 IEEE 7th International Conference on Cloud Computing*, IEEE, 2014.
22. Wu, H., *et al.*, Network security for virtual machine in cloud computing, in: *5th International Conference on Computer Sciences and Convergence Information Technology*, IEEE, 2010.
23. Riddle, A.R. and Chung, S.M., A survey on the security of hypervisors in cloud computing, in: *2015 IEEE 35th International Conference on Distributed Computing Systems Workshops*, IEEE, 2015.
24. Tank, D., Aggarwal, A., Chaubey, N., Virtualization vulnerabilities, security issues, and solutions: a critical study and comparison. *Int. J. Inf. Technol.*, 1–16, 2019.
25. Ebrahim, M., Khan, S., Khalid, U.B., Symmetric Algorithm Survey: A Comparative Analysis. *Int. J. Comput. Appl.*, 61, 12–19, January 2013.
26. Somorovsky, J., Heiderich, M., Jensen, M., Schwenk, J., Gruschka, N., Lo Iacono, L., All Your Clouds Are Belong to Us: Security Analysis of Cloud Management Interfaces, in: *Proceedings of the 3rd ACM Workshop on Cloud Computing Security Workshop (CCSW '11)*, ACM, New York, NY, USA, pp. 3–14, 2011, https://dx.doi.org/10.1145/2046660.2046626.
27. Wang, M. and Que, Y., The Design and Implementation of Passwords Management System Based on Blowfish Cryptographic Algorithm. *IEEE Comput. Sci. Technol. App. IFCSTA*, 2, 24–28, Chongqing, December 2009.
28. Palaniswamy, N., Dugar M, D., Jain, D.K., Sarabhoje, R., Enhanced Blowfish Algorithm using Bitmap Image Pixel Plotting for Security Improvisation. *Educ. Technol. Computer (ICETC)*, 1, V1-533-V1-538, Shanghai, June 2010.
29. Semwal, P. and Sharma, M.K., Comparative study of different cryptographic algorithms for data security in cloud computing, in: *2017 3rd International Conference on Advances in Computing, Communication & Automation (ICACCA)(Fall)*, IEEE, 2017.
30. Cao, Y.-. and Fu, C., An Efficient Implementation of RSA Digital Signature Algorithm, in: *IEEE Wireless Communications Networking and Mobile Computing (WiCOM)*, pp. 1–4, Dalian, October 2008.
31. Si, H., Cai, Y., Cheng, Z., An Improved RSA Signature Algorithm based on Complex Numeric Operation Function. *IEEE Challenges Environ. Sci. Comput. Eng. (CESCE)*, 2, 397–400, China, March 2010.

32. Zheng, Y.-H., Zhu, Y.-F., Xu, H., An Application of Low Private Exponent Attack on RSA, in: *IEEE Computer Science & Education (ICCSE)*, pp. 1864–1866, Nanning, July 2009.
33. Somani, U., Lakhani, K., Mundra, M., Implementing Digital Signature with RSA Encryption Algorithm to Enhance the Data Security of Cloud in Cloud Computing, in: *IEEE Parallel Distributed and Grid Computing (PDGC)*, pp. 211–216, Solan, October 2010.
34. Dharmakeerthi, T.D., *A Study on Secure File Storage in Cloud Computing using Cryptography*, April 2020.
35. Mather, T., Kumaraswamy, S., Latif, S. Cloud Security and Privacy: An Enterprise Perspective on Risks and Compliance, in: *O'Reilly Media, Inc.*, Sebastopol, CA, USA, pp. 1–312, 2009, https://www.oreilly.com/library/view/cloud-security-and/9780596802769/.
36. Takahashi, T., Blanc, G., Kadobayashi, Y., Fall, D., Hazeyama, H., Matsuo, S., Enabling secure multitenancy in cloud computing: challenges and approaches, in: *Future Internet Communications (BCFIC), 2012 2nd Baltic congress on Vilnius*, pp. 72–9, 2012, doi:10.1109/BCFIC.2012.6217983.
37. Zhou, M., Zhang, R., Xie, W., Qian, W., Zhou, A., Security and privacy in cloud computing: a survey, in: *Semantics Knowledge and Grid (SKG). 2010 Sixth International Conference on Beijing*, pp. 105–12, 2010, doi:10.1109/SKG.2010.19.
38. Panth, D., Mehta, D., Shelgaonkar, R., A survey on security mechanisms of leading cloud service providers. *Int. J. Comput. Appl.*, 98, 1, 34–7, July 2014.
39. Akinbi, A., Pereira, E., Beaumont, C., Evaluating security mechanisms implemented on public platform-as-a-service cloud environments case study: Windows azure, in: *Internet Technology and Secured Transactions (ICITST), 2013 8th International Conference for London*, pp. 162–7, 2013, doi:10.1109/ICITST.2013.6750183.
40. Ristov, S. and Gusev, M., Security evaluation of open source clouds, in: *EUROCON, 2013*, pp. 73–80, IEEE, Zagreb, 2013, doi:101109/EUROCON20136624968.
41. Booth, G., Soknacki, A., Somayaji, A., Cloud security: attacks and current defenses, in: *2013 8th Annual Symposium on Information Assurance*, Albany, NY, June 2013.
42. Joseph, A.O., Jaspher, G., Kethrine, W., Security of real time cloud service providers: a survey, in: *Electronics and Communication Systems (ICECS). 2014 International Conference on Coimbatore*, pp. 1–5, 2014, doi:10.1109/ECS.2014.6892555.
43. Alenezi, A. *et al.*, The Impact of Cloud Forensic Readiness on Security. *CLOSER.*, 2017.
44. Nanavati, M., Colp, P., Aiello, B., Warfield, A., Cloud security: a gathering storm. *Commun. ACM*, 57, 5, 70–9, May 2014. http://dx.doi.org/10.1145/2593686.

45. Deshmukh, R.V. and Devadkar, K.K., Understanding DDos attack & its effect in cloud environment. *Procedia Comput. Sci.*, 49, 202–10, 2015. ISSN 1877-0509.
46. Kandias, M., Virvilis, N., Gritzalis, D., The insider threat in cloud computing. *Crit. Inf. Infrastruct. Secur.*, 6983, 93–103, 2013. doi:10.1007/978-3-642-41476-3_8.

21

The Transformative Influence of Industry 4.0 and Hyper Artificial Intelligence on Human Resource Management

Rashmi Kumari* **and Sujata Priyambada Dash**

Department of Management, Birla Institute of Technology, Mesra, Ranchi, India

Abstract

The market's economic importance is evident, and organizations must continuously improve their competitive edge to maintain their market presence. This involves strategically allocating resources to investments and ensuring efficient operation and growth. The human resource (HR) management (HRM) division has embraced digital transformation, integrating artificial intelligence (AI) technology to enhance recruitment processes. AI allows organizations to efficiently identify suitable candidates for specific roles, streamlining the recruitment process and optimizing HR strategies. This shift toward strategic and tech-enabled HR practices aligns with the evolving demands of the competitive market landscape, saving valuable time and resources for core operational activities. AI is revolutionizing the HR sector, enhancing efficiency and competitiveness in the digital age. It streamlines the hiring process, streamlines the interview process, and enhances overall HRM functions. AI can handle tasks like career planning, employee orientation, and training programs with precision and efficacy. This integration leads to increased productivity and accuracy in HR tasks. The influence of Industry 4.0 and AI on HRM procedures is significant. This study examines the profound impact of AI and Industry 4.0 technologies on HRM practices, revealing both the advantages and challenges that they pose to traditional HR practices. This critical examination of the intersection between Industry 4.0, AI, and HRM is crucial in understanding the evolving dynamics of the modern workplace and the pivotal role technology plays in reshaping HR functions and strategies.

**Corresponding author*: rashmik@bitmesra.ac.in

Pradosh Kumar Gantayat, Sandeep Kumar Panda, S. Balamurugan and Sheng-Lung Peng (eds.) Hyper-Intelligent Networks: Exploring the Future of Connectivity for Society 5.0, (455–482) © 2026 Scrivener Publishing LLC

Keywords: Human resource management, artificial intelligence, Industry 4.0, technology, digital transformation

21.1 Introduction

The human species is constantly evolving, reflecting the dynamic nature of our existence. With each passing day, our evolution presents us with fresh challenges and opportunities, driving the development of new requirements. This perpetual evolution creates a continuous demand for advancements in technology, information, and information management to address these emerging needs effectively. Organizations across various industries are compelled to keep pace with these evolving trends, fostering a culture of innovation and adaptability. As technology evolves, businesses must embrace change to not only survive but flourish in this rapidly changing landscape. By recognizing and responding to the shifting demands of technology, organizations position themselves to not only survive but also thrive in a competitive market. Consequently, those who effectively harness these technological advancements can differentiate themselves, expand their reach, and conduct business operations in a highly efficient manner. The ability to adapt to the changing technological landscape presents organizations with the opportunity to drive growth, foster innovation, and enhance their overall performance. Thus, embracing change and adapting to technological shifts enable organizations to remain competitive and achieve sustainable success in an ever-evolving business environment.

Human resource management (HRM) plays a crucial role within the institution, serving as one of the fundamental mechanisms through which employees shape their skills, conduct, and mindset to align with the organizational goals. This essential function is strategically positioned within one of the central pillars of the institution's structure, ensuring its effective implementation and impact [1, 2]. Therefore, when business owners create their HRM procedures, they try to be receptive to new ideas, educate themselves, and help staff members become more adept at managing information. Thus, in knowledge-based economies, human resource (HR) practices are crucial [3, 4]. The primary goal of HRM in businesses is to enhance the knowledge, abilities, and skills of the human element while also focusing on shaping their attitude, behavior, contribution, and performance [5]. Because an organization's ability to survive is determined by the caliber of its current people resources and how they are used dynamically [6].

According to Tewari and Pant, the utilization of artificial intelligence (AI) in conjunction with Industry 4.0 in the HR department of businesses has made it possible for organizations to control their managerial and operational procedures, boost productivity, and cut expenses [7]. This is due to the fact that smart automation technologies have become increasingly necessary for institutions in recent times. The goal of this study is to clarify the ideas behind Industry 4.0 and AI while also highlighting how these two trends are affecting HRM. The current research was covered in the study on the influence of Industry 4.0 and AI on HRM. The studies detailed in Table 21.1 offer a review of the extensive study identifying the pivotal contributions of Industry 4.0 and AI in shaping the future landscape of the HR sector. Through a thorough examination of the literature, a plethora of findings have emerged, illuminating the profound impact that these technologies are poised to have on various facets of HR practices in the times ahead.

Table 21.1 Summary of previous studies.

S. no.	Year of publication	Name of authors	Research findings
1	2023	Chowdhury *et al.*	The aim of the current study was to create AI applications for HRM. To provide an extensive understanding of the resources available within the corporate environment, the diligent researchers undertook an extensive literature analysis. This in-depth research encompassed a wide array of topics crucial to the field, including international business to gain insights into global market trends and opportunities, information management to explore efficient data handling techniques, general management practices for overall organizational effectiveness, operational management strategies to streamline day-to-day operations, and HRM for a deeper understanding of employee engagement and talent optimization. The review revealed that companies could not adopt AI applications and reap the benefits of doing so solely with technical resources; additional research was required to guarantee that employees are adequately informed.
2	2023	Pereira *et al.*	The effects of AI applications on HRM practices and organizational performance were examined by the researchers, with a focus on the health sector. Their investigation yielded information about the organizational and financial benefits that the health sector can derive from the use of AI applications.

(*Continued*)

Table 21.1 Summary of previous studies. (*Continued*)

S. no.	Year of publication	Name of authors	Research findings
3	2023	Ibrahimagaoglu	The requirement for companies to stack and process HR information in cyberspace has been increasingly crucial in today's technologically driven world. This growing need has prompted researchers to delve into the realm of electronic human resources management, seeking to explore the various complexities and possibilities that come with managing HR functions in a digital landscape. The definition, goals, forms, significance, evolution, phases, benefits, and drawbacks of electronic HRM (e-HRM) were all disclosed by the researcher in this study.
4	2023	Yilmaz and Yilmaz	Researchers looked into how Industry 4.0 might affect HRM in their study. They examined the impact of Industry 4.0 on HRM functions by outlining numerous theories related to it. They came to the conclusion that digital transformation had a remarkable impact on HRM practices.
5	2023	Ugurlu and Dogan	The study's authors provided further details on the topic of digital HRM, conceptualized the change of HRM, and examined how technological developments have affected the hiring process. They stated that web-based HRM technology, intranet portals, and online platforms were the most significant results of digitalization in the HRM industry. The researcher emphasized that new applications and viewpoints to the traditional business practices and procedures were brought about by this circumstance and would continue to be brought about.
6	2023	Akca	The objective of this research was to investigate how talent management uses AI applications. AI applications were discovered to have a substantial positive impact on the company and its workforce in the areas of talent acquisition, data collection and analysis, workplace productivity enhancement, employee workload reduction, and cost containment.

(*Continued*)

Table 21.1 Summary of previous studies. (*Continued*)

S. no.	Year of publication	Name of authors	Research findings
7	2023	Anayat	The previously mentioned study offers a comprehensive theoretical overview of the topic and makes beneficence to the field of AI in HRM. The investigation showed that machine learning (ML), natural language processing (NLP), machine vision, and recommendation systems were among the AI technologies used for specific purposes in HRM operations. Furthermore, in a comprehensive study that delved into the integration of AI into HRM practices, it was revealed that various key areas of HRM benefitted from the application of AI technology. These areas encompassed the automated induction process, which streamlines and enhances new employee onboarding, as well as skill development and training initiatives that leverage AI algorithms to personalize learning experiences and optimize employee growth.
8	2023	Seyidzade	In order to ascertain the significance of digital transformation with regard to HRM functions in businesses, the author of the paper performed a survey and looked into advances in the sector. The study came to the conclusion that digital transformation has good effects on businesses, especially in the area of human resources management.
9	2023	Murugesan *et al.*	The study's authors looked at artificial intelligence's contributions to HR digitization and its uses in Industry 4.0. The results showed that the foundation of sustainable growth was hierarchical organization research. Improvements in safety and well-being were considered crucial components of AI use in HR.
10	2022	Ming	The current study examined how ML is being applied to HRM, an area that is growing and has a lot of promise to improve the effectiveness and performance of HRM systems.
11	2022	Pal *et al.*	ML techniques were used by the authors of the current study to classify resumes, aid in skill extraction, and present a range of talents under pertinent job profile categories. The resume classification tool will improve e-recruitment's use and efficacy. This particular approach will help businesses and save time and effort during the hiring procedure.
12	2022	Van Noordt *et al.*	The researchers found that, whereas AI was frequently used to enhance internal management and the delivery of public services, its application in policy decision-making remained constrained.

(*Continued*)

Table 21.1 Summary of previous studies. (*Continued*)

S. no.	Year of publication	Name of authors	Research findings
13	2022	Pan *et al.*	The authors of the current study looked into the connection between the hiring practices of AI-adopting businesses and the behavioral restrictions placed on them. To gain a better understanding of various constraints and potential opportunities, the study integrated transaction cost theory with the technology, organization, and environment model. The study's conclusions showed that, while regulatory support and technological proficiency encouraged the use of AI, businesses' perceptions of its complexity hindered its spread.
14	2022	Karaboga and Karaboga	Researchers conducted a bibliometric analysis of digitalization and digital technologies in HRM, identifying three main domains: e-HRM Approach, HR Analytics, and Industry 4.0, Smart HR Practices and Performance Relationship. The integration of digital technologies in HRM is a pioneering area in academia, with a surge in interest and scholarly inquiry due to its relevance in the contemporary HR landscape. The study emphasizes the critical role of digital transformation in reshaping traditional HR paradigms and practices, underscoring the need for continuous exploration. Digital technologies have the potential to revolutionize HR operations, drive efficiency, foster innovation, and enhance organizational performance, thus highlighting the need for further studies and developments in this burgeoning field.
15	2022	Orucoglu	The impact of digitization and Industry 4.0 on HRM functions was investigated by the researcher. Industry 4.0 is significantly impacting HRM, with advanced technologies streamlining recruitment, employee training, performance reviews, and industrial relations. Data analytics and AI-driven systems provide real-time feedback, enhancing employee development and productivity. Job analysis and design processes benefit from automation, leading to more efficient roles. Career development frameworks adapt to digital skills, and job evaluation and compensation structures reflect market value. HR information systems and digital tools enhance administrative processes, allowing HR professionals to focus on strategic initiatives and employee development. Wearable technology and Internet-of-Things devices monitor workplace conditions, and data analytics provide actionable insights into workforce performance and organizational effectiveness.

(*Continued*)

Table 21.1 Summary of previous studies. (*Continued*)

S. no.	Year of publication	Name of authors	Research findings
16	2022	Toprak *et al.*	The researchers looked into how AI is used in HRM in their study. Additionally, they provided a conceptual examination of the impact of AI on HRM and highlighted the benefits and drawbacks of AI in HRM operations through the development of AI applications.
17	2022	Suseno *et al.*	The study examined the impact of high-performance work systems on the relationships among HR managers' beliefs, AI anxiety, and change preparedness for AI adoption. Consistent with the study findings, HR managers' attitudes and anxiety levels regarding artificial intelligence were significantly influenced by how prepared their companies were to use AI. The researchers conducted a detailed study where they discovered a significant correlation between individuals' preexisting beliefs and their attitudes toward AI. Those who held optimistic views were found to display a higher level of acceptance toward AI technology, contrasting with those who expressed deeper concerns and hesitations regarding its implications and applications. To provide an understanding of HR managers' preparedness for AI adoption, they merged their views on AI, their concerns about it, and their impressions of putting high-performance work systems in place inside the organization.
18	2022	Gong *et al.*	Using AI technology, the researchers in their study created a module for pay estimation with the goal of enhancing HRM through information management. The previously mentioned module enhanced skills using a backpropagation neural network in accordance with candidates' resumes and industrial expertise. The investigation led to the establishment of an intelligent human resource management system (HRMS) and an AI-based HRMS, which improved HRM efficiency.
19	2022	Rahman *et al.*	The current study successfully developed and implemented a cutting-edge, innovative blockchain-powered performance evaluation system specifically designed for monitoring and enhancing employee performance within a corporate setting. This groundbreaking technology comes with a myriad of assurances, highlighting its key features of confidentiality, security, and reliability. The system ensures the anonymity of employees while safeguarding their sensitive performance data, guaranteeing a trustworthy and tamper-proof environment for performance assessments.

(*Continued*)

Table 21.1 Summary of previous studies. (*Continued*)

S. no.	Year of publication	Name of authors	Research findings
20	2021	Tiwari *et al.*	The connection between AI and HR functions as well as the various tasks performed by the HR department were examined in this study. The analysis' findings showed a favorable relationship between various elements, including innovation and simplicity of use, indicating that AI has an impact on both.
21	2021	Vrontis *et al.*	This study looked at how AI, robotics, and other cutting-edge technologies affect HRM. The findings show that there are a number of potentials for HRM as well as major ethical and technological problems.
22	2021	Wei and Jin	The aim of this study was to improve the HRM system by combining an optimized GM model and a backpropagation NN model.
23	2021	Qamar *et al.*	This study conducted a thorough assessment of the literature on AI in HRM. The study produced a unique idea map between AI and HRM that outlined how AI could be applied to improve understanding of HRM decision-making processes. The researchers also provided a more thorough understanding of the moral challenges associated with AI's use in HRM. To help with the shift toward ethical AI, they proposed a basic framework that is suggestive and may be used to combine ethical practices and methodologies.
24	2021	Zhu and Usman	The current study used ML technology to manage and analyze HR data in contemporary firms. The HR system was ML technology, which also reduced the business volume and raised the management and efficacy of HR.
25	2021	Kumari and Hemalatha	The study in Chennai examined AI technologies in HRM practices and employees' perceptions. Using a sociological survey, HR experts and IT sector employees were involved. The research revealed no favorable attitudes toward AI systems and identified obstacles to their implementation.

(*Continued*)

Table 21.1 Summary of previous studies. (*Continued*)

S. no.	Year of publication	Name of authors	Research findings
26	2020	Qin *et al.*	The study that is being referenced here extensively leveraged the semantic representations present at the word level, the perceptual acuity of individuals, and their overall job-related experiences, amalgamating this critical data to craft a highly sophisticated and innovative framework cantered around recurrent neural networks for the explicit purpose of facilitating a more efficient and accurate matching process between job applicants and their potential roles. The previously mentioned approach has the potential to reduce reliance on physical work and increase employability.
27	2020	Uğur and Güner	The author of the current study described the digital apps used in HR procedures as well as the challenges these applications presented. It was stated that employees' work in the pertinent processes was made easier and faster by the digital applications employed in HR procedures.
28	2020	Şendogdu	This study analyzes the impact of Industry 4.0 advancements on HRM. The role that robotic resources play in our daily lives and the necessity of the idea of robotic resource management were also covered in the study.
29	2020	Bayarcelik	The study reviews the impact of digital transformation on HRM, revealing that artificial intelligence automates talent development, accelerates HR processes, and increases productivity by evaluating employee data.
30	2020	Parsehyan	The ongoing research delves into the numerous advantages that HR 4.0 offers in terms of digital compliance, shedding light on the vast potential that AI holds within recruitment, screening, interviewing, and training procedures. This investigation identifies how integrating AI into these critical HR functions not only streamlines processes but also enhances efficiency and accuracy.
31	2020	Samarasinghe and Medis	In order to shed light on the impact of AI on the field of HRM, this comprehensive study delved into the vast knowledge areas and insights put forth by a diverse range of prominent experts and scholars who have dedicated their careers to understanding the evolving role of technology in the realm of HRM.

(*Continued*)

Table 21.1 Summary of previous studies. (*Continued*)

S. no.	Year of publication	Name of authors	Research findings
32	2020	Jawad	The study introduces a cutting-edge website-based HRMS designed to streamline the management of employee activity information. This comprehensive system showcases significant advancements in efficiency and performance, particularly in the realm of data storage and management.
33	2020	Tewari and Pant	In the pursuit of shedding light on the transformative impact of AI within the realm of HRM, this comprehensive study conducted an in-depth analysis of the contributions and research findings of numerous respected experts and thought leaders in the field. By examining and synthesizing the diverse perspectives and insights of these prominent specialists, the study aimed to provide a detailed exploration of how AI is revolutionizing various aspects of HRM practices, ranging from recruitment and talent management to performance evaluation and employee engagement strategies.
34	2020	Nawaz	The study explores AI's potential in HRM, analyzing 23 Scopus articles from 1991 to 2020. It identifies nine HRM activities that could benefit from AI application, enhancing efficiency and customer satisfaction.
35	2019	Rykun	The research reveals that AI has transformed HRM areas, including recruitment, by reducing labor-intensive tasks like CV sorting, candidate selection, and employee training.
36	2019	Necula and Strîmbei	The study developed an architecture for semantic web technology and data science for talent training, demonstrating higher classification impact compared to regression analysis, random forest, and Support Vector Machines (SVM), efficiently marking resume data.
37	2019	Yawalkar	The aforementioned study described the function of artificial intelligence in HRM as well as potential benefits and drawbacks.
38	2019	Ciftcioglu *et al.*	This study clarified the relation between HRM and Industry 4.0. It also described the challenges that would need to be overcome in light of the potential changes to business life that innovations brought about by Industry 4.0 could bring about in terms of technology.
39	2019	Sekeroglu and Özer	The study reviews AI and technology's impact on HRM, revealing its role in candidate selection and fostering a bias-free recruitment process.

(*Continued*)

Table 21.1 Summary of previous studies. (*Continued*)

S. no.	Year of publication	Name of authors	Research findings
40	2019	Aksu and Surgevil	The study delves into the concept of digital competence, shedding light on the essential skills that organizations are increasingly seeking in the modern technological era. These sought-after competencies encompass a wide range of abilities, including but not limited to digital literacy, the capacity for information analysis, adaptability to self-improvement, proficiency in problem-solving, and the vital attribute of digital emotional intelligence.
41	2019	Alkan	The study provides a comprehensive definition of ML, a cutting-edge technology that enables computers to learn from data and make predictions. It delves into various sub-concepts within ML, including supervised learning, where the model is trained on labeled data; unsupervised learning, where the model identifies patterns without labeled data; semi-supervised learning, which combines elements of supervised and unsupervised learning; reinforcement learning, which involves a system learning through trial and error; and intensive learning methods. The research suggests a notable trend toward an increased utilization of ML in managing industry changes.
42	2019	Tambe *et al.*	This research showed how AI applications in HRM problems, such as hiring and selection, are becoming more and more common and have significantly reduced the cost and time required to accomplish the stated tasks.
43	2018	Thite *et al.*	The current study proposed an HRMS algorithm and recruitment management system built on blockchain. The results showed that there were clear benefits to the recommended system over the current recruitment methods.
44	2018	Jarrahi	The study sheds light on the profound and far-reaching influence that AI exerts on various facets of organizational operations and strategies. It underscores how the integration of AI technologies impacts decision-making processes, shapes management methodologies, revolutionizes knowledge management practices, and ultimately shapes consumer outcomes in multifaceted ways. This includes enhancing service quality perceptions among consumers through personalized experiences and ensuring higher levels of satisfaction by streamlining operational efficiencies.

(*Continued*)

Table 21.1 Summary of previous studies. (*Continued*)

S. no.	Year of publication	Name of authors	Research findings
45	2018	Onik *et al.*	The research sheds light on the key challenges faced by business and technology leaders as they navigate the shift toward digitalization. One significant hurdle is the need for HR departments to play an important role in facilitating the adoption of a digital mindset among employees. This involves not just embracing digital tools and technologies but also fostering a culture that is conducive to innovation and continuous learning in the digital realm. Additionally, another obstacle highlighted in the research pertains to the transformation of employee experiences through the effective utilization of digital platforms and applications. By leveraging these technological tools, organizations can enhance employee engagement, streamline processes, and create a more dynamic and agile workforce.

Source: Author's representation

21.2 Methodology

This section highlights the integration of artificial intelligence and deep learning techniques in Human Resource Management to support the objectives of Industry 4.0.

21.2.1 Human Resource Management

To optimize resources, HR departments are implementing digital tools including cloud computing, AI, and data analysis [8]. Chatbots, digital technologies, and AI have become commonplace in HRM. The following roles of AI in HRM are performed by it:

- *Recruitment:* In the comprehensive research article by Amla Malhotra in 2017, it was highlighted that only about 40% of businesses and industry sectors have implemented AI technologies. Noteworthy companies like SAT, Facebook, and GE have integrated various digital tools into their recruitment procedures, leveraging AI for tasks such as assessing candidates, conducting interviews, and pinpointing emerging talent within the talent pool [8]. For instance, AI algorithms enable hiring managers to swiftly review and evaluate job applications, ensuring a quicker response time for applicants seeking opportunities within these innovative institutions. Additionally, having a reliable chat box system or automated answering machine in place is paramount for swiftly addressing inquiries and resolving any issues that may arise throughout the recruitment process within a business setting. Such automation tools not only streamline the hiring workflow but also enhance the overall candidate experience by facilitating efficient communication and providing timely assistance whenever needed. Therefore, the strategic integration of AI technologies in the recruitment domain is proving to be a game-changer for progressive organizations aiming to optimize their talent acquisition processes and stay ahead in the competitive market landscape.

- *Screening and Interview Process:* AI has revolutionized the interviewing process by streamlining it through the application of word or voice pattern evaluations. This innovative implementation of AI technology not only expedites the interview process but also enhances the overall experience for candidates seeking employment opportunities. In modern recruitment practices, AI-based software tools play a pivotal role in conducting digital interviews that are both efficient and informative. Specifically, the utilization of software applications like Amy and Clara has become increasingly prevalent within business environments. These advanced tools effectively manage and coordinate interview schedules and meetings, exemplifying the significant impact of AI on optimizing organizational processes.

Moreover, leveraging AI software for digital interviews signifies a shift toward a more sophisticated and tech-savvy approach to talent acquisition. By automating various stages of the interview process, organizations demonstrate their commitment to embracing technological advancements to enhance the recruitment experience for both recruiters and candidates. The inclusion of AI technology in interview processes presents numerous benefits, including increased efficiency, reduced bias, and improved accuracy in evaluating candidate qualifications. As businesses strive to stay competitive and innovative in their recruitment strategies, the integration of AI software for conducting interviews serves as a strategic advantage that fosters productivity and effectiveness in the selection of top talent.

- *Lessen the Administrative Burden*: HR professionals play a vital role within companies, as they are responsible for a wide range of tasks crucial to organizational success. In today's fast-paced business world, technology and AI have become valuable tools that businesses utilize to support their HR departments. By employing AI, companies are able to streamline processes, increase efficiency, and ultimately alleviate the burden on HR staff. This modern approach not only simplifies administrative duties but also enhances the overall productivity of HR functions within an organization.

- *Selecting:* The researcher, Rajesh, conducted a comprehensive study investigating the potential of AI in revolutionizing the recruitment and selection process within HRM. Rajesh delved into the ways in which AI could streamline the task of HR managers by swiftly identifying the most suitable candidates for various roles within an organization. By implementing AI tools, employers strive to optimize their recruitment strategies by harnessing the power of technological advancements to efficiently evaluate applicants and match them with positions that align with their skills and competencies [9].
- *Reduce Discrimination:* In the contemporary landscape, AI is increasingly playing a pivotal role in mitigating biases and favoritism prevalent in recruitment processes, thereby significantly enhancing transparency within work environments. This transformative use of AI technology is revolutionizing the traditional methods of personnel selection by introducing data-driven decision-making to the recruitment process. Through the deployment of sophisticated AI tools and algorithms, organizations are now equipped to objectively analyze resumes and job descriptions, paving the way for a more inclusive and merit-based hiring process. By leveraging AI applications, such as resume screening software powered by ML models, companies can streamline their recruitment workflows and identify the most qualified candidates based on an impartial evaluation of their qualifications and skills. This innovative approach not only fosters a more equitable employment landscape but also empowers organizations to recruit diverse talent pools and foster an inclusive work culture that values meritocracy and fairness. The strategic integration of AI in parsing job descriptions and evaluating candidate profiles signifies a significant shift toward enhancing the overall efficiency and integrity of

recruitment practices, ultimately leading to a more transparent and accountable workplace environment.

- *Strengthen Workplace Learning:* In the contemporary global landscape, the integration of digital and computer technology within business operations has become increasingly vital and prevalent. Leveraging these advanced technological tools enables businesses to uncover and capitalize on the hidden functions that can significantly enhance their overall performance and competitiveness. By harnessing the power of computers and modern technologies, organizations can effectively streamline their processes, optimize decision-making, and gain valuable insights through sophisticated data analysis. This empowerment allows companies to stay ahead of the curve by providing real-time feedback to employees and trainees, facilitating continuous learning and development within the workforce [10].

21.2.2 Artificial Intelligence

The first introduction of AI was made in 1956 by McCarthy *et al.* However, Alan Turing, an English mathematician and computer scientist, began researching AI in 1950 [11, 12]. But even with the early scientists' significant contributions [11], the fundamental concept of AI was originally proposed by James in 1890.

In essence, AI emulates the intricate workings of the human brain and translates it into a computational framework, thereby enabling machines to replicate cognitive functions. AI's capacity to learn, generalize, uncover, and derive novel insights greatly enhances comprehension of intricate relationships. Consequently, AI technology elevates human intelligence beyond its inherent constraints in this aspect, opening up boundless possibilities. Presently, the widespread adoption of AI across diverse sectors such as finance, health, safety, voice processing, NLP, production, and HRM underscores its transformative impact. For instance, AI-driven solutions are revolutionizing financial systems by increasing efficiency and accuracy [13, 14]. Similarly, AI-powered tools are enhancing healthcare outcomes by facilitating data-driven diagnoses and treatment strategies [15, 16]. Moreover, the integration of AI in safety protocols is advancing risk management practices and ensuring workplace security [17, 18]. Additionally, AI's application in voice and NLP is refining communication

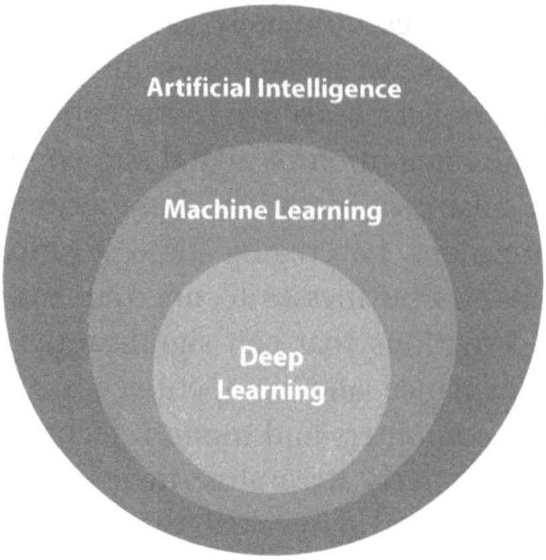

Figure 21.1 AI components.

channels and streamlining information exchange [19–22]. Furthermore, AI is optimizing production processes by enhancing operational efficiencies and resource utilization [23, 24]. Lastly, AI-driven tools are transforming HRM practices by automating routine tasks and enabling data-informed decision-making [25–27]. The pervasive influence of AI underscores its immense potential to revolutionize various industries by augmenting human capabilities and driving innovation.

AI consists of two primary components, as illustrated in Figure 21.1. To ensure a better grasp of the notion of AI, it is therefore also required to be familiar with the concepts of ML and deep learning (DL).

21.2.3 Machine Learning

ML is a subfield of AI that includes pattern recognition and numerical learning. ML is a system that is capable of learning and guarantees the structural development and analysis of algorithms that can make predictions based on data. Rather than simply applying and following standard program commands without any interpretation, the aforementioned algorithms operate by building a model to generate data-based predictions and decision mechanisms based on the information from the model data inputs [28].

The concept of ML is first explained with supervised learning, which is the process of gathering information from interconnected systems and arranging it in a predetermined sequence. Secondly, unsupervised learning involves studying data from systems whose interactions have not yet been identified and sorted in groups. Thirdly, semi-supervised learning that is partially supervised combines elements of both supervised and uncontrolled learning. Put differently, it is an approach to learning that makes use of both annotated big data and annotated little data. Lastly, reinforced learning occurs when the teacher determines whether or not the information that was learned as a result of the system's operation is accurate.

21.2.4 Deep Learning

Nowadays, DL is a popular model in the sound and image processing fields that was created in 2006 using AI techniques. Architecturally speaking, it has a multi-layer structure that allows it to hold a lot of concealed information. When data flow across the network, a DL model automatically picks up on and summarizes pertinent information. According to Eker *et al.*, the term "deep" refers to the number of layers in the network, meaning that, as the number of layers increases, so does the depth of the network [29].

When ML and DL technologies are compared, it is evident that ML operates in a single layer, whereas DL operates concurrently in multiple layers. In an attempt to determine a single process outcome depending on the size and complexity of the system, DL employs many ML algorithms simultaneously and interprets the results. For example, when working on image recognition tasks involving Earth and Mars, it is essential to distinctly categorize images of these two planets. In the realm of ML, it becomes crucial to imbue our computational models with the collective knowledge accrued by humanity over time as a means to enhance their learning capabilities. Introducing a hypothesis statement aids in outlining the key features unique to Earth and Mars that we aim to highlight within the model. These distinguishing characteristics serve as vital input for our system; for instance, an image with an orange hue is likely to be categorized as Mars, while the presence of water typically signals that the image represents Earth. Despite its independent learning capabilities, DL is still able to discern the nuanced differences between various characteristics without human intervention. In essence, DL is able to autonomously acquire knowledge and develop its own set of rules. For example, when presented with images of Earth and Mars, the DL system is capable of highlighting key discrepancies in color, form, and other distinguishing features. It is remarkable how the system can adapt and evolve by leveraging its innate abilities, thereby demonstrating its capacity to operate without the need for traditional human input or guidance.

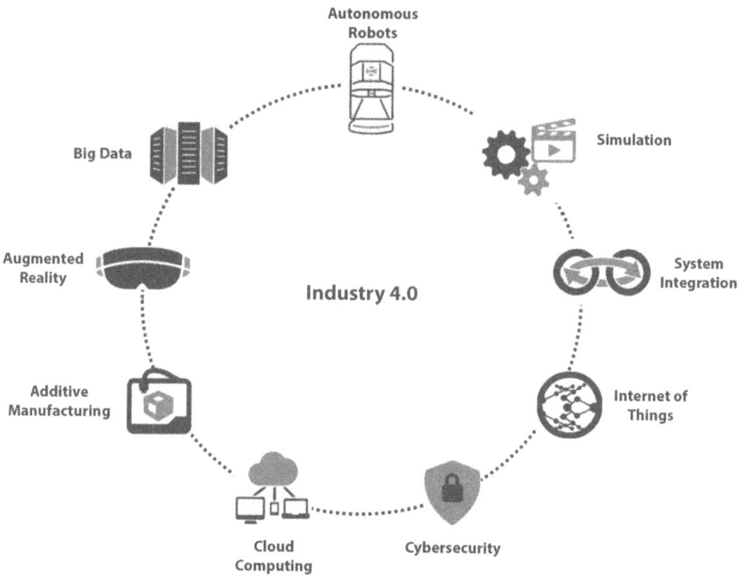

Figure 21.2 Industry 4.0.

21.2.5 Industry 4.0

Industry 4.0, often known as the Fourth Industrial Revolution, refers to the corporate environment where machines and people are integrated through a digital value chain and are connected by real-time data [30]. Industry 4.0 aims to develop systems that generate data with a high degree of automation by creating a corporate environment where workers will be replaced by robots with intelligence comparable to that of humans. A few of the technologies that Industry 4.0 links human and machine activities to are depicted in Figure 21.2.

21.3 Results and Discussion

Digital business solutions in HR have increased due to Industry 4.0, the influx of Gen Z workers, and the growing number of Y-generation individuals in the workforce. Institutions are now forced to shift their HR procedures to digital platforms as a result of this shift, which has rendered digitalization in HR essential. For instance, Vodafone Turkey's digitalization of development programs and improvements in the sphere of education were recognized by the Great Place to Work Institute as deserving of special honors in the categories of "Digital Transformation in HR" and "Diversity." The Vodafone Red Academy Learning Center has been using cutting-edge learning technology with 3,300 Vodafone, 7,500 dealers, and 18,000 sub-dealer personnel to reach a target population of about 29,000 people since 2015. Through a variety of applications, including the Orientation Program Discovered, Leadership and Talent Development Programs, Specialization and Functional Development, and Strategic Development Programs, it consistently promotes its workers' professional growth with digital technology. Another example is the "Over Sea (DenizAşırı)" program, which was introduced in Turkey for the first time in the online internship space. The significance of digitalization was demonstrated in 2017 when the aforementioned Deniz Bank initiative won the "Most Innovative HR Technologies" award [31]. This indicates the significance of digitization for HR on a worldwide level.

AI plays a major role in HRM and is beginning to appear in practically every industry. Applications of AI in human resources can choose the best individuals for the suitable jobs and responsibilities while also lightening the administrative staff's workload. Additionally, they can recommend appropriate training for staff members to gain new abilities. The HR department can then use the analyses and reports generated by AI to develop a proper career plan for each employee of the organization. It also helps to lessen the likelihood of mistakes happening, avoid breakdowns in other units' workflow, and enable more effective staff engagement [32].

21.4 AI and HRM

AI is used in various HR applications, from learning HRM skills to assessing employee performance. One of the primary HR procedures is recruitment, which may be extremely expensive, even for a medium-sized organization. Future strategic plans of the organization may be impacted if this process is mismanaged or encounters problems. These are serious consequences. Exams and interviews have resulted in significant expenses and lost time for the organization trying to sort through hundreds of applications to find the employee candidate most qualified for any given position and pick the candidate who has the necessary skills from among them. AI seems to be a useful tool for HR in this situation. These days, the process of identifying potential employees that ought to be the initial stage of the recruitment process is conducted *via* the institution's website or intermediary websites rather than through one-on-one applications. The resumes that job seekers upload to these websites form a database that will be utilized in the process of choosing the best applicant for the organization. AI-based technologies take the candidate's resume and job description as input. A ML algorithm is defined as the generic learning function Y = f (X), whereby an AI tool predicts future values of "Y" based on new examples of input variables "X," such as the HR data pertaining to the most suitable job matches for candidates who are available for the algorithm's training. The AI-based technology must learn the unknown function f from data using ML methods. To put it another way, AI-based candidate identification tools make use of recently created job postings to screen the company's resume databases, which may contain a large number of resumes, and bring qualified applicants to the recruiter's notice. More advanced technologies allow you to upload profiles of people who match the specific keywords that recruiters have detected into the application monitoring software and visit social media sites like Facebook, LinkedIn, and others at a predetermined regularity. Similar contextual search and matching algorithms are used by both tool types to examine a large number of resumes [3].

Another way that AI has affected this process is shown in the exams and interviews that were done prior to getting in touch with the HR department and adding any workload to it. Mya chatbots serve as one illustration of this. Mya Systems, an enterprise and innovation business, developed this chatbot that interviews job applicants online. After the interview, the chatbot grades the applicant and uploads the results to the Mya application system. If the candidate has impressed Mya as a consequence of this report being submitted, then Mya will make sure that the candidate meets with the human resources recruitment team to start the following parts of the process. Additionally, it guarantees that the employee candidate receives the relevant information throughout the recruitment process. One of the most popular programs used by medium and large sized institutions HR departments is called Mya, which saves the organization 70% of time when hiring new employees [33]. Many IT companies check all employee emails and internal communication portal correspondence before a deadline, look over the sentences created by employees and the words and emojis that they use, alert the HR department to employee commitment, offer recommendations tailored to the individual to increase their commitment, and generate reports.

21.5 Industry 4.0 and HRM

In order to foster innovation and learning inside their organizational structure, organizations should rethink their human resources procedures in Industry 4.0, including performance management, compensation, staffing, and training and development methods. In this sense, it is important to make sure that new production capacities are developed in order to enable businesses to grow and replenish their resource bases and to successfully adapt to the rapid advancements in technology.

21.5.1 Performance Management

The system for assessing performance needs to support innovation and learning in Industry 4.0. As a result, the organization should prioritize the behavior-based approach, the result-based strategy, and employee career development. Employees must receive regular performance updates in order to be motivated. In addition, having quantitative performance evaluation matrices is crucial to assessing performance in a more impartial manner. Standardizing the institution's performance standards and communicating to staff members what is expected of them are key components of a successful evaluation process. It is defined as measuring real performance, contrasting actual performance with the set performance standards, assessing the problem and talking to the staff about it, and taking necessary corrective action.

21.5.2 Payroll System

One area where the digitalization of HRM is evident in compensation is the payroll system. When we look at the payroll calculation system, we can see that there are legal constraints on the calculations. This computation can be completed more quickly, more affordably, and with fewer errors if it is carried out by a program. These programs make it simple to handle compensation, even in organizations with thousands of workers. These technologies, known as digital remuneration, allow for precise completion of the aforementioned computations, which would have been costly had errors been made in the social rights, advance payment, enforcement, and other deductions calculations. These systems allow workers to make requests like advance payments for their bosses' approval *via* the system. Payrolls authorized in digital archives can also be preserved. The more HRM becomes digitalized, the more important the corporate portal becomes. Our top example in this regard is the TofaşGo project, which was created by the Tofaş corporation, a pioneer in many industries in Turkey. The Tofaş company created a corporate mobile and web platform for this initiative, bringing all of its employees together in one location. Through the aforementioned Industry 4.0 project, Tofaş has access to numerous HRM processes, including managing employee fund requests, payroll, annual leave requests, employee monitoring, time management report monitoring, job openings in Koç group companies, and application monitoring for these positions [34].

21.5.3 Manpower Planning

Organizations must enhance their hiring procedures since putting the wrong person in a position and having them make a mistake there could result in significant expenses for the organization. Therefore, during the applicant selection process, institutions should concentrate on utilizing psychometric tests to ascertain candidates' inventive behaviors and receptivity to innovation. As a result, the organization builds a strong foundation for its personnel system. Additional factors that universities should take into account and test during applicant interviews include creativity, adaptability, active imagination, intellectual curiosity, and openness to new experiences. Employers who consider these factors while hiring people will find it easier to adjust to the developments brought about by Industry 4.0 [31]. One of the most significant advancements in the hiring process with Industry 4.0 is the application of AI. The utilization of AI technologies in these procedures guarantees expedited and cost-effective completion of these activities. The Mya AI Recruitment Assistant is one of the most notable instances that are now in use. According to applications submitted by organizations utilizing the Mya Artificial Intelligence Recruitment Assistant, employees who handle hiring save 75% of their working hours. In addition, it was observed that candidates' satisfaction with Mya during the job interview process was 9.8 out of 10. The AI recruitment assistant Mya is used in the hiring process by the multinational cosmetics firm L'Oréal. Since September 2018, AI has been effectively used in the US, England, and France to handle a variety of recruitment tasks. L'Oréal has successfully leveraged its AI program to enhance the efficiency of candidate selection, particularly through the evaluation of over a million applications annually. The utilization of this technology has significantly increased the capacity to identify well-suited individuals for various roles within the company. Nilesh Bhoite, Head of HR & Digital at L'Oréal, mentioned that during job interviews with a substantial number of applicants, the AI system demonstrated remarkable efficiency by effectively engaging with 92% of candidates and achieving an outstanding 100% satisfaction rate. This data underscores the positive impact and benefits of integrating AI into the recruitment process at L'Oréal. The organization's commitment to adopting innovative solutions such as AI reflects its dedication to optimizing talent acquisition practices and ensuring the best possible outcomes for both candidates and the company. By embracing cutting-edge technology like AI, L'Oréal continues to set a high standard in modern recruitment strategies, showcasing its proactive approach toward advancing HR processes and fostering a more streamlined and effective hiring journey for all stakeholders involved. The candidates have given us very great comments, expressing how simple the system is to use and how special they feel. One area of HRM where digitization is reflected in compensation is the payroll system. When we look at the payroll calculation system, we can see that there are legal constraints on the calculations. This computation can be completed more quickly, more affordably, and with fewer errors if it is carried out by a program. These programs make it simple to handle compensation, even in organizations with thousands of workers. These platforms, known as digital remuneration, are used in the aforementioned computations, where errors might occur in the social rights, advance payment, enforcement, and other calculations.

21.5.4 Training and Development

Training programs must be created by institutions with the goal of enhancing creative thinking, lifelong learning, and Industry 4.0 development. It is advised that training programs be designed with numerous assignments in mind for institutional staff members. It is recommended that the training program be designed to help individuals build their competencies rather than something that is specifically connected to their employment. Instead of being brief, these training sessions ought to be ongoing and long-term. In addition, it is recommended that employees at institutions receive guiding and on-the-job training from the moment they begin employment in order to enhance their collaborative and decision-making skills [31].

21.5.5 Management by Objectives

It is noticeable that among many assessment methodologies, management by objectives has become more and more popular. This method, known as a performance evaluation, focuses on attaining pre-established objectives through the collaborative process of setting and assessing goals. It emphasizes the importance of aligning individual performance with overall targets, ensuring a clear direction for both the evaluation process and the achievement of desired outcomes. In this program, management and staff decide how to have mutual discussions, declare ideas, and come to decisions by consensus. Furthermore, this program's continuous feedback mechanism enables managers and staff to keep an eye on operations and adjust regulations as needed. Therefore, it can be inferred that the management by objectives method is consistent with Industry 4.0 when it comes to performance evaluation.

21.6 Conclusion

Each of the products or services used by people changes as a result of technological advancements. Businesses that are able to adapt to this transformation will thrive, whereas others will gradually lose market share. It is a fact that needs to be acknowledged that companies seeking to thrive must prioritize their people over consumers, goods, and services. The best employee who can benefit the company can be chosen and trained by a human resources department that is strategically placed and organized. On the other hand, the opposite circumstance can spell disaster for the organization.

The current study looked into how AI and Industry 4.0 technology affected HRM. After conducting a literature survey, it was discovered that Industry 4.0 has several benefits, including the ability to save time and money, impartial assessment, less work, higher productivity, and data analysis and collection for HRM functions within organizations, including hiring and placement, integration and orientation, performance management, training and development management, career management, and wage management. In light of the growing human population, Industry 4.0 and AI technologies have emerged as some of the most crucial instruments for integrating AI into HR operations within a company and identifying qualified job candidates. Thus, it became clear that the majority of enterprises' manual operations had been replaced by chatbots, robots, automation, DL, ML, etc. This transition was new and gradual, but it was also expected to gain traction and continue to evolve. However, the comprehensive literature evaluation emphasized that new economic sectors will arise and the requirement for human capital would decline. Furthermore, a negative impact was assessed to be the organizational culture and employees' prejudiced attitude toward the use of AI and Industry 4.0 technologies, as well as their perception of their use as complex. It is anticipated that the data gathered from reading 45 recent papers will add to the body of knowledge.

21.7 Future Research Directions

Although there are now few recognized consequences of Industry 4.0 and AI on people and procedures, it is certain that these technologies will proliferate and advance in the future. In the realm of HRM, the landscape of information and its related facets, including information management, information processing systems, and information technology, is poised to experience considerable shifts, transformations, and advancements. These elements are anticipated to evolve in response to the ever-changing demands and expectations within the field. As such, there is a growing emphasis on the concept of e-HRM, signaling a shift toward digitalization and technology integration in HR practices. The anticipated changes indicate a journey toward modernization and optimization of HR processes, with the recognition that technology plays a crucial role in shaping the future of HRM practices. The forthcoming developments are projected to bring about enhanced efficiencies, streamlined workflows, and improved accessibility to HR-related information and services. As we move forward into this digital era, it becomes increasingly evident that the integration of Industry 4.0 and AI will have a profound impact on how businesses manage their HR. The rapid evolution of technology means that traditional HR practices are becoming outdated, making way for innovative approaches that rely heavily on data-driven decision-making and automation. This shift toward a more tech-savvy HR landscape not only promises increased efficiency and productivity but also raises questions about the role of human intervention in an environment driven by intelligent machines. The concept of unmanned HR, once a distant possibility, now seems like an inevitable reality as we witness the relentless march of technology in reshaping the workplace. It is becoming clear that organizations that embrace and adapt to these changes will have a competitive edge in attracting and retaining top talent in a future, where HR and technology merge seamlessly.

References

1. Öğüt, A., Akgemci, T., Tahir Demirsel, M., Stratejik Insan Kaynaklari Yönetimibağlaminda Örgütlerde Işgören Motivasyonu Süreci. *Selçuk Üniversitesi Sosyal Bilimler Enstitüsü Dergisi*, 12, 277–290, 2004.
2. Saridakis, G., Lai, Y., Cooper, C.L., Exploring the relationship between HRM and firm performance: A meta-analysis of longitudinal studies. *Hum. Resource Manage. Rev.*, *27*, 1, 87–96, 2017.
3. Kulkarni, S.B. and Che, X., Intelligent software tools for recruiting. *J. Int. Technol. Inf. Manage.*, *28*, 2, 2–16, 2019.
4. Ertaş, A., *Dijital insan kaynakları yönetimi*, Efe Akademik Yayıncılık, İstanbul, 2023.
5. Özçelik, A.O., Sadullah, O., Uyargil, C., *İnsan kaynakları yönetimi (İ.Ü.)*, İstanbul, Beta Yayınevi, 2021.

6. Tripathi, R.T. and Singh, P.K., A study on innovative practices in digital human resource management, in: *Proceedings of the National Conference Digital Transformation of Business in India: Opportunities and Challenges*, Dehradun, pp. 1–13, 2017, March.
7. Tewari, I. and Pant, M., Artificial intelligence reshaping human resource management: A review, in: *2020 IEEE International Conference on Advent Trends in Multidisciplinary Research and Innovation (ICATMRI)*, IEEE, pp. 1–4, 2020, December.
8. Amla, M. and Malhotra, P.M., Digital transformation in HR. *Int. J. Interdiscip. Multi. Stud. (IJIMS)*, *4*, 3, 536–544, 2017.
9. Rajesh, S., Being Human in the Age of AI Can We Draw a Line? *NHRD Netw. J.*, *11*, 3, 74–80, 2018.
10. Albert, E.T., AI in talent acquisition: a review of AI-applications used in recruitment and selection. *Strategic HR Rev.*, *18*, 5, 215–221, 2019.
11. Kırılmaz, S.K. and Ateş, C., İşe alımlarda yapay zekâ kullanımı: kavramsal bir değerlendirme. *J. Bus. Trade*, *2*, 1, 37–48, 2021.
12. Soleimani, M., Intezari, A., Taskin, N., & Pauleen, D., Cognitive biases in developing biased Artificial Intelligence recruitment system. *Proceedings of the 54th Hawaii International Conference on System Sciences*, 5091–5099, 2021.
13. Şengüler, H. and İnel, M.N., An empirical study based on artificial intelligence for determining brand value based on financial data. *Sosyoekonomi*, *53*, 30, 395–424, 2021.
14. Arda, E. and Küçükkocaoğlu, G., Stock price predictions using artificial intelligence methods. *J. Res. Economics Polit. Finance*, *2*, 6, 565–586, 2021.
15. Ullah, A., Şahin, C.B., Dinler, O.B., Khan, M.H., Aznaoui, H., Heart disease prediction using various machines learning approach. *J. Cardiovasc. Dis. Res.*, *12*, 3, 379–391, 2021.
16. Batur, C., & Diri, B., Identifying predictive genes for sequence classification using artificial immune recognition system. *Online J. Sci. Technol.*, 8, 4, 58–66, 2018 October.
17. Dinler, O.B. and Şahin, C.B., Prediction of phishing web sites with deep learning using WEKA environment. *Avrupa Bilim ve Teknoloji Dergisi*, 24, 35–41, 2021. https://doi.org/10.31590/ejosat.901465.
18. Şahin, C. B., Deep-Immune-Network Model for Vulnerable Clone Detection. *Manchester Journal of Artificial Intelligence and Applied Sciences (MJAIAS)*, 3, 1, 2022. Retrieved from https://www.mjaias.co.uk/mj-en/article/view/51.
19. Korkmaz, Y. and Boyacı, A., A comprehensive Turkish accent/dialect recognition system using acoustic perceptual formants. *Appl. Acoust.*, *193*, 108761, 2022.
20. Batur Dinler, O. and Aydin, N., An optimal feature parameter set based on gated recurrent unit recurrent neural networks for speech segment detection. *Appl. Sci.*, *10*, 4, 1273, 2020.

21. Lauriola, I., Lavelli, A., Aiolli, F., An introduction to deep learning in natural language processing: Models, techniques, and tools. *Neurocomputing, 470*, 443–456, 2022.
22. Ning, J., [Retracted] Natural Language Processing Technology Used in Artificial Intelligence Scene of Law for Human Behavior. *Wirel. Commun. Mob. Comput., 2022*, 1, 6606588, 2022.
23. Çiçek, Y., Uludag, A., Gülbandılar, E., Şeker pancarı üretiminde kullanılan yapay zekâ teknikleri. *Eskişehir Türk Dünyası Uygulama ve Araştırma Merkezi Bilişim Dergisi*, 3, 2, 54–59, 2022.
24. Dikel, S. and Öz, M., Artificial intelligence (AI) application in aquaculture, in: *ISPEC 10th International Conference on Agriculture, Animal Sciences and Rural Development*, 2022.
25. Ming, L., [Retracted] A Deep Learning-Based Framework for Human Resource Recommendation. *Wirel. Commun. Mob. Comput., 2022*, 1, 2377143, 2022.
26. Vrontis, D., Christofi, M., Pereira, V., Tarba, S., Makrides, A., Trichina, E., Artificial intelligence, robotics, advanced technologies and human resource management: a systematic review, in: *Artificial Intelligence and International HRM*, pp. 172–201, 2023.
27. Wei, G. and Jin, Y., Human resource management model based on three-layer BP neural network and machine learning. *J. Intell. Fuzzy Syst., 40*, 2, 2289–2300, 2021.
28. Gardner, M.W. and Dorling, S.R., Artificial neural networks (the multilayer perceptron)—a review of applications in the atmospheric sciences. *Atmos. Environ., 32*, 14–15, 2627–2636, 1998.
29. Eker, E., Kayri, M., Ekinci, S., Izci, D., A new fusion of ASO with SA algorithm and its applications to MLP training and DC motor speed control. *Arabian J. Sci. Eng., 46*, 3889–3911, 2021.
30. Samarasinghe, K.R. and Medis, A., Artificial intelligence based strategic human resource management (AISHRM) for industry 4.0. *Glob. J. Manage. Bus. Res., 20*, 2, 7–13, 2020.
31. Çiftçioğlu, B.A., Mutlu, M., Katırcıoğlu, S., Endüstri 4.0 Ve İnsan Kaynaklari Yönetiminin İlişkisi. *Bandırma Onyedi Eylül Üniversitesi Sosyal Bilimler Araştırmaları Dergisi, 2*, 1, 31–53, 2019.
32. Yawalkar, M.V.V., A study of artificial intelligence and its role in human resource management. *Int. J. Res. Anal. Rev. (IJRAR), 6*, 1, 20–24, 2019.
33. Bulut, A. and Dinler, O.B., The effect of industry 4.0 and artificial intelligence on human resource management. *Uluslararası Doğu Anadolu Fen Mühendislik ve Tasarım Dergisi, 5*, 2, 143–166, 2023.
34. Ogoo Blog, (2017). Tofaş mobil intranetle iç iletişimde dijital dönüşüm, http://blog.ogoodigital.com/tofasmobil-intranetle-ic-iletisimde-dijital-donusum/ (Date of Access: 17.09.2024).

Index

Also of Interest

Check out these published and forthcoming titles in the "Industry 5.0 Transformation Applications" series from Scrivener Publishing

Cyber-Physical Systems for Innovating and Transforming Society 5.0
Edited by Tanupriya Choudhury, Abhijit Kumar, Ravi Tomar, S. Balamurugan and Ankit Vishnoi
Forthcoming 2025. ISBN 978-1-394-19771-2

Distributed Time-Sensitive Systems
Edited by Tanupriya Choudhury, Rahul Kumar Singh, Ravi Tomar, S. Balamurugan, J. C. Patni
Published 2025. ISBN 978-1-394-19772-9

Generative Artificial Intelligence
Concepts and Applications
Edited by R. Nidhya, D. Pavithra, Manish Kumar, A. Dinesh Kumar, and S. Balamurugan
Published 2025. ISBN 978-1-394-20922-4

Intelligent Robots and Cobots
Concepts and Applications for Industry 5.0 Transformation
Edited by Ramasamy V, S. Balamurugan, and Sheng-Lung Peng
Published 2025. ISBN 978-1-394-19817-7

Smart Factories for Industry 5.0 Transformation
Edited by R. Nidhya, Manish Kumar, S. Karthik, Rishabh Anand and S. Balamurugan
Published 2025. ISBN 978-1-394-19995-2

Optimized Computational Intelligence Driven Decision-Making
Theory, Application and Challenges
Edited by Hrudaya Kumar Tripathy, Sushruta Mishra, Minakhi Rout, S. Balamurugan and Samaresh Mishra
Published 2024. ISBN 978-1-394-24253-5

Welding Practices for Industry 5.0
Edited by Syed Quadir Moinuddin, Shaik Himam Saheb, Ashok Kumar Dewangan, Muralimohan Cheepu and S. Balamurugan
Published 2024. ISBN 978-1-394-17241-2

Metaverse and Immersive Technologies
An Introduction to Industrial, Business and Social Applications
Edited by Chandrashekhar A, Shaik Himam Saheb, Sandeep Kumar Panda, S. Balamurugan and Sheng-Lung Peng
Published 2023. ISBN 978-1-394-17454-6

www.scrivenerpublishing.com

Printed in the USA/Agawam, MA
September 16, 2026

910661.160